AA

1001
GREAT
FAMILY PUBS

Pictures in this book come from the AA's own library (AA WORLD TRAVEL LIBRARY): Jim Henderson 311; Caroline Jones 2; Simon McBride 309; Tom Mackie 113, 115, 225; Andy Midgley 5; Rick Strange 4; Wyn Voysey 335

Cover photographs: Front Cover: ltl Crooked Billet, Stoke Row; tl Photodisc; tc AA World Travel Library/Tom Mackie; tr AA World Travel Library/Rich Newton; rtr AA World Travel Library/Alex Kouprianoff; bottom Rising Sun; Back Cover: tl AA World Travel Library/Chris Coe; tl Photodisc; tc AA World Travel Library/James Tims; tr Crooked Billet, Stoke Row; rtr AA World Travel Library/Wyn Voysey; lbl AA World Travel Library/M Birkitt; bl AA World Travel Library/Mike Hayward; bc AA World Travel Library/Richard Ireland; br AA World Travel Library; rbr AA World Travel Library/EA Bowness

Design by Jamie Wiltshire, Typeset/Repro by Servis Filmsetting Ltd, Manchester, Printed by Everbest, China, Editor: Denise Laing

Pub descriptions have been contributed by the following team of writers: Phil Bryant, Neville Chalkley, Alice Gardner, David Halford, Judith Hope, Julia Hynard, Denise Laing, Philip Moss, Derryck Strachan. Published by AA Publishing, a trading name of Automobile Association Developments Limited, whose registered office is Southwood East, Apollo Rise, Farnborough, Hampshire GU14 0JW. Registered number 1878835.

A CIP catalogue for this book is available from the British Library.

ISBN-10 074954 2659   ISBN-13 978-0-7495-4265-8   A02147
Maps prepared by the Cartography Department of The Automobile Association. Maps © Automobile Association Developments Limited 2005.

This product includes mapping data licensed from Ordnance Survey® with the permission of the Controller of Her Majesty's Stationery Office.
© Crown copyright 2005. All rights reserved. Licence number 399221.

Sample entry

① NEWTOWN **NEWTOWN ARMS** ◆◆◆◆

④ Small Village XX11 1XX
☎ 01234 567890 🖹 01234 567891
e-mail: newtownarms@village.com
⑤ Dir: *Telephone for directions.* **Map Ref:** *TT33* **②**

This 16th-century village inn is situated in a picturesque village. The mainly traditional menu includes roast beef; steak, kidney and mustard pie; fresh halibut grilled with lime and coriander butter, but also very hot chilli seafood linguine. Among the bar snacks are jacket potatoes, baguettes and sandwiches.

⑥ OPEN: 11.15-11 (Sun 11-3, 7-10.30)Closed 25-26 Dec
⑦ BAR MEALS: L served all week 11.30-2 D served all week 6.30-9 Av main course £5.99 **RESTAURANT:** L served all **⑧** week 11.30-1.45 D served all week 7-8.45 Av 3 course à la carte £14 **BREWERY/COMPANY:** Freehouse ♀: 9 **⑨**
⑩ CHILDREN'S FACILITIES: menu, portions, games, high-chairs, food/bottle warming, outdoor play area, slide, climbing frame, fort, family room **GARDEN:** Large grassed area with tables
NOTES: No dogs (ex guide dogs), Parking 100 **⑪**
⑫ ROOMS: 6 en suite s£45 d£60

---

① GUIDE ORDER This guide is divided into regions. Within each region counties are listed alphabetically. To find a particular county refer to page opposite. Locations and pub names are listed alphabetically. Some village pubs prefer to be initially located under the nearest town, in which case the village name is included in the address and directions.

② MAP REFERENCE The map reference is based on the National Grid and can be used with the map at the beginning of each region.

③ SYMBOLS See below.

④ ADDRESS AND POSTCODE Street name plus the postcode. If necessary the name of the village is included (see 1 above). This may be up to five miles from the named location.

⑤ DIRECTIONS Directions are supplied by the proprietor. Please telephone for directions where none are supplied.

⑥ OPEN The opening times and closed dates of the establishment.

⑦ BAR MEALS indicates the times and days when bar food can be ordered, and may show the average price of a main course as supplied by the proprietor. Please be aware that last

orders could vary by up to 30 minutes.

⑧ RESTAURANT indicates the times and days when food can be ordered from the restaurant, and may show the average cost of a 3-course á la carte meal and a 3- or 4-course fixed-price menu as supplied by the proprietor. Last orders may be approximatley 30 minutes before the times stated.

⑨ BREWERY/COMPANY The name of the Brewery or Company to which the pub is tied. Free house indicates an independently owned pub.

⑩ CHILDREN'S FACILITIES as listed

⑪ NOTES We indicate whether dogs are welcome, information about the pub garden, parking and credit cards. We only indicate places which do not take credit cards.

⑫ ROOMS Only accommodation that has been inspected by The AA, RAC, VisitBritain, VisitScotland or the Welsh Tourist Board is included. AA Stars and Diamonds are shown at the beginning of an entry. Small Stars and Diamonds appearing under ROOMS indicates that the accommodation has been inspected by one of the other organisations. Please see below for an explanation of ratings.

AA Classifications and Awards

Establishments in the guide with Stars ★ or Diamonds ◆ shown next to their name have been inspected and rated by the AA. The Star system for Hotels ranges from 1 to 5, with a Quality Assessment score to differenciate between hotels with the same star rating. The Diamond system for B&Bs also ranges from 1 to 5. The best of both types of establishment are shown in red. A Rosette award is shown where the food is particularly good. Restaurants with Rooms are local or national destinations for eating out which also offer accommodation. For more detailed explanations of our ratings please see the AA website www.theAA.com.

Symbols

★ **Stars**
The rating for Hotel accommodation

 Rosettes
The AA's food award

 Restaurants with Rooms
Category of inspected accommodation

◆ **Diamonds.** The rating for Bed and Breakfast accommodation

 Indicates that a pub serves a minimum of four main dishes with sea fish as the main ingredient.

♀ Indicates the number of wines available by the glass

🍺 Denotes the principle beers sold

Contents

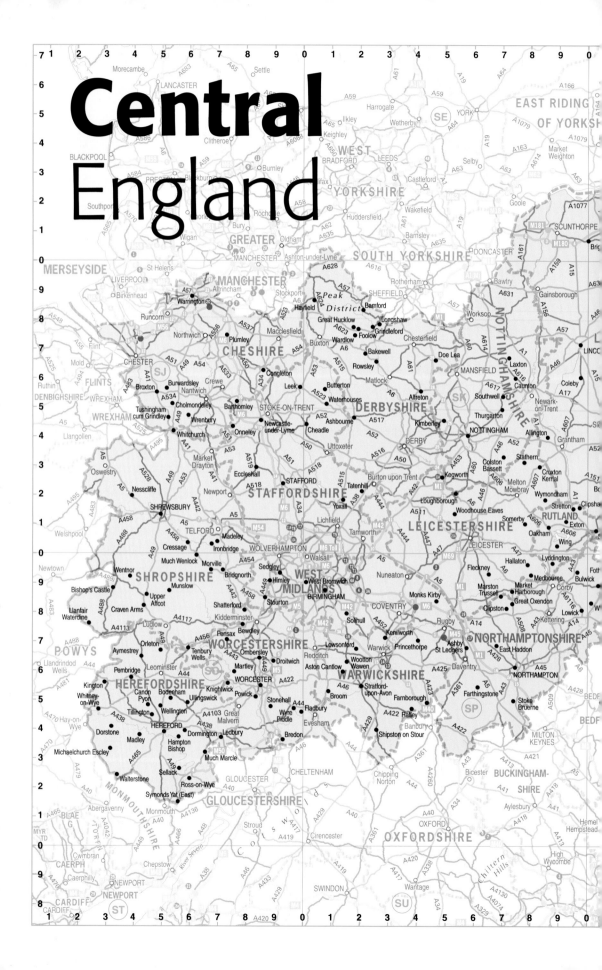

The Central England region includes the urban conurbations of Birmingham, Coventry, Leicester and Nottingham, providing an exciting and culturally diverse nightlife, as well as the delightful cathedral towns of Hereford, Lincoln and Worcester, and the historic county towns of Chester, Shrewsbury and Warwick, distinguished by their beautiful and ancient architecture.

The heart of England's finest natural feature is the Peak District, which takes in parts of six counties. It was Britain's first National Park, established in 1951, and is the starting point of the Pennine Way, a long distance trail stretching 270 miles along the Pennine Ridge through the Yorkshire Dales and the Cheviot Hills to the Scottish Borders.

The region is renowned for its castles and caverns; fine china from the Staffordshire Potteries, and fruit from the orchards of Hereford and Worcestershire. Major attractions include the likes of Alton Towers, Drayton Manor Park, Chatsworth House, Althorp and the town of Stratford-upon-Avon, feted for its associations with Shakespeare. It also boasts the smallest county in England: Rutland.

Top tipples

Herefordshire has been at the centre of cider making for centuries and the world's largest cider mill, Bulmers, is located in Hereford, pressing some 80,000 tonnes of cider apples annually from the region's 10,000 acres of orchards. You can explore the history of cider making at Hereford's Cider Museum & King Offa Distillery in Ryelands Street, and sample the King Offa cider brandy, apple aperitif and cider liqueur produced at the museum.

Burton-on-Trent in Staffordshire is the capital of British beer brewing. The waters of the Trent were found to be particularly good for brewing, given their high levels of dissolved salts, and at one time a quarter of all the beer sold in Britain was made here. If you're interested in the history of brewing, pay a visit to the Bass Museum.

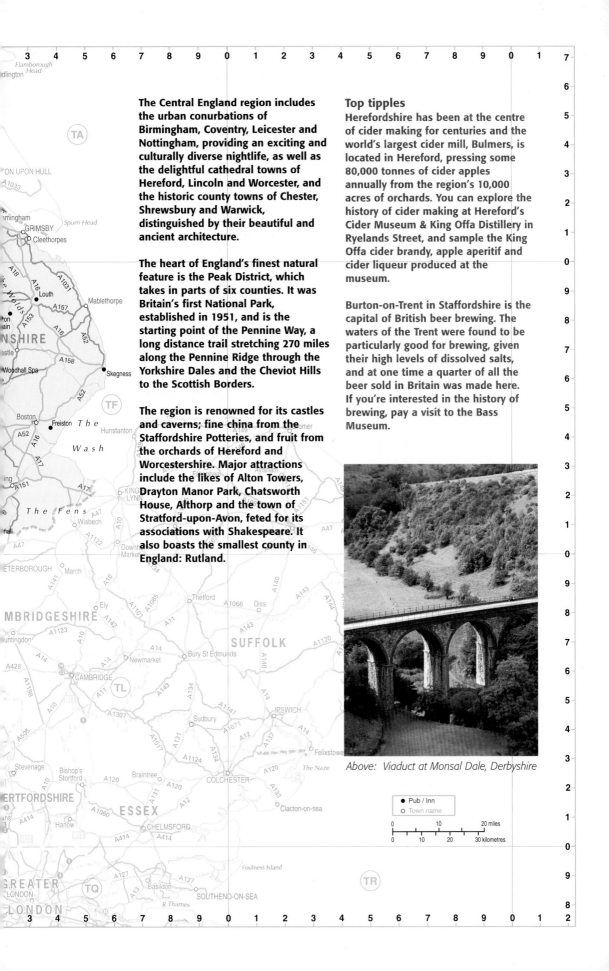

Above: Viaduct at Monsal Dale, Derbyshire

● Pub / Inn
○ Town name

0   10   20 miles
0   10   20   30 kilometres

BARTHOMLEY   THE WHITE LION INN

CW2 5PG
☎ 01270 882242 ▤ 01270 873348
Map Ref: SJ75

Dating from 1614, this half-timbered and thatched inn with character bars is in a lovely rural setting, and has associations with the English Civil War. It offers bar food ranging from hot beef banjo, tuna mayonnaise, and pâté with toast, to more substantial dishes such as pie with peas, mash and gravy, and a daily roast with creamed potatoes and vegetables. Strictly no chips!

OPEN: 11.30-11 (Thurs 5-11, Sun 12-10.30)
BAR MEALS: L served Fri-Wed 12-2 Av main course £5
BREWERY/COMPANY: Burtonwood 🍺: Burtonwood Bitter, Top Hat & Guest ales. **CHILDREN'S FACILITIES:** portions, food/bottle warming **NOTES:** Dogs allowed: On leads, not in bar during lunch, Parking 20

BROXTON   THE COPPER MINE

Nantwich Rd CH3 9JH
☎ 01829 782293
Dir: *A41 from Chester, L at rdbt onto A534, pub 0.5m on R.* *Map Ref:* SJ45

Convenient for Cheshire Ice Cream Farm, the 14th-century Beeston Castle, and the Candle Factory at Cheshire Workshops, this pub has a conservatory with fine views of the surrounding countryside and is newly refurbished. Favourite dishes on the new menu from the 'new' owners, who owned the pub in the 1990s, include halibut with mustard rarebit, sea bass with smoked oysters, crispy roasted duck with orange liqueur sauce and a whole rack of honey-glazed pork ribs. Patio and lawn with mature trees.

OPEN: 12-3 6-11 (Sun 12-10.30) **BAR MEALS:** L served all week 12-2.30 D served Tue-Sun 6.30-9.30 Av main course £6.95 **RESTAURANT:** L served all week 12-2.30 D served Tue-Sun 6.30-9.30 Av 3 course à la carte £15
BREWERY/COMPANY: Free House 🍺: Worthington Cream Flow, Pedigree & Banks Real Ale.
CHILDREN'S FACILITIES: menu, portions, high-chairs, food/bottle warming, outdoor play area **GARDEN:** Large patio area with flower gardens & lawns **NOTES:** No dogs (ex guide dogs), Parking 80

BURWARDSLEY   THE PHEASANT INN ★★ ◈◈ ♀

CH3 9PF
☎ 01829 770434 ▤ 01829 771097
e-mail: reception@thepheasant-burwardsley.com
Dir: *From Chester A41 to Whitchurch, after 4m L to Burwardsley. Follow signs 'Cheshire Workshops'.* *Map Ref:* SJ55

A delightful old sandstone inn tucked away in a beautiful rural setting with lofty views over the Cheshire plain. This traditional country inn is cosy indoors with reputedly the largest log fire in the county, while outside a flower-filled courtyard is ideal for summer evening drinks. The half-timbered former farmhouse makes a great setting for a bar that boasts sophisticated cooking and well-kept ales.

OPEN: 11-11 **BAR MEALS:** L served all week 12-2.30 D served all week 6.30-9.30 Av main course £9
RESTAURANT: L served all week 12-2.30 D served all week 6.30-9.30 Av 3 course à la carte £18
BREWERY/COMPANY: Free House 🍺: Weetwood Old Dog, Eastgate, Outhouse, Best. ♀: 7 **CHILDREN'S FACILITIES:** menu, licence, high-chairs, food/bottle warming, baby changing, outdoor play area **GARDEN:** Ten tables, views of the Cheshire Plains **NOTES:** No dogs (ex guide dogs), Parking 40
ROOMS: 10 en suite 2 family rooms s£65 d£80

CHOLMONDELEY THE CHOLMONDELEY ARMS ♦♦♦ 🍽 🍷

SY14 8HN
☎ 01829 720300 📠 01829 720123
e-mail: guy@cholmondeleyarms.co.uk
Dir: *On A49, between Whitchurch & Tarporley.*
Map Ref: *SJ55*

Formerly the village school, the Cholmondeley Arms is set in countryside close to historic Cholmondeley Castle. The school closed in 1982, re-opening as a pub six years later, much to the relief of locals who, due to a passionately teetotal 19th century Marquess of Cholmondeley, had been publess for 100 years. Since then it has gone from strength to strength, gaining plaudits and awards for its hand-pumped beers and excellent home-made food.

OPEN: 11-3 7-11 Closed: 25 Dec **BAR MEALS:** L served all week 12-2.30 D served all week 7-10 Av main course £15 **RESTAURANT:** L served all week 12-2.30 D served all week 7-10 **BREWERY/COMPANY:** Free House **🍺:** Marston's Pedigree, Adnams Bitter, Banks's, Everards Tiger Best. **🍷:** 7 **CHILDREN'S FACILITIES:** menu, high-chairs, food/bottle warming, baby changing, outdoor play area **GARDEN:** Lrg lawns **NOTES:** Dogs allowed, Parking 60 **ROOMS:** 6 en suite 1 family room s£50 d£65

CONGLETON THE EGERTON ARMS HOTEL ♦♦♦♦ 🍽 🍷

Astbury Village CW12 4RQ
☎ 01260 273946 📠 01260 277273
e-mail: egertonastbury@totalise.co.uk
Dir: *Telephone for directions.* ***Map Ref:*** *SJ86*

This 16th-century village inn is situated in the picturesque village of Astbury, adjacent to the 11th-century church. The mainly traditional menu includes roast topside of beef; steak, kidney and mustard pie; fresh halibut grilled with lime and coriander butter, but also very hot chilli seafood linguine. Among the bar snacks are jacket potatoes, baguettes and sandwiches. As well as Robinson's ales there is a large selection of malt whiskies and gins. All the 6 en suite bedrooms are attractive and well equipped.

OPEN: 11.15-11 (Sun 11-3, 7-10.30) **BAR MEALS:** L served all week 11.30-2 D served all week 6.30-9 Av main course £5.99 **RESTAURANT:** L served all week 11.30-1.45 D served all week 7-8.45 Av 3 course à la carte £14 Av 3 course fixed price £13.95 **BREWERY/COMPANY:** Robinsons **🍺:** Robinsons Old Stockport, Double Hop, Robinson Best Bitter. **🍷:** 9 **CHILDREN'S FACILITIES:** menu, portions, games, high-chairs, food/bottle warming, outdoor play area, slide, climbing frame, Fort, family room **GARDEN:** Large grassed area with tables **NOTES:** No dogs (ex guide dogs), Parking 100 **ROOMS:** 6 en suite s£45 d£60

PLOUGH INN HOTEL 🍽 🍷

Macclesfield Rd, Eaton CW12 2NH
☎ 01260 280207 📠 01260 298458
e-mail: info@plough-eaton.co.uk
Dir: *on A536 (Congleton to Macclesfield road)*
Map Ref: *SJ86*

Like a giant jigsaw puzzle, an ancient Welsh barn was transported here in hundreds of pieces to become a marvellously atmospheric restaurant adjoining this Elizabethan inn. From the specials menu come poached fresh salmon and prawn salad; and lamb Henry with mash. The carte offers lightly grilled turbot with lemon butter, and fillet steak cooked at the table. Apple crumble and custard is a typical dessert.

OPEN: 11-11 (Sun 12-10.30) **BAR MEALS:** L served all week 12-2.30 D served all week 5.30-9.30 (Sun 12-8.30) Av main course £7.95 **RESTAURANT:** L served all week 12-2.30 D served all week 6-9.30 (Sun 12-8.30) Av 3 course à la carte £22 Av 3 course fixed price £14.95 **BREWERY/COMPANY:** Free House **🍺:** Boddingtons, Hydes, Moore Houses, Storm Brew. **🍷:** 8 **CHILDREN'S FACILITIES:** portions, high-chairs, food/bottle warming **GARDEN:** Secret garden **NOTES:** No dogs, Parking 58 **ROOMS:** 8 en suite s£50 d£70 (♦♦♦♦)

PLUMLEY THE GOLDEN PHEASANT HOTEL

Plumley Moor Rd WA16 9RX
☎ 01565 722261 ▤ 01565 722125
Dir: *From M6 J19, take A556 signed Chester.*
2m turn L at signs for Plumley/Peover. Through
Plumley, after 1m pub opposite rail station.
Map Ref: *SJ77*

In the heart of rural Cheshire, the hotel has a
large restaurant, bar area (that also serves
food), public bar, children's play area and
bowling green. The menu offers a wide choice,
from sirloin steak to cod Véronique, from Cajun
chicken sizzler to crab and coriander fishcakes,
and from bangers and mash to penne
arabbiata. Real ales are pulled from the
attractive handpumps installed by J.W. Lees, one
of the country's few remaining independent
family breweries, with its own cooperage.

OPEN: 11-11 (Sun 12-10.30) **BAR MEALS:** L served all
week 12-2.30 D served all week 6-9.30 (Sat 12-9.30, Sun
12-8.30) Av main course £6.95 **RESTAURANT:** L served all
week 12-2.30 D served all week 6-9.30 (Sat 12-9.30, Sun
12-8.30) Av 3 course à la carte £18 Av 2 course fixed price
£10 **BREWERY/COMPANY:** J W Lees **◖:** J W Lees Bitter,
GB Mild & Moonraker. **♀:** 15
CHILDREN'S FACILITIES: menu, portions, licence, games,
high-chairs, food/bottle warming, baby changing, outdoor play
area, Play area in large garden **GARDEN:** Seating front and
back of pub **NOTES:** Water, No dogs (ex guide dogs),
Parking 80

TUSHINGHAM CUM GRINDLEY BLUE BELL INN

SY13 4QS
☎ 01948 662172 ▤ 01948 662172
Dir: *On the A41 N of Whitchurch.*
Map Ref: *SJ54*

In what must be a unique tale from the
annals of pub-haunting, this 17th-century,
black and white magpie building that oozes
character with its abundance of beams, open
fires and horse brasses was once haunted by
the spirit of a duck. Believe that or not, the
Blue Bell remains a charming characterful
pub with well-kept ales. Look to the
blackboards for today's specials. Under new
ownership, so reports are welcome.

OPEN: 12-3 6-11 (Sun 12-3, 7-11) Rest: 25 Dec Closed
eve **BAR MEALS:** L served Tue-Sun 12-2 D served all week
6-9 Av main course £6.50 **RESTAURANT:** L served all week
12-2 D served all week 7-9 **BREWERY/COMPANY:** Free
House **◖:** Hanby Ales, Ansells Mild & Guest Beers.
CHILDREN'S FACILITIES: portions, games, food/bottle
warming, outdoor play area **GARDEN:** Picnic benches
NOTES: Dogs allowed: in bar, in garden, water, Parking 20

WARRINGTON RING O BELLS

Old Chester Rd, Daresbury WA4 4AJ
☎ 01925 740256 ▤ 01925 740972
Map Ref: *SJ68*

'Alice in Wonderland' author Lewis Carroll
was born in Daresbury, his father being the
village curate. Formerly a grand old
farmhouse, it became a pub in 1872, its
name presumed to reflect patronage by
thirsty church bellringers. Fresh fish is the
house speciality, so you may see blackened
salmon, halibut, tuna steak or whole seabass.
Popular too are chicken with Camembert;
lamb and apricot pie; and Hot Hobs - filled
baguettes. Daily changing chalkboards display
daily specials.

OPEN: 11-11 (Sun 12-10.30) Closed: 25 Dec Eve
BAR MEALS: L served all week 12-10 D served all week
12-10 (Sunday) 12-9.30 Av main course £6.95
RESTAURANT: L served all week 12-10 D served all week
12-10 (Sunday 12-9.30) **◖:** Tetley Greenalls, Scottish
Courage Theakstons, Courage Directors & John Smiths, Guest
Ales. **♀:** 24 **CHILDREN'S FACILITIES:** menu, high-chairs,
family room **GARDEN:** Terraced garden, seating for 130
people **NOTES:** No dogs (ex guide dogs), Parking 100

WRENBURY   THE DUSTY MILLER ♀

CW5 8HG
☎ 01270 780537
e-mail: admin@dustymiller-wrenbury.com
Map Ref: SJ54

A black and white lift bridge, designed by Thomas Telford, completes the picture postcard setting for this beautifully converted 16th-century mill building beside the Shropshire Union canal. The current landlord is the great-grandson of Arthur Summer, who ran the mill up until the Second World War. The menu might offer naturally smoked fresh haddock and prawns baked in a Staffordshire oatcake, glazed with melting cheddar cheese; slow roast duck breast with Cumberland sauce and garlic mash; or parsnip and cheddar lattice pie with a spicy tomato sauce.

OPEN: 11.30-3 6.30-11 **BAR MEALS:** L served Tues-Sun 12-2 D served all week 6.30-9.30 (Sun 12-2.30, 7-9) Av main course £10 **RESTAURANT:** L served all week 12-2 D served all week 6.30-9.30 🍺: Robinsons Best Bitter, Double Hop, Old Tom, Hatters Mild & Hartleys XB. ♀: 12 **CHILDREN'S FACILITIES:** menu, portions, high-chairs, food/bottle warming **GARDEN:** Canalside garden accessed via footbridge **NOTES:** Dogs allowed: in bar, in garden, Water, Kennel, Parking 60

ALFRETON   WHITE HORSE INN 🐑 ♀

Badger Ln, Woolley Moor DE55 6FG
☎ 01246 590319 📠 01246 590319
e-mail: info@the-whitehorse-inn.co.uk
Dir: From A632 (Matlock/Chesterfield rd) take B6036. Pub 1m after Ashover. From A61 take B6036 to Woolley Moor. **Map Ref:** SK45

Situated on an old toll road, close to Ogston Reservoir, this 18th-century inn has outstanding views over the Amber Valley. The bar food menu offers such dishes as Thai fish cakes, braised belly pork and black pudding, or chicken Stroganoff - as well as an extensive range of sandwiches.

OPEN: 12-3 6-11 (Sun 12-10.30, all day summer wknds) **BAR MEALS:** L served all week 12-2 D served Tues-Sat 6-9 Sun 12-5.30/6 Av main course £7.50 **RESTAURANT:** L served all week 12-2 D served Tues-Sat 6-9 Sun 12-5.30/6 Av 3 course à la carte £16 **BREWERY/COMPANY:** Free House 🍺: Jennings Cumberland, Adnams Broadside, Blacksheep, 1744. ♀: 8 **CHILDREN'S FACILITIES:** menu, portions, licence, games, high-chairs, food/bottle warming, Adventure playground, football pitch, sand pit **GARDEN:** Large patio with picnic benches **NOTES:** Dogs allowed, Parking 50

ASHBOURNE   DOG & PARTRIDGE COUNTRY INN ★★ 🐑 ♀

Swinscoe DE6 2HS
☎ 01335 343183 📠 01335 342742
e-mail: dogpart@fsbdial.co.uk
Dir: Telephone for directions. **Map Ref:** SK14

This pub has a particular claim to fame: it was extended in 1966 to accommodate the Brazilian World Cup football team, who practised in a nearby field. Its extensive menus offer such dishes as halibut in Pernod, and ostrich steak in a whisky and cream sauce, alongside all the traditional favourites. Vegetarians are well catered for, and a local speciality is a Staffordshire oatcake with a choice of fillings accompanied by red cabbage, beetroot and salad.

OPEN: 11-11 **BAR MEALS:** L served all week 11-11 D served all week **RESTAURANT:** L served all week 11-11 D served all week **BREWERY/COMPANY:** Free House 🍺: Greene King Old Speckled Hen & Ruddles County, Hartington Best, Wells Bombardier, Scottish Courage Courage Directors. **CHILDREN'S FACILITIES:** menu, portions, high-chairs, food/bottle warming, baby changing, board games, sandpit, highchairs, family room **GARDEN:** Good patio area with lovely views **NOTES:** Dogs allowed: in bar, in garden, in bedrooms, Parking 50 **ROOMS:** 29 en suite 16 family rooms s£50 d£75

ASHBOURNE   THE GREEN MAN ROYAL HOTEL ◆◆◆

St Johns St DE6 1GH
☎ 01335 345783 📄 01335 346613
Dir: *In town centre off A52.* **Map Ref:** *SK14*

Located in the heart of Ashbourne, this 18th-century coaching inn has two bars, the Johnson and the Boswell, and recently came under new management. One of Britain's few remaining gallows still stands outside. The bars combine modernity with tradition, and the pub can cater for up to 200 guests.

OPEN: 11-11 (Sun 12-10.30) Closed: Dec 25 & Jan 1
BAR MEALS: L served all week 12-3.00 D served all week 6-9 (Sun Sandwiches 12-3) Av main course £12
BREWERY/COMPANY: Free House 🍺: Marston's Pedigree.
CHILDREN'S FACILITIES: menu, high-chairs, food/bottle warming **GARDEN:** courtyard **NOTES:** No dogs (ex guide dogs), Parking 12 **ROOMS:** 18 en suite 1 family room s£40 d£60

BAKEWELL   THE MONSAL HEAD HOTEL ★★ 🐑 🍷

Monsal Head DE45 1NL
☎ 01629 640250 📄 01629 640815
e-mail: Christine@monsalhead.com
Dir: *A6 from Bakewell towards Buxton. 1.5m to Ashford. Follow Monsal Head signs, B6465 for 1m.* **Map Ref:** *SK26*

Set at the heart of the Peak District National Park, the Monsal Head is ideal for walkers, and has superb views of the hills and dales. The hotel complex includes a real ale pub, with flagstone floors and a roaring fire in winter. The menu provides a flexible choice of dishes. There's also a light snack menu and daily blackboard specials.

OPEN: 11.30-11 (Sun 12-10.30) Closed: 25 Dec
BAR MEALS: L served all week 12-9.30 D served all week Sunday 12-9 Av main course £9 **RESTAURANT:** L served (Sat-Sun) 12-9.30 D served all week 7-9.30 Sunday 12-9 Av 3 course à la carte £16 **BREWERY/COMPANY:** Free House 🍺: Timothy Taylor Landlord, Whim Hartington IPA, Abbeydale Moonshine. 🍷: 15 **CHILDREN'S FACILITIES:** menu, portions, high-chairs, food/bottle warming, baby changing **NOTES:** Dogs allowed, Parking 20
ROOMS: 7 en suite 1 family room s£40 d£40

BAMFORD   YORKSHIRE BRIDGE INN ★★

Ashopton Rd S33 0AZ
☎ 01433 651361 📄 01433 651361
e-mail: mr@ybridge.force9.co.uk
Dir: *A57 from M1, L onto A6013, pub 1m on R.* **Map Ref:** *SK28*

The inn dates from 1826 and takes its name from an old packhorse bridge on the Derwent River. It's also close to Ladybower Reservoir, scene of the Dambusters' rehearsals before their raid. In winter the bars provide a cosy sanctuary, while in summer you can sit in the courtyard or beer garden. Food is available in the bar and dining room from a comprehensive menu.

OPEN: 11-11 **BAR MEALS:** L served all week 12-2 D served all week 6-9 Av main course £7.25
RESTAURANT: L served all week 12-2 D served all week 6-9.30 **BREWERY/COMPANY:** Free House 🍺: Blacksheep, Old Peculier, Stones Bitter, Worthington Creamflow.
CHILDREN'S FACILITIES: menu, high-chairs, food/bottle warming, baby changing, outdoor play area **GARDEN:** Walled courtyard, numerous seating areas **NOTES:** Dogs allowed, Parking 40 **ROOMS:** 14 en suite 3 family rooms s£47 d£64

DOE LEA HARDWICK INN

Hardwick Park S44 5QJ
☎ 01246 850245 ▤ 01246 856365
e-mail: Batty@hardwickinn.co.uk
*Dir: M1 J29 take A6175. 0.5m L (signed
Stainsby/Hardwick Hall). After Stainsby, 2m L at
staggered junction. Follow brown Tourist Board
signs.* **Map Ref:** *SK46*

Built in 1607 from locally quarried sandstone by the
south gate of Hardwick Hall, the pub has been in the
same family since 1928. All meals are freshly prepared,
with a menu offering a choice of steaks, roasts and
freshly delivered fish.

OPEN: 11.30-11 **BAR MEALS:** L served all week
11.30-9.30 D served all week Mon 11.30-9 Av main
course £6.50 **RESTAURANT:** L served Tues- Sun 12-2
D served Tues-Sat 7-9 Sun 12-2 Av 3 course à la carte
£16.50 **BREWERY/COMPANY:** Free House 🍺: Scottish
Courage Theakston Old Peculier & XB, Greene King Old
Speckled Hen & Ruddles County, Marston's Pedigree.
CHILDREN'S FACILITIES: menu, portions, high-chairs,
food/bottle warming, outdoor play area, family room
GARDEN: pond & picnic table, extensive lawns
NOTES: No dogs (ex guide dogs)

FOOLOW THE BULLS HEAD INN

S32 5QR
☎ 01433 630873 ▤ 01433 631738
e-mail: wilbnd@aol.com
Dir: Just off A623, N of Stoney Middleton.
Map Ref: *SK17*

Family-owned inn set in a conservation village in the
heart of the Peak District National Park. It has flagstone
floors, roaring fires and an inglenook fireplace in the
oak-panelled dining room, and is a welcoming venue
for walkers and their dogs. Dishes like minted lamb
casserole, and battered cod and chips from the regular
menu are supplemented by specials such as roast sea
bass with fennel, and wild boar steak with orange
game sauce.

OPEN: 12-3 6.30-11 **BAR MEALS:** L served Tue-Sun 12-2
D served Tue-Sat 6.30-9 **RESTAURANT:** L served Tue-Sun
12-2 D served Tue-Sat 6.30-9 (Sunday 12-2, 5-8)
Av 3 course à la carte £18 **BREWERY/COMPANY:** Free
House 🍺: Black Sheep Best, Marston's Pedigree, Tetley Bitter,
Fuller's London Pride. **CHILDREN'S FACILITIES:** menu,
high-chairs, food/bottle warming **NOTES:** Dogs allowed:
Water, Parking 20

GREAT HUCKLOW THE QUEEN ANNE ◆◆◆ ♓

Great Hucklow, nr Tideswell SK17 8RF
☎ 01298 871246
e-mail: mal@thequeen.net
*Dir: A623 turn off at Anchor pub toward
Bradwell, 2nd R to Great Hucklow.*
Map Ref: *SK17*

A warm welcome awaits at this traditional
country free house with its log fires, good
food, and an ever-changing range of cask
ales. The inn dates from 1621, and a licence
has been held for 300 years. Comfortable en
suite bedrooms make an ideal base for
exploring the spectacular Peak District
National Park. Bar food ranges from freshly-
made sandwiches to grills, and includes
favourites like steak and ale pie, beef stew
and Yorkshire pudding, and chicken jalfrezi.

OPEN: 12-2.30 6-11 (Sat 11.30-11, Sun 7-10.30)
BAR MEALS: L served Mon-Sun 12-2 D served Mon-Sun
6.30-8.30 **BREWERY/COMPANY:** Free House
🍺: Mansfield Cask Ale, Shaws, Storm Brewery, Kelham Island.
♓: 7 **CHILDREN'S FACILITIES:** portions, games, high-chairs,
food/bottle warming **GARDEN:** Lawn overlooking the hills
NOTES: Dogs allowed: in bar, in garden, in bedrooms,
Parking 30 **ROOMS:** 2 en suite d£55

GRINDLEFORD THE MAYNARD ARMS ★★★

Main Rd S32 2HE
☎ 01433 630321 📠 01433 630445
e-mail: info@maynardarms.co.uk
Dir: *From M1 take A619 into Chesterfield, then onto Baslow. A623 to Calver, R into Grindleford.*
Map Ref: *SK27*

In the heart of the Peak District National Park, this stone-built inn overlooks the Derwent Valley. The interior design is up-to-the-minute, and the menus are equally in tune with modern thinking. This means that in the bar there are likely to be crispy potato skins, chilli beef, and grilled mackerel fillet as starters, to be followed by penne pasta, savoury beef olives, or even an all-day breakfast. In the restaurant one can start with shredded smoked chicken on a herb salad with balsamic dressing; or warm black pudding and Stilton on a crisp salad; then roast pheasant with chasseur sauce; braised lamb shank in a tomato and white wine bean casserole; or poached medallions of escolar with a mushroom, grape and wine cream sauce. There are daily specials too.

OPEN: 11-3 5.30-11 (Sun 12-10.30)
BAR MEALS: L served all week 12-2 D served all week 6-9.30 Av main course £6.95 **RESTAURANT:** L served Sun-Fri 12-2 D served all week 7-9.30 Av 3 course fixed price £22.90 **BREWERY/COMPANY:** Free House 🍺: Interbrew Boddingtons Bitter, Greene King Old Speckled Hen, Marston's Pedigree, Timothy Taylor Landlord. **CHILDREN'S FACILITIES:** portions, licence, high-chairs, food/bottle warming
GARDEN: Well kept gardens **NOTES:** No dogs (ex guide dogs), Parking 60 **ROOMS:** 10 en suite 2 family rooms s£69 d£79

HAYFIELD THE ROYAL HOTEL ♀

Market St SK22 2EP
☎ 01663 741721 📠 01663 742997
e-mail: enquiries@royalhayfield.co.uk
Dir: *Off the A624.* **Map Ref:** *SK08*

A fine-looking, 1755-vintage building in a High Peak village that itself retains much of its old-fashioned charm. The oak-panelled Windsor Bar has log fires when you need them, and serves a constantly changing roster of real ales, bar snacks and selected dishes, while the dining room usually offers sausage and mash, vegetable chow mein, grilled gammon steak, glazed lamb hock, T-bone steak, mixed grill, and wholetail scampi in breadcrumbs. Kinder Scout and the fells look impressive from the hotel patio.

OPEN: 11-11 **BAR MEALS:** L served all week 12-2.15 D served all week 6-9.15 Av main course £7
RESTAURANT: L served all week D served all week Av 3 course à la carte £16 **BREWERY/COMPANY:** Free House 🍺: Hydes, Tetleys, San Miguel. ♀: 8
CHILDREN'S FACILITIES: menu, portions, games, high-chairs, food/bottle warming, baby changing, family room
GARDEN: Patio, seats 80 **NOTES:** No dogs, Parking 70

LONGSHAW FOX HOUSE ♀

S11 7TY
☎ 01433 630374 📠 01433 637102
Dir: *Leave M1 at J29 and follow signs for Chesterfield. Travel towards Baslow & Bakewell. At Baslow roundabout turn right on to A621 towards Sheffield, turn left after 5 miles on to B6054 and head towards Hathersage. The pub is at junction of B6954/A625.* **Map Ref:** *SK27*

A delightfully original 17th-century coaching inn and, at 1,132 feet above sea level, one of the highest pubs in Britain. There was a time when, during particularly hard winters, the tap room would be covered in straw and the sheep given its shelter. The Longshaw dog trials also originated here, after an argument between farmers and shepherds as to who owned the best dog. A simple menu lists sandwiches, starters, Sunday roasts, and mains like chicken and ham pie, ground Scottish beefsteak burger, and lamb - this time in the form of cutlets.

OPEN: 11-11 (Sun 12-10.30) **BAR MEALS:** L served all week 12-5 D served all week 5-10 (Sun 12-9.30) Av main course £7 **RESTAURANT:** L served all week 12-5 D served all week 5-10 (Sun 12-9.30) **BREWERY/COMPANY:** Vintage Inns 🍺: Bass, Stones, Blacksheep, John Smiths. ♀: 16
CHILDREN'S FACILITIES: portions, licence, high-chairs, food/bottle warming, baby changing **GARDEN:** Patio area
NOTES: No dogs (ex guide dogs), Parking 80

ROWSLEY THE GROUSE & CLARET ♀

Station Rd DE4 2EB
☎ 01629 733233 ▤ 01629 735194
Dir: *On A6 between Matlock & Bakewell.*
Map Ref: *SK26*

This pub is handy for touring the Peak District and the several historic towns close by, and Haddon Hall and Chatsworth House are only a few minutes' drive away. The name of the pub is taken from a kind of fishing fly, and is very popular with local fly fishermen. Appetising menu features such perennial favourites as liver and sausage sizzler, Thai prawns, various pies and traditional Sunday roast.

OPEN: 11-11 (Sun 12-10.30) **BAR MEALS:** L served all week 12-10 D served all week Av main course £7 **RESTAURANT:** L served all week 12-10 D served all week **BREWERY/COMPANY:** W'hampton & Dudley ◖: Marston's Pedigree, Mansfield, Bank's Bitter. ♀: 12 **CHILDREN'S FACILITIES:** menu, high-chairs, food/bottle warming, baby changing, outdoor play area **GARDEN:** Food served outside, great views **NOTES:** No dogs, Parking 60

WARDLOW THE BULL'S HEAD AT WARDLOW 🐑 ♀

SK17 8RP
☎ 01298 871431
Map Ref: *SK17*

Located in the heart of the Peak National Park, this pub has stood next to one of the country's oldest drovers' routes for over 300 years. Largely unaltered inside, it is decorated with antique prints, clocks, coach lamps, brass and copperware. Expect lamb shanks with creamy onion sauce; halibut; trout; vegetarian lasagne; and a selection of steaks. To follow, try profiteroles, or Bakewell pudding with cream.

OPEN: 11.30-3 6.30-11 **BAR MEALS:** L served Sat-Sun 11.30-3 D served all week 6.30-9.30 **RESTAURANT:** L served Sat-Sun 11.30-3 D served all week 6.30-9.30 **BREWERY/COMPANY:** Free House ◖: Scottish Courage John Smith's, Carlsberg-Tetley Tetley's Smooth. **CHILDREN'S FACILITIES:** menu, portions, high-chairs, food/bottle warming, outdoor play area, family room **GARDEN:** Grassed area, tables, seating **NOTES:** No dogs (ex guide dogs), Parking 50, No credit cards

AYMESTREY THE RIVERSIDE INN ♀

HR6 9ST
☎ 01568 708440 ▤ 01568 709058
e-mail: theriverside@btinternet.com
Dir: *On A4110 between Hereford & Knighton.*
Map Ref: *SO46*

An attractive half-timbered Welsh longhouse, dating from 1580, set on the banks of the River Lugg in the heart of the Welsh Marches. The interior, with its low beams and log fires, provides a relaxing atmosphere reflecting 400 years of hospitality. Real ales and ciders from local brewers are carefully selected, and good wines match specialities such as home-made steak and kidney pudding in the bar, or roast haunch of local venison on sweet and sour red cabbage in the restaurant.

OPEN: 11-3 6-11 Open All day in summer Closed: Dec 25 **BAR MEALS:** L served all week 12-2 D served all week 7-9 Av main course £7.95 **RESTAURANT:** L served all week 12-2 D served all week 7-9 **BREWERY/COMPANY:** Free House ◖: Wye Valley Seasonal, Wood Seasonal. ♀: 7 **CHILDREN'S FACILITIES:** portions, high-chairs **GARDEN:** Overlooks river, landscaped **NOTES:** Dogs allowed, Parking 40 **ROOMS:** 5 en suite 3 family rooms s£40 d£65 (♦♦♦♦)

BODENHAM ENGLAND'S GATE INN

HR1 3HU
☎ 01568 797286 🖺 01568 797768
Map Ref: SO55

A pretty black and white coaching inn dating from around 1540, with atmospheric beamed bars and blazing log fires in winter. A picturesque garden attracts a good summer following, and so does the food. The menu features such dishes as pan fried lamb steak with apricot and onion marmalade, roasted breast of duck with parsnip mash and spinach and wild rice cakes with peppers on a chilli and tomato salsa.

OPEN: 11-11 (Sunday 12-10.30) **BAR MEALS:** L served all week 12-2.30 D served all week 6-9.30 Av main course £9.95 **RESTAURANT:** L served all week 12-2.30 D served all week 6-10 (Sun 12-3, 6-9) Av 3 course à la carte £15 **BREWERY/COMPANY:** Free House 🍺: Marston's Pedigree, Wye Valley Bitter & Butty Bach. **CHILDREN'S FACILITIES:** menu, portions, high-chairs, food/bottle warming **GARDEN:** Large sunken garden with large patio area **NOTES:** Dogs allowed: Water, Parking 100

CANON PYON THE NAGS HEAD INN ◆◆◆ 🐑

HR4 8NY
☎ 01432 830252
Dir: Telephone for directions. **Map Ref:** SO44

Four hundred years old, with flagstone floors, open fires and exposed beams to prove it. A comprehensive menu might entice you into starting with smoked salmon wrapped around asparagus spears, then to try chicken breast with apricots in creamy white wine sauce, beef Stroganoff, or monkfish tail fillets in a port, mushroom and bacon sauce. Vegetarian options include stuffed peppers and tagliatelle. Curry nights and Sunday carvery. The large garden features a children's adventure playground.

OPEN: 11-2.30 6-11 **BAR MEALS:** L served Tue-Sun 12-2.30 D served all week 6.30-9.30 (Sun 12-9) **RESTAURANT:** L served Tue-Sun 12-2.30 D served all week 6.30-9.30 Sun 12-9 **BREWERY/COMPANY:** Free House 🍺: Fuller's London Pride, Boddingtons. **CHILDREN'S FACILITIES:** menu, portions, high-chairs, food/bottle warming, outdoor play area, Adventure playground. Safe and secure **GARDEN:** Beer garden, patio, table seating for 60 **NOTES:** in bar, in garden, in bedrooms, No dogs (ex guide dogs), Parking 50 **ROOMS:** 6 en suite 1 family room s£35 d£45

DORMINGTON YEW TREE INN 🐑

Len Gee's Restaurant, Priors Frome HR1 4EH
☎ 01432 850467 🖺 01432 850467
e-mail: len@lengees.info
Dir: A438 Hereford to Ledbury, turn at Dormington towards Mordiford, 0.5m on L. **Map Ref:** SO54

This former hop pickers' pub has panoramic views over Hereford towards the Black Mountains of Wales. The menu features classic European dishes, as well as a splendid carvery, with four joints of meat and a wide selection of vegetables. Try the tempting fish specials, including baked red snapper with lime butter and chargrilled shark with chilli oil and peppers.

OPEN: 12-2 7-11 (Closed Tue Jan-Mar) **BAR MEALS:** L served all week 12-2 D served all week 7-9 Av main course £8.95 **RESTAURANT:** L served all week 12-2 D served all week 7-9 Av 3 course à la carte £18 Av 3 course fixed price £14.95 **BREWERY/COMPANY:** Free House 🍺: Carlsberg-Tetley Tetley, Wye Valley, Greene King Old Speckled Hen. **CHILDREN'S FACILITIES:** menu, portions, high-chairs, food/bottle warming **GARDEN:** Terraced with views of Black Mountains **NOTES:** Dogs allowed, Waterbowls, Parking 40

DORSTONE THE PANDY INN ⍦

HR3 6AN
☎ 01981 550273 ▤ 01981 550277
Dir: *Off B4348 W of Hereford.* **Map Ref:** *SO34*

Oliver Cromwell was a frequent visitor to the Pandy, the oldest inn in Herefordshire, built in 1185 to house workers building Dorstone Church. Alongside the usual pub favourites, the South African owners offer traditional dishes from back home (bobotie and bredie) along with duck stirfry, courgette bake with goats' cheese, pork fillet with apricots, and lamb's liver with mash and onions, plus various hot and cold desserts.

OPEN: 12-3 6-11 (Mon 6-11 only, Sat 12-11, Sun 12-10.30) **BAR MEALS:** L served Tue-Sun 12-2.30 D served all week 7-9.30 Av main course £9.50
RESTAURANT: L served Tue-Sun 12-2.30 D served all week 7-9.30 **BREWERY/COMPANY:** Free House ◀: Wye Valley Butty Bach & Dorothy Goodbody. ⍦: 15
CHILDREN'S FACILITIES: menu, portions, licence, games, food/bottle warming, baby changing, outdoor play area, swings **GARDEN:** Large garden, lots of benches and tables
NOTES: Dogs allowed: in garden, Parking 50

HAMPTON BISHOP THE BUNCH OF CARROTS ⍦

HR1 4JR
☎ 01432 870237 ▤ 01432 870237
e-mail: bunchofcarrotts@buccaneer.co.uk
Dir: *From Hereford take A4103, A438, then B4224.* **Map Ref:** *SO53*

Friendly pub with real fires, old beams and flagstones. Its name comes from a rock formation in the River Wye which runs alongside the pub. There is an extensive menu plus a daily specials board, a carvery, salad buffet and simple bar snacks. Readers reports welcome.

OPEN: 11-3 6-11 **BAR MEALS:** L served all week 12-2.30 D served all week 6-10 (Sun 9pm) **RESTAURANT:** L served all week 12-2 D served all week 6-10
BREWERY/COMPANY: Free House ◀: Bass, Hook Norton, Directors, Theakstons. ⍦: 11
CHILDREN'S FACILITIES: menu, high-chairs, outdoor play area **NOTES:** Dogs allowed, Parking 100

HEREFORD THE CROWN & ANCHOR ⍦

Cotts Ln, Lugwardine HR1 4AB
☎ 01432 851303 ▤ 01432 851637
e-mail: c_a@oz.co.uk
Dir: *2 miles from Hereford city centre on A438, turn left into Lugwardine down Cotts Lane.*
Map Ref: *SO53*

Old Herefordshire-style black-and-white pub with quarry tile floors and a large log fire, just up from the bridge over the River Lugg. Among the many interesting specials you might find fillets of Torbay sole with mussels and white wine, mushrooms in filo pastry with wild mushroom and marsala sauce, seafood tagliolini, supreme of chicken stuffed with wild mushrooms and chestnuts with cranberry and white wine sauce, or Brother Geoffrey's pork sausages with juniper and red wine sauce and mash. A long lunchtime sandwich list is available.

OPEN: 12-11 Closed: 25 Dec **BAR MEALS:** L served all week 12-2 D served all week 7-10 Av main course £9
BREWERY/COMPANY: Enterprise Inns ◀: Worthington Bitter, Theakstons XB, Timothy Taylors Landlord, Marstons Pedigree. ⍦: 8 **CHILDREN'S FACILITIES:** menu
GARDEN: Patio area with tables and lots of plants
NOTES: No dogs (ex guide dogs), Parking 30

KINGTON THE STAGG INN & RESTAURANT ⊛⊛ ♉

Titley HR5 3RL
☎ 01544 230221 📠 231390
e-mail: reservations@thestagg.co.uk
Dir: *Between Kington & Presteigne on the B4355.* **Map Ref:** *SO25*

Situated at the meeting point of two drovers'

roads (the Mortimer Trail and Offa's Dyke), the pub was originally named The Balance. Fireplaces with real fires, a bread oven, and antique furniture all add to the atmosphere. Food is served in the homely bar with its wood burner and jug collection, or in the separate informal dining room. Seasonal cartes may start with red mullet with fennel and sauce vièrge and continue with rack of Marches lamb

OPEN: 12-3 6.30-11 (Sun 12-3) Closed: 1st 2wks Nov & 1wk Feb **BAR MEALS:** L served Tue-Sun 12-2 D served Tue-Sat 6.30-10 Av main course £7.90 **RESTAURANT:** L served Tue-Sat 12-2 D served Tue-Sat 6.30-10 Av 3 course à la carte £23 **BREWERY/COMPANY:** Free House
🍺: Hobsons Town Crier, Old Henry, and Best Bitter, Bass.
♉: 10 **CHILDREN'S FACILITIES:** games, high-chairs, food/bottle warming **GARDEN:** Food served outside
NOTES: Dogs allowed, Parking 20

LEDBURY THE FEATHERS HOTEL ★★★ ⊛ 🐑 ♉

High St HR8 1DS
☎ 01531 635266 📠 01531 638955
e-mail: mary@feathers-ledbury.co.uk
Dir: *S from Worcester A449, E from Hereford A438, N from Gloucester A417.* **Map Ref:** *SO73*

The Feathers is a distinctive building on Ledbury High Street with striking black and white timbered frontage. The fine old inn retains it oak beams, panelled walls and open log fires. Try fresh grilled Cornish plaice with cider carrots and crispy pancetta. Locally sourced meats are a feature, appearing in dishes such as medallions of local pork tenderloin.

OPEN: 11-11 (Sun 12-10.30) **BAR MEALS:** L served all week 12-2 D served all week 7-9.30 Av main course £14
RESTAURANT: L served all week 12-2 D served all week 7-9.30 Av 3 course à la carte £25 **BREWERY/COMPANY:** Free House 🍺: Coors Worthington's Bitter, Interbrew Bass, Fuller's London Pride, Old Speckled Hen. ♉: 18
CHILDREN'S FACILITIES: games, high-chairs, family room **GARDEN:** Courtyard garden, fountain, gazebo **NOTES:** No dogs (ex guide dogs), Parking 30 **ROOMS:** 19 en suite 3 family rooms s£79.50 d£99.50

THE VERZON ★★ ⊛ ♉

Trumpet HR8 2PZ
☎ 01531 670381 📠 01531 670830
e-mail: info@theverzon.co.uk
Dir: *Situated 2.5 miles west of Ledbury on the A438 towards Hereford.* **Map Ref:** *SO73*

In February 2004 new owners took over the running of this impressive former Georgian farmhouse. Hops, apple orchards and cattle - the farming hallmarks of Herefordshire - provide the theme in the Hop Bar. Beer-battered Cornish cod, flat-cap mushroom rigatoni with Parmesan, and toasted bagel with smoked salmon and scrambled egg give a good idea of what's offered. The Vintage Sports Car Club meets here on the last Thursday of every month, and the terrace has wonderful views of the Malvern Hills.

OPEN: 8-11 Closed: 26 Dec **BAR MEALS:** L served all week 12-2 D served all week 7-9 Av main course £12
RESTAURANT: L served all week 12-2 D served all week 7-9 Av 3 course à la carte £27 🍺: Hook Norton Best Bitter, Tetley Best, Spitfire Kentish Ale. ♉: 7
CHILDREN'S FACILITIES: menu, portions, licence, high-chairs, food/bottle warming **GARDEN:** Large terrace and lawn, views of Malvern Hill **NOTES:** Parking 100
ROOMS: 8 en suite 1 family room s£45 d£88

MADLEY THE COMET INN

Stoney St HR2 9NJ
☎ 01981 250600
e-mail: thecometinn@yahoo.co.uk
Dir: *approx 6m from Hereford on the B4352.*
Map Ref: *SO43*

Located on a prominent corner position and set in two and a half acres, this black and white 19th-century inn was originally three cottages, and retains many original features and a roaring open fire. A simple, hearty menu includes steak and ale pie, shank of lamb, grilled gammon, chicken curry, cod in crispy batter, mushroom stroganoff, and a variety of steaks, baguettes, and jacket potatoes.

OPEN: 12-2 7-11 (Open all day Fri-Sun & BHs) Mon Lunch **BAR MEALS:** L served all week 12-2 D served Mon-Sun 7-9 Av main course £7 **RESTAURANT:** L served all week 12-2 D served Mon-Sat 7-9 **BREWERY/COMPANY:** Free House ◖: Hook Norton Best Bitter, Wye Valley Bitter, Tetley Smooth Flow. **CHILDREN'S FACILITIES:** menu, portions, high-chairs, food/bottle warming, outdoor play area **GARDEN:** Large garden with shrubs **NOTES:** No dogs (ex guide dogs), Parking 40

MICHAELCHURCH ESCLEY THE BRIDGE INN ♀

HR2 0JW
☎ 01981 510646 ▤ 01981 510646
e-mail: embengiss@yahoo.co.uk
Dir: *from Hereford take A465 towards Abergavenny, then B4348 towards Peterchurch. Turn L at Vowchurch for village.* **Map Ref:** *SO33*

By Escley Brook, at the foot of the Black Mountains and close to Offa's Dyke, there are 14th-century parts to this oak-beamed family pub: the dining room overlooks the garden, abundant with rose and begonias, and the river - an ideal area for walkers and nature lovers. Speciality dishes include steak and kidney with crispy dumplings.

OPEN: 12-2.30 6-11 (Sun 12-10.30) Closed: 25 Dec **BAR MEALS:** L served Tue-Sun 12-2 D served all week 7-9.15 **RESTAURANT:** L served Tue-Sun 12-2 D served all week 7-9.30 **BREWERY/COMPANY:** Free House ◖: Wye Valley Beers, Interbrew Flowers, Adnams. ♀: 12 **CHILDREN'S FACILITIES:** menu, portions, food/bottle warming, outdoor play area, fenced, rope swing **GARDEN:** Large riverside patio, fenced garden, heaters **NOTES:** Dogs allowed: in bar, in garden, water, Parking 25

MUCH MARCLE THE SLIP TAVERN ♀

Watery Ln HR8 2NG
☎ 01531 660246
Dir: *Follow signs off A449 at Much Marcle junction.* **Map Ref:** *SO63*

Curiously named after a 1575 landslip which buried the local church, this country pub is delightfully surrounded by cider apple orchards. An attractive conservatory overlooking the award-winning garden, where summer dining is popular, and there's also a cosy bar.

OPEN: 11.30-2.30 6.30-11 (Sun 12-3, 7-10.30) **BAR MEALS:** L served all week 11.30-2.30 D served all week 6.30-9.00 Av main course £8.50 **RESTAURANT:** L served all week 11.30-2 D served all week 6.30-9.30 Av 3 course à la carte £17.50 **BREWERY/COMPANY:** Free House ◖: John Smiths, Hook Norton, Tetleys Smooth Flow, Ausells. ♀: 8 **CHILDREN'S FACILITIES:** menu, outdoor play area, climbing frame, swings **GARDEN:** Large terrace seating 50, lawns/flowerbeds **NOTES:** No dogs, Parking 45

ORLETON THE BOOT INN

SY8 4HN
☎ 01568 780228 ▯ 01568 780228
e-mail: thebootorleton@hotmail.com
Dir: Follow the A49 S from London (approx 7 miles) to the B4362 (Woofferton), 1.5 miles off B4362 turn L. The Boot Inn is in the centre of the village. **Map Ref:** *SO46*

This 16th-century black and white timbered inn has a peaceful atmosphere undisturbed by music or games. In winter a blazing fire in the inglenook warms the bar, where an appetising selection of snacks and sandwiches extends the menu along with a list of specials: fish mixed grill, rack of lamb, local game in season, and cheese and lentil loaf.

OPEN: 12-3 6-11 (Sun 12-3, 6-10.30)
BAR MEALS: L served Tue-Sun 12-2 D served all week 7-9 Av main course £5 **RESTAURANT:** D served all week 7-9 Av 3 course à la carte £13 **BREWERY/COMPANY:** Free House ◖: Hobsons Best, Local Real Ales.
CHILDREN'S FACILITIES: menu, portions, licence, games, high-chairs, food/bottle warming, outdoor play area
GARDEN: Lawn, BBQ area **NOTES:** Dogs allowed: Water, Parking 20

PEMBRIDGE THE CIDER HOUSE RESTAURANT

Dunkerton's Cider Mill, Luntley HR6 9ED
☎ 01544 388161 ▯ 01544 388654
Dir: W on A44 from Leominster, L in Pembridge centre by New Inn, 1m on L.
Map Ref: *SO35*

A converted, half-timbered 16th-century barn with natural oak beams, and beautiful views over rolling countryside. Susie and Ivor Dunkerton started the restaurant after years of cider-making on the farm, and are dedicated to fresh local produce and home cooking. Expect carrot and apple soup with sesame bread; leek and almond tartlet with sorrel sauce; or organic Hereford beef, cider and parsley pie with red onion relish. Breads, cakes and desserts all made on the premises.

OPEN: 10-5 Please telephone first Closed: 1 Oct - Easter
BAR MEALS: L served Wed-Sat 12-2.30 Av main course £10 **RESTAURANT:** L served Mon-Sat 12-2.30 None Av 3 course à la carte £18.50 **BREWERY/COMPANY:** Free House ◖: Caledonian Golden Promise.
CHILDREN'S FACILITIES: portions, high-chairs, food/bottle warming **GARDEN:** Terrace overlooking fields
NOTES: No dogs (ex guide dogs), Parking 30

NEW INN 🐑

Market Square HR6 9DZ
☎ 01544 388427 ▯ 01544 388427
Dir: From M5 J7 take A44 W through Leominster towards Llandrindod Wells.
Map Ref: *SO35*

A black and white timbered inn at the centre of a picture-postcard village full of quaint cottages. It dates from the early 14th century, and is one of the oldest pubs in England, once used as the local courthouse and reputedly haunted. Full of old beams, wonky walls and worn flagstones. The menu lists home-cooked dishes such as creamed kidneys on toast, duck breast in port and cranberry sauce, port cider casserole with sage dumplings, fish and chips, seafood stew, and T-bone steak in Stilton sauce.

OPEN: 11-2.30 6-11 (3 pm in Summer)
BAR MEALS: L served all week 12-2 D served all week 7-9.30 **RESTAURANT:** 12-2 7-9.30
BREWERY/COMPANY: Free House ◖: Fuller's London Pride, Kingdom Bitter, Wood Shropshire Lad, Black Sheep Best. **CHILDREN'S FACILITIES:** portions, high-chairs, food/bottle warming, family room **GARDEN:** Patio, seating under the Market Sq **NOTES:** No dogs (ex guide dogs), Parking 25

ROSS-ON-WYE THE MOODY COW

Upton Bishop HR9 7TT
☎ 01989 780470
Map Ref: SO52

An old stone-built inn with an L-shaped configuration and a patio area out front offering plenty of shady seating in summer.

Beyond the rustic bar are two further rooms; the Fresco is set up for informal eating at wooden tables with raffia woven chairs and displays of cow-themed pieces. The Snug is the place to relax on comfy sofas by the wood-burning fire. The restaurant forms the other leg of the 'L', a converted barn with blue glazing, exposed beams and carpeted floors. One extensive menu serves all, supplemented by daily blackboard specials.

OPEN: 12-2.30 6.30-11 (Sun 12-3) **BAR MEALS:** L served Tues-Sun 12-2 D served Tues-Sat 6.30-9.30 Av main course £10.95 **RESTAURANT:** L served Tues-Sun 12-2 D served Tues-Sat 6.30-9.30 Av 3 course à la carte £18.95 **BREWERY/COMPANY:** Free House 🍺: Cats Whiskers, Hook Norton Best, Wye Valley Best. ♟: 7 **CHILDREN'S FACILITIES:** menu, portions, games, high-chairs, food/bottle warming **GARDEN:** Patio area with iron table, chairs, parasols **NOTES:** Dogs allowed: in bar, water provided, Parking 40

SELLACK THE LOUGH POOL INN

HR9 6LX
☎ 01989 730236 📠 01989 730462
Dir: A49 from Ross-on-Wye toward Hereford, side rd signed Sellack/Hoarwithy, pub 3m from R-on-W. *Map Ref:* SO52

A typical Herefordshire black and white, half-timbered pub dating from the late 1500s. A lawned garden with pond and waterfowl among weeping willows are just across a quiet country lane. The restaurant at the rear has wooden tables, smart place settings, a large fireplace and well-trained staff. The daily carte is honest, rustic, and eminently satisfying.

OPEN: 11.30-2.30 6.30-11 (Sun 12-2 7-10.30) Closed: 25 Dec, 26 Dec (eve) **BAR MEALS:** L served all week 12-2 D served all week 7-9.15 Av main course £12.50 **RESTAURANT:** L served all week 12-2 D served all week 7-9.15 Av 3 course à la carte £23 **BREWERY/COMPANY:** Free House 🍺: Wye Valley, Scottish Courage John Smiths, Greene King Ruddles Country & Old Speckled Hen. ♟: 10 **CHILDREN'S FACILITIES:** menu, portions, high-chairs, food/bottle warming, family room **GARDEN:** Lawn outside pub **NOTES:** Dogs allowed: in bar, in garden, water, Parking 40

SYMONDS YAT (EAST) THE SARACENS HEAD INN ◆◆◆◆

HR9 6JL
☎ 01600 890435 📠 01600 890034
e-mail: email@saracensheadinn.co.uk
Map Ref: SO51

Riverside inn on the east bank of the glorious Wye, situated by the ancient hand ferry which

has been in use for 250 years. Handy for exploring the Wye Valley and Forest of Dean. Wide range of home-made bar food and restaurant dishes includes chargrilled chicken breast with port and Stilton sauce, grilled whole seabass, Highland fillet filled with haggis, poached greenlip mussels, Herefordshire beef in ale pie, monkfish kebab, and prawn and black bean stir-fry.

OPEN: 11-11 **BAR MEALS:** L served all week 12-2.30 D served all week 7-9.15 Av main course £8 **RESTAURANT:** D served all week 7-9.15 **BREWERY/COMPANY:** Free House 🍺: Scottish Courage Theakstons Best & Old Peculier, Old Speckled Hen, Wye Valley Hereford Pale Ale, Marston's Pedigree. ♟: 7 **CHILDREN'S FACILITIES:** menu **GARDEN:** 2 riverside terraces **NOTES:** Dogs allowed: in bar, in garden, Parking 38 **ROOMS:** 11 en suite 1 family room s£48 d£69

TILLINGTON THE BELL

HR4 8LE
☎ 01432 760395 📠 01432 760580
e-mail: beltill@aol.com
Map Ref: *SO44*

Popular family-run pub in an area renowned for its apple orchards and fruit farms - a good base for exploring the scenic countryside of the Welsh Borders. Plenty of character features inside, including a new English oak floor in the lounge bar. Good and appetising menu features fresh cod in batter, pork fillet medallions, Mrs Jessop's lamb cutlets, pheasant supreme, and mussels steamed with fresh herbs and Indian spices. Various grills and a choice of 'winter warmer' dishes such as flamed rib-eye steak and beef, and Wye Valley ale and mushroom pie.

OPEN: 11-3 6-11 (All day Sat, til 5 Sun) **BAR MEALS:** L served all week 12-2.15 D served Mon-Sat 6-9.15 Sun 12-2.30 Av main course £7.50 **RESTAURANT:** L served all week 12-2.15 D served Mon-Sat 6-9.15 Av 3 course à la carte £20 🍺: London Pride, Hereford Bitter, other local ales. **CHILDREN'S FACILITIES:** menu, portions, games, high-chairs, food/bottle warming, outdoor play area, tree-house, tunnel, swings, slide **GARDEN:** Small paved area & large lawn with tables **NOTES:** Dogs allowed: in bar, Parking 60

ULLINGSWICK THREE CROWNS INN ◉◉ ♉

HR1 3JQ
☎ 01432 820279 📠 01432 820279
e-mail: info@threecrownsinn.com
Dir: *From Burley Gate rdbt take A465 toward Bromyard, after 2m L to Ullingswick, L after 0.5m, pub 0.5m on R.* **Map Ref:** *SO54*

An unspoilt country pub in deepest rural Herefordshire, where food sources are so local their distance away is referred to in fields, rather than miles. A hand-written sign even offers to buy surplus garden fruit and veg from locals. New parterres in the garden give additional space for growing more varieties of herbs, fruit and vegetables that are not easy, or even possible, to buy commercially. There's even a pea whose provenance can be traced back to some that Lord Carnarvon found in a phial in Tutankhamun's tomb. The menus change daily, but there is always fish, such as line-caught poached monkfish and proscuito with celeriac mousse and haricot blanc. Soufflés often appear too. Meat dishes have included braised belly of Berkshire pork, marinated lamb rumb with kidney kebab, and confit of Gressingham duck.

OPEN: 12-2.30 7-11 (May-Aug 12-3, 6-11) Closed: 2wks from Dec 25 **BAR MEALS:** L served all week 12-3 D served all week 7-10.30 **RESTAURANT:** L served all week 12-2 D served all week 7-9.30 **BREWERY/COMPANY:** Free House 🍺: Hobsons Best, Wye Valley Butty Bach & Dorothy Goodbody's. ♉: 9 **CHILDREN'S FACILITIES:** portions, games, high-chairs, food/bottle warming, baby changing, Mother & Baby changing facility **GARDEN:** Formal garden with patio, heaters **NOTES:** except when food is being served in bar, No dogs (ex guide dogs), Parking 20

WALTERSTONE CARPENTERS ARMS ♉

HR2 0DX
☎ 01873 890353
Dir: *Off the A465 between Hereford & Abergavenny at Pandy.* **Map Ref:** *SO32*

There's plenty of character in this 300-year-old free house located on the edge of the Black Mountains where the owner, Mrs Watkins, was born. Here you'll find beams, antique settles and a leaded range with open fires that burn all winter. Popular options include home-made faggots with mashed potatoes and mushy peas; or cod and prawn pie. A vegetarian selection and home-made desserts are also available.

OPEN: 12-3 7-11 **BAR MEALS:** L served all week 12-3 D served all week 7-9.30 **RESTAURANT:** 12-3 7-9.30 **BREWERY/COMPANY:** Free House 🍺: Wadworth 6X. **CHILDREN'S FACILITIES:** menu, outdoor play area, family room **NOTES:** Dogs by arrangement only, Parking 20, No credit cards

WELLINGTON THE WELLINGTON

HR4 8AT
☎ 01432 830367
e-mail: thewellington@hotmail.com
Dir: *Take Wellington turning between Hereford & Leominster on the A49.* **Map Ref:** *SO44*

A Victorian country pub, with original open fireplaces, antique furniture, and a good selection of real ales and local ciders. A meal from the changing restaurant menu might be locally smoked salmon with beetroot and lime relish; Herefordshire rib-eye steak with Roquefort butter; and treacle tart with clotted cream. Local sausages are a speciality; there is also a bar menu offering an enticing range of lighter meals, and a good value children's section.

OPEN: 12-3 6-11 (Sun 12-3, 7-10.30)
BAR MEALS: L served Tue-Sun 12-2 D served Mon-Sat 7-10 Av main course £11.50 **RESTAURANT:** L served Tue-Sun 12-2 D served Mon-Sat 7-10 Av 3 course à la carte £20 Av 2 course fixed price £6.95 : Hobsons, Wye Valley Butty Bach, Coors Hancocks HB, Guest Real Ales.
CHILDREN'S FACILITIES: menu, portions, games, high-chairs, food/bottle warming, outdoor play area, high chairs
GARDEN: Beer garden, play area, ample seating
NOTES: Dogs allowed: in bar, in garden, Water, Parking 20

WHITNEY-ON-WYE RHYDSPENCE INN ★★

HR3 6EU
☎ 01497 831262 ▤ 01497 831751
e-mail: info@rhydspence-inn.co.uk
Dir: *N side of A438 1m W of Whitney-on-Wye.* **Map Ref:** *SO24*

In the 14th century it was a manorial hall house, but by Tudor times it had become an inn used by Welsh and Irish drovers taking the Black Ox Trail to markets as far away as London. Fillet of Hereford steak, Welsh lamb, peppered venison, and grilled Dover sole are near certainties, along with grills, hot and spicy curry, and vegetarian options. Ask for the interesting explanation of the pub's name.

OPEN: 11-2.30 7-11 Closed: 2 wks in Jan
BAR MEALS: L served all week 11-2 D served all week 7-9.30 Av main course £8.50 **RESTAURANT:** L served all week 11-2 D served all week 7-9.30 Av 3 course à la carte £23 **BREWERY/COMPANY:** Free House ◖: Robinsons Best, Interbrew Bass. **CHILDREN'S FACILITIES:** menu, high-chairs, baby changing, family room **GARDEN:** 2/3 acres, mostly lawn **NOTES:** No dogs (ex guide dogs), Parking 30
ROOMS: 7 en suite s£37.50 d£75

CROXTON KERRIAL PEACOCK INN

1 School Ln NG32 1QR
☎ 01476 870324 ▤ 01476 870171
e-mail: peacockcroxton@globalnet.co.uk
Dir: *Situated on A607, 3m from Junct with A1.* **Map Ref:** *SK82*

300-year-old coaching inn situated on the edge of the Vale of Belvoir with its historic castle only a mile away. Noted for its lovely views and garden, the pub attracts walkers, equestrians and anglers. Everything is prepared on the premises and the menu is noted for its quality fish and chips. Other options may include Aberdeen Angus steak, lasagne and a range of celebrated Sunday roasts. The salad dressing, made from the chef's own recipe, is a particular favourite with customers.

OPEN: 12-3.30 6-11 **BAR MEALS:** L served all week 12-3.30 D served all week 6.30-10 **RESTAURANT:** L served all week 12-3.30 D served all week 6.30-10
BREWERY/COMPANY: Free House ◖: Scottish Courage John Smith's, Timothy Taylor Landlord and guest beers.
CHILDREN'S FACILITIES: portions, licence, high-chairs
GARDEN: 1.5 acres of landscaped garden **NOTES:** Dogs allowed: Water, Parking 40

FLECKNEY THE OLD CROWN ♀

High St LE8 8AJ
☎ 0116 2402223
e-mail: old-crown-inn@fleckney7.freeserve.co.uk
Map Ref: SP69

Close to the Grand Union Canal and Saddington Tunnel, a traditional village pub that is especially welcoming to hiking groups and families. Choose from a variety of platters, grills, baguettes, burgers, jacket potatoes and more. Chef's Specials include lamb in a red wine and plum sauce, poached salmon, lamb and mint pudding, and pork in a mushroom and brandy sauce.

OPEN: 11-11 (Sun 12-10.30) **BAR MEALS:** L served all week 12-2 D served Tue-Sat 5-9 Av main course £8 **RESTAURANT:** L served all week 12-2 D served Tue-Sat 8-9 **BREWERY/COMPANY:** Everards Brewery 🍺: Everards Tiger & Beacon, Scottish Courage Courage Directors, Adnams Bitter, Greene King Abbot Ale. **CHILDREN'S FACILITIES:** menu, portions, games, high-chairs, food/bottle warming, baby changing, outdoor play area, playhouse, family room **GARDEN:** Wonderful views **NOTES:** Dogs allowed, Parking 60, No credit cards

HALLATON THE BEWICKE ARMS ♀

1 Eastgate LE16 8UB
☎ 01858 555217 📠 01858 555598
Dir: S of A47 between Leicester & junction of A47/A6003. **Map Ref:** SP79

On Easter Monday 1770, a local chatelaine was saved from being gored by a raging bull when a hare ran across the bull's path. She arranged for two hare pies and a generous supply of ale be made available to the parish poor each succeeding Easter Monday at the pub. These days a typical menu may include local gammon with home-made chips. The climbing frame and gardens are child friendly, as indeed are the foot-long fish fingers offered on the junior menu.

OPEN: 12-3 6-11 (Open all day Sun, Winter 7-11) Closed: Easter Monday **BAR MEALS:** L served all week 12-2 D served Mon-Sat 7-9.30 (Food on Sun May-Oct) Av main course £8.95 **RESTAURANT:** L served all week 12-2 D served Mon-Sat 7-9.30 Av 3 course à la carte £16.25 **BREWERY/COMPANY:** Free House 🍺: Grain Store Brewery, IPA Flowers, Grainstore Triple B. ♀: 18 **CHILDREN'S FACILITIES:** menu, Play area **GARDEN:** Patio with picnic benches, pond **NOTES:** No dogs (ex guide dogs), Parking 20

KEGWORTH CAP & STOCKING

20 Borough St DE74 2FF
☎ 01509 674814
Dir: Village centre (chemist on LHS. Turn left and left again to Borough St). **Map Ref:** SK42

A traditional, unspoilt country pub with comfortable, old-fashioned rooms and authentic features. Its award-winning garden has a barbecue area and pétanque piste, as well as a children's play area. Appetising food includes soups, rolls (some hot) and burgers for the snack seeker; pizzas and ploughman's for those with a little more appetite; and, for the truly hungry, Hungarian goulash, chicken curry, beef stroganoff, or vegetarian green lentil curry. Thai chicken, and minty lamb appear as specials. Bass is served from the jug.

OPEN: 11.30-2.30 6.30-11 Sun (12-2.30,7-10.30) **BAR MEALS:** L served all week 11.30-1.45 D served all week 6.30-8.45 (Sun 12-1.45, 7-8.45) Av main course £6.25 **BREWERY/COMPANY:** Punch Taverns 🍺: Bass & Greene King IPA. **CHILDREN'S FACILITIES:** portions, food/bottle warming, outdoor play area, enclosed lawn, family room **GARDEN:** Enclosed walled garden, patio, conservatory **NOTES:** Dogs allowed: in bar, in garden, Water, Parking 4, No credit cards

LOUGHBOROUGH THE SWAN IN THE RUSHES ♀

21 The Rushes LE11 5BE
☎ 01509 217014 📄 01509 217014
e-mail: tynemill@tynemill.co.uk
Dir: On A6 (Derby road). **Map Ref:** SK51

A 1930s tile-fronted real ale pub with two drinking rooms, a cosmopolitan atmosphere and no frills. Ten ales always available, including six guests. Two annual beer festivals, acoustic open-mic nights, folk club, and skittle alley. Simple menu lists dishes like Lincolnshire sausages, chilli, Kefalonian meat pie, or vegetables a la creme. Baguettes, jacket potatoes, and ploughman's also available.

OPEN: 11-11 (Sun 12-10.30) **BAR MEALS:** L served all week 12-2.30 D served Mon-Fri 6-8.30 Av main course £5.95 **BREWERY/COMPANY:** Tynemill Ltd
◀: Archers Golden, Carlsberg-Tetley Tetley Bitter, Castle Rock Gold, Guest Ales. ♀: 17
CHILDREN'S FACILITIES: food/bottle warming, children welcome until 8.30pm, family room **NOTES:** Dogs allowed, Water if required, Parking 16

MARKET HARBOROUGH THE QUEENS HEAD INN 🐑 ♀

Main St, Sutton Bassett LE16 8HP
☎ 01858 463530
e-mail: queens.head@freeuk.com
Dir: Heading towards Colby L into Uppingham Road. **Map Ref:** SP78

This community-owned traditional English pub, overlooking the beautiful Welland valley, offers real ales, bar meals, a separate restaurant and an enclosed garden which has been extensively improved by the new owners. More than 30 main courses include a good choice of fish dishes such as red snapper, fresh tuna, haddock and cod. Well-kept real ales are like Timothy Taylor's and Adnams are always available.

OPEN: 12-2.30 5-11 (Sat 12-11.30, Sun 12-10.30)
BAR MEALS: L served all week 12-2.30 D served all week 5-9.30 Av main course £10.75 **RESTAURANT:** L served all week 12-2.30 D served all week 7-11 (All day Sat & Sun) Av 3 course à la carte £17 **BREWERY/COMPANY:** Free House ◀: Adnams, Timothy Taylor Landlord & Greene King IPA. **CHILDREN'S FACILITIES:** menu, portions, high-chairs, food/bottle warming, baby changing **GARDEN:** patio, BBQ, food served outside **NOTES:** No dogs (ex guide dogs), Parking 20

MEDBOURNE THE NEVILL ARMS

12 Waterfall Way LE16 8EE
☎ 01858 565288 📄 01858 565509
e-mail: nevillarms@hotmail.com
Dir: From Northampton take A508 to Market Harborough then B664 for 5m.L for Medbourne. **Map Ref:** SP89

Warm golden stone and mullioned windows make this traditional old coaching inn, in its riverside setting by the village green, truly picturesque. Popular pub garden has its own dovecote and is a great attraction for children who like to feed the ducks. Handy for visiting Rutland Water, Burghley House, Bosworth Field and Stamford. A choice of appetising home-made soups, spicy lamb with apricots, smoked haddock and spinach bake, and pork in apple cream and cider are typical examples

of the varied menu. Easter Monday is the right time to catch the spectacular bottle-kicking contest against nearby Hallaton.

OPEN: 12-2.30 6-11 (Sun 12-3, 7-10.30) Rest: 25 Dec, 31 Dec Closed eve **BAR MEALS:** L served all week 12-2 D served all week 7-9.45 Sun 12-3 & 7-9.30 Av main course £5.95 **BREWERY/COMPANY:** Free House
◀: Fuller's London Pride, Adnams Bitter, Greene King Abbot Ale, Guest Beers. **CHILDREN'S FACILITIES:** menu, portions, games, high-chairs, food/bottle warming, family room **GARDEN:** Chairs/tables available, seating by river **NOTES:** No dogs (ex guide dogs), Parking 30

SOMERBY STILTON CHEESE INN

High St LE14 2QB
☎ 01664 454394
Map Ref: *SK71*

At the heart of a working village in beautiful countryside, this sandstone building dates from the 16th century. The same menus service both bar and restaurant areas, with good selections to be found on the specials boards. Try smoked cod with parsley sauce; trout with a honey and almond glaze; wild boar and apple sausages with cider sauce; or medallions of pork fillet with Marsala and apple sauce. Interesting selection of vegetarian specials and a good range of real ales.

OPEN: 12-3 6-11 **BAR MEALS:** L served all week 12-2 D served all week 6-9 (Sun 7-9) Av main course £6.75 **RESTAURANT:** L served all week 12-2 D served all week 6-9 Av 3 course à la carte £13.50 **BREWERY/COMPANY:** Free House **◀:** Grainstore Ten Fifty, Brewster's Hophead, Belvoir Star, Carlsberg-Tetley Tetley's Cask. **♀:** 10

CHILDREN'S FACILITIES: menu, portions, high-chairs, food/bottle warming, family room **GARDEN:** Small patio, seats around 20 **NOTES:** in garden, No dogs (ex guide dogs), Parking 14

STATHERN RED LION INN

Red Lion St LE14 4HS
☎ 01949 860868 ▤ 01949 861579
e-mail: info@theredlioninn.co.uk
Dir: *From A1 take sign for A52 Nottingham. L off A52 signposted Belvoir Castle, Redmile. Follow road for 2/3 miles. Stathern is on your L.*
Map Ref: *SK73*

The young team at the Red Lion is passionate about traditional pub values, aiming to serve excellent food, beer and wine in a friendly and enjoyable atmosphere. Following a recent refurbishment, you'll discover a traditional stone-floored bar and an informal lounge with a comfy sofa, magazines and newspapers. There's also an informal dining area and an elegant dining room. Produce from the best local suppliers is used to create a daily-changing menu, which might include loin of venison with parsnip mash, red cabbage and elderberry sauce; smoked haddock and Welsh rarebit with bubble and squeak; or peppered goat's cheese with roasted cherry tomatoes.

OPEN: 12-3 6-11 (Sat 12-11, Sun 12-5.30) Closed: 26 Dec, 1 Jan **BAR MEALS:** L served all week 12-2 D served Mon-Sat 7-9.30 Sun 12-3 Av main course £10.95 **RESTAURANT:** L served all week 12-2 D served Mon-Sat 7-9.30 Sun 12-3 Av 3 course à la carte £21 Av 3 course fixed price £11.50 **◀:** Grainstore Olive Oil, Brewster's VPA, Exmoor Gold. London Pride. **♀:** 8 **CHILDREN'S FACILITIES:** menu, portions, games, high-chairs, food/bottle warming, outdoor play area, baby crockery, toys **GARDEN:** Enclosed, decking area, tables, heaters **NOTES:** Dogs allowed: Water, Parking 25

WOODHOUSE EAVES THE PEAR TREE INN

Church Hill LE12 8RT
☎ 01509 890243 ▤ 01509 890243
Dir: *Village centre.* **Map Ref:** *SK51*

Family-run inn at the centre of a lovely village in the beauty spot known as Charnwood Forest. It is noted for freshly-cooked starters and such main dishes as home-made steak and ale pie, wild salmon and pan-fried swordfish. Vegetarian dishes might be mushroom stroganoff or spicy provençale. There are excellent local walks.

OPEN: 12-3 6-11 (Sat 12-11, Sun 12-11.30) **BAR MEALS:** L served all week 12-2 D served Mon-Sun 6-9.30 Av main course £6.95 **RESTAURANT:** L served all week 12-2 D served Mon-Sat 6-9.30 **BREWERY/COMPANY:** Punch Taverns **◀:** Burton Ale, Jennings Cumberland, Flowers, Robinsons Best. **♀:** 10 **CHILDREN'S FACILITIES:** menu, portions, high-chairs, food/bottle warming, family room **GARDEN:** Patio area and lawn **NOTES:** No dogs, Parking 50

THE WHEATSHEAF INN

Brand Hill LE12 8SS
☎ 01509 890320 📠 01509 890891
e-mail: wheatsheaf.woodhouse@virgin.net
Dir: *M1 Jct 22 follow directions for Quorn.*
Map Ref: *SK51*

Around 1790, local quarrymen wanted their own pub, so they built this, with its distinctive archway through to what is now the car park and garden. In addition to daily specials, the appealing quarterly-changing menu has seasonal game and venison, fish and chips, burgers, Woodhouse smokies and fresh fish delivered daily, salads and vegetarian dishes.

OPEN: 12-2.30 6-11 **BAR MEALS:** L served Mon-Sat 12-2 D served Mon-Sat 7-9.30 Av main course £9
RESTAURANT: L served all week 12-2 D served Mon-Sat 7-9.30 (Sun L 12-2.30) Av 3 course à la carte £15
BREWERY/COMPANY: Free House 🍺: Greene King Abbot Ale, Interbrew Bass, Timothy Taylor Landlord, Adnams Broadside. 🍷: 14 **CHILDREN'S FACILITIES:** portions, food/bottle warming, baby changing **GARDEN:** Enclosed patio with seating, picnic tables **NOTES:** Dogs allowed: Water, Parking 70

WYMONDHAM THE BERKELEY ARMS 🍷

59 Main St LE14 2AG
☎ 01572 787587 📠 01572 787587
e-mail: dawnpetherick@handbag.com
Map Ref: *SK81*

Equidistant from Oakham and Melton Mowbray in the heart of the countryside, lies this chef-managed country inn. Inside, a bar of exposed stonework and original beams, non-smoking dining-room and a garden that is popular with families and walkers. Typically, bar lunches might include garlic chicken and chorizo sausage with roast tomato and basil ciabatta, while dinner might offer seared calves' liver on a truffle spinach with horseradish mash and truffle oil.

OPEN: 12-3 6-11 (Closed Mon & Tue Lunch)
BAR MEALS: L served Thu-Sun 12-2 D served Wed-Sat 6-9 Av main course £8.50 **RESTAURANT:** L served Wed-Sun 12-2 D served Wed-Sat 6-9 Av 3 course fixed price £14
BREWERY/COMPANY: Pubmaster 🍺: Marstons Pedigree, Greene King IPA & Guest Ale. 🍷: 10 **CHILDREN'S FACILITIES:** portions, high-chairs **GARDEN:** Food served outside **NOTES:** Dogs allowed, Parking 40

ALLINGTON THE WELBY ARMS 🐑 🍷

The Green NG32 2EA
☎ 01400 281361 📠 01400 281361
Dir: *From Grantham take either A1 north, or A52 west. Allington is 1.5m.* **Map Ref:** *SK84*

Taking its name from the Welby family who used to own the village, the pub provides a quiet haven for travellers who wish to escape from the nearby A1. With its views across the village green towards Allington Manor, this is quite an oasis - a proper village pub within reach of historic houses and market towns. In order to exploit fresh, seasonal local produce, the menu changes frequently, but typical choices include steak and mushroom pie, rack of lamb, pork schnitzel, vegetable lasagne, and several fish dishes. An excellent range of real ales is available in the comfortable bar, along with 15 malt whiskies.

OPEN: 12-2.30 6-11 (Sun 12-4 6-10.30)
BAR MEALS: L served all week 12-2 Av main course £8.95
RESTAURANT: L served all week 12-2 D served all week 6.30-9.30 **BREWERY/COMPANY:** Free House 🍺: Scottish Courage John Smith's, Interbrew Bass, Timothy Taylor Landlord, Greene King Abbot. 🍷: 8
CHILDREN'S FACILITIES: portions, high-chairs, food/bottle warming **GARDEN:** Terrace with tables and chairs
NOTES: No dogs (ex guide dogs), Parking 35

BOURNE THE WISHING WELL INN

Main St, Dyke PE10 0AF
☎ 01778 422970 ▤ 01778 394508
Dir: *Inn 1.5m from A15, 12m from A1,*
Colsterworth rdbt. **Map Ref:** *TF02*

Village inn dating back 300 years, with old oak beams and two inglenook fireplaces in the bar and restaurant areas. The place is named after the wishing well in the smaller of the two restaurants. Outside is an attractive beer garden and children's play area, plus a paddock where an annual family fun day is held. Favourite dishes are village grills, jumbo cod, steak and ale pie, and minted lamb chops.

OPEN: 11-3 6-11 **BAR MEALS:** L served all week 12-2 D served all week 6.30-9 Av main course £8 **BREWERY/COMPANY:** Free House ◾: Greene King Abbot Ale, Everards Tiger Bitter, 3 Guests. **CHILDREN'S FACILITIES:** menu, portions, licence, games, high-chairs, food/bottle warming, outdoor play area **NOTES:** No dogs, Parking 100

BRIGG THE JOLLY MILLER

Brigg Rd, Wrawby DN20 8RH
☎ 01652 655658 ▤ 01652 657506
Dir: *1.5m E of Brigg on the A18, on L.*
Map Ref: *TA00*

Popular country inn situated a few miles south of the Humber estuary. Pleasant bar and dining area fitted out in traditional pub style. Saturday night entertainment and facilities for christenings, weddings and other functions. Children are particularly welcome, with a swing, slide, roundabout and climbing frame in the garden, as well as a children's menu. Straightforward dishes offer the likes of chilli, curry and Sunday lunches.

OPEN: 3-11 (Thu-Sun 12-11) **BAR MEALS:** L served all week 12 D served all week 8 Av main course £5 **BREWERY/COMPANY:** Free House ◾: Two changing guest ales. **CHILDREN'S FACILITIES:** menu, portions, games, high-chairs, food/bottle warming, baby changing, outdoor play area, swing, slide round about & climbing frame **GARDEN:** outdoor eating, patio **NOTES:** No dogs, Parking 40

COLEBY THE BELL INN ♀

3 Far Ln LN5 0AH
☎ 01522 810240 ▤ 01522 811800
Dir: *8m S of Lincoln on A607. In Coleby village turn right at church.* **Map Ref:** *SK96*

One of the three original buildings that became today's rural Bell Inn actually was a pub, built in 1759. The dining area is also divisible by three - a brasserie, a restaurant, and a terrace room. Main courses include braised shoulder of lamb on Greek-style potatoes; steamed steak and mushroom pudding; and smoked tofu and sweet potato strüdel. A separate fish and seafood menu offers grilled haddock on a sweet potato, goat's cheese and aubergine gâteau.

OPEN: 11.30-3 5.30-11 (Sun 11.30-10.30) Closed: 2-4 Jan **BAR MEALS:** L served all week 12-2.30 D served all week 5.30-9 (Sun 12-8) Av main course £12.50 **RESTAURANT:** L served all week 12-2.30 D served all week 5.30-9.30 Av 3 course à la carte £25 **BREWERY/COMPANY:** Pubmaster ◾: Interbrew Bass, Carlsberg-Tetley Bitter, Batemans XB, Wadworths 6X. ♀: 7 **CHILDREN'S FACILITIES:** menu, portions, high-chairs, food/bottle warming **GARDEN:** Enclosed by fence, decking area, heaters **NOTES:** Dogs allowed: in bar, Parking 40

DONINGTON ON BAIN THE BLACK HORSE ◆◆◆ ♉

Main Rd LN11 9TJ
☎ 01507 343640 📠 01507 343640
e-mail: barrett@blackhorse1125.freeserve.co.uk
Map Ref: *TF28*

Ideal for walkers, this old-fashioned country pub is set in a small village in the heart of the Lincolnshire Wolds on the Viking Way. A large grassed area surrounded by trees is ideal for enjoying a drink or dining al fresco on sunny days. The specials are chalked up on a blackboard and include the likes of Black Horse pasta, fresh Grimsby haddock in beer batter, Viking grill, many varieties of sausage and mash, seafood platter and steaks, as well as a good selection of vegetarian options.

OPEN: 12-2.30 7-11 (Closed Mon Lunch) Rest: 25 Dec Closed eve **BAR MEALS:** L served all week 12-2 D served all week 7-9 Av main course £6.50 **RESTAURANT:** L served Tue-Sun 12-2 D served all week 7-9 Av 3 course à la carte £12.50 **BREWERY/COMPANY:** Free House ◖: John Smiths, Greene King, Tom Woods. **CHILDREN'S FACILITIES:** menu, portions, high-chairs **GARDEN:** Large grassed area surrounded by trees **NOTES:** Dogs allowed: in garden, in bedrooms, Water provided, pre book for bedrooms, Parking 80 **ROOMS:** 8 en suite 2 family rooms s£26 d£44

EWERBY FINCH HATTON ARMS

43 Main St NG34 9PH
☎ 01529 460363 📠 01529 461703
e-mail: bookings@finchhatton.fsnet.co.uk
Dir: *from A17 to Kirkby-la-Thorne, then 2m NE. Also 2m E of A153 between Sleaford & Anwick.*
Map Ref: *TF14*

Originally known as the Angel Inn, this 19th-century pub was given the family name of Lord Winchelsea who bought it in 1875. After a chequered history and a short period of closure, it reopened as a new-style pub/restaurant in the 1980s. The extensive, varied menu offers such dishes as salmon, sweet and sour chicken, steak and kidney pie, and sea bass. Real ales include Major Bitter from the Riverside micro-brewery in Wainfleet All Saints.

OPEN: 11.30-2.30 6.30-11 Closed: 25-26 Dec **BAR MEALS:** L served all week 11.30-2.30 D served all week 6.30-11 **RESTAURANT:** L served all week 11.30-2.30 D served all week 6.30-11 **BREWERY/COMPANY:** Free House ◖: Everards Tiger Best, Dixons Major. **CHILDREN'S FACILITIES:** portions, games, high-chairs, food/bottle warming, baby changing **NOTES:** No dogs (ex guide dogs), Parking 60 **ROOMS:** 8 en suite s£44 d£66 (★★)

FREISTON KINGS HEAD

Church Rd PE22 0NT
☎ 01205 760368
Dir: *from Boston take A52 towards Skegness. 3m turn R at Haltoft End to Freiston.*
Map Ref: *TF34*

Originally two cottages, this village pub is renowned for its prize-winning hanging baskets and colourful window boxes. Inside, you can relax by an open fire and enjoy straightforward wholesome bar food. Home-made pies are a speciality and include steak and kidney, chicken and mushroom, and rabbit. Also look out for Grimsby cod or haddock. The blackboard specials change on a weekly basis. Birdwatchers come from far and near to visit the newly opened RSPB reserve at Freiston Shore.

OPEN: 11-2.30 7-11 (Sun 12-3 7.30-10.30) **BAR MEALS:** L served Tues-Sun 12-2 D served Tues-Sat 7-9 Av main course £7.75 **RESTAURANT:** L served Tue-Sun 12-2 D served Wed-Sat 7-9 Av 3 course à la carte £17 **BREWERY/COMPANY:** Batemans ◖: Batemans XB & Dark Mild, Worthington Cream Flow. **CHILDREN'S FACILITIES:** portions, high-chairs, food/bottle warming **NOTES:** No dogs (ex guide dogs), Parking 30, No credit cards

FROGNALL   THE GOAT ♀

155 Spalding Rd PE6 8SA
☎ 01778 347629
e-mail: goat.frognall@virgin.net
Dir: *A1 to Peterborough, A15 to Market Deeping, old A16 to Spalding, pub about 1.5m from jct of A15 & A16.* **Map Ref:** *TF11*

Welcoming country pub dating from the 17th century, with an open fire, large beer garden and plenty to amuse the kids. Real ale is taken seriously, with four different guest cask ales each week. Also on offer are 25 single malt whiskies, plus mulled wine in winter and sangria in summer. The chef's home-made selection includes pork in sweet and sour sauce, curry of the day, and leek and mushroom crumble.

OPEN: 11-2.30 6-11 (Sun 12-3, 7-10.30) Closed: 25 Dec
BAR MEALS: L served all week 12-2 D served all week 6.30-9.30 **RESTAURANT:** L served all week 12-2 D served all week 6.30-9.30 **BREWERY/COMPANY:** Free House
🍺: 4 Guest Cask Ales change each week. ♀: 14
CHILDREN'S FACILITIES: menu, high-chairs, outdoor play area, action tree, adventure frame, swings, family room
GARDEN: Covered patio, beer garden, seats approx 90
NOTES: No dogs, Parking 50

LINCOLN   WIG & MITRE ✿ ♀

30/32 Steep Hill LN2 1TL
☎ 01522 535190 ▤ 01522 532402
e-mail: email@wigandmitre.com
Dir: *Town centre adjacent to cathedral and Lincoln Castle car park, at the top of Steep Hill.*
Map Ref: *SK97*

Located in the upper part of medieval Lincoln, at the top of Steep Hill, this pub-restaurant offers continuous service from 8am to around midnight every day, all year round. Food choices range from sandwiches to set three course meals, with a wide variety of individual dishes in between. Expect Thai crab cakes with a lemon grass and coriander butter sauce; saddle of venison (served rare) and fish of the day.

OPEN: 8am-midnight **BAR MEALS:** Food served all week 8am-11pm Av main course £13.95 **RESTAURANT:** Food served all week 8am-11pm Av 3 course à la carte £26 Av 3 course fixed price £13.95 **BREWERY/COMPANY:** Free House 🍺: Greene King, Marstons Pedigree & Ruddles Best.
♀: 34 **CHILDREN'S FACILITIES:** portions, games, high-chairs, food/bottle warming **NOTES:** Dogs allowed: in bar

LOUTH   MASONS ARMS 🐑 ♀

Cornmarket LN11 9PY
☎ 01507 609525 ▤ 0870 7066450
e-mail: ron@themasons.co.uk
Map Ref: *TF38*

Situated in the Cornmarket, this former posting inn dates from 1725 and some relics of its past association with the Masons can be found on doors and windows. Today it is under new ownership but still provides a 'downstairs' for informal eating and an 'upstairs' where the à la carte menu features steaks, sautéed duck breast, and fresh Bateman's beer-battered Grimsby haddock. Well-kept real ales complement the mainly traditional fare.

OPEN: 10-11 12-10.30 (Sun 12-10.30)
BAR MEALS: L served all week 12-2 D served Mon-Sat 6-9 Av main course £7.95 **RESTAURANT:** L served Sun 12-2 D served Fri-Sat 7-9.30 Av 3 course à la carte £10
BREWERY/COMPANY: Free House 🍺: Timothy Taylor Landlord, Marston's Pedigree, Samuel Smiths, Batemans XB Bitter. ♀: 9 **CHILDREN'S FACILITIES:** menu, portions, licence, high-chairs, food/bottle warming **NOTES:** No dogs, Parking 7

SKEGNESS THE VINE HOTEL ★★★

Vine Rd, Seacroft PE25 3DB
☎ 01754 763018 & 610611 ▤ 01754 769845
e-mail: info@thevinehotel.com
Map Ref: *TF56*

Ivy-covered Victorian hotel, converted from a farmhouse and bought by Harry Bateman in

1928. Now this charming hostelry offers a fine selection of Bateman ales, silver service in the restaurant and comfortable accommodation, attracting lots of weddings. Once a haunt of poet Alfred Lord Tennyson, who has given his name to The Tennyson Lounge. Specialities include Grimsby fish and chips, and Batemans beef and ale pie.

OPEN: 11-11 (Sun 12-10.30) **BAR MEALS:** L served all week 12.15-2.15 D served all week 6.30-9.15 Sat-Sun all day Av main course £5.95 **RESTAURANT:** L served all week 12.30 D served all week 6.30-9.30 Sun 12-2.30 Av 3 course à la carte £21 **BREWERY/COMPANY:** Batemans
🍺: Batemans XB & XXXB, Mild. **CHILDREN'S FACILITIES:** menu, portions, licence, high-chairs, food/bottle warming **GARDEN:** Secluded **NOTES:** Dogs allowed, Parking 50 **ROOMS:** 24 en suite 3 family rooms s£50 d£80

STAMFORD THE BLUE BELL INN

Shepherds Walk Belmesthorpe PE9 4JG
☎ 01780 763859
Dir: *2 m N of Stamford on the A6121 Bourn Road, turn R for Belmesthorpe and pub is on the L.* **Map Ref:** *TF00*

Now firmly established under its new owners, this charming 17th-century free house with its open fires and ghost stories is said to have played host to Lady Godiva. Greene King, Old Speckled Hen and Summer Lightning are among the choices to wash down an appetising selection of home-made dishes. Expect steak and ale pie; chicken curry with pilau rice and naan bread; mushroom Stroganoff with rice; or wholetail scampi with tartare sauce.

OPEN: 12-2.30 6-11 **BAR MEALS:** L served all week 12-2 D served Mon-Sat 6.30-9.00 Av main course £6.50 **RESTAURANT:** L served all week 12-2 D served Mon-Sat 6.30-9 Av 4 course fixed price £15 **BREWERY/COMPANY:** Free House 🍺: Interbrew Bass, Greene King Old Speckled Hen, Summer Lightning, Abbott. **CHILDREN'S FACILITIES:** menu, portions, licence, high-chairs, food/bottle warming, outdoor play area **GARDEN:** Panoramic views **NOTES:** No dogs (ex guide dogs), Parking 30

THE GEORGE OF STAMFORD ★★★ ◉ 🐑 ♟

71 St Martins PE9 2LB
☎ 01780 750750 ▤ 01780 750701
e-mail: reservations@georgehotelofstamford.com
Dir: *take A1 N from Peterborough. From A1 roundabout signposted B1081 Stamford, down hill to lights. Hotel on L.* **Map Ref:** *TF00*

The George we see today is essentially 16th century, but if the crypt underneath the cocktail bar is anything to go by, its origins are certainly medieval. The famous gallows inn sign straddling the road outside once implied a warm welcome for the bona fide traveller, but to the highwayman it was intended as a warning: leave our customers alone! Informal meals are served in the light and airy Garden Lounge, the York Bar, or outside in the ivy-clad courtyard. In the magnificent antique oak-panelled restaurant, a three-course meal might be chicken liver parfait with orange and redcurrant sauce, medley of grilled seafood and shellfish with jasmine bisque and braised leeks, and a dessert from the trolley.

OPEN: 11-2.30 6-11 (Sat-Sun open all day from 11) **BAR MEALS:** L served all week 7-11 Av main course £8.95 **RESTAURANT:** L served all week 12.30-2.30 D served all week 7.30-10.30 Av 3 course à la carte £33 Av 2 course fixed price £17.50 **BREWERY/COMPANY:** Free House 🍺: Adnams Broadside, Fuller's London Pride, Greene King Ruddles Bitter. ♟: 15 **CHILDREN'S FACILITIES:** portions, high-chairs, food/bottle warming, baby changing, baby sitter by arrangement, cots **GARDEN:** Sunken lawn, 200 year-old Mulberry tree **NOTES:** Dogs allowed: dog pack, towel, blanket, feeding mat, Parking 120 **ROOMS:** 47 en suite 20 family rooms s£78 d£110

Northamptonshire

Lincolnshire continued

WOODHALL SPA VILLAGE LIMITS MOTEL

Stixwould Rd LN10 6UJ
☎ 01526 353312 📠 01526 353312
e-mail: enquiries@villagelimits.com
Dir: *On reaching roundabout on main street of Woodhall Spa follow directions for Petwood Hotel. 500 yrds further on same road.*
Map Ref: TF16

The once-fashionable Woodhall Spa, with its grand hotels, grew up after iodine- and bromide-rich waters were discovered by chance in the 19th century. Traditional pub food in the motel's restaurant and bar includes steaks, grilled gammon, chargrilled chicken, wholetail scampi, grilled rainbow trout, battered and smoked haddock, and salads. Real ales include Tom Wood's Best Bitter from the Highwood brewery, Barnetby. In World War II, the famous Dambusters requisitioned nearby Petwood House for their Officers' Mess.

OPEN: 12-2.30 6-11 **BAR MEALS:** L served all week 12-2 D served all week 6-9 **RESTAURANT:** L served all week 12-2 D served all week 6.30-9 **BREWERY/COMPANY:** Free House 🍺: Bateman XB, Black Sheep Best, Barnsley Bitter, Carlsberg-Tetley Tetley's Smooth Flow. **CHILDREN'S FACILITIES:** menu, portions, food/bottle warming **GARDEN:** Enclosed garden with superb views **NOTES:** No dogs (ex guide dogs), Parking 30 **ROOMS:** 8 en suite 1 family room s£37.50 d£60

ASHBY ST LEDGERS THE OLDE COACH HOUSE INN ♀

CV23 8UN
☎ 01788 890349 📠 01788 891922
e-mail: oldcoachhouse@traditionalfreehouses.com
Dir: *M1 J18 follow signs A361/Daventry. Village on L.* **Map Ref:** SP56

A late 19th-century farmhouse and outbuildings, skilfully converted into a pub with dining areas, accommodation and meeting rooms, set in a village that dates way back to the Domesday Book of 1086. The village was home to Robert Catesby, one of the Gunpowder plotters. Beer is taken seriously here with up to eight regularly changing real ales and legendary beer festivals. The pub also serves fresh, high quality food in comfortable surroundings, featuring game casserole, seafood linguine, massive mixed grills, Australian butterfish, grilled seabass, and summer barbecues.

OPEN: 12-11 (Sun 12-10.30) **BAR MEALS:** L served all week 12-2.30 D served all week 6-9.30 **RESTAURANT:** L served all week 12-2 D served all week 6-9.30 **BREWERY/COMPANY:** Free House 🍺: Everards Original, Everards Tiger, Fuller's London Pride, Hook Norton Best. ♀: 8 **CHILDREN'S FACILITIES:** menu, portions, games, high-chairs, food/bottle warming, baby changing, large wooden adventure playground, family room **GARDEN:** Landscaped garden **NOTES:** No dogs (ex guide dogs), Parking 50 **ROOMS:** 6 en suite 1 family room s£51 d£65 (♦♦♦)

BULWICK THE QUEEN'S HEAD 🐑 ♀

Main St NN17 3DY
☎ 01780 450272
Dir: *Just off the A43 nr Corby, 12m from Peterborough, 2m from Dene Park.*
Map Ref: SP99

Overlooking the village church, this charming country pub dates back to the 17th century. The cosy interior boasts four open fireplaces, wooden beams and flagstone floors in a warren of small rooms. Relax by the fire or on the patio with a pint of quality ale such as Black Sheep, Spitfire or Jennings Sneck Lifter, and some hearty pub food from the bar or à la carte menu. Dishes could include squid with linguini nero; chicken stuffed with Tillegio cheese wrapped in Parma ham; monkfish and scallops on a rosemary skewer; and pan-fried calves' liver served with pancetta mash and red onion marmalade. For a truly traditional pub meal try one of the selection of home-made pies. The new landlord looks likely to continue the good work in this welcoming hostelry.

OPEN: 12-2.30 6-11 **BAR MEALS:** L served Tue-Sun 12-2 D served Tue-Sat 6-9 Av main course £9.95 **RESTAURANT:** L served Tue-Sun 12-2 D served Tue-Sat 6-9 Av 3 course fixed price £20 **BREWERY/COMPANY:** Free House 🍺: Timothy Taylor Landlord, Greene King Old Speckled Hen, Fullers London Pride, Jennings Sneck Lifter. ♀: 9 **CHILDREN'S FACILITIES:** menu, portions, high-chairs, food/bottle warming **GARDEN:** Food served outside. Patio area **NOTES:** Dogs allowed: Water provided, Parking 40

CLIPSTON   THE BULLS HEAD

Harborough Rd LE16 9RT
☎ 01858 525268
Dir: *On B4036 S of Market Harborough.*
Map Ref: *SP78*

American airmen once pushed coins between the beams as a good luck charm before bombing raids, and the trend continues with foreign paper money pinned all over the inn. In addition to its good choice of real ales, the pub has an amazing collection of over 500 whiskies. The menu offered by the new tenants includes shark steaks, whole sea bass, hot toddy duck, and steak pie.

OPEN: 11.30-3 5.30-11 (Open Sat & Sun all day in summer) **BAR MEALS:** L served all week 12-2 D served all week 6.30-9.00 (Sat 6.30-9.30) Av main course £7.95
RESTAURANT: L served all week 11.30-2 D served all week 6.30-9.30 Av 3 course à la carte £17.50
BREWERY/COMPANY: Free House 🍺: Tiger, Becon, Guest Beers & Seasonal. **CHILDREN'S FACILITIES:** menu, portions, licence, high-chairs, food/bottle warming, baby changing
GARDEN: Patio & Lawned Area **NOTES:** Dogs allowed: in bar, in garden, Parking 40

EAST HADDON   RED LION HOTEL

NN6 8BU
☎ 01604 770223 📠 01604 770767
Dir: *7m NW of Northampton on A428, 8m from J18 of M1. Midway between Northampton & Rugby.* *Map Ref:* *SP66*

Near to Althorpe Park, this 17th-century thatched inn boasts a walled side garden filled with lilac, roses and fruit trees. The cosy, traditionally furnished interior has oak panelled settles, cast-iron framed tables and recessed china cabinets. A fresh, innovative menu is available in the elegant dining room, with an emphasis on fish and seafood. Start your meal with seared lime-marinated scallops with a vodka cucumber dressing; wild mushroom and lentil parfait; or teriyaki chicken and duckling terrine with plum chutney. Equally imaginative main courses include tilapia gateau with a mixed fish mousseline; pan-fried loin of sword fish with roasted apple and citrus compote and lemon butter sauce; and seared loin of venison with a dark cherry jus. The bar menu offers hearty choices like trio of sausages on mash with onion gravy or deep fried Brie.

OPEN: 11-2.30 6-11 Closed: Dec 25
BAR MEALS: L served all week 12.15-2 D served Mon-Sat 7-9.30 Av main course £12 **RESTAURANT:** L served all week 12.15-2 D served Mon-Sat 7-9.30 Av 3 course à la carte £27 Av 3 course fixed price £21
BREWERY/COMPANY: Charles Wells 🍺: Wells Eagle IPA, & Bombardier, Adnams Broadside, Red Stripe. ♀: 7
CHILDREN'S FACILITIES: portions, games, high-chairs, food/bottle warming **GARDEN:** Large lawns and well maintained flower beds **NOTES:** No dogs (ex guide dogs), Parking 40

FARTHINGSTONE   THE KINGS ARMS

Main St NN12 8EZ
☎ 01327 361604 📠 01327 361604
e-mail: paul@kingsarms.fsbusiness.co.uk
Dir: *from M1 take A45 W, at Weedon join A5 then R on road signed Farthingstone.*
Map Ref: *SP65*

This cosy 18th-century Grade II listed inn is tucked away in unspoilt countryside near Canons Ashby (NT), adorned with a collection of stone gargoyles. Excellent real ales are served here. The menu is short and consists of things like British cheese platters, sausage and mash, or Yorkshire pudding filled with steak and kidney or beef in Guinness. The landlord also sells cheeses and a variety of speciality regional foods.

OPEN: 12-3 7-11 (Lunchtime wknds only) Rest: Mon-Fri open evenings only **BAR MEALS:** L served Sat-Sun 12-2 Av main course £6.50 **BREWERY/COMPANY:** Free House
🍺: Hook Norton, Timothy Taylor Landlord, Shepherd Neame Spitfire Premium Ale, Jennings Bitter.
CHILDREN'S FACILITIES: portions, games, food/bottle warming, books, puzzles, games available, games room, family room **GARDEN:** Many plants, herb garden, innovative design **NOTES:** Dogs allowed: in bar, in garden, in bedrooms, Water, Parking 20, No credit cards

FOTHERINGHAY   THE FALCON INN 🌹 ♀

PE8 5HZ
☎ 01832 226254 📠 01832 226046
Dir: *N of A605 between Peterborough &*
Oundle. *Map Ref:* *TL09*

The Falcon and chef/patron Ray Smikle are
members of the Huntsbridge Inns group, each

member producing innovative yet affordable food in a
relaxing pub environment. This attractive 18th-century
stone-built inn is set in a garden recently redesigned by
landscape architect Bunny Guinness. Settle in the locals'
tap bar, the smart rear dining room or the conservatory
extension and choose from the blackboard snack
selection or the seasonal carte.

OPEN: 11.30-3 6-11 (Sun 12-3,7-10.30)
BAR MEALS: L served all week 12-2.15 D served all week
7-9.30 Av main course £9.50 **RESTAURANT:** L served all
week 12-2.15 D served all week 6.30-9.30 Av 3 course à la
carte £24 Av 2 course fixed price £11.75
BREWERY/COMPANY: Free House 🍺: Adnams Bitter, Greene
King IPA, Scottish Courage John Smith's, Nethergate. ♀: 15
CHILDREN'S FACILITIES: menu, portions, food/bottle warming,
toys, highchairs **GARDEN:** Good views of Fotheringhay Church
NOTES: No dogs (ex guide dogs), Parking 30

GREAT OXENDON   THE GEORGE INN 🐑 ♀

LE16 8NA
☎ 01858 465205 📠 01858 465205
Dir: *Telephone for directions.* *Map Ref:* *SP78*

A dining pub up on a bank by the side of the
road. Good quality, reasonably priced food
served in the bar includes snacks, light bites
and the more substantial sirloin steak au
poivre, loin of lamb Florentine, and roast fillet
of cod with crispy bacon. Dinner options
include roast fillet of salmon on chive mash,
baked breadcrumbed escalope of chicken
Savoyarde, and pan-fried duck breast.
Vegetarians should ask for a list of what's
available.

OPEN: 11.30-3 6-11 Rest: Sun Closed eve
BAR MEALS: L served all week 12-2.30 D served Mon-Sat
7-10 (Closed Sun pm) Av main course £8.95
RESTAURANT: L served Tues-Sun 12-2.30 D served Mon-Sat
7-10 Av 3 course à la carte £25 Av 3 course fixed price
£14.95 **BREWERY/COMPANY:** Free House 🍺: Interbrew
Bass, Adnams Bitter. ♀: 9
CHILDREN'S FACILITIES: portions, games, high-chairs,
food/bottle warming **GARDEN:** Large formal, large patio for
dining **NOTES:** Dogs allowed: in garden, in bedrooms, Water,
Parking 34

LOWICK   THE SNOOTY FOX 🐑 ♀

NN14 3BH
☎ 01832 733434 📠 01832 733931
e-mail: thesnootyfox@btinternet.com
Dir: *off the A14 5m E of Kettering on A6116.*
Straight over at 1st roundabout and L into
Lowick. *Map Ref:* *SP98*

Exquisite carved beams are among the more
unusual features at this 16th-century building
which has been a pub since 1700. Originally
the manor house, it is supposedly haunted by
a horse and its rider killed at the Battle of
Naseby. The new operators now specialise in
grill and rotisserie cooking, so check out the
rack of Cornish lamb, Gloucester Old Spot
pork belly, sirloin steaks, and others. Fresh
Cornish fish is also a feature, as is a good
wine list.

OPEN: 12-3 6-11 (25-26 Dec & 1 Jan Closed eve)
BAR MEALS: L served all week 12-2 D served all week
6.30-9.30 Av main course £11 **RESTAURANT:** L served all
week 12-2 D served all week 6.30-9.30 Av 3 course à la
carte £25 🍺: Jennings Cumberland, Greene King IPA, Fullers
London Pride, Morland Old Speckled Hen & Morland Original.
♀: 7 **CHILDREN'S FACILITIES:** games, high-chairs,
food/bottle warming, baby changing **GARDEN:** Small lawned
area at front of property **NOTES:** Dogs allowed: Parking 100

MARSTON TRUSSELL THE SUN INN ★★ ⊗ 🐑 ♀

Main St LE16 9TY
☎ 01858 465531 📠 01858 433155
e-mail: manager@suninn.com
Dir: *S of A4304 between Market Harborough &*
Lutterworth. **Map Ref:** *SP68*

Chef/patron Paul Elliott has taken over this late

17th-century dining pub in the heart of the Leicestershire countryside. Here you'll find roaring winter fires, a friendly welcome, well-kept ales and a carefully chosen wine list. In the non-smoking restaurant, expect traditional and exotic cuisine to suit all tastes. In summer, al fresco meals are served on the paved front patio.

OPEN: 12-2 6-11 Closed: Dec 26, Jan 2
BAR MEALS: L served Mon-Sun 12-1.45 D served all week 7-9.30 Sun 12-2 Av main course £16.50
RESTAURANT: L served Mon-Sun 12-1.45 D served all week 7-9.30 Av 3 course à la carte £26.50 Av 3 course fixed price £27.50 **BREWERY/COMPANY:** Free House 🍺: Bass, Hook Norton Best, Marstons Pedigree, Charles wells Bombardier.
♀: 8 **CHILDREN'S FACILITIES:** menu, portions, games, high-chairs, baby changing **GARDEN:** Front patio, seating for 20 **NOTES:** No dogs (ex guide dogs), Parking 60
ROOMS: 20 en suite 2 family rooms s£59 d£69

NORTHAMPTON THE FOX & HOUNDS ♀

Main St, Great Brington NN7 4JA
☎ 01604 770651 📠 01604 770164
e-mail: althorpcoachinn@aol.com
Dir: *Telephone for directions.* **Map Ref:** *SP76*

Located just a mile from Althorp House, ancestral home of the Spencer family, the Fox

and Hounds is a much photographed stone and thatch coaching inn dating from the 16th century. Its many charms include a pretty courtyard and garden, real fires, numerous guest ales and a reputation for quality food. Expect plenty of game in season, Sunday roasts and main courses ranging from Drambuie fillet or stuffed chicken breast. Vegetarian dishes and salad selections also available.

OPEN: 11-11 (Sun 12-10.30) **BAR MEALS:** L served all week 12-2.30 D served all week 6.30-9.30 Av main course £5.85
RESTAURANT: L served all week 12-2.30 D served all week 6.30-9.30 Av 3 course à la carte £19.95 🍺: Green King IPA, Speckled Hen, Fullers London Pride, Abbot Ale. ♀: 8
CHILDREN'S FACILITIES: menu, portions, games, high-chairs, food/bottle warming, books, crayons **GARDEN:** Secluded wall area, lots of trees **NOTES:** Dogs allowed: in bar, in garden, water bowls, toys, dog chews, Parking 50

OUNDLE THE MONTAGU ARMS 🐑

Barnwell PE8 5PH
☎ 01832 273726 📠 01832 275555
e-mail: ianmsimmons@aol.com
Dir: *off A605 opposite Oundle slip Rd, access*
to A605 via A14 or A1. **Map Ref:** *TL08*

Originally three cottages built in 1601 for workmen constructing the nearby manor house, The Montagu Arms is now one of Northamptonshire's oldest inns. Overlooking the brook and village green in the royal village of Barnwell, the inn has a large garden well equipped for children's play. The extensive menu offers fajitas, nachos and chimichangas as well as chargrilled steaks, rack of lamb, and chicken breast in puff pastry shell with Stilton sauce. Good fish dish selection Fridays and Saturdays.

OPEN: 12-3 6-11 (Sat-Sun all day) **BAR MEALS:** L served all week 12-2.30 D served all week 7-10 Av main course £7
RESTAURANT: L served all week 12-2.30 D served all week 7-10 **BREWERY/COMPANY:** Free House 🍺: Adnams Broadside, Southwold Bitter, Interbrew Flowers IPA & Original, Hop Back Summer Lightning.
CHILDREN'S FACILITIES: menu, portions, high-chairs, food/bottle warming, baby changing, outdoor play area, swings, play area **GARDEN:** Large lawn, ample benches
NOTES: No dogs (ex guide dogs), Parking 25

Northamptonshire continued

STOKE BRUERNE   THE BOAT INN

NN12 7SB
☎ 01604 862428 📠 01604 864314
e-mail: info@boatinn.co.uk
Dir: *Just off A508.* **Map Ref:** *SP74*

Traditional thatched canalside inn run by the same family since 1877, located by a working

lock and opposite a popular canal museum. Inside are cosy bars with open fires and flagstones. Dishes range from Cajun red snapper and minted lamb shank to Boat Inn burger and grilled sirloin steak. Good range of jacket potatoes with fillings such as Greenland prawns and chicken tikka mayonnaise.

OPEN: 9-11 (3-6 closed Mon-Thu in winter)
BAR MEALS: L served all week 9.30-9 D served all week
RESTAURANT: L served Tue-Sun 12-2 D served all week 7-9 Sun 12-2. 6.30-8.30 Av 3 course fixed price £16
BREWERY/COMPANY: Free House 🍺: Banks Bitter, Marstons Pedigree, Adnams Southwold, Frog Island Best.
CHILDREN'S FACILITIES: menu, portions, licence, high-chairs, food/bottle warming **GARDEN:** Table and grass area by canal **NOTES:** Dogs allowed: in bar, in garden, water, Parking 50

WADENHOE   THE KING'S HEAD

Church St PE8 5ST
☎ 01832 720024
e-mail: lou@kingzed.co.uk
Map Ref: *TL08*

A peaceful 16th-century stone free house, located beside the River Nene. The pub boasts a partly thatched roof, oak beams, quarry-tiled floors and an inglenook fireplace. The public bar is just the place to enjoy a quiet pint of Adnams, or to sample the selection of malt whiskies and fine wines. Diners will appreciate the relaxed atmosphere of the lounge bar or cottage room, whilst in summer you might be tempted to enjoy al fresco dining against a background of boats drifting past on the river. Bar meals range from soup with farmhouse bread to large filled rolls and jacket potatoes.

In the evening, the cooking shifts up a notch, and typical main dishes include roast Gressingham duck, chicken breast with Stilton and New Zealand green-lipped mussels, and roast trout with Brazil nuts and Pernod jus. Cheesecake, syllabub, and fruit crumble are amongst the home-made puddings.

OPEN: 12-3 All day on wknds during sunny weather 7-11 (Wed-Sat 12-3, 6.30-11, Sun 12-4) **BAR MEALS:** L served all week 12-2 D served Wed-Sat 7-9 (Sun 12-2) Av main course £6.50 **RESTAURANT:** L served all week D served Wed-Sat 7-9 **BREWERY/COMPANY:** Free House 🍺: Adnams, Timothy Taylor Landlord, Oakham JHB, Adnams Broadside. **CHILDREN'S FACILITIES:** portions, games, high-chairs, food/bottle warming, baby changing **GARDEN:** Large paddock, children must be supervised, courtyard, patio, seating **NOTES:** Dogs allowed: in bar, in garden, water, Parking 20

CAUNTON   CAUNTON BECK ♀

NG23 6AB
☎ 01636 636793 📠 01636 636828
e-mail: cautonbeck@aol.com
Dir: *5m NW of Newark on A616.*
Map Ref: *SK76*

This pub-restaurant is no ordinary establishment—it opens for breakfast at 8am and offers a continuous service right through until midnight. It's a 16th-century cottage, set amid herb gardens and a dazzling rose arbour. Greene King, Ruddles and John Smith's beers complement the extensive international wine list and regularly changing blackboard menus.

OPEN: 8am-midnight **BAR MEALS:** L served all week 8am-11pm D served all week 8am-11pm Av main course £13.50 **RESTAURANT:** L served all week 8am-11pm D served all week 8am-11pm Av 3 course à la carte £24 Av 3 course fixed price £13.95 **BREWERY/COMPANY:** Free House 🍺: Greene King Ruddles Best, Scottish Courage John Smith's, Springhead Best Bitter. ♀: 22
CHILDREN'S FACILITIES: portions, licence, games, high-chairs, food/bottle warming **GARDEN:** Terrace & lawns **NOTES:** Dogs allowed: in bar, in garden, Parking 30

COLSTON BASSETT   THE MARTINS ARMS INN

School Ln NG12 3FD
☎ 01949 81361 ▯ 01949 81039
Dir: *From M1 J22 take A50 then A46 N towards Newark. Colston Bassett is E of Cotgrave OR J21A M1 then A46 to Newark.*
Map Ref: *SK73*

If you think you've seen this classic 18th-century inn somewhere before, you may well be right. The award-winning Martins Arms often features on both local and national television. It was converted from a 17th-century farmhouse to an inn during the middle years of the 19th century by local Squire Martin, hence its name. Today, this listed building in the Vale of Belvoir has a country house feel to it, with period furnishings, traditional hunting prints and seasonal fires in the Jacobean fireplace. The acre of landscaped grounds - backing on to National Trust land - includes a herb garden and well-established lawns. Regional ingredients are a feature of the menu, with a classic ploughman's lunch comprising Melton Mowbray pork pie, Colston Bassett Stilton or Cheddar, home-cured ham, pickles and bread.

OPEN: 12-3 6-11 Rest: 25 Dec Closed eve
BAR MEALS: L served all week 12-2 6-10 Av main course £11.50 **RESTAURANT:** L served all week 12-2 D served Mon-Sat 6-9.30 Sun 12-1.30
BREWERY/COMPANY: Free House ▯: Marston's Pedigree, Interbrew Bass, Greene King Abbot Ale, Timothy Taylor Landlord. ▯: 7 **CHILDREN'S FACILITIES:** portions, food/bottle warming, family room **GARDEN:** Acre of landscaped garden with 80 covers **NOTES:** Dogs allowed: Only in garden; water available, Parking 35

KIMBERLEY   THE NELSON & RAILWAY INN

12 Station Rd NG16 2NR
☎ 0115 938 2177
Dir: *1m N of J26 M1.* **Map Ref:** *SK44*

The landlord of 34 years gives this 17th-century pub its distinctive personality. Next door is the Hardy & Hanson brewery that supplies many of the beers, but the two nearby railway stations that once made it a railway inn are now sadly derelict. A hearty menu includes monster mixed grill, a feast of sausage, and chicken curry, plus a choice of rolls and sandwiches.

OPEN: 11-11 (Sun 12-10.30) **BAR MEALS:** L served all week 12-2.30 D served all week 5.30-9 (Sun 12-6) **RESTAURANT:** L served all week 12-2.30 D served all week 5.30-9 (Sun 12-6) **BREWERY/COMPANY:** Hardy & Hansons ▯: Hardys, Hansons Best Bitter, Classic, Cool & Dark. **CHILDREN'S FACILITIES:** menu, licence, high-chairs, food/bottle warming, family room **GARDEN:** Food served outdoors, patio/terrace **NOTES:** Dogs allowed: water provided, Parking 50

LAXTON   THE DOVECOTE INN

Moorhouse Rd NG22 0NU
☎ 01777 871586 ▯ 01777 871586
e-mail: dovecoteinn@yahoo.co.uk
Dir: *Telephone for directions.* **Map Ref:** *SK76*

Set in the only village that still uses the 'three field system', (pop into the local Visitor Centre to find out what that is), this 18th-century pub is an ideal stopping point for walkers. Dishes on offer include chicken stuffed with asparagus in a smokey bacon and cream sauce; roast rack of lamb in a rosemary, mint, onion and mushroom gravy; and mushroom Stroganoff and seafood platter. There is also a range of light bites - baguettes, sandwiches and jacket potatoes.

OPEN: 11.30-3 6.30-11.30 (Fri-Sat 6-11.30)
BAR MEALS: L served all week 12-2 D served all week 6.30-9.30 Av main course £9 **RESTAURANT:** L served all week 12-2 D served all week 6.30-9.30
BREWERY/COMPANY: Free House ▯: Mansfield Smooth, Banks Smooth, Marston's Pedigree. ▯: 10
CHILDREN'S FACILITIES: menu, portions, high-chairs, food/bottle warming **GARDEN:** Table & chairs in front garden **NOTES:** Dogs allowed: in bar, Parking 45
ROOMS: 2 en suite s£35 d£50 (♦♦♦♦)

NOTTINGHAM LINCOLNSHIRE POACHER ♀

161-163 Mansfield Rd NG1 3FR
☎ 0115 941 1584
Dir: *M1 J26. Town centre.* **Map Ref:** *SK53*

Traditional wooden-floored town pub with settles and sturdy wooden tables. Bustles with real ale fans in search of the 12 real ales on tap - regular brewery evenings and wine tastings. Also, good cider and 70 malt whiskies - a great drinkers pub. Large summer terrace.

OPEN: 11-11 (Sun 12-10.30) Closed: Jan 1
BAR MEALS: L served all week 12-8 D served Mon-Fri (Mon 12-3, Fri 12-3 & 5-7, Sun 12-4) Av main course £5.50
BREWERY/COMPANY: Tynemill Ltd 🍺: Bateman XB, XXXB, Castle Rock, JHB. ♀: 6 **CHILDREN'S FACILITIES:** menu, family room **GARDEN:** beer garden, food served in garden
NOTES: Dogs allowed

YE OLDE TRIP TO JERUSALEM ♀

1 Brewhouse Yard, Castle Rd NG1 6AD
☎ 0115 9473171
e-mail: yeoldtrip@hardysandhansons.plc.uk
Map Ref: *SK53*

Allegedly Britain's oldest pub, and also one of the most unusual, with parts of it penetrating deep into the sandstone of Castle Rock. In Middle English, a 'tryppe' was a resting place, as Richard the Lionheart's Crusaders would have known, since they 'trypped' here in 1189. Having only just left the castle above, en route for the Holy Land, one can understand why it took them so long. The caves were once used for brewing, with malting taking place in the Rock Lounge which, like the Museum Room, has a sixty-foot chimney piercing the rock above. Most gustatory wishes are met by a menu which runs from sandwiches, jackets, burgers and salads, to main courses typified by giant meat- or vegetable-filled Yorkshire puddings, chicken tikka masala, salmon Florentine, steak and Kimberley ale pie, and red pepper and mushroom lasagne (one of several vegetarian options). Don't leave without seeing the 'cursed galleon'. The last three people to clean it died mysteriously. Spooky.

OPEN: 11-11 (Sun 12-10.30) **BAR MEALS:** L served all week 11-6 D served None (Sun 12-6) Av main course £6.50 **BREWERY/COMPANY:** 🍺: Hardys & Hansons Kimberley Best Bitter, Best Mild, Ye Olde Trip Ale, Kimberly Cool. ♀: 11 **CHILDREN'S FACILITIES:** portions, licence, family room **GARDEN:** Seating in front & rear courtyard **NOTES:** No dogs (ex guide dogs)

SOUTHWELL FRENCH HORN 🐑 ♀

Main St, Upton NG23 5ST
☎ 01636 812394 📠 01636 815497
e-mail: duckstock@hotmail.com
Map Ref: *SK65*

An 18th-century former farmhouse handy for visiting the racecourse and nearby Southwell Minster. It offers real ales, 24 wines by the glass and good food. Seafood is a speciality and popular seafood evenings are held on a Thursday. Typical dishes are grilled red mullet with lobster and mango curry, and wild sea bass with green bean salad and saffron vinaigrette. Children are welcome and there is a large enclosed garden to the rear.

OPEN: 11.30-3 5.30-11 **BAR MEALS:** L served all week 12-2.15 D served all week 6-9.30 Sun 12-4 Av main course £10.50 **RESTAURANT:** L served Sun-Mon, Wed-Sat 12-2.30 D served Tue-Sat 7-9.30 Sun 12-4 Av 3 course à la carte £21.50 Av 3 course fixed price £12 🍺: Directors, Adnams. ♀: 24 **CHILDREN'S FACILITIES:** portions, licence, games, high-chairs, food/bottle warming **GARDEN:** Large enclosed garden **NOTES:** Dogs allowed: in bar, in garden, Water, Parking 100

THURGARTON THE RED LION

Southwell Rd NG14 7GP
☎ 01636 830351
Dir: *On A612 between Nottingham & Southwell.* **Map Ref:** *SK64*

This 16th-century inn was once a monks' alehouse. It has recently been refurbished and a sunny parlour added. The extensive bar menu offers beef and Guinness casserole, chicken tikka masala, grilled salmon, vegetable lasagne and a good choice of salads. Specials might include lobster thermidor, or venison, black cherry and port casserole. Look for the 1936 Nottingham Guardian cutting on the wall that reports the murder of a previous landlady by her niece!

OPEN: 11.30-2.30 6.30-11 (Open all day Sat-Sun & BHs)
BAR MEALS: L served all week 12-2 D served all week 7-10 Sat&Sun 12-9.30 Av main course £6.95
RESTAURANT: L served all week 12-2 D served all week 7-10 **BREWERY/COMPANY:** Free House 🍺: Greene King Abbot Ale, Jenning Cumberland, Carlsberg-Tetley, Black Sheep.
CHILDREN'S FACILITIES: menu, portions, high-chairs, food/bottle warming **GARDEN:** Large spacious, well kept
NOTES: in bar, No dogs (ex guide dogs), Parking 40

CLIPSHAM THE OLIVE BRANCH

Main St LE15 7SH
☎ 01780 410355 📠 01780 410000
e-mail: info@theolivebranchpub.com
Dir: *2m off A1 at Ram Jam Inn junction, 10m N of Stamford.* **Map Ref:** *SK91*

In 1890 three farm cottages were knocked together to form an ale house, and offered to the disgruntled villagers by the local squire who had closed the original pub. Thus the appropriately-named Olive Branch came into being. In 1999 the pub was saved from closure by three young men, who divided their responsibilities according to their strengths: the chef, for excellence in ingredients and cooking; the sommelier, for the growing range of drinks - from quality wines and real ales to farmhouse ciders; and the general manager for maintaining service standards front-of-house and in the restaurant. An attractive front garden and terrace, and an interior full of locally made furniture and artists' works (all for sale) set the scene. For atmosphere, add log fires, books, sloe gin, mulled wine and chestnuts in winter; and barbecues, home-made lemonade and garden skittles in summer.

OPEN: 12-3.30 6-11 (Sun 12-6 only, summer Sat 12-11) Closed: 26 Dec 1 Jan **BAR MEALS:** L served all week 12-2 D served Mon-Sat 7-9.30 Sun 12-3 Av main course £11.50
RESTAURANT: L served all week 12-2 D served Mon-Sat 7-9.30 Av 3 course à la carte £21.50 Av 3 course fixed price £12.50 **BREWERY/COMPANY:** 🍺: Grainstore 1050 & Olive Oil, Fenland, Brewster's. ♀: 15 **CHILDREN'S FACILITIES:** portions, games, high-chairs, food/bottle warming **GARDEN:** Gravelled area, pergola, BBQ area, lawn
NOTES: Dogs allowed: in bar, in garden, Parking 15

EXTON FOX & HOUNDS

LE15 8AP
☎ 01572 812403 📠 01572 812403
Map Ref: *SK91*

This late 17th-century former coaching inn stands on Exton's village green. There's a large walled garden for al fresco summer dining, and the pub is just a short drive from Rutland Water. Jacket potatoes and filled ciabattas feature on the casual lunch menu, beside an extensive choice of traditional Italian pizzas. Other dishes include pan-fried calves' liver and bacon; chicken with roasted peppers and linguine; and grilled halibut with Mediterranean vegetables.

OPEN: 11-3 6-11 **BAR MEALS:** L served all week 12-2 D served all week 6.30-9 No food Sun eve Av main course £9 **RESTAURANT:** L served all week 12-2 D served all week 6.30-9 Av 3-course à la carte £18
BREWERY/COMPANY: Free House 🍺: Greene King IPA, Grainstore Real Ales, John Smiths Smooth. ♀: 8
CHILDREN'S FACILITIES: menu, portions, games, high-chairs, food/bottle warming, outdoor play area **GARDEN:** Large walled garden & patio area **NOTES:** Dogs allowed: in bar, in garden, in bedrooms, water, Parking 20

LYDDINGTON   OLD WHITE HART ♀

51 Main St LE15 9LR
☎ 01572 821703 ▤ 01572 821965
Dir: *On A6003 between Uppingham and
Corby, take B672.* **Map Ref:** *SP89*

This honey-coloured 17th-century stone pub
stands by the green in an attractive village
high above the Welland Valley, close to good
walks and Rutland Water. Interesting, freshly
prepared food is served in the cosy main bar
with its heavy beams, dried flower
arrangements, traditional furnishings and
splendid log fire - and in the adjoining dining
areas. The blackboard menu may offer
starters such as warm salad of smoked
bacon, black pudding and cherry tomatoes
topped with grilled Slipcote cheese and
balsamic dressing. Follow these with deep-

fried Grimsby haddock and chips; home-made steak
and kidney pudding; or wild mushroom and asparagus
risotto. Ambitious evening carte. There is flower-filled
rear garden with 10 pétanque pitches, also a patio
with heaters and a marquee in the summer.

OPEN: 12-3 6.30-11 Closed: 25 Dec
BAR MEALS: L served all week 12-2 D served Mon-Sat
6.30-9 Av main course £12 **RESTAURANT:** L served all
week 12-2 D served Mon-Sat 6.30-9 Av 3 course à la carte
£20 Av 3 course fixed price £12.95
BREWERY/COMPANY: Free House ◖: Greene King IPA &
Abbot Ale, Timothy Taylor Landlord. ♀: 7
CHILDREN'S FACILITIES: portions, games, high-chairs,
food/bottle warming **GARDEN:** Beer garden, heated patio
area, marquee **NOTES:** No dogs (ex guide dogs), Parking 50

OAKHAM   BARNSDALE LODGE HOTEL ★★★ ✿ ♀

The Avenue, Rutland Water, North Shore LE15
8AH
☎ 01572 724678 ▤ 01572 724961
e-mail: enquiries@barnsdalelodge.co.uk
Map Ref: *SK80*

An Edwardian-style hotel overlooking Rutland

Water in the heart of this picturesque little county. Its
rural connections go back to its 17th-century origins as
a farmhouse, but nowadays modern comforts and
hospitality are offered. Real ales including local brews
are served in the bar.

OPEN: 7-11 **BAR MEALS:** L served all week 12.15-2.15
D served all week 7-9.45 Av main course £10
RESTAURANT: L served all week 12.15-2.15 D served all
week 7-9.45 Av 3 course à la carte £35
BREWERY/COMPANY: Free House ◖: Rutland Grainstore,
Marstons Pedigree, Scottish Courage Courage Directors,
Theakston Best Bitter. ♀: 8 **CHILDREN'S FACILITIES:** menu,
high-chairs, food/bottle warming, baby changing, swings, slide,
croquet, crazy golf **GARDEN:** Courtyard, established garden
with lawns **NOTES:** Dogs allowed: in bar, in garden,
in bedrooms, water, Parking 280 **ROOMS:** 46 en suite
4 family rooms s£75 d£99.50

STRETTON   RAM JAM INN ★★ ✿ 🍵 ♀

The Great North Rd LE15 7QX
☎ 01780 410776 ▤ 01780 410361
e-mail: rji@rutnet.co.uk
Dir: *On A1 northbound carriageway past
B1668 turn off, through service station into
hotel car park.* **Map Ref:** *SK91*

The inn is believed to have acquired its present name in
the 18th century when the landlord's sign advertised
'Fine Ram Jam', though no one is quite sure what that
might have been. Today, the informal café-bar and bistro
exudes warmth, and in summer the patio, overlooking
the paddock and orchard, is set for outdoor dining.

OPEN: 7am-11pm Closed: 25 Dec **BAR MEALS:** L served
all week 12-9.30 D served all week Av main course £8.95
RESTAURANT: L served all week 12-9.30 D served all week
Av 3 course à la carte £18 **BREWERY/COMPANY:** Free
House ◖: Fuller's London Pride, Scottish Courage John
Smith's Cask and Smooth. ♀: 11 **CHILDREN'S FACILITIES:**
menu, portions, games, high-chairs, food/bottle warming, baby
changing, outdoor play area, Lrg outside area **GARDEN:** Patio
set for open air dining **NOTES:** Dogs allowed: in garden,
Parking 64 **ROOMS:** 7 en suite 1 family room s£47 d£57

WING KINGS ARMS ◆◆◆◆ ♀

Top St LE15 8SE
☎ 01572 737634 ▤ 01572 737255
e-mail: enquiries@thekingsarms-wing.co.uk
Dir: *1m off A6003 between Uppingham &
Oakham.* **Map Ref:** *SK80*

Built from local stone and Collyweston roofing

slates, the Kings Arms is a traditional, family-run inn
dating back to 1649. Just two miles from Rutland
Water, it makes an ideal base from which to tour
England's smallest county. The bar, in the oldest part of
the building, is full of atmosphere with flagstone floors,
low beams, and welcoming winter fires. Half of the
bedrooms are built in the old village bakery, and the
largest room features the original bread ovens.

OPEN: 12-3 (Summer, open all day wknds) 6-11
BAR MEALS: L served all week 12-2 D served all week
6.30-9 Av main course £9.50 **RESTAURANT:** L served all
week 12-2 D served all week 6.30-9 Av 3 course à la carte
£20 **BREWERY/COMPANY:** Free House ◖: Grainstore,
Pedigrees & Guest Beers. ♀: 7 **CHILDREN'S FACILITIES:**
menu, portions, high-chairs, play area in garden **GARDEN:** Lrg
lawn **NOTES:** in garden, No dogs, Parking 25 **ROOMS:** 8
en suite 4 family rooms s£50 d£80

BISHOP'S CASTLE BOARS HEAD ◆◆◆ ♀

Church St SY9 5AE
☎ 01588 638521 ▤ 01588 630126
e-mail: sales@boarsheadhotel.co.uk
Map Ref: *SO38*

One of Bishop's Castle's oldest buildings, this
former coaching inn received its first full
licence in 1642. Legend tells that it escaped
burning during the Civil War because half the
King's men were drinking here, while the rest
were out vandalising the town. The exposed
beams are genuine, and a chimney contains
a priest hole. The inn is celebrated for its
lunchtime steak, chicken and sausage sizzlers,
while scrumpy pork, lamb shank, salmon
béarnaise, and paella appear on the carte.

OPEN: 11.30-11 (Sun 12-10.30) **BAR MEALS:** L served all
week 12-2 D served all week 6.30-9.30 (Sun 12-9.30)
Av main course £7 **RESTAURANT:** L served all week 12-2
D served all week 6.30-9.30 Av 3 course à la carte £12.50
BREWERY/COMPANY: Free House ◖: Scottish Courage
Courage Best & Courage Directors & regular guests. ♀: 8
CHILDREN'S FACILITIES: menu, portions, licence, games,
high-chairs, food/bottle warming, Highchairs, cot
NOTES: in bedrooms, No dogs (ex guide dogs), Parking 20
ROOMS: 4 en suite 1 family room s£38 d£60

BRIDGNORTH THE BEAR ♀

Northgate WV16 4ET
☎ 01746 763250
e-mail: thebearinn@aol.com
Dir: *From High Street (Bridgnorth) go through
Northgate (sandstone archway) and the pub is
on the L.* **Map Ref:** *SO79*

Traditional Grade II listed hostelry in one of
the loveliest of the Severn-side towns. The
way it clings to the top of a high sandstone
cliff gives it an almost continental flavour.
 A former coaching inn, the award-winning
Bear boasts two carpeted bars which are

characterised by whisky-water jugs, gas-type wall
lamps and wheelback chairs.
 Good quality, appetising menu offers the likes of
ham, egg and chips, braised lamb shank, wild
mushroom and spinach risotto, and salmon and herb
fishcakes. Daily-changing real ales and a choice of
seven malts.

OPEN: 11-3 5-11 (Sun 7-10.30) **BAR MEALS:** L served all
week 12-2 Av main course £5.50
BREWERY/COMPANY: Enterprise Inns ◖: Changing guest
ales. **GARDEN:** Food served outside **NOTES:** Dogs allowed:
Parking 18

CRAVEN ARMS   THE SUN INN

Corfton SY7 9DF
☎ 01584 861239 & 861503
e-mail: normanspride@aol.com
Dir: *on the B4368 7m N of Ludlow.*
Map Ref: *SO48*

Family-run pub in beautiful Corvedale, first licensed in 1613. Landlord Norman Pearce brews his own Corvedale beers, using local borehole water, and sells them bottled and from the barrel. Landlady Teresa Pearce cooks all the meals, which are served with four to six vegetables or a freshly cut salad, and the produce is locally sourced. Dishes include beef in Corvedale Ale, and lamb Shrewsbury. The pub puts on small beer festivals at Easter and August bank holidays.

OPEN: 12-2.30 6-11 **BAR MEALS:** L served all week 12-2 D served all week 6-9.30 (Sun 12-3, 7-9) Av main course £7.25 **RESTAURANT:** L served all week 12-2 D served all week 6-9.30 (Sun 12-3, 7-9) **BREWERY/COMPANY:** Free House ◀: Corvedale Normans Pride, Secret Hop, Dark & Delicious, Julie's Ale. ♀: 14 **CHILDREN'S FACILITIES:** menu, portions, licence, games, high-chairs, food/bottle warming, swings, highchairs **GARDEN:** 4 benches with tables, pretty views **NOTES:** Dogs allowed: in bar, water, Parking 30

CRESSAGE   THE RIVERSIDE INN

Cound SY5 6AF
☎ 01952 510900 ▤ 01952 510980
Dir: *On A458 Shrewsbury-Bridgnorth rd.*
Map Ref: *SJ50*

In three acres of garden alongside the River Severn, this extensively refurbished coaching inn offers river view dining both outdoors and in a modern conservatory. The single menu serves both dining areas and spacious bar, furnished and decorated in haphazard country style.

Traditional pub dishes include hot crab pâté and mushrooms with Shropshire blue cheese, followed by local lamb noisettes with parsnip chips, and salmon fishcakes with hollandaise.

Exotic alternatives follow the lines of Peking duck pancakes with hoisin sauce, "Pee-kai" chicken breasts with satay sauce, and spinach, sorrel and Mozzarella parcels.

OPEN: 12-3 6-11 **BAR MEALS:** L served all week 12-2.30 D served all week 6.30-9.30 Av main course £7.50 **RESTAURANT:** L served all week 12-2.30 D served all week 7-9.30 Av 3 course à la carte £22 **BREWERY/COMPANY:** Free House ◀: Various cask ales & regular guest beers. **CHILDREN'S FACILITIES:** menu, outdoor play area, family room **GARDEN:** beer garden, patio, outdoor eating **NOTES:** Dogs allowed: Parking 100

IRONBRIDGE   THE GROVE INN ♦♦♦

10 Wellington Rd, Coalbrookdale TF8 7DX
☎ 01952 433269 ▤ 01952 433269
e-mail: frog@fat-frog.co.uk
Dir: *J6 M54, follow signs for Ironbridge.*
Map Ref: *SJ60*

Tucked away in a basement of the Grove hotel, the Fat Frog Restaurant brings a Provençale flavour to the Ironbridge Gorge. With its red check tablecloths, the restaurant is filled with French murals, mannequins and skeletons - not to mention the resident ghost! Owner/chef Johnny Coleau serves a varied selection of English, continental and vegetarian dishes that include fillet au poivre; supreme de saumon citron; and entrecôte Forestière.

OPEN: 12-2.30 5.30-11 (Sun 12-5.30) **BAR MEALS:** L served all week 12.30-2 D served Mon-Sat 6.30-8.30 (Sun 12-3) Av main course £8.95 **RESTAURANT:** L served all week 12.30-2 D served Mon-Sat 7-9.30 (Sun 12-3) Av 3 course fixed price £21.50 **BREWERY/COMPANY:** Free House ◀: Banks Original, Traditional, Harp Irish, Hoegarden. **CHILDREN'S FACILITIES:** portions, high-chairs, food/bottle warming, baby changing **GARDEN:** Large lawned flowered garden **NOTES:** Dogs allowed: in bar, in garden, in bedrooms, water, food if required, Parking 12 **ROOMS:** 5 en suite 2 family rooms s£30 d£45

THE MALTHOUSE ◆◆◆◆ ♀

The Wharfage TF8 7NH
☎ 01952 433712 ▯ 01952 433298
e-mail: enquiries@malthousepubs.co.uk
Dir: *Telephone for directions.* **Map Ref:** *SJ60*

The Malthouse is set on the banks of the River Severn in Ironbridge, a village renowned for its spectacular natural beauty and award-winning museums, and now a designated UNESCO World Heritage Site. The pub, a converted malthouse located only 250 yards from the bridge's main visitor centre, has been an inn since the turn of the 20th century. It has been refurbished, and now offers six rooms above a popular jazz bar with live music from Wednesday to Saturday.

OPEN: 11-11 (Sun 12-3 6-10.30) Closed: 25-26 Dec **BAR MEALS:** L served all week 12-2.30 D served all week 6-9.30 Av main course £8 **RESTAURANT:** L served all week 12-2 D served all week 6.30-9.45 Av 3 course à la carte £21.20 **BREWERY/COMPANY:** Inn Partnership **◀:** Flowers Original, Boddingtons, Tetley. ♀: 10 **CHILDREN'S FACILITIES:** menu, portions, games, high-chairs, food/bottle warming, baby changing **NOTES:** No dogs, Parking 15 **ROOMS:** 6 en suite 2 family rooms s£55 d£60

LLANFAIR WATERDINE THE WATERDINE ◆◆◆◆◆ ✿✿ ♀

LD7 1TU
☎ 01547 528214 ▯ 01547 529992
Dir: *4m NW of Knighton, just off the Newtown road, turn R in Lloyney, over bridge, follow road to village, last on left opposite church.*
Map Ref: *SO27*

It was in the lounge bar of what was then called the Red Lion that Col John (later Lord) Hunt planned his ascent of Everest in 1953. Built in the second half of the 16th century, The Waterdine is surrounded by peaceful, beautiful countryside. The views from the garden are superb, and at its foot runs the England-Wales border in the form of the River Teme. The pub's owner is renowned chef, Ken Adams.

OPEN: 12-3 7-11 Closed: 1 wk Winter 1wk Spring Rest: Sunday closed eve **BAR MEALS:** L served Tue-Sun 12-2 D served Tue-Sat 7-9 Av main course £7 **RESTAURANT:** L served Tue-Sun 12-1.45 D served Tue-Sat 7-9 Av 3 course à la carte £25.50 Av 3 course fixed price £26 **BREWERY/COMPANY:** Free House **◀:** Jack Snipe, Wood Shropshire Legends, Parish Bitter & Shropshire Lad. ♀: 8 **GARDEN:** Quiet walled garden, good views **NOTES:** No dogs, Parking 12 **ROOMS:** 3 en suite s£50 d£90

MADELEY THE NEW INN

Blists Hill Victorian Town, Legges Way TF7 5DU
☎ 01952 588892 ▯ 01952 243447
e-mail: rhamundy@btinternet.com
Dir: *Between Telford & Broseley.*
Map Ref: *SJ60*

Here's something different - a Victorian pub that was moved brick by brick from the Black Country and re-erected at the Ironbridge Gorge Open Air Museum. The building remains basically as it was in 1890, and customers can buy traditionally brewed beer at five-pence farthing per pint - roughly £2.10 in today's terms - using pre-decimal currency bought from the bank. The mainly traditional menu includes home-made soup, steak and kidney pudding, and ham and leek pie.

OPEN: 11-4 Closed: Dec 24-25 **BAR MEALS:** L served all week 12-2.30 Av main course £5 **RESTAURANT:** L served all week 12-2.30 Av 3 course fixed price £10 **BREWERY/COMPANY:** **◀:** Banks Bitter, Banks Original, Pedigree. **CHILDREN'S FACILITIES:** menu, portions, high-chairs, food/bottle warming, outdoor play area, family room **GARDEN:** Food served outside **NOTES:** No dogs (ex guide dogs), Parking 300

MORVILLE ACTON ARMS

WV16 4RJ
☎ 01746 714209 📠 01746 714102
e-mail: acton-arms@madfish.com
Dir: *On A458, 3m W of Bridgnorth.*
Map Ref: *SO69*

Successive landlords have all frequently seen the apparition making this one of Britain's most haunted pubs. Described as 'like a sheet flicking from one door to another', the spectre may be a former abbot of Shrewsbury who lived in the village in the 16th century. There's nothing spectral about the food, though, with completely worldly dishes such as salmon, halibut or plaice fillets; lamb shanks; venison pie; or lamb in honey and ginger.

OPEN: 11.30-2.30 (all day during Summer and Sat, Sun) 6-11 **BAR MEALS:** L served all week 12-2 D served all week 6-9 All day Sat/Sun **RESTAURANT:** L served all week 12-2.30 D served all week 7-9.30 All day Sat/Sun **BREWERY/COMPANY:** W'hampton & Dudley 🍺: Bank's Hanson's Mild & Banks Bitter. **CHILDREN'S FACILITIES:** menu, portions, high-chairs, food/bottle warming, outdoor play area, toys, bouncy castle (weather permitting) **GARDEN:** Large area with benches & seats **NOTES:** Dogs allowed: in bar, water, Parking 40

MUCH WENLOCK THE GEORGE & DRAGON

2 High St TF13 6AA
☎ 01952 727312
Dir: *On A458 halfway between Shrewsbury & Bridgnorth.* *Map Ref:* *SO69*

There's a remarkable collection of brewery memorabilia, including over 500 water jugs hanging from the ceiling, in this historic Grade II listed building. Adjacent to the market square, Guildhall and ruined priory, the inn's cosy and inviting atmosphere makes this an obvious choice for locals and visitors alike. Expect a good range of popular dishes, with snacks (sandwiches, baguettes, Ploughmans etc) available at lunch time then dinner, which offers Thai chicken curry; chicken breast in apricot, mead and cream; or salmon poached in dill and white wine.

OPEN: 12-3 (Wknds & summer June-Sep all day) 6-11 (Fri-Sun 12-11, 12-10.30) **BAR MEALS:** L served Mon-Sun 12-2.00 D served Mon-Tue, Thur-Sat 6-9.00 Av main course £7.95 **RESTAURANT:** L served Mon-Sun 12-2.00 D served Mon-Tue, Thur-Sat 6.30-9.00 Av 3 course à la carte £16.95 **BREWERY/COMPANY:** 🍺: Greene King Abbot Ale, Old Speckled Hen & IPA, Adnams Broadside, Hobsons Town Crier. **CHILDREN'S FACILITIES:** menu **NOTES:** No dogs (ex guide dogs)

WENLOCK EDGE INN

Hilltop, Wenlock Edge TF13 6DJ
☎ 01746 785678 📠 01746 785285
e-mail: info@wenlockedgeinn.co.uk
Dir: *4.5m from Much Wenlock on B4371.*
Map Ref: *SO69*

This inn perches at one of the highest points of Wenlock Edge's dramatic wooded ledge. Originally a row of 17th-century quarrymen's cottages, the cosy interior contains a small country-style dining room and several bars, one with a wood-burning stove. Outside, a furnished patio takes full advantage of the views stretching across Apedale to Caer Caradoc and the Long Mynd. Start your meal with Bantry Bay mussels; home-made chicken liver pâté; or oak smoked salmon,

followed by a hearty main course like home-made steak and ale pie or roast vegetable and blue Stilton wellington. Puddings include warm chocolate brioche pudding with rich chocolate sauce; and the pub favourite sticky toffee pudding with home-made toffee sauce. The lunchtime menu offers freshly baked baguette sandwiches as well as a range of hot dishes.

OPEN: 12-2.30 6.30-11 Closed: 24-26 Dec **BAR MEALS:** L served Wed-Sun 12-2 D served Wed-Sun 7-9 Av main course £9 **RESTAURANT:** L served Wed-Sun 12-2 D served Wed-Sun 7-9 Av 3 course à la carte £16 **BREWERY/COMPANY:** Free House 🍺: Hobsons Best & Town Crier. **CHILDREN'S FACILITIES:** menu, portions, high-chairs, food/bottle warming **GARDEN:** Patio area with furniture, stunning views **NOTES:** Dogs allowed: in bar, in garden, in bedrooms, water, toys, chews, Parking 50

MUNSLOW THE CROWN COUNTRY INN ◆◆◆◆

SY7 9ET
☎ 01584 841205 📄 01584 841255
e-mail: info@crowncountryinn.co.uk
Dir: *On B4368 between Craven Arms & Much Wenlock.* **Map Ref:** *SO58*

Previously a Shropshire 'Hundred House' where Judge Jeffries is said to have presided, the Grade II listed Crown is noted for its sturdy oak beams, flagstone floors and large inglenook fireplace, which is the central feature of the main bar area. Handy for Wenlock Edge and the Long Mynd and visiting Ironbridge, Ludlow or the Severn Valley Railway.

OPEN: 12-2.00 6.30-11 Closed: 25 Dec
BAR MEALS: L served Tue-Sun 12-2 D served Tue-Sun 6.30-9 Av main course £11 **RESTAURANT:** L served Tue-Sun 12-2 D served Tue-Sun 6.30-9 Av 3 course à la carte £20 **BREWERY/COMPANY:** Free House Holden's Black Country Bitter, Black Country Mild, Woods Parish Bitter, Holden's Golden Glow & Holden's Special Bitter.
CHILDREN'S FACILITIES: menu, portions, licence, games, high-chairs, food/bottle warming, outdoor play area
GARDEN: Large garden with grassed and patio areas
NOTES: Dogs allowed: in bar, water, Parking 20
ROOMS: 3 en suite 1 family room s£40 d£60

NESSCLIFFE THE OLD THREE PIGEONS INN 🐑 ♀

SY4 1DB
☎ 01743 741279 📄 01743 741259
Dir: *On A5 London road, 8m W of Shrewsbury.*
Map Ref: *SJ31*

A 600-year-old inn built of ship's timbers, sandstone, and wattle and daub, set in two acres of land looking towards Snowdonia and the Bretton Hills. There is a strong emphasis on fish, with a choice of many seasonal dishes, and it is a venue for gourmet club and lobster evenings. Characteristic dishes include seafood platter, duck and cranberry, braised oxtails, liver and bacon, chicken Merango, and oak-smoked haddock.

OPEN: 12-3 6-11 **BAR MEALS:** L served all week 12-2.30 D served all week 6.30-9.30 Av main course £7
RESTAURANT: L served all week 12-2.30 D served all week 6.30-9.30 Av 3 course à la carte £18
BREWERY/COMPANY: Free House ◀: Shropshire Gold, Archers & guest ale. ♀: 10 **CHILDREN'S FACILITIES:** menu
GARDEN: Lawn, lake, excellent views **NOTES:** Dogs allowed: Parking 50

SHREWSBURY WHITE HORSE INN

Pulverbatch SY5 8DS
☎ 01743 718247
Dir: *7m past the Nuffield Hospital.*
Map Ref: *SJ41*

Some 8 miles south of Shrewsbury off the A49, a cruck-structured building houses this fine old inn which was mentioned in the Domesday Book. Up to 40 main dishes are on offer every day, ranging from salmon, plaice and haddock in various guises to home-made steak and ale pie, whole lamb shanks and half a dozen speciality curries. Grills include chicken, gammon and various cuts of steak: a daily special might be beef bourguignon.

OPEN: 12-2.30 6-11 Rest: (Summer open till 4pm weekends) **BAR MEALS:** L served all week 12-2.30 D served all week 7-9.30 Av main course £7.50
RESTAURANT: L served all week 12-2 D served all week 7-9.30 Av 3 course à la carte £15.95
BREWERY/COMPANY: Enterprise Inns ◀: Local Salopian ales. **CHILDREN'S FACILITIES:** menu **GARDEN:** patio area, seats 12 **NOTES:** No dogs (ex guide dogs), Parking 50

UPPER AFFCOT THE TRAVELLERS REST INN ♀

SY6 6RL

☎ 01694 781275 📠 01694 781555

e-mail: reception@travellersrestinn.co.uk

Dir: On A49. **Map Ref:** SO48

Traditional south Shropshire inn located between Church Stretton and Craven Arms. Customers come some distance to enjoy the friendly atmosphere, great range of real ales and good pub meals, which are served right through from lunch till 9pm. Food options include freshly made sandwiches, jacket potatoes, dragon's fire curry, mixed grill, and vegetable lasagne. Finish with an old-fashioned pudding like treacle sponge or apple pie with custard.

OPEN: 11-11 Sun 12-10.30 **BAR MEALS:** L served all week 11.30 D served all week 8.30 Av main course £7 🍺: Wood Shropshire Lad, Hobsons Best Bitter, Bass, Guiness. ♀: 14 **CHILDREN'S FACILITIES:** menu, portions, licence, high-chairs, baby changing **NOTES:** Dogs allowed: in bar, Parking 50 **ROOMS:** 12 en suite 4 family rooms s£35 d£55

WENTNOR THE CROWN INN

SY9 5EE

☎ 01588 650613 📠 01588 650436

e-mail: crowninn@wentnor.com

Dir: From Shrewsbury A49 to Church Stretton, follow signs over Long Mynd to Asterton, R to Wentnor. **Map Ref:** SO39

Standing in the shadow of the famous Long Mynd, in an area with vast potential for walking and other outdoor pursuits, the Crown is a traditional, unspoilt 17th-century coaching inn with log fires, beams and horse brasses. Sophisticated meals are served in the bar and non-smoking restaurant: pork tenderloin filled with marinated fruits, pan-fried breast of duck with a burnt orange sauce, and grilled sea bass with couscous are typical of the choices.

OPEN: 12-3 (Summer wknds all day) 7-11 (Sat 12-3 6-11, Sun 10.30) Closed: Dec 25 **BAR MEALS:** L served all week 12-2 D served all week 7-9 **RESTAURANT:** L served all week 12-2 D served all week 7-9 **BREWERY/COMPANY:** Free House 🍺: Hobsons, Greene King Old Speckled Hen, Salopian Shropshire Gold. **CHILDREN'S FACILITIES:** menu, outdoor play area **NOTES:** No dogs, Parking 20

WHITCHURCH THE HORSE & JOCKEY

Church St SY13 1LB

☎ 01948 664902 📠 01948 664902

e-mail: andy-thelwell@yahoo.co.uk

Dir: In town centre next to church. **Map Ref:** SJ54

Coaching inn built on Roman ruins and extended between the 17th and 19th centuries. Inside you'll find exposed beams, an open fire and a menu offering a vast array of dishes. You can select from the carte, grill or easy eating menus, plus there's a list of pizzas. Typical dishes might be stuffed best end of lamb with honey and port sauce, pan-fried chicken with brandy, cream and coarse grain mustard, and mushroom tortellini.

OPEN: 11.30-2.30 6-11 **BAR MEALS:** L served Tues-Sun 11.30-2.30 D served Tues-Sun 6-10 **RESTAURANT:** L served Tues-Sun 11.30-2.30 D served Tues-Sun 6-10 **BREWERY/COMPANY:** Pubmaster 🍺: Interbrew Worthington, Scottish Courage John Smith's, Stella Artois, Fosters. **CHILDREN'S FACILITIES:** menu **GARDEN:** Patio and grassed area, with wooden benches **NOTES:** No dogs (ex guide dogs), Parking 10

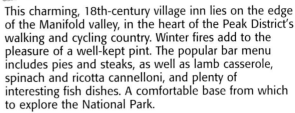

BUTTERTON THE BLACK LION INN

ST13 7SP
☎ 01538 304232
Dir: *From A52 (between Leek & Ashbourne)*
take B5053. **Map Ref:** *SK05*

This charming, 18th-century village inn lies on the edge of the Manifold valley, in the heart of the Peak District's walking and cycling country. Winter fires add to the pleasure of a well-kept pint. The popular bar menu includes pies and steaks, as well as lamb casserole, spinach and ricotta cannelloni, and plenty of interesting fish dishes. A comfortable base from which to explore the National Park.

OPEN: 12-3 7-11 Rest: Mon Closed lunch
BAR MEALS: L served Tues-Sun 12-2 D served all week 7-9
RESTAURANT: L served Tues-Sun 12-2 D served all week 7-9.30 **BREWERY/COMPANY:** Free House 🍺: Scottish Courage Theakston Best, Interbrew Bass, Everards Tiger Best, Timothy Taylor. 🍷: 10 **CHILDREN'S FACILITIES:** menu, family room **NOTES:** No dogs (ex guide dogs), Parking 30

CHEADLE THE QUEENS AT FREEHAY

Counslow Rd, Freehay ST10 1RF
☎ 01538 722383 📠 01538 722383
Dir: *Two miles from Alton Towers.*
Map Ref: *SK04*

Located just 3.5 miles from Alton Towers, The Queens was transformed a few years ago from a run-down pub into a popular, award-winning eating house. The freshly cooked meals include fish and game in season - usually found on the specials board - along with a range of choices from the grill with classic sauces (chasseur, Diane) as optional extras. Home-made beef and Guinness pie or Moroccan lamb tagine are representative of the dishes elsewhere on the menu.

OPEN: 12-2.30 6-11 Closed: 25-26 Dec, 31 Dec(eve), 1 Jan (eve) **BAR MEALS:** L served all week 12-2 D served all week 6-9.30 (Sun 12-2.30, 6.30-9.30) Av main course £9.95 **RESTAURANT:** L served all week 12-2 D served all week 6-9.30 Av 3 course à la carte £18 Av 3 course fixed price £9.95 **BREWERY/COMPANY:** Free House 🍺: Draught Bass, Draught Worthington Bitter. **CHILDREN'S FACILITIES:** menu, portions, food/bottle warming **GARDEN:** Small garden with four benches **NOTES:** No dogs, Parking 30

ECCLESHALL THE GEORGE

Castle St ST21 6DF
☎ 01785 850300 📠 01785 851452
e-mail:
information@thegeorgeinn.freeserve.co.uk
Map Ref: *SJ82*

A family-run, 16th-century former coaching inn with its own micro-brewery, where the owners' son produces award-winning Slater's ales. Occasional beer festivals are held, and the menu features a good, wide variety of dishes, including lamb steak in a gin and redcurrant sauce, half chicken with barbecue sauce and steak and kidney pie cooked in the inn's prize ale. A selection of salads, jackets and sandwiches is also available.

OPEN: 11-11 (12-10.30 Sun) Closed: 25 Dec
BAR MEALS: L served all week 12-9.30 D served all week 6-9.45 **RESTAURANT:** L served all week 12-2.30 D served all week 6-9.45 **BREWERY/COMPANY:** Free House 🍺: Slaters Ales. **CHILDREN'S FACILITIES:** menu, high-chairs, food/bottle warming **NOTES:** Dogs allowed: Parking 30

HIMLEY CROOKED HOUSE 🐑

Coppice Mill DY3 4DA
☎ 01384 238583 🖺 01384 214911
Dir: *Telephone for directions. 1.5m east along B4176 off A449.* **Map Ref:** *SO89*

One of Britain's most aptly-named pubs, this really is a crooked house. It was built as a farmhouse in 1765, but when mineshafts beneath collapsed in the mid-19th century, it was condemned, but finally saved by Banks' Brewery. Kids in particular love the wonky grandfather's clock, and ball-bearings that appear to roll uphill, while adults find them quite unsettling after a few pints! The perfectly upright menu lists grills, salads, rotisserie chicken, and giant battered cod.

OPEN: 11.30-2.30 Opening hours apply to Mon-Thu 5-11 Open all day Mar-Oct **BAR MEALS:** L served Mon-Sun 12-2 D served Mon-Sun 6-9 Av main course £7.50 **RESTAURANT:** L served Mon-Sun 12-2 D served Mon-Sun 6-9 **BREWERY/COMPANY:** 🍺: Bank's. **CHILDREN'S FACILITIES:** menu, licence, games, high-chairs, food/bottle warming, outdoor play area, play area, changing facilities **GARDEN:** Patio area with tables **NOTES:** Dogs allowed: in bar, in garden, water, Parking 40

LEEK ABBEY INN 🍷

Abbey Green Rd ST13 8SA
☎ 01538 382865 🖺 01538 398604
e-mail: martin@abbeyinn.co.uk
Dir: *Telephone for directions.* **Map Ref:** *SJ95*

Set in beautiful countryside on the Staffordshire moorlands, this 17th-century inn is on the outskirts of Leek, and handy for the potteries of Stoke-on-Trent. It is also conveniently close to Alton Towers and Tittesworth Reservoir, and with its spacious bars and restaurant, and large terrace, it is an ideal destination for a meal or a drink.

OPEN: 11-2.30 6.30-11 (Sun 12-3 7-10.30) **BAR MEALS:** L served all week 11-2 D served all week 6.30-9 Av main course £4 **BREWERY/COMPANY:** Free House 🍺: Interbrew Bass. 🍷: 8 **CHILDREN'S FACILITIES:** menu, licence, outdoor play area **NOTES:** No dogs (ex guide dogs), Parking 30

THREE HORSESHOES INN ★★ ✿ 🍷

Buxton Rd, Blackshaw Moor ST13 8TW
☎ 01538 300296 🖺 01538 300320
Dir: *Telephone for directions.* **Map Ref:** *SJ95*

A sprawling creeper-covered inn geared to catering for visitors and locals in three smart eating outlets. Choose from the traditional décor and food of the bar carvery, the relaxed atmosphere of the brasserie, and the more formal restaurant. The award-winning menu offers dishes ranging from traditional (tournedos Rossini; bangers and mash) to steamed monkfish in banana leaf or Thai duck curry.

OPEN: 12-3 6-11 **BAR MEALS:** L served all week 12-2 D served all week 6.30-9 Av main course £7.25 **RESTAURANT:** L served Sun 12.30-1.30 D served Sun-Fri 6.30-9 **BREWERY/COMPANY:** Free House **CHILDREN'S FACILITIES:** menu, outdoor play area **NOTES:** No dogs (ex guide dogs), Parking 100 **ROOMS:** 7 en suite

NEWCASTLE-UNDER-LYME   MAINWARING ARMS ♀

Whitmore ST5 5HR
☎ 01782 680851 📠 01782 680224
e-mail: info@mannersrestaurant.co.uk
Map Ref: SJ84

A welcoming old creeper-clad inn on the Mainwaring family estate. Crackling log fires set the scene at this very traditional country retreat, where daily blackboard specials support the popular bar menu. Expect freshly-made sandwiches, home-made steak and kidney pie, pork and leek sausages with chive mash, grilled plaice with mustard sauce, or battered cod with chips and mushy peas.

OPEN: 12-11 (Sun 12-10.30) **BAR MEALS:** L served all week 12-2.30 D served all week 6-8.30 Av main course £5 **BREWERY/COMPANY:** Free House 🍺: Boddingtons, Marstons Pedigree, Bass plus guest ales. **GARDEN:** Patio seats 25-30, food served outside **NOTES:** Dogs allowed: only when food service is over, Parking 60

ONNELEY   THE WHEATSHEAF INN ♦♦♦♦ ♀

Barhill Rd CW3 9QF
☎ 01782 751581 📠 01782 751499
e-mail: thewheatsheaf.inn@virgin.net
Dir: On the A525 between Madeley & Woore, 6.5m W of Newcastle Under Lyme.
Map Ref: SJ74

Overlooking the local golf course and village cricket ground, this recently renovated wayside inn has been a hostelry since 1769. Solid oak beams, roaring log fires and distinctive furnishings are a fine setting for some fine dining. Specials include Chateaubriand roast, steamed halibut steak on buttered spinach, pan-fried kangaroo, and chicken breast in smoked bacon with creamy grape and cheese sauce. Bar meals also available.

OPEN: 12-2.30 6-11 **BAR MEALS:** L served all week 12-2.30 D served all week 6-9.30 Av main course £6 **RESTAURANT:** D served all week 6.30-9.30 Av 3 course à la carte £15 **BREWERY/COMPANY:** Free House 🍺: Bass, Worthington, Guest Ales. **CHILDREN'S FACILITIES:** menu **GARDEN:** Food served outside **NOTES:** No dogs, Parking 60 **ROOMS:** 6 en suite s£65 d£69

STAFFORD   THE HOLLYBUSH INN ♀

Salt ST18 0BX
☎ 01889 508234 📠 01889 508058
e-mail: geoff@hollybushinn.co.uk
Dir: Telephone for directions. **Map Ref:** SJ92

Reputedly the second oldest licensed inn in the country - with a building that may well

date from the 12th century - the heavy beams and straw-thatched roof of the Hollybush Inn make this easy to believe. Carved beams, open fires, attractive prints and cosy alcoves characterise the comfortably old-fashioned interior. It boasts another distinction too: the present landlord's son became a joint licensee at just 18 years and 6 days old - making him the youngest person to be granted a license. Geoff Holland still loves serving good food and drink to discerning customers.

OPEN: 12-2.30 6-11 (open all day Sat-Sun) **BAR MEALS:** L served all week 12-2 D served all week 6-9.30 **BREWERY/COMPANY:** Free House 🍺: Boddingtons, Pedigree & Guest Ales. ♀: 12 **CHILDREN'S FACILITIES:** menu, portions, food/bottle warming **GARDEN:** Large lawned garden with seatings **NOTES:** Dogs allowed: in garden, water provided, Parking 25

STOURTON   THE FOX INN

Bridgnorth Rd DY7 5BL
☎ 01384 872614 & 872123 ▤ 01384 877771
Map Ref: SO88

Remote pub with a warm atmosphere, attracting walkers from many nearby rambling areas. Smart conservatory, good value food.

OPEN: 11.30-3 5-11 open all day weekends
BAR MEALS: L served all week 12.30-2.15
D served Tue-Sat Late Sun lunch 3-5.30pm
RESTAURANT: L served Tue Av 3 course à la carte
£25 ◖: Bathams Ale, Enville Ale.
CHILDREN'S FACILITIES: menu, portions, high-chairs, food/bottle warming, baby changing
NOTES: No dogs (ex guide dogs)

TATENHILL   HORSESHOE INN ♀

Main St DE13 9SD
☎ 01283 564913 ▤ 01283 511314
Dir: From A38 at Branston follow signs for
Tatenhill. **Map Ref:** SK22

Probably five to six hundred years old, this historic pub retains much original character, including evidence of a priest's hiding hole. In winter, log fires warm the bar and family area. In addition to home-made snacks like chilli con carne, and Horseshoe brunch, there are sizzling rumps and sirloins, chicken curry, moussaka, battered cod with chips and mushy peas, and a pasta dish of the week. And specials too - beef bourguignon, or steak and kidney pudding, for instance.

OPEN: 11-11 **BAR MEALS:** L served all week 2-9.30
D served all week 12-9.30 Av main course £6.50
RESTAURANT: L served all week 12-9.30 D served all week
12-9.30 **BREWERY/COMPANY:** W'hampton & Dudley
◖: Marstons Pedigree, Banks Original, Stella Artois, Fosters.
♀: 9 **CHILDREN'S FACILITIES:** menu, outdoor play area,
play area, pets corner, family room **GARDEN:** Small enclosed
garden with fish pond **NOTES:** Dogs allowed: water,
Parking 70

WATERHOUSES   YE OLDE CROWN ◆◆

Leek Rd ST10 3HL
☎ 01538 308204
Map Ref: SK05

A traditional village local, Ye Olde Crown dates from around 1648 when it was built as a coaching inn. Sitting on the bank of the River Hamps, it's also on the edge of the Peak District National Park and the Staffordshire moorlands. Inside are original stonework and interior beams, and open fires are lit in cooler weather. Sample menu includes roast beef, steak and kidney pie, chicken tikka masala, battered cod, and tuna pasta bake. Homely accommodation includes an adjacent cottage.

OPEN: 11.30-3 6.30-11 (Sun 12-3, 6.30-11) Closed:
Dec 25 Rest: Sunday closed eve in Jan-Feb
BAR MEALS: L served all week 12-2 D served all week 7-9
Av main course £7 **BREWERY/COMPANY:** Free House
◖: Carlsberg-Tetley Tetley Bitter, Burton Ale.
CHILDREN'S FACILITIES: menu **NOTES:** (overnight by
arrangement), No dogs (ex guide dogs), Parking 30
ROOMS: 7 bedrooms 6 en suite s£32.50 d£65

YOXALL THE CROWN

Main St DE13 8NQ
☎ 01543 472551
Dir: *On A515 N of Lichfield.* **Map Ref:** *SK11*

In a picturesque village, this pub is reputedly over 250 years old: its name possibly deriving from its former use as the local courthouse. Within easy reach of Uttoxeter racecourse and Alton Towers it's a great spot to enjoy locally sourced, home-cooked food prepared by the landlord. Expect on the regularly changing menu such lunchtime bites as a breakfast brunch and hot filled baguettes whilst evening options such as steak and Guinness pie are supplemented by offerings posted on the chalkboard.

OPEN: 11.30-3 5.30-11 (Sat-Sun & BHs open all day)
BAR MEALS: L served all week 12-2 D served Mon-Sat 6.30-9 Av main course £6.50
BREWERY/COMPANY: Marstons ◖: Marston's Pedigree, Stella Artois. **CHILDREN'S FACILITIES:** menu **NOTES:** Dogs allowed: in bar, in garden, Parking 20

ASTON CANTLOW KING'S HEAD 🐑 ♀

21 Bearley Rd B95 6HY
☎ 01789 488242 ▯ 01789 488137
Map Ref: *SP16*

Shakespeare's parents were married in the ancient village of Aston Cantlow and had their wedding breakfast at the King's Head. It is a restored, timbered, black and white Tudor pub flanked by a huge spreading chestnut tree with a large, hedged beer garden and an attractive terrace for summer use. Inside are all the elements you hope to find in an old inn: wooden settles, oak tables, an inglenook fireplace and a flagstone floor. The new management places an emphasis on quality food and wine with a cheerful service. Food is freshly prepared from a menu that changes every 6-8 weeks, but the King's Head duck supper is still a firm favourite. Other choices may include pot roast, and poussin with lemon, ginger and green olives. Fish dishes are represented by grilled kingfish with pineapple salsa and peppercorn butter, and whole Dover sole. There are well-kept real ales and a small, eclectic wine list.

OPEN: 11-3 (Summer open all day) 5.30-11 Rest: 25 Dec open 12-2 only **BAR MEALS:** L served all week 12-2.30 D served all week 7-10 Av main course £11.50
RESTAURANT: L served all week 12-2.30 D served all week 7-10 Av 3 course à la carte £20
BREWERY/COMPANY: Furlong ◖: Greene King Abbot Ale, Fuller's London Pride, Best Bitter, Black Sheep. ♀: 8
CHILDREN'S FACILITIES: portions, games, high-chairs, food/bottle warming **GARDEN:** Large hedged beer garden, food in summer **NOTES:** Dogs allowed: in bar, in garden, water, Parking 60

BROOM BROOM TAVERN ♀

High St B50 4HL
☎ 01789 773656 ▯ 01789 772983
e-mail: richard@distinctivepubs.freeserve.co.uk
Dir: *N of B439 W of Stratford-upon-Avon.*
Map Ref: *SP05*

Charming brick and timber 16th-century inn, reputedly haunted by a cavalier killed on the cellar steps. The same menu is offered in the bar and restaurant. 'Tavern Favourites' include home-made steak and kidney pie and the Tavern crispy duck supper, while 'Your Local Butcher' may offer fillet or sirloin steak, rack of lamb, calves' liver, or Sunday roast. Legend has it that William Shakespeare and friends fell asleep under a tree outside the Broom, after losing a drinking contest nearby.

OPEN: 11.30-2.30 5.30-11 **BAR MEALS:** L served all week 12-2 D served all week 6.30-9 Av main course £8.50
RESTAURANT: L served all week 12-2 D served all week 6.30-9 Av 3 course à la carte £15
BREWERY/COMPANY: Greene King ◖: Green King IPA, Adnams Bitter, Rotation Ale. ♀: 20
CHILDREN'S FACILITIES: menu **GARDEN:** Front lawn with picnic tables **NOTES:** No dogs (ex guide dogs), Parking 30

FARNBOROUGH THE INN AT FARNBOROUGH

OX17 1DZ
Map Ref: SP44

Dating from around 1700, the Inn at Farnborough is a Grade II listed free house set in an historic and picturesque village, ideally placed for a relaxing lunch or dinner after a visit to the nearby National Trust property of Farnborough Hall or the Civil War battleground at Edge Hill. Originally the butcher's house, the pub serves local Hook Norton ales and menus of high-quality British produce and meats, some of which are organic. Dishes are prepared with refined touches of foreign lands: roast rump of Lighthorne lamb, for example, is served with Moroccan spiced vegetables. Fish too is well represented with sautéed scallops, mussels and prawns; and roast sea bass with Japanese lime and ginger. Lunches can be as simple as a ploughman's or filled ciabatta roll, while a fixed price menu offers excellent choice and value. Families welcome, with smaller portions for children always available.

OPEN: 12-3 6-11 all day Sat/Sun **BAR MEALS:** L served all week 12-3 D served all week 6-11 all day Sat/Sun Av main course £12.95 **RESTAURANT:** L served all week 12-3 D served all week 6-11 all day Sat/Sun Av 3 course à la carte £22.95 Av 3 course fixed price £12.95 **◖:** Abbot Ale, Spitfire, Budwar, Hook Norton Best. **♀:** 14
CHILDREN'S FACILITIES: portions, licence, games, high-chairs, food/bottle warming, baby changing
GARDEN: sunny, stylish, terraced garden **NOTES:** Dogs allowed: in bar, in garden, dog bowls, Parking 40

KENILWORTH CLARENDON HOUSE

High St CV8 1LZ
☎ 01926 857668 ▤ 01926 850669
e-mail: info@clarendonhousehotel.com
Dir: From A452 pass castle, turn L into Castle Hill and continue into High Street.
Map Ref: SP27

The original (1430) timber-framed Castle Tavern is incorporated within the hotel, still supported by the oak tree around which it was built. Big, comfortable sofas indoors and a heated patio outside. From the brasserie menu: Thai chicken curry and rice, salad of pigeon and pancetta, honey and lemon dressing, and kedgeree fishcakes, light curry sauce and quails' eggs. The specials board might feature pan-fried wild boar steak with crushed parsnips, roasted baby onions and cranberry and thyme jus.

OPEN: 11-11 (Sun 12-10.30) Closed: 25-26 Dec, 1 Jan
BAR MEALS: L served all week 12-10 D served all week 12-10 Av main course £9.50 **RESTAURANT:** L served all week 12-10 D served all week 12-10 Av 3 course à la carte £18 **BREWERY/COMPANY:** Old English Inns **◖:** Greene King Abbot Ale, IPA. **CHILDREN'S FACILITIES:** menu
GARDEN: Patio garden seats about 100. Outdoor heating
NOTES: Dogs allowed: in bar, in garden, in bedrooms, Parking 35 **ROOMS:** 22 en suite 2 family rooms s£57.50 d£79.50 (★★)

LOWSONFORD FLEUR DE LYS ♀

Lapworth St B95 5HJ
☎ 01564 782431 ▤ 01564 782431
e-mail: Fleurdelys.solihull@laurelpubco.com
Dir: A34 (Birmingham to Stratford).
Map Ref: SP16

Converted from three cottages and a mortuary and located alongside the Stratford-upon-Avon Canal, this 17th-century pub boasts a galleried dining room and atmospheric bars with low beams and real log fires. Fleur de Lys pies were originally made here. The style is casual dining with steak and Guinness pie, wild boar pie, free-range sausages with bubble and squeak and traditional fish and chips among the wholesome dishes. The large canalside garden is the ideal place to enjoy a drink or meal. Ideal for children, and there's even a safe fenced area for the under 8s.

OPEN: 9-11 (Sun 9-10.30) **BAR MEALS:** L served all week 12-10 D served all week Sun 12-9 Av main course £7
BREWERY/COMPANY: **◖:** Interbrew Flowers Original & IPA, Guest Ale. **♀:** 16 **CHILDREN'S FACILITIES:** menu, portions, high-chairs, food/bottle warming, outdoor play area, Fenced area for uder 8's **GARDEN:** Lrg canalside
NOTES: Dogs allowed: in bar, in garden, water, Parking 150

MONKS KIRBY THE BELL INN

Bell Ln CV23 0QY
☎ 01788 832352 ▤ 01788 832352
e-mail: belindagb@aol.com
Dir: *Off The Fosseway junction with B4455.*
Map Ref: SP48

The Spanish owners of this quaint, timbered inn, originally a priory gatehouse and brewhouse cottage, describe it as 'a corner of Spain in the heart of England'. Not surprisingly, there's a strong emphasis on Mediterranean cuisine and an extensive tapas menu. Choose from a wide range of steak dishes, pasta or paellas, or perhaps choose from the wide-ranging selection of seafood dishes—halibut Malagena, lobster Sarafina, deep-fried langoustines, monkfish cooked in a clay dish, or fresh poached salmon among them.

OPEN: 12 2.30 7-11 Closed: 26 Dec, 1 Jan
BAR MEALS: L served Tue-Sun 12-2.30 D served all week 7-11 closed Monday Av main course £12.50
RESTAURANT: L served Tue-Sun 12-2.30 D served all week 7-11 Av 3 course à la carte £30
BREWERY/COMPANY: Free House **◖:** Boddingtons.
♀: 127 **CHILDREN'S FACILITIES:** portions, high-chairs, food/bottle warming **GARDEN:** overlooks a stream & buttercup meadow **NOTES:** No dogs

PRINCETHORPE THE THREE HORSESHOES ♀

Southam Rd CV23 9PR
☎ 01926 632345
Dir: *On A423 at X of B4455 & B4453.*
Map Ref: SP47

Traditional coaching inn, built about 1856, on the Fosse Way. It has a large garden with a range of children's play equipment overlooking open countryside. Beams, horse brasses and log fires characterise the bar, where a blackboard menu of home-cooked food is available. Why not enjoy a Sunday lunch in the inviting atmosphere?

OPEN: 11.30-2.30 6-11 (Sun 12-11) Closed: 25 Dec
BAR MEALS: L served all week 12-2.00 D served all week 6-9.30 **RESTAURANT:** L served all week 12-2 D served all week 6-11 **BREWERY/COMPANY:** Free House **◖:** Ruddles Best, John Smiths, Bombadier, Pedigree.
CHILDREN'S FACILITIES: menu, portions, high-chairs, food/bottle warming, slide, fort, swings **GARDEN:** Large eating area, patio **NOTES:** No dogs (ex guide dogs), Parking 50 **ROOMS:** 4 en suite s£25 d£50 (♦♦♦) no children overnight

RATLEY THE ROSE AND CROWN ♀

OX15 6DS
☎ 01295 678148
Dir: *Follow Edgehill signs, 7 miles N of Banbury or 13m SE of Stratford-On-Avon on A422.*
Map Ref: SP34

Following the Battle of Edgehill in 1642, a Roundhead was discovered in the chimney of this 11th (or 12th)-century pub and beheaded in the hearth. His ghost reputedly haunts the building. Enjoy the peaceful village location and the traditional pub food, perhaps including beef and ale pie, scampi and chips, chicken curry and the Sunday roast.

OPEN: 12-2.30 6.30-11 Sun (12-3.30, 7-11)
BAR MEALS: L served all week 12-2 D served all week 7-9 Av main course £10.50 **RESTAURANT:** L served Tue-Sun D served Tue-Sat 7-9.30 Av 3 course à la carte £18
BREWERY/COMPANY: Free House **◖:** Wells Bombardier & Eagle IPA, Greene King Old Speckled Hen & guest ale. **♀:** 8
CHILDREN'S FACILITIES: menu **GARDEN:** Garden with wooden benches **NOTES:** Dogs allowed: in bar, in garden, in bedrooms, Water, Fireplace, Parking 4

SHIPSTON ON STOUR THE RED LION ♦♦♦♦ ♀

Main St, Long Compton CV36 5JS
☎ 01608 684221 🖨 01608 684221
e-mail: redlionhot@aol.com
Dir: On A3400 between Shipston on Stour & Chipping Norton. Map Ref: SP24

A Grade II listed stone-built coaching inn dating from 1748, located in an area of outstanding natural beauty and ideally situated for such major attractions as Stratford upon Avon, Warwick, Oxford and the Cotswold Wildlife Park. With past tales of witches in the village and a nearby prehistoric stone circle, there is much to interest the historian as well as the rambler. The inside retains an old world charm with log fires, stone walls and oak beams yet offers the modern facilities expected today. The menu is extensive and caters for all tastes from interesting sandwiches, baguettes, and light bites to an à la carte candlelit dinner.

OPEN: 11-2.30 (Sun 12-3, 7-10.30) 6-11
BAR MEALS: L served all week 12-2 D served all week 7-9 Av main course £8 **RESTAURANT:** L served all week 12-2 D served all week 7-9 Av 3 course à la carte £15
BREWERY/COMPANY: Free House 🍺: Hook Norton Best, Websters Bitter, Theakston Best, Adnams.
CHILDREN'S FACILITIES: menu, portions, games, high-chairs, food/bottle warming, outdoor play area, large garden/play equipment **GARDEN:** Large garden with views of surrounding hills **NOTES:** Dogs allowed: in bar, in garden, in bedrooms, Parking 60 **ROOMS:** 5 en suite 1 family room s£40 d£60

WHITE BEAR HOTEL ♀

High St CV36 4AJ
☎ 01608 661558 🖨 01608 662612
e-mail: whitebearhot@hotmail.com
Map Ref: SP24

This former coaching inn, parts of which date from the 16th century, has a Georgian façade overlooking the market place. It is a lively pub serving good food and fine ales, and the two beamed bars are full of character. A typical menu might include Gloucester Old Spot pork chop with ginger and soy sauce; marinated sea bass with thyme, lemon and bacon; and tomato and spinach risotto. A good selection of sandwiches, baguettes and snacks is available at lunchtime.

OPEN: 11-11 (Sun 12-10.30) **BAR MEALS:** 12-2 6.30-9.30
RESTAURANT: 12-2 6.30-9.30
BREWERY/COMPANY: Punch Taverns 🍺: Marstons Pedigree, Interbrew Bass & Guest Ales.
CHILDREN'S FACILITIES: portions, high-chairs, food/bottle warming **GARDEN:** Patio, food served outside
NOTES: Dogs allowed: in bar, water, Parking 20

STRATFORD-UPON-AVON THE DIRTY DUCK

Waterside CV37 6BA
☎ 01789 297312 🖨 01789 293441
Map Ref: SP25

Frequented by members of the Royal Shakespeare Company from the nearby theatre, this traditional, partly Elizabethan inn has a splendid raised terrace overlooking the River Avon. In addition to the interesting range of real ales, a comprehensive choice of food is offered. Light bites, pastas, salads and mains at lunchtime, plus pub classics and 'make it special' dishes at night, from rustic sharing bread with herbs, garlic and olives to roast rack of lamb.

OPEN: 11-11 (Sun 12-10.30) **BAR MEALS:** L served all week 12-3 D served Mon-Sat 5.30-11 Av main course £6
RESTAURANT: L served all week 12-2 D served Mon-Sat 5.30 Av 3 course à la carte £15
BREWERY/COMPANY: Whitbread 🍺: Flowers Original, Morland Old Speckled Hen, Wadworth 6X. **GARDEN:** terrace overlooking theatre garden and river **NOTES:** Dogs allowed: at manager's discretion

WOOTTON WAWEN THE BULLS HEAD

Stratford Rd B95 6BD
☎ 01564 792511 📠 795803
e-mail: enquiries@thebullshead.co.uk
Dir: On A3400. **Map Ref:** SP16

This impressive 14th-century inn has recently been extensively refurbished. Originally converted from two large cottages, the building still retains plenty of atmosphere. Low beams, open fires and old pews set the scene in the bar and snug areas, and the style continues in the 'great hall' restaurant. Outside, you'll find a lawned garden and paved patio, surrounded by mature trees. The Bulls Head offers a warm welcome, with quality food at sensible prices. The bar menu sets the pace with choices like warmed tuna pannini with roasted red onions and smoked peppers; or peanut and coriander satay chicken wrap with mixed leaves. In the restaurant, smoked haddock brandade with Parma ham, poached egg and mayonnaise might precede braised lamb shank with crushed new potatoes and Puy lentil cassoulet; seared calves' liver with caramelised spring onions, Roquefort mash and black pudding; or baked cod supreme with fennel and olive crust.

OPEN: 11-11 (Sun 12-10.30) **BAR MEALS:** L served all week 12-2.30 D served all week 7-9.30 (Sun 12-4) **RESTAURANT:** L served all week 12-2.30 D served Mon-Sat 7-9.30 (Sun 12-4) Av 3 course à la carte £23 **BREWERY/COMPANY:** W'hampton & Dudley ◀: Marston's Pedigree, Banks Bitter plus guest ales. **CHILDREN'S FACILITIES:** portions, games, high-chairs, food/bottle warming **GARDEN:** Lawned area & paved patio surrounded by trees **NOTES:** No dogs (ex guide dogs), Parking 30

BIRMINGHAM THE PEACOCK

Icknield St, Forhill, nr King's Norton B38 0EH
☎ 01564 823232 📠 01564 829593
Map Ref: SP08

Despite its out of the way location, at Forhill just outside Birmingham, the Peacock keeps very busy serving traditional ales and a varied menu (booking essential). Blackboards display the daily specials, among which you might find braised partridge on a bed of pheasant sausage and mash, whole sea bass with crab, grilled shark steak with light curry butter, pan-fried sirloin steak with mild mushroom and pepper sauce, or lamb fillet with apricot and walnut stuffing. Several friendly ghosts are in residence, and one of their tricks is to disconnect the taps from the barrels. Large gardens with two patios.

OPEN: 11-11 (Sun 12-10.30) **BAR MEALS:** L served all week 11 D served all week 10 Av main course £7.95 **RESTAURANT:** L served all week 12-10 D served all week 6.30-9.30 **BREWERY/COMPANY:** ◀: Hobsons Best Bitter, Theakstons Old Peculier, Enville Ale. **GARDEN:** Patio at front, food served outside **NOTES:** No dogs, Parking 100

SEDGLEY BEACON HOTEL & SARAH HUGHES BREWERY ♀

129 Bilston St DY3 1JE
☎ 01902 883380 📠 01902 883381
Map Ref: SO99

Little has changed in 150 years at this traditional brewery tap, which still retains its Victorian atmosphere. The rare snob-screened island bar serves a taproom, snug, large smoke-room and veranda. Proprietor John Hughes reopened the adjoining Sarah Hughes Brewery in 1987, 66 years after his grandmother became the licensee. Flagship beers are Sarah Hughes Dark Ruby, Surprise and Pale Amber, with guest bitters also available. Lunchtime cheese and onion cobs are the only food.

OPEN: 12-2.30 (Sat & Sun 12-3) 5.30-10.45 (Fri 5.30-11, Sat 6-11, Sun 7-10.30) **BREWERY/COMPANY:** ◀: Sarah Hughes Dark Ruby, Surprise & Pale Amber, Selection of Guest Beers and seasonal products. ♀: 8 **CHILDREN'S FACILITIES:** food/bottle warming, outdoor play area, roundabout, slide, climbing frame, family room **GARDEN:** Beer garden with benches, tables&play area **NOTES:** Dogs allowed: in bar, water, Parking 50, No credit cards

West Midlands continued

SOLIHULL   THE BOAT INN

222 Hampton Ln, Catherine-de-Barnes B91 2TJ
☎ 0121 705 0474 ◽ 0121 704 0600
e-mail: steven-hickson@hotmail.com
Map Ref: *SP17*

Village pub with a small, enclosed garden located right next the canal in Solihull. Real ales are taken seriously and there are two frequently changing guest ales in addition to the regulars. There is also a choice of 14 wines available by the glass. Fresh fish is a daily option and other favourite fare includes chicken cropper, Wexford steak, and beef and ale pie.

OPEN: 12-11 Sun 12-10.30 **BAR MEALS:** L served all week 12-9.30 D served all week 12-9.30 Av main course £7.95
🍺: Tetleys, Directors, 2 gueat ales. ♀: 14
CHILDREN'S FACILITIES: menu, portions, licence, games, high-chairs, food/bottle warming, baby changing, family room
GARDEN: Small enclosed garden with tables & chairs
NOTES: No dogs (ex guide dogs), Parking 90

WEST BROMWICH   THE VINE

Roebuck St B70 6RD
☎ 0121 5532866 ◽ 0121 5255450
e-mail: bharat@sukis.co.uk
Dir: *Telephone for directions.* **Map Ref:** *SP09*

Well-known, family-run business renowned for its good curries and cheap drinks. For over 26 years this typically Victorian alehouse has provided the setting for Suki Patel's eclectic menu. Choose from a comprehensive range of Indian dishes (chicken tikka masala, goat curry, lamb saag), a barbecue menu and Thursday spit roast, offered alongside traditional pub meals like sausage and chips, chicken and ham pie or toasted sandwiches. The Vine boasts the Midlands' only indoor barbeque.

OPEN: 11.30-2.30 5-11 (Fri-Sun all day)
BAR MEALS: L served all week 12-2 D served all week 5-10.30 Av main course £4.25 **RESTAURANT:** D served all week 5-10.30 **BREWERY/COMPANY:** Free House
🍺: Bannks, Brew XI. **CHILDREN'S FACILITIES:** menu, portions, games, food/bottle warming, outdoor/indoor play area, family room **GARDEN:** Large beer garden, play area
NOTES: No dogs (ex guide dogs)

BEWDLEY   HORSE & JOCKEY

Far Forest DY14 9DX
☎ 01299 266239 ◽ 01299 266227
e-mail: info@horseandjockey-farforest.co.uk
Map Ref: *SO77*

Serving fresh food sourced from local farms and cooked with imagination, this peaceful

country pub, which was first licensed in 1838, is dedicated to maintaining traditional practices of hospitality - and thanks to the owners' enthusiasm and dedication, it is now a deservedly successful dining destination. Restoration of the premises some years ago uncovered oak beams, floorboards, an inglenook fireplace, and a glass-covered well.

OPEN: 12-3 6-11 open all day May-Sep
BAR MEALS: L served Tue-Sun 12-2.30 D served Tue-Sun 6-9.30 Sun 12-4 Av main course £7.50
RESTAURANT: L served Sun 12-2.30 D served all week 6-9.30 Sun 12-4 Av 3 course à la carte £13.95
BREWERY/COMPANY: Free House 🍺: Hobsons Best, Bombadier, Stella, Boddingtons. **CHILDREN'S FACILITIES:** menu, licence, games, high-chairs, food/bottle warming, outdoor play area, table football, air hockey, family room
GARDEN: Large lawn, play area, seating, good views
NOTES: Dogs allowed: in garden only, Parking 50

THE MUGHOUSE INN & ANGRY CHEF RESTAURANT

12 Severnside North DY12 2EE
☎ 01299 402543 🗎 01299 402543
e-mail: drew@mughousebewdley.co.uk
Map Ref: SO77

Historic pub located on the glorious River Severn. The inn's name dates back to the 17th century when 'mug house' was a popular term for an alehouse. Seating area at the front directly overlooks the water and is a favourite spot with customers in the summer months. Many popular walks in the nearby Wyre Forest. Lunchtime bar menu offers the likes of beer battered cod, steak and Guinness Mug Pie, and home-made faggots.

OPEN: 12-11 Sun 12-10.30 **BAR MEALS:** L served all week 12-2.30 (Sun 12.30-6) Av main course £5.95 **RESTAURANT:** D served Tue-Sat 7-9 Sunday lunch Carvery 12.30-6 Av 3 course à la carte £23 🍺: Timothy Taylor's Landlord, Mugs Gayme plus 2 guest beers. ♀: 7 **CHILDREN'S FACILITIES:** menu, licence, food/bottle warming, family room **GARDEN:** food served at lunchtime **NOTES:** Dogs allowed: water

BREDON FOX & HOUNDS INN & RESTAURANT

Church St GL20 7LA
☎ 01684 772377 🗎 01684 772377
Dir: M5 J9 into Tewkesbury take B4080 towards Pershore. Bredon 3m. Map Ref: SO93

Resplendent with colourful, over-flowing hanging baskets in summer, this pretty 16th-century thatched pub is located close to the River Avon. Food is served in the bar areas and dining lounge, including blackboard specials, lunchtime bar snacks and the main menu. Favourite dishes include chicken Caribbean, pork tenderloin, pasta carbonara, and the daily fresh fish selection, as well as filled hot and cold baguettes, and various tasty ploughman's.

OPEN: 11.30-3 6-10.30 (Sun 12-3, 6-10.30) Rest: 25/26 Dec closed eve **BAR MEALS:** L served all week 12-2 D served all week 6.30-9.30 Av main course £7 **RESTAURANT:** L served all week 12-2 D served all week 6.30-9.30 Av 3 course à la carte £20 **BREWERY/COMPANY:** Whitbread 🍺: Banks, Marstons Pedigree, Old Speckled Hen. **GARDEN:** Small shaded garden with BBQ area **NOTES:** No dogs (ex guide dogs), Parking 35

DROITWICH THE CHEQUERS

Cutnall Green WR9 0PJ
☎ 01299 851292 🗎 01299 851744
Dir: Telephone for directions. Map Ref: SO86

This charming country pub is decorated in traditional style, with an open fire, timbered bar and richly-coloured furnishings. The effect is cosy and welcoming - a good place to linger over numerous real ales, fine wines and perhaps a meal from the extensive menu. Dishes range from lunch light bites through to dinner dishes such honey-roast breast of Gressingham duck, with confit red cabbage, potato wedges, cinnamon sage and apple jus; and whole grilled lemon sole, with crushed potatoes, rocket salad, tomato, garlic and dill.

OPEN: 12-3 6-11 Closed: 25-26 Dec, (31 Dec, 1Jan), 2 Jan **BAR MEALS:** L served all week 12-2 D served all week 6.30-9.15 **RESTAURANT:** L served all week 12-2 D served all week 6.30-9.15 **BREWERY/COMPANY:** Enterprise Inns 🍺: Timothy Taylors, Banks Pedigree, Banks Bitter, Banks Mild. ♀: 11 **CHILDREN'S FACILITIES:** menu, family room **GARDEN:** Large garden with benches, flower borders **NOTES:** Dogs allowed: in garden, Parking 75

FLADBURY CHEQUERS INN

Chequers Ln WR10 2PZ
☎ 01386 860276 ▤ 01386 861286
Dir: *Off A4538 between Evesham and Pershore.* **Map Ref:** *SO94*

The Chequers is a 14th-century inn with plenty of beams and an open fire, tucked away in a pretty village with views of the glorious Bredon Hills. Local produce from the Vale of Evesham provides the basis for home-cooked dishes offered from the monthly-changing menu, plus a choice of daily specials. A lawned garden overlooks open fields.

OPEN: 11-3 6-11 **BAR MEALS:** L served all week 12-2 D served Mon-Sat 6.30-10 **RESTAURANT:** L served all week 12-2 D served Mon-Sat 6.30-10
BREWERY/COMPANY: Free House 🍺: Hook Norton Best, Scottish Courage Directors, Fuller's London Pride, Wyre Piddle Piddle In The Wind. **GARDEN:** Lawned garden with open field views **NOTES:** No dogs, Parking 28

KNIGHTWICK THE TALBOT 🍷

WR6 5PH
☎ 01886 821235 ▤ 01886 821060
e-mail: admin@the-talbot.co.uk
Dir: *A44 through Worcester, 8m W turn onto B4197.* **Map Ref:** *SO75*

The business rule KISS - Keep It Simple, Stupid - definitely applies in the bar of this 15th-century coaching inn. Real ales called This, That, Wot and T'other are all brewed on the premises with hops grown in the parish. In fact, everything bar the fresh fish, which comes from Wales and Cornwall, is made here from local ingredients, or from produce grown in the 'chemical free' garden. And that includes preserves, breads and black pudding. At lunchtime, have a ploughman's by all means, but why not try fresh crab blinis and garlic mayonnaise, pheasant breast with tarragon sauce, and treacle hollygog? The beamed lounge bar leads to an arboured patio and riverside lawn.

OPEN: 11-11 (Sun 12-10.30) Rest: Dec 25 Closed eve
BAR MEALS: L served all week 12-2 D served all week 6.30-9.30 (Sun 7-9) Av main course £13.95
RESTAURANT: L served all week 12-2 D served all week 6.30-9.30 (Sun 7-9) Av 3 course à la carte £26 Av 3 course fixed price £22.95 **BREWERY/COMPANY:** Free House 🍺: Teme Valley This, That, T'Other, City of Cambridge Hobsons Choice. **CHILDREN'S FACILITIES:** Highchairs, Cot **GARDEN:** Riverside grass area **NOTES:** Dogs allowed: in bar, in garden, Parking 50 **ROOMS:** 11 en suite 3 family rooms s£40 d£75 (★★)

MARTLEY ADMIRAL RODNEY INN ◆◆◆◆ 🐑

Berrow Green WR6 6PL
☎ 01886 821375 ▤ 01886 822048
e-mail: rodney@admiral.fslife.co.uk
Dir: *From M5 Junc 7, take A44 signed Bromyard & Leominster. After approx 7m at Knightwick turn R onto B4197, Inn 1.5m on L at Berrow Green.* **Map Ref:** *SO76*

Early 17th-century farmhouse-cum-alehouse, named after the man who taught Nelson. It is on the Worcester Way footpath, and has wonderful views of the Malvern Hills. Lunch choices include hot dishes such as lamb shank, fish and chips, rack of ribs, chilli con carne. The evening menu offers the likes of peppered duck breast with grilled figs, and crispy lemon thyme chicken with chestnut mushrooms. The bread is made on the premises.

OPEN: 11-3 5-11 (Mon open 5-11pm, open all day Sat, Sun) **BAR MEALS:** L served Tues-Sun 12-2 D served all week 6.30-9 Av main course £6.50
RESTAURANT: L served Sun D served Mon-Sun 7-9 Av 3 course à la carte £22.50 **BREWERY/COMPANY:** Free House 🍺: Wye Valley Bitter, local guest beers eg. Quaff from Woods in Shropshire. **CHILDREN'S FACILITIES:** menu, portions, licence, games, high-chairs, food/bottle warming, baby changing **GARDEN:** Seating, grass area, terrace **NOTES:** Dogs allowed: in bar, in garden, water, Parking 40 **ROOMS:** 3 en suite s£40 d£55

OMBERSLEY CROWN & SANDYS ARMS

Main Rd WR9 0EW
☎ 01905 620252 📠 01905 620769
e-mail:
richardeverton@crownandsandys.co.uk
Dir: Telephone for directions. **Map Ref:** SO86

A classy establishment run by Richard Everton, who also has his own village deli and wine shop. Original beams and fireplaces co-exist rather well alongside modern furniture in the trendy open-plan bar/bistro and stylish restaurant. Regular 'wine dinners' and theme evenings add to the appeal. Freshly-made sandwiches, baguettes and hot dishes are available at lunchtime. Main dishes, which are changed every week, always include a wide choice of fresh market fish and seafood, such as scallops, sea bass, monkfish, lemon sole and cod. Other main courses include prime English steak filled with Shropshire blue cheese wrapped in bacon, with port and mushroom sauce. Shropshire beers are on tap in the bar.

OPEN: 11-3 5-11 **BAR MEALS:** L served all week 11.30-2.30 D served all week 6-10 Sun all day to 9.30 Av main course £9.45 **RESTAURANT:** L served all week 11.30-2.30 D served all week 6-10 Av 3 course à la carte £15.95 **BREWERY/COMPANY:** Free House 🍺: Quaff, IPA, Shropshire Lad, guest ale. ♀: 10 **CHILDREN'S FACILITIES:** portions, games, high-chairs, food/bottle warming, baby changing **GARDEN:** Large beer garden, Japanese style terrace **NOTES:** No dogs (ex guide dogs), Parking 100

THE KINGS ARMS

Main Rd WR9 0EW
☎ 01905 620142 📠 01905 620142
e-mail: kaombersley@btconnect.com
Dir: Just off A449. **Map Ref:** SO86

After the Battle of Worcester in 1651, the fleeing King Charles II probably needed a stiff drink, and reputedly made this his first stop. It was old even then, dating as it does from 1411. Black-and-white-timbered externally, with an inviting, dimly lit interior with lots of nooks and crannies, flagstone floors, and blazing fires in winter. On warmer days customers spill out into the pretty walled garden to eat at tables among the flowers. A tempting selection of modern pub food is available, with the day's fresh fish listed on a blackboard. A fish fixture is seafood platter for two, typically including lobster, crab, oysters, king prawns, langoustines and smoked salmon. Other options are fillet of beef Wellington with rich red sauce (again for two); fillet of pork with bacon and rosemary; braised lamb in Bordeaux with boulangère potatoes; mushroom and leek shepherd's pie with goat's cheese mash; and Jerusalem artichoke, lemon and thyme crumble. Some interesting real ales are served too.

OPEN: 11-3 5.30-11 (Sun all day) Closed: 25 Dec **BAR MEALS:** L served all week 12-2.15 D served all week 6-10 Av main course £9 **RESTAURANT:** L served all week 12-2.15 D served all week 6-10 Av 3 course à la carte £9 **BREWERY/COMPANY:** Free House 🍺: Banks's Bitter, Marston's Pedigree, Cannon Royall Arrowhead, Morrells Varsity. ♀: 10 **CHILDREN'S FACILITIES:** portions, food/bottle warming, baby changing **GARDEN:** Walled garden **NOTES:** No dogs (ex guide dogs), Parking 60

PENSAX THE BELL INN

WR6 6AE
☎ 01299 896677
Dir: From Kidderminster A456 to Clows Top, B4202 towards Abberley, pub 2m on L.
Map Ref: SO76

Friendly rural local offering five real ales by the jug at weekends to extend the choice available. There's also a beer festival held at the end of June. Home-made dishes are prepared from seasonal local produce - steaks, liver and onions, and home-cooked ham with free-range eggs. Superb views are enjoyed from the garden, and great local walks. Walkers and cyclists are welcome. Look out for the bargain lunchtime menu.

OPEN: 12-2.30 5-11 (Sun 12-10.30) Rest: Mon Closed lunch except BH's **BAR MEALS:** L served Tues-Sun 12-2 D served all week 6-9 Sun 12-4 Av main course £6.25 **RESTAURANT:** L served Tue-Sun 12-2 D served all week 6-9 Sun 12-4 **BREWERY/COMPANY:** Free House 🍺: Timothy Taylor Best Bitter, Hobsons Best, Hook Norton Best, Cannon Royall. **CHILDREN'S FACILITIES:** outdoor play area, family room **GARDEN:** Food served outside **NOTES:** Dogs allowed: Parking 20

POWICK THE HALFWAY HOUSE INN

Bastonford WR2 4SL
☎ 01905 831098
Dir: *From A15 J7 take A4440 then A449.*
Map Ref: *SO85*

Situated on the A449 between Worcester and Malvern, this delightful pub is just a few minutes' drive from the picturesque spa town of Malvern, a popular centre for exploring the Malvern Hills. The menu choice ranges from Herefordshire fillet steak or roasted Gressingham duck breast to baked fillet of Scottish salmon and spinach, ricotta and beef tomato lasagne. Under new management.

OPEN: 12-3 6-11 **BAR MEALS:** L served Mon-Sun 12-2 D served Mon-Sun 6-9 Av main course £9 **RESTAURANT:** L served Mon-Sun 12-2 D served Mon-Sun 6-9 Av 3 course à la carte £25 **BREWERY/COMPANY:** Free House 🍺: Abbot Ale, St Georges Bitter, Fuller's London Pride, Timothy Taylor. **CHILDREN'S FACILITIES:** outdoor play area, Enchanted tree play area in garden **GARDEN:** Lawn area **NOTES:** No dogs (ex guide dogs), Parking 30

STONEHALL THE FRUITERER'S ARMS

Stonehall Common WR5 3QG
☎ 01905 820462 ▯ 01905 820501
e-mail: thefruiterersarms@btopenworld.com
Dir: *2m from J7 M5. Stonehall Common is 1.5m from St Peters Garden Centre Norton.*
Map Ref: *SO84*

Pub on Stonehall Common, once frequented by the area's fruit pickers. Four guest ales are rotated weekly, and there's a main menu, specials menu and Sunday menu offered in the bar, restaurant, garden pavilion and garden. Favourite dishes include Swiss chicken with Alpine cheese, fillet of lamb with Madeira and rosemary, and the fresh fish of the day. The garden is large and has a purpose-built play area for children.

OPEN: 12-3 6-11 (all day Sunday. Saturday in Summer) **BAR MEALS:** L served all week 12-2 D served all week 6-9.15 Av main course £10 **RESTAURANT:** L served all week 12-2.30 D served all week 6-9.15 all day Sundays Av 3 course à la carte £20 Av 2 course fixed price £10.95 🍺: Bass, Malvern Hills Black Pear, Hobsons Bitter. **CHILDREN'S FACILITIES:** menu, portions, licence, games, high-chairs, food/bottle warming, baby changing, outdoor play area, wood chipping base, 50mtr zip wire. **GARDEN:** 1.7 acres, 50 seat wooden pavillion, seats **NOTES:** Dogs allowed: in garden, watering station, Parking 35

TENBURY WELLS THE FOUNTAIN HOTEL 🐑 ♉

Oldwood, St Michaels WR15 8TB
☎ 01584 810701 ▯ 01584 819030
e-mail: enquiries@fountain-hotel.co.uk
Dir: *1M out of Tenbury Wells on the A4112 Leominster Road.* **Map Ref:** *SO56*

A 17th-century inn complete with black-and-white timbered exterior, and traditional country atmosphere. Alcohol was first sold here in 1855, when there was horse racing on adjacent Oldwood Common. Now run by Russell Allen, and his wife, Michaela, the inn has been winning plaudits for its quality food and real ales. Book a table near the 1000-gallon aquarium.

OPEN: 9-11 **BAR MEALS:** L served all week 9-9 D served all week 9-9 Av main course £8.95 **RESTAURANT:** L served all week 12.00-10pm D served all week 21-10pm **BREWERY/COMPANY:** Free House 🍺: Black Sheep Best, Fuller's London Pride, Adnams Broadside, Fountain Ale. ♉: 8 **CHILDREN'S FACILITIES:** menu, portions, licence, high-chairs, food/bottle warming, outdoor play area, swings, slides, assault course, trampoline, family room **GARDEN:** Large, secluded. Patio area with heaters **NOTES:** No dogs (ex guide dogs), Parking 60 **ROOMS:** 11 en suite 3 family rooms s£49.95 d£49.95 (♦♦♦♦)

PEACOCK INN

WR15 8LL
☎ 01584 810506 📠 01584 811236
e-mail: jamesvidler@btconnect.com
Dir: *A456 from Worcester then A443 to Tenbury Wells. Inn is 1.25m E of Tenbury Wells.*
Map Ref: *SO56*

A 14th-century coaching inn overlooking the River Teme, with a sympathetic extension made even more attractive by colourful hanging baskets. The relaxing bars and oak-panelled restaurant are enhanced by oak beams, dried hops and open log fires, while upstairs you might encounter the ghost of Mrs Brown, a former landlady. Local market produce plays a pivotal role in the menus.

OPEN: 12.30-3 6-11 **BAR MEALS:** L served all week 12-2.15 D served all week 6.30-9.30 Av main course £14 **RESTAURANT:** L served all week 12-2.15 D served all week 7-9.30 Av 3 course à la carte £20 Av 3 course fixed price £13.45 **BREWERY/COMPANY:** Free House 🍺: Hobsons Best Bitter, Adnams Bitter, Old Hooky. ♀: 10 **CHILDREN'S FACILITIES:** menu, portions, high-chairs, food/bottle warming, Highchairs **GARDEN:** Overlooks River Teme **NOTES:** Dogs allowed: in bar, in garden, Parking 30 **ROOMS:** 6 en suite s£60 d£70

WORCESTER THE SALMON'S LEAP

42 Severn St WR1 2ND
☎ 01905 726260 📠 01905 724151
e-mail: bernardwalker@thesalmonsleap.freeserve.co.uk
Dir: *In City centre, opposite Royal Worcester Porcelain Museum. From M5 J7 follw signs for Museum & Cathedral.* **Map Ref:** *SO85*

Quiet family pub, less than five minutes' walk from the cathedral, offering a regularly changing selection of cask ales from around the country and good quality pub food. Favourite dishes include smoked fish platter, home-made chicken and mushroom pie and a choice of steaks. The beer garden has a fenced off children's area with play equipment and a bouncy castle in summer. Saturday night barbecues, from 6pm, are a regular event in fine weather.

OPEN: 11.30-11 (Oct-Apr closed Mon lunch - open 5) **BAR MEALS:** L served all week 12-7.30 D served all week 12-7.30 Av main course £5.50 **RESTAURANT:** L served all week 12-7.30 D served all week 12-7.30 🍺: Timothy Taylor, 5 other guest ales. **CHILDREN'S FACILITIES:** menu, licence, games, high-chairs, outdoor play area, Fenced area & equipment; bouncy castle-summer, family room **GARDEN:** Adjacent to pub **NOTES:** Dogs allowed: in bar, except in restaurant; water, Parking 3

WYRE PIDDLE THE ANCHOR INN ♀

Main St WR10 2JB
☎ 01386 552799 📠 01386 552799
e-mail: ngreen32@btinternet.com
Dir: *From M5 J6 take A4538 S towards Evesham.* **Map Ref:** *SO94*

An impressive half-timbered inn on the banks of the Avon, standing in gardens that overlook the pleasure craft moored by the water's edge. Old world in style, the 400-year-old building features a cosy lounge with original low-timbered ceiling, old coaching prints around the walls and an inglenook fireplace decorated with horse brasses. The dining room enjoys a panoramic view out over the river and countryside. The asparagus supper is very popular when in season, as is local game.

OPEN: 12-3 6-11 (Easter & Aug BH & Sun open all day) **BAR MEALS:** L served all week 12-2 D served all week 7-9 Av main course £7.50 **RESTAURANT:** L served all week 12-2 D served all week 7-9 Av 3 course à la carte £15 **BREWERY/COMPANY:** Enterprise Inns 🍺: Banks bitter, Timothy Taylor landlord, Marston's Pedigree, Piddle Ale. ♀: 22 **CHILDREN'S FACILITIES:** menu **GARDEN:** River Avon at bottom, wonderful views **NOTES:** No dogs, Parking 10

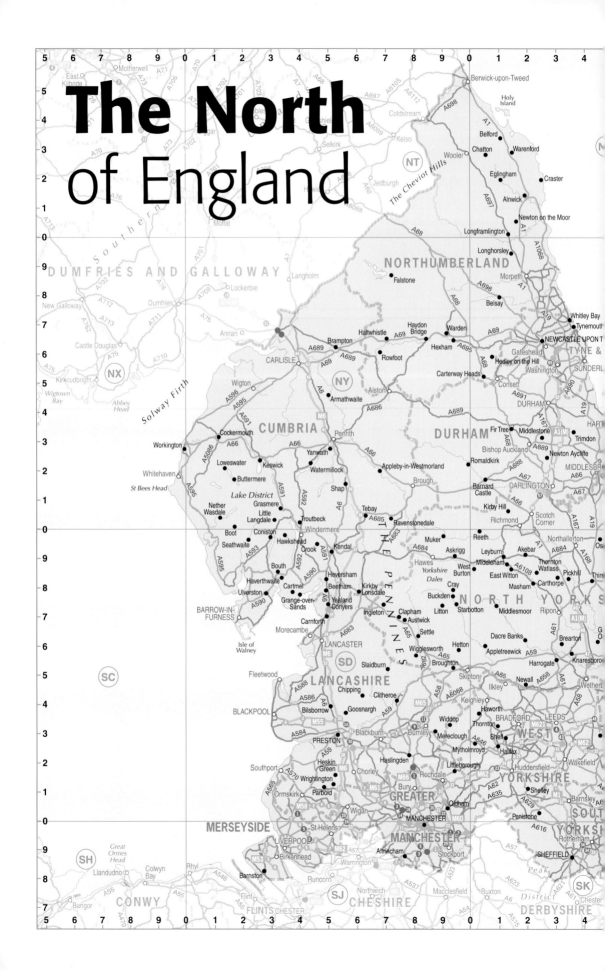

The big industrial cities of the north – Liverpool, Manchester, Leeds, Sheffield, Bradford and Newcastle – have shaken off much of their dour image in recent decades and in parts have enough cultural cachet to challenge the capital. Blackpool is Europe's top seaside resort attracting six million plus visitors annually; York and Durham are two of England's finest cathedral cities, and genteel towns like Harrogate, Windermere and Haworth offer all that's best in tea shops and literary associations. Fabulous natural landscapes take in the Lake District, the Yorkshire Dales, and the North York Moors National Park. The North Pennines, spanning Northumberland, Durham and Cumbria, is the country's most recently declared 'Area of Outstanding National Beauty'.

Favourite tourist attractions in the region are Flamingo Land Theme Park; Pleasureland in Southport; Beamish, the North of England Open Air Museum; Merseyside Maritime Museum, The National Museum of Photography, Film & Television; The National Railway Museum; Castle Howard, and Windermere Lake Cruises.

Top tipples

An extraordinary episode in the region's drinking history began during World War I when Carlisle's brewing industry and alcohol outlets were brought under state control. It was Lloyd George's initiative; he was then in charge of munitions and troubled by the outbreaks of drunkenness when munitions factory workers from Gretna descended on the town en masse. The State Management Scheme was ultimately rather successful, producing good beer and fine public houses, and the locals were quite sad when the brewery and pubs were sold off in 1971.

For those interested in traditionally brewed regional beers, the following companies offer brewery tours: Jennings Castle Brewery at Cockermouth in Cumbria, Theakston Working Brewery & Visitor Centre at Masham, North Yorkshire (home to the legendary Old Peculier), and the York Brewery Co Ltd, within York city walls, where the ticket price includes a complimentary pint.

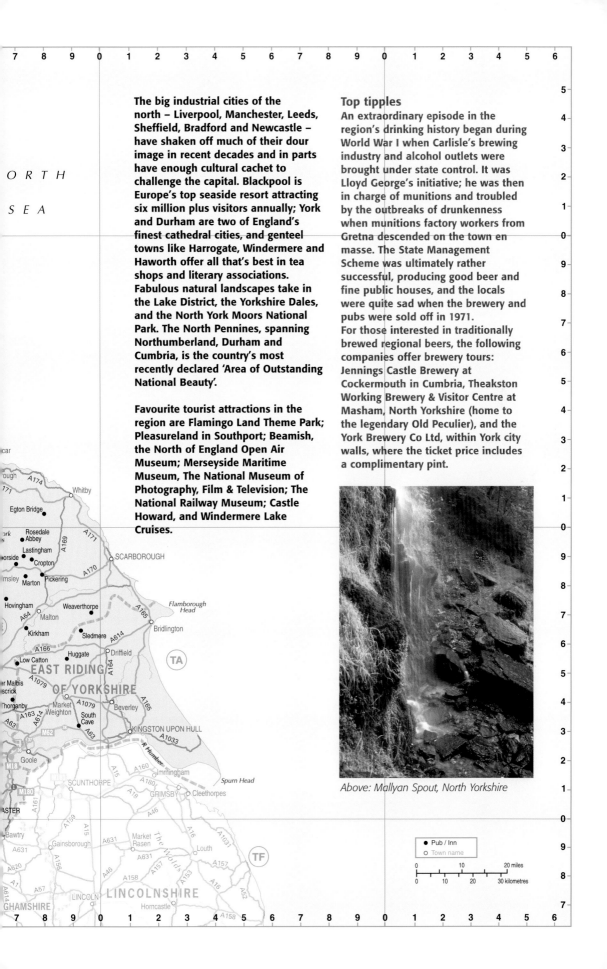

Above: Mallyan Spout, North Yorkshire

Pub / Inn
Town name

0   10   20 miles
0 10 20 30 kilometres

APPLEBY-IN-WESTMORLAND   THE NEW INN

Brampton Village CA16 6JS
☎ 017683 51231
Map Ref: NY62

At the heart of Brampton village with splendid Pennine views, a charming 18th-century inn with oak beams and an original range. One menu serves the bar and dining room with all home-cooked fare, from regulars like steak and ale pie and Cumberland sausage to specials of battered haddock, fisherman's platter and home-made mushroom balti.

OPEN: 12-3 7-11 **BAR MEALS:** L served all week 12-2 D served all week 7-9 Av main course £6.50
RESTAURANT: L served all week 12-2 D served all week 7-9
BREWERY/COMPANY: Free House 🍺: Black Sheep, Charles Wells Bombardier, John Smiths.
CHILDREN'S FACILITIES: menu, portions, food/bottle warming, family room **GARDEN:** Food served outside
NOTES: In the garden only, No dogs, Parking 16, No credit cards

TUFTON ARMS HOTEL ♇

Market Square CA16 6XA
☎ 017683 51593 📄 017683 52761
e-mail: info@tuftonarmshotel.co.uk
Map Ref: NY62

Set in the heart of the beautiful Eden Valley, this 16th-century, family-run coaching inn is

renowned for its hospitality. Its sturdy presence is a landmark in the centre of this medieval market town. Restored to its former Victorian splendour, there are rich drapes, period paintings and elegant furniture. The stylish conservatory restaurant overlooks a cobbled mews courtyard and the cuisine is an appealing blend of classical and modern, with fresh local meat, game, fish and seafood appearing on the menu.

OPEN: 11-11 Closed: 25-26 Dec **BAR MEALS:** L served all week 12-2 D served all week 7-9 Av main course £6.95
RESTAURANT: L served all week 12-2 D served all week 7-9 Av 3 course à la carte £19 Av 3 course fixed price £24.50
BREWERY/COMPANY: Free House 🍺: Tufton Arms Ale, Coors Worthington Bitter, Interbrew Flowers & Boddingtons, Tennants. ♇: 15 **CHILDREN'S FACILITIES:** portions, high-chairs, food/bottle warming **NOTES:** Dogs allowed: in bar, in bedrooms, Parking 15

ARMATHWAITE   THE DUKES HEAD HOTEL ♇

Front St CA4 9PB
☎ 016974 72226
Dir: A6, turn at Armathwaite turning.
Map Ref: NY54

This has been a pub since the building of the Settle to Carlisle railway, and for the past 15 years the Lynch family have welcomed walkers, climbers, anglers, and all who appreciate comfort and courtesy. Meals could include roast duckling with apple sauce and stuffing; home-made salmon and coley fishcakes with the pub's own tartare sauce; braised pheasant and venison casserole; and filo parcels filled with a chestnut pûrée, mushroom and hazelnut stuffing.

OPEN: 12-3 5.30-11 Closed: 25 Dec
BAR MEALS: L served all week 12-1.45 D served all week 6.15-9 Av main course £10 **RESTAURANT:** L served all week 12-1.45 D served all week 6.15-9 Av 3 course à la carte £18 **BREWERY/COMPANY:** Pubmaster 🍺: Jennings Cumberland Ale, Carlsberg-Tetley Tetley's Bitter. ♇: 6
CHILDREN'S FACILITIES: portions, high-chairs, food/bottle warming **GARDEN:** Lawned area surrounded by trees
NOTES: Dogs allowed: in back bar, in garden, in bedrooms, water, Parking 26

BEETHAM   THE WHEATSHEAF HOTEL ◆◆◆◆ 🐑 ♀

LA7 7AL
☎ 015395 62123 📠 015395 64840
e-mail: wheatsheaf@beetham.plus.com
Dir: On A6 5m N of J35. *Map Ref:* SD47

This family owned and run free house offers a tranquil retreat of uncomplicated charm.

The 16th-century former coaching inn stands beside the church in the attractive village of Beetham, tucked away off the A6. Throughout the inn you'll find personal touches like fresh flowers and table decorations, as well as local and national newspapers and magazines. Lunchtime bar meals include ciabatta sandwiches.

OPEN: 11.30-3 5.30-11 (Sun 12-3, 6-10.30)
BAR MEALS: L served all week 12-2 D served all week 6-9 Av main course £17.95 **RESTAURANT:** L served all week 12-2 D served all week 6-9 Av 3 course à la carte £18.50
BREWERY/COMPANY: Free House 🍺 Jennings Cumberland Ale & Bitter, Guest Ales. ♀: 8
CHILDREN'S FACILITIES: menu, high-chairs, food/bottle warming **GARDEN:** small outside seating area **NOTES:** in bar, in garden, Water, No dogs, Parking 40
ROOMS: 6 en suite 1 family room s£55 d£40

BOOT   BROOK HOUSE INN 🐑 ♀

CA19 1TG
☎ 019467 23288 📠 019467 23160
e-mail: stay@brookhouseinn.co.uk
Map Ref: NY10

Family-run inn located in the heart of Eskdale with glorious views and fabulous walking

country all around. The owners take great pride in the quality of their food, beer and accommodation, and they make all their own bread, marmalade, jams, desserts and sauces. Fresh, seasonal produce is the basis of the dishes - local where possible. Specials include baked Esthwaite water trout wrapped in pastry, and braised leg of local organic mutton with Armagnac and prune sauce.

OPEN: 11-11 Closed: 25 Dec **BAR MEALS:** L served all week 12-5.30 D served all week 5.30-8.30 Av main course £8 **RESTAURANT:** L served all week 12-4.30 D served all week 6-8.30 🍺: Theakstons Best, Timothy Taylors Landlord + up to 4 guest ales. ♀: 8
CHILDREN'S FACILITIES: menu, portions, licence, games, high-chairs, food/bottle warming, baby changing, family room
GARDEN: Terrace with seating; views across valley
NOTES: in bar, Parking 25 **ROOMS:** 7 en suite s£40 d£60 (◆◆◆◆)

THE BURNMOOR INN ♀

CA19 1TG
☎ 019467 23224 📠 019467 23337
e-mail: stay@burnmoor.co.uk
Map Ref: NY10

The whole family is welcome at this traditional 16th-century free house nestling at the foot of Scafell Pike - including the dog! In

cooler weather a log fire burns in the beamed bar and the pub attracts many hill walkers. The restaurant dates back to 1578, but there's also a new conservatory and dining area with spectacular views of the western fells.

OPEN: 11-11 **BAR MEALS:** L served all week 11-5 D served all week 6-9 Sun 11-5, 6-8.30 Av main course £7.50
RESTAURANT: L served all week 11-5 D served all week 6-9 Sun 11-5, 6-8.30 Av 3 course à la carte £17.50
BREWERY/COMPANY: Free House 🍺 Jennings Cumberland, Bitter, Worthingtons, Roosters Brewery. ♀: 8
CHILDREN'S FACILITIES: menu, portions, licence, games, high-chairs, food/bottle warming, baby changing, outdoor play area, swings, ropes, climbing frame, slide, family room
GARDEN: Part paved part grassed, seating 40 people
NOTES: Dogs allowed: in bar, in garden, in bedrooms, dog blankets, water, Parking 30 **ROOMS:** 9 en suite 2 family rooms s£30 d£60 (◆◆◆)

BOUTH THE WHITE HART INN ⚲

LA12 8JB
☎ 01229 861229 ▤ 01229 861229
e-mail: nigelwhitehart@aol.com
Map Ref: SD38

The Bouth of today reposes quietly in the Lake District National Park, although once it had an occasionally noisy gunpowder factory. When this closed in 1928 villagers turned to woodland industries and farm labouring instead, and some of their tools now adorn this 17th-century coaching inn. Ever-changing specials may include pork medallions in port and mushroom sauce; homemade lamb and apricot pie; or fresh haddock in light beer batter. The upstairs restaurant looks out over woods, fields and fells, while the horseshoe-shaped bar offers six real ales, including Cumbrian brews.

OPEN: 12-2 6-11 **BAR MEALS:** L served Wed-Sun 12-2 D served Mon-Sun 6-8.45 Av main course £7.45 **RESTAURANT:** 12-2 D served Wed-Sun 6-8.45 Av 3 course à la carte £17 **BREWERY/COMPANY:** Free House ◧: Black Sheep Best, Jennings Cumberland Ale, Tetley, Yates Bitter. **CHILDREN'S FACILITIES:** menu, licence, games, high-chairs, food/bottle warming, baby changing, Playground Opposite, family room **GARDEN:** West facing terrace **NOTES:** No dogs (ex guide dogs), Parking 30

BRAMPTON ABBEY BRIDGE INN

Lanercost CA8 2HG
☎ 016977 2224 ▤ 016977 42184
e-mail: info@abbeybridge.co.uk
Map Ref: NY56

The pub is located by the bridge over the River Irthing, 400 metres from Lanercost Priory (1166), a mile from Hadrian's Wall and half a mile from Naworth Castle. In the 19th century the Naworth family were deeply involved in the Temperance Movement, so the Black Bull, as it was then, lost its licence until the 1960s. Now the pub has three bar areas, one specifically for walkers where dogs are welcome, a main bar area and a restaurant/lounge. The menu offers local and British favourites using locally supplied produce. Look out for flaky fish pie, marinated pork with coriander, and chicken and apricot casserole.

OPEN: 12-3 6-11 **BAR MEALS:** L served all week 12-2 D served Wed-Sun 6-9 **RESTAURANT:** L served all week 12-2 D served Wed-Sun 6.30-9 Av 3 course à la carte £15 ◧: Black Sheep Special, Yates Bitter, Coniston Bluebird XB, Carlsberg-Tetley Tetley Smooth. **CHILDREN'S FACILITIES:** portions, games, high-chairs, food/bottle warming, baby changing **GARDEN:** Terraced garden, bridge & grass area **NOTES:** Dogs allowed: in bar, in garden, in bedrooms, Parking 20

BUTTERMERE BRIDGE HOTEL ★★★ ⚲

CA13 9UZ
☎ 017687 70252 ▤ 017687 70215
e-mail: enquiries@bridge-hotel.com
Dir: Take B5289 from Keswick.
Map Ref: NY11

Spend a weekend at this 18th-century former coaching inn and enjoy its stunning location in an area of outstanding natural beauty between Buttermere and Crummock Water. Main courses from the restaurant include sliced duck breast served with a confit of leg with a honey and orange glaze; or poached plaice roulade. The bar menu offers Cumberland hotpot, Cumberland sausage and a good range of vegetarian choices. For smaller appetites there's a good selection of salads, sandwiches and toasties.

OPEN: 10.30-11 (open all day in summer) **BAR MEALS:** L served all week 12-2.30 D served all week 6-9.30 Av main course £6 **RESTAURANT:** D served all week 7-8.30 Av 5 course fixed price £21 **BREWERY/COMPANY:** Free House ◧: Theakston's Old Peculier, Black Sheep Best, Interbrew Flowers IPA, Tirrell Old Faithfull. ⚲: 6 **CHILDREN'S FACILITIES:** menu, portions, licence, high-chairs, food/bottle warming, baby changing **NOTES:** Dogs allowed: in garden, in bedrooms, Parking 60 **ROOMS:** 21 en suite s£60 d£60

CARTMEL   THE CAVENDISH

LA11 6QA
☎ 015395 36240 ▤ 015395 36243
e-mail: jmsmcwh@aol.com
Dir: M6 J36 take A590 follow signs for Barrow in Furness, Cartmel is signposted. In village take 1st R.
Map Ref: SD37

Cartmel's oldest hostelry, and the only one to be built within the village walls, dates from the 15th century. Now managed by new owners who welcome families with children and dogs, the pub's oak beams, log fires, low ceilings and uneven floors create a traditional cosy atmosphere. Bar food also follows traditional lines, ranging from soup and sandwiches to bangers and mash. Locally bought and freshly cooked produce feature in typical restaurant dishes such as fillet steak, sea bass and local ostrich. Top quality real ales and a good selection of malt whiskies. Tree-lined garden overlooking a stream.

OPEN: 11.30-11 (Sun 12-10.30) **BAR MEALS:** L served all week 12-2 D served all week 6-9 Sun 12-6 Av main course £7.25 **RESTAURANT:** L served all week 12-2 D served all week 6-9 Av 3 course à la carte £18
BREWERY/COMPANY: Free House ◪: John Smiths, Cumberland, Bombadier, Theakstons.
CHILDREN'S FACILITIES: menu, portions, games, high-chairs, food/bottle warming **GARDEN:** Tree lined adjoining & overlooking stream **NOTES:** Dogs allowed: in bar, Parking 25

COCKERMOUTH   THE TROUT HOTEL ★★★ ⊛ 🐑 ♀

Crown St CA13 0EJ
☎ 01900 823591 ▤ 01900 827514
e-mail: enquiries@trouthotel.co.uk
Map Ref: NY13

Dating from about 1670 and once a private house, the Trout became a hotel in 1934. The hand-carved oak staircase and marble fireplace are among the many striking features, and the bedrooms are comfortable and well-equipped. Interesting range of starters, old favourites and snacks. Main courses include sea bass, Thai green curry, and grilled sirloin steak, while flaked salmon open sandwich, minute steak baguette, and tuna and cheese melt feature among the lighter options.

OPEN: 11-11 **BAR MEALS:** L served all week 9.30-9.30 D served all week **RESTAURANT:** L served Sat & Sun 12-2 D served all week 7-9.30 **BREWERY/COMPANY:** Free House ◪: Jennings Cumberland Ale, Theakston Bitter, John Smiths, Marston's Pedigree. ♀: 12
CHILDREN'S FACILITIES: menu, portions, games, high-chairs, food/bottle warming **GARDEN:** Riverside garden, food served outside **NOTES:** No dogs, Parking 50
ROOMS: 43 en suite 1 family room s£59.95 d£109

CONISTON   BLACK BULL INN & HOTEL 🐑 ♀

1 Yewdale Rd LA21 8DU
☎ 015394 41335 ▤ 015394 41168
e-mail: i.s.bradley@btinternet.com
Map Ref: SD39

Built at the time of the Spanish Armada, this old coaching inn has a lovely village setting, by the beck and in the shadow of the Old Man. Real ales are brewed on the premises, and excellent food is served in both the bar and restaurant. Fish dishes include fresh whitebait, Morecombe Bay shrimps and a daily special; meat courses range from straightforward Cumberland sausages to the more complex pheasant and chicken breast stuffed with haggis and black pudding, wrapped in bacon and served with a red wine sauce.

OPEN: 11-11 (Sun 12-10.30) Closed: Dec 25
BAR MEALS: L served all week 12-9.30 D served all week
RESTAURANT: L served By appointment D served all week 6-9 **BREWERY/COMPANY:** Free House ◪: Coniston Bluebird, Old Man Ale, Opium, Blacksmith & XB.
CHILDREN'S FACILITIES: menu, portions, licence, games, high-chairs, food/bottle warming, baby changing, family room
GARDEN: Riverside patio outside **NOTES:** Dogs allowed: in bar, in garden, in bedrooms, dog beds and meals, Parking 12

CROOK   THE SUN INN ♈

LA8 8LA
☎ 01539 821351 ▯ 01539 821351
Dir: *off the B5284.*
Map Ref: *SD49*

A warmly welcoming inn dating from 1711, The Sun is steeped in tradition with winter fires and a summer terrace overlooking rolling countryside. The best local ingredients are used to create a variety of dishes, such as venison steak with wild mushroom sauce, game casserole, and fell-bred steaks. The bar snack and regular menus are supplemented by daily specials, and fresh fish is also featured.

OPEN: 12-2.30 6-11 (Sat 12-11, Sun 12-10.30)
BAR MEALS: L served all week 12-2.15 D served all week 6-8.45 Av main course £7 **RESTAURANT:** L served all week 12-2.30 D served all week 6-9 Av 3 course à la carte £18
BREWERY/COMPANY: Free House ◀: Theakston, Scottish Courage John Smith's, Courage Directors, Wells Bombardier.
♈: 14 **CHILDREN'S FACILITIES:** menu, portions, games, high-chairs, baby changing **GARDEN:** Terrace **NOTES:** Dogs allowed: in bar, in garden, Parking 20

GRANGE-OVER-SANDS   HARE & HOUNDS COUNTRY INN 🐑 ♈

Bowland Bridge LA11 6NN
☎ 015395 68333 ▯ 015395 68993
Dir: *M6 onto A591, L after 3m onto A590, R after 3m onto A5074, after 4m sharp L & next L after 1m.* **Map Ref:** *SD47*

Wonderfully located in Bowland Bridge in the beautiful Winster Valley, with stunning views over Cartmel Fell, this 17th-century coaching inn is 10 minutes from Lake Windermere. The traditional atmosphere is enhanced by flagstone floors, exposed oak beams, and ancient pews warmed by open fires. The bar menu has the usual ploughman's, baguettes with various fillings, salads and hot plates such as chicken curry, Cumberland sausage and mash, or home-made pies in shortcrust pastry. Children have their own menu, or portions served from the adult version; outside, they will appreciate the play area and swings in the lovely garden, with its fruit trees, rare trees, shrubs and plants.

OPEN: 11-11 (Sun 12-10.30) **BAR MEALS:** L served all week 12-2.30 D served all week 6-9 Av main course £7.50 **RESTAURANT:** L served all week 12-2.30 D served all week 6-9 Av 3 course à la carte £15 Av 3 course fixed price £8.50 **BREWERY/COMPANY:** Free House ◀: Black Sheep, Jennings, Boddingtons. ♈: 10
CHILDREN'S FACILITIES: menu, portions, games, high-chairs, food/bottle warming, baby changing, outdoor play area, Swings, Tables, Grassed Area, family room **GARDEN:** Orchard with tables and hard area with tables **NOTES:** No dogs (ex guide dogs), Parking 80

GRASMERE   THE TRAVELLERS REST INN ♈

Keswick Rd LA22 9RR
☎ 015394 35604 ▯ 017687 72309
e-mail: stay@lakedistrictinns.co.uk
Dir: *From M6 take A591 to Grasmere, pub 0.5m N of Grasmere.* **Map Ref:** *NY30*

Originally three miners' cottages, the inn dates back over 500 years. It's full of character inside and surrounded by beautiful scenery outside, with stunning views from the beer garden. A good range of beers and an extensive menu of traditional home-cooked fare is offered.

OPEN: 12-11 (Sun 12-10.30) **BAR MEALS:** L served all week 12-3 D served all week 6-9.30 (Mar-Oct, 12-9.30) Av main course £8 **RESTAURANT:** L served all week 12-3 D served all week 6-9.30 (Mar-Oct, 12-9.30) Av 3 course à la carte £16 **BREWERY/COMPANY:** Free House ◀: Jennings Bitter, Cumberland Ale, & Sneck Lifter, Jennings Cocker Hoop.
♈: 10 **CHILDREN'S FACILITIES:** menu, portions, games, high-chairs, outdoor play area, family room **GARDEN:** beer garden, stunning views, picnic tables **NOTES:** Dogs allowed: in bar, in garden, in bedrooms, water bowls provided, Parking 60

HAVERTHWAITE RUSLAND POOL HOTEL RESTAURANT & BAR

LA12 8AA
☎ 01229 861384 ▤ 01229 861425
e-mail: enquires@ruslandpool.co.uk
Dir: M6 J36 take A590 towards Barrow-in-Furness for 17m and the hotel is on the R of the A590 Westbound. **Map Ref:** *SD38*

Previously known as the Dicksons Arms, the Rusland Pool has been a pub, a cafe, a restaurant and private cottages. Close by is Lakeland, offering some of England's finest scenery, perfect for touring by car and exploring on foot. Only a stone's throw from this traditional coaching inn is magnificent Morecambe Bay with its winding channels of water and vast expanses of sand. The menu includes chef's specials which might feature local mallard breast, lemon sole, Lakeland

Herdwick lamb Henry, and asparagus and pine nut risotto.

OPEN: 11-11 **BAR MEALS:** L served all week 12-9 D served all week Av main course £8.95
RESTAURANT: L served all week 12-9 D served all week
BREWERY/COMPANY: Free House ▣: Tetleys, Boddingtons. **CHILDREN'S FACILITIES:** menu, licence, games, high-chairs, food/bottle warming, outdoor play area, Wild Animal Park, Aquarium, Windermere **GARDEN:** Terraced area overlooking Woodland **NOTES:** Dogs allowed: in bar, in garden, in bedrooms, Water on request, Parking 35

HAWKSHEAD KINGS ARMS HOTEL ◆◆◆

The Square LA22 0NZ
☎ 015394 36372 ▤ 015394 36006
e-mail: info@kingsarmshawkshead.co.uk
Map Ref: *SD39*

This charming 16th-century pub overlooks a village square that William Worsdworth, John

Ruskin and Beatrix Potter would all have known well. Main course dinner choices are likely to include steak and ale pie and local fell-bred minted lamb steaks. Lunchtime is when to order a 5oz rump steak sandwich, gammon, chips and salad, or chicken curry and rice.

OPEN: 11-11 (Sun 12-10.30) Rest: 25 Dec Closed eve
BAR MEALS: L served all week 12-2.30 D served all week 6-9.30 Av main course £7.50 **RESTAURANT:** L served all week 12-2.30 D served all week 6-9.30
BREWERY/COMPANY: Free House ▣: Carlsberg-Tetley Bitter, Black Sheep Best, Yates, Hawkshead Bitter.
CHILDREN'S FACILITIES: menu, portions, licence, games, high-chairs, food/bottle warming, Highchairs
GARDEN: Walled area, picnic tables **NOTES:** Dogs allowed: in bar, in garden, in bedrooms, water **ROOMS:** 9 bedrooms 8 en suite 3 family rooms s£39 d£68

QUEENS HEAD HOTEL ★★ ❀ ♈

Main St LA22 0NS
☎ 015394 36271 ▤ 015394 36722
e-mail: enquiries@queensheadhotel.co.uk
Dir: M6 J36 A590 to Newby Bridge. Take 1st R, 8m to Hawkshead. **Map Ref:** *SD39*

This hotel was already old when William Wordsworth attended the local grammar school. The surrounding lakes and fells provide many of the ingredients used in meals, including Esthwaite Water trout, Graythwaite estate pheasant, and Herdwick sheep. At lunch there are sandwiches, salads, light bites, grills and main meals, such as Westmoreland pie.

OPEN: 11-11 (Sun 12-10.30) **BAR MEALS:** L served all week 12-2.30 D served all week 6.15-9.30
RESTAURANT: L served all week 12-2.30 D served all week 6.15-9.30 **BREWERY/COMPANY:** Frederic Robinson ▣: Robinsons Hartleys XB, Cumbrian Way, Double Hop. ♈: 11 **CHILDREN'S FACILITIES:** menu, licence, games, high-chairs, food/bottle warming, family room
NOTES: No dogs (ex guide dogs), Parking 14
ROOMS: 14 bedrooms 11 en suite 2 family rooms s£47.50 d£84

THE SUN INN ◆◆◆◆

Main St LA22 0NT
☎ 015394 36236 ▤ 015394 36155
Dir: N on M6 J36, take A591 to Ambleside, then B5286 to Hawkshead. S on M6 J40, take A66 to Keswick, A591 to Ambleside, then B5286 to Hawkshead. Map Ref: SD39

The Sun is a listed 17th-century coaching inn at the heart of the village where Wordsworth went to school. Inside are two resident ghosts - a giggling girl and a drunken landlord - and outside a paved terrace with seating for 32. Traditional local food is served - lamb chops on black pudding mash in the bar and sea bass on leek and potato mash in the restaurant; look out too for bangers and mash with Cumberland sausage.

OPEN: 11-11 Sun 12-10.30 **BAR MEALS:** L served all week 12-2.30 D served all week 6.15-9.30 Av main course £6.50
RESTAURANT: D served all week 6.30-9
BREWERY/COMPANY: Free House 🍺: Barn Gates Cracker, Jennings, Hesket & Newmarket plus two guest ales.
CHILDREN'S FACILITIES: menu, portions, licence, high-chairs, food/bottle warming, family room **GARDEN:** beer garden, paved terrace, seating **NOTES:** Dogs allowed: in bar **ROOMS:** 8 en suite (◆◆◆◆)

HEVERSHAM BLUE BELL HOTEL 🐑

Princes Way LA7 7EE
☎ 015395 62018 ▤ 015395 62455
e-mail: stay@bluebellhotel.co.uk
Dir: On A6 between Kendal & Milnthorpe.
Map Ref: SD48

Originally a vicarage for the old village, this hotel dates back as far as 1460. Heversham is an ideal base for touring the scenic Lake District and Yorkshire Dales, but pleasant country scenery can also be viewed from the hotel's well-equipped bedrooms. The charming lounge bar, with its old beams, is the perfect place to relax with a drink or enjoy one of the meals available on the menu, including potted shrimps, sirloin steak, Cumbrian game pie and Isle of Man crab.

OPEN: 11-11 **BAR MEALS:** L served all week 11-9 D served all week 6-9 (Sun 11-8) Av main course £7.95
RESTAURANT: L served all week 11-9 D served all week 7-9 (Sun 11-8) Av 3 course à la carte £17
BREWERY/COMPANY: Samuel Smith 🍺: Samuel Smith Old Brewery Bitter. **CHILDREN'S FACILITIES:** menu, portions, games, high-chairs, food/bottle warming, baby changing, Changing room, Childrens Menu, family room **GARDEN:** Quiet garden, decoratively furnished **NOTES:** Dogs allowed: in bar, in bedrooms, Parking 100 **ROOMS:** 21 en suite 4 family rooms s£39 d£79 (★★)

KENDAL THE GILPIN BRIDGE INN ◆◆◆ 🐑

Bridge End, Levens LA8 8EP
☎ 015395 52206 ▤ 015395 52444
Dir: Telephone for directions. Map Ref: SD59

Good food is the chief attraction at this convivial pub which has seen a few changes in the last year. A garden with tables, chairs

and children's play area has been added by the new landlord. It offers the likes of home-made steak and ale pie, roast duckling, 16oz T-bone steak, and 'The Gilpin Grill' - a true meat feast - served in both the bar and restaurant at reasonable prices. Lunch is now available in the restaurant throughout the week.

OPEN: 11.30-2.30 5.30-11 (Open all day Summer, BHs)
BAR MEALS: L served all week 11.30-2 D served all week 5.30-9 (Sun 12-9) Av main course £5.50
RESTAURANT: L served all week 11.30-2 D served all week 6-9 Sun 12-9 Av 3 course à la carte £13.50 Av 2 course fixed price £4.95 **BREWERY/COMPANY:** 🍺: Robinsons Best Bitter, Old Stockport Hartleys XB.
CHILDREN'S FACILITIES: menu, portions, licence, games, high-chairs, food/bottle warming, outdoor play area, Wooden play equipment, family room **NOTES:** Dogs allowed: in garden, Parking 60 **ROOMS:** 10 en suite 2 family rooms s£40 d£55

KESWICK THE HORSE & FARRIER INN 🐑 ♀

Threlkeld Village CA12 4SQ
☎ 017687 79688 📠 017687 79824
e-mail: enquiries@horseandfarrier.com
Dir: *Telephone for directions.* **Map Ref:** *NY22*

Ever popular with fell walkers, this stone inn has stood here for over 300 years. There's a

relaxed, welcoming atmosphere in the traditional-style bars and non-smoking restaurant, decorated with hunting prints and warmed by a cheerful log fire. Menus are packed with seasonal and local produce, and all meals are freshly prepared to order. Lunchtime brings an appealing selection of platter sandwiches and hot dishes, whilst dinner might include spiced Scottish salmon on red pepper cous cous.

OPEN: 11-11 (Sun 12-10.30) **BAR MEALS:** L served all week 12-2 D served all week 6-9 **RESTAURANT:** L served all week 12-2 D served all week 6-9 **BREWERY/COMPANY:** Jennings
🍺: Jennings Bitter, Cocker Hoop, Sneck Lifter, Cumberland Ale & Guest Ale. ♀: 13 **CHILDREN'S FACILITIES:** menu, portions, games, high-chairs, food/bottle warming, family room
GARDEN: Long garden with views of Blencathra Mountain
NOTES: in bar, Parking 60 **ROOMS:** 9 en suite 1 family room s£35 d£70 (♦♦♦♦)

KIRKBY LONSDALE THE WHOOP HALL ★★ ♀

Skipton Rd LA6 2HP
☎ 015242 73632 📠 015242 72154
e-mail: info@whoophall.co.uk
Dir: *From M6 take A65. Pub 1m SE of Kirkby Lonsdale.* **Map Ref:** *SD67*

16th-century converted coaching inn, once the kennels for local foxhounds. In an imaginatively converted barn you can relax and enjoy Yorkshire ales and a good range of dishes based on local produce. Oven baked fillet of sea bass with tagliatelle verdi and tiger prawns, and stir-fried honey roast duck with vegetables and water chestnuts are among the popular favourites. The bar offers traditional hand-pulled ales and roaring log fires, while outside is a terrace and children's area.

OPEN: 7-11 **BAR MEALS:** L served all week 12-6 D served all week 6-10 Av main course £5 **RESTAURANT:** L served all week 12-2.30 D served all week 5-10 Av 3 course à la carte £15 Av 3 course fixed price £17
BREWERY/COMPANY: Free House 🍺: Black Sheep, Greene King IPA, Tetley Smooth, Caffreys. ♀: 14
CHILDREN'S FACILITIES: menu, licence, outdoor play area, Adventure playground. Changing facilities, family room
GARDEN: Terrace & lawn areas with good views
NOTES: Dogs allowed: in garden, in bedrooms, Water provided, Parking 120 **ROOMS:** 25 en suite s£67.50 d£85

LITTLE LANGDALE THREE SHIRES INN ★★

LA22 9NZ
☎ 015394 37215 📠 015394 37127
e-mail: enquiries@threeshiresinn.co.uk
Dir: *Turn off A593, 2.3m from Ambleside at 2nd junct signposted for The Langdales. 1st L 0.5m, Hotel 1m up lane.* **Map Ref:** *NY30*

This traditional Cumbrian slate and stone building was erected in the 1880s, when it

provided a resting place for those travelling over the Hardknott and Wrynose passes. Relax on the terrace which overlooks a mountain stream. The interior has bare beams and brickwork in the bar, and floral country-house décor in other rooms. Children are catered for with the usual favourites; dogs are welcome in the bar but not in the hotel.

OPEN: 11-11 (Sun 12-10.30) (Dec-Jan 12-3, 8-10.30) Closed: Dec 25 **BAR MEALS:** L served all week 12-2 D served all week 6-8.45 **RESTAURANT:** D only, served all week 6.30-8 **BREWERY/COMPANY:** Free House
🍺: Jennings Best & Cumberland, Ruddles County, Coniston Old Man, Hawkshead Bitter. **CHILDREN'S FACILITIES:** menu, licence, high-chairs, food/bottle warming, baby changing, high chairs, baby changing facilities **GARDEN:** Terrace and gardens next to stream **NOTES:** Dogs allowed: in bar, in garden, Parking 20 **ROOMS:** 10 en suite 1 family room s£36 d£72

LOWESWATER KIRKSTILE INN ◆◆◆◆

CA13 0RU
☎ 01900 85219 ▯ 01900 85239
e-mail: info@kirkstile.com
Dir: *Telephone for directions.* **Map Ref:** *NY12*

Beautifully situated, with superb views across
Cumbrian fells, this fine inn has been providing

food, drink and shelter for over 400 years. The Kirkstile is
the ideal spot to enjoy a jar of local real ale, and since
June 2003 has been making its own. You can eat and
drink anywhere you like, and the menu offers the likes
of Cumberland sausage casserole, Lakeland steak and
Melbreak ale pie, and baked lamb shoulder.

OPEN: 11-11 Closed: 25 Dec **BAR MEALS:** L served all
week 12-2 D served all week 6-9 Av main course £8
RESTAURANT: D served all week 6-9 Av 3 course à la carte
£14 **BREWERY/COMPANY:** Free House ◖: Jennings Bitter,
Coniston Bluebird, Yates Bitter. **CHILDREN'S FACILITIES:**
menu, portions, licence, high-chairs, food/bottle warming, baby
changing, baby changing facilities, toys & books, family room
GARDEN: Located away from road with river running by
NOTES: Dogs allowed: in bar, in garden, water, allowed in
some bedrooms, Parking 40 **ROOMS:** 11 bedrooms
9 en suite 2 family rooms s£40 d£70

NETHER WASDALE THE SCREES INN

CA20 1ET
☎ 019467 26262 ▯ 019467 26262
e-mail: info@thescreesinnwasdale.com
Dir: *E of A595 between Whitehaven &
Ravenglass.* **Map Ref:** *NY10*

Nestling in the scenic Wasdale valley and
close to Wastwater, this welcoming 300-year-
old inn with its en suite bedrooms, cosy log
fire, choice of real ales and large selection of
malt whiskies makes an excellent base for
walking, mountain biking, swimming or
diving. The menu offers home-baked steak
and kidney pie, grilled halibut, and goat's
cheese strudel filled with roast parsnips,
celeriac, leek and apple. There is a children's
menu; also a good choice of sandwiches at
lunchtime.

OPEN: 12-11 **BAR MEALS:** L served all week 12-3
D served all week 6-9 Av main course £7
RESTAURANT: L served all week 12-3 D served all week 6-9
Av 3 course à la carte £12 **BREWERY/COMPANY:** Free
House ◖: Black Sheep Best, Yates Bitter, Worthington's Bitter,
Derwent. **CHILDREN'S FACILITIES:** menu, portions, licence,
games, high-chairs, food/bottle warming **GARDEN:** Seating
area to front & side of pub, BBQ area **NOTES:** Dogs allowed:
in bar, in garden, in bedrooms, Water, Parking 30

RAVENSTONEDALE BLACK SWAN HOTEL 🐑 ♀

CA17 4NG
☎ 015396 23204 ▯ 015396 23604
e-mail: reservations@blackswanhotel.com
Dir: *M6 J38 take A685 E towards Brough.*
Map Ref: *NY70*

Ravenstonedale is a peaceful, unspoilt village
in the upper Eden Valley, lying between the

Lake District and Yorkshire Dales National Park. The
hotel is a grand Lakeland stone affair built around
1899. An à la carte menu is complemented by daily
specials, and an extensive bar menu. Wednesdays are
fish specials days, although there is always a good
selection of fish available. The sheltered garden leads
to a natural riverside glade.

OPEN: 9am-11pm (Sun 12-10.30) **BAR MEALS:** L served
all week 12-2.00 D served all week 6-9 snack menu all day
Av main course £8 **RESTAURANT:** L served all week
12-2.00 D served all week 7-9 Av 3 course à la carte £15
BREWERY/COMPANY: Free House ◖: Black Sheep,
Scottish Courage John Smith's, Dent, Derwent. ♀: 8
CHILDREN'S FACILITIES: menu, portions, licence, games,
high-chairs, food/bottle warming **GARDEN:** River & garden
NOTES: Dogs allowed: in bar, in garden, in bedrooms,
Parking 40 **ROOMS:** 12 bedrooms 11 en suite
2 family rooms s£40 d£45 (★★)

THE FAT LAMB COUNTRY INN ★★

Crossbank CA17 4LL
☎ 015396 23242 ▤ 015396 23285
e-mail: fatlamb@cumbria.com
Dir: *On A683 between Sedbergh and Kirkby Stephen.* **Map Ref:** *NY70*

Dating from the 1600s, this is a sprawling

country inn with solid grey stone stone walls and its own nature reserve. Faced with bar snack, carte or fixed price dinner menu, all possibilities are tempting. The informal garden doubles as a pleasant eating area, and the private nature reserve, set just behind the pub, offers 15 acres of peace and beauty.

OPEN: 11-2 6-11 **BAR MEALS:** L served all week 12-2 D served all week 6-9 Av main course £6.50
RESTAURANT: L served all week 12-2 D served all week 6-9 Av 3 course à la carte £16 Av 4 course fixed price £20
BREWERY/COMPANY: Free House 🍺: Cask Condition Tetley's Bitter. **CHILDREN'S FACILITIES:** menu, portions, high-chairs, food/bottle warming, baby changing, outdoor play area, Garden with sandpit & playhouse **GARDEN:** Open grassed area surrounded by shrubs **NOTES:** Dogs allowed: in bar, in garden, in bedrooms, Parking 60 **ROOMS:** 12 en suite 4 family rooms s£44 d£36

KINGS HEAD HOTEL ◆◆◆

CA17 4NH
☎ 015396 23284
e-mail: enquiries@kings-head.net
Dir: *Ravenstonedale is less that 10 mins (7 miles) from J38 Tebay on A685 & 6 miles from Kirkby Stephen.* **Map Ref:** *NY70*

With a history dating from the 16th century, in its time this building has served as an inn, a court and jail, cottages, a temperance hotel and latterly licensed premises again. The Kings Head retains its old world charm and traditional values, with cask ales, 45 malt whiskies, home-cooked local produce and real log fires. There are interesting 'Specials', a salad bar, and a chargrill.

OPEN: 11-3 6-11 (Fri-Sat Open all day Spring & Summer)
BAR MEALS: L served all week 12-2 D served all week 6-9 Av main course £7.50 **RESTAURANT:** L served all week 12-2 D served all week 6-9 Av 3 course à la carte £15.50 🍺: Black Sheep, Dent, Carlsberg-Tetley Tetley's Imperial, Over 100 Guest Ales. **CHILDREN'S FACILITIES:** menu, portions, licence, high-chairs, food/bottle warming, family room **GARDEN:** By river, offset from building, tree canopy **NOTES:** Dogs allowed: in bar, in garden, in bedrooms, Water, food bowls, Parking 10 **ROOMS:** 3 bedrooms 2 en suite 1 family room s£35 d£50

SEATHWAITE   NEWFIELD INN

LA20 6ED
☎ 01229 716208
e-mail: paul@seathwaite.freeserve.co.uk
Dir: *A590 toward Barrow, then R onto A5092, becomes A595, follow for 1m, R at Duddon Bri, 6m to Seathwaite.* **Map Ref:** *SD29*

Located in Wordsworth's favourite Duddon Valley, this early 17th-century building has been a farm and a post office in the past. The interior boasts a real fire, oak beams and a stunning slate floor. The menu encompasses homemade cuisine, including shortcrust steak pie, lasagne, vegetarian spicy bean casserole, local beef steaks, and an ever-changing specials board. The garden offers some stunning views of the fells and there is an enclosed children's play area.

OPEN: 11-11 Rest: variations over Christmas & New Year
BAR MEALS: L served all week 12-9 D served all week 12-9 Av main course £6 **RESTAURANT:** L served all week 12-9 D served all week 12-9 Av 3 course à la carte £14
BREWERY/COMPANY: Free House 🍺: Scottish Courage Theakston Old Peculier, Jennings Cumberland Ale, Coniston Bluebird, Caledonian Deuchars IPA.
CHILDREN'S FACILITIES: menu, portions, games, high-chairs, food/bottle warming, outdoor play area, large enclosed grass area **GARDEN:** Sheltered, seating for 40, stunning views
NOTES: Dogs allowed: in bar, in garden, water, Parking 30

SHAP GREYHOUND HOTEL ♀

Main St CA10 3PW
☎ 01931 716474 📠 01931 716305
e-mail:
postmaster@greyhoundshap.demon.co.uk
Dir: *Telephone for directions.* **Map Ref:** *NY51*

Built as a coaching inn in 1684, the

Greyhound is a welcoming sight for travellers after crossing Shap Fell. It offers a choice of up to eight real ales and a good selection of wines. From the specials board expect dishes like braised haunch of venison in red wine; roast fillet of haddock with a pesto crust and spicy salsa; or wild mushroom mille-feuille with a Parmesan wafer. There is a good choice of children's dishes, and a snack menu at lunchtime.

OPEN: 11-11 **BAR MEALS:** L served all week 12-2 D served all week 6-9 Av main course £8 **RESTAURANT:** L served all week 12-2 D served all week 6-9 Av 3 course à la carte £15 **BREWERY/COMPANY:** Free House ◀: Carlsberg-Tetley Bitter, Young's Bitter, Greene King Old Speckled Hen, Jennings Bitter plus Guest Ales. ♀: 8 **CHILDREN'S FACILITIES:** menu, portions, licence, high-chairs, food/bottle warming, baby changing **GARDEN:** Food served outside **NOTES:** Dogs allowed: in bar, Parking 30

TEBAY CROSS KEYS INN ♦♦♦

CA10 3UY
☎ 015396 24240 📠 015396 24240
e-mail: www.stay@crosskeys-tebay.co.uk
Dir: *Just off J38 M6. Along A685 to Kendal.*
Map Ref: *NY60*

A little gem of a free house, allegedly haunted by the ghost of Mary Baynes, the Tebay Witch, still looking for her black cat which was savagely disposed of by a former landlord. An extensive lunch and evening menu is available in both the restaurant and bar.

OPEN: 12-3 6-11 (Open all day Fri-Sun)
BAR MEALS: L served all week 12-2.30 D served all week 6-9 Av main course £6.75 **RESTAURANT:** L served all week 12-2.30 D served all week 6-9 **BREWERY/COMPANY:** Free House ◀: Black Sheep Cask, Carlsberg-Tetley Tetley's Cask, Smooth & Imperial. **CHILDREN'S FACILITIES:** menu, licence, games, high-chairs, food/bottle warming, baby changing, outdoor play area, Lrg grass play area **GARDEN:** Lrg patio area, lrg lawned area **NOTES:** Dogs allowed: in bar, Parking 50 **ROOMS:** 6 bedrooms 3 en suite s£25 d£45

TROUTBECK QUEENS HEAD HOTEL ♦♦♦♦ ♀

Townhead LA23 1PW
☎ 015394 32174 📠 015394 31938
e-mail: enquiries@queensheadhotel.com
Dir: *M6 J36, A590/591 westbound towards Windermere, R at mini-rdbt onto A592 signed Penrith/Ullswater, pub 2m on R.*
Map Ref: *NY40*

The Queens Head enjoys stunning views across the Garburn Pass and its rambling rooms are full of character, with solid beams, open fires, ancient carved settles and stone-flagged floors. Old prints adorn the walls of a bar servery created from an Elizabethan four-poster bed. The children's menu might include steak, ale and mushroom cobbler; or fettuccine pasta with chicken strips, basil and mushrooms.

OPEN: 11-11 (Sun 12-10.30) Closed: 25 Dec
BAR MEALS: L served all week 12-2 D served all week 6.30-9 Av main course £12.50 **RESTAURANT:** L served all week 12-2 D served all week 6.30-9 Av 3 course à la carte £22 Av 4 course fixed price £15.50 **BREWERY/COMPANY:** Free House ◀: Interbrew Boddingtons Bitter, Coniston Bluebird, Old Man Bitter, Jennings Cumberland Ale. **CHILDREN'S FACILITIES:** licence, high-chairs, food/bottle warming, baby changing **NOTES:** No dogs (ex guide dogs), Parking 100 **ROOMS:** 14 en suite s£60 d£85

ULVERSTON FARMERS ARMS

Market Place LA12 7BA
☎ 01229 584469
e-mail: roger@farmersrestaurant-
thelakes.co.uk
Map Ref: SD27

A warm welcome is extended to locals and visitors alike at this lively 16th-century inn located at the centre of the attractive, historic market town. The town is host to many festivals so there is always something of interest going on. Inside the visitor will find a comfortable and relaxing beamed front bar with an open fire in winter. Landlord Roger Chattaway takes pride in serving quality food; his Sunday lunches are famous, and at other times the varied and tempting specials menu lists roast Barbary duck, moules marinière,

chargrilled large king prawns with garlic and chillies, and stir-fried marinated chicken in a sesame Cantonese sauce. The lunchtime choice includes hot and cold sandwiches, baguettes or ciabatta, and various salads.

OPEN: 10-11 **BAR MEALS:** L served all week 11.30-3 D served all week 5.30-8.30 Av main course £6.50
RESTAURANT: L served all week 11.30-3 D served all week 5.30-8.30 Av 3 course à la carte £12
BREWERY/COMPANY: Free House ◀: Scottish Courage Directors & Theakston Best Bitter, Timothy Taylor Landlord, Hawkshead Best Bitter. **CHILDREN'S FACILITIES:** menu, outdoor play area, family room **GARDEN:** Patio garden, outdoor heaters and canopy **NOTES:** No dogs

WATERMILLOCK BRACKENRIGG INN ◆◆◆◆

CA11 0LP
☎ 017684 86206 ▤ 017684 86945
e-mail: enquiries@brackenrigginn.co.uk
Dir: From M6 motorway (Jcn 40) take the A66 (signed Keswick). Then take A592 signed Ullswater. Located six miles from M6 and Penrith. **Map Ref:** NY42

The Brackenrigg makes the most of its elevated position, with sweeping views across Lake Ullswater and the surrounding fells. Cumbrian food and drink are very much to the fore, the bar menu offering Cumberland sausage (made in the village). In fine weather you can sit on the terrace and enjoy the fabulous scenery.

OPEN: 12-11 (Sun 12-10.30) Nov-Mar closed btwn 3-5pm (Mon-Fri) **BAR MEALS:** L served all week 12-2.30 D served all week 6.30-9 **RESTAURANT:** L served all week 12-2.30 D served all week 6.30-9 **BREWERY/COMPANY:** Free House ◀: Theakstons Best, Jennings Cumberland, Black Sheep Special, Coniston Bluebird. ♀: 12
CHILDREN'S FACILITIES: menu, portions, licence, high-chairs, food/bottle warming, high chair, cot **GARDEN:** Garden has views of Ullswater & the valley **NOTES:** Dogs allowed: in bar, water provided, Parking 40 **ROOMS:** 17 en suite 8 family rooms s£32 d£54

WORKINGTON THE OLD GINN HOUSE

Great Clifton CA14 1TS
☎ 01900 64616 ▤ 01900 873384
e-mail: enquiries@oldginnhouse.co.uk
Dir: 3 miles from Workington, 4 miles from Cockermouth, just off the A66. **Map Ref:** NY02

In the 17th century, when this old Lakeland inn was a farm, wool was treated in a process known as ginning, in what is today's unusual rounded Ginn Room bar. The buildings, separated by an attractive courtyard, are full of character, yet their modern facilities have been carefully integrated. An example is the main dining area, whose glazed-butter yellows, bright check curtains and terracotta tiles create a warm Mediterranean glow. Hearty home-made soups; braised shoulder of lamb with

garlic and mint; pork and Stilton and other home-made pies; sea bass with mushroom risotto; plus steaks and specials characterise the menu. Sink into a sofa in the cosy lounge and read one of the magazines or books provided. The Old Ginn House is a good focal point for a tour of the many attractions of the Western Lakes and Fells.

OPEN: 12-2 6-11 Closed: 24-26 Dec, 1 Jan
BAR MEALS: L served all week 12-1.45 D served all week 6-9.30 Av main course £7.95 **RESTAURANT:** L served all week 12-1.45 D served all week 6-9.30 ◀: Jennings Bitter, Murphy's Stout, John Smiths Bitter.
CHILDREN'S FACILITIES: menu, portions, games, high-chairs, food/bottle warming **GARDEN:** Courtyard **NOTES:** No dogs (ex guide dogs), Parking 40 **ROOMS:** 20 en suite s£45 d£60 (◆◆◆◆)

Cumbria continued

YANWATH — THE YANWATH GATE INN

CA10 2LF
☎ 01768 862386 📠 01768 864006
e-mail: deanchef@hotmail.com
Map Ref: NY52

The Yanwath Gate Inn has been offering hospitality in the North Lakes since 1687. Nowadays however, the busy kitchen is the driving force as the award-winning new owner/chef Dean El-Taher dishes up a contemporary international cuisine. This is the place to enjoy a pint of Black Sheep bitter while you choose something from the appetising menu. Mediterranean-style breads are baked fresh each morning, together with handmade pastas and carefully flavoured olive oils. A tapas menu on the bar, and a cosy reading area, ensure a relaxed mood for diners wishing to eat either in the bar by the log fire, or to take a table in one of the two restaurants. Each dish is cooked and prepared to order, and the regularly changing menus make full use of plentiful local produce.

OPEN: 12-2.30 6.30-11 Closed: Jan **BAR MEALS:** L served all week 12-2 D served all week 6-9 Av main course £10.50 **RESTAURANT:** L served all week 12-2 D served all week 6-9.15 Av 3 course à la carte £20 Av 2 course fixed price £7.50 **BREWERY/COMPANY:** Free House 🍺: Black Sheep Bitter, Jennings Cumberland Bitter, Scottish Courage John Smith's Smooth. **CHILDREN'S FACILITIES:** menu, licence, high-chairs **GARDEN:** Secluded terrace, lawns, landscaped garden **NOTES:** No dogs (ex guide dogs), Parking 20

BARNARD CASTLE — THE MORRITT ARMS HOTEL ★★★ ⊛ ♇

Greta Bridge DL12 9SE
☎ 01833 627232 📠 01833 627392
e-mail: relax@themorritt.co.uk
Dir: *At Scotch Corner take A66 towards Penrith, after 9m turn at Greta Bridge. Hotel over bridge on L.* **Map Ref:** NZ01

The present building began life in the 17th-century as a farmhouse, although buried underneath are the remains of a Roman settlement. Charles Dickens researched Nicholas Nicklelby here in 1839, his stay commemorated by the Dickens Bar. There is a formal restaurant, or, for more informal meals choose the bar, Pallatts bistro, or the landscaped gardens.

OPEN: 11-11 **BAR MEALS:** L served all week 12-3 D served all week 6-9.30 Av main course £8 **RESTAURANT:** L served all week 12-3 D served all week 7-9 Av 3 course à la carte £26 Av 4 course fixed price £21 **BREWERY/COMPANY:** Free House 🍺: John Smith's, Timothy Taylor Landlord, Black Sheep Best, Cumberland Ale. ♇: 20 **CHILDREN'S FACILITIES:** menu, portions, licence, games, high-chairs, food/bottle warming, baby changing, outdoor play area, swings, slide, grass area, family room **GARDEN:** Terraced, traditional garden with walk ways **NOTES:** Dogs allowed: in bar, in garden, in bedrooms, water, Parking 100 **ROOMS:** 23 en suite s£59.50 d£87.50

FIR TREE — DUKE OF YORK RESIDENTIAL COUNTRY INN

DL15 8DG
☎ 01388 762848 📠 01388 767055
e-mail: suggett@firtree-crook.fsnet.co.uk
Dir: *on A68 trunk road to Scotland, 12m W of Durham City.* **Map Ref:** NZ13

A former drovers' and coaching inn on the old York to Edinburgh coach route, this 18th-century white-painted inn has a collection of flint arrowheads, axes and Africana. Typical food includes home-made steak and kidney pie, pork Zaccharoff, fresh cod in Black Sheep beer batter, and soups that are so popular, people often ask for the recipe. Large landscaped beer garden.

OPEN: 11-2.30 6.30-10.30 **BAR MEALS:** L served all week 12-2 D served all week 6.30-9 Av main course £7.50 **RESTAURANT:** L served all week 12-2 D served all week 6.30-9 Av 3 course à la carte £20 **BREWERY/COMPANY:** Free House 🍺: Black Sheep, Worthington, Stones, Carling. **CHILDREN'S FACILITIES:** menu, portions, licence, high-chairs, food/bottle warming, outdoor play area **GARDEN:** Garden at rear of pub, patio area **NOTES:** in garden, water, No dogs (ex guide dogs), Parking 65

MIDDLESTONE SHIP INN

Low Rd DL14 8AB
☎ 01388 810904
e-mail: graham@snaithg.freeserve.co.uk
Dir: On B6287 Kirk Merrington to Coundon
Road. *Map Ref:* NZ23

Beer drinkers will appreciate the string of
CAMRA accolades received by this family-run
pub on the village green. In the last three
years regulars could have sampled well over
500 different beers. Ask about the pub's
challenge for regulars to visit as many pubs
as possible with 'ship' in their name. Home-
cooked food in the bar and restaurant. The
rooftop patio has spectacular views over the
Tees Valley and Cleveland Hills.

OPEN: 4-11 (Thur-Sat 12-11 Sun 12-10)
BAR MEALS: L served Fri-Sun 12-2.30 D served Mon,
Wed-Sat 5-9 (Sun 12-2) **RESTAURANT:** L served Fri-Sun
12-2.30 D served Mon, Wed-Sat 5-9 (Sun 12-2) 🍺: Timothy
Taylor Landlord & 5 Guest Ales.
CHILDREN'S FACILITIES: menu, games, high-chairs,
food/bottle warming, outdoor play area, Swings on village
green, family room **GARDEN:** Village green **NOTES:** Dogs
allowed: in bar, in garden, Parking 6, No credit cards

NEWTON AYCLIFFE BLACKSMITHS ARMS ♀

Preston le Skerne, (off Ricknall Lane) DL5 6JH
☎ 01325 314873
Map Ref: NZ22

As its name suggests, this traditional pub was
originally a blacksmith's shop dating from
around 1800. It is set in isolated farmland
outside the new town of Newton Aycliffe. It
has an excellent reputation locally as a good
dining pub, coupled with the helpful and
friendly environment. There's a weekly-
changing range of real ales, as many as 150
each year, supporting micro-breweries
wherever possible. The beer garden is a
popular summer attraction, with a play area
to keep the children amused.

OPEN: 12-3 6-11 (Sun-10.30) Closed: 25 Dec 1 Jan
BAR MEALS: L served Tue-Sun 11.30-2 D served Tue-Sun
6-9.30 (Sun 12-2, 7-9) **BREWERY/COMPANY:** Free House
🍺: Ever changing selection of real ales. ♀: 10
CHILDREN'S FACILITIES: menu, high-chairs, food/bottle
warming, baby changing, outdoor play area, Toys, Swings &
Climbing Frames **GARDEN:** Fully enclosed rural setting, 0.75
acre **NOTES:** No dogs (ex guide dogs), Parking 25

ROMALDKIRK ROSE AND CROWN ★★ 🌸🌸 ♀

DL12 9EB
☎ 01833 650213 📠 01833 650828
e-mail: hotel@rose-and-crown.co.uk
Dir: 6m NW from Barnard Castle on B6277.
Map Ref: NY92

Built in 1733, the Rose and Crown has old
oak beams, a large dog grate with a roaring

fire in the fireplace, and lots of brass, copper and old
photographs in the wood-panelled bar. Good quality
bar lunches range from traditional pub food with an
individual twist (ploughman's with local cheese; steak,
kidney and mushroom pie made with Theakston's ale)
to more sophisticated fare.

OPEN: 11.30-3 5.30-11 Closed: Dec 24-26
BAR MEALS: L served all week 12-1.30 D served all week
6.30-9.30 Av main course £10 **RESTAURANT:** L served all
week 12-1.30 D served all week 7.30-9 Av 4 course fixed price
£26 **BREWERY/COMPANY:** Free House 🍺: Theakston Best,
Black Sheep Best. ♀: 10 **CHILDREN'S FACILITIES:** menu,
portions, licence, games, high-chairs, food/bottle warming,
Changing area, high chairs, games, books **GARDEN:** Tables at
front of Inn **NOTES:** Dogs allowed: in garden, in bedrooms,
Parking 24 **ROOMS:** 12 en suite 2 family rooms s£75 d£110

Co Durham continued

TRIMDON THE BIRD IN HAND

Salters Ln TS29 6JQ
☎ 01429 880391
Map Ref: NZ33

Village pub nine miles west of Hartlepool with fine views over surrounding countryside from an elevated position. There's a cosy bar and games room, stocking a good choice of cask ales and guest beers, a spacious lounge and large conservatory restaurant. Traditional Sunday lunch goes down well, as does breaded plaice and other favourites. In summer you can sit outside in the garden, which has a roofed over area for climbing plants.

OPEN: 12-11 Sun 12-10.30 Closed Mon-Thurs 4-7
BAR MEALS: L served Tues-Sun 12-3 D served Tues-Sun 7-9 Av main course £3.50 **CHILDREN'S FACILITIES:** menu, portions, games, high-chairs, food/bottle warming, Eating, family room **GARDEN:** Enclosed area with gazebo type roof
NOTES: Dogs allowed: in bar, Parking 30

ALTRINCHAM THE BULLS HEAD & LODGE

Wicker Ln, Hale Barns WA15 0HG
☎ 0161 903 1300 🖹 0161 903 1301
e-mail: lodge@bullshead.co.uk
Dir: Exit Junct6 M56. Turn Left at slip road and follow through centre, Wicker Lane is on the L.
Map Ref: SJ78

Usefully located for Manchester city centre and the airport, The Bulls Head offers a varied menu plus daily-changing specials. The atmosphere is friendly and informal, and there is an extensive range of wines and beers.

OPEN: 11-11 **BAR MEALS:** L served all week 12-2 D served all week (Sun 12.30-7) **RESTAURANT:** L served all week 12-2 D served all week 6-9 (Sun 12.30-7)
🍺: Robinsons, Cumbria Way, XB, Hatters Mild. 🍷: 6
CHILDREN'S FACILITIES: menu, portions, licence, games, high-chairs, food/bottle warming, baby changing, outdoor play area, Climbing Apparatus & Slide, family room
GARDEN: Spacious with seating & bowling green
NOTES: Parking 80 **ROOMS:** 21 en suite 4 family rooms s£55 d£55

LITTLEBOROUGH THE WHITE HOUSE

Blackstone Edge, Halifax Rd OL15 0LG
☎ 01706 378456
Map Ref: SD91

High on the Pennines, 1,300 feet above sea level, with panoramic views of the moors and Hollingworth Lake far below, this old coaching house dates from 1671. The pub is on the Pennine Way, which is popular with walkers and cyclists who sup on Theakston's and regular guest ales, and on Sundays can benefit from an all-day menu. Blackboard specials regularly include fresh fish: plaice, marlin and grilled tuna, a seafood medley. Also various grilled steaks, 'lamb Henry' and steak and kidney pie.

OPEN: 12-3 6-11.30 Closed: 25 Dec
BAR MEALS: L served all week 12-2 D served all week 6.30-9 **BREWERY/COMPANY:** Free House 🍺: Timothy Taylor Landlord, Theakstons Bitter, Exmoor Gold.
CHILDREN'S FACILITIES: menu, portions, high-chairs, food/bottle warming **NOTES:** No dogs, Parking 44

MANCHESTER DUKES 92

14 Castle St, Castlefield M3 4LZ
☎ 0161 839 8646 📠 0161 832 3595
e-mail: dukes92@freenet.co.uk
Dir: Town centre. *Map Ref:* SJ89

Beautifully-restored 19th-century stable building with a vast patio beside the 92nd lock of the Duke of Bridgewater canal, opened in 1762. The interior is full of surprises, with minimalist décor downstairs and an upper gallery displaying local artistic talent. The renowned cheese and pâté counter is a great draw, offering a huge range of British and continental cheeses, along with a salad selection, and a choice of platters for sharing.

OPEN: 11-11 (Fri-Sat 11-12, Sun12-10.30) Closed: 25-26 Dec, 1 Jan **BAR MEALS:** L served all week 12-3 D served Sun-Thurs 5-8 **RESTAURANT:** L served all week 12-3 D served Mon-Fri 5-8 **BREWERY/COMPANY:** Free House 🍺: Interbrew Boddingtons Bitter.
CHILDREN'S FACILITIES: menu, high-chairs
GARDEN: Large front and back patio with seating
NOTES: No dogs (ex guide dogs), Parking 30

THE QUEEN'S ARMS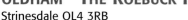

6 Honey St, Cheetham M8 8RG
Map Ref: SJ89

The Queen's is part of a loose grouping of real ale pubs in Manchester's Northern Quarter. The original tiled frontage shows that it was once allied to the long-vanished Empress Brewery. Its clientele spans the socio-economic spectrum from 'suits' to bikers to pensioners, all seemingly happy with the heavy rock on the jukebox. Food is available, but it's the brewed, distilled and fermented products that attract, including an impressive 'menu' of bottled lagers, fruit beers, vodkas and wines.

OPEN: 12-11 (Sun 12-10.30, 25 Dec 12-3, 7.30-10.30) **BAR MEALS:** L served all week 12-8 D served all week After 5-bookings preferred Av main course £3.50 🍺: Timothy Taylors Landlord, Phoenix Bantam.
CHILDREN'S FACILITIES: portions, licence, food/bottle warming, outdoor play area, Garden-parents must supervise
GARDEN: Lawn & seated veranda **NOTES:** Dogs allowed: in bar, No credit cards

OLDHAM THE ROEBUCK INN

Strinesdale OL4 3RB
☎ 0161 624 7819 📠 0161 624 7819
e-mail: smhowarth1@aol.com
Dir: From Oldham take A62 then A672 towards Ripponden. 1m turn R at Moorside PH into Turf Pit Lane. Pub 1m. *Map Ref:* SD90

Historic inn located on the edge of Saddleworth Moor in the rugged Pennines. The upstairs room was originally used as a Sunday school and a mortuary where bodies recovered from the nearby reservoirs were often brought. Fare includes grilled plaice, large fresh haddock with mushy peas, steak Diane, braised loin of lamb and sea bass.

OPEN: 12-2.30 5-12 **BAR MEALS:** L served all week 12-2.15 D served all week 5-9.30 (Sun 12-8.15) Av main course £7.50 **RESTAURANT:** L served all week 12-2.15 D served all week 5-9.30 (Sun 12-8.15) Av 3 course à la carte £12.50 Av 3 course fixed price £8.95
BREWERY/COMPANY: Free House 🍺: Boddingtons Smoothflow, Draft Bass. 🍷: 8
CHILDREN'S FACILITIES: menu, portions, games, high-chairs, food/bottle warming, baby changing, outdoor play area, Play area **NOTES:** Dogs allowed: Parking 40

Greater Manchester continued

THE WHITE HART INN ◉◉ ♀

Stockport Rd, Lydgate OL4 4JJ
☎ 01457 872566 ▤ 01457 875190
e-mail: charles@thewhitehart.co.uk
Dir: *From Manchester A62 to Oldham. R onto bypass, A669 through Lees. Inn 500yds past Grotton brow of hill turn R onto A6050.*
Map Ref: *SD90*

Local landowner John Buckley built the White Hart in 1788. The vast cellars were originally used to brew beer; and, in time, various parts of the buildings saw service as a prison, a school, and weavers' cottages. During the Second World War the top floor was used as a Home Guard lookout post, whilst the cellars did duty as an air raid shelter. Now, quality is the keynote, with cooking based on the best available local produce. Starters on the combined brasserie/restaurant menu include home-smoked salmon and sweet potato cake; or a home-made corned beef terrine. To follow, try pan-fried pheasant with roast chestnuts, mushrooms and potatoes; or asparagus and wild mushroom tart with poached egg.

OPEN: 12-11 (Sun 1-10.30) **BAR MEALS:** L served all week 12-2.30 D served all week 6-9.30 Sun 1-7.30 Av main course £14 **RESTAURANT:** L served Sun 1-3.30 D served Tue-Sat 6.30-9.30 Av 3 course à la carte £26 **BREWERY/COMPANY:** Free House ◧: Timothy Taylor Landlord, J W Lees Bitter, Carlsberg-Tetley Bitter, Interbrew Bass Bitter. ♀: 10 **CHILDREN'S FACILITIES:** portions, high-chairs, food/bottle warming, baby changing **GARDEN:** Lawned garden with view of Saddleworth Moor **NOTES:** No dogs (ex guide dogs), Parking 70

BILSBORROW   OWD NELL'S TAVERN 🐑 ♀

Guy's Thatched Hamlet, Canal Side PR3 0RS
☎ 01995 640010 ▤ 01995 640141
e-mail: info@guysthatchedhamlet.com
Dir: *Telephone for directions.* **Map Ref:** *SD53*

Owd Nell's is part of Guy's thatched hamlet, which also includes Guy's Lodge, crown green bowling, craft shops and a late night dance venue. The tavern, a 16th-century former farmhouse, offers a wide selection of guest ales, malt whiskies and wines by the glass. Favourite dishes are stuffed mushrooms, Aberdeen Angus steaks, oysters, lobster, pasta and pizza.

OPEN: 11-11 Closed: 25 Dec **BAR MEALS:** L served all week 11-10.30 D served all week 11-10.30 Av main course £5 **RESTAURANT:** L served all week 12-2.30 D served all week 5.30-10.30 Sunday 12.00-10.30 Av 3 course à la carte £15 Av 2 course fixed price £6 **BREWERY/COMPANY:** Free House ◧: Interbrew Boddingtons Bitter & Flowers, Jennings Bitter, Castle Eden Ale, Owd Nells Bitter. ♀: 40 **CHILDREN'S FACILITIES:** menu, portions, games, high-chairs, food/bottle warming, baby changing, outdoor play area, tunnels, swings, see-saw, family room **GARDEN:** Patio areas by the Lancaster Canal, 200 seats **NOTES:** Dogs allowed: in bar, in garden, water, Parking 300

CARNFORTH   DUTTON ARMS

Station Ln, Burton LA6 1HR
☎ 01524 781225 ▤ 01524 782662
Dir: *from M6 take A6 signed Milnthorpe (Kendal), 3m before Milnthorpe turn R signed Burton/Holme.* **Map Ref:** *SD47*

Close to a host of tourist attractions, including Morecambe Bay, the Lancashire Canal and the Northern Yorkshire Dales, the Dutton Arms was originally the Station Hotel serving the nearby mainline station, and was built in 1860.

OPEN: 10-3.30 6-11 **BAR MEALS:** L served all week 11-2.30 D served all week 6-9.30 Av main course £11 **RESTAURANT:** L served all week 12-2 D served all week 6-9 Av 3 course à la carte £11 **BREWERY/COMPANY:** Free House ◧: Interbrew Boddingtons, Black Sheep & Guest Beer. **CHILDREN'S FACILITIES:** menu, portions, high-chairs, food/bottle warming, baby changing, outdoor play area, changing room, play area inside and out, family room **GARDEN:** Lawned area with adventure playground **NOTES:** in bar, in garden, Water, No dogs (ex guide dogs), Parking 30

CHIPPING DOG & PARTRIDGE

Hesketh Ln PR3 2TH
☎ 01995 61201 ▯ 01995 61446
Map Ref: *SD64*

Dating back to 1515, this comfortably modernised rural free house in the Ribble Valley enjoys wonderful views of the surrounding fells. The barn has been converted into an additional dining area, and the emphasis is on home-made food using local produce. Diners can choose from bar snacks, or à la carte in the restaurant. The latter includes roast local duckling, home-made steak and kidney pie, and jumbo scampi in batter. Vegetarians are well catered for.

OPEN: 11.45-3 6.45-11 (Sun 11.45-10.30)
BAR MEALS: L served all week 12-1.45 D served all week
RESTAURANT: L served all week 12-1.30 D served all week 7-9 Sun luncheon 12-3, A la carte 3.30-8.30
BREWERY/COMPANY: Free House ◖: Carlsberg-Tetley.
CHILDREN'S FACILITIES: menu, portions, high-chairs, food/bottle warming **NOTES:** No dogs (ex guide dogs), Parking 30

CLITHEROE ASSHETON ARMS ☉ ♀

Downham BB7 4BJ
☎ 01200 441227 ▯ 01200 440581
e-mail: asshetonarms@aol.com
Dir: *From A59 take Chatburn turn. In Chatburn follow signs for Downham.* **Map Ref:** *SD74*

The Assheton Arms (named after Lord Clitheroe's family who own the whole village) offers a single bar, and sectioned rooms house an array of solid oak tables, wing back settees, window seats, an original stone fireplace, and a large blackboard listing the interesting range of daily dishes on offer. The pub is well placed for a wild moorland walk up Pendle Hill, which looms high above the village.

OPEN: 12-3 7-11 (summer Sun open all day) Closed: 1st wk in Jan **BAR MEALS:** L served all week 12-2 D served all week 7-10 Av main course £9
BREWERY/COMPANY: Enterprise Inns ◖: Marstons Pedigree, Interbrew Boddingtons Bitter. ♀: 18
CHILDREN'S FACILITIES: menu, portions, games, high-chairs, food/bottle warming **NOTES:** Dogs allowed: in bar, Parking 12

GOOSNARGH THE BUSHELL'S ARMS ♀

Church Ln PR3 2BH
☎ 01772 865235 ▯ 01772 865235
Dir: *Take A6 N to Garstang, R onto Whittingham Lane, after 3m L into Church Lane. The pub is on R of village green.*
Map Ref: *SD53*

Dr Bushell was a philanthropic Georgian who built his villagers not just a hospital but this pub too. The owner previously managed an IT company, but has had a long-standing ambition to run a pub. A collection of main courses may include salmon fillet topped with a rarebit crust, pork loin filled with black pudding and forcemeat, Goosnargh chicken breast, roasted lamb rump, beer-battered cod, The Bushell's burger, or pie of the day. Ideal walking country.

OPEN: 12-2.30 5-11 **BAR MEALS:** L served Tue-Sun 12-2 D served Tue-Sun 6-9 (Sun 12-8) Av main course £5.50
RESTAURANT: L served Tue-Sun 12-2 D served Tue-Sun 6-9 (Sun 12-8) Av 3 course à la carte £17.50 Av 3 course fixed price £9.95 **BREWERY/COMPANY:** Enterprise Inns ◖: Timothy Taylor Landlord, Boddingtons Cask, Old Speckled Hen Cask Tetleys. ♀: 15 **CHILDREN'S FACILITIES:** portions, food/bottle warming **GARDEN:** Secluded garden with lawns & flower beds **NOTES:** Dogs allowed: in bar, water & toys, Parking 10

HASLINGDEN FARMERS GLORY

Roundhill Rd BB4 5TU
☎ 01706 215748 🖹 01706 215748
Dir: *7 miles equidistant from Blackburn, Burnley and Bury, 1.5m from M66.*
Map Ref: *SD72*

Stone-built 350-year-old pub situated high above Haslingden on the edge of the Pennines. Formerly a coaching inn on the ancient route to Whalley Abbey, it now offers locals and modern A667 travellers a wide-ranging traditional pub menu of steaks, roasts, seafood, pizzas, pasta, curries and sandwiches. Live folk music every Wednesday and a large beer garden with ornamental fishpond.

OPEN: 12-3 7-11.30 **BAR MEALS:** L served all week 12-2.30 D served all week 7-9.30 Av main course £6.50
RESTAURANT: L served all week 12-2.30 D served all week 7-9.30 Av 3 course à la carte £12
BREWERY/COMPANY: Pubmaster ◖: Carlsberg-Tetley Tetley Bitter, Marston's Pedigree, Greene King IPA, Jennings.
CHILDREN'S FACILITIES: menu, portions, games, high-chairs, food/bottle warming, baby changing **GARDEN:** 1/2 acre, fixed seating, ornamental fish pond **NOTES:** No dogs (ex guide dogs), Parking 60

HESKIN GREEN FARMERS ARMS ♀

85 Wood Ln PR7 5NP
☎ 01257 451276 🖹 01257 453958
e-mail: andy@farmersarms.co.uk
Dir: *On B5250 between M6 & Eccleston.*
Map Ref: *SD51*

Long, creeper-covered country inn with two cosy bars decorated in old pictures and farming memorabilia. Once known as the Pleasant Retreat, this is a family-run pub proud to offer a warm welcome. Typical dishes include steak pie, fresh salmon with prawns and mushroom, halibut, rack of lamb and chicken curry.

OPEN: 12-11 (Sun close 10.30) **BAR MEALS:** L served all week 12-9.30 D served all week Av main course £7.50
RESTAURANT: L served all week 12-9.30 D served all week Av 3 course à la carte £13
BREWERY/COMPANY: Enterprise Inns ◖: Timothy Taylor Landlord, Pedigree, Interbrew Flowers IPA & Boddingtons, Carlsberg-Tetley. ♀: 7 **CHILDREN'S FACILITIES:** menu, outdoor play area **NOTES:** Dogs allowed: Parking 50
ROOMS: 5 en suite s£35 d£50 (♦♦♦)

MERECLOUGH KETTLEDRUM INN & RESTAURANT ♀

302 Red Lees Rd BB10 4RG
☎ 01282 424591 🖹 01282 424591
Dir: *from Burnley town centre, past Burnley FC, 2.5m, 1st pub on L.* **Map Ref:** *SD83*

The Kettledrum is an inviting and well-kept country inn with superb views of the famous Pendle Hill, below which lived Mother Demdike and Mother Chattox, accused in 1652 of witchcraft and taken to Lancaster to be hanged. In addition to traditional pub food there are dishes like venison sausage, Gressingham duck breast, seafood tagliatelle, braised knuckle of lamb, steaks, wild mushroom risotto, and gnocchi. A separate fish section on the menu lists fillet of Scotch salmon, baked mackerel fillet, and Thai green tiger prawn curry.

OPEN: 12-3 6-11 (Sun open all day)
BAR MEALS: L served all week 12-2.30 D served all week 6-9 Av main course £7 **RESTAURANT:** L served all week 12-2.30 D served all week 6-9 Av 3 course à la carte £12
BREWERY/COMPANY: Pubmaster ◖: Black Sheep, John Smiths. ♀: 12 **CHILDREN'S FACILITIES:** menu, portions, high-chairs, food/bottle warming, family room
GARDEN: Seating Area **NOTES:** No dogs (ex guide dogs), Parking 30

PARBOLD THE EAGLE & CHILD

Maltkiln Ln L40 3SG
☎ 01257 462297 📄 01257 464718
Dir: *From M6 J27 to Parbold. At bottom of Parbold Hill turn R on B5246 to Hilldale. Then 4th L to Bispham Green.* **Map Ref:** *SD41*

The emphasis at this dining pub is firmly placed on good ales, cider, and varied freshly cooked food. The pub's name is an allusion to the story of Lord Derby's illegitimate child. The baby was placed in a nearby eagle's nest, rescued by the childless Lady Derby and raised as one of the family. Nowadays, flagged floors, coir matting, and oak settles grace the interior, and the interesting range of light meals includes sandwiches with side salad and chips.

OPEN: 12-3 5.30-11 (Sun 12-10.30) Rest: 25 Dec Closed eve **BAR MEALS:** L served all week 12-2 D served all week 6-8.30 Sun 12-8.30 Av main course £9.50 **RESTAURANT:** L served all week 12-2 D served all week 6-8.30 Fri&Sat 6-9, Sun 12-8.30 Av 3 course à la carte £20 **BREWERY/COMPANY:** Free House 🍺: Moorhouses Black Cat, Thwaites Bitter, 5 changing guest beers. ⚲: 6 **CHILDREN'S FACILITIES:** menu, portions, high-chairs, food/bottle warming, family room **GARDEN:** Large patio, wooden benches, bowling green **NOTES:** Dogs allowed: in bar, Parking 50

PRESTON CARTFORD COUNTRY INN & HOTEL

Little Eccleston PR3 0YP
☎ 01995 670166 📄 01995 671785
Map Ref: *SD52*

This old, pleasantly rambling three-storey inn guards a historic toll bridge over the tidal River Wyre. Inside, an open log fire may be blazing, and there's always pool, darts or dominoes to be played. A good range of food on the bar menu includes sandwiches, pizzas (evenings only), jacket potatoes, salads, chicken and bacon pasta, lamb Henry and seafood platter. Meals can also be taken outside overlooking the river, along part of which runs a four-mile walk that conveniently starts and finishes at the pub.

OPEN: 12-3 (Sun 12-10.30) 6.30-11 (Open 6.30 in summer) **BAR MEALS:** L served all week 12-2 D served all week 6.30-9.30 Av main course £5 **RESTAURANT:** L served all week D served all week **BREWERY/COMPANY:** Free House 🍺: Hart Beers, Fullers London Pride, Moorhouse, Guest ales. **CHILDREN'S FACILITIES:** menu, high-chairs, food/bottle warming, outdoor play area, climbing frame and slide, family room **NOTES:** Dogs allowed: in bar, Parking 60

SLAIDBURN HARK TO BOUNTY INN

Townend BB7 3EP
☎ 01200 446246 📄 01200 446361
e-mail: manager@hark-to-bounty.co.uk
Dir: *From M6 J31 take A59 to Clitheroe then B6478, through Waddington, Newton and onto Slaidburn.* **Map Ref:** *SD75*

A family-run 13th century inn known as The Dog until 1875 when Bounty, the local squire's favourite hound, disturbed a post-hunt drinking session with its loud baying. Traditional favourites include home-made fish, and steak and kidney pies, vegetable and cheese crumble, and grilled fillet of haddock topped with tomatoes and Lancashire cheese, supplemented by pastas and curries from the chalkboards.

OPEN: 11-11 **BAR MEALS:** L served all week 12-2 D served all week 6-9 Sun 12-2.30, 6-8 Av main course £8.50 **RESTAURANT:** L served Tue-Sun 12-2 D served Tue-Sat 6-9 Sun 12-2.30, 6-8 Av 3 course fixed price £15.95 **BREWERY/COMPANY:** Scottish Courage 🍺: Theakston Old Peculier, Scottish Courage Courage Directors & 1 guest ale (changed monthly). **CHILDREN'S FACILITIES:** menu, portions, licence, high-chairs, food/bottle warming, baby changing **GARDEN:** Large enclosed area **NOTES:** Dogs allowed: in bar, in garden, in bedrooms, except during food service, Parking 25

Lancashire continued

WRIGHTINGTON   THE MULBERRY TREE ⑥⑥ 🐑 ♀

WN6 9SE
☎ 01257 451400 ▤ 01257 451400
Dir: *Jct 27 off M6 turn into Mossy Lea Road
2m on the right.* **Map Ref:** *SD51*

Former Roux brothers' head chef Mark Prescott has been ranked in Great Britain's top ten of contemporary chefs, so it's no surprise that The Mulberry Tree is a sought-after venue for discerning diners. The bar menu has speciality sandwiches at lunchtime. The dinner menu continues with interesting, accomplished dishes. There's a specials board as well.

OPEN: 12-3 6-11 Closed: 26 Dec, 1 Jan
BAR MEALS: L served Mon-Sun 12-2 D served Mon-Sun 6-9.30 All day Sun, Fri-Sat 6-10 Av main course £12.95
RESTAURANT: L served all week 12-2 D served all week 6-10 Sun 12-3 Av 3 course à la carte £25.95 Av 3 course fixed price £17.95 **BREWERY/COMPANY:** Free House
🍺: Interbrew Flowers IPA. ♀: 8
CHILDREN'S FACILITIES: portions, high-chairs
NOTES: No dogs, Parking 100

YEALAND CONYERS   THE NEW INN

40 Yealand Rd LA5 9SJ
☎ 01524 732938
e-mail: charlottepinder@hotmail.com
Dir: *Join A6 between Carnforth & Milnthorpe, 3m then L after Yealand Conyers sign, 0.25m to pub.* **Map Ref:** *SD57*

An ivy-clad 17th-century building situated in a picturesque village on the edge of the Lake District. Good beers and home-cooked food are served in the oak-beamed bar, non-smoking dining room or in the garden. Popular dishes include Cumberland sausage; fresh salmon fillet with cream, Chardonnay and herb sauce; and lentil and red pepper curry. There is an excellent dessert menu and a good range of snacks.

OPEN: 11.30-11 (Sun 12-10.30) **BAR MEALS:** L served all week 11.30-9.30 D served all week Sun 12-9.30 Av main course £8 **RESTAURANT:** L served all week 11.30-9.30 D served all week 11.30-9.30 Sun 12-9.30
BREWERY/COMPANY: Frederic Robinson 🍺: Hartleys XB, Robinson's Seasonal Bitter, Old Tom.
CHILDREN'S FACILITIES: menu, portions, high-chairs, food/bottle warming **NOTES:** Dogs allowed: in bar, in garden, water, Parking 50

BARNSTON   FOX AND HOUNDS 🐑 ♀

Barnston Rd CH61 1BW
☎ 0151 6487685
Dir: *From M53 J4 take A5137 to Heswell. R to Barnston on B5138.* **Map Ref:** *SJ28*

Situated in the conservation area of Barnston, the decor of this pub is true to its origins, featuring an assortment of 1920s/1930s memorabilia. Much of the Edwardian building's character has been preserved, including pitch pine woodwork and leaded windows. Alongside a superb range of bar snacks, including platters, toasted sandwiches and baked potatoes, expect favourites such as fish and chips, steak pies, lamb shank and cod and prawn crumble.

OPEN: 11-11 (Sun 12-10.30) **BAR MEALS:** L served all week 12-2 Av main course £5.70
BREWERY/COMPANY: Free House 🍺: Websters Yorkshire Bitter, Theakston, Best & Old Peculier, Marstons Pedigree & two guest beers. ♀: 11 **CHILDREN'S FACILITIES:** portions, games, food/bottle warming, baby changing, family room
GARDEN: Lots of flowers & baskets **NOTES:** Dogs allowed: in bar, in garden, except at lunchtime, Parking 60

ALNWICK MASONS ARMS ♀

Stamford, Nr Rennington NE66 3RX
☎ 01665 577275 📠 01665 577894
e-mail: bookings@masonsarms.net
Dir: *3.5m from A1 on B1340.* **Map Ref:** *NU11*

This 200-year-old coaching inn has been tastefully modernised and is a useful staging post for visitors to Hadrian's Wall, Lindisfarne and the large number of nearby golf courses. Substantial home-cooked food is available in the bar and restaurant, using the best of local produce. Expect Orkney herrings with oatcakes, game casserole, seafood lasagne and chicken with orange and lemon sauce.

OPEN: 12-2 6.30-11 (Sun 12-2 7-10.30)
BAR MEALS: L served all week 12-2 D served all week 6.30-9 Av main course £6.50 **RESTAURANT:** L served all week 12-2 D served all week 7-9 Av 3 course à la carte £7
BREWERY/COMPANY: Free House ◀: Scottish Courage John Smith's, Theakston Best, Secret Kingdom, Gladiator.
♀: 12 **CHILDREN'S FACILITIES:** menu, portions, licence, high-chairs, food/bottle warming, family room
NOTES: No dogs (ex guide dogs), Parking 50
ROOMS: 12 en suite 3 family rooms s£40 d£54 (♦♦♦♦)

BELFORD BLUE BELL HOTEL 🐑

Market Place NE70 7NE
☎ 01668 213543 📠 01668 213787
e-mail: bluebell@globalnet.co.uk
Map Ref: *NU13*

A long-established, creeper-clad coaching inn in the centre of Belford. Just off the A1 it is convenient for exploring Northumberland's magnificent coastline and the Cheviot Hills. The inn offers a friendly, relaxed atmosphere, and a good range of real ales. There's an elegant restaurant as well as the more informal surroundings of the bar and buttery. Three acres of garden include an orchard and vegetable garden.

OPEN: 11-2.30 6.30-11 **BAR MEALS:** L served all week 11-2 D served all week 6.30-9 Av main course £9.50
RESTAURANT: L served Sun 12-2 D served all week 7-8.45 Av 3 course à la carte £27 Av 5 course fixed price £25
BREWERY/COMPANY: Free House ◀: Interbrew Boddingtons Bitter, Northumbrian Smoothe, Calders, Tetleys Smooth. **CHILDREN'S FACILITIES:** menu, portions, games, high-chairs, food/bottle warming, family room **GARDEN:** 3 acres **NOTES:** No dogs (ex guide dogs), Parking 17
ROOMS: 17 en suite s£36 d£82 (★★★)

BELSAY THE HIGHLANDER ♀

NE20 0DN
☎ 01661 881220
e-mail: highlander@encore-retail.co.uk
Dir: *(On A696, 2m S of Belsay & 4m N of Ponteland).* **Map Ref:** *NZ07*

This popular, flower-adorned roadside hostelry, with its log fires, plain wooden tables and cosy interior, is now under new management. A good range of food is on offer: for starters, choose from smoked salmon and cream cheese cornets; or deep fried whitebait, perhaps followed by pork tenderloin in a cream, apple and cider sauce; casserole of beef served on a bed of mashed potato; haggis, neeps and tatties; or roasted red pepper lasagne.

OPEN: 11-11 (Sun 12-10.30) **BAR MEALS:** L served all week 12-6 D served all week 6-9.30 Av main course £6.75
BREWERY/COMPANY: Enterprise Inns ◀: John Smiths, Tetleys & Guest ale. ♀: 11 **CHILDREN'S FACILITIES:** menu, portions, high-chairs, food/bottle warming **GARDEN:** Heated Patio area with secure garden at rear **NOTES:** Dogs allowed: in bar, water available, Parking 60

CARTERWAY HEADS THE MANOR HOUSE INN

DH8 9LX
☎ 01207 255268
Dir: *A69 W from Newcastle, L onto A68 then S for 8m. Inn on R.* **Map Ref:** *NZ05*

This small family-run free house enjoys spectacular views across open moorland and the Derwent Reservoir from its lonely position high on the A68. The cosy stone-walled bar, with its log fires, low-beamed ceiling and massive timber support, offers a good range of well-kept real ales and around 70 malt whiskies. Built circa 1760, the inn has a succession of dining areas, and a huge collection of mugs and jugs hangs from the beams in the candlelit restaurant. The menu is not overwhelmingly large, and only the best quality ingredients, locally sourced where possible, are used. Typical dishes include Cumberland sausage and mash; crayfish and mushroom crepes; filo baskets of king prawns and mussels; roast duck breast; and various steaks. Home-made puddings are a feature, as is the choice of up to 16 local cheeses.

OPEN: 11-11 Rest: 25 Dec closed evening
BAR MEALS: L served all week 12-9.30 D served all week Av main course £11 **RESTAURANT:** L served all week 12-2.30 D served all week 7-9.30 (Sun 9) Av 3 course à la carte £19 **BREWERY/COMPANY:** Free House
🍺: Theakstons Best, Mordue Workie Ticket, Greene King Ruddles County, Scottish Courage Courage Directors. ♀: 12
CHILDREN'S FACILITIES: menu, portions, licence, high-chairs, food/bottle warming **GARDEN:** Small picnic area
NOTES: Dogs allowed: in bar, in bedroom by arrangement, Parking 60 **ROOMS:** 4 en suite s£38 d£60 (♦♦♦♦)

CHATTON THE PERCY ARMS HOTEL

Main Rd NE66 5PS
☎ 01668 215244 🖷 01668 215277
Dir: *From Alnwick take A1 N, then B6348 to Chatton.* **Map Ref:** *NU02*

Traditional 19th-century former coaching inn, situated in the heart of rural Northumberland. Expect a warm traditional pub welcome, as well as a selection of fine beers, wines and tempting food. Bar menu includes Aberdeen Angus steaks, deep-fried haddock, steak and kidney pie and a wide selection of fish and seafood dishes.

OPEN: 11-11 (Sun12-10.30) **BAR MEALS:** L served all week 12-2.30 D served all week 6.30-9.30 Av main course £7 **RESTAURANT:** L served all week 12-2.30 D served all week 6.30-9.30 **BREWERY/COMPANY:** Free House 🍺: Jenkins Beers. ♀: 8
CHILDREN'S FACILITIES: menu, portions, licence, games, high-chairs, food/bottle warming, baby changing
GARDEN: patio/terrace, front beer garden **NOTES:** No dogs, Parking 30

CRASTER COTTAGE INN ♦♦♦

Dunstan Village NE66 3SZ
☎ 01665 576658 🖷 01665 576788
e-mail: enquiries@cottageinnhotel.co.uk
Dir: *NW of Howick to Embleton road.*
Map Ref: *NU21*

In an Area of Outstanding Natural Beauty, easily accessible from the A1, this 18th-century inn is located in a hamlet close to the sea. There is a beamed bar, Harry Hotspur Restaurant, conservatory, loggia and patio. One menu serves all - a comprehensive choice of snacks, full meals, kids' and vegetarian options, supplemented by daily specials. Local ingredients are used wherever possible in dishes such as seafood platter, Craster fish stew and whole joint of lamb.

OPEN: 11-12 **BAR MEALS:** L served all week 12-2.30 D served all week 6-9.30 Av main course £9.50
RESTAURANT: L served all week 12-2.30 D served all week 6-9.30 **BREWERY/COMPANY:** Free House 🍺: Belhaven 80/-, Wylam Bitter, John Smiths. ♀: 12
CHILDREN'S FACILITIES: menu, portions, high-chairs, food/bottle warming, outdoor play area, Outside play area, adventure play ground **GARDEN:** Patio area with 6 acres of lawn & woodland **NOTES:** No dogs (ex guide dogs), Parking 60 **ROOMS:** 10 en suite s£39 d£69

EGLINGHAM TANKERVILLE ARMS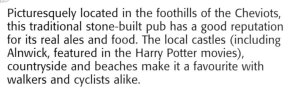

NE66 2TX
☎ 01665 578444 🖷 01665 578444
Dir: *B6346 from Alnwick.* **Map Ref:** *NU11*

Picturesquely located in the foothills of the Cheviots, this traditional stone-built pub has a good reputation for its real ales and food. The local castles (including Alnwick, featured in the Harry Potter movies), countryside and beaches make it a favourite with walkers and cyclists alike.

OPEN: 12-2 7-11 (Times may vary, ring for details) Closed: 25 Dec **BAR MEALS:** L served all week 12-2 D served all week 6-9 **RESTAURANT:** L served all week 12-2 D served all week 6-9 Av 3 course à la carte £20
BREWERY/COMPANY: Free House 🍺: Greene King Ruddles Best, Scottish Courage Courage Directors, Black Sheep Best, Mordue Workie Ticket.
CHILDREN'S FACILITIES: portions, high-chairs, food/bottle warming, baby changing, outdoor play area, Changing facilities
GARDEN: Country garden, seating for 25, good views
NOTES: No dogs (ex guide dogs), Parking 15

FALSTONE THE BLACKCOCK INN ♦♦♦ ♀

NE48 1AA
☎ 01434 240200
e-mail: blackcock@falstone.fsbusiness.co.uk
Dir: *Off unclassified rd from Bellingham (accessed from A68 or B6320).*
Map Ref: *NY78*

A traditional 18th-century stone-built inn, close to Kielder Reservoir and Forest, with some lovely walks accessible from the village. The pub is also handy for the Rievers Cycle Route. Old beams and open log fires make for a cosy atmosphere, and food is served in the bar, lounge and dining area alongside a good choice of beers. Dishes are based on the best local produce, ranging from snacks to steaks, with fish and vegetarian options. Try one of the Yorkshire puddings with a variety of fillings.

OPEN: 11-3 6-11 (Winter 7-11) **BAR MEALS:** L served all week 11-2 D served all week 7-9 Av main course £6.95
RESTAURANT: L served all week D served Fri-Sun 7-9 Av 3 course à la carte £16 **BREWERY/COMPANY:** Free House 🍺: Blackcock Ale, Wylam Bitter, Theakston Cool Cask, Magnet Ale. ♀: 8 **CHILDREN'S FACILITIES:** menu, portions, high-chairs, food/bottle warming, outdoor play area, Swings, climbing frame, family room **GARDEN:** lawn, flower beds, picnic benches **NOTES:** Dogs allowed: in bar, in garden, in bedrooms, Parking 20 **ROOMS:** 5 en suite 1 family room s£35 d£55

THE PHEASANT ♦♦♦♦

Stannersburn NE48 1DD
☎ 01434 240382 🖷 01434 240382
e-mail: enquiries@thepheasantinn.com
Dir: *From A68 onto B6320, or from A69, B6079, B6320, follow signs 'Kielder Water'.*
Map Ref: *NY78*

This 17th-century free house is close to Kielder Water, and some of Northumberland's most unspoilt countryside. The snug interior has a wealth of beams, exposed stone walls and open fires. Century old photographs are a tribute to the local community and a way of life long vanished. With its mellow pine furniture and warm terracotta walls, the restaurant is a relaxing environment in which to enjoy a good selection of traditional home-cooked food.

OPEN: 11-3 6-11 (opening times vary, ring for details) Closed: Dec 25-26 **BAR MEALS:** L served all week 12-2.30 D served all week 7-9 **RESTAURANT:** L served all week 12-2.30 D served all week 7-9 Sun 12-2, 8-
BREWERY/COMPANY: Free House 🍺: Theakston Best, Marstons Pedigree, Timothy Taylor Landlord, Greene King Old Speckled Hen. **CHILDREN'S FACILITIES:** portions, games, high-chairs, food/bottle warming, baby changing, outdoor play area, Open garden, small stream with bridge, family room
GARDEN: Grassed courtyard, stream running through
NOTES: Dogs allowed: in garden, By arrangement only, Parking 30 **ROOMS:** 8 en suite 1 family room s£40 d£70

HALTWHISTLE MILECASTLE INN

Military Rd, Cawfields NE49 9NN
☎ 01434 321372
e-mail: clarehind@aol.co.uk
Dir: *Leave A69 at Haltwhistle, pub about 2 miles from Haltwhistle at junction with B6318.*
Map Ref: *NY76*

Spectacular views from the gardens towards Hadrian's Wall are a treat for tourists arriving at this stone-built rural inn. The beamed bar has open fires and even a resident ghost. New owners have developed a menu strong on the likes of game pie, venison, pheasant, steaks, gammon, Whitby scampi, seafood medley and other fish, as well as vegetarian dishes.

OPEN: 12-2.30 Nov-Mar 12-3, 6-11 6.30-11 Mar-Nov 12-11
BAR MEALS: L served all week 12-3 D served all week 6-9
RESTAURANT: L served Sun 12-2.30 D served Sun-Sat 7-9
BREWERY/COMPANY: Free House ◀: Northumberland Castle, Carlsberg-Tetley Tetley Bitter, Marsdens Pedigree, Old Speckled Hen. **CHILDREN'S FACILITIES:** menu, portions, food/bottle warming **GARDEN:** Walled with benches, seats 25 **NOTES:** in garden, No dogs (ex guide dogs), Parking 30

HAYDON BRIDGE THE GENERAL HAVELOCK INN

Ratcliffe Rd NE47 6ER
☎ 01434 684376 🖷 01434 684283
e-mail: GeneralHavelock@aol.com
Dir: *On A69, 7m west of Hexham.*
Map Ref: *NY86*

Not far from Hadrian's Wall, this 19th-century roadside inn was built as a private house in 1840 but has been licensed since 1890. The restaurant, in a converted barn at the back, overlooks the River Tyne, as does the tranquil south-facing patio framed by trees and potted plants. Ingredients are sourced locally for the no-nonsense pub food.

OPEN: 12-2.30 7-11 **BAR MEALS:** L served Tue-Sun 12-2 D served Tue-Sat 7-9 Av main course £8
RESTAURANT: L served Tue-Sun 12-2 D served Tue-Sat 7-9 Av 3 course à la carte £23 Av 3 course fixed price £14.25
BREWERY/COMPANY: Free House ◀: Hesket Newmarket, Courage Directors, Wylam Magic, Helvellyn Gold.
CHILDREN'S FACILITIES: portions, games, high-chairs, food/bottle warming **GARDEN:** Patio area on river bank, lots of plants **NOTES:** Dogs allowed: in bar, in garden

---

HEDLEY ON THE HILL THE FEATHERS INN

NE43 7SW
☎ 01661 843607 🖷 01661 843607
Map Ref: *NZ05*

From its hilltop position, this small stone-built free house overlooks the splendid adventure country of the Cheviots. The three-roomed pub is well patronised by the local community, but strangers, too, are frequently charmed by its friendly and relaxed atmosphere. Families are welcome, and a small side room can be booked in advance if required. Old oak beams, coal fires and rustic settles set the scene and there's a good selection of traditional pub games like shove ha'penny and bar skittles. The stone walls are decorated with local photographs of rural life. Although the pub has no garden, food and

drinks can be served at tables on the green in good weather. The menus change regularly, and the imaginative home cooking includes an extensive choice of vegetarian meals. Expect spiced lentil and vegetable hotpot with naan bread, gingered salmon cakes with coriander salsa, pork casseroled with tarragon and Dijon mustard, and seafood pancake. An appetising range of puddings. Coach parties by arrangement.

OPEN: 12-3 6-11 (Sun 12-3, 7-10.30) Closed: Dec 25
BAR MEALS: L served Sat-Sun 12-2.30 D served Tue-Sun 7-9 Av main course £8.10 **BREWERY/COMPANY:** Free House ◀: Mordue Workie Ticket, Big Lamp Bitter, Fuller's London Pride, Yates Bitter.
CHILDREN'S FACILITIES: portions, licence, food/bottle warming, family room **GARDEN:** Tables outside at the front
NOTES: Water, No dogs (ex guide dogs), Parking 12

HEXHAM DIPTON MILL INN ♀

Dipton Mill Rd NE46 1YA
☎ 01434 606577
e-mail: glb@hexhamshire.co.uk
Dir: *2m S of Hexham on HGV route to Blanchland (B6306) (Dipton Mill Rd).*
Map Ref: *NY96*

This quintessential country pub with a millstream running through its garden and real fires warming the bar in winter is in serious walking country near Hadrian's Wall and other Roman sites. The low-ceilinged, panelled bar has a quiet, friendly atmosphere with red upholstered furniture adding to the general cosiness. Food is served evening and lunch-times with all dishes being freshly prepared.

OPEN: 12-2.30 6-11 (Sun 12-4, 7-10.30) Closed: 25 Dec
BAR MEALS: L served all week 12-2.15 D served all week 6.30-8.30 Sun 12-2.15, 7.30-8.30 Av main course £6
BREWERY/COMPANY: Free House 🍺: Hexhamshire Shire Bitter, Old Humbug, Devil's Water, Devil's Elbow & Whapweasel. ♀: 11 **CHILDREN'S FACILITIES:** menu, licence, food/bottle warming **GARDEN:** Grassed and terraced area, small aviary **NOTES:** No dogs (ex guide dogs), No credit cards

MINERS ARMS INN

Main St, Acomb NE46 4PW
☎ 01434 603909
Dir: *17m W of Newcastle on A69, 2m W of Hexham.* **Map Ref:** *NY96*

Close to Hadrian's Wall in a peaceful village, this charming 18th-century pub has stone walls, beamed ceilings and open fires. Real ales are a speciality, as is good home-cooked food. There is no jukebox or pool table, so visitors will have to entertain themselves with conversation, and some choices from a menu that includes lasagne, curry, Italian chicken, steak and kidney pie, chilli, and a special trifle. Good setting for cyclists and walkers, and the garden has an aviary.

OPEN: 5-11 Sat 12-11, Sun 12-10.30 Easter, Summer, Xmas Hols 12-11 all wk **BAR MEALS:** L served all week 12-9 D served all week 5-9 Sun 12-5.30 Av main course £5.35
RESTAURANT: L served all week 12-9 D served all week 5-9 Sunday 12-5.30 **BREWERY/COMPANY:** Free House 🍺: Jennings Best, Yates, Northumberland Smooth, Durham White Velvet. **CHILDREN'S FACILITIES:** menu, portions, games, high-chairs, food/bottle warming, family room **GARDEN:** Secluded sun trap beer garden, seating, BBQ **NOTES:** Dogs allowed: in bar, in garden, water, No credit cards

LONGFRAMLINGTON THE ANGLERS ARMS

Weldon Bridge NE65 8AX
☎ 01665 520271 570655 📠 01665 570041
e-mail: johnyoung@anglersarms.fsnet.co.uk
Map Ref: *NU10*

A traditional old coaching inn dating from the 1760s, standing by picturesque Weldon Bridge over the River Coquet. Assiduous attention by management and staff apart, what helps to give it a warm and friendly atmosphere are the little touches found at every turn - antiques, bric-a-brac, hand-painted wall tiles and, not unexpectedly, fishing memorabilia. Speaking of fishing, residents may do so for free on the inn's own one-mile stretch of river. Typical dishes at the bar, or in the decidedly sophisticated old Pullman railway carriage restaurant, are home-made steak and ale pie, Northumbrian sausage Lyonnaise, mixed grill, steaks, chicken in bacon, grilled rainbow trout, and balti curry. For some, a hot beef sandwich with rich onion gravy and French fries might be sufficient, with a pint of one of the ever-changing real ales.

OPEN: 11-3 6-11 **BAR MEALS:** L served all week 12-2 D served all week 6-9.30 Av main course £8
RESTAURANT: L served all week 12-2 D served all week 6-9.30 🍺: Worthington, Carling, Boddingtons & 3 Guest Ales.
CHILDREN'S FACILITIES: menu, portions, licence, high-chairs, food/bottle warming, outdoor play area, Play area in garden, climbing frame, family room **GARDEN:** Well looked after 0.5 acre garden **NOTES:** Dogs allowed: in garden, in bedrooms, Parking 30 **ROOMS:** 5 en suite 1 family room (♦♦♦♦)

LONGHORSLEY LINDEN TREE ♀

Linden Hall NE65 8XF
☎ 01670 500033 📄 01670 500001
e-mail: stay@lindenhall.co.uk
Dir: *Off the A1 on the A697 1m N of
Longhorsley.* **Map Ref:** *NZ19*

Originally two large cattle byres, this popular bar takes
its name from the linden trees in the grounds of
Linden Hall Hotel, an impressive Georgian mansion.
Straightforward meals range from aubergine and
broccoli bake, braised lamb shank, or medallions of
pork, to grilled salmon, or poached smoked cod fillets.

OPEN: 11-11 (Sun 12-10.30) Closed: 1 Jan
BAR MEALS: L served all week 12-2 D served all week
6-9.30 Av main course £18.95 **RESTAURANT:** L served all
week 12.00-2.00 D served all week 6-9.30
BREWERY/COMPANY: Free House 🍺: Worthingtons,
Worthington 1744, Pedigree. ♀: 7
CHILDREN'S FACILITIES: menu, portions, games, high-chairs,
food/bottle warming, baby changing **GARDEN:** Large open
court yard **NOTES:** Dogs allowed: in garden, in bedrooms,
Parking 200

NEWTON ON THE MOOR COOK AND BARKER INN ♀

NE65 9JY
☎ 01665 575234 📄 01665 575234
Dir: *0.5m from A1 S of Alnwick.*
Map Ref: *NU10*

Traditional Northumbrian inn located in a
picturesque village with outstanding views

over the coast. Good quality fare, including some
exotic specialities, a welcoming atmosphere, and
various characterful features make the Cook and
Barker a popular dining destination. Eat lunch in the
beer garden when the weather suits. In the evening,
an à la carte menu may include courses like pot roast
lamb shank on a basil and rosemary mash.

OPEN: 12-3 6-11 **BAR MEALS:** L served all week 12-2
D served all week 6-9 Av main course £6.95
RESTAURANT: L served all week 12-2 D served all week 7-9
Av 3 course à la carte £25 Av 3 course fixed price £19.50
BREWERY/COMPANY: Free House 🍺: Timothy Taylor
Landlord, Theakstons Best Bitter, Fuller's London Pride,
Batemans XXXB. ♀: 12 **CHILDREN'S FACILITIES:** portions,
high-chairs, food/bottle warming, family room
GARDEN: Pretty area with lots of space for children
NOTES: No dogs (ex guide dogs), Parking 60

ROWFOOT THE WALLACE ARMS 🐑

NE49 0JF
☎ 01434 321872 📄 01434 321872
Map Ref: *NY66*

The pub was rebuilt in 1850 as the Railway
Hotel at Featherstone Park station, when the
now long-closed Haltwhistle-Alston line
(today's South Tyne Trail) was engineered. It
changed to the Wallace Arms in 1885. All
around is great walking country, and just half
a mile away is Featherstone Castle in its
beautiful parkland. Nothing pretentious on
the menu, just good, modestly-priced
haddock fillet in beer batter, salmon fillet in
lemon and tarragon sauce, steak and ale pie,
grilled sirloin steak, and smoked haddock and
prawn pasta. There are light snacks, burgers
and sandwiches, if you prefer.

OPEN: 11-3 4-11 (opening times vary, ring for details)
BAR MEALS: L served all week 12-2 D served all week 6-9
Av main course £6.50 **RESTAURANT:** L served all week
12-2 D served all week 6-9 Av 3 course à la carte £15
BREWERY/COMPANY: Free House 🍺: Hook Norton Old
Hooky, Young's Special, Greene King IPA, Greene King Abbot
Ale. **CHILDREN'S FACILITIES:** menu, portions, high-chairs,
food/bottle warming **GARDEN:** Large lawn surrounded by
stone wall **NOTES:** in garden, No dogs (ex guide dogs),
Parking 30

WARDEN   THE BOATSIDE INN

NE46 4SQ
☎ 01434 602233 601061
Dir: *Just off A69 west of Hexham, follow signs to Warden Newborough & Fourstones.*
Map Ref: *NY96*

This attractive stone pub nestles beneath

Warden Hill Iron Age fort and sits next to where the North and South Tyne rivers meet. The name comes from the rowing boat that ferried people across the river before the bridge was built. A popular destination for walkers, the inn promises real ale and good food cooked from local produce. Expect dishes such as fish pie, mussels, liver and bacon casserole and chicken curry.

OPEN: 11-3 6-11 **BAR MEALS:** L served all week 12-2 D served all week 6.30-9.30 Av main course £7 **RESTAURANT:** L served all week 12-2 D served all week 6.30-9.30 **BREWERY/COMPANY:** Free House 🍺: Jennings, Cumberland, Cumberland Cream, Jennings Bitter. **CHILDREN'S FACILITIES:** menu, portions, high-chairs, food/bottle warming **GARDEN:** Paved patio with lawn area, hanging baskets **NOTES:** Dogs allowed: in bar, in garden, water, Parking 70

WARENFORD   WARENFORD LODGE

NE70 7HY
☎ 01668 213453 📠 01668 213453
e-mail: warenfordlodge@aol.com
Dir: *100yds E of A1,10m N of Alnwick.*
Map Ref: *NU12*

By the original toll bridge over the Waren Burn, this 200-year-old coaching inn was once on the Great North Road. The A1, as it later became, today by-passes the village, leaving the pub a welcome stone's throw away. Inside, one is struck by the thick stone walls, and open fires blazing away on colder days. Once owned by the Dukes of Northumberland, the pub's windows and plasterwork show family crests. Visitors and locals alike enjoy the atmosphere and award-

winning Northumbrian dishes. Book ahead to avoid disappointment.

OPEN: 12-2 Closed Sun Eve, Mon-Tue(Nov-Easter) 7-11 Closed: 25/26 Dec, 1 Jan-31 Jan **BAR MEALS:** L served Sat-Sun 12-1.30 D served Tues-Sun 7-9.30 Av main course £7.20 **RESTAURANT:** L served Sat-Sun 12-1.30 D served Tues-Sun 7-9.30 Av 3 course à la carte £15.20 **BREWERY/COMPANY:** Free House 🍺: Scottish Courage John Smith's. 🍷: 8 **CHILDREN'S FACILITIES:** portions, food/bottle warming **GARDEN:** More a field than a garden **NOTES:** No dogs (ex guide dogs), Parking 60

NEWCASTLE UPON TYNE   SHIREMOOR HOUSE FARM 🍷

Middle Engine Ln, New York NE29 8DZ
☎ 0191 257 6302 📠 0191 2578602
Map Ref: *NZ26*

Situated in converted farm buildings, this pub offers large bars serving a wide range of ales and pub food. Try Jarrow River Catcher or Theakston Best Bitter to go with sizzling strips of chicken with sweet chilli sauce; steak, ale and mushroom casserole; and fillet of salmon with prawn and dill sauce. There is a covered patio with heaters for chilly evenings.

OPEN: 11-11 **BAR MEALS:** L served all week 12 D served all week 10 Av main course £6.95 **RESTAURANT:** L served all week D served all week Av 3 course à la carte £18 🍺: Timothy Taylor's Landlord, Mordue Workie Ticket, Theakston BB, John Smiths. 🍷: 12 **CHILDREN'S FACILITIES:** menu, licence, high-chairs, food/bottle warming, baby changing, family room **GARDEN:** Covered patio with heaters and lighting **NOTES:** No dogs (ex guide dogs), Parking 120

Tyne & Wear continued

TYNEMOUTH COPPERFIELDS

Grand Hotel, Hotspur St NE30 4ER
☎ 0191 293 6666 ▤ 0191 293 6665
e-mail: info@grandhotel-uk.com
Dir: *On NE coast, 10m from
Newcastle-upon-Tyne.* ***Map Ref:*** *NZ36*

Copperfields bar is part of the Grand Hotel at Tynemouth, and is set on a cliff top commanding some of the most stunning views of natural coastline in the country. It was a frequent haunt of Stan Laurel of Laurel and Hardy fame. Traditional home-cooked meals served in the bar include North Shields cod and chips, steak and mushroom pie and popular roast dinners.

OPEN: 12-11 Sun 12-10.30 **BAR MEALS:** L served all week 12-3 D served all week 3-8 Av main course £5.50 **RESTAURANT:** L served all week 12-3 D served Mon-Sat 6.30-9.45 Av 3 course à la carte £25 Av 3 course fixed price £17 **◖:** Durham Magus, Bass '9', Workie Ticket.
CHILDREN'S FACILITIES: menu, portions, licence, games, high-chairs, food/bottle warming, baby changing
NOTES: No dogs (ex guide dogs), Parking 16

WHITLEY BAY THE WATERFORD ARMS ♉

Collywell Bay Rd, Seaton Sluice NE26 4QZ
☎ 0191 237 0450 & 0191 296 5287
Dir: *From A1 N of Newcastle take A19 at
Seaton Burn then follow signs for A190 to
Seaton Sluice.* ***Map Ref:*** *NZ37*

The building dates back to 1899 and is situated close to the small local fishing harbour, overlooking the North Sea. Splendid beaches and sand dunes are within easy reach, and the pub is very popular with walkers. Seafood dishes are the speciality, including a whale-sized cod or haddock and chips, seafood feast, and salmon.

OPEN: 12-11 (Sun 12-10.30) **BAR MEALS:** L served all week 12-9 D served all week Av main course £3
RESTAURANT: L served all week 12-9 D served all week Av 3 course à la carte £13
BREWERY/COMPANY: Pubmaster **◖:** Tetleys, John Smiths, Guest Ales. **CHILDREN'S FACILITIES:** menu
GARDEN: Food served outside **NOTES:** No dogs, Parking 90

HUGGATE THE WOLDS INN ◆◆◆

YO42 1YH
☎ 01377 288217
e-mail: huggate@woldsinn.freeserve.co.uk
Dir: *S off A166 between York & Driffield.*
Map Ref: *SE85*

Probably the highest inn on the Yorkshire

Wolds, which explains Wolds Topper, a 'mixed grill to remember'. Sixteenth-century in origin, with tiled roofs and white-painted chimneys, the inn's wood-panelled interior has open fires, gleaming brassware and a bar serving baguettes, sandwiches and main dishes such as seafood platter, and pork chop and mushrooms. The restaurant offers grills, steak pie, rack of lamb, beef Bourguignonne, fillet of plaice and Scottish salmon fillet.

OPEN: 12-2 (May-Sept open Sun at 6) 6.30-11 (Oct-May closed Fri lunch) **BAR MEALS:** L served Tue-Thurs, Sat, Sun 12-2 D served Tues-Sun 6.30-9.30 Av main course £6
RESTAURANT: L served Tue-Thur, Sat & Sun 12-2 D served Tues-Sun 6.30-9.30 Sun 6.30-9 Av 3 course à la carte £17
BREWERY/COMPANY: Free House **◖:** Carlsberg-Tetley Tetley Bitter, Timothy Taylor Landlord, Black Sheep.
CHILDREN'S FACILITIES: menu, portions, high-chairs, food/bottle warming **GARDEN:** Large & contained
NOTES: in garden, No dogs (ex guide dogs), Parking 50
ROOMS: 3 en suite s£26 d£36

LOW CATTON THE GOLD CUP INN ♀

YO41 1EA
☎ 01759 371354
Dir: *1m S of A166 or 1m N of A1079, E of York.* **Map Ref:** *SE75*

Historic coaching inn in the centre of a small village. A popular dining venue for almost 50 years, the pub boasts some striking features. The oak tables and matching booths were made specifically for the original restaurant, reputedly from a single oak tree. Dishes on the varied menu range from Gold Cup Cajun chicken and seafood pie, to roast rack of lamb and venison daube.

OPEN: 12-3 6-11 (Sat 12-11, Sun 12-10.30) Rest: Mon closed lunchtime **BAR MEALS:** L served Sun, Tue-Sat 12-2 D served all week 6-9.30 (12-9.30 wknds) Av main course £6 **RESTAURANT:** L served Sun D served all week 6-9.30 12-9.30 Av 3 course à la carte £16 Av 2 course fixed price £9.75 **BREWERY/COMPANY:** Free House 🍺: Tetley, John Smiths. ♀: 10 **CHILDREN'S FACILITIES:** menu, portions, high-chairs, food/bottle warming, outdoor play area **NOTES:** in bar, No dogs (ex guide dogs), Parking 60, No credit cards

SLEDMERE THE TRITON INN ♀

YO25 3XQ
☎ 01377 236644
e-mail: info@thetritoninnsledmere.co.uk
Dir: *Leave A166 at Garton on the Wolds, take B1252 to Sledmere.* **Map Ref:** *SE96*

An 18th-century coaching inn set in the shadow of historic Sledmere House, halfway between York and the coast on the scenic route to Bridlington. It makes an ideal base for touring the wolds, moors and coast. A log fire burns in the oak-panelled bar and home-made food is freshly prepared to order. Options range from sandwiches and baked potatoes to Thai prawns in batter, lamb chops in redcurrant and rosemary, and brandy peppered steak.

OPEN: 12-3 5-11 (12-11 Sat/Sun) Closed: Mons 1 Oct-31 Mar **BAR MEALS:** L served all week 12-2 D served Mon-Thurs 5.30-8 Fri/Sat 5.30-9, Sun 12-3 Av main course £6 **RESTAURANT:** L served all week 12-2 D served Mon-Sat 5.30-8 Av 3 course à la carte £16 **BREWERY/COMPANY:** Free House 🍺: Timothy Taylor's Landlord/Camerons Creamy, rotating guest ales, Mansfield Dark. **CHILDREN'S FACILITIES:** menu, portions, games, high-chairs, food/bottle warming, baby changing, board games, books **GARDEN:** Front & rear terrace with tables & chairs **NOTES:** Dogs allowed: in bar, in garden, water bowl, Parking 35

SOUTH CAVE THE FOX AND CONEY INN ♦♦♦♦ ♀

52 Market Place HU15 2AT
☎ 01430 422275 📠 01430 421552
e-mail: foxandconey@aol.com
Dir: *4 miles E of M62 on A63. 4 miles N of Brough mainline railway.* **Map Ref:** *SE93*

Right in the heart of South Cave, this family run pub dates from 1739 and is probably the oldest building in the village. The inn, which is handy for walkers on the nearby Wolds Way, was known simply as The Fox until William Goodlad added the Coney (rabbit) in 1788. Jacket potatoes, salads and baguettes supplement varied hot dishes like steak in ale pie, chicken curry, seafood platter and mushroom Stroganoff.

OPEN: 11.30-2.30 4.30-11 **BAR MEALS:** L served all week 11.30-2 D served all week 5.30-9.30 (Sun 12-3.30, 5.30-9) Av main course £6 **RESTAURANT:** L served all week 11.30-2 D served all week 5.30-9.30 **BREWERY/COMPANY:** Enterprise Inns 🍺: Timothy Taylors Landlord, Scottish Courage John Smith's & Theakston Cool Cask, Deuchers IPA, Guest Beers. ♀: 15 **CHILDREN'S FACILITIES:** menu, portions, high-chairs, food/bottle warming, baby changing, family room **GARDEN:** Seats approx 30 **NOTES:** No dogs (ex guide dogs), Parking 22 **ROOMS:** 12 en suite 2 family rooms s£42 d£55

ACASTER MALBIS THE SHIP INN

Moor End YO23 2UH
☎ 01904 703888 🖨 01904 705609
Dir: *From York take A1036 south, after Dringhouses take follow signs for Bishopthorpe and then Acaster Malbis.* **Map Ref:** *SE54*

The Ship is a 17th-century coaching house in a village setting on the outskirts of York, overlooking the River Ouse. A choice of home-made dishes is served in a conservatory-style eating area, and an à la carte menu in the Wheel House Restaurant. Typical options include cod in beer batter, steak, gammon, pizzas, and vegetarian lasagne. There is a large riverside beer garden.

OPEN: 11-11 (Sun 12-10.30) Oct-Feb Mon-Wed closed daytime Rest: Oct-Feb Closed Mon-Wed daytime **BAR MEALS:** L served all week 12-2.30 D served all week 4.30-8 Av main course £6.75 **RESTAURANT:** D served Fri-Sun 7-9.30 Av 3 course à la carte £19 Av 3 course fixed price £15 **BREWERY/COMPANY:** Enterprise Inns
🍺: Marston's Pedigree, Theakstons Best, John Smiths Cask, Tetley. **CHILDREN'S FACILITIES:** menu, portions, games, high-chairs, food/bottle warming, baby changing, outdoor play area, Wooden climbing frame, tyre swing, Ch Room, family room **GARDEN:** Large garden with benches and tables
NOTES: Dogs allowed: Water, Parking 60

AKEBAR THE FRIAR'S HEAD 🐑 ♟

Akebar Park DL8 5LY
☎ 01677 450201 450591 🖨 01677 450046
Dir: *Take A684 from Leeming Bar Motel (on A1). W towards Leyburn for 7m. Friar's Head is in Akebar Park.* **Map Ref:** *SE19*

Originally a farm and adjoining cottages, this is a typical stone-built Yorkshire Dales pub in Lower Wensleydale with lovely south-facing views over a golf course and farmland. The well-stocked bar, hand-pulled Yorkshire ales and blazing log fire make it perfect for relaxing after an invigorating walk in the hills. Diners eat in a flower-filled conservatory beneath trailing vines.

OPEN: 10-2.30 6-11.30 (Sun 7-10.30) **BAR MEALS:** L served all week 12-2.30 D served all week 6-11 Av main course £8 **RESTAURANT:** L served all week 12-2.30 D served all week 6-10 Av 3 course à la carte £18 **BREWERY/COMPANY:** Free House 🍺: Scottish Courage John Smith's & Theakston Best Bitter, Black Sheep Best.
♟: 14 **CHILDREN'S FACILITIES:** portions, high-chairs, food/bottle warming, Seated and dining with adults **GARDEN:** Terrace overlooks green, next to golf course **NOTES:** No dogs (ex guide dogs), Parking 60

APPLETREEWICK THE CRAVEN ARMS

BD23 6DA
☎ 01756 720270
e-mail: cravenapple@aol.com
Dir: *From Skipton take A59 towards Harrogate, B6160 N. Village signed on R. (Pub just outside village).* **Map Ref:** *SE06*

Built as a farm by Sir William Craven (a Lord Mayor of London) in the late 1500s, and later a weaving shed and courthouse, this ancient building retains its original beams, flagstone floors and magnificent Dales fireplace. The village stocks are still outside, with spectacular views of the River Wharfe and Simon's Seat. Home-made soup, steak pie with ale and mushrooms, cheesy cottage pie, traitor's pie (Lancashire hotpot in a giant Yorkshire pudding), local sausages, baguette sandwiches - these are all among the wholesome fare on offer.

OPEN: 11.30-3 6.30-11 (Sat & BHs 11.30-11, Sun 12-10.30) **BAR MEALS:** L served all week 11.30-2.30 D served all week 6.30-9 Sat 11.30-9, Sun 12-9 Av main course £5.50 **BREWERY/COMPANY:** Free House 🍺: Black Sheep, Tetley, Old Bear Original, Old Bear Hibernator.
CHILDREN'S FACILITIES: menu, portions, high-chairs, food/bottle warming, outdoor play area **GARDEN:** Walled grass beer garden, hill views **NOTES:** Dogs allowed: in bar, in garden, Parking 35

ASKRIGG KINGS ARMS

Market Place DL8 3HQ
☎ 01969 650817 ▯ 01969 650856
e-mail: kingsarms@askrigg.fsnet.co.uk
Dir: *N off A684 between Hawes & Leyburn.*
Map Ref: *SD99*

At the heart of the Yorkshire Dales, Askrigg's pub was known as The Drovers in the TV series 'All Creatures Great and Small'. Built in 1762 as racing stables and converted to a pub in 1860, today it boasts a good range of real ales and an extensive menu and wine list. There is a spectacular inglenook fireplace in the main bar.

OPEN: 11-3 6-11 (Sat 11-11, Sun 12-10.30)
BAR MEALS: L served all week 12-2 D served all week 6.30-9 Av main course £8.50 **RESTAURANT:** D served Fri-Sat 7-9 Av 3 course à la carte £17
BREWERY/COMPANY: Free House ◖: Scottish Courage John Smiths, Black Sheep, Guest Ales, Theakstons Best Bitter.
CHILDREN'S FACILITIES: menu **GARDEN:** Paved courtyard
NOTES: Dogs allowed: in bar, water provided

AUSTWICK THE GAME COCK INN

The Green LA2 8BB
☎ 015242 51226 ▯ 015242 51028
Map Ref: *SD76*

In the glorious surroundings of the Three Peaks, this cosy village pub draws a good local crowd. Everything on the menu is home cooked and freshly prepared in-house, and among the main dishes are venison casserole, lamb shoulder, battered haddock, and pork with black pudding. Sandwiches and bar snacks are also available, and there is a large rear garden with play area, popular in summer.

OPEN: 11.30-3 6-11 (All day Sun) **BAR MEALS:** L served all week 11.30-2 D served all week 6-9 (Sun 12-9) Av main course £7.95 **RESTAURANT:** L served all week 11.30-2 D served all week 6-9 (Sun 12-9) Av 3 course à la carte £13.50 **BREWERY/COMPANY:** ◖: Thwaites Best Bitter & Smooth. **CHILDREN'S FACILITIES:** menu, portions, high-chairs, food/bottle warming, outdoor play area, Play area and bird avairy in garden, family room **GARDEN:** large beer garden **NOTES:** in garden, No dogs (ex guide dogs), Parking 6

BREARTON MALT SHOVEL INN

HG3 3BX
☎ 01423 862929
Dir: *From A61 (Ripon/Harrogate) take B6165 towards Knaresborough. Turn at Brearton - 1.5m.* **Map Ref:** *SE36*

The oldest building in a very old village, The Malt Shovel has been at the heart of this small farming community since 1525. The rural setting has some good examples of ancient strip farming and, although the pub is surrounded by rolling farmland, it's just 15 minutes from Harrogate and within easy reach of Knaresborough or Ripon. A collection of beer mugs, horse brasses and hunting scenes decorates the heavily-beamed rooms leading off the carved oak bar, and you can enjoy a quiet game of dominoes or shove ha'penny without any electronic intrusions. The blackboard menu has something for everyone. Expect roast pork with crackling and apple sauce; warm chicken salad; and a good selection of fish dishes like pan-fried sea bass with herb butter. Vegetarians are well catered for too, with goat's cheese and chargrilled vegetables; or spinach and mushroom lasagne are typical.

OPEN: 12-2.30 6.45-11 (Sun 12-2.30, 7-10.30)
BAR MEALS: L served Tue-Sun 12-2 D served Tue-Sat 7-9 Av main course £6.50 **BREWERY/COMPANY:** Free House ◖: Daleside Nightjar, Durham Magus, Black Sheep Best, Theakston Masham. ♀: 20
CHILDREN'S FACILITIES: portions, high-chairs, food/bottle warming, baby changing **NOTES:** Dogs allowed: in bar, Parking 20, No credit cards

BROUGHTON   THE BULL ♀

BD23 3AE
☎ 01756 792065
e-mail: janeneil@thebullatbroughton.co.uk
Dir: On A59 3m from Skipton on A59.
Map Ref: SD95

Like the village itself, the pub is part of the 3,000-acre Broughton Hall estate, owned by the Tempest family for 900 years. The chef/manager was enticed from his much acclaimed former establishment to achieve similar high standards here. His compact, thoughtful menu offers slow-roasted ham shank glazed with orange and honey, crab and lobster risotto, and chargrilled chicken breast with herby cream cheese.

OPEN: 12-3 5.30-11 (Sun 12-8) **BAR MEALS:** L served all week 12-2 D served Mon-Sat 6-9 (Sunday 12-6.30)
RESTAURANT: L served all week 12-2 D served Mon-Sat 6-9 Sun 12-6.30 Av 3 course à la carte £16
BREWERY/COMPANY: Free House ◖: Scottish Courage, John Smith's Smooth, Bull Bitter (Local), Guest Ales.
CHILDREN'S FACILITIES: menu, games, high-chairs, food/bottle warming, family room **NOTES:** Dogs allowed: in bar, in garden, water, dog biscuits, Parking 60

BUCKDEN   THE BUCK INN ★★ ❀❀ 🐑 ♀

BD23 5JA
☎ 01756 760228 ▤ 01756 760227
e-mail: info@thebuckinn.com
Dir: From Skipton take B6265, then B6160.
Map Ref: SD97

Set in the heart of 'Calendar Girls' country, this

Georgian inn counts among its regulars some of the ladies who thought up the idea. The inn sits at the foot of Buckden Pike, facing south across the village green surrounded by picturesque stone cottages, and enjoying panoramic Dales views. The cosy bar has lots of charm and character, and the spacious Courtyard restaurant has two AA Rosettes.

OPEN: 11-11 **BAR MEALS:** L served all week 12-2 D served all week 6.30-9 Av main course £8.95
RESTAURANT: D served all week 6.30-9 Av 3 course à la carte £17 Av 4 course fixed price £23.95
BREWERY/COMPANY: Free House ◖: Black Sheep Bitter, Old Peculiar, Timothy Taylor's Landlord, Copper Dragon.
♀: 10 **CHILDREN'S FACILITIES:** menu, portions, high-chairs, food/bottle warming **GARDEN:** Patio **NOTES:** Dogs allowed: in bar, in bedrooms, Parking 40 **ROOMS:** 14 en suite 2 family rooms s£41 d£82

CARTHORPE   THE FOX & HOUNDS 🐑 ♀

DL8 2LG
☎ 01845 567433 ▤ 01845 567155
Dir: Off A1, signposted on both northbound & southbound carriageways. Map Ref: SE38

Tucked away just off the A1 this neat 200-year-old free house, run by the Fitzgerald family for 20 years, was once the village smithy. In fact, the old anvil and other tools of the trade can still be seen in the dining room. There are midweek set-price lunch and dinner menus, as well as specials from the blackboard. Sunday lunch might include roast loin of pork with apple sauce and stuffing.

OPEN: 12-2.30 7-11 Closed: 1st wk Jan
BAR MEALS: L served Tue-Sun 12-2 D served Tue-Sat 7-10 Sun 7-9.30 Av main course £10 **RESTAURANT:** L served Tue-Sun 12-2 D served Tue-Sun 7-9.30 Av 3 course à la carte £16 Av 3 course fixed price £13.95
BREWERY/COMPANY: Free House ◖: Black Sheep Best, Worthington's Bitter. **CHILDREN'S FACILITIES:** portions, games, high-chairs, food/bottle warming **NOTES:** No dogs (ex guide dogs), Parking 22

CLAPHAM NEW INN ♀

LA2 8HH
☎ 01524 251203 🖨 251496
e-mail: info@newinn-clapham.co.uk
Dir: On A65 in Yorkshire Dale National Park.
Map Ref: SD76

Family-run 18th-century coaching inn located in a peaceful Dales village beneath Ingleborough, one of Yorkshire's most famous summits. There are plenty of good walks from the pub. Honest, wholesome food is served in the non-smoking dining room.

OPEN: 11-11 (Winter open 11-3, 6.30-11)
BAR MEALS: L served all week 12-2 D served all week 6.30-8.30 (Sun 6.30-8) Av main course £8.95
RESTAURANT: L served all week 12-2 D served all week 6.30-8.30 (Sun 6.30-8) Av 3 course à la carte £20 Av 4 course fixed price £20 **BREWERY/COMPANY:** Free House **🍺:** Black Sheep Best, Carlsberg-Tetley Tetley Bitter, Copper Dragon Pippin, Dent Fellbeck. ♀: 18
CHILDREN'S FACILITIES: menu, portions, high-chairs, food/bottle warming, Baby changing facilities
GARDEN: Riverside seats, beer garden **NOTES:** Dogs allowed: in bar, in garden, in bedrooms, water, Parking 35

CRAY THE WHITE LION INN ♀

Cray BD23 5JB
☎ 01756 760262 🖨 761024
e-mail: admin@whitelioncray.com
Map Ref: SD97

Renowned as a 'tiny oasis' of hospitality, this family-owned, traditional inn is the highest pub in Wharfedale, and offers a warm and friendly welcome. The tastefully restored former drovers' hostelry remains faithful to its origins with old beams, log fires and stone-flagged floors. Hand-pulled ales and home-cooked food complete the picture: try home-made venison casserole, oven-roasted duck breast with raspberry and redcurrant sauce or vegetable lasagne topped with goats' cheese, along with various lighter bites at lunchtime.

OPEN: 11-11 Closed: 25 Dec **BAR MEALS:** L served all week 12-2 D served all week 5.45-8.30 Av main course £8
BREWERY/COMPANY: Free House **🍺:** Daleside Blonde, Moorhouse Pendle witches Brew, Premier Bitter, Timothy Taylor Landlord. ♀: 9 **CHILDREN'S FACILITIES:** menu, portions, food/bottle warming, family room **GARDEN:** Beer garden with 10 trestle tables **NOTES:** Dogs allowed: in bar, in garden, in bedrooms, water, Parking 20 **ROOMS:** 8 en suite 1 family room s£40 d£60 (♦♦♦)

CROPTON THE NEW INN ♀

YO18 8HH
☎ 01751 417330 🖨 01751 417582
e-mail: info@croptonbrewery.co.uk
Map Ref: SE78

With the award-winning Cropton micro-brewery in its own grounds, this family-run free house on the edge of the North York Moors National Park is popular with locals and visitors alike. Meals are served in the restored village bar, and in the elegant Victorian restaurant: New Inn lamb joint, speciality sausages, steak and Scoresby Stout pie, fisherman's pie, Whitby cod, salmon, and plenty more.

OPEN: 11-11 **BAR MEALS:** L served all week 12-2 D served all week 6-9 Av main course £8
RESTAURANT: L served all week 12-2 D served all week 6-9 **BREWERY/COMPANY:** Free House **🍺:** Cropton Two Pints, Monkmans Slaughter, Thwaites Best Bitter, Yorkshire Moors Bitter. ♀: 7 **CHILDREN'S FACILITIES:** menu, portions, games, high-chairs, food/bottle warming, outdoor play area, family room **GARDEN:** Beer garden **NOTES:** Parking 50
ROOMS: 10 en suite 2 family rooms s£39 d£54 (♦♦♦)

DACRE BANKS THE ROYAL OAK INN

Oak Ln HG3 4EN
☎ 01423 780200 📄 781748
e-mail: enquiries@theroyaloak.uk.com
Dir: *From A59 (Harrogate/Skipton) take B6451 towards Pateley Bridge.* **Map Ref:** *SE16*

In the heart of Nidderdale, this family-run free

house was built in 1752. With its open fires and timbered beams, the Royal Oak offers fine Yorkshire ales and home-cooked meals. There's also an attractive rear garden. The snack menu includes hot baguettes and jacket potatoes.

OPEN: 11.30-3 5-11 (Sun 12-3, 7-10.30)
BAR MEALS: L served all week 11.30-2 D served all week 6.30-9 Av main course £9.95 **RESTAURANT:** L served all week 11.30-2 D served all week 6.30-9 Av 3 course à la carte £17 Av 3 course fixed price £12.95
BREWERY/COMPANY: Free House ◖: Rudgate Yorkshire Dales & Special, Black Sheep Best, Royal Oak Dacre Ale, Carlsberg-Tetley Tetley's Mild.
CHILDREN'S FACILITIES: portions, food/bottle warming **GARDEN:** Garden at rear overlooks river **NOTES:** in bar, No dogs (ex guide dogs), Parking 15 **ROOMS:** 3 en suite s£35 d£55 (♦♦♦♦)

EAST WITTON THE BLUE LION

DL8 4SN
☎ 01969 624273 📄 01969 624189
e-mail: bluelion@breathemail.net
Map Ref: *SE18*

From the end of the 18th century onwards, coach travellers and drovers journeying through Wensleydale have been refuelling at the Blue Lion. Probably largely unchanged since then, its stone façades have featured in the sixties-based TV series 'Heartbeat'. The bar with its open fire and flagstone floor, and the restaurant, candlelit in the evening, are both perfect settings.

OPEN: 11-11 **BAR MEALS:** L served all week 12-2.15 D served all week 7-9.30 Av main course £12
RESTAURANT: L served Sun 12-2.15 D served all week 7-9.30 Av 3 course à la carte £22.90
BREWERY/COMPANY: Free House ◖: Black Sheep Riggwelter, Scottish Courage Theakston Old Peculier. ♀: 12
CHILDREN'S FACILITIES: portions, high-chairs, food/bottle warming **GARDEN:** Lrg lawn, beautiful views **NOTES:** Dogs allowed: in bar, in garden, in bedrooms, Parking 30

EGTON BRIDGE HORSESHOE HOTEL ♀

YO21 1XE
☎ 01947 895245
Dir: *From Whitby take A171 towards Middlesborough. Village signed in 5m.*
Map Ref: *NZ80*

An 18th-century country inn by the River Esk,

and handy for the North Yorkshire Moors Railway. Inside are oak settles and tables, local artists' paintings and, depending on the weather, an open fire. Lunchtime bar food includes sandwiches in malted granary bread, and hot baguettes. More substantial are lamb fillet with bubble and squeak or warm pigeon breast salad with raspberry vinegar.

OPEN: 11.30-3 6.30-11 (All day Sat, Sun&BH's in Summer) Closed: 25 Dec **BAR MEALS:** L served all week 12-2 D served all week 7-9 Av main course £7.50
RESTAURANT: L served all week 12-2 D served all week 7-9
BREWERY/COMPANY: Free House ◖: Scottish Courage & John Smiths, Durham, Whitby, Nick Staford. ♀: 7
CHILDREN'S FACILITIES: menu, portions, games, high-chairs, food/bottle warming, baby changing, family room
GARDEN: Beautiful garden on banks of River Esk
NOTES: Dogs allowed: in bar, in garden, water provided, Parking 25

ESCRICK BLACK BULL INN ◆◆◆

Main St YO19 6JP
☎ 01904 728245 🗎 01904 728154
e-mail: blackbullhotel@btconnect.com
Dir: *From York follow the A19 for 5m, enter Escrick, take second L up main street, premises located on the L.* **Map Ref:** *SE64*

Situated in the heart of a quiet village, this 19th-century pub is within easy reach of York racecourse and the historic city centre. The sea is also nearby, as evidenced by the fish selection: red snapper, scampi or haddock may be found on the menu. Other dishes might include Moroccan chicken, steak and ale pie, oriental salmon, fillet steak Rossini, or chicken and vegetable pie.

OPEN: 12-3 5-11 (Sun all day) **BAR MEALS:** L served all week 12-2.30 D served all week 6-9.30 Av main course £6.95 **RESTAURANT:** L served all week 12-2.30 D served all week 6-9.30 Av 3 course à la carte £15 🍺: John Smiths, Tetleys, Carlsberg, Stella. ♀: 7 **CHILDREN'S FACILITIES:** menu, games, high-chairs, food/bottle warming, family room **NOTES:** No dogs (ex guide dogs), Parking 10 **ROOMS:** 10 en suite 2 family rooms s£45 d£65

GREAT OUSEBURN THE CROWN INN ♀

Main St YO26 9RF
☎ 01423 330430 🗎 01423 331095
Map Ref: *SE46*

The Crown remembers the days when regular visitors were cattle drovers and large parties of fishermen on coach outings from the coast. Barrett's Great Canadian Circus would winter in the village; the circus band was under the direction of Ambrose Tiller who went on to found the world-renowned dancing troupe the 'Tiller Girls'. The Crown prides itself on offering a wide choice of imaginative dishes prepared from the finest, mostly local fish, seafood, meat and game. The new brasserie has increased the dining opportunities with competitively priced two or three course meals including a half bottle of wine, while the bar still offers its good value two course menu. Be prepared for a leisurely browse through the various menus and weekly changing specials board as the range of dishes, too numerous to single out, need careful consideration. In keeping with the range and standard of the cuisine there is an extensive wine list personally selected by the owners.

OPEN: 12-2 5-11 (Sat 11-11, Sun 12-10.30, BHs all day) Closed: 25 Dec Rest: Mon-Fri Closed lunch **BAR MEALS:** L served Sat-Sun D served all week 5-9.30 (Sat 12-5, Sun 12-9) Av main course £6 **RESTAURANT:** L served Sat-Sun D served all week 5-9.30 (Sat 12-9.30, Sun 12-9) Av 3 course à la carte £22 **BREWERY/COMPANY:** Free House 🍺: Black Sheep Best, Scottish Courage, John Smith's, Hambeltons Best Bitter. ♀: 10 **CHILDREN'S FACILITIES:** menu, high-chairs, food/bottle warming, baby changing **GARDEN:** Paved, walled area **NOTES:** No dogs (ex guide dogs), Parking 60

HARROGATE THE BOARS HEAD HOTEL ★★★ ♀

Ripley Castle Estate HG3 3AY
☎ 01423 771888 🗎 01423 771509
e-mail: reservations@boarsheadripley.co.uk
Dir: *On the A61 Harrogate/Ripon road, the Hotel is in the centre of Ripley village.*
Map Ref: *SE35*

An old coaching inn situated at the heart of the Ripley Castle Estate, the Boars Head has been luxuriously furnished by Sir Thomas and Lady Ingilby to create an impressive hotel. The bar/bistro welcomes guests old and new to sample the range of creative and award-winning dishes. The walled courtyard situated to the rear of the hotel is a bonus in summer when guests can dine outside.

OPEN: 11-11 Sun 12-10.30 (Winter Mon-Sat 11-3, 5-11) (Winter Sun 12-3, 5-10.30) **BAR MEALS:** L served all week 12-2.30 D served all week 6.30-10 Winter-lunch served 2pm Av main course £9.95 **RESTAURANT:** L served all week 12-2 D served all week 7-9.30 Av 3 course fixed price £29 **BREWERY/COMPANY:** Free House 🍺: Scottish Courage Theakston Best & Old Peculier, Daleside Crackshot, Hambleton White Boar, Daleside Old Leg Over. ♀: 9 **CHILDREN'S FACILITIES:** menu, portions, games, high-chairs, food/bottle warming, baby changing, Under 6, not in bar pm. Changing facilities **GARDEN:** Courtyard area **NOTES:** Overnight in bedrooms only, No dogs (ex guide dogs), Parking 45 **ROOMS:** 25 en suite s£99 d£120

HETTON THE ANGEL

BD23 6LT
☎ 01756 730263 ▤ 01756 730363
e-mail: info@angelhetton.co.uk
Dir: *From A59 take B6265 towards Grassington/Skipton.* **Map Ref:** *SD95*

A stone-built Dales inn with a history going back over 500 years. Specialities are fresh fish, Dales-bred lamb, beef and seasonal game.

OPEN: 12-3 6-10.30 Closed: Dec 25, Jan 1
BAR MEALS: L served all week 12-2 D served all week 6-9 (Sat 6-10) Av main course £9.50 **RESTAURANT:** L served Sun 12-2 D served Mon-Sat 6-9 Av 3 course à la carte £27.50 Av 3 course fixed price £18.50
BREWERY/COMPANY: Free House ◖: Blacksheep Bitter, Taylor Landlord, Warefdale Folly, Golden Dragon Bitter. ♀: 24
CHILDREN'S FACILITIES: portions, games, high-chairs, food/bottle warming **GARDEN:** Terrace in front of pub
NOTES: No dogs (ex guide dogs), Parking 56
ROOMS: 5 en suite s£120 d£120

HOVINGHAM THE WORSLEY ARMS HOTEL ★★★

Main St YO62 4LA
☎ 01653 628234 ▤ 01653 628130
e-mail: worsleyarms@aol.com
Dir: *From A1 take A64 towards Malton, L onto B1257 signed Slingsby & Hovingham. 2m to Hovingham.* **Map Ref:** *SE67*

In 1841 Sir William Worsley tried to create a spa to rival Bath, but his guests disliked the muddy track between his new hotel and spa house. The spa failed. The hotel, however, survived and, together with the pub, forms part of the historic Hovingham Hall estate. The pub offers two places to eat: the Restaurant and the Cricketer's Bar.

OPEN: 12-2.30 7-11 **BAR MEALS:** L served all week 12-2 D served all week 7-10 **RESTAURANT:** L served Sun 12-2 D served all week 7-10 **BREWERY/COMPANY:** Free House ◖: Scottish Courage John Smith's, Hambleton Stallion. ♀: 20
CHILDREN'S FACILITIES: menu, portions, games, high-chairs **GARDEN:** Formal and open gardens, mahogany furniture
NOTES: Dogs allowed: in bar, in garden, in bedrooms, Parking 30 **ROOMS:** 20 en suite 2 family rooms s£60 d£100

INGLETON MARTON ARMS HOTEL ◆◆◆◆

Thornton-in-Lonsdale LA6 3PB
☎ 01524 241281 ▤ 01524 242579
e-mail: mail@martonarms.co.uk
Dir: *At junction A65/A687. Take the road opposite the A687, take the first or second left. The Marton Arms is situated opposite the Church of St Oswald.* **Map Ref:** *SD67*

A former coaching inn once patronised by Sir Arthur Conan Doyle, located opposite the Norman church where he was married. Real beers and over 300 Scottish malt whiskies are stocked and there's a comprehensive menu. Food options range through sandwiches, snacks, regular dishes and daily specials, such as greenlip mussels with white wine and garlic, and game pie with home-made chips. The speciality selection of pizzas and burgers is also available to takeaway.

OPEN: 11-11 (Sun 12-10.30) **BAR MEALS:** L served all week 12-2 D served all week 6-9 Av main course £3
RESTAURANT: L served all week 12-3 D served all week 6-9 ◖: Timothy Taylor Golden Best, Black Sheep Bitter, Theakstons, Cains. ♀: 8 **CHILDREN'S FACILITIES:** menu, portions, games, high-chairs, food/bottle warming, baby changing
GARDEN: Lawned garden with tables and shrubs
NOTES: No dogs (ex guide dogs), Parking 40
ROOMS: 12 en suite 1 family room s£42 d£64

KILBURN   THE FORRESTERS ARMS HOTEL ◆◆◆

YO61 4AH
☎ 01347 868386 & 868550 📄 01347 868386
e-mail:
paulcussons@forrestersarms.fsnet.co.uk
Map Ref: SE57

Sturdy stone former-coaching inn still offering ten comfortable rooms for travellers passing close by the famous White Horse of Kilburn on the North York Moors. The cosy lower bar has some of the earliest oak furniture by Robert Thompson, with his distinctive mouse symbol on every piece. Evidence of the inn's former stables can be seen in the upper bar. Steak and ale pie, pheasant casserole, homemade lasagne and lamb chops are popular dishes.

OPEN: 11-11 **BAR MEALS:** L served all week 12-2.30 D served all week 6.30-9 Av main course £7
RESTAURANT: L served all week 12-2.30 D served all week 6.30-9 Av 3 course à la carte £9.95
BREWERY/COMPANY: Free House 🍺: Scottish Courage John Smiths, Carlsberg-Tetley Tetley's, Hambleton.
CHILDREN'S FACILITIES: menu, portions, high-chairs, food/bottle warming **NOTES:** Dogs allowed: in bar, in garden, in bedrooms, Dog bowl, biscuits, Parking 40
ROOMS: 10 en suite 2 family rooms s£40 d£52

KIRBY HILL   THE SHOULDER OF MUTTON INN

DL11 7JH
☎ 01748 822772 📄 01325 718936
e-mail: info@shoulderofmutton.net
Dir: 4m N of Richmond, 6m from A1 A66 J at Scotch Corner. **Map Ref:** NZ10

A 200-year-old traditional inn in an elevated position overlooking Holmedale. Log fires burn in the bar areas, while the separate Stable restaurant retains its original beams. Choose whether to eat here or in the bar; the well-priced set menu offers traditional fare with a modern influence - prawn, celery and apple cocktail then poached salmon with prawn and rose butter, for example. The à la carte is just as reasonable - halibut with asparagus & bacon or venison with black pudding would be typical mains.

BAR MEALS: L served Sat-Sun 12-2 D served Wed-Sun 7-9
RESTAURANT: L served Sat-Sun 12-2 D served Wed-Sun 7-9 Av 3 course à la carte £22 Av 3 course fixed price £17.95
BREWERY/COMPANY: Free House 🍺: Scottish Courage John Smiths, Jennings Cumberland Ale, Black Sheep Best.
CHILDREN'S FACILITIES: menu, portions, food/bottle warming **GARDEN:** Paved **NOTES:** Dogs allowed: in bar, in garden, in bedrooms, Parking 22 **ROOMS:** 5 en suite 1 family room s£39 d£49 (◆◆◆)

KIRKBYMOORSIDE   GEORGE & DRAGON HOTEL ★★ ♀

17 Market Place YO62 6AA
☎ 01751 433334 📄 01751 432933
e-mail: georgeatkirkby@aol.com
Dir: Just off A170 between Scarborough & Thirsk in centre of the Market Town.
Map Ref: SE68

heart of Kirkbymoorside. The pub has changed quite dramatically over the years - the restaurant used to be the brewhouse. Sports enthusiasts will appreciate the collection of rugby and cricket memorabilia in the bar, including photographs, autographs, prints and other paraphernalia. A good variety of food is available, from snacks and blackboard specials in the bar to candlelit dinners in Knights' Restaurant or the bistro.

OPEN: 10-11 **BAR MEALS:** L served all week 12-2.15 D served all week 6.30-9.15 **RESTAURANT:** L served all week 12-2.15 D served all week 6.30-9.15 Av 3 course à la carte £18 **BREWERY/COMPANY:** Free House 🍺: Black Sheep Best, Tetley and changing guest beers. ♀: 10
CHILDREN'S FACILITIES: menu, portions, high-chairs, food/bottle warming, baby changing **GARDEN:** Walled garden, herb garden **NOTES:** Dogs allowed: in bar, Parking 15 **ROOMS:** 18 en suite 2 family rooms s£49 d£79

A 17th-century former coaching inn offering a haven of warmth, refreshment and rest in the

THE LION INN ♀

Blakey Ridge YO62 7LQ
☎ 01751 417320 📠 01751 417717
e-mail: info@lionblakey.co.uk
Dir: *From A170 follow signs 'Hutton le Hole/Castleton'. 6m N of Hutton le Hole.*
Map Ref: *SE68*

The Lion stands 470m above sea level, the fourth highest inn in England, with breathtaking views over the beautiful North York Moors National Park. The friendly, cosy interior with beamed ceilings, 4ft-thick stone walls and blazing fires makes up for the isolated location. Typical chef's specials are T-bone steak, steak and mushroom pie, and tournedos Rossini. Other choices on the extensive à la carte menu offer fish and chicken options, while varied vegetarian and children's menus cater for every need.

OPEN: 10-11 **BAR MEALS:** L served all week 12-10 D served all week 12-10 Av main course £6.95 **RESTAURANT:** L served Sun only 12-7 D served all week 7-10 Av 3 course à la carte £18 Av 3 course fixed price £10.95 **BREWERY/COMPANY:** Free House 🍺: Scottish Courage Theakston Blackbull, XB & Old Peculiar, Scottish Courage John smith's Bitter, Greene King Old Speckled Hen. ♀: 9 **CHILDREN'S FACILITIES:** menu, portions, high-chairs, food/bottle warming, baby changing **GARDEN:** Large garden, picnic benches, well **NOTES:** Dogs allowed: in bar, in garden, in bedrooms, Parking 200 **ROOMS:** 10 bedrooms 8 en suite 3 family rooms s£18 d£50 (♦♦♦)

KIRKHAM   STONE TROUGH INN ✿ 🐑 ♀

Kirkham Abbey YO60 7JS
☎ 01653 618713 📠 01653 618819
e-mail: info@stonetroughinn.co.uk
Dir: *1 1/2m off A64, between York & Malton.*
Map Ref: *SE76*

Stone-built country inn high above Kirkham Priory and the River Derwent. The stone 'trough' of the pub's name stands at the entrance: it originally supported a cross erected by a knight in the 12th century to commemorate his son; the cross eventually disappeared, leaving behind the base with its depression. Today's owners offer friendliness, hospitality, and excellent real ales, while building a deserved reputation for fine eating.

OPEN: 12-2.30 6-11 (Sun 11.45-10.30) Closed: Dec 25 **BAR MEALS:** L served Tues-Sun 12-2 D served Tues-Sun 6.30-8.30 Av main course £8.95 **RESTAURANT:** L served Sun 12-2.15 D served Tue-Sat 6.45-9.30 Av 3 course à la carte £24 **BREWERY/COMPANY:** Free House 🍺: TetleyCask, Timothy Taylor Landlord, Black Sheep Best, Malton Brewery Golden Chance. ♀: 9 **CHILDREN'S FACILITIES:** menu, portions, games, high-chairs, food/bottle warming, Patio and lawn **NOTES:** No dogs (ex guide dogs), Parking 100

KNARESBOROUGH   THE GENERAL TARLETON INN ★★★ ✿✿ 🐑 ♀

Boroughbridge Rd, Ferrensby HG5 0PZ
☎ 01423 340284 📠 01423 340288
e-mail: gti@generaltarleton.co.uk
Dir: *On A6055, on crossroads in Ferrensby.*
Map Ref: *SE35*

Traditional 18th-century coaching inn conveniently close to the A1 and many of Yorkshire's top attractions. It takes its name from Sir Banastre Tarleton, a distinguished 18th-century war hero and politician. Surrounded by glorious North Yorkshire countryside, the General Tarleton offers a rambling, low-beamed bar with open fires and a popular covered courtyard where you may choose to eat. The menu is impressive and wide ranging. There is an extensive and impressive wine list.

OPEN: 12-3 6-11 **BAR MEALS:** L served all week 12-2.15 D served all week 6-9.30 Av main course £10 **RESTAURANT:** L served Sun 12-1.45 D served Mon-Sat 6-9.30 Av 3 course fixed price £29.50 **BREWERY/COMPANY:** Free House 🍺: Black Sheep Best, Timothy Taylors Landlord. ♀: 16 **CHILDREN'S FACILITIES:** menu, portions, games, high-chairs, food/bottle warming **GARDEN:** Garden improvement in progress **NOTES:** Parking 37 **ROOMS:** 14 en suite s£74.95 d£84.90

LASTINGHAM **BLACKSMITHS ARMS**

YO62 6TL
☎ 01751 417247
e-mail: blacksmithslastingham@hotmail.com
Map Ref: SE79

A 17th-century, stone-built inn in an idyllic village within the North York Moors National

Park. Opposite is the church, whose Saxon crypt attracts up to thirty thousand visitors each year. Many, no doubt, pop into the pub as well, which must delight the new owners. Main courses on the menu include roast topside of beef with Yorkshire pudding; half a crispy roast duck with orange sauce; and cottage pie with peppers. And there are daily specials.

OPEN: 12-3.30 6-11 (Mar-Nov open 10.30-11)
BAR MEALS: L served all week 12-2.15 D served all week 7-9 10.30-12 (snacks), 2.30-5.30 (light meals)
RESTAURANT: L served all week 12-2 D served all week 7-9.15 **BREWERY/COMPANY:** Free House 🍺: Theakstons Best Bitter, Marston's Pedigree, Black Bull Bitter, Lastingham Best Bitter. **CHILDREN'S FACILITIES:** portions, high-chairs, food/bottle warming **GARDEN:** Cottage garden seating 32, decking seats 20 **NOTES:** No dogs (ex guide dogs)

LEYBURN **SANDPIPER INN** ♀

Market Place DL8 5AT
☎ 01969 622206 📄 01969 625367
e-mail: hsandpiper@aol.com
Dir: From A1 take A684 to Leyburn.
Map Ref: SE19

The oldest building in Leyburn, dating back to around 1640, has been a pub for just 30 years and an outstanding one since its purchase in 1999 by the Harrison family. With a beautiful summer garden, a bar, snug and dining room within, the bar and restaurant menus offer an exciting and varied mix of traditional and more unusual dishes.

OPEN: 11.30-3 6.30-11 (Sun 12-3, 6.30-10.30) Closed: 2wks Jan **BAR MEALS:** L served all week 12-2.30 D served all week 6.30-9.00 (Fri-Sat 6.30-9.30, Sun 7-9) Av main course £13.95 **RESTAURANT:** L served all week 12-2.30 D served all week 6.30-9 Fri-Sat 6.30-9.30, Sun 12-2, 7-9 **BREWERY/COMPANY:** Free House 🍺: Black Sheep Best, Black Sheep Special, Daleside, Theakstons Hogshead. ♀: 8 **CHILDREN'S FACILITIES:** high-chairs, food/bottle warming, family room **GARDEN:** Terrace area to front **NOTES:** Dogs allowed: in bar, in 'snug area', Parking 6

LITTON **QUEENS ARMS**

BD23 5QJ
☎ 01756 770208
e-mail: queensarmslitton@mserve.net
Dir: From Skipton: Northvale Road, follow for 15 miles. Signposted. *Map Ref:* SD97

Early 16th-century inn in a remote corner of the Yorkshire Dales, now brewing its own Litton Ale with spring water from the neighbouring hillside. Two-foot thick walls, low ceilings, beams and coal fires give the place a traditional, timeless feel. A good range of food incorporates plenty of fish, including Wharfedale trout and grilled halibut, home-made pies, including rabbit and game, pork fillet, chicken supreme, a hefty mixed grill, vegetarian and children's dishes.

OPEN: 12-3 7-11 Closed: 3 Jan-1Feb
BAR MEALS: L served Tue-Sun, BH Mon's 12-2 D served Tue-Sun, BH 7-9 Av main course £6.95
RESTAURANT: L served Tue-Sun 12-2 D served Tue-Sun 7-9 Av 3 course à la carte £17.50 **BREWERY/COMPANY:** Free House 🍺: Litton Ale, Tetleys, plus guest ales.
CHILDREN'S FACILITIES: menu, portions, games, high-chairs, food/bottle warming, baby changing, family room
GARDEN: Beer garden, outdoor eating, patio **NOTES:** Dogs allowed: in bar, Parking 10

MARTON THE APPLETREE COUNTRY INN ♀

YO62 6RD
☎ 01751 431457 🗎 01751 430190
e-mail: appletreeinn@supanet.com
Dir: *From Kirkby Moorside on A170 turn right after one mile, follow road for two miles to Marton.* **Map Ref:** *SE78*

In a tiny village within a spit of the North Yorks Moors, this self-styled dining pub, 17th century in origin, has a shop attached selling a cornucopia of home-made edible goodies. Modern British food is evidenced by thin tomato tart with olives and herbs; grilled black bream with salad Niçoise and balsamic orange reduction; and Cheddar and wild mushroom tagliatelle. Good Yorkshire beers are on draught. Visitors may like to know that the head chef/proprietor is called Trajan, after the Roman emperor.

OPEN: 12-2.30 6.30-11 (Sun 12-3, 7-10.30) Closed: 2 weeks Jan **BAR MEALS:** L served Wed-Sun 12-2 D served Wed-Mon 6.30-9 (Sun 12-2.30, 7-9) Av main course £8.50 **RESTAURANT:** L served Wed-Sun 12-2 D served Wed-Mon 6.30-10 (Sun 12-12.30, 7-9) Av 3 course à la carte £23.50 **BREWERY/COMPANY:** Free House 🍺: Scottish Courage John Smiths Cask, Guest ales; Malton, York, Daleside. ♀: 12 **CHILDREN'S FACILITIES:** portions, high-chairs, food/bottle warming **GARDEN:** Patio, seats 16, adjoining orchard **NOTES:** No dogs (ex guide dogs), Parking 30

MASHAM KINGS HEAD HOTEL ★★ ♀

Market Place HG4 4EF
☎ 01765 689295 🗎 01765 689070
e-mail: masham.kingshead@snr.co.uk
Map Ref: *SE28*

Overlooking Masham's spacious market square with its cross and maypole, this 18th-century, three-storey former posting house and excise office is a perfect base for touring the Yorkshire Dales. Pancetta-wrapped chicken breast, cod on lemon and Chardonnay risotto, and glazed pork loin and baked apple will all be found on the menu, plus specials too. Real ales are on tap. A new barn conversion has doubled the number of bedrooms, and includes one fully fitted for the disabled guest.

OPEN: 11-11 **BAR MEALS:** L served all week 12-3 D served all week 6-10 Av main course £8 **RESTAURANT:** L served all week 12-3 D served all week 6-10 **BREWERY/COMPANY:** 🍺: Scottish Courage Theakstons Best Bitter, Black Bull & Old Peculier, Guest Ales. ♀: 14 **CHILDREN'S FACILITIES:** menu, portions, games, high-chairs, food/bottle warming, baby changing **GARDEN:** Georgian patio style **NOTES:** Dogs allowed: in garden, Water **ROOMS:** 23 en suite s£50 d£65

MIDDLEHAM BLACK SWAN HOTEL 🐑

Market Place DL8 4NP
☎ 01969 622221 🗎 01969 622221
e-mail: blackswanmiddleham@breathe.com
Map Ref: *SE18*

Built in 1640, this Grade II listed building is decorated with original oak beams and a log fire. It overlooks Middleham market square, with the beer garden at the rear backing on to the castle. Situated in a famous racing area, horses can be seen passing the front every morning on their way to the gallops. Traditional country cooking results in dishes like local rack of lamb, beef in Old Peculier ale and roast partridge or pheasant. Many circular walks of varying lengths can begin here.

OPEN: 11-3.30 6-11 (open all day Sat-Sun summer) **BAR MEALS:** L served all week 12-2 D served all week 6.30-9 Av main course £6 **RESTAURANT:** L served all week 12-2 D served all week 6.30-9 Av 3 course à la carte £17 **BREWERY/COMPANY:** Free House 🍺: Scottish Courage John Smiths, Theakstons Best Bitter, Black Bull, Old Peculier & Guest Beers. **CHILDREN'S FACILITIES:** menu, games, high-chairs, food/bottle warming, baby changing, family room **GARDEN:** Patio and lawn with benches, tables **NOTES:** Dogs allowed: in bar, in bedrooms, Dogs by appointment

MIDDLESMOOR   CROWN HOTEL ♀

HG3 5ST
☎ 01423 755204
Dir: *Telephone for directions.* **Map Ref:** *SE07*

The original building dates back to the 17th century; today it offers the chance to enjoy a good pint of local beer by a cosy, roaring log fire, or in a sunny pub garden. Stands on a breezy 900ft hilltop with good views towards Gouthwaite Reservoir. Ideal for those potholing or following the popular Nidderdale Way.

OPEN: 12-2.30 7-11 **BAR MEALS:** L served Mon-Sun 12-2.30 D served Mon-Sat 7-8.30 Av main course £6.95 **RESTAURANT:** L served all week 12-2.30 D served all week 7-9 **BREWERY/COMPANY:** Free House 🍺: Black Sheep Best, Worthingtons Smooth, Theakstons Bitter. ♀: 20 **CHILDREN'S FACILITIES:** menu, portions, high-chairs, food/bottle warming **NOTES:** Dogs allowed: in bar, in garden, in bedrooms, Water, Parking 10

MUKER   THE FARMERS ARMS ♀

DL11 6QG
☎ 01748 886297
Dir: *From Richmond take A6108 towards Leyburn, turn R onto B6270.* **Map Ref:** *SD99*

The last remaining pub - of three - in this old lead-mining village at the head of beautiful Swaledale, and a popular resting place for walkers on the Pennine Way and Coast-to-Coast route. With several miles under the belt, refuel with home-made steak pie, chicken alla Romana, deep-fried cod, liver and onions, or vegetable tandoori masala, aided and abetted by a pint of Castle Eden's Nimmos XXXX. Children's and smaller meals are also available.

OPEN: 11-11 Sun 12-10.30 **BAR MEALS:** L served all week 12-2.30 D served all week 7-8.50 Av main course £7 **BREWERY/COMPANY:** Free House 🍺: Theakston Best & Old Peculiar, John Smith's, Nimmo's XXXX, Black Sheep. ♀: 10 **CHILDREN'S FACILITIES:** menu, portions, high-chairs, food/bottle warming **GARDEN:** Cobbled area with flower beds **NOTES:** Dogs allowed: Water Provided, Parking 6

OSMOTHERLEY   QUEEN CATHERINE HOTEL ♦♦

7 West End DL6 3AG
☎ 01609 883209
e-mail: queencatherine@yahoo.co.uk
Map Ref: *SE49*

Named after Henry VIII's wife, Catherine of Aragon, who left her horse and carriage here while sheltering from her husband with nearby monks. There is no sense of menace around this friendly hotel nowadays, believed to be the only one in Britain bearing its name, and visitors can enjoy a well-cooked meal: monkfish tails, crab-stuffed chicken breast, lamb shank with minted gravy, Icelandic cod, and Whitby breaded scampi are all on the menu.

OPEN: 12-3 6-11 (open all day Sat-Sun) **BAR MEALS:** L served all week 12-2 D served all week 6-9 **RESTAURANT:** L served all week 12-2 D served all week 6-9 🍺: Hambleton Ales-Stud, Stallion, Bitter, Goldfield. **CHILDREN'S FACILITIES:** menu, portions **NOTES:** Dogs allowed: in bar, Water **ROOMS:** 5 en suite s£25 d£50

PICKERING   FOX & HOUNDS COUNTRY INN ★★ ⊛ 🐑 ♀

Sinnington YO62 6SQ
☎ 01751 431577 📄 01751 432791
e-mail: foxhoundsinn@easynet.co.uk
Dir: *3m W of town, off A170.* *Map Ref:* *SE78*

Sinnington is one of Yorkshire's loveliest
villages, with a little river running through its
centre, banks of daffodils in the spring, and a
maypole on the village green. It makes an entirely
appropriate setting for this handsome 18th-century
coaching inn with its oak-beamed ceilings, old wood
panelling and open fires. Imaginative modern cooking
is served in the well-appointed non-smoking dining
room. Fish dishes are a strength of the specials board.

OPEN: 12-2.30 6-11 (Sun 12-2.30, 6-10.30)
BAR MEALS: L served all week 12-2 D served all week 6.30-9
(Sun 6.30-8.30) Av main course £8 **RESTAURANT:** L served
all week 12-2 D served all week 6.30-9 (Sun 6.30-8.30)
Av 3 course à la carte £22 **BREWERY/COMPANY:** Free
House 🍺: Camerons Bitter, Black Sheep Special, Worthingtons
Creamflow. ♀: 7 **CHILDREN'S FACILITIES:** menu, portions,
high-chairs, food/bottle warming, baby changing **GARDEN:**
Lawn with tree feature, herb garden **NOTES:** Dogs allowed:
in bar, in garden, in bedrooms, Outside kennel if req., Parking 30
ROOMS: 10 en suite 1 family room s£49 d£70

THE WHITE SWAN ★★ ⊛ 🐑 ♀

Market Place YO18 7AA
☎ 01751 472288 📄 01751 475554
e-mail: welcome@white-swan.co.uk
Dir: *In Market Place between church & steam
railway station.* *Map Ref:* *SE78*

Built in 1532, then extended to become a coaching inn
on the York to Whitby road. The owners and staff take
great pride in their service, with careful attention to
every detail - where else are you encouraged to ask for
something you fancy that may not be on the menu?
Ingredients are the best Yorkshire has to offer, and
seafood comes freshly landed from Whitby.

OPEN: 10-3 6-11 **BAR MEALS:** L served all week 12-2
D served all week 7-9 **RESTAURANT:** L served all week
12-2 D served all week 7.00-9 **BREWERY/COMPANY:** Free
House 🍺: Black Sheep Best & Special, Goldfield Hambleton
Ales, Yorkshire Moors Cropton Brewery. ♀: 10
CHILDREN'S FACILITIES: menu, portions, games, high-chairs,
food/bottle warming, family room **GARDEN:** Beautifully
planted terrace **NOTES:** Dogs allowed: in bar, in garden,
in bedrooms, Parking 35 **ROOMS:** 12 en suite
2 family rooms s£75 d£130

PICKHILL   NAGS HEAD COUNTRY INN ★★ ♀

YO7 4JG
☎ 01845 567391 📄 01845 567212
e-mail:
enquiries@nagsheadpickhill.freeserve.co.uk
Dir: *1m E of A1(4m N of A1/A61 junction). W
of Thirsk.* *Map Ref:* *SE38*

Former coaching inn with beamed ceilings, stone-
flagged floors and cosy winter fires. The original
building, dating back to the 17th century, has been
extended and modernised over the years but still
retains the feel and atmosphere of a traditional English
country local. Bar and restaurant meals are chosen
from a single menu that changes with the seasons to
make the most of available produce.

OPEN: 11-11 **BAR MEALS:** L served all week 12-2 D served
all week 6-9.30 Av main course £10 **RESTAURANT:** L served
all week 12-2 D served all week 7-9.30
BREWERY/COMPANY: Free House 🍺: Hambleton Bitter &
Goldfield, Black Sheep Best & Special, John Smiths Cask, Old
Peculiar. **CHILDREN'S FACILITIES:** portions, high-chairs,
food/bottle warming **GARDEN:** Secluded wall area with
seating area **NOTES:** Dogs allowed: in garden, in bedrooms,
Water and toys, Parking 40 **ROOMS:** 16 en suite
1 family room s£45 d£70

REETH CHARLES BATHURST INN ◆◆◆◆

Arkengarthdale DL11 6EN
☎ 01748 884567 & 884265 ▤ 01748 884599
e-mail: info@cbinn.co.uk
Map Ref: *SE09*

Located in remote and beautiful Arkengarthdale, the most northerly of the Yorkshire Dales, this 18th-century inn is ideal for walkers, located as it is close to the halfway point of the Coast-to-Coast Walk. Food is fresh, with the ingredients purchased locally, then prepared and cooked on the premises. The menu is written up daily on a striking mirror. Game comes from the surrounding moors, and fish from Hartlepool is delivered five times a week.

OPEN: 11-11 (Closed Mon-Thurs at lunch) Closed: End Nov-Feb **BAR MEALS:** L served all week 12-2 D served all week 6.30-9 **RESTAURANT:** L served all week 12-2 D served all week 6.30-9 **BREWERY/COMPANY:** Free House **◀:** Scottish Courage Theakstons, John Smiths Bitter & John Smiths Smooth, Black Sheep Best & Riggwelter. **CHILDREN'S FACILITIES:** menu, portions, games, high-chairs, food/bottle warming, outdoor play area, swings, climbing Frame & Seesaw **NOTES:** Dogs allowed: in bar, in bedrooms, Parking 50 **ROOMS:** 18 en suite s£60 d£75

ROSEDALE ABBEY THE MILBURN ARMS HOTEL ★★ ✿ 🐑

YO18 8RA
☎ 01751 417312 ▤ 01751 417541
e-mail: info@millburnarms.co.uk
Dir: *A170 W from Pickering 3m, R at sign to Rosedale then 7m N.* **Map Ref:** *SE79*

Dating back to 1776 and hidden deep in the folds of the spectacular North York Moors National Park, this charming country house hotel is a perfect retreat from the hustle and bustle of the modern world. Rosedale is great for walking, and close by are some of Yorkshire's best-loved attractions, including Castle Howard, Rievaulx Abbey and the region's famous steam railway.

OPEN: 11.30-3 6-11 Closed: 25 Dec **BAR MEALS:** L served all week 12-2.15 D served all week 6.30-9 Av main course £8 **RESTAURANT:** L served Sun 12-2.30 D served all week 7-9 Av 3 course à la carte £30 **BREWERY/COMPANY:** Free House **◀:** Black Sheep Best, Carlsberg-Tetley Tetely Bitter, John Smith's, Stella. **CHILDREN'S FACILITIES:** menu, portions, games, high-chairs, food/bottle warming, baby changing **GARDEN:** Large grassed lawn area to side and front **NOTES:** No dogs (ex guide dogs), Parking 60 **ROOMS:** 13 en suite 3 family rooms s£47.50 d£40

SETTLE GOLDEN LION HOTEL ◆◆◆◆ 🐑 ♀

Duke St BD24 9DU
☎ 01729 822203 ▤ 01729 824103
e-mail: info@goldenlion.yorks.net
Dir: *In the town centre opposite Barclays bank.*
Map Ref: *SD86*

This former coaching inn has been the silent witness to incalculable comings and goings in Settle's old market since around 1640. Its cosy, fire-warmed bar and comfy bedrooms often meet the needs of travellers on the spectacular Settle-Carlisle railway line. Fresh sandwiches, toasted baguettes and other breads, and stone-baked pizzas are available at lunchtime, while the carte usually features cornfed chicken wrapped in prosciutto ham; and fresh poached salmon with scallop and prawn sauce.

OPEN: 11-11 **BAR MEALS:** L served all week 12-2.30 D served all week 6-10 Av main course £7 **RESTAURANT:** L served all week 12-2.30 D served all week 6-10 Av 3 course à la carte £14 **BREWERY/COMPANY:** Thwaites **◀:** Thwaites Bitter, Bomber, Thoroughbred, Smooth & Guest beers. **♀:** 9 **CHILDREN'S FACILITIES:** menu, portions, licence, high-chairs, food/bottle warming **GARDEN:** Patio with picnic benches & umbrellas **NOTES:** in bar, Water, No dogs, Parking 14 **ROOMS:** 12 bedrooms 10 en suite 2 family rooms s£32 d£57

STARBOTTON   FOX & HOUNDS INN ♀

BD23 5HY
☎ 01756 760369 ▤ 01756 760867
Dir: *On B6160 N of Kettlewell.*
Map Ref: *SD97*

Situated in a picturesque limestone village in
Upper Wharfedale, this ancient pub was
originally built as a private house. Much of its
trade comes from the summer influx of
tourists and those tackling the long-distance
Dales Way nearby. Make for the cosy bar, with
its solid furnishings and flagstones, and enjoy
a pint of Black Sheep or one of the guest
ales. The menu has a traditional British focus:
expect steak and ale pie, lamb shank, pork
medallions in brandy and mustard sauce and
a selection of steaks. There is also a choice of
vegetarian dishes.

OPEN: 11.30-3 5.30-10.30 (Open all day Sat-Sun) (BHs
open lunch only) **BAR MEALS:** L served all week 12-2.30
D served all week 5.30-9 Sun 12-8.15 Av main
course £6.50 **BREWERY/COMPANY:** Free House ◖: Black
Sheep, Timothy Taylor Landlord, Tetleys, Boddingtons & Guest
Beers. ♀: 8 **CHILDREN'S FACILITIES:** menu, portions,
food/bottle warming **GARDEN:** Patio with 10 tables
NOTES: Dogs allowed: in bar, in garden, in bedrooms,
Parking 15

THIRSK   THE CARPENTERS ARMS 🐑 ♀

YO7 2DP
☎ 01845 537369 ▤ 01845 537889
e-mail: karen@karenlouise.fsnet.co.uk
Dir: *2m outside Thirsk on the A170.*
Map Ref: *SE48*

An 18th-century inn in the pretty hamlet of
Felixkirk, just outside Thirsk, where the writer
and vet, James Herriott, had his surgery. The
friendly and welcoming bistro is a sea of
coloured checked cloths, with carpenters'
tools dangling from the ceiling, old-fashioned
toy hot-air balloons, and an array of what are
best summed up as knick-knacks. The
restaurant is given a more formal feel by
white linen cloths and napkins, crystal glasses
and stylish, locally made furniture.

OPEN: 11.30-3 6.30-11 Closed: 25 Dec, 1 Jan(eve), 2-9
Jan **BAR MEALS:** L served all week 12-2 D served all week
7-9 **RESTAURANT:** L served Mon-Sun 12-2 D served
Mon-Sun 7-9 Av 3 course à la carte £25 Av 2 course fixed
price £15.95 **BREWERY/COMPANY:** Free House ◖: Black
Sheep Bitter, Timothy Taylor Landlord, Greene King Old
Speckled Hen. ♀: 10 **CHILDREN'S FACILITIES:** portions,
high-chairs, food/bottle warming, baby changing
NOTES: No dogs (ex guide dogs), Parking 50

THORGANBY   THE JEFFERSON ARMS

Main St YO19 6DA
☎ 01904 448316 ▤ 01904 449670
Dir: *Telephone for directions.* **Map Ref:** *SE64*

Dating from 1730, this beautiful public house
is set in a delightful rural setting just a few
miles from the centre of York. It is lavishly
decorated in Gothic style, reminiscent of an old manor
house, and overlooking a patio beer garden with
fishpond, fountain and waterfall. Lengthy menus list
house specialities such as loin of lamb on a bed of
bacon and spinach, rump steak on cracked pepper
mash with caramelised onions and Madeira sauce and
spaghetti with salmon and prawns.

OPEN: 12-2 6-11 **BAR MEALS:** L served Tue-Sun 12-2
D served all week 6-9 **RESTAURANT:** L served all week
12-2 D served all week 6-9 **BREWERY/COMPANY:** Free
House ◖: Scottish Courage John Smiths, Black Sheep Best,
Theakston Cool Cask, Black Bull.
CHILDREN'S FACILITIES: menu, high-chairs, baby changing
GARDEN: Side of pub with fish pond and fountain
NOTES: No dogs (ex guide dogs), Parking 55

THORNTON WATLASS THE BUCK INN ★

HG4 4AH
☎ 01677 422461 📠 01677 422447
e-mail: buckwatlass@btconnect.com
*Dir: From A1 at Leeming Bar take A684 to
Bedale, then B6268 towards Masham. Village
2m on R, hotel by cricket green.* **Map Ref:** *SE28*

After 16 years of running the Buck, Margaret

and Michael Fox still strive to maintain the warm
welcome and relaxed atmosphere that keeps people
coming back. The inn overlooks the village green and
cricket pitch (the pub is the boundary), facing the old
stone cottages of this peaceful village.

OPEN: 11-11 (Sun 12-10.30) Rest: Dec 25 closed eve
BAR MEALS: L served all week 12-2 D served all week 6-9.30
(Sun 12-9.30) Av main course £10 **RESTAURANT:** L served
all week 12-2 D served all week 6.30-9.30 Av 3 course à la
carte £18.50 Av 3 course fixed price £12.50
BREWERY/COMPANY: Free House 🍺: Theakston Best, Black
Sheep Best, John Smith's & Guest beers. ♀: 6
CHILDREN'S FACILITIES: menu, portions, games, high-chairs,
food/bottle warming, baby changing, outdoor play area,
Outdoor swings, slide, climbing frame **GARDEN:** Food served
outside **NOTES:** Dogs allowed: Water, Parking 40
ROOMS: 7 bedrooms 5 en suite s£50 d£60

WASS WOMBWELL ARMS

YO61 4BE
☎ 01347 868280
e-mail: thewombwellarms@aol.com
*Dir: From A1 take A168 to A19 junct. Take York
exit, then L after 2.5m, L at Coxwold to
Ampleforth. Wass 2m.* **Map Ref:** *SE57*

The building was constructed around 1620 as
a granary, probably using stone from nearby
Byland Abbey, and it became an ale house in
about 1645. A series of stylishly decorated
rooms provide the setting for bistro-style
cooking. Local suppliers have been
established for all the produce used: at least
three vegetarian dishes are offered daily
along with a good choice of fresh fish,
including Whitby cod. Popular options are
steak, Guinness and mushroom pie, country

rabbit, and game casserole. Great location for those
walking the North Yorks National Park.

OPEN: 12-2.30 7-11 (closed Sun eve in winter & all Mon)
BAR MEALS: L served all week 12-2 D served all week
7-9.30 Av main course £9.95 **RESTAURANT:** L served all
week 12-2 D served all week 7-9 Av 3 course à la carte
£18.95 **BREWERY/COMPANY:** Free House 🍺: Black
Sheep Best, Timothy Taylor Landlord, Cropton Two Pints. ♀: 9
CHILDREN'S FACILITIES: menu, portions, high-chairs,
food/bottle warming **GARDEN:** Gravel beer garden, seats
approx 25 **NOTES:** No dogs (ex guide dogs), Parking 15

WEAVERTHORPE THE STAR COUNTRY INN

YO17 8EY
☎ 01944 738273 📠 01944 738273
e-mail: starweaverthorpe@aol.com
*Dir: 12m E of Malton to Sherborn Village,
traffic lights on A64, turn R at the lights.
Weaverthorpe 4m. Star Inn on the Junct facing.*
Map Ref: *SE97*

Situated in the heart of the Yorkshire Wolds, this
brightly-shining Star has expanded over the years to
incorporate adjoining cottages housing an extended
dining area and comfortable accommodation for
overnight guests. The rustic facilities of bar and dining
room, with large winter fires and a welcoming,
convivial atmosphere, complement food cooked to
traditional family recipes using fresh local produce.

OPEN: 12-3 7-11 **BAR MEALS:** L served Wed-Mon 12-2
D served Wed-Mon 7-9.30 (Sun 12-3) Av main course £7.50
RESTAURANT: L served Wed-Mon 12-2 D served Wed-Mon
7-9.30 (Sun 12-3) Av 3 course à la carte £15
BREWERY/COMPANY: Free House 🍺: Carlsberg-Tetley Tetley
Bitter, Scottish Courage John Smith's, Wold Top.
CHILDREN'S FACILITIES: menu, portions, high-chairs,
food/bottle warming **NOTES:** Dogs allowed: in bar, Parking 30
ROOMS: 3 en suite 1 family room s£30 d£50 (♦♦♦)

Yorkshire, North continued

WEST BURTON   FOX & HOUNDS

DL8 4JY
☎ 01969 663111 ▤ 01969 663279
Dir: *A468 between Hawes and Leyburn, 1/2 mile east of Aysgarth.* **Map Ref:** *SE08*

Overlooking the village green in the unspoilt village of West Burton, this inn offers log fires and home cooking. Hand-pulled ales on offer at the bar include Black Sheep and Old Peculiar. The new owners continue to provide traditional pub food to accompany your pint: dishes such as steak and kidney pie, curry and lasagne will fortify you for country walks or visits to nearby waterfalls, castles or cheese-tasting at the Wensleydale Creamery.

OPEN: 11-11 (winter closed 2-6) **BAR MEALS:** L served all week 12-2 D served all week 6-9 Av main course £6.50
RESTAURANT: L served all week 12-2 D served all week 6.30-9 Av 3 course à la carte £15
BREWERY/COMPANY: Free House ◀: Black Sheep, Old Peculier, John Smiths, Tetleys.
CHILDREN'S FACILITIES: menu, portions, games, high-chairs, food/bottle warming, baby changing, family room
NOTES: Dogs allowed: Parking 6

WIGGLESWORTH   THE PLOUGH INN

BD23 4RJ
☎ 01729 840243 ▤ 01729 840638
e-mail: sue@ploughinn.info
Dir: *From A65 between Skipton & Long Preston take B6478 to Wigglesworth.* **Map Ref:** *SD85*

This traditional 18th-century country inn is ideally placed for exploring the Yorkshire Dales and the Forest of Bowland. The bar has oak beams and an open fire, and the conservatory restaurant has fine views across the hills.

OPEN: 11-3 6-11 **BAR MEALS:** L served all week 12-2 D served all week 7-9 (From 6 at busy times) Av main course £8.50 **RESTAURANT:** L served all week 12-2 D served all week 7-9 Av 3 course à la carte £19.50 Av 2 course fixed price £6.50 **BREWERY/COMPANY:** Free House ◀: Carlsberg-Tetley Tetley Bitter, Black Sheep Best.
CHILDREN'S FACILITIES: menu, portions, games, high-chairs, food/bottle warming, family room **GARDEN:** Large area with views over Yorkshire Dales **NOTES:** No dogs (ex guide dogs), Parking 70 **ROOMS:** 12 en suite 3 family rooms s£47 d£70 (★★)

DONCASTER   WATERFRONT INN

Canal Ln, West Stockwith DN10 4ET
☎ 01427 891223
Map Ref: *SE50*

Built in the 1830s overlooking the Trent Canal basin and the canal towpath, the pub is now popular with walkers. Nearby is a marina. Real ales and good value food that includes pasta with home-made ratatouille, broccoli and cheese bake, deep fried scampi, half honey-roasted chicken, and home-made lasagne. On Sundays there's a carvery as well. Serves over 40 real ales and ciders at its annual May Bank Holiday beer festival. There's also a children's menu.

OPEN: 11.30-11 **BAR MEALS:** L served all week 12-2.30 D served all week 5.30-8.30 **RESTAURANT:** L served all week 12-2.30 D served all week 5.30-8.30
BREWERY/COMPANY: Enterprise Inns ◀: Scottish Courage John Smith Cask, Black Sheep, Timothy Taylors, Charles Wells Bombardier Premium Bitter.
CHILDREN'S FACILITIES: menu, outdoor play area, Wooden play area **NOTES:** Dogs allowed: Water provided, Parking 30

PENISTONE THE FOUNTAIN INN ♀

Wellthorne Ln, Ingbirchworth S36 7GJ
☎ 01226 763125 🖹 01226 761336
e-mail: reservations@fountain-inn.co.uk
Dir: *Exit M1 Junction 37. Take A628 to Manchester then take A629 to Huddersfield.*
Map Ref: *SE20*

Busy but friendly and informal country inn with stylish, cosy interior. Famous for the local choir which gathers here every Christmas and brings a countrywide following, it is also next door to 'Last of the Summer Wine' country. Favourite bar meals include ale-braised steak, shoulder of lamb, Fountain grill, and bean fajitas, with a good fish choice ranging around buttered haddock, crab linguini, and salmon and prawn fishcakes.

OPEN: 11.45-2.30 5-11 Closed: 25 Dec
BAR MEALS: L served all week 12-2 D served all week 5-9.30 Av main course £9.50 🍺: Tetleys Cask, Theakstons Best, Black Sheep, John Smith Smooth. ♀: 9
CHILDREN'S FACILITIES: menu, family room
GARDEN: Enclosed patio, only drinks served
NOTES: in garden, No dogs (ex guide dogs), Parking 45

SHEFFIELD THE FAT CAT

23 Alma St S3 8SA
☎ 0114 249 4801 🖹 0114 249 4803
e-mail: enquiries@thefatcat.co.uk
Dir: *Telephone for directions.* **Map Ref:** *SK38*

150-year-old listed building, bought by its current owner 23 years ago and acknowledged as Sheffield's first real ale free house. Cosy fires have been reintroduced and a beer garden opened. The award-winning Fat Cat has its own brewery, and at least four of its draught beers are featured in the pub, which is said to be haunted. The keenly priced food always includes a variety of vegetarian and gluten-free fare as well as daily specials. The menu changes weekly. Consistently one of the top-rated urban pubs in Britain - and deservedly so.

OPEN: 12-3 5.30-11 (Sun 7-10.30, Fri & Sat 12-11) Closed: Dec 25-26 **BAR MEALS:** L served all week 12-2.30 D served Mon-Fri 6-7.30 Av main course £3
BREWERY/COMPANY: Free House 🍺: Timothy Taylor Landlord, Kelham Island Bitter, Pale Rider, Pride of Sheffield.
CHILDREN'S FACILITIES: family room **GARDEN:** Hard surface walled area, flower beds, heaters **NOTES:** Dogs allowed: in bar, in garden, No credit cards

---

HALIFAX THE ROCK INN HOTEL ★★★

Holywell Green HX4 9BS
☎ 01422 379721 🖹 01422 379110
e-mail: reservations@rockinnhotel.com
Dir: *From M62 J24 follow signs for Blackley, L at x-rds, approx 0.5m on L.* **Map Ref:** *SE01*

Substantial modern extensions have transformed this attractive 17th-century wayside inn into a thriving hotel and conference venue in the scenic valley of Holywell Green. All day dining in the brasserie-style conservatory is truly cosmopolitan.

OPEN: 11-11 **BAR MEALS:** L served all week 12-2.30 D served all week 5-6 **RESTAURANT:** L served all week, D served all week 🍺: Black Sheep, Taylor Landlord, John Smiths. **CHILDREN'S FACILITIES:** menu, portions, games, high-chairs, food/bottle warming, changing facilities
GARDEN: Terrace, surrounded by fields **NOTES:** Dogs allowed, water, Parking 120 **ROOMS:** 30 en suite

SHIBDEN MILL INN ◆◆◆◆

Shibden Mill Fold HX3 7UL
☎ 01422 365840 🖷 01422 362971
e-mail: shibdenmillinn@zoom.co.uk
Map Ref: SE02

This whitewashed free house is tucked into a leafy hollow of the Shibden Valley, with a stream rushing noisily nearby. The 17th-century inn has been sympathetically renovated to retain its original charm. Open fires and soft cushions make the low-beamed bar a cosy place to relax, and there's a wide choice of traditional ales to accompany bar meals like shepherd's pie tart or grilled smoked salmon with bubble and squeak. Meanwhile, crisp napery and candlelit tables give the restaurant a certain rustic elegance. It's the ideal setting in which to sample the contemporary English menu and extensive wine list. Expect braised beef with glazed parsnips and shallot sauce; grilled sea bass with crab tart and artichokes; and herb and potato dumplings with curried spinach and peas. And, if you can't face the drive home, you could always stop over in one of the twelve individually decorated en suite bedrooms!

OPEN: 12-2.30 5.30-11 **BAR MEALS:** L served all week 12-2 D served all week 6-9.30 Av main course £11.50 **RESTAURANT:** L served all week 12-2 D served all week 6-9.30 **BREWERY/COMPANY:** Free House 🍺: John Smiths, Theakston XB, Shibden Mill, Stella Artois. 🍷: 12 **CHILDREN'S FACILITIES:** menu, portions, games, high-chairs, food/bottle warming, high chairs, colouring materials, board games **GARDEN:** Walled garden with heated patio **NOTES:** in garden only, No dogs, Parking 200 **ROOMS:** 12 en suite s£65 d£80

HAWORTH   THE OLD WHITE LION HOTEL ★★ 🐑 🍷

Main St BD22 8DU
☎ 01535 642313 🖷 01535 646222
e-mail: enquiries@oldwhitelionhotel.com
Dir: Turn off A629 onto B6142, hotel 0.5m past Haworth Station. **Map Ref:** SE03

300-year-old former coaching inn located at the top of a cobbled street, close to the Brontë Museum and Parsonage. Traditionally furnished bars offer a welcome respite from the tourist trail. Theakston ales, and a wide range of generously served snacks and meals are on offer. Jacket potatoes, giant Yorkshire puddings and specials also available. Comfortable bedrooms.

OPEN: 11-11 **BAR MEALS:** L served all week 11.30-2.30 D served all week 5.30-9.30 (Sat & Sun 12-9.30) Av main course £6.25 **RESTAURANT:** L served Sun 12-2.30 D served all week 7-9.30 Av 3 course à la carte £19 Av 3 course fixed price £14 **BREWERY/COMPANY:** Free House 🍺: Theakstons Best & Green Lable, Carlsberg-Tetley Tetley Bitter, Scottish Courage John Smith's, Websters. **CHILDREN'S FACILITIES:** menu, high-chairs, food/bottle warming **NOTES:** No dogs (ex guide dogs), Parking 9 **ROOMS:** 14 en suite 2 family rooms

LEDSHAM   THE CHEQUERS INN

Claypit Ln LS25 5LP
☎ 01977 683135 🖷 01977 680791
Dir: Between A1 & A656 above Castleford.
Map Ref: SE42

Quaint creeper-covered inn located in an old estate village in the countryside to the east of Leeds. Unusually, the pub is closed on Sunday because the one-time lady of the manor was offended by drunken farm workers on her way to church more than 160 years ago. Inside are low beams and wooden settles, giving the pub the feel of a traditional village establishment.

OPEN: 11-3 5-11 (Sat 11-11) **BAR MEALS:** L served Mon-Sat 12-2.15 D served Mon-Sat 5.30-9.45 Av main course £9.45 **BREWERY/COMPANY:** Free House 🍺: Theakston Best, John Smiths, Brown Cow, Timothy Taylor Landlord. **CHILDREN'S FACILITIES:** family room **GARDEN:** outdoor eating, patio **NOTES:** Dogs allowed: Parking 35

MYTHOLMROYD SHOULDER OF MUTTON ♀

New Rd HX7 5DZ
☎ 01422 883165
Dir: *A646 Halifax to Todmorden, in Mytholmroyd on B6138, opp train station.*
Map Ref: *SE02*

Character Pennines pub next to a trout stream and ideally placed for the popular 50-mile Calderdale Way. The pub's reputation for real ales and hearty food using locally sourced ingredients remains intact after 30 years of ownership. The menu ranges from beef cooked in Guinness to vegetarian dishes.

OPEN: 11.30-3 7-11 (Sat 11.30-11, Sun 12-10.30)
BAR MEALS: L served all week 11.3-2 D served Wed-Mon 7-8.15 Av main course £3.99 **RESTAURANT:** L served all week 11.30-2 D served Wed-Mon 7-8.15 ◖: Black Sheep, Boddingtons, Flowers, Taylor Landlord. ♀: 10
CHILDREN'S FACILITIES: menu, portions, high-chairs, food/bottle warming, outdoor play area, family room
GARDEN: Riverside garden with floral display, seating
NOTES: Dogs allowed: in bar, in garden, Water, Treats, Parking 25, No credit cards

NEWALL THE SPITE

LS21 2EY
☎ 01943 463063
Map Ref: *SE14*

'There's nowt but malice and spite at these pubs', said a local who one day did the unthinkable - drank in both village hostelries, renowned for their feuding landlords. The Traveller's Rest, which became The Malice, is long closed, but the Roebuck has survived as The Spite. Salmon mornay, haddock, scampi, steak and ale pie, ostrich fillet and speciality sausages are likely to be on offer.

OPEN: 12-3 6-11 (Sat 12-11, Sun 12-10.30)
BAR MEALS: L served all week 12-5 D served (Tue-Thu 6-8.30, Fri-Sat 6-9) Av main course £6.50
RESTAURANT: L served all week 11.30-2 D served (Tue-Thu 6-8.30, Sat 6-9) 6-9 **BREWERY/COMPANY:** Unique Pub Co ◖: John Smiths, Tetleys, Bombardier, Worthington Creamflow.
CHILDREN'S FACILITIES: menu **GARDEN:** Food served outside. Lawned area **NOTES:** Dogs allowed: Water provided, Parking 50

SHELF DUKE OF YORK ♀

West St, Stone Chair HX3 7LN
☎ 01422 202056 ▤ 01422 206618
e-mail: katrina@dukeofyork.co.uk
Dir: *M62 J25 to Brighouse. Take A644 N. Inn 500 yds on R after Stone Chair roundabout.*
Map Ref: *SE12*

A vast array of brassware and bric-a-brac adorns this 17th-century former coaching inn located between Bradford and Halifax, and the atmosphere is lively and friendly. Expect classic dishes such as beef bourguignon, grilled fillet steak with peppercorn sauce, and braised lamb Henry with orange mashed potatoes and rosemary broth. The pub carries a wide range of cask ales.

OPEN: 11.30-11.30 (Sun 12-10.30) **BAR MEALS:** L served all week 12-2.30 D served all week 5-9.30
RESTAURANT: L served all week 12-2.30 D served all week 5-9.30 Av 3 course fixed price £11.95
BREWERY/COMPANY: Whitbread ◖: Landlord, Landlady, J W Lees, Tetleys & Guest beer. ♀: 15
CHILDREN'S FACILITIES: high-chairs **GARDEN:** Patio at front with chairs **NOTES:** in bar, Parking 30

SHELLEY   THE THREE ACRES INN 🐑 ♇

HD8 8LR
☎ 01484 602606 ▤ 01484 608411
e-mail: 3acres@globalnet.co.uk
Dir: *From Huddersfield take A629 then B6116, take L turn for village.* **Map Ref:** *SE21*

With its commanding views over the Pennines,

reputation for quality food and welcoming atmosphere, this charming inn is a longstanding favourite. Dine in the bar, or in the restaurant - a charming and elaborately decorated room featuring bare beams, ornamental plates and a corner filled with antique books. An exhaustive selection of dishes ranging from traditional to oriental, all freshly prepared to order, can be sampled from the menus.

OPEN: 12-3 7-11 (Sat 7-11 only) Closed: 25 Dec
BAR MEALS: L served all week 12-2 D served all week 7-9.45 Av main course £12.95 **RESTAURANT:** L served Sun-Fri 12-2 D served all week 7-9.45 Av 3 course à la carte £25 **BREWERY/COMPANY:** Free House ◖: Timothy Taylor Landlord, Adnams Bitter, Black Sheep, Tetley Smooth. ♇: 9
CHILDREN'S FACILITIES: portions, high-chairs, food/bottle warming **GARDEN:** Covered terrace **NOTES:** No dogs (ex guide dogs), Parking 100

THORNTON   RING O'BELLS ♇

212 Hilltop Rd BD13 3QL
☎ 01274 832296 ▤ 01274 831707
e-mail: enquiries@theringobells.com
Dir: *From M62 take A58 for 5m, R at crossroads onto A644, after 4.5m follow signs for Denholme, on to Well Head Rd into Hilltop Rd.* **Map Ref:** *SE03*

Pennine pub set high above the village of Thornton, where the Brontë sisters were born while their father was curate here. Stunning views over dramatic moorland up to 30 miles on a clear day. The building is a conversion of a Wesleyan chapel and two former mill workers' cottages, and the ghost of a former priest is rumoured to still be in residence.

OPEN: 11.30-3.30 5.30-11 (Sun 12-4.30, 6.30-10.30) Closed: Dec 25 **BAR MEALS:** L served all week 12-2 D served all week 5.30-9.30 Av main course £8.95
RESTAURANT: L served all week 12-2 D served all week 7-9.30 (Sun 6.15-8.45) Av 2 course fixed price £9.95
BREWERY/COMPANY: Free House ◖: Scottish Courage John Smiths & Courage Directors, Black Sheep & Black Sheep Special. ♇: 10 **CHILDREN'S FACILITIES:** menu, portions, high-chairs, food/bottle warming, baby changing
NOTES: No dogs (ex guide dogs), Parking 25

WIDDOP   PACK HORSE INN

HX7 7AT
☎ 01422 842803 ▤ 01422 842803
Dir: *Off A646 & A6033.* **Map Ref:** *SD93*

A converted laithe farmhouse dating from the 1600s, 300 yards from the Pennine Way and popular with walkers. 130 single malts available.

OPEN: 12-3 7-11 Rest: Oct-Easter Closed lunchtimes during the week **BAR MEALS:** L served all week 12-2 D served Tue-Sun 7-10 Av main course £6.95
RESTAURANT: D served Sat 7-9.30
BREWERY/COMPANY: Free House ◖: Thwaites, Theakston XB, Morland Old Speckled Hen, Blacksheep Bitter.
CHILDREN'S FACILITIES: menu **NOTES:** Dogs allowed: Parking 40

Ashness Bridge, Cumbria, in Autumn

South & East England

The southeast region is dominated by the capital but also stretches up to the wild corners of the Fenlands and down across the water to the Channel Islands. Large cities, other than London, are the seaports of Portsmouth and Southampton, otherwise the county towns tend to be small and historic, but no less influential, with centres of academic excellence at Cambridge and Oxford, and major league cathedrals like Canterbury and Winchester. Other key ports are Felixstowe, Harwich and Dover, and the coast is dotted with popular seaside resorts: Yarmouth, Lowestoft, Southend, Margate, Brighton and Bournemouth. Diverse natural features include The Fens, Constable Country, the New Forest, The Needles and the South Downs.

The majority of the country's top tourist attractions are located in the region, including Madame Tussaud's; the Tower of London; the Natural History Museum; Legoland, Windsor; Chessington World of Adventure; the Science Museum; Canterbury Cathedral; Windsor Castle; Westminster Abbey; St Paul's Cathedral; London Zoo; the Victoria & Albert Museum; Thorpe Park; the British Museum, and the Tate Galleries.

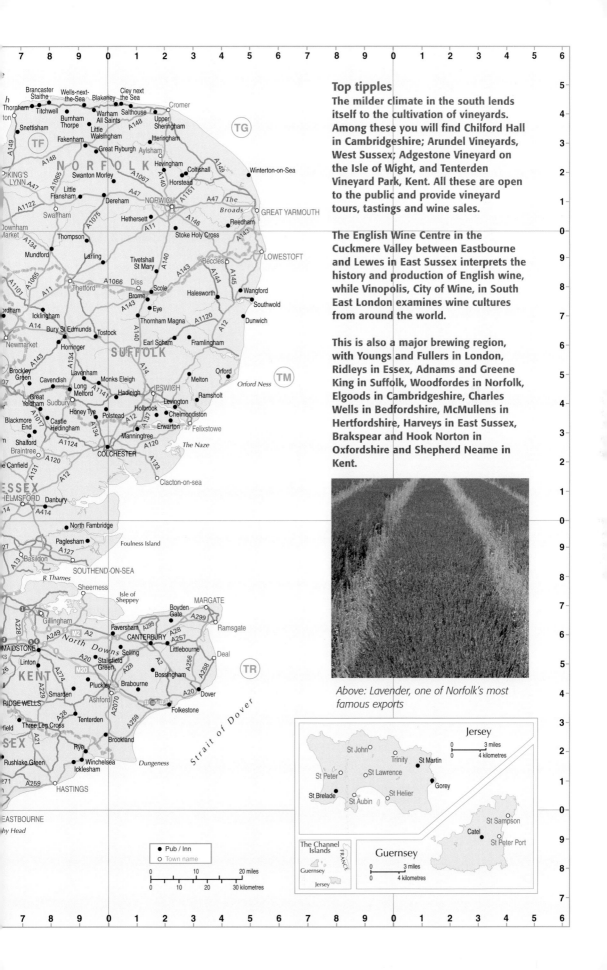

Top tipples

The milder climate in the south lends itself to the cultivation of vineyards. Among these you will find Chilford Hall in Cambridgeshire; Arundel Vineyards, West Sussex; Adgestone Vineyard on the Isle of Wight, and Tenterden Vineyard Park, Kent. All these are open to the public and provide vineyard tours, tastings and wine sales.

The English Wine Centre in the Cuckmere Valley between Eastbourne and Lewes in East Sussex interprets the history and production of English wine, while Vinopolis, City of Wine, in South East London examines wine cultures from around the world.

This is also a major brewing region, with Youngs and Fullers in London, Ridleys in Essex, Adnams and Greene King in Suffolk, Woodfordes in Norfolk, Elgoods in Cambridgeshire, Charles Wells in Bedfordshire, McMullens in Hertfordshire, Harveys in East Sussex, Brakspear and Hook Norton in Oxfordshire and Shepherd Neame in Kent.

Above: Lavender, one of Norfolk's most famous exports

Map labels

NORFOLK
SUFFOLK
ESSEX
KENT
SEX

NORWICH
IPSWICH
COLCHESTER
CHELMSFORD
SOUTHEND-ON-SEA
LOWESTOFT
GREAT YARMOUTH
MAIDSTONE
CANTERBURY
MARGATE
HASTINGS
EASTBOURNE
KING'S LYNN

Brancaster Staithe, Thornham, Titchwell, Wells-next-the-Sea, Blakeney, Cley next the Sea, Cromer, Snettisham, Burnham Thorpe, Warham All Saints, Little Walsingham, Salthouse, Upper Sheringham, Fakenham, Great Ryburgh, Itteringham, Aylsham, Hevingham, Coltishall, Winterton-on-Sea, Swanton Morley, Horstead, Little Fransham, Dereham, The Broads, Hethersett, Reedham, Swaffham, Thompson, Stoke Holy Cross, Mundford, Larling, Tivetshall St Mary, Beccles, Wangford, Thetford, Diss, Scole, Halesworth, Southwold, Brome, Eye, Icklingham, Thornham Magna, Dunwich, Bury St Edmunds, Tostock, Earl Soham, Framlingham, Newmarket, Horringer, Orford, Brockley Green, Cavendish, Lavenham, Monks Eleigh, Melton, Orford Ness, Long Melford, Hadleigh, Levington, Ramsholt, Great Yeldham, Sudbury, Honey Tye, Holbrook, Chelmondiston, Blackmore End, Castle Hedingham, Polstead, Erwarton, Felixstowe, Shalford, Manningtree, The Naze, Braintree, Canfield, Danbury, North Fambridge, Paglesham, Foulness Island, Basildon, Sheerness, Isle of Sheppey, Boyden Gate, Ramsgate, Gillingham, Faversham, Selling, Littlebourne, Deal, Linton, Stalisfield Green, Bossingham, Pluckley, Brabourne, Dover, Smarden, Ashford, Folkestone, Three Leg Cross, Tenterden, Brookland, Rye, Winchelsea, Icklesham, Rushlake Green, Dungeness, Thorpe, Downham Market

Legend

● Pub / Inn
○ Town name

0 10 20 miles
0 10 20 30 kilometres

Channel Islands insets

Jersey

St John, Trinity, St Martin, St Peter, St Lawrence, St Brelade, St Aubin, St Helier, Gorey

0 3 miles
0 4 kilometres

The Channel Islands — FRANCE, Guernsey, Jersey

Guernsey

St Sampson, Catel, St Peter Port

0 3 miles
0 4 kilometres

BROOM THE COCK

23 High St SG18 9NA
☎ 01767 314411 ▯ 01767 314284
Dir: *Off B658 SW of Biggleswade.*
Map Ref: *TL14*

Unspoilt to this day with its intimate, quarry-tiled rooms with latched doors and panelled walls, this 17th-century establishment is known as 'The Pub with no Bar'. Real ales are served straight from casks racked by the cellar steps. A straightforward pub grub menu includes home-made cottage pie, casseroles and chilli. There is a camping and caravan site at the rear of the pub.

OPEN: 12-3 6-11 (Sat 12-4, Sun 12-4)
BAR MEALS: L served all week 12-2.30 D served Mon-Sat 7-9 **RESTAURANT:** L served all week 12-2.30 D served Mon-Sat 7-9.30 **BREWERY/COMPANY:** Greene King
◀: Greene King Abbot Ale, IPA & Ruddles County.
CHILDREN'S FACILITIES: menu, portions, high-chairs, food/bottle warming, outdoor play area, family room
GARDEN: 12 tables on patio, lawn area **NOTES:** Dogs allowed: in bar, Parking 30

KEYSOE THE CHEQUERS

Pertenhall Rd, Brook End MK44 2HR
☎ 01234 708678 ▯ 01234 708678
e-mail: Chequers.keysoe@tesco.net
Dir: *On B660 N of Bedford.* *Map Ref:* *TL06*

In a quiet village, a 15th-century inn characterised by original beams and an open stone fireplace. Take a ridge-top walk for fine views of Graffham Water in anticipation of a warm welcome, good real ale and some fine pub food. Food served in the bar includes chicken curry, fried scampi, steak in a grain mustard cream sauce, chicken breast stuffed with Stilton in a chive sauce, or salads, sandwiches and ploughman's. Good wine list. A play area in the garden, overlooked by a rear terrace, is an added summer attraction.

OPEN: 11.30-2.30 6.30-11 **BAR MEALS:** L served Wed-Mon 12-2 D served Wed-Mon 7-9.45
BREWERY/COMPANY: Free House ◀: Hook Norton Best, Fuller's London Pride. **CHILDREN'S FACILITIES:** menu, portions, high-chairs, food/bottle warming, outdoor play area, play tree in garden, family room **GARDEN:** Patio & grassed area fenced off from car park **NOTES:** No dogs (ex guide dogs), Parking 50

LINSLADE THE GLOBE INN

Globe Ln, Old Linslade LU7 2TA
☎ 01525 373338 ▯ 01525 850551
Dir: *A5 S to Dunstable, follow signs to Leighton Buzzard (A4146).* *Map Ref:* *SP92*

Licensed in 1830 as an official beer shop, this charming, family-friendly whitewashed pub

stands by the Grand Union Canal, close to the River Ouzel. It was originally frequented by navvies digging the canal, and is rumoured to be the pub where the nearby Great Train Robbery was planned in 1963. Seafood dishes are a speciality, as are pies and puddings. Weddings and other functions catered for.

OPEN: 11-3 (Jan-Feb 12-3, 6-11, Summer 11-11) 6-11 (Sun 12-10.30) **BAR MEALS:** L served all week 12-9 D served all week 12-9 Av main course £7.50
RESTAURANT: L served all week 12-3 D served all week 6-9 (Sun 12-9) Av 3 course à la carte £20
BREWERY/COMPANY: Greene King ◀: Greene King Abbott Ale, Old Speckled Hen, IPA & Ruddles County Ale, Hook Norton. ♀: 16 **CHILDREN'S FACILITIES:** menu, portions, games, high-chairs, swings, slides, Wendy house, fenced-off area **GARDEN:** Large, seats approx 200 **NOTES:** Dogs allowed: in bar, in garden, Water, Parking 150

RADWELL THE SWAN INN ♀

Felmersham Rd MK43 7HS
☎ 01234 781351
e-mail: stewartmcgre@aol.com
Dir: Off A6 N of Bedford. *Map Ref:* TL05

Dating back over 300 years, this stone and thatch built inn is located in a country setting by the River Ouse, which offers some of the best fishing in the south of England. It's a good location for walkers, and there's a large garden at the rear ideal for families. Traditional favourites include fisherman's breakfast and home-cooked steak and kidney pie, while among the specialities of the house are herb-crusted lamb cutlets and vegetable Wellington.

OPEN: 11-11 (Sun 12-5) **BAR MEALS:** L served all week 12-2.30 D served all week 6.30-9 Sun 12-4.30 Av main course £7 **RESTAURANT:** L served all week 12-2.30 D served all week 6.30-9 Sun 12-4.30 Av 3 course à la carte £16 **BREWERY/COMPANY:** Charles Wells ◀: Wells Eagle & Bombardier. ♀: 7 **CHILDREN'S FACILITIES:** portions, games, high-chairs, food/bottle warming, outdoor play area **NOTES:** Dogs allowed: in bar, Parking 25

SOUTHILL THE WHITE HORSE NEW 🐾 ♀

High St SG18 9LD
☎ 01462 813364
e-mail: jack@ravenathexton.f9.co.uk
Map Ref: TL14

A village pub retaining traditional values, yet happily accommodating the needs of non-smokers, children and those who like sitting outside on cool days (the patio has heaters). Locally renowned for its chargrilled steaks from the Duke of Buccleuch's Scottish estate. Other main courses include Cajun chicken, chargrilled pork loin steaks, Whitby Bay scampi, and stuffed breaded plaice. Old Warden Park and its Shuttleworth Collection of old planes is nearby.

OPEN: 11-3 6-11 (Sun 12-10.30, all day BH's) **BAR MEALS:** L served all week 12-2 D served all week 6.10-10 (Sun 12-9) Av main course £7.50 ◀: Greene King IPA, London Pride, Speckled Hen, Flowers. ♀: 22 **CHILDREN'S FACILITIES:** menu, games, high-chairs, food/bottle warming, baby changing, outdoor play area, climbing frame with swings and slides **GARDEN:** Large grassed area with trees & seating **NOTES:** Dogs allowed: in garden, water, Parking 40

STANBRIDGE THE FIVE BELLS ♀

Station Rd, Stanbridge LU7 9JF
☎ 01525 210224 📠 01525 211164
e-mail: fivebells@traditionalfreehouses.com
Dir: Off A505 E of Leighton Buzzard.
Map Ref: SP92

A stylish and relaxing setting for a drink or a meal is offered by this white-painted 400-year-old village inn, which has been delightfully renovated and revived. The bar features lots of bare wood as well as comfortable armchairs and polished, rug-strewn floors. The modern decor extends to the bright, airy 75-cover dining room. There's also a spacious garden with patio and lawns. Hosts Emma Moffitt and Andrew Mackenzie offer bar meals, set menus and a carte choice for diners. The bar menu typically includes dishes such as smoked chicken, sun-dried tomato and pine nut salad; battered fish, chips and mushy peas; baked courgettes stuffed with goat's cheese and mint with a mixed salad; rib eye steak with fries; and chicken, ham, leek and mushroom pie. From the pudding menu, look out for chocolate and orange torte and raspberry crème brûlée - and be tempted!

OPEN: 12-3 5-11 **BAR MEALS:** L served all week 12-2.30 D served all week 7-9 **RESTAURANT:** L served all week 12-2.30 D served all week 7-9 Av 3 course fixed price £15 **BREWERY/COMPANY:** ◀: Interbrew Bass, Wadworth 6X, Hook Norton Best Bitter, Well's Bombardier. ♀: 8 **CHILDREN'S FACILITIES:** menu, games, high-chairs, outdoor play area, slide, climbing wall, swing etc **GARDEN:** Large, traditional garden. Patio area **NOTES:** No dogs, Parking 100

Bedfordshire continued

TILSWORTH   THE ANCHOR INN

1 Dunstable Rd LU7 9PU
☎ 01525 210289 🖷 01525 211578
e-mail: tonyanchorinn@aol.com
Map Ref: *SP92*

The only pub in a Saxon street village, the Anchor dates from 1878. The restaurant is a recent addition to the side of the pub, and the whole building has recently been refurbished. The licensees pride themselves on their fresh food and well-kept ales. Hand-cut steaks are particularly popular (they buy the meat at Smithfield, butcher it and hang it themselves). An acre of garden includes patio seating, an adventure playground and a barbecue.

OPEN: 12-11 **BAR MEALS:** L served all week 12-2.30 6-10 (Sun 12-4) Av main course £9 **RESTAURANT:** L served all week 12-2.30 6-10 (Sun 12-4) Av 3 course à la carte £25 **BREWERY/COMPANY:** Greene King ◖: Green King IPA, Abbot Ale, Wadworth 6X. ♀: 8 **CHILDREN'S FACILITIES:** menu, portions, games, high-chairs, food/bottle warming, outdoor play area, Adventure playground, family room **GARDEN:** 1acre+ of garden, seats, bbq, patio **NOTES:** No dogs (ex guide dogs), Parking 30

ALDWORTH   THE BELL INN

RG8 9SE
☎ 01635 578272
Dir: *Just off B4009 (Newbury-Streatley rd).*
Map Ref: *SU57*

One might be surprised to discover that an establishment not offering even egg and chips can hold its own in a world of smart dining pubs and modish gastropubs. Well, be surprised. The Bell not only survives, it positively prospers and, to be fair, it does serve some food, if only hot, crusty, generously filled rolls. And since it is one of the few truly unspoiled country pubs left, and serves cracking pints of Arkell's, West Berkshire and guest real ales, this alimentary limitation has been no disadvantage. The Bell is old, very old, beginning life in 1340 as a five-bay cruck-built manor hall. It has reputedly been in the same family for 200 years: ask Mr Macaulay, the landlord - he's been here for thirty of them, and he has no plans to change it from the time warp it is. A 300-year-old, one-handed clock still stands in the taproom, and the rack for the spit-irons and clockwork roasting jack are still over the fireplace. Taller customers may bump their heads at the glass-panelled bar hatch.

OPEN: 11-3 6-11 Closed: Dec 25 **BAR MEALS:** L served Tue-Sun 11-2.50 D served Tue-Sun 6-10.50 **BREWERY/COMPANY:** Free House ◖: Arkell's Kingsdown, 3B, West Berkshire Old Tyler & Maggs Magnificent Mild, Guest Beer. **CHILDREN'S FACILITIES:** food/bottle warming **GARDEN:** Peaceful, old fashioned **NOTES:** Dogs allowed: in bar, On leads, Parking 12, No credit cards

ASHMORE GREEN   THE SUN IN THE WOOD ♀

Stoney Ln RG18 9HF
☎ 01635 42377 🖷 01635 528392
e-mail: suninthewood@aol.com
Dir: *A34 Robin Hood rndbt, L to Shaw, at mini rndbt R then 7th L into Stoney Lane, 1.5m, pub on L.* **Map Ref:** *SU56*

Standing in the shadow of tall trees, this popular, extensively refurbished pub occupies a delightful woodland setting and yet is only a stone's throw from the centre of Newbury. Stone floors, plenty of wood panelling and various prints by Renoir and Monet add to the appeal. The extensive choice of food includes fillet steak Rossini, pan-fried calves liver, and sea bass fillets. Freshly baked baguettes are available in the bar from Tuesday to Saturday.

OPEN: 12-2.30 6-11 **BAR MEALS:** L served Mon-Sun 12-2 D served Mon-Sat 6.30-9.30 Av main course £11.50 **RESTAURANT:** L served Mon-Sun 12-2 D served Mon-Sat 6.30-9.30 Av 3 course à la carte £20 **BREWERY/COMPANY:** Wadworth ◖: Wadworth 6X & Henrys Original IPA, Badger Tanglefoot. ♀: 10 **CHILDREN'S FACILITIES:** menu, portions, games, high-chairs, food/bottle warming, baby changing, outdoor play area, swings, slides, climbing frame **GARDEN:** Lovely country garden among national woodland **NOTES:** No dogs, Parking 60

BOXFORD   THE BELL AT BOXFORD

Lambourn Rd RG20 8DD
☎ 01488 608721 ▯ 01488 608749
e-mail: paullavis@lycos.co.uk
Dir: *A338 toward Wantage, R onto B4000,*
take 3rd L to Boxford. **Map Ref:** *SU47*

A mock Tudor country pub at the heart of the
glorious Lambourn Valley, renowned for its picturesque
downland scenery. The 22-mile Lambourn Valley Way
runs through the village. Relax in the cosy bar with its
choice of real ales, and peruse the impressive wine list
(champagne by the glass!) and the bistro-style
blackboard menu that changes daily. Heated terraces
for outdoor dining.

OPEN: 11-3 6-11 (Sat 6.30-11, Sun 7-10.30)
BAR MEALS: L served all week 12-2 D served all week 7-10
Av main course £10.95 **RESTAURANT:** L served all week
12-2 D served all week 7-10 Av 3 course à la carte £25
Av 2 course fixed price £11.95 **BREWERY/COMPANY:** Free
House ◀: Morrells Oxford, Badger Tanglefoot, Interbrew Bass,
Scottish Courage Courage Best. ⏶: 60 **CHILDREN'S**
FACILITIES: portions, games, food/bottle warming
GARDEN: Heated terraces hold 80 people **NOTES:** Dogs
allowed: in bar, in garden, in bedrooms, Parking 36

CHIEVELEY   THE CRAB AT CHIEVELEY

North Heath, Wantage Rd RG20 8UE
☎ 01635 247550 ▯ 01635 247440
e-mail: info@crabatchieveley.com
Dir: *Off B4494 N of Newbury.* **Map Ref:** *SU47*

This attractive thatched dining pub enjoys an
outstanding location with lovely views across
the West Berkshire Downs. Fish and seafood are the
speciality here, with over 30 dishes and blackboard
specials as well. Meals are served in the bar and non-
smoking restaurant, as well as in the gardens.

OPEN: 11-11 (Sun 12-10.30) **BAR MEALS:** L served all
week 12-2.30 D served all week 6-10
RESTAURANT: L served all week 12-2.30 D served all week
6-10 Av 3 course fixed price £16
BREWERY/COMPANY: Free House ◀: Fullers London
Pride, Boddingtons, West Berkshire, Black Sheep. ⏶: 14
CHILDREN'S FACILITIES: menu, portions, games, high-chairs,
food/bottle warming, 2 garden areas, patio, terrace
GARDEN: Seating and terrace with BBQ & marquee
NOTES: Dogs allowed: in bar, in garden, in bedrooms,
Parking 60

COOKHAM DEAN   CHEQUERS INN BRASSERIE

Dean Ln SL6 9BQ
☎ 01628 481232 ▯ 01628 481237
e-mail: info@chequers-inn.com
Dir: *From A4094 in Cookham High St take R*
fork after r'way bridge into Dean Lane. Pub in
1m. **Map Ref:** *SU88*

Historic pub with oak beams and open fire,
tucked away between Marlow and
Maidenhead in one of the prettiest villages in
the Thames Valley. The writer Kenneth
Grahame, who wrote 'The Wind in the
Willows', spent his childhood here. Striking
Victorian and Edwardian villas around the
green set the tone, whilst the surrounding
wooded hills and dales have earned
Cookham Dean a well-earned reputation as a
centre for good walks. Today, the Chequers offers
carefully-chosen wines and a good selection of ales.
Supplementing the varied menu is a daily-changing
blackboard which may offer the likes of roast
monkfish, Parma ham and cauliflower purée; whole
plaice with lemon and prawn butter; or roast lamb
shank with bay leaves, garlic, lentils, mash and red
wine sauce.

OPEN: 11-3 5.30-11 Closed: Dec 25
BAR MEALS: L served all week 12-2.30 D served all week
6-9.30 **BREWERY/COMPANY:** Free House ◀: Wadworth
6X, Greene King Morland Original, Ruddles County. ⏶: 7
CHILDREN'S FACILITIES: portions, licence, high-chairs,
food/bottle warming **GARDEN:** Small lawned area with
benches and parasols **NOTES:** in bar, Water, Parking 50

CURRIDGE THE BUNK INN

RG18 9DS
☎ 01635 200400 📠 01635 200336
e-mail: alison@thebunkinn.co.uk
*Dir: M4 J13/A34 N towards Oxford then 1st slip rd then R for 1m. R at T-jnct, 1st R signposted Curridge. **Map Ref:** SU47*

Not so long ago local builders used to bunk off to this now smart, considerably extended inn with beams, brasses, log fire and attractive bar. There are starters such as carrot and coriander soup, and deep-fried Brie with apple and cider chutney. Recent main courses include Mediterranean vegetable crumble, and half shoulder of lamb with Singapore noodles, chilli and plum sauce. Nine blackboard specials daily.

OPEN: 11-11 **BAR MEALS:** L served all week 12-2.30 D served all week 7-10 Av main course £13
RESTAURANT: L served all week 12-2.30 D served all week 7-10 Av 0 course fixed price £25
BREWERY/COMPANY: Free House 🍺: Arkells 3B, Wadworth 6X, Fuller's London Pride. 🍷: 6
CHILDREN'S FACILITIES: menu, portions, games, high-chairs, food/bottle warming, baby changing, outdoor play area
NOTES: Dogs allowed: in bar, in garden, Parking 38

EAST GARSTON THE QUEENS ARMS ♦♦♦ 🍷

Newbury Rd RG17 7ET
☎ 01488 648757 📠 01488 648642
e-mail: queensarms@barbox.net
Map Ref: SU37

A charming 19th-century village inn enjoying a close association with the racing world of the Lambourn Valley. Jockeys, trainers and punters fill its bar and restaurant on Newbury race days, and the food lives up to expectations. A large terrace and garden are ideal for summer, complete with BBQ area, and an adventure playground appeals to children. The new landlord has extended the range of beers available and the dining capacity.

OPEN: 11-11 (Closed on 25 Dec at 2pm)
BAR MEALS: L served all week 11 D served all week 10 Av main course £8.50 **RESTAURANT:** L served all week 11-11 D served all week 7-11 Av 3 course à la carte £15
BREWERY/COMPANY: Free House 🍺: Fuller's London Pride, Wadworths 6X. 🍷: 12
CHILDREN'S FACILITIES: menu, portions, high-chairs, outdoor play area, activity area, adventure play area
GARDEN: Large garden, terrace, BBQ area **NOTES:** Dogs allowed: in bar, in garden, in bedrooms, Parking 40
ROOMS: 14 en suite 4 family rooms s£40 d£60

HUNGERFORD THE CROWN & GARTER ♦♦♦♦ 🍷

Inkpen Common RG17 9QR
Map Ref: SU36

A 17th-century pub reputedly visited by James I on his way to see his mistress. Nearby is Inkpen Beacon, at 975 feet England's highest chalk hill, topped by the

famous gibbet and surrounded by outstanding scenery. Today's gibbet is modern, one of several that have stood here since the first was erected in 1676 to hang two murderers. That one eventually rotted away through lack of use; the second was struck by lightning, while the third lasted nearly a hundred years until toppled by gales in 1949.

OPEN: 12-3 5.30-11 (Sun 7-10.30) **BAR MEALS:** L served Wed-Sun 12-2 D served all week 6.30-9.30
RESTAURANT: L served Wed-Sun 12-2 D served all week 6.30-9.30 Av 3 course à la carte £20 🍺: Mr Chubbs, Moonlight, Good Old Boy, Murphys. 🍷: 6
CHILDREN'S FACILITIES: menu, portions, games, high-chairs, food/bottle warming, outdoor play area **GARDEN:** Fenced garden **NOTES:** Dogs allowed: in bar, Parking 30
ROOMS: 8 en suite bedrooms s£50 d£70

KNOWL HILL BIRD IN HAND COUNTRY INN ♀

Bath Rd RG10 9UP
☎ 01628 826622 & 822781 ▤ 01628 826748
e-mail: sthebirdinhand@aol.com
Dir: *On A4, 5m W of Maidenhead, 7m E of Reading.* **Map Ref:** *SU87*

A fascinating old inn that has remained in the same family for three generations. Dating back to the 14th century, its features include a main bar whose oak panelling came from a Scottish castle. In the building that is now the Forge Bar, George III stopped in the late 1700s and granted a royal charter to the landlord in gratitude for the hospitality shown him. This tradition of warm welcome and friendly service lives on to this day.

OPEN: 11-3 6-11 (Sun 12-4, 7-10:30) **BAR MEALS:** L served all week 12-2.30 D served all week 6.30-10 Av main course £9.95 **RESTAURANT:** L served all week 12-2.30 D served all week 7-10 **BREWERY/COMPANY:** Free House ◖: Brakspear Bitter, Fuller's London Pride, Pedigree. ♀: 12 **CHILDREN'S FACILITIES:** menu, portions, high-chairs, food/bottle warming, baby changing **GARDEN:** Garden next to patio with fountain **NOTES:** Dogs allowed: in bar, in garden, in bedrooms, Parking 86 **ROOMS:** 15 en suite 1 family room s£60 d£70 (★★★)

READING THE FLOWING SPRING NEW ♀

Henley Rd, Playhatch RG4 9RB
☎ 0118 969 3207
e-mail: flowingspring@aol.com
Map Ref: *SU77*

A lovely country pub overlooking the Thames flood plain at the point where the Chiltern Hills strike out north east towards Bedfordshire. The proprietor likes his establishment to be known as "a pub that serves good food, rather than a restaurant that serves lousy beer". Representative dishes on the combined bar/restaurant menu include home-made curries, shoulder of lamb, and rib-eye steaks. It's a Fullers pub, so Chiswick, London Pride and ESB are all well kept on tap.

OPEN: 11.30-11 **BAR MEALS:** L served Mon-Sun 12-2.30 D served Wed-Sat 6.30-9.30 Av main course £6 ◖: London Pride, ESB, Chiswick. ♀: 7 **CHILDREN'S FACILITIES:** menu, high-chairs, food/bottle warming, outdoor play area **GARDEN:** Large garden bounded by streams **NOTES:** Dogs allowed: in bar, Parking 40

SONNING BULL INN ♀

High St RG4 6UP
☎ 01189 693901 ▤ 01189 691057
e-mail: bullinn@accommodatinginn.co.uk
Dir: *Telephone for directions.* **Map Ref:** *SU77*

In 'Three Men in a Boat', published in 1889, Jerome K. Jerome called the 16th-century Bull 'a veritable picture of an old country inn'. Were he to return, he'd find little changed. The setting alongside the church is still splendid, and it still has its beams, tiled floors and winter log fires. The extensive menu, though, is bang up to date, with Thai green chicken curry, goat's cheese and red pepper cannelloni, Brie and cranberry parcel, tuna pasta bake, and vegetarian, vegan, gluten-free and dairy-free options.

OPEN: 11-3 5.30-11 (Sat-Sun all day) **BAR MEALS:** L served all week 12-2 D served all week 6.30-9 (All day Sat-Sun) Av main course £10.25 **RESTAURANT:** L served all week 12-2 D served all week 6.30-9.30 Av 3 course à la carte £18.50 **BREWERY/COMPANY:** Gales ◖: Gale's HSB, Best, Butser Bitter. **CHILDREN'S FACILITIES:** portions, licence, games, food/bottle warming, family room **GARDEN:** Patio area **NOTES:** Dogs allowed: in bar, Dog Bowls, Parking 20

Berkshire continued

THEALE   THATCHERS ARMS ♀

North St RG7 5EX
☎ 0118 930 2070 📠 0118 930 2070
Dir: *Telephone for directions.* **Map Ref:** *SU67*

A warm, friendly country pub in a rural area, The Thatchers Arms is surrounded by many footpaths and lanes for walkers. Although in a small hamlet, the pub is only a five minute drive from the M4. There are good garden facilities and a separate patio area. The menu features a range of good steaks, and a variety of fish and seafood dishes. The new licensees are keen to attract a wide ranging clientele, with many family facilities available, and senior citizens day on Wednesday.

OPEN: 12-2.30 (Sat 12-3, 6-11, Sun 12-3, 7-10.30) 5.30-11 **BAR MEALS:** L served all week 12-2 D served all week 7-9.30 Av main course £10 **RESTAURANT:** L served all week 12-2 D served all week 7-9.30
BREWERY/COMPANY: 🍺: Fuller's London Pride, Spitfire, Green King IPA, John Smiths Smooth. ♀: 8
CHILDREN'S FACILITIES: menu, portions, games, high-chairs, food/bottle warming **NOTES:** Dogs allowed: in bar, in garden, Water, Parking 15

WORLD'S END   THE LANGLEY HALL INN 🐑 ♀

RG20 8SA
☎ 01635 248332 📠 01635 248571
Dir: *From J13 M4/Chieveley J A34, N towards Oxford on A34. Take Chieveley & Beedon sliproad, L then immediately R onto Oxford Rd. Langley Hall is 1.5m on L.* **Map Ref:** *SU47*

Friendly, family-run bar/restaurant with a reputation for freshly prepared food, real ales and a good selection of wines. Fresh fish dishes vary according to the daily catch - maybe pan-fried crevettes, grilled Dover sole, quick fried squid, or steamed sea bass. Other favourites are braised lamb, beef stir-fry, and Thai chicken curry. Outside there is a large patio and garden, completely enclosed for the safety of children and dogs, plus a petanque court for fine weather use.

OPEN: 11-3 5.30-12 (Fri-Sat 11-12, Sun 11-7) Closed: 26 Dec, 1 Jan **BAR MEALS:** L served Mon-Sun 12-2.30 D served Mon-Sat 6.30-10 (Sun 12.30-4) Av main course £10
RESTAURANT: L served Mon-Sun 12-2.30 D served Mon-Sat 6.30-10 (Sun 12-4) Av 3 course à la carte £20 🍺: West Berkshire Brewery - Good Old Boy, Mr Chubbs, Lunchtime Bitter, Youngs. ♀: 24 **CHILDREN'S FACILITIES:** portions, licence, high-chairs, food/bottle warming, 12yrs Mon-Fri
GARDEN: Enclosed patio&garden; petanque during summer
NOTES: Dogs allowed: in bar only, Parking 25
ROOMS: 3 en suite bedrooms s£40 d£50 (♦♦♦♦)

ASTON CLINTON   THE OAK ♀

119 Green End St HP22 5EU
☎ 01296 630466 📠 01296 631796
e-mail: wayne@welgate.freeserve.co.uk
Dir: *Entry via Brook St, off the A41.*
Map Ref: *SP81*

Thatched, 500-year-old former coaching inn, with flagstone floors, inglenook fireplace and bags of traditional charm. Set in the old part of the village, it offers a good garden and a wide-ranging menu. The new owners are keen to welcome children of all ages, making this an enjoyable venue for a family visit. Expect traditional pub favourites, alongside tuna citron and seafood tagliatelle.

OPEN: 11.30-2.30 6-11 (Sun 12—3, 6-11 Open all day Sat-Sun in summer) **BAR MEALS:** L served all week 12-2 D served all week 6-9.30 Av main course £5.25
RESTAURANT: L served all week 12-2 D served all week 6-9.30 **BREWERY/COMPANY:** Fullers 🍺: Fullers London Pride, Fullers ESB plus one guest beer. ♀: 6
CHILDREN'S FACILITIES: menu, portions, high-chairs, food/bottle warming, outdoor play area, Large garden
GARDEN: Food served outside **NOTES:** Dogs allowed: Water, Parking 30

BEACONSFIELD THE ROYAL STANDARD OF ENGLAND

Brindle Ln, Forty Green HP9 1XT
☎ 01494 673382 ▤ 01494 523332
Dir: *A40 to Beaconsfield. R at Church rndbt onto B474 towards Penn. L onto Forty Green Rd, then 1m.* **Map Ref:** *SU99*

Dating from the 12th century, this welcoming country inn has striking stained glass windows, beams, flagstone floors, and a large inglenook fireplace. Situated in a part of the world renowned for Civil War battles and skirmishes, the inn became a Royalist headquarters, and it was this that led to its splendid and impressive name. The inn is a perfect base for walking and even better for recuperating after a long hike, cooling your blisters and refuelling with such dishes as braised venison steak with caramelised pears, slow-cooked lamb marinated in mint and honey, sea bass fillet with tarragon and tomato velouté, or the pub's renowned beef and Owd Roger ale pie. The specials board might include green spring vegetable frittata or duck breast with ginger citrus sauce - good sandwiches too and desserts like knickerbocker glory are well worth making room for. A range of real ales including Marston's powerful Owd Roger - not suitable for drivers!

OPEN: 11-3 5.30-11 (Sun 12-3, 7-10.30)
BAR MEALS: L served all week 12-2.15 D served all week 6.30-9.15 Av main course £10
BREWERY/COMPANY: Free House ◗: Marston's Pedigree, Brakspear Bitter, Fuller's London Pride, Greene King.
CHILDREN'S FACILITIES: licence, family room
GARDEN: Paved seating area with floral borders
NOTES: in garden, Water, No dogs (ex guide dogs), Parking 90

BUCKINGHAM THE OLD THATCHED INN ♀

Adstock MK18 2JN
☎ 01296 712584 ▤ 01296 715375
Map Ref: *SP63*

Licensed since 1702, this thatched and beamed 17th-century inn has come through a refurbishment with its traditional beams and inglenook fireplace intact. A modern conservatory and the timbered lounge provide a choice of eating place where the menu plus specials and light bites is offered. Pork and sage sausages, Imam Bayildi aubergine with apricot, onions and pine nuts, fresh oven-baked cod, Caribbean chicken, steak and kidney pudding; and rod caught rainbow trout are all part of an interesting menu. Desserts include blood orange mousse torte and apple and rhubarb crumble.

OPEN: 12-3 6-11 (open all day bank holidays & weekends)
BAR MEALS: L served all week 12-2.35 D served all week 6-9.30 (Sat 12-9.30, Sun 12-9) Av main course £10.95
RESTAURANT: L served all week 12-2.30 D served all week 6-9.30 Av 3 course à la carte £20 ◗: Hook Norton Best, Bass, Hook Norton Seasonals. ♀: 8
CHILDREN'S FACILITIES: menu, portions, licence, games, high-chairs, food/bottle warming, highchairs **GARDEN:** Floral terrace with tables, lawned area **NOTES:** Dogs allowed: in bar, in garden, Water provided, Parking 20

CHALFONT ST GILES IVY HOUSE 🐑 ♀

London Rd HP8 4RS
☎ 01494 872184 ▤ 01494 872870
Dir: *On A413 2m S of Amersham & 1.5m N of Chalfont St Giles.* **Map Ref:** *SU99*

A beautiful 18th-century brick and flint inn which, from the mid-19th to the mid-20th centuries, was owned by the same family. The recent addition of five luxury en suite bedrooms has effectively made it a real inn again. Inside the pub itself, beams, open fires, books, brass and armchairs create a warm, relaxing atmosphere.

OPEN: 12-3.30 6-11 (Sat 12-11, Sun 12-10.30)
BAR MEALS: L served all week 12-2.30 D served all week 6.30-9.30 (Sat 12-9.30, Sun 12-9) **RESTAURANT:** L served all week 12-2.30 D served all week 6.30-9.30 Av 3 course à la carte £24 **BREWERY/COMPANY:** Free House ◗: Fuller's London Pride, Brakspear Bitter, Wadworth 6X, Hook Norton Old Hooky. ♀: 20 **CHILDREN'S FACILITIES:** menu, portions, games, high-chairs, food/bottle warming, baby changing, colouring sheets & pens **GARDEN:** Courtyard & garden with outstanding views **NOTES:** Dogs allowed: in bar, in garden, not in restaurant, Parking 45

CUDDINGTON THE CROWN

Spurt St HP18 0BB
☎ 01844 292222
e-mail: david@thecrowncuddington.co.uk
Dir: *Telephone for directions.* **Map Ref:** *SP71*

Having successfully run Annie Bailey's bar-cum-brasserie in Cuddington for a number of

years, the Berrys turned their attention to improving the Crown, a delightful Grade II listed pub nearby. Customers will find plenty of character inside, with a popular locals' bar and several low-beamed dining areas filled with charming prints and the glow of evening candlelight. A choice of beers on tap, an extensive wine list and an eclectic menu add to the enjoyment of a visit here.

OPEN: 12-3 6-11 (All day Sun) **BAR MEALS:** L served all week 12-2.30 D served all week 6.30-10 (Sun 12-8) Av main course £10 **RESTAURANT:** L served all week 12-2.30 D served all week 6.30-10 (Sun 12-8) Av 3 course à la carte £20 Av 3 course fixed price £20
BREWERY/COMPANY: Fullers ◀: Fullers London Pride, Adnams. ♀: 9 **CHILDREN'S FACILITIES:** menu, portions, games, food/bottle warming, baby changing **GARDEN:** Small patio area **NOTES:** No dogs (ex guide dogs), Parking 12

DENHAM THE SWAN INN ♀

Village Rd UB9 5BH
☎ 01895 832085 ▤ 01895 835516
Dir: *From A412 follow signs for Denham. Jct 17 M25 or Jct 1 M40.* **Map Ref:** *TQ08*

A Georgian double-fronted, wisteria-clad inn in the pretty, unspoiled village of Denham is everyone's idea of the ideal country pub; secluded and peaceful, it is only minutes away from suburban London and two motorways. Inside, a log fire and private dining room are equally suitable for intimate dinners or business meetings, while a thriving bar welcomes locals and city folk alike. All tastes are catered for, from a quick sandwich to serious eating; popular choices are twice-baked Roquefort soufflé with watercress salad and braised lamb shank.

OPEN: 11-11 Sun 12-10.30 **BAR MEALS:** L served all week 12-2.30 D served all week 7-10 (Sun L 12-3) Av main course £11.50 **RESTAURANT:** L served all week 12-2.30 D served all week 7-10 (Sun L 12-3) Av 3 course à la carte £21.50 ◀: Directors, Courage Best, Morrells Oxford Blue, Fosters. ♀: 13 **CHILDREN'S FACILITIES:** portions, high-chairs, food/bottle warming **GARDEN:** Terrace on 2 levels **NOTES:** Dogs allowed: Water, Parking 12

FARNHAM COMMON THE FORESTERS ♀

The Broadway SL2 3QQ
☎ 01753 643340 ▤ 01753 647524
e-mail: barforesters@aol.com
Map Ref: *SU98*

There's a real buzz at the Foresters - formerly the Foresters Arms, which was built in the

1930s to replace a Victorian building. Located close to Burnham Beeches, a large woodland area famous for its coppiced trees, it offers a combination of good drinking and a busy restaurant renowned for the quality of its food. The daily menu might include pan-roasted duck breast with carrot and parsnip rosti; leek, sweetcorn and ricotta roulade with tomato grilled aubergine; or fresh haddock and chips.

OPEN: 11-11 Mon-Sat 12-10.30 Sun
BAR MEALS: L served all week 12-2.30 D served all week 6.30-10 Food all day Sat & Sun Av main course £10.50
RESTAURANT: L served all week 12-2.30 D served all week 6.30-10 Sat 12-10, Sun 12.30-9 Av 3 course à la carte £20
BREWERY/COMPANY: Simply ◀: Fullers London Pride, Draught Bass, Youngs Special Bitter, Carling. ♀: 9
CHILDREN'S FACILITIES: portions **NOTES:** Dogs allowed: in bar, Water provided

FRIETH   THE PRINCE ALBERT

RG9 6PY
☎ 01494 881683
e-mail: lacysti@aol.com
Dir: *From Marlow take Oxford Road.*
Map Ref: *SU79*

Difficult to improve on the description submitted for this guide by the new owners: 'Nestling in the Chiltern valley close to Hambledon and Marlow, the Prince Albert is a small, traditional family-run pub offering fresh home-cooked food at reasonable prices. A short wine list offers half a dozen choices from around the world. There is no music, no cigarette machine, and no TV; just a friendly reception and warm open fires. Soups, filled

baguettes, stews, chillis, curries and pies are all made in-house with traceable local ingredients.'

OPEN: 11.30-11 **BAR MEALS:** L served Mon-Sun 12-9.30 D served all week 12-9.30 Sun 12-5.30 Av main course £5.95 **BREWERY/COMPANY:** Brakspear
🍺: Brakspear Bitter, Special.
CHILDREN'S FACILITIES: menu, portions, food/bottle warming, family room **GARDEN:** Food served outside
NOTES: Dogs allowed: in bar, Parking 20, No credit cards

GREAT MISSENDEN   THE GEORGE INN

94 High St HP16 0BG
☎ 01494 862084 📠 01494 865622
Dir: *Off A413 between Aylesbury & Amersham.*
Map Ref: *SP80*

Established as a coaching inn in 1483, the George has always had strong ties with

nearby Missenden Abbey. The small, cosy bars boast a wealth of old beams and fireplaces. The restaurant offers a relaxed non-smoking environment for lunchtime sandwiches, baguettes and jacket potatoes, as well as hot dishes like home-made steak and kidney pie, seasonal game, or tomato and Mozzerella tortellini.

OPEN: 11-11 (Sun 12-3, 7-10.30) **BAR MEALS:** L served all week 12-2.30 D served Mon-Sat 6.30-9.30 Av main course £7.50 **RESTAURANT:** L served all week 12-2.30 D served Mon-Sat 6.30-9.30 Av 3 course à la carte £15
BREWERY/COMPANY: Inn Partnership 🍺: Adnams Bitter, Adnams Broadside, Interbrew Flowers Original.
CHILDREN'S FACILITIES: menu, portions, high-chairs, food/bottle warming, outdoor play area, Fenced, with bark chipping, climbing frame **GARDEN:** Beer garden & patio
NOTES: Dogs allowed: in bar, in garden, Water, Parking 25

THE POLECAT INN   ♀

170 Wycombe Rd, Prestwood HP16 0HJ
☎ 01494 862253 📠 01494 868393
e-mail: polecatinn@btinternet.com
Dir: *On the A4128 between Great Missenden and High Wycombe.* **Map Ref:** *SP80*

Small, low-beamed rooms with rug-strewn floors radiate from the central bar of this charming 17th-century free house in the Chiltern Hills. There are open fires in the winter months, and a three-acre garden with tables for alfresco summer eating. Local ingredients and herbs from the garden are the foundation of the wide-ranging menu and daily blackboard specials, with food freshly prepared on the premises. Besides the range of sandwiches, ploughman's and jacket potatoes, lunchtime snacks include sausages

in French bread, and hot roast beef in stotty bread. There's also a full menu at midday and in the evenings, with starters like terrine of chicken and asparagus in Parma ham with charred olive bread, and smoked trout ramekin. Main dishes include lamb shank with Puy lentils, grilled swordfish with mango and chilli coulis, and feta and spinach pie with salad and garlic bread.

OPEN: 11.30-2.30 6-11 (Sun 12-3) Closed: Dec 25-26, Jan 1 **BAR MEALS:** L served all week 12-2 D served Mon-Sat 6.30-9 Av main course £8.50 **BREWERY/COMPANY:** Free House 🍺: Marston's Pedigree, Bass, Greene King Old Speckled Hen, Interbrew Flowers IPA. ♀: 16
CHILDREN'S FACILITIES: portions, food/bottle warming, outdoor play area, family room **NOTES:** Dogs allowed: in bar, in garden, Parking 40, No credit cards

The Rising Sun

Little Hampden HP16 9PS
☎ 01494 488393 & 488360 📠 01494 488788
e-mail: sunrising@rising-sun.demon.co.uk
Dir: *From A413 N of Gt Missenden take Rignall Rd on L (signed Princes Risborough) 2.5m turn R signed 'Little Hampden only'.* *Map Ref:* SP80

You'll find this 250-year-old country inn tucked away in the Chiltern Hills surrounded by beech woods and glorious scenery. A network of footpaths begins just outside the front door, so it's a perfect base for country walks. Reached down a single track no-through-road, the pub is seemingly miles from anywhere, yet London is only 40 minutes away by train from nearby Great Missenden. The proprietor prides himself on a well-run, clean and welcoming establishment, which is strictly non-smoking throughout; booking is advisable. An interesting menu offers starters which can double as snacks and an extensive à la carte selection for lunch and dinner.

OPEN: 11.30-3 (Sun 12-3 only) 6.30-10
BAR MEALS: L served Tue-Sun 12-2 D served Tue-Sat 7-9 (Sun L 12-2) Av main course £9.95
RESTAURANT: L served Tue-Sun 12-2 D served Tue-Sat 7-9 Av 3 course à la carte £19.95 **BREWERY/COMPANY:** Free House 🍺: Adnams, Brakspear Bitter, Marstons Pedigree, Old Speckled Hen. **CHILDREN'S FACILITIES:** menu, portions, food/bottle warming **GARDEN:** Fence enclosed garden with seating area **NOTES:** Water, No dogs (ex guide dogs), Parking 20

KINGSWOOD   Crooked Billet

Ham Green HP18 0QJ
☎ 01296 770239 📠 01296 770094
e-mail: info@crookedbillet.com
Dir: *On A41 between Aylesbury & Bicester.*
Map Ref: SP61

Located in peaceful Buckinghamshire countryside, this 200-year-old pub is believed to be haunted by Fair Rosamund, a girlfriend of Charles I. A change of hands has resulted in extensive and tempting menus, both à la carte and fixed price. Starters may include, risotto of sea scallops with wild mushrooms, and leek and egg baked pots. Among the main courses can be found pan-fried monkfish or duck breast, fillet of lamb, or wild venison, all with unusual but delectable-sounding accompaniments. Sandwiches made from home-made bread are a lighter option.

OPEN: 11-11 **BAR MEALS:** L served all week 12-6 6-9 Sun 12-8 Av main course £12.50 **RESTAURANT:** L served all week 12-6 D served all week 6-9 Sun 12-8 Av 3 course à la carte £25 **BREWERY/COMPANY:** 🍺: Hook Norton, Worthington 1744, London Pride. **CHILDREN'S FACILITIES:** menu, portions, high-chairs, food/bottle warming, outdoor play area **GARDEN:** Large seated area surrounded by woodland **NOTES:** No dogs (ex guide dogs), Parking 50

LONG CRENDON   The Angel Inn 🌹 🍷

47 Bicester Rd HP18 9EE
☎ 01844 208268 📠 01844 202497
Dir: *A418 to Thame, B4011 to L Crendon, Inn on B4011.* *Map Ref:* SP60

Gastro-pub status is conceded to this 16th-century coaching inn, which dishes up great food in the air-conditioned conservatory or out on the patio or sun terrace. Wattle and daub walls and inglenook fireplaces testify to the inn's age, and there's plenty of character too in the assorted scrubbed pine and oak tables set on light wooden floors. Real ales are served, along with cocktails, Champagne and wine by the glass.

OPEN: 12-3 7-10 Rest: Sun Closed eve
BAR MEALS: L served all week 12-3 D served Mon-Sat 7-9.30 Av main course £12.50 **RESTAURANT:** L served all week 12-2.30 D served Mon-Sat 7-9.30 Av 3 course à la carte £25 **BREWERY/COMPANY:** Free House 🍺: Oxford Blue, IPA, Brakes Beer. 🍷: 11
CHILDREN'S FACILITIES: portions, high-chairs, food/bottle warming **GARDEN:** Patio, terrace at rear of pub **NOTES:** in garden, water, No dogs (ex guide dogs), Parking 25

MARLOW THE KINGS HEAD

Church Rd, Little Marlow SL7 3RZ
☎ 01628 484407 📠 01628 484407
Dir: M40 J4 take A4040 S 1st A4155.
Map Ref: SU88

This flower-adorned pub, only 10 minutes from the Thames Footpath, dates back to 1654. It has a cosy, open-plan interior with original beams and open fires. From sandwiches and jacket potatoes, the menu extends to the likes of sea bass with ginger, sherry and spring onions, lamb shank with rich minty gravy, mash and fresh vegetables, pheasant casserole, tuna and Mozzarella fish-cakes, and stir-fry duck with plum sauce.

OPEN: 11-3 5-11 (Sat-Sun 11-11) **BAR MEALS:** L served all week 12-2.15 D served all week 6.30-9.30 Sunday 12-8 Av main course £8.25 **RESTAURANT:** L served all week 12-2.15 D served all week 6.30-9.30 Sunday 12-8 Av 3 course à la carte £14
BREWERY/COMPANY: Enterprise Inns 🍺: Brakspear Bitter, Fuller's London Pride, Rebellion IPA, Timothy Taylor Landlord.
CHILDREN'S FACILITIES: menu, portions, high-chairs, food/bottle warming, baby changing **GARDEN:** Safely behind pub, lots of tables & chairs **NOTES:** No dogs (ex guide dogs), Parking 50

OVING THE BLACK BOY

Church Ln HP22 4HN
☎ 01296 641258 📠 01296 641271
e-mail: theblackboyoving@aol.com
Map Ref: SP72

There are 30 tables in the huge garden of this old pub. On the same land, long before the green-fingered brigade got to work, Cromwell and his soldiers camped here before sacking nearby Bolebec Castle during the Civil War. Prisoners were put in the pub's cellars, and one unfortunate who died in custody now haunts the building. Don't let that deter you from enjoying a range of Aberdeen Angus steaks, pheasant, chicken ballotine, venison sausages, sea bream or freshwater perch.

OPEN: 12-3 6-11 **BAR MEALS:** L served Tues-Sun 12-2 D served Tues-Sat 6.30-9 Sun 12-2.30 Av main course £11.75 **RESTAURANT:** L served Tues-Sun 12-2 D served Tues-Sat 6.30-9 Sun 12-2.30 Av 3 course à la carte £20 🍺: Spitfire, Youngs Bitter, Batemans Bitter, Adnams Bitter. 🍷: 10 **CHILDREN'S FACILITIES:** menu, portions, games, food/bottle warming **GARDEN:** Large garden with pergolas&views of Aylesbury **NOTES:** Dogs allowed: in bar, Water, Parking 20

WEST WYCOMBE THE GEORGE AND DRAGON HOTEL

High St HP14 3AB
☎ 01494 464414 📠 01494 462432
e-mail: enq@george-and-dragon.co.uk
Dir: On A40, close to M40. *Map Ref: SU89*

Built on the site of a 14th-century hostelry, this 18th-century former coaching inn in a National Trust village has welcomed generations of visitors. Indeed, some from a bygone era are rumoured still to haunt its corridors - notably Sukie, a servant girl. The hotel is reached through a cobbled archway and comprises a delightful jumble of whitewashed, timber-framed buildings. The range of real ales is excellent, and a varied menu offers something for everybody.

OPEN: 11-2.30 5.30-11 (Sun 12-3, 7-10.30, Sat 12-3, 5.30-11) **BAR MEALS:** L served all week 12-2 D served all week 6-9.30 Av main course £8
BREWERY/COMPANY: Unique Pub Co 🍺: Scottish Courage Courage Best, Wells Bombardier Premium, Greene King Abbot Ale, Adnams Broadside. 🍷: 12
CHILDREN'S FACILITIES: menu, portions, high-chairs, food/bottle warming, outdoor play area, Climbing frame, swings, family room **GARDEN:** Large garden adjacent to car park **NOTES:** Dogs allowed: in bar, in garden, in bedrooms, Water, Parking 35

127

Buckinghamshire continued

WOOBURN COMMON CHEQUERS INN ★★ ⬡ ⌣

Kiln Ln HP10 0JQ
☎ 01628 529575 📠 01628 850124
e-mail: info@chequers-inn.com
Dir: M40 J2 through Beaconsfield towards H Wycombe.1m turn L into Broad Lane. Inn 2.5m.
Map Ref: SU98

Just two miles from the M40 at Junction 2, it's hard to believe that this deeply rural inn is only 24 miles by road from central London. Built in the 17th century, with a massive oak post and beam bar, it's a splendidly snug spot on a cold winter's night and delightful when sitting out with a drink on balmy summer evenings. Bedroom accommodation is convenient, up-to-date and thoroughly comfortable.

OPEN: All day **BAR MEALS:** L served all week 12-2.30 D served all week 6.30-9.30 Av main course £10 **RESTAURANT:** L served all week 12-2.30 D served all week 7-9.30 **BREWERY/COMPANY:** Free House 🍺: Ruddles, IPA, Abbot, Tanners Jack. ⌣: 12 **CHILDREN'S FACILITIES:** portions, licence, high-chairs, food/bottle warming **GARDEN:** Large with tables & chairs; bbq in summer **NOTES:** No dogs (ex guide dogs), Parking 60 **ROOMS:** 17 en suite bedrooms 1 family room

BARRINGTON THE ROYAL OAK

West Green CB2 5RZ
☎ 01223 870791 📠 01223 870791
Dir: From Barton off M11 S of Cambridge 1 mile. Map Ref: TL34

Rambling timbered and thatched 13th-century pub, the oldest thatched inn in England. Overlooks village green (which coincidentally, is the largest in England) and provides a wide range of fish and Italian dishes.

OPEN: 12-2.30 (Sun 12-10.30) 6-11 **BAR MEALS:** L served all week 12-2.30 D served Mon- Sat 6.30-9 Sun 12-3.30, Fri&Sat 6.30-9.30 Av main course £10 **RESTAURANT:** L served Wed-Sat 12-2.30 D served Wed-Sat 6.30-9 Fri&Sat 6.30-9.30 Av 3 course à la carte £22 **BREWERY/COMPANY:** Old English Inns 🍺: IPA Potton Brewery, Adnams, Everards, Elgoods. **CHILDREN'S FACILITIES:** portions, games, high-chairs, food/bottle warming **GARDEN:** Overlooking village green **NOTES:** No dogs (ex guide dogs), Parking 50

ELTON THE BLACK HORSE 🐑 ⌣

14 Overend PE8 6RU
☎ 01832 280240 📠 01832 280875
Dir: Off A605 (Peterborough to Northampton rd). Map Ref: TL09

The Black Horse is within easy lunching distance of the Peterborough business park,

and a genuine village inn. Its warm country atmosphere is at odds with its history: Harry Kirk, the landlord here in the 1950s, was an assistant to Tom and Albert Pierrepoint, Britain's most famous hangmen; Harry's son is now said to haunt the bar. It was also once the village jail. The delightful one-acre rear garden overlooks Elton's famous church.

OPEN: 12-3 6-11 open all day summer **BAR MEALS:** L served all week 12-2 D served Mon-Sat 6-9 Av main course £9.95 **RESTAURANT:** L served all week 12-2 D served Mon-Sat 6-9 Av 3 course à la carte £20 **BREWERY/COMPANY:** Free House 🍺: Bass, Everards Tiger, Nethergate, Archers. ⌣: 14 **CHILDREN'S FACILITIES:** menu, portions, high-chairs, baby changing, outdoor play area, family room **GARDEN:** Food served outside. Patio area **NOTES:** Dogs allowed: in the garden only. Water provided, Parking 30

FENSTANTON KING WILLIAM IV ♀

High St PE28 9JF
☎ 01480 462467 📠 01480 468526
e-mail: kingwilliam@thefen.fsnet.co.uk
Dir: *Off A14 between Cambridge &*
Huntingdon (J27). **Map Ref:** *TL36*

Originally three 17th-century cottages, this
rambling, part cream-painted, part red brick
inn is in the centre of the village, adjacent to
an old clock tower. Inside are low beams, a
lively bar and the plant-festooned Garden
Room. Tourists, visitors on business and
locals all call by for a traditional bar meal or
something perhaps a little more sophisticated
from the carte menu. Expect creamed leek
and saffron tart, Thai vegetable curry, calves'
liver and grilled fillet of Scottish salmon
among a varied choice of main courses.

OPEN: 11-3.30 6-11 (Sun 12-10.30) from Easter open all
day **BAR MEALS:** L served all week 12-2.15 D served
Mon-Sat 7-9.45 Sun 12-3.30 Av main course £5.80
RESTAURANT: L served all week 12-2.15 D served Mon-Sat
7-9.45 Av 3 course à la carte £21
BREWERY/COMPANY: Greene King 🍺: Greene King Abbot
Ale & IPA, Guest Ales. ♀: 9
CHILDREN'S FACILITIES: menu, games, high-chairs,
food/bottle warming **GARDEN:** Patio area **NOTES:** Dogs
allowed: in bar, Water, Parking 14

FORDHAM WHITE PHEASANT ♀

CB7 5LQ
☎ 01638 720414
e-mail: whitepheasant@whitepheasant.com
Dir: *From Newmarket. A142 to Ely, approx 5*
miles to Fordham Village. On L as you enter
Fordham. **Map Ref:** *TL67*

Named after a protected white pheasant
killed by a previous landlord, this white-
painted, 17th-century free house is set in a
Fenland village between Newmarket and Ely.
Rug-strewn wooden floors, tartan fabrics, soft
lighting and scrubbed, candlelit tables
characterise the interior. Food ranges from
sandwiches and salads to a restaurant carte.
Home-cured meat and fish is a speciality,
alongside mussels steamed in Norfolk beer,
and pan-fried fillet of gilthead bream with roasted
aubergine and tomato dressing.

OPEN: 12-3 6-11 (Sun 7-10.30) Closed: 25-30, 1 Jan
BAR MEALS: L served all week 12-2.30 D served all week
6-9.30 Av main course £12 **RESTAURANT:** L served all
week 12-2.30 D served all week 6-10.30 Av 3 course à la
carte £25 **BREWERY/COMPANY:** Free House
🍺: Woodforde's Nelson's Revenge, Norfolk Nog, Admirals
Reserve, Wherry. ♀: 14 **CHILDREN'S FACILITIES:** portions,
games, high-chairs, food/bottle warming **GARDEN:** Pleasant
area, child friendly **NOTES:** No dogs (ex guide dogs),
Parking 30

GOREFIELD WOODMANS COTTAGE 🐑 ♀

90 High Rd PE13 4NB
☎ 01945 870669 📠 01945 870631
e-mail: magtuck@aol.com
Dir: *3m NW of Wisbech.* **Map Ref:** *TF41*

Popular pub run by a hard-working brother
and sister team. Their efforts have paid off,
and Woodmans Cottage remains a successful
local with well-kept beers and a good choice
of locally-sourced food. Established favourites
include seafood platter, Chinese rack of ribs,
lamb and mushroom with red wine, minty
lamb shank, nut roast, the mega mix grill, and
Cajun chicken. There is also an award-
winning sweet trolley.

OPEN: 11-2.30 7-11 Closed: 25 Dec
BAR MEALS: L served all week 12-2.30 D served all week
7-10 Av main course £7.50 **RESTAURANT:** L served all
week 12-2.30 D served all week 7-10 Av 3 course à la carte
£20 **BREWERY/COMPANY:** Free House 🍺: Greene King
IPA & Abbot Ale, Interbrew Worthington Bitter.
CHILDREN'S FACILITIES: menu, portions, games, high-chairs,
food/bottle warming, outdoor play area **GARDEN:** walled
patio area **NOTES:** No dogs (ex guide dogs), Parking 40

HUNTINGDON   THE OLD BRIDGE HOTEL ★★★ ◉◉ ♀

1 High St PE29 3TQ
☎ 01480 424300 🖨 01480 411017
e-mail: oldbridge@huntsbridge.co.uk
Dir: *Signposted from A1 & A14.*
Map Ref: *TL27*

Owned by the Huntsbridge partnership of

chefs, who manage four dining pubs in and around Huntingdon, Oliver Cromwell's home town. Décor throughout acknowledges its original 18th-century character, from the panelled dining room and main lounge with their fine fabrics, quality prints and comfortable chairs, to the bedrooms. Walls in the more informal Terrace dining area are all hand-painted.

OPEN: 11-11 (Sun 12-10.30) **BAR MEALS:** L served all week 12-2.30 D served all week 6.30-10.30 Av main course £10 **RESTAURANT:** L served all week 12-2.30 D served all week 6.30-10.30 Av 3 course à la carte £25 Av 2 course fixed price £12 **BREWERY/COMPANY:** 🍺: Adnams Best, Hobsons Choice, Bateman XXXB. ♀: 15 **CHILDREN'S FACILITIES:** menu, portions, games, high-chairs, food/bottle warming **GARDEN:** Drinks served only **NOTES:** in bar, in garden, in bedrooms, No dogs (ex guide dogs), Parking 60 **ROOMS:** 24 en suite 1 family room s£85 d£125

NEWTON   THE QUEEN'S HEAD ♀

CB2 5PG
☎ 01223 870436
Dir: *6m S of Cambridge on B1368, 1.5m off A10 at Harston, 4m from A505.* **Map Ref:** *TL44*

This quintessentially English pub, dating back to 1680 (though the cellar is much older), stands in the heart of the village by the green, a few miles south of Cambridge. There are no fruit machines or piped music to interrupt the lively conversation in the two small bars; nor for 40 years has there been a menu - or specials 'whatever they might be'. Hot alternatives for lunch are limited to home-made soup, Aga-baked potatoes with cheese and butter, and toast with beef dripping. A dozen varieties of cut-to-order sandwiches - such as roast beef, smoked

ham, salmon, cheese - are made with the freshest brown bread and butter; you could try a Humphrey (banana with lemon and sugar) for a change. Evening meals consist of soup and cold platters. Ales are dispensed direct from the barrel in studious avoidance of modernisation.

OPEN: 11.30-2.30 6-11 (Sun 12-2.30, 7-10.30) Closed: 25 Dec **BAR MEALS:** L served all week 11.30-2.15 D served all week 6-9.30 Sun 7.30-9.30 **BREWERY/COMPANY:** Free House 🍺: Adnams Southwold, Broadside, Fisherman, Bitter & Regatta. ♀: 8 **CHILDREN'S FACILITIES:** portions, food/bottle warming, Games room, family room **NOTES:** Dogs allowed: in bar, Water, Parking 15, No credit cards

STRETHAM   THE LAZY OTTER 🐾 ♀

Cambridge Rd CB6 3LU
☎ 01353 649780 🖨 01353 649314
e-mail: swilkinson110454@aol.com
Dir: *Telephone for directions.* **Map Ref:** *TL57*

With its large beer garden and riverside restaurant overlooking the marina, the Lazy Otter lies just off the A10 between Ely and Cambridge. The pub's location beside the Great Ouse river makes it very popular in summer. Typical dishes include jumbo cod, lemon sole topped with crab meat, or fisherman's medley, as well as a selection of steaks and grills. The marina holds 30 permanent boats, as well as up to 10 day boats.

OPEN: 11-11 **BAR MEALS:** L served all week 12-2.30 D served all week 6-9.30 Av main course £7.50 **RESTAURANT:** L served all week 12-2.30 D served all week 6-9.30 🍺: Marston's Pedigree, Wadsworth 6X, Interbrew Flowers IPA, Scottish Courage John Smith's & Courage Best. ♀: 8 **CHILDREN'S FACILITIES:** menu, portions, high-chairs, food/bottle warming, outdoor play area **GARDEN:** Large beer garden along river front **NOTES:** No dogs, Parking 50

THRIPLOW THE GREEN MAN

Lower St SG8 7RJ
☎ 01763 208855 📠 01763 208431
e-mail: greenmanthriplow@ntlworld.com
Dir: *1m W of junction 10 on M11.*
Map Ref: TL44

A rejuvenated early 19th-century pub standing at the heart of a quaint rural village famous for its annual daffodil weekend and pig race. It offers fixed-price menus and guest ales that change regularly. Typical evening dishes include braised shoulder of lamb and foie gras, and roast duck breast, while the lunchtime selection might include goats' cheese and roast pepper cannelloni. Picnic tables in the large landscaped garden encourage al fresco meals.

OPEN: 12-2.30 6-11 **BAR MEALS:** L served Tue-Sun 12-2.30 D served Tue-Sat 7-9.30 (Sun 12-3) Av main course £8 **RESTAURANT:** 12-2.30 D served Tue-Sat 7-9.30 **BREWERY/COMPANY:** Free House 🍺: Eccleshall Slaters Original, Hop Back Summer Lightning, Batemans XXXB, Milton Klas Act. **CHILDREN'S FACILITIES:** portions, high-chairs **NOTES:** No dogs (ex guide dogs), Parking 12

BLACKMORE END THE BULL INN 🐑 ♀

CM7 4DD
☎ 01371 851037 📠 01371 851037
Map Ref: TL73

Off the beaten track in the heart of tranquil north Essex, not far from the showpiece village of Finchingfield, star of a thousand kitchen calendars. Now in new hands, this traditional village pub, created from two 17th-century cottages and an adjoining barn, is full of original beams and open hearths, and overlooks farmland. Herbs used in the kitchen are grown in the attractive garden. Word of mouth, rather than advertising, guarantees its continuing popularity with locals and visitors. The no-nonsense menu caters for most tastes with a good choice of starters such as broccoli and Stilton soup, deep-fried whitebait, nachos, or crispy mushrooms, backed up with main courses including steaks, rack of ribs, fish and seafood, sausage and mash, spaghetti arrabbiata, and Thai chicken curry and rice. On Sundays there's a set-price lunch with similar starters, traditional roasts and a selection of sweets of the toffee apple and pecan pie, and chocolate pudding variety.

OPEN: 12-3 6-11 **BAR MEALS:** L served all week 12-3 D served all week 7-9 Sun 12-3, 6-9 Av main course £6.95 **RESTAURANT:** L served Tue-Sun 12-2.30 D served Mon-Sun 6-9 Av 3 course à la carte £12 **BREWERY/COMPANY:** Free House 🍺: Greene King IPA, Abbot Ale, Adnams Best, London Pride. ♀: 6 **CHILDREN'S FACILITIES:** menu, portions, games, high-chairs, food/bottle warming, high chairs, toys, books, family room **GARDEN:** beer garden, outdoor eating, BBQ **NOTES:** No dogs (ex guide dogs), Parking 36

CASTLE HEDINGHAM THE BELL INN ♀

St James St CO9 3EJ
☎ 01787 460350
e-mail: bell-inn@ic24.net
Dir: *On A1124 N of Halstead, R to Castle Hedingham.* *Map Ref:* TL73

The Bell dates from the 15th century and was the principle coaching inn on the Bury St Edmunds to London route. The pub has been in the same family since 1967 and still has beams, wooden floors, open fires and gravity-fed real ale straight from the barrel. Other features are the barrel-vaulted function room, walled garden and vine-covered patio. Monday is fish night (try it barbecued), while other favourites are smoked prawns, shepherds pie and treacle tart.

OPEN: 11.30-3 Open all day Friday 6-11 (Sun 12-3, 7-10.30) Closed: 25 Dec(eve) **BAR MEALS:** L served all week 12-2 D served all week 7-9.30 Av main course £7.50 **BREWERY/COMPANY:** Grays 🍺: Mild Adnams Broadside, Greene King IPA, Adnams Bitter. ♀: 7 **CHILDREN'S FACILITIES:** menu, games, high-chairs, food/bottle warming, baby changing, outdoor play area, swings, high chairs, nappy changing facilities, family room **GARDEN:** Large walled orchard garden **NOTES:** Dogs allowed: by arrangement only, Parking 15

CLAVERING   THE CRICKETERS

CB11 4QT
☎ 01799 550442 📠 01799 550882
e-mail: cricketers@lineone.net
Dir: *From M11 J10 take A505 E. Then A1301, B1383. At Newport take B1038.*
Map Ref: *TL43*

Owned and run by the parents of celebrity chef Jamie Oliver - who grew up and worked in the kitchen here - this popular 16th-century inn is at the heart of a beautiful and unspoilt Essex village. Cricketing memorabilia abounds in the bars and restaurant with their beamed ceilings and log fires that serve to create a friendly atmosphere. The choice of food is extensive and varied.

OPEN: 10.30-11 Closed: 25-26 Dec **BAR MEALS:** L served all week 12-2 D served all week 7-10 **RESTAURANT:** L served all week 12-2 D served all week 7-10 Av 3 course à la carte £26 Av 3 course fixed price £26 **BREWERY/COMPANY:** Free House 🍺: Adnams Bitter, Carlsberg-Tetley Tetley Bitter. ♀: 10 **CHILDREN'S FACILITIES:** menu, portions, high-chairs, food/bottle warming, outdoor play area, Fenced patio, family room **GARDEN:** One patio and one courtyard **NOTES:** No dogs, Parking 100 **ROOMS:** 14 en suite bedrooms s£70 d£100 (♦♦♦♦)

COLCHESTER   THE ROSE & CROWN HOTEL ★★★ 🏵️🏵️

East St CO1 2TZ
☎ 01206 866677 📠 01206 866616
e-mail: info@rose-and-crown.com
Dir: *From M25 J28 take A12 N & follow signs for Colchester.* *Map Ref:* *TL92*

Situated in the heart of Britain's oldest town, this splendid 14th-century posting house retains much of its Tudor character. With ancient timbers, smartly decorated bedrooms, and wide-ranging menus, this popular destination has a daily log fire during the winter season to add to its air of warmth. Part of the bar is made of cell doors from the old jail that was once on the site. The focus is on fresh seafood, with other options such as

rack of lamb, calves' liver and bacon, breast of duck with orange sauce, or seared venison fillet.

OPEN: 12-2 7-11 **BAR MEALS:** L served all week 12-2 D served all week 7-10 Av main course £9 **RESTAURANT:** L served all week 12-2 D served Mon-Sat 7-9.45 Av 3 course à la carte £20 **BREWERY/COMPANY:** Free House 🍺: Carlsberg-Tetley Tetley's Bitter, Rose & Crown Bitter, Adnams Broadside. **CHILDREN'S FACILITIES:** menu, portions, high-chairs, food/bottle warming, baby changing, family room **NOTES:** No dogs (ex guide dogs), Parking 50 **ROOMS:** 31 en suite 2 family rooms s£80 d£87

DANBURY   THE ANCHOR

Runsell Green CM3 4QZ
☎ 01245 222457 📠 01245 222457
e-mail: anchordanbury@ukonline.co.uk
Dir: *From Chelmsford take the A414 towards Danbury, pub is 50yds from the main road behind Runsell Green village green.*
Map Ref: *TL70*

This lovely 16th-century black and white timbered pub may once have been a smithy. Nowadays roaring winter fires and a wealth of low-beamed ceilings creates a welcoming atmosphere, with settees and armchairs in the Dog Bar for those who prefer a quiet drink with man's best friend. Nearby nature reserves make the Anchor a popular choice for walkers. Menu choices include T-bone steak; liver and bacon casserole; and spinach and red pepper lasagne.

OPEN: 12-3 6-11 (Fri-Sun 12-11) **BAR MEALS:** L served all week 12-2.30 D served all week 6-9.30 Sun 12-4 Av main course £8.95 **RESTAURANT:** L served all week 12-2.30 D served all week 6-9.30 Av 3 course à la carte £17 **BREWERY/COMPANY:** Ridley & Sons 🍺: Ridleys IPA, Rumpus, Old Bob & Prospect. ♀: 6 **CHILDREN'S FACILITIES:** menu, portions, games, high-chairs, outdoor play area, Large grassed play area with benches **GARDEN:** Lawned front garden & patio with benches **NOTES:** Dogs allowed: in bar, Water, Parking 50

ELSENHAM THE CROWN

The Cross, High St CM22 6DG
☎ 01279 812827
Dir: M11 J8 towards Takeley L at traffic lights.
Map Ref: TL52

A pub for 300 years, with oak beams, open fireplaces and Essex pargetting at the front. The menu, which has a large selection of fresh fish, might offer cottage pie with cheese topping, gammon steak, three cheese pasta bake, steak and kidney pie, baked trout with almonds and honey, steak and mushroom pie, home-made burgers, and steaks cooked to order.

OPEN: 11-3 Sun 12-4, 7-10.30) 6-11
BAR MEALS: L served all week 12-2 D served Tue-Sat 7-9 Av main course £8.50 **RESTAURANT:** L served all week 12-2 D served Tue-Sat 7-9 Av 3 course à la carte £16
BREWERY/COMPANY: ◖: Youngs PA, Adnams Broadside, Spitfire & Guest Beers. **CHILDREN'S FACILITIES:** menu, high-chairs, food/bottle warming, Play area
GARDEN: enclosed grassed area, tables patio garden
NOTES: Dogs allowed: in bar, in garden, Water, Parking 28

GREAT YELDHAM THE WHITE HART

Poole St CO9 4HJ
☎ 01787 237250 ▯ 01787 238044
e-mail: reservations@whitehartyeldham.co.uk
Dir: On A1017 between Haverhill & Halstead.
Map Ref: TL73

A picturesque timber-framed house and former coaching inn now celebrating its 500th birthday. Located in rural Essex, it has the additional attractions of a large landscaped garden through which runs a tributary of the River Colne. Originally built in the 17th century, the last refurbishment was conducted in consultation with English Heritage to ensure authenticity, and the interior is full of character.

OPEN: 11am-3pm Sun 12-3pm 6pm-11pm Sun 7-10.30pm
BAR MEALS: L served all week 12-2pm D served all week 6.30-9.30 Sun 7-9.30pm **RESTAURANT:** L served all week 12-2 D served all week 6.30-9.30 Sun evening from 7pm Av 3 course à la carte £27.50 Av 2 course fixed price £10.50
BREWERY/COMPANY: Free House ◖: Guest ales (Local & Nationwide), Bottled Belgian Ales. ♀: 12
CHILDREN'S FACILITIES: portions, licence, games, high-chairs, food/bottle warming, Toy box, changing room
GARDEN: Landscaped, large patio area, small river
NOTES: No dogs (ex guide dogs), Parking 40

LITTLE CANFIELD THE LION & LAMB

CM6 1SR
☎ 01279 870257 ▯ 01279 870423
e-mail: info@lionandlamb.co.uk
Dir: M11 J8 B1256 towards Takeley.
Map Ref: TL52

There's a friendly welcome at this traditional country pub restaurant, with its soft red bricks, oak beams and winter log fires. Handy for Stansted airport and the M11, the pub's charm and individuality make it a favourite for business or leisure. Choices from the bar menu include steak and ale pie, local sausages and York ham salad, while the restaurant offers, perhaps, braised lamb shanks with a ragout of white beans, or wild mushroom risotto. There is a separate fresh fish board.

OPEN: 11-11 (Sun 12-10.30) **BAR MEALS:** L served all week 11-10 D served all week 11-10 (Sun 12-10) Av main course £12.50 **RESTAURANT:** L served all week 11-10 D served all week 11-10 (Sun 12-10) Av 3 course à la carte £22.50 Av 3 course fixed price £16 **BREWERY/COMPANY:** Ridley & Sons ◖: Ridleys IPA, Old Bob, Prospect & Seasonal Beers. ♀: 10 **CHILDREN'S FACILITIES:** menu, portions, games, high-chairs, food/bottle warming, baby changing, outdoor play area, Garden, Wendy house, baby changing facility **GARDEN:** Lrg enclosed garden over-looking farmland **NOTES:** No dogs (ex guide dogs), Parking 50

MANNINGTREE THE MISTLEY THORN HOTEL

High St, Mistley CO11 1HE
☎ 01206 392821 ▤ 01206 392133
e-mail: sherrisingleton@aol.com
Map Ref: TM13

Historic pub in the centre of Mistley, which stands on the estuary of the River Stour near Colchester and is the only surviving Georgian port in England today. A previous pub on the same site was the scene of 17th-century witch trials conducted by the self-appointed 'Witchfynder General', Matthew Hopkins. The Mistley Thorn Hotel reopened early in 2004 after a complete refurb.

OPEN: 12-11 **BAR MEALS:** L served all week 12-2.30 D served all week 7-10 Av main course £9.50
RESTAURANT: L served all week 12-2.30 D served Mon-Sat 7-9.30 **BREWERY/COMPANY:** Free House ◀: Greene King IPA, Adnams, St. Peters. ♉: 8
CHILDREN'S FACILITIES: menu, portions, games, high-chairs, food/bottle warming, baby changing **NOTES:** Dogs allowed: in bar, Parking 6

NORTH FAMBRIDGE THE FERRY BOAT INN

Ferry Ln CM3 6LR
☎ 01621 740208
e-mail: sylviaferryboat@aol.com
Dir: From Chelmsford take A130 S then A132 to South Woodham Ferrers, then B1012. R to village. **Map Ref:** TQ89

A 500-year-old inn on the River Crouch, close to the Essex Wildlife Trust's 600-acre sanctuary, with wonderful walks. Low beams and log fires characterise the interior, and there is reputed to be a poltergeist in residence. Typical pub fare includes dishes such as steak and kidney pie, and smoked haddock.

OPEN: 11.30-3 7-11 (Sun 12-4 7-10.30)
BAR MEALS: L served all week 12-2 D served all week 7-9.30 (Sun 12-2.45, 7-9) Av main course £7
RESTAURANT: L served all week 12-1.30 D served all week 7-9 Av 3 course à la carte £15 **BREWERY/COMPANY:** Free House ◀: Shepherd Neame Bishops Finger, Spitfire & Best Bitter. **CHILDREN'S FACILITIES:** menu, high-chairs, food/bottle warming, outdoor play area, swings, toys, books, family room **GARDEN:** Acre, grassed, benches **NOTES:** Dogs allowed: in bar, Parking 30 **ROOMS:** 6 en suite bedrooms 3 family rooms s£30 d£40 (♦♦♦)

PAGLESHAM PLOUGH & SAIL

East End SS4 2EQ
☎ 01702 258242 ▤ 01702 258242
Map Ref: TQ99

Charming, weather-boarded, 17th-century dining pub on the bracing Essex marshes, within easy reach of the rivers Crouch and Roach. For over 300 years this has been a meeting place for the farming, fishing and sailing communities. Inside are pine tables, brasses and low beams, giving the place a quaint, traditional feel. The attractive, well-kept garden has an aviary and is a popular spot during the summer months. Renowned for its good quality food and fresh fish dishes, including fresh skate, tuna steaks, steak and Stilton pie, and Dover sole.

OPEN: 11.30-3 6.45-11 **BAR MEALS:** L served all week 12-2.15 D served all week 7-9.30 **RESTAURANT:** L served all week 12-2.15 D served all week 7-9.30
BREWERY/COMPANY: Free House ◀: Greene King IPA, Ridleys, Mighty Oak, Fuller's London Pride. ♉: 10
CHILDREN'S FACILITIES: menu, play area in garden
GARDEN: Large garden with aviary **NOTES:** No dogs, Parking 30

RADWINTER THE PLOUGH INN

CB10 2TL

☎ 01799 599222

Dir: *4m E of Saffron Walden, at Jct of B2153 & B2154.* **Map Ref:** *TL63*

An Essex woodboard exterior, old beams and a thatched roof characterise this listed inn, once frequented by farm workers. A recent refurbishment program has added a 50-seat restaurant, and turned the Plough from a purely local village pub into a destination gastro-pub, without losing too much of the village pub feel. A typical menu includes the likes of smoked haddock parcels, lamb noisettes, partridge, duck breast, and a variety of home-made pies.

OPEN: 12-3 6-11 (Sun 7-10.30) **BAR MEALS:** L served all week 12-2 D served Mon-Sat 6.30-9 (Sun 12-2.30, Sat 6.30-9.30) **RESTAURANT:** L served all week 12-2 D served Mon-Fri 6.30-9 (Sun 12-2.30, Sat 6.30-9.30) **BREWERY/COMPANY:** Free House **◖:** Adnams Best, IPA, Abbot Ale, Greene King Mild. **♀:** 7 **CHILDREN'S FACILITIES:** menu, portions, high-chairs, food/bottle warming **GARDEN:** Food served outside **NOTES:** Dogs allowed: in bar, Water, Parking 28

SHALFORD THE GEORGE INN NEW

The Street CM7 5HH

☎ 01371 850207 ▤ 01371 851355

e-mail: info@thegeorgeshalford.com

Map Ref: *TL72*

A hundred years ago there were five pubs in Shalford, but the George Inn, which dates back some 500 years, is the one and only now. It's a traditional village pub, with oak beams and open fires, surrounded by lovely countryside. The menu is written up on the blackboard daily, including steaks, chicken breast specialities and popular Oriental and Indian dishes. Fish goes down well too, particularly battered plaice, cod Mornay, and salmon en croute.

OPEN: 12-2 6.30-11 closed Mon evening Nov-Mar **BAR MEALS:** L served all week 12-2.30 Av main course £4.95 **RESTAURANT:** L served all week 12-2.30 D served Mon-Sat 6.30-9.30 Av 3 course à la carte £11.95 **◖:** Greene King IPA, Fullers London Pride, Stella Artois, Guiness. **CHILDREN'S FACILITIES:** portions, high-chairs, food/bottle warming **GARDEN:** Patio **NOTES:** No dogs (ex guide dogs), Parking 25

WENDENS AMBO THE BELL

Royston Rd CB11 4JY

☎ 01799 540382

Dir: *Near Audley End train station.*

Map Ref: *TL53*

Formerly a farmhouse and brewery, this 16th-century timber-framed building is set in a pretty Essex village close to Audley End House. The pub is surrounded by extensive gardens, which have now been landscaped from the summer terrace down to the children's mini golf. The cottage-style rooms have low ceilings and open fires in winter. An allegedly friendly ghost, Mrs Goddard, is also in residence. The kitchen offers smoked haddock florentine, fillet steak with Madeira, mushroom and red wine sauce and chicken with pan fried mushrooms in a tarragon sauce.

OPEN: 11.30-2.30 5-11 (Fri-Sun all day) **BAR MEALS:** L served all week 12-2 D served Mon-Sat 6-9 Av main course £7.85 **RESTAURANT:** L served all week 12-2 D served Mon-Sat 7-9 Av 3 course à la carte £19 **BREWERY/COMPANY:** Free House **◖:** Adnams Bitter, Ansells Mild, Adnams Broadside, Ripley's IPA. **CHILDREN'S FACILITIES:** licence, several acres of garden **NOTES:** Dogs allowed: in bar, in garden, Water, Parking 40

TWICKENHAM THE WHITE SWAN

Riverside TW1 3DN
☎ 020 8892 2166
e-mail: whiteswan@massivepub.com

A traditional pub, the White Swan has been trading here on the Thames since 1690. Outside is a pleasant riverside garden, which attracts plenty of custom in the summer. A popular setting for barbecues and family gatherings. The pub fills up rapidly when there is rugby at Twickenham and an annual charity raft race on the river in July. Typical dishes include calves' liver, bacon and mash, cottage pie, fresh beer-battered cod and chips, steak and sausage and mash.

OPEN: 11-3 (Summer: 11-11, Sun 12-10.30) 5.30-11 (Fri-Sat 11-11, Sun 12-10.30) **BAR MEALS:** L served all week 12-2.30 D served all week 7-10 Av main course £6.50 ◖: IPA, Bombadier, Spitfire, Directors.
CHILDREN'S FACILITIES: portions, food/bottle warming
GARDEN: 15 benches overlooking river **NOTES:** Dogs allowed: in bar

CATEL HOTEL HOUGUE DU POMMIER ★★★ ❁ ♀

Hougue Du Pommier Rd GY5 7FQ
☎ 01481 256531 ▤ 01481 256260
e-mail:
hotel@houguedupommier.guernsey.net

Translated as 'Apple Tree Hill,' this lovely inn dates back to 1712 and stands amid ten

acres of orchards from which cider was once produced. The Tudor Bar used to be the stables of a farmhouse. Expect a varied choice of dishes, including, perhaps, caramelised sea bass on lemon and cracked pepper risotto, and roast lobster with champagne, Cognac and English mustard gratin.

OPEN: 10.30-11.45 **BAR MEALS:** L served all week 12-2.15 D served all week 6.30-9 Av main course £6.45
RESTAURANT: D served all week 6.30-9 Av 3 course à la carte £24.50 Av 5 course fixed price £19.75 ◖: John Smith's, Extra Smooth, Guernsey Best Bitter. ♀: 8
CHILDREN'S FACILITIES: menu, portions, licence, games, high-chairs, food/bottle warming, baby changing
GARDEN: Ten acres, pitch & putt, BBQ, swimming pool
NOTES: No dogs (ex guide dogs), Parking 60
ROOMS: 43 en suite bedrooms 5 family rooms s£36 d£72

ALRESFORD THE GLOBE ON THE LAKE 🐑 ♀

The Soke, Broad St SO24 9DB
☎ 01962 732294 ▤ 01962 736211
e-mail: duveen-conway@supanet.com
Dir: Telephone for directions. **Map Ref:** SU53

In an outstanding setting on the banks of a reed-fringed lake and wildfowl sanctuary, The Globe is a convivial hostelry facing a prime Hampshire waterscape. The lake was created by Bishop de Lucy in the 12th century as a fish pond, and the great weir remains to this day an outstanding piece of medieval engineering. An inn on the site since then was probably all but destroyed during Alresford's great fire of 1689. The Globe was rebuilt as a coaching inn, sitting at the bottom of the town's superb Georgian main street. Waterfowl frequent the garden,

sunbathing between the picnic benches or by the children's playhouse. Inside the bar, a log fire blazes on cooler days, while a smart dining room and unusual garden room share the stunning outlook over the water. In summer freshly prepared food can be enjoyed in the garden and on the heated rear terrace.

OPEN: 11-3 Summer Sat-Sun allday 6-11 Winter Sun 12-8 Closed: 25-26 Dec **BAR MEALS:** L served all week 12-2 D served all week 6.30-9.30 Winter Sun til8 Av main course £8.25 **RESTAURANT:** L served all week 12-2 D served all week 6.30-9 Winter Sun til7
BREWERY/COMPANY: Unique Pub Co ◖: Wadworth 6X, Scottish Courage Directors, Henley Brakspear Bitter, Fuller's London Pride. ♀: 20 **CHILDREN'S FACILITIES:** menu, portions, high-chairs, baby changing, outdoor play area, over 14 in bar, play house, family room **GARDEN:** Large lakeside garden **NOTES:** No dogs (ex guide dogs)

AXFORD THE CROWN INN

RG25 2DZ
☎ 01256 389492 📠 01256 389149
e-mail: thecrowninn.axford@virgin.net
Dir: *Telephone for directions.* **Map Ref:** *SU64*

Small country inn set at the northern edge of the pretty Candover Valley. A selection of real ales is the ideal accompaniment to ginger and lemongrass chicken skewers, chilli con carne or barbequed ribs plus blackboard specials, all cooked to order and served in the two bars or in the dining area. Pie of the day is always worth a try too. A large garden for the summer.

OPEN: 12-3 6-11 Apr-Oct (Sat 12-11 Sun 12-10.30)
BAR MEALS: L served all week 12-2.30 D served all week 6.30-9.30 Av main course £8 **RESTAURANT:** L served all week 12-2.30 D served all week 6.30-9 (Fri Sun 9.30, Sun 8.30) **BREWERY/COMPANY:** Free House 🍺: Becketts Whitewater, Triple FFF Alton Pride, Cheriton Potts Ale, Wadworth 6X. 🍷: 7 **CHILDREN'S FACILITIES:** menu, games, high-chairs, food/bottle warming **GARDEN:** Large Patio, Garden **NOTES:** Dogs allowed: in bar, in garden, Water, Parking 30

BASINGSTOKE HODDINGTON ARMS

Upton Grey RG25 2RL
☎ 01256 862371 📠 01256 862371
e-mail: monca777@aol.com
Dir: *Telephone for directions.* **Map Ref:** *SU65*

Log fires and 18th-century beams contribute to the relaxing atmosphere at this traditional pub, which is located near the duck pond at Upton Grey, Hampshire's best kept village for several years. In addition to a choice of bar snacks and a set price menu of the day, blackboard specials include the likes of cod and pancetta fish cake, minted lamb casserole, and home-cooked Hoddington pies. There's also a peaceful rear terrace and garden.

OPEN: 12-3 6-11 **BAR MEALS:** L served Mon-Sun 12-2 D served Mon-Sat 7-9.30 Av main course £8
RESTAURANT: L served Mon-Sun 12-2 D served Mon-Sun 7-9.30 Av 3 course à la carte £19 Av 2 course fixed price £10 **BREWERY/COMPANY:** Greene King 🍺: Greene King IPA, Old Speckled Hen, Ruddles Best, Fosters. 🍷: 7 **CHILDREN'S FACILITIES:** menu, portions, games, high-chairs, food/bottle warming, outdoor play area, family room **GARDEN:** Large patio with play area **NOTES:** Dogs allowed: in bar, in garden, Water, Parking 30

BENTWORTH THE SUN INN

Sun Hill GU34 5JT
☎ 01420 562338
Map Ref: *SU64*

This delightful flower-decked pub is located down a narrow lane on the edge of Bentworth village; it's the first building in or the last one out, depending on which way you are travelling, and always seems to come as a surprise. The two original cottages have been opened up to make three interconnecting rooms, each with its own log fire and authentic brick/wood floors. Lots of pews, settles and scrubbed pine tables add to the relaxed atmosphere.

OPEN: 12-3 6-11 (Sun 12-10.30) **BAR MEALS:** L served all week 12-2 D served all week 7-9.30
BREWERY/COMPANY: Free House 🍺: Cheriton Pots Ale, Ringwood Best & Old Thumper, Brakspear Bitter, Fuller's London Pride. **CHILDREN'S FACILITIES:** menu, high-chairs, food/bottle warming, family room **NOTES:** Dogs allowed: in bar, in garden, Water

BROCKENHURST   THE FILLY INN

Lymington Rd, Setley SO42 7UF
☎ 01590 623449 📠 01590 623449
e-mail: pub@fillyinn.co.uk
Map Ref: *SU30*

One of the most picturesque, cosy traditional pubs in the heart of the New Forest. Locals attest to frequent sightings of George, the resident ghost, thought to be a long-dead, repentant highwayman. The far from spooky menu offers a wide range of bar snacks of baguettes and filled jacket potatoes, as well as home-cooked English ham with egg and chips, beef lasagne and home-baked pies of the day.

OPEN: 10-11 **BAR MEALS:** L served all week 10-2.15 D served all week 6.30-10 **RESTAURANT:** L served all week 10-2.15 D served all week 6.30-10 Av 3 course à la carte £19.50 **BREWERY/COMPANY:** Free House ◖: Ringwood Best, Old Thumper, Badger Tanglefoot. **CHILDREN'S FACILITIES:** menu, portions, games, high-chairs, food/bottle warming, outdoor play area, garden **GARDEN:** About 0.75 acres of lawn **NOTES:** Dogs allowed: in bar, in garden, in bedrooms, Water, Parking 90 **ROOMS:** 6 bedrooms 5 en suite s£55 d£65 (♦♦♦) no children overnight

BROOK   THE BELL INN ★★★ ❀

SO43 7HE
☎ 023 80812214 📠 023 80813958
e-mail: bell@bramshaw.co.uk
Dir: *From M27 J1 (Cadnam) take B3078 signed Brook, 0.5m on R.* **Map Ref:** *SU21*

Dating from 1782, this handsome listed inn is part of Bramshaw Golf Club and has remained in the same family for its entire history. The inn, a free house with Ringwood and Courage real ales, retains many period features, particularly the imposing inglenook fireplace in the bar and the beamed bedrooms in the oldest part of the building. The quality of cuisine is a source of pride, reflected in a bar menu that changes daily.

OPEN: 11-11 (Sun 12-10.30) **BAR MEALS:** L served all week 12-2.30 D served all week 6.30-9.30 Av main course £8.95 **RESTAURANT:** L served all week 12-2 D served all week 6.30-9.30 Av 3 course fixed price £14.95 **BREWERY/COMPANY:** Free House ◖: Ringwood Best, Scottish Courage Courage Best, John Smiths, Worthington. **CHILDREN'S FACILITIES:** menu, portions, games, high-chairs, food/bottle warming, baby changing, play area in garden, family room **NOTES:** in garden, No dogs (ex guide dogs), Parking 60 **ROOMS:** 25 en suite bedrooms s£65 d£90

CHALTON   THE RED LION ♈ 🍷

PO8 0BG
☎ 023 92592246 📠 023 92596915
e-mail: redlionchalton@aol.com
Dir: *Just off A3 between Horndean & Petersfield. Take exit near Queen Elizabeth Country Park.* **Map Ref:** *SU71*

Thatched and immaculately maintained, Hampshire's oldest pub dates back to 1147, and was originally a workshop for craftsmen building the Norman church opposite. Imaginative dishes from the daily menu include guinea fowl in Calvados, teriyaki beef and fresh Mahi Mahi fish in coconut, as well as the usual pub snacks. Large garden has spectacular views of the South Downs.

OPEN: 11-3 6-11 Rest: 25-26 Dec closed evening **BAR MEALS:** L served all week 12-2 D served Mon-Sat 6.30-9.30 Av main course £8.75 **RESTAURANT:** L served all week 12-2 D served Mon-Sat 6.30-9.30 **BREWERY/COMPANY:** Gales ◖: Gales Butser, Winter Brew, GB & HSB. 🍷: 20 **CHILDREN'S FACILITIES:** menu, portions, games, high-chairs, food/bottle warming, outdoor play area, family dining room, family room **GARDEN:** Spectacular views over South Downs **NOTES:** Dogs welcome in public bar & garden, Parking 80

CHAWTON · THE GREYFRIAR ♀

Winchester Rd GU34 1SB
☎ 01420 83841
e-mail: info@thegreyfriar.co.uk
Dir: Chawton lies just off the A31 near Alton. Access to Chawton via the A31/A32 J. Sign posted Jane Austen's House. Map Ref: SU73

Built well over 400 years ago, the interior architecture clearly shows origins as a terrace of cottages. By 1847 the building was a 'beer shop', and by 1871 it had become a proper pub, the Chawton Arms. In 1894 a licence was granted in the name of the Greyfriar. The simple lunch menu offers freshly-baked baguettes, ploughman's, Greyfriar burger and haddock and chips, for example, while on the daily main menu tuna, shark and mahi mahi may appear, alongside sirloin, fillet and rump steaks, sausage and mash and Thai curries - all fresh and home made. Opposite the pub is Jane Austen's house, a museum since 1949.

OPEN: 12-11 (Mon-Fri 12-11, Sun 12-10.30)
BAR MEALS: L served all week 12-2 D served Mon-Sat 7-9.30 Av main course £8.95 **RESTAURANT:** L served all week 12-2 D served Mon-Sat 7-9.30 🍺: Fuller's London Pride, Chiswick & ESB, Seasonal Ales. ♀: 7
CHILDREN'S FACILITIES: menu, portions, games, food/bottle warming, outdoor play area **GARDEN:** Paved area, sun trap, picnic tables **NOTES:** Dogs allowed: in bar, in garden, Water, Parking 16

DAMERHAM · THE COMPASSES INN ♦♦♦♦  ♀

SP6 3HQ
☎ 01725 518231 📠 01725 518880
e-mail: info@compassesinn.net
Dir: From Fordingbridge (A338) follow signs for Sandleheath/Damerham. Or signs from B3078. Map Ref: SU11

Located in the village centre overlooking the cricket pitch, this 300-year-old coaching inn was once almost self-sufficient, with its own brew tower, dairy, butchery and well. Atmosphere a-plenty in both of the bars, and in the cottagey bedrooms which, with their proximity to famous chalk rivers, are named after famous trout flies.

OPEN: 11-3 6-11 (all day Sat, Sun 12-4, 7-10.30)
BAR MEALS: L served all week 12-2.30 D served all week 7-9.30 Sun 7-9 Av main course £7.95 **RESTAURANT:** L served all week 12-2.30 D served all week 7-9.30 Sun 7-9 Av 3 course à la carte £17 **BREWERY/COMPANY:** Free House 🍺: Ringwood Best, Hop Back Summer Lightning, Interbrew Bass. ♀: 8 **CHILDREN'S FACILITIES:** menu, portions, licence, high-chairs, food/bottle warming, baby changing, swings & see saw **GARDEN:** Large garden, water feature **NOTES:** Dogs allowed: in bar, in garden, By arrangement, Parking 30
ROOMS: 6 en suite bedrooms 1 family room s£39.50 d£69

DUMMER · THE QUEEN INN ♀

Down St RG25 2AD
☎ 01256 397367 📠 01256 397601
Dir: from M3 J7, follow signs to Dummer. Map Ref: SU54

You can dine by candlelight at this 16th-century village pub, with its low beams and huge open log fire. Everything is home made, from the soup and light bites to the famous fish and chips with beer batter, fresh crab cakes, and prime steaks. The steak and kidney pudding is only for the heartier appetite!

OPEN: 11.30-2.30 6-11 (Sun 12-3 7-10.30)
BAR MEALS: L served all week 12-2.30 D served all week 6-9.30 **RESTAURANT:** L served all week 12-1.30 D served all week 6-9.30 **BREWERY/COMPANY:** Unique Pub Co 🍺: Courage Best & John Smiths, Fuller's London Pride, Old Speckled Hen. ♀: 8 **CHILDREN'S FACILITIES:** portions, high-chairs, food/bottle warming **GARDEN:** Benches, tables, chairs **NOTES:** No dogs (ex guide dogs), Parking 20

EAST MEON   YE OLDE GEORGE INN

Church St GU32 1NH
☎ 01730 823481 📄 01730 823759
Dir: *S of A272 (Winchester/Petersfield). 1.5m from Petersfield turn L opp church.*
Map Ref: *SU62*

In a lovely village on the River Meon, a charming 15th-century inn close to a magnificent Norman church, and near to Queen Elizabeth Country Park. Its open fires, heavy beams and rustic artefacts create an ideal setting for relaxing over a good choice of real ales or enjoying freshly prepared bar food. A new team took over at the beginning of 2004, so reports on their progress are welcomed.

OPEN: 11-3 (Sun 12-3, 7-10.30) 6-11
BAR MEALS: L served all week 12-2 D served all week 7-9
RESTAURANT: L served all week 12-2 D served all week 7-9
BREWERY/COMPANY: Hall & Woodhouse 🍺: Badger Best, Tanglefoot & King & Barnes Sussex.
CHILDREN'S FACILITIES: menu, family room
GARDEN: Patio Area **NOTES:** Dogs allowed: Parking 30

EASTON   THE CHESTNUT HORSE

SO21 1EG
☎ 01962 779257 📄 01962 779037
Dir: *From M3 J9 take A33 towards Basingstoke, then B3047. Take 2nd R, then 1st L.* **Map Ref:** *SU53*

A delightful dining pub with a beautiful village setting in the Itchen Valley surrounded by thatched cottages. There's plenty of 16th-century character in the open fires and low-beamed ceilings, which are hung with old beer mugs and chamber pots; intimate dining areas are divided by standing timbers. The Chestnut Horse is great for walkers, with the Three Castles Path passing right by.

OPEN: 11-3 5.30-11 (Sun eve Winter closes at 6pm)
BAR MEALS: L served all week 12-2.30 D served all week 6.30-9.30 **RESTAURANT:** L served all week 12-2.30 D served all week 6.30-9.30 Av 2 course fixed price £9.95
BREWERY/COMPANY: Free House 🍺: Interbrew Bass, Scottish Courage Courage Best, Chestnut Horse Special, Fuller's London Pride. 🍷: 9 **CHILDREN'S FACILITIES:** menu, portions, food/bottle warming **GARDEN:** Decked patio, heaters **NOTES:** Dogs allowed: in bar, in garden, Water, Parking 40

CRICKETERS INN

SO21 1EJ
☎ 01962 779353 📄 01962 779010
e-mail: info@cricketers-easton.com
Dir: *M3 J9, A33 towards Basingstoke. Turn R at Kingsworthy onto B3047. 0.75m turn R.*
Map Ref: *SU53*

The regulars liked this pub so much, they bought it! Under the new ownership of three devoted former customers, this traditional free house, in a pretty village close to the River Itchen is thriving. Regularly changing guest ales from all over the UK combined with hearty food and a good atmosphere makes this a popular establishment. There is an extensive bar snack menu, or a varied carte, offering many accomplished dishes, including whole plaice with prawn and

lobster bisque sauce, Thai chicken, 'Curry of the week' and the house speciality - ribs with a variety of accompaniments.

OPEN: 12-3 6-11 (Sun 12-3 7-10.30)
BAR MEALS: L served all week 12-2 D served Mon-Sat 7-9 Av main course £7.95 **RESTAURANT:** L served all week 12-2 D served Mon-Sat 7-9 **BREWERY/COMPANY:** Free House 🍺: Ringwood, Otter, Changing guest ales.
CHILDREN'S FACILITIES: menu, portions, high-chairs, food/bottle warming **GARDEN:** Paved patio at front **NOTES:** Dogs allowed: Parking 16

EAST TYTHERLEY STAR INN ◆◆◆◆

SO51 0LW
☎ 01794 340225 ▯ 01794 340225
e-mail: info@starinn-uk.com
Dir: 5m N of Romsey off A3057. Take L turn Dunbridge B3084. Left for Awbridge & Lockerley. Through Lockerley then 1m. **Map Ref:** *SU22*

An award-winning 16th-century country inn adjoining the village cricket ground, on a quiet road between Romsey with its abbey, and the cathedral city of Salisbury. Dine where you like, in the bar, at dark-wood tables in the main dining room, or outside on the patio, where you can also play chess on a king-sized board. There are two menus, the carte and the classical.

OPEN: 11-2.30 6-11 Closed: 26 Dec
BAR MEALS: L served Tue-Sun 12-2 D served Tue-Sun 7-9
RESTAURANT: L served Tue-Sun 12-2 D served Tue-Sun 7-9
Av 3 course à la carte £20 **BREWERY/COMPANY:** Free House ◀: Ringwood Best plus guest beers. ♀: 10
CHILDREN'S FACILITIES: portions, games, high-chairs, food/bottle warming, outdoor play area **GARDEN:** Patio area, country garden with furniture. **NOTES:** Dogs allowed: in bar, in garden, Water bowl, Parking 60 **ROOMS:** 3 en suite bedrooms 2 family rooms s£50 d£70

FORDINGBRIDGE THE AUGUSTUS JOHN

116 Station Rd SP6 1DG
☎ 01425 652098
e-mail: peter@augustusjohn.com
Dir: Telephone for directions. **Map Ref:** *SU11*

Named after the renowned British painter who lived in the village (the pub was also his local), this unassuming brick building has developed a reputation as a smart dining venue. The daily changing menu is based on seasonally available produce. Liver and bacon with mash, steak and Guinness casserole, and rack of lamb are favourite dishes along with daily fresh fish and vegetarian specialities such as baked avocado with fresh tomato and basil concasse.

OPEN: 11.30-3.30 6-12 **BAR MEALS:** L served all week 11.30-2 D served all week 6.30-9 Av main course £10
RESTAURANT: L served all week 11.30-2 D served all week 6.30-9 Av 3 course à la carte £18
BREWERY/COMPANY: Eldridge Pope ◀: Bass, Tetley, Flowers IPA. ♀: 8 **CHILDREN'S FACILITIES:** menu, portions, high-chairs, food/bottle warming, outdoor play area
NOTES: Dogs allowed: in bar, Parking 40

FRITHAM THE ROYAL OAK

SO43 7HJ
☎ 02380 812606 ▯ 02380 814066
e-mail: royaloakfritham@btopenworld.com
Map Ref: *SU21*

Unaltered for some 100 years, this small, thatched 17th-century traditional country pub

is deep in the New Forest and maintains its long tradition of preferring conversation to the distractions of juke box and fruit machines. With open fires and overlooking the forest and its own working farm, it is ideally located for walkers and ramblers, with ploughman's lunches and home-baked quiches to munch on, and home-made evening meals on two nights per week. The garden has lovely views of the valley, and a pétanque terrain.

OPEN: 11-3 6-11 (Sat 11-11, Sun 12-11)
BAR MEALS: L served all week 12-2.30 D served 2 days a wk winter only 7-9 Av main course £5
BREWERY/COMPANY: Free House ◀: Ringwood Best & Fortyniner, Hop Back Summer Lightning, Palmers Dorset Gold.
CHILDREN'S FACILITIES: food/bottle warming, baby changing **GARDEN:** Large, countryside views, ample benches **NOTES:** Dogs allowed: in bar, in garden, Water, biscuits, No credit cards

IBSLEY   OLD BEAMS INN ♀

Salisbury Rd BH24 3PP
☎ 01425 473387
Dir: *On A338 between Ringwood & Salisbury.*
Map Ref: SU10

The cruck beam is clearly visible from the outside of this thatched, 14th-century building. In addition to the restaurant there is also a popular buffet counter. Located in the Avon Valley and handy for the New Forest.

OPEN: 12-11 Sun 12-10.30   **BAR MEALS:** L served all week 12-9 D served all week Av main course £6.50
RESTAURANT: 1 Av 3 course à la carte £15
BREWERY/COMPANY: Greene King 🍺: IPA, Ringwood. ♀: 24
CHILDREN'S FACILITIES: menu, family room
GARDEN: Outdoor eating **NOTES:** Parking 120

LYMINGTON   MAYFLOWER INN ♀

Kings Saltern Rd SO41 3QD
☎ 01590 672160 📠 01590 679180
e-mail: info@themayflower.uk.com
Dir: *A337 towards New Milton, L at rdbt by White Hart, L to Rookes Ln, R at mini-rdbt, pub 0.75m.* **Map Ref:** *SZ39*

Solidly built mock-Tudor inn by the water's edge with views over the Solent and Lymington River. It's a favourite with yachtsmen and walkers with dogs, and welcomes families with its purpose-built play area for children and on-going summer barbecue, weather permitting. The bar menu offers sandwiches, light meals, main meals and puds. For dinner in the non-smoking restaurant, expect starters such as antipasto

platter or seared scallops; and mains like roasted duck sizzler.

OPEN: 11-11 (Sun 12-10.30) **BAR MEALS:** L served all week 12-9.30 D served all week 6.30-9.30 Av main course £7 **RESTAURANT:** L served all week 12-9.30 D served all week 6.30-9.30 Av 3 course à la carte £20
BREWERY/COMPANY: Enterprise Inns 🍺: Ringwood Best, Fuller's London Pride, Greene King Abbot Ale & Old Speckled Hen. ♀: 8 **CHILDREN'S FACILITIES:** menu, portions, high-chairs, food/bottle warming, large garden with play area
GARDEN: Large lawns, decking area **NOTES:** Dogs allowed: in bar, in garden, in bedrooms, Water, baskets, Parking 30

LYNDHURST   THE TRUSTY SERVANT 🐑

Minstead SO43 7FY
☎ 02380 812137
Map Ref: *SU30*

Popular New Forest pub overlooking the village green, retaining many original Victorian features. The famous sign is taken from a 16th-century Winchester scholar's painting portraying the qualities of an ideal college servant. The six en suite bedrooms are named after Sherlock Holmes, whose creator Sir Arthur Conan Doyle is buried in Minstead church, and the locally-connected kings William I and II.

OPEN: 11-11 (Sun 12-10.30) **BAR MEALS:** L served all week 12-2.30 D served all week 7-10
RESTAURANT: L served all week 12-2.30 D served all week 7-10 **BREWERY/COMPANY:** Enterprise Inns 🍺: Ringwood Best, Fuller's London Pride, Wadworth 6X, Gale's HSB.
CHILDREN'S FACILITIES: menu, portions, high-chairs, food/bottle warming, family room **GARDEN:** Heated barn area seats 30, picnic benches **NOTES:** Dogs allowed: in bar, in garden, Water, Parking 16

MAPLEDURWELL   THE GAMEKEEPERS

Tunworth Rd RG25 2LU
☎ 01256 322038 ▤ 01256 322038
e-mail: phil_costello64@hotmail.com
Dir: *3m from J6 M3. Turn R at the Hatch pub on A30 towards Hook. Gamekeepers is signposted.* **Map Ref:** *SU65*

A very rural location for this 19th-century pub, which has a large secluded garden and, unusually, a well at its centre. An extensive menu is offered and all the food is made on the premises. Expect the likes of monkfish and tiger prawns in a creamy garlic sauce, duck breast on a bed of ginger and coriander noodles, or tenderloin of pork in sage and onion gravy. Game is also a feature in season.

OPEN: 12-3 6-11 **BAR MEALS:** L served all week 12-2.30 D served all week 6.30-9.30 Sun 12-3 Av main course £10.75 **RESTAURANT:** L served all week 12-2.30 D served all week 6.30-9.30 Sun 12-3 Av 3 course à la carte £21.50 **BREWERY/COMPANY:** Hall & Woodhouse ◖: Badger Best, Tanglefoot, Sussex Ales, Badgers Smooth. ♀: 12 **CHILDREN'S FACILITIES:** menu, high-chairs, food/bottle warming **GARDEN:** Large, secluded garden area **NOTES:** Dogs allowed: in garden, Water, Parking 50

MEONSTOKE   THE BUCKS HEAD

Bucks Head Hill SO32 3NA
☎ 01489 877313
Dir: *by the jct of A32 & B2150.*
Map Ref: *SU61*

Surrounded by fields and woodland, this beautiful 16th-century inn on the banks of the River Meon is popular with locals as well as visitors. This is ideal walking country, with Old Winchester Hill and the former Meon Valley Railway walking trail nearby. Old Speckled Hen, Ruddles County and regular guest beers are served beside open fires in the two character bars, and there's a range of home-cooked meals.

OPEN: 11-3 6-11 (Summer-open all day) **BAR MEALS:** L served all week 12-1.45 D served Mon-Sat 7-8.45 Sun 12-2.30 Av main course £6.95 **RESTAURANT:** L served all week 12-1.45 D served all week 7-8.45 sun 12-2.30 **BREWERY/COMPANY:** Greene King ◖: Old Speckled Hen, Ruddles County, IPA, Guest Beer (changes regularly). **CHILDREN'S FACILITIES:** menu, portions, family room **GARDEN:** Riverside garden on village green **NOTES:** Dogs allowed: in bar, in garden, Water provided, Parking 40

MICHELDEVER   HALF MOON & SPREAD EAGLE ♀

Winchester Rd SO21 3DG
☎ 01962 774339 ▤ 01962 774834
e-mail: r_c_tolfree@btopenworld.com
Dir: *Take A33 from Winchester towards Basingstoke. After 5m turn L after petrol station. Pub 0.5m on R.* **Map Ref:** *SU53*

Old drovers' inn located in the heart of a pretty thatched and timbered Hampshire village, overlooking the cricket green. The pub, comprising three neatly furnished interconnecting rooms, has a real local feel and has reverted to its old name having been the Dever Arms for eight years. An extensive menu ranges through Sunday roasts, Moon burgers, honeyed salmon supreme with lime courgettes, fresh battered cod, and half shoulder of minted lamb.

OPEN: 12-3 6-11 (Sun 7-10.30) **BAR MEALS:** L served all week 12-2 D served all week 6-9 Fri & Sat food served til 9.30 Av main course £10 **RESTAURANT:** L served all week 12-2 D served all week 6-9 Av 3 course à la carte £19 **BREWERY/COMPANY:** Greene King ◖: Greene King IPA Abbot Ale, XX Mild and guest ales. ♀: 7 **CHILDREN'S FACILITIES:** menu, high-chairs, outdoor play area, animals, play equipment **GARDEN:** Patio area, tables, chairs, grass area **NOTES:** Dogs allowed: in bar, in garden, Water, Parking 20

NORTH WALTHAM   THE FOX ♀

RG25 2BE
☎ 01256 397288 ▤ 01256 398564
e-mail: info@thefox.org
Dir: *From M3 J7 take A30 towards Winchester.*
Village signposted on R. Take 2nd signed rd.
Map Ref: *SU54*

Built as three farm cottages in 1624, this peaceful village pub is situated down a quiet country lane enjoying splendid views across fields and farmland. Its three large flat gardens also have attractive flower beds. The menu changes monthly to reflect the seasonal produce available.

OPEN: 11-12 (all day w/end) **BAR MEALS:** L served all week 12.30-2.30 D served all week 6.30-10 Av main course £8 **RESTAURANT:** L served all week 12.30-2.30 D served all week 6.30-10 Av 3 course à la carte £19.50 **BREWERY/COMPANY:** 🍺: Scottish Courage Courage Best, Gales HSB, Oakleaf Farmhouse, Bombardier. ♀: 11 **CHILDREN'S FACILITIES:** menu, portions, licence, high-chairs, food/bottle warming, outdoor, activity area **GARDEN:** Large, flat grass area, countryside views **NOTES:** Dogs allowed: in bar, Water, Parking 40

PORTSMOUTH & SOUTHSEA   THE STILL & WEST 🐑 ♀

2 Bath Square, Old Portsmouth PO1 2JL
☎ 023 92821567 ▤ 02302 826560
Dir: *Bath Square, top of Broad Street.*
Map Ref: *SZ69*

Nautically themed pub close to HMS Victory and enjoying excellent views of Portsmouth Harbour and the Isle of Wight. Built in 1504, the main bar ceilings are hand-painted with pictures relating to local shipping history. Plenty of fish on the menu including trout, black beam, seafood paella, and the famous Still & West fish grill of fresh fish and mussels.

OPEN: 12-11 Rest: Mon-Sat 10-11, Sun 11-10.30 **BAR MEALS:** L served all week 12-3 Sun L 12-4 Av main course £5.95 **RESTAURANT:** L served all week 12-2.30 D served all week 6-9 Av 3 course à la carte £17 **BREWERY/COMPANY:** Gales 🍺: HSB, GB, Butsers, Stella. ♀: 7 **CHILDREN'S FACILITIES:** menu, portions, high-chairs, food/bottle warming, baby changing room **GARDEN:** Food served outside. Overlooks harbour **NOTES:** In the garden only, No dogs (ex guide dogs)

ROCKBOURNE   THE ROSE & THISTLE 🐑 ♀

SP6 3NL
☎ 01725 518236
e-mail: enquiries@roseandthistle.co.uk
Dir: *Rockbourne is signposted from B3078 and*
from A354. **Map Ref:** *SU11*

Two long, low whitewashed cottages, dating from the 16th century, were converted nearly 200 years ago to create this downland village pub, still full of charming original features. It is a picture postcard pub if ever there was one, with a stunning rose arch, flowers around the door and a delightful village setting. Open fires make it a cosy retreat in colder weather, while the summer sun brings visitors into the neat front garden.

OPEN: 11-3 6-11 Oct-Apr closed Sun from 8 **BAR MEALS:** L served all week 12-2.30 D served all week 6.30-9.30 Sun seasonal variation Av main course £12 **RESTAURANT:** L served all week 12-2.30 D served all week 6.30-9.30 Sun seasonal variation Av 3 course à la carte £18 **BREWERY/COMPANY:** Free House 🍺: Fuller's London Pride, Adnams Broadside, Wadworth 6X, Hop Back Summer Lightning. ♀: 18 **CHILDREN'S FACILITIES:** portions, licence, high-chairs, food/bottle warming **GARDEN:** An English country garden **NOTES:** No dogs (ex guide dogs), Parking 28

ROMSEY THE DUKES HEAD

Greatbridge Rd SO51 0HB
☎ 01794 514450 ▤ 01794 518102
Map Ref: SU32

This rambling 400-year-old pub, covered in flowers during the summer, nestles in the Test Valley just a stone's throw from the famous trout river. Main courses might be braised oxtail in red wine topped with a gratinée creamy mash; pan-fried duck breast served on a bed of wilted spinach with a red wine sauce spiked with raspberries, or trout fillet with a beurre blanc sauce. Light lunches are available, and there is a very extensive wine list. Everything is made on the premises, except puff pastry and bread.

OPEN: 11-11 **BAR MEALS:** L served Tue-Sun 12-2.30 D served all week 6-9.30 Av main course £10.35 **RESTAURANT:** L served all week 12-2.30 D served all week 6-9 Av 3 course à la carte £22 **BREWERY/COMPANY:** Free House ☎: Fuller's London Pride, Greene King IPA, Courage Directors. ♉: 8 **CHILDREN'S FACILITIES:** portions, food/bottle warming **GARDEN:** Large garden near river, approx 60 seats **NOTES:** Dogs allowed: in bar, in garden, Parking 50

THE MILL ARMS ◆◆◆◆

Barley Hill, Dunbridge SO51 0LF
☎ 01794 340401 ▤ 01794 340401
e-mail: millarms@aol.co.uk
Map Ref: SU32

This 18th century coaching inn is set in a picturesque Test Valley village. The inn is surrounded by colourful gardens and offers a warm welcome inside, with its flagstone floors, oak beams and open fires; there's even a skittle alley with its own private bar to hire! The fun continues with the selection of real ales: Test Tickler is specially brewed for the pub, or how about a pint of Mottisfont Meddler? The wide selection of food includes traditional pub favourites, as well as a range of steaks and salads. Starters include crab cakes on a sweet chilli sauce, followed by home-made steak and ale pie; or pan-fried duck breast with apricot and thyme gravy.

OPEN: 12-3 (open all day Fri-Sun) 6-11 **BAR MEALS:** L served all week 12-2.30 D served all week 6-9.30 **RESTAURANT:** L served all week D served all week **BREWERY/COMPANY:** Free House ☎: Dunbridge Test Tickler, Mottisfont Meddler. **CHILDREN'S FACILITIES:** menu, portions, high-chairs, food/bottle warming, outdoor play area, Wendy house & bouncy castle **GARDEN:** Large garden, patio area **NOTES:** Dogs allowed: in bar, in garden, Water, Parking 90 **ROOMS:** 6 en suite s£50 d£50

ROWLAND'S CASTLE THE FOUNTAIN INN ◆◆◆◆

34 The Green PO9 6AB
☎ 023 9241 2291 ▤ 02392 412 291
e-mail: fountaininn@amserve.com
Map Ref: SU71

Once a coach house, and now a lovingly refurbished Georgian building on a village green. Owned by one-time Van Morrison band member Herbie Armstrong, who holds frequent live music gigs here. New menus from a Savoy-trained chef offer 'real' corned beef, parsnip and carrot hash; and potted Selsey crab and prawns at both lunchtime and dinner. Some dishes, like beetroot risotto, broad beans and Parmesan, for instance, appear for dinner only.

OPEN: 12-2.30 5-11 (Fri-Sun 12-11) **BAR MEALS:** L served Tue-Sun 12-3 D served Tue-Sat 6-10.30 **RESTAURANT:** L served Tue-Sun 12-3 D served Tue-Sat 6-10.30 ☎: Ruddles IPA, Abbot, Ruddles Cask, Kronenberg 1994. **CHILDREN'S FACILITIES:** portions, high-chairs, outdoor play area, slides swings & climbing frame **GARDEN:** Enclosed back garden, eight tables **NOTES:** Dogs allowed: in bar, in garden, in bedrooms, Parking 20 **ROOMS:** 4 en suite 1 family room s£25 d£50

ST MARY BOURNE THE BOURNE VALLEY INN

SP11 6BT
☎ 01264 738361 📄 01264 738126
e-mail:
bournevalleyinn@wessexinns.fsnet.co.uk
Map Ref: SU45

Located in the charming Bourne valley, this popular traditional inn is the ideal setting for conferences, exhibitions, weddings and other notable occasions. The riverside garden abounds with wildlife, and children can happily let off steam in the special play area. Typical menu includes deep fried Brie or a cocktail of prawns, followed by rack of lamb with a redcurrant and port sauce, salmon and prawn tagliatelle, steak and mushroom pie, crispy haddock and chips and warm duck salad.

OPEN: 11-11 **BAR MEALS:** L served all week 12-2 D served all week 7-9 **RESTAURANT:** L served all week 12-2 D served all week 7-9.30 **BREWERY/COMPANY:** Free House 🍺: Draught Bass, Flowers, Brakspeare.
CHILDREN'S FACILITIES: menu, portions, licence, high-chairs, food/bottle warming, outdoor play area, Outdoor play, climbing area **GARDEN:** Riverside, secluded garden **NOTES:** Dogs allowed: in bar, Water & biscuits provided, Parking 50 **ROOMS:** 9 en suite s£50 d£60 (♦♦♦)

SOUTHAMPTON THE WHITE STAR TAVERN & DINING ROOMS ♗

28 Oxford St SO14 3DJ
☎ 020 8082 1990 📄 023 8090 4982
e-mail: manager@whitestartavern.co.uk
Map Ref: SU41

Located in the historic and sensitively restored part of the city close to Ocean Village and the marina, what was formerly a seafarers' hotel is a blend of old and new; a cosy bar area with original flagstone floors and fireplaces, and a stylish panelled dining room with huge windows. The tavern prides itself on a frequently changing modern British menu using fresh and locally sourced ingredients. Quality dishes include terrine of Dorset ham and parsley, crab and cucumber risotto, and confit lamb shoulder. On sunny days patrons can enjoy a cocktail and watch the world go by while dining alfresco on pavement seating.

OPEN: 12-11 Closed: 25-26 Dec, 1 Jan
BAR MEALS: L served all week 12-3 D served all week 3pm Fri & Sat Av main course £13 **RESTAURANT:** L served all week 12-3 D served all week 6.30-10.30 Sun 12-9 Av 3 course à la carte £20 🍺: London Pride, Bass. ♗: 8
CHILDREN'S FACILITIES: portions, high-chairs, food/bottle warming **NOTES:** No dogs (ex guide dogs)

SPARSHOLT THE PLOUGH INN ♗

Main Rd SO21 2NW
☎ 01962 776353 📄 01962 776400
Dir: From Winchester take B3049(A272) W, take L turn to village of Sparsholt. The Plough Inn is 1m down the lane. **Map Ref:** SU43

The Plough became an alehouse around 150 years ago. The main bar and dining areas blend together very harmoniously, helped by judicious use of farmhouse-style pine tables, a mix of wooden and upholstered seats, collections of agricultural implements, stone jars, wooden wine box end-panels and dried hops. The dining tables to the left of the entrance have a view across open fields to wooded downland. Booking is definitely advised for any meal.

OPEN: 11-3 6-11 (Sun 12-3, 6-10.30) Closed: 25 Dec
BAR MEALS: L served all week 12-2 D served all week 6-9 Av main course £10 **RESTAURANT:** L served all week 12-2 D served all week 6-9 Av 3 course à la carte £22.50
BREWERY/COMPANY: Wadworth 🍺: Wadworth Henry's IPA, 6X, Farmers Glory & Old Timer. ♗: 12
CHILDREN'S FACILITIES: menu, high-chairs, food/bottle warming, outdoor play area, play fort, donkey paddock, family room **GARDEN:** Patio, Lawn, Play Area **NOTES:** Dogs allowed: in bar, on leads, Parking 90

STOCKBRIDGE THE PEAT SPADE

Longstock SO20 6DR
☎ 01264 810612
e-mail: peat.spade@virgin.net
Dir: *Telephone for directions.* **Map Ref:** *SU33*

Tucked away in the Test Valley close to Hampshire's finest chalk stream is this red-brick and gabled Victorian pub with unusual paned windows. It offers an informal atmosphere in which to enjoy a decent pint of Hampshire ale and a satisfying meal chosen from the menu which might include salmon, haddock and scallop fish pie; local pork medallions with hoi sin sauce; or baked goat's cheese with sweet potatoes and parsley oil dressing. Good use of local organic produce.

OPEN: 11.30-3 6.30-11 Closed: Dec 25-26 & 31Dec-1 Jan Rest: Sun closed eve **BAR MEALS:** L served Tue-Sun 12-2.30 D served Tue-Sun 7-9.30 **RESTAURANT:** L served Tue-Sun 12-2 D served Tue-Sun 7-9.30
BREWERY/COMPANY: Free House ◀: Ringwood Best, Ringwood 49er & guest ales.
CHILDREN'S FACILITIES: portions, games, food/bottle warming **GARDEN:** Raised terrace, teak seating, lawn area **NOTES:** Dogs allowed: in bar, on a lead, Parking 22, No credit cards

STRATFIELD TURGIS THE WELLINGTON ARMS ★★★

RG27 0AS
☎ 01256 882214 📄 01256 882934
e-mail: wellington.arms@virgin.net
Dir: *On A33 between Basingstoke & Reading.*
Map Ref: *SU65*

Standing at an entrance to the ancestral home of the Duke of Wellington, this 17th-century former farmhouse is now a Grade II listed hotel with some period bedrooms in the original building. Well-kept real ales go down well with a good range of snacks, sandwiches, omelettes, pastas, ploughman's and salads in the bar. A changing carte in the restaurant may offer main courses such as pan-fried cod fillet on aubergine mash, Chinese-style duck stir fry, and blue cheese and leek tart with salad.

OPEN: 11-11 (Sun 12-10.30) **BAR MEALS:** L served all week 12-2.30 D served all week 6-10
RESTAURANT: L served Sun-Fri 12-2 D served Mon-Sat 6.30-9.30 **BREWERY/COMPANY:** Woodhouse Inns ◀: Badger Best Bitter & Tanglefoot.
CHILDREN'S FACILITIES: portions, high-chairs, food/bottle warming **NOTES:** Dogs allowed: in garden, in bedrooms, Parking 60 **ROOMS:** 30 en suite bedrooms 2 family rooms s£65 d£75

WARSASH THE JOLLY FARMER COUNTRY INN

29 Fleet End Rd SO31 9JH
☎ 01489 572500 📄 01489 885847
e-mail: mail@thejollyfarmeruk.com
Dir: *Exit M27 Jct 9, head towards A27 Fareham, turn R onto Warsash Rd Follow for 2m then L onto Fleet End Rd.* **Map Ref:** *SU40*

Not far from the Hamble river, this pub has an Irish landlord with a famous sense of humour - you won't miss the multi-coloured classic car parked outside. The pub also has its own golf society and cricket team. The bars are furnished in rustic style with farming equipment on walls and ceilings, there's a patio for al fresco eating, and a purpose-built children's play area. The menu offers local fish, salads and grills, as well as specialities like medallions of beef fillet with brandy and peppercorn sauce.

OPEN: 11-11 **BAR MEALS:** L served all week 12-2.30 D served all week 6-10 Av main course £6.95
RESTAURANT: L served all week 12-2.30 D served all week 6-10 Av 3 course à la carte £15
BREWERY/COMPANY: Whitbread ◀: Gale's HSB, Fuller's London Pride, Interbrew Flowers IPA.
CHILDREN'S FACILITIES: menu, portions, games, high-chairs, food/bottle warming, outdoor play area, Swings, See-saw, Wendy house, castle, family room **GARDEN:** Large play area **NOTES:** Dogs allowed: in bar, Water, Parking 50

WHITCHURCH   THE RED HOUSE INN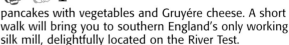

21 London St RG28 7LH
☎ 01256 895558
Dir: *From M3 or M4 take A34 to Whitchurch.*
Map Ref: *SU44*

A busy 16th-century coaching inn with quaint flagstones and gnarled beams, the Red House is set near the centre of this small Hampshire town. The friendly, open plan layout includes a locals' bar and a stylish dining room with stripped pine floor, large mirror and old fireplace. This is one of the growing fraternity of chef-owned free houses where diners can expect to find first-rate ingredients cooked in an imaginative modern style. Typical main dishes include wild sea bass with courgette cake; New Zealand lamb with spinach and roast pepper mousse; and buckwheat pancakes with vegetables and Gruyére cheese. A short walk will bring you to southern England's only working silk mill, delightfully located on the River Test.

OPEN: 11.30-3 6-11 (Sun 12-3, 7-10.30)
BAR MEALS: L served all week 12-2 D served all week 6.30-9.30 Av main course £10.50 **RESTAURANT:** L served all week 12-2 D served all week 6.30-9.30 Av 3 course à la carte £27.50 Av 3 course fixed price £30
BREWERY/COMPANY: Free House 🍺: Cheriton Diggers Gold & Pots Ale, Itchen Valley Fagins, Hop Back Summer Lightning. **CHILDREN'S FACILITIES:** menu, portions, food/bottle warming, outdoor play area, Wendy house, garden, family room **GARDEN:** Large, 25 seat patio
NOTES: Dogs allowed: in bar, in garden, except in restaurant, Parking 25

WATERSHIP DOWN INN 🍷

Freefolk Priors RG28 7NJ
☎ 01256 892254
Dir: *On B3400 between Basingstoke & Andover.* *Map Ref:* *SU44*

Enjoy an exhilarating walk on Watership Down before relaxing with a pint of well-kept local ale at this homely 19th-century inn named after Richard Adams' classic tale of rabbit life. The menu choices range from sandwiches, jacket potatoes, salads and ploughman's through to lamb cooked in a tomato, onion and herb sauce; breast of chicken in a creamy cider sauce with mushrooms and apples; and vegetable Bourguignon. But don't expect any rabbit dishes!

OPEN: 11.30-3.30 6-11 Rest: 25/26/31 Dec Evening
BAR MEALS: L served all week 12-2.30 D served all week 6-9.30 (Sun 12-2.30 & 7-8.30) Av main course £6.95
BREWERY/COMPANY: Free House 🍺: Oakleaf Bitter, Butts Barbus Barbus, Triple FFF Pressed Rat & Warthog, Hogs Back TEA. 🍷: 8 **CHILDREN'S FACILITIES:** menu, portions, high-chairs, food/bottle warming, outdoor play area, Fully enclosed, newly upgraded **GARDEN:** Beer garden, patio, heaters **NOTES:** No dogs, Parking 18

WHITSBURY   THE CARTWHEEL INN 🍷

Whitsbury Rd SP6 3PZ
☎ 01725 518362 📄 01725 518886
e-mail: thecartwheelinn@lineone.net
Dir: *Off A338 between Salisbury & Fordingbridge.* *Map Ref:* *SU11*

Handy for exploring the New Forest, visiting Breamore House and discovering the remote Mizmaze on the nearby downs, this extended, turn-of-the-century one-time wheelwright's and shop has been a pub since the 1920s. Venue for a beer festival held annually in August, with spit-roast pigs, barbecues, Morris dancing and a range of 30 real ales. Popular choice of well kept beers in the bar too. Home-made food on daily specials boards - steak and kidney pudding, fisherman's pie and chicken curry. Like their postcard says: "Off the beaten track, but never in a rut!"

OPEN: 11-3 5.30-11 all day Sat/Sun
BAR MEALS: L served all week 12-3 D served all week 6-9.30 Av main course £6.50 **BREWERY/COMPANY:**
🍺: Ringwood 49er, Old Thumper, Ringwood Best, Smiles.
🍷: 15 **CHILDREN'S FACILITIES:** menu, outdoor play area
GARDEN: Lawn, rockery borders **NOTES:** Dogs allowed: Water, Parking 25

WICKHAM GREENS RESTAURANT & PUB

The Square PO17 5JQ
☎ 01329 833197
e-mail: DuckworthGreens@aol.com
Map Ref: SU51

Prominent on a corner of Wickham's picturesque square, this mock-Tudor pub has been run by Frank and Carol Duckworth for 20 years. Fresh ingredients are obligatory in everything, from starters like smoked duck salad with pear chutney, to main dishes such as slow-roasted belly pork with grain mustard mash and red wine sauce, and Scottish salmon fillet drizzled with truffle oil.

OPEN: 11-3 6-11 (Summer Sun all day)
BAR MEALS: L served Tues-Sun 12-2 D served Tues-sun 6-9 Sun 12-3, 6-8.30 Av main course £10.50
RESTAURANT: L served Tues-Sun 12-2 D served Tues-Sun 6-9 Sun 12-3, 6-8.30 Av 3 course à la carte £22.50
BREWERY/COMPANY: Free House ◀: Fullers London Pride, Hopback Summer Lightning, Bass. ♀: 10
CHILDREN'S FACILITIES: portions, high-chairs, food/bottle warming **GARDEN:** Safe area, views & access to River Meon
NOTES: No dogs (ex guide dogs), Parking 200

ALDBURY THE VALIANT TROOPER

Trooper Rd HP23 5RW
☎ 01442 851203 ▤ 01442 851071
Dir: A41 at Tring junct, follow railway station signs, 0.5m and at village green turn R then 200yds on L. *Map Ref:* SP91

Family-run free house in a pretty village surrounded by the Chiltern Hills, where hikers, cyclists and dogs are all made welcome. Local and guest beers feature, and interesting daily specials from the blackboard are hot and spicy chicken stir fry; beef fillet Stroganoff; steak, kidney and ale pie; and shark and tuna Breton. The Duke of Wellington is rumoured to have held a tactical conference at the pub - hence the name.

OPEN: 11-11 (Sun 12-10.30) **BAR MEALS:** L served all week 12-2.30 D served Tue-Sat 6.30-9.15
RESTAURANT: L served Tue-Sun 12-2 D served Tue-Sun 6.30-9.15 **BREWERY/COMPANY:** Free House ◀: Fuller's London Pride, Scottish Courage John Smith's, Marston's Pedigree, Greene King Ruddles Best.
CHILDREN'S FACILITIES: menu, outdoor play area, large garden, wendy house, high chairs, family room **NOTES:** Dogs allowed: Parking 36

ASHWELL BUSHEL & STRIKE

Mill St SG7 5LY
☎ 01462 742394 ▤ 01462 743768
e-mail: graeme@375aol
Map Ref: TL23

Wooden floors, leather chesterfields and open fires in winter characterise the main bar of this popular inn, which stands in the shadow of Ashwell's Norman church tower. The restaurant is a conversion of the old school hall with its vaulted roof and oak floor. Try a traditional lamb and vegetable-filled Hertfordshire Pasty, braised lamb shank on ratatouille, seafood pie, or chicken breast with a wild mushroom and basil mousse. Spotted Dick and apple crumble are often among the sweet selections.

OPEN: 11.30-3 6-11 (all day Sun) **BAR MEALS:** L served all week 12-2.30 D served all week 7-9.30 Sun 12-4, 7-9 Av main course £7.50 **RESTAURANT:** L served all week 12-2.30 D served all week 7-9.30 Av 3 course à la carte £19
BREWERY/COMPANY: Charles Wells ◀: Charles, Old Speckled Hen, Broadside, Bombadier. ♀: 7
CHILDREN'S FACILITIES: menu, portions, games, high-chairs, food/bottle warming **GARDEN:** Large garden, patio, tables, benches **NOTES:** Dogs allowed: in bar only, Water, Parking 40

THE THREE TUNS

High St SG7 5NL
☎ 01462 742107 ▤ 01462 743662
e-mail: claire@tuns.co.uk
Map Ref: TL23

There are many original features in this 19th-century inn, providing an old-world atmosphere in the heart of Ashwell village. The hotel was completely refurbished in 1998, and the chefs have established an excellent local reputation for home-cooked food, and the menus are changed daily. Typical choices include cubed pork in paprika sauce; Scotch salmon fillet with hollandaise sauce; or cheese and mushroom omelette.

OPEN: 11-11 (Sun 12-10.30) **BAR MEALS:** L served all week 12-2.30 D served all week 6.30-9.30 Av main course £10 **RESTAURANT:** L served all week 12-2.30 D served all week 6.30-9.30 Av 3 course à la carte £18 **BREWERY/COMPANY:** Greene King ◖: Greene King IPA, Ruddles, Abbot. ♀: 7 **CHILDREN'S FACILITIES:** menu, portions, games, high-chairs, food/bottle warming, outdoor play area, family room **GARDEN:** Large, terrace at top, seats around 100 **NOTES:** Dogs allowed: in bar, in garden, Parking 20

BARLEY   THE FOX & HOUNDS

High St SG8 8HU
☎ 01763 848459 ▤ 01763 849274
e-mail: thefoxbarley@aol.com
Dir: A505 onto B1368 at Flint Cross, pub 4m.
Map Ref: TL43

Set in a pretty village, this former 17th-century hunting lodge is notable for its pub sign which extends across the lane. It has real fires, a warm welcome and an attractive garden. The menu offers a good range of standards such as Cumberland sausage, sirloin steak, gammon, scampi and chilli, while for something lighter there are sandwiches, baguettes, home-made burgers, garlic bread with cheese, and potato boats with chilli and sour cream.

OPEN: 12-11 (Sun 12-10.30) **BAR MEALS:** L served all week 12-3 D served all week 6-9 Sun 12-5 Av main course £5 **RESTAURANT:** 12-3 6-9 **BREWERY/COMPANY:** Punch Taverns ◖: IPA, 6X. ♀: 8 **CHILDREN'S FACILITIES:** menu, portions, games, food/bottle warming, outdoor play area **GARDEN:** "L" shaped garden with tables and chairs **NOTES:** Dogs allowed: in bar, Parking 25

BUNTINGFORD   THE SWORD IN HAND

Westmill SG9 9LQ
☎ 01763 271356
e-mail: heather@swordinhand.ndo.co.uk
Dir: Off A10 1.5m S of Buntingford.
Map Ref: TL32

Early 15th-century inn, once the home of the Scottish noble family, Gregs. The pub's name is taken from a motif within their family crest. The dining room looks out over open countryside, and offers a regularly changing menu. This may include Barbary duck Wellington with red wine and cranberry sauce, roasted garlic and herb rack of lamb, fillet steak topped with melted Stilton, breast of pheasant wrapped in bacon on honey-soused winter vegetables, or salmon fillet wrapped in Parma ham with tomato and basil sauce.

OPEN: 12-3 Open Mon L in Summer) 5.30-11 **BAR MEALS:** L served Tue-Sun 12-2.30 D served Tue-Sun 6.30-9.30 Av main course £10 **RESTAURANT:** L served Tue-Sun 12-2.30 D served Tue-Sun 6.30-9.30 Av 3 course à la carte £20 **BREWERY/COMPANY:** Free House ◖: Greene King IPA, Young's Bitter, Shephard & Neame Spitfire, Batemans & Guest Ales. **CHILDREN'S FACILITIES:** menu, portions, high-chairs, food/bottle warming, outdoor play area, large garden for ball games, play area **GARDEN:** Large, beautiful view, patio area, pergola **NOTES:** Dogs allowed: in bar, in garden, Parking 25

FLAUNDEN THE BRICKLAYERS ARMS

Hogpits Bottom HP3 0PH
☎ 01442 833322 🖹 834841
e-mail: goodfood@bricklayersarms.co.uk
Dir: M1 J8 through H Hempstead to Bovington then follow Flaunden sign. M25 J18 through Chorleywood to Chenies/Latimer then Flaunden.
Map Ref: TL00

This traditional country pub with its low beams, exposed brickwork and open fires has been extensively renovated and refurbished by its new owners, who have many years of experience in the trade. It is popular with walkers and locals, as well as those who enjoy relaxing in the delightful garden in the summer months.

OPEN: 11.30-11.30 **BAR MEALS:** L served all week 12-2 D served all week 6-9.30 Av main course £13
RESTAURANT: L served all week 12-3 D served all week 6-9.30 Av 3 course à la carte £23
BREWERY/COMPANY: Free House 🍺: Old Speckled Hen, Brakspear Bitter, Ringwood Old Thumper, Marston's Pedigree.
🍷: 12 **CHILDREN'S FACILITIES:** menu, portions, high-chairs, food/bottle warming **GARDEN:** Sunny & secluded
NOTES: Dogs allowed: in bar, in garden, Water, Parking 40

HEMEL HEMPSTEAD ALFORD ARMS

Frithsden HP1 3DD
☎ 01442 864480 🖹 01422 876893
e-mail: info@alfordarms.co.uk
Map Ref: TL00

Despite the traditional trappings - wooden floors, quarry tiles, log fires, old furniture and pictures - the Alford Arms has a light modern feel. It is a Victorian pub in the hamlet of Frithsden surrounded by National Trust woodland, and in summer you can sit outside on the terrace overlooking the green.

OPEN: 11-11 (Sun 12-10.30) Closed: 25-26 Dec
BAR MEALS: L served all week 12-2.30 D served all week 7-10 (Sun 12-3) Av main course £11.50
RESTAURANT: L served all week 12-2.30 D served all week 7-10 (Sun 12-3) Av 3 course à la carte £21.75
BREWERY/COMPANY: Free House 🍺: Marstons Pedigree, Brakspear, Interbrew Flowers & Morrells Oxford Blue. 🍷: 13
CHILDREN'S FACILITIES: portions, high-chairs, food/bottle warming **GARDEN:** Terrace with tables overlooking green
NOTES: Dogs allowed: in bar, in garden, Water provided, Parking 25

HEXTON THE RAVEN

SG5 3JB
☎ 01582 881209 🖹 01582 881610
e-mail: jack@ravenathexton-f9.co.uk
Dir: Telephone for directions. Map Ref: TL13

Named after Ravensburgh Castle up in the neighbouring hills, this neat 1920s pub has

comfortable bars and a large garden with terrace and play area. The traditional pub food menu is more comprehensive than many, with baguettes, filled jackets, pork ribs, steaks from the Duke of Buccleuch's Scottish estate, surf and turf, ribs, hot chicken and bacon salad, Mediterranean pasta bake and a whole lot more. Daily specials are on the blackboard.

OPEN: 11-3 6-11 (Sun 12-10.30) **BAR MEALS:** L served all week 12-2 D served all week 6-10 Av main course £7.50
RESTAURANT: L served all week 12-2 D served all week 6-10 **BREWERY/COMPANY:** Enterprise Inns 🍺: Greene King Old Speckled Hen, Fullers London Pride, Greene King IPA. 🍷: 16 **CHILDREN'S FACILITIES:** menu, games, high-chairs, food/bottle warming, baby changing, outdoor play area **GARDEN:** Table & chair seating for 50, benches & tables **NOTES:** Dogs allowed in the garden only. Water provided, Parking 40

LITTLE HADHAM THE NAGS HEAD

The Ford SG11 2AX

☎ 01279 771555 ▤ 01279 771555

*Dir: M11 J8 take A120 towards Puckeridge & A10. At lights in Little Hadnam turn L. Pub 0.75m on R. **Map Ref:** TL42*

This 16th-century former coaching inn has also been a brewery, bakery and Home Guard arsenal in its time. Internal features are an oak-beamed bar and a restaurant area with open brickwork and an old bakery oven. Fish is a speciality and 20 fish main courses are offered - maybe poached skate wing with black butter, or cod in Abbot batter. Alternatively you might choose Swiss lamb joint, farmhouse grill or vegetarian harvest pie.

OPEN: 11-2.30 6-11 (Sun 12-3.30 7-10.30) Rest: Dec 25-26 Closed eve **BAR MEALS:** L served all week 12-2 D served all week 6-9 Sun 7-9, Fri-Sat 6-9.30 Av main course £6.95 **RESTAURANT:** L served all week 12-2 D served all week 6-9 Sun 7-9, Fri-Sat 6-9.30 Av 3 course à la carte £16 **BREWERY/COMPANY:** Greene King ▣: Greene King Abbot Ale, IPA, Old Speckled Hen & Ruddles County Ale, Marstons Pedigree. **CHILDREN'S FACILITIES:** menu, high-chairs, food/bottle warming **GARDEN:** Patio area at front of pub; courtyard

OLD KNEBWORTH THE LYTTON ARMS

Park Ln SG3 6QB

☎ 01438 812312 ▤ 01438 817298

e-mail: thelyttonarms@btinternet.com

*Dir: From A1(M) take A602. At Knebworth turn R at rail station. Follow signs 'Codicote'. Pub 1.5m on R. **Map Ref:** TL22*

Popular with ramblers, horse-riders and cyclists in picturesque north Hertfordshire countryside, this 1877 Lutyens-designed inn claims to have served over 4,000 real ales in 14 years. Recently refurbished, inside and out, the Lytton offers ten cask-conditioned real ales changing daily, a selection of light bites and a daily specials board. Food options may include home-made pies, sausages, liver and bacon, curries, seafood pasta, and battered fish and chips.

OPEN: 11-11 (Sun 12-10.30) **BAR MEALS:** L served Mon-Sun 12-2.30 D served Mon-Sat 7-9.30 Sun 12-5 Av main course £7.50 **RESTAURANT:** L served Mon-Sun 12-2.30 D served Mon-Sat 6.30-9.30 Sun 12-5 **BREWERY/COMPANY:** Free House ▣: Fuller's London Pride, Adnams Best Bitter, Broadside, Wherry. ♀: 30 **CHILDREN'S FACILITIES:** menu, portions, licence, high-chairs, food/bottle warming, baby changing **GARDEN:** Large umbrella protected decking **NOTES:** Dogs allowed: Water, Parking 40

ST ALBANS ROSE & CROWN

10 St Michael St AL3 4SG

☎ 01727 851903 ▤ 01727 761775

e-mail: ruth.courtney@ntlworld.com

***Map Ref:** TL10*

Traditional 16th-century pub situated in a beautiful part of St Michael's 'village', opposite the entrance to Verulanium Park and the Roman Museum. It has a classic beamed bar with a huge inglenook, and a summer patio filled with flowers. The new landlord is continuing to offer the pub's distinctive range of American deli-style sandwiches, which are served with potato salad, kettle crisps and pickled cucumber. The "Cotton Club", for example, has a roast beef, ham, Swiss cheese, mayo, tomato, onion, lettuce and horseradish mustard filling.

OPEN: 11.30-3 (Open all day Sun) 5.30-11 (Open all day Sat from Easter-Oct) **BAR MEALS:** L served Mon-Sat 12-2 12.30-2.30 Av main course £5 **BREWERY/COMPANY:** Pubmaster ▣: Adnams Bitter, Carlsberg-Tetley Tetley Bitter, Fuller's London Pride, Courage Directors. ♀: 8 **CHILDREN'S FACILITIES:** portions, licence, food/bottle warming **GARDEN:** Tables, hanging baskets etc **NOTES:** Dogs allowed: in bar, in garden, Water, Parking 6

WELLPOND GREEN NAG'S HEAD ◆◆◆◆

SG11 1NL
☎ 01920 821424
*Dir: Telephone for directions. **Map Ref:** TL42*

The Nag's Head is a family-run free house in a sleepy hamlet in pretty rolling countryside, half a mile off the A120. The menu offers a variety of seafood and fish main courses, including skate wing, mussels, and lemon sole. Other popular dishes are calves' liver with sautéed onions and bacon; breast of duck with an orange and brandy sauce; vegetarian stirfry flavoured with ginger and served with pilau rice; and grilled lamb cutlets. Comfortable accommodation in attractive en suite bedrooms.

OPEN: 12-2.30 6-11 **BAR MEALS:** L served Tue-Sun 12-2 D served Mon-Sat 6.30-9.30 Av main course £6.95
RESTAURANT: L served Tue-Sun 12-2 D served Mon-Sat 6.30-9.30 Av 3 course à la carte £18
BREWERY/COMPANY: Free House ◀: Greene King IPA & Ruddles County. **CHILDREN'S FACILITIES:** portions, high-chairs, food/bottle warming, outdoor play area, Swings
GARDEN: Lawn, full size boules pitch, Patio
NOTES: No dogs (ex guide dogs), Parking 28
ROOMS: 5 en suite 1 family room s£50 d£70

GOREY CASTLE GREEN PUB AND BISTRO

La Route de la Cote JE3 6DR
☎ 01534 853103 ▤ 01534 853103
e-mail: castlegreenpub@hotmail.com

A superbly located pub overlooking Gorey harbour and, in turn, overlooked by dramatic Mont Orgueil Castle. What may rank as Jersey's most famous setting can be enjoyed from the terrace, during the summer at least, while dining on the pan-Pacific-style dishes produced by Australian chef/manager Stephen Mills. Examples include marinated duck breast with cumin-scented vegetable spaghetti and passion fruit sauce, aromatic herb-poached mahi mahi with warm salad, and open lasagne with roasted organic vegetables and spiced plum tomato sauce.

OPEN: 11-11 **BAR MEALS:** L served all week 12-2.30 D served all week 6-9 Av main course £12
RESTAURANT: L served all week 12-2.30 D served all week 6-9 Av 3 course à la carte £25 ◀: Stella, Directors, Fosters, John Smith Extra Smooth. **CHILDREN'S FACILITIES:** menu
NOTES: No dogs (ex guide dogs)

ST BRELADE LA PULENTE HOTEL ▾

La Route de la Pulente JE3 8HG
☎ 01534 744487 ▤ 01534 498846
Dir: West side of the Island, along the 5 mile road

Amazing sea views, open fires on chilly days and a welcoming atmosphere at all times are promised at this friendly pub. The artistic bar and rustic restaurant are complemented in summer by a balcony and terrace where freshly-caught fish can be enjoyed along with choices from the specials menu: seafood platter, crab salad, fruits de mer, and perhaps garlic and herb chicken on cracked-pepper mash, green vegetable stew, and Caesar salad. Live music on Sunday afternoons in summer.

OPEN: 11-11 **BAR MEALS:** L served all week 12-2.20 D served Mon-Sat 6-8.20 Av main course £6.50
RESTAURANT: L served all week 12-2.20 D served Mon-Sat 6-8.20 Av 3 course à la carte £12 **BREWERY/COMPANY:**
◀: Interbrew Bass Bitter, Scottish Courage Theakstons Best, Stella, Kronenbourg 1664. ▾: 11
CHILDREN'S FACILITIES: menu **NOTES:** No dogs (ex guide dogs), Parking 30

Jersey continued

ST MARTIN ROYAL HOTEL

La Grande Route de Faldouet JE3 6UG
☎ 01534 856289 ▤ 01534 857298
e-mail: johnbarker@jerseymail.co.uk

Situated in the parish of St Martin, this friendly local has log fires in winter and a sunny beer garden in which to relax during the summer months. Nearby are the delights of St Catherine's Bay. Among the traditional favourites here are rack of spare ribs, braised lamb shank, fresh grilled Jersey plaice and spaghetti bolognaise. There are also filled jacket potatoes, chicken and chargrilled dishes and ploughman's lunches. Chef Isaac Pestana will prepare seafood platters on request.

OPEN: 9.30-11.30 Sun 11-11.30 **BAR MEALS:** L served all week 12-2.15 D served Mon-Sat 6-8.30 Sun 12-2.15 Av main course £8.50 **RESTAURANT:** L served all week 12-2.15 D served Mon-Sat 6-8.30 Sun 12-2.15 summer open on Sunday Evenings Av 3 course à la carte £15 **◖:** Fosters, John Smiths Smooth, Theakstons cool, Guiness. **♈:** 9 **CHILDREN'S FACILITIES:** menu, portions, games, high-chairs, food/bottle warming, baby changing, outdoor play area **NOTES:** No dogs, Parking 80

BOSSINGHAM THE HOP POCKET

The Street CT4 6DY
☎ 01227 709866 ▤ 01227 709866
e-mail: forgan50@aol.com
Map Ref: TR14

Birds of prey and an animal corner for children are among the more unusual attractions at this family pub in the heart of Kent. Canterbury is only five miles away and the county's delightfully scenic coast and countryside are within easy reach. All meals are cooked to order, using fresh produce. Expect supreme of chicken, spicy salmon, Cajun beef, chilli nachos and mushroom Stroganoff. Extensive range of sandwiches and omelettes.

OPEN: 11-3 6.30-11 **BAR MEALS:** L served Tue-Sun 12-2.30 D served Mon-Sun 7-9.15 Sunday 12-4 & 6.30-9 Av main course £9.25 **RESTAURANT:** L served Tue-Sun 12-2.30 D served Mon-Sun 7-9.15 Av 3 course à la carte £17.50 Av 3 course fixed price £16 **◖:** London Pride, Shepherd Neame Admiral. **CHILDREN'S FACILITIES:** menu, portions, high-chairs, food/bottle warming **NOTES:** Dogs allowed: in bar, Parking 30, No credit cards

BOYDEN GATE THE GATE INN

North Stream CT3 4EB
☎ 01227 860498
Dir: From Canterbury on A28 turn L at Upstreet. *Map Ref:* TR26

This rural retreat is surrounded by marshland and pasture, with a beautiful garden overlooking a stream populated by ducks and geese. On display is the Chislet Horse, which the locals will explain better than this guide! Inside, quarry-tiled floors and pine furniture feature in the family-friendly interconnecting bars. It might be a challenge to decide on what to eat, since the huge menu offers a wide range of snacks and sustaining meals.

OPEN: 11-2.30 6-11 (Sun 12-4, 7-10.30) **BAR MEALS:** L served all week 12-2 D served all week 6-9 Av main course £5.95 **BREWERY/COMPANY:** Shepherd Neame **◖:** Shepherd Neame Master Brew, Spitfire & Bishops Finger, Seasonal Beers. **♈:** 11 **CHILDREN'S FACILITIES:** portions, games, high-chairs, food/bottle warming, baby changing, family room **GARDEN:** By the side of stream **NOTES:** Dogs allowed: in bar, in garden, Water & dog biscuits, Parking 14, No credit cards

BRABOURNE THE FIVE BELLS ♀

The Street TN25 5LP
☎ 01303 813334 📠 01303 814667
e-mail: five.bells@lineone.net
Dir: 5m E of Ashford. **Map Ref:** *TR14*

Named after those rung out from the village church, this 16th-century inn lies below the scarp slope of the North Downs. Its old beams, inglenook fireplace and traditional upholstery help create a welcoming and hospitable atmosphere - and no piped music to spoil it. The garden is delightful. Extensive menus include fresh fish of the day, and home-made specialities such as steak and kidney pie, Wienerschnitzel, and chicken curry, plus snacks, salads and a children's menu.

OPEN: 11.30-3 6.30-11 **BAR MEALS:** L served all week 12-2 D served all week 7-10 Av main course £9 **RESTAURANT:** L served all week 12-2 D served all week 7-10.30 Av 3 course à la carte £18.20 **BREWERY/ COMPANY:** Free House 🍺: Shepherd Neame Master Brew, Wells Bombardier, Interbrew Bass, Greene King IPA. ♀: 8 **CHILDREN'S FACILITIES:** menu, outdoor play area, slide, see-saw, swing **GARDEN:** Lawn, seating for 80 persons **NOTES:** Dogs allowed: in bar, in garden, Water, Parking 65

BROOKLAND WOOLPACK INN

TN29 9TJ
☎ 01797 344321
Map Ref: *TQ92*

Partly built from old ship timbers and set in Kentish marshland, this 15th-century cottage inn was originally a beacon-keeper's house, and is particularly popular with birdwatchers. One of the long Victorian tables has penny games carved into the top. Home-made wholesome pub food includes steak pie, chicken Kiev, pork chops, lasagne, grilled trout, a variety of steaks, and the usual sandwiches, jackets and ploughmans. See the blackboard for specials.

OPEN: 11-3 6-11 (Open all day Sat & Sun) **BAR MEALS:** L served all week 12-2 D served all week 6-9 **BREWERY/COMPANY:** Shepherd Neame 🍺: Shepherd Neame Spitfire Premium Ale, Master Brew Bitter. **CHILDREN'S FACILITIES:** menu, portions, high-chairs, food/bottle warming, baby changing, outdoor play area, play area, animals, family room **GARDEN:** Large beer garden with 2 tables **NOTES:** Dogs allowed: Water, Parking 30

CANTERBURY THE OLD COACH HOUSE ♀

A2 Barnham Downs CT4 6SA
☎ 01227 831218 📠 01227 831932
Dir: 7M S of Canterbury on A2. Turn at Jet Petrol Station. **Map Ref:** *TR15*

A former stop on the original London to Dover coaching route, and listed in the 1740 timetable, this inn stands some 300 metres from the Roman Way. Noteworthy gardens with home-grown herbs and vegetables, weekend spit-roasts, and unabashed continental cuisine mark it as an auberge in the finest Gallic tradition. Food options include seafood, venison and other game in season, plus perhaps rib of beef with rosemary, pot au feux, and grilled lobster with brandy sauce.

OPEN: 11-11 **BAR MEALS:** L served all week 12-2.30 D served all week 6.30-9 **RESTAURANT:** L served all week 12-2 D served all week 6.30-9 **BREWERY/COMPANY:** Free House 🍺: Interbrew Whitbread Best Bitter. **CHILDREN'S FACILITIES:** menu **GARDEN:** Large sand pit, seating **NOTES:** Dogs allowed: Parking 60 **ROOMS:** 10 en suite (★★)

CHIDDINGSTONE CASTLE INN

TN8 7AH
☎ 01892 870247 ▤ 01892 870808
e-mail: info@castleinn.co.uk
Dir: *S of B2027 between Tonbridge & Edenbridge.* ***Map Ref:*** *TQ54*

The Castle's picturesque mellow brick exterior

has served, over the years, as a much favoured film set: 'Elizabeth R', 'Room with a View', 'The Life of Hogarth' and 'The Wicked Lady' all featured scenes shot here. The building dates back to 1420 and is full of nooks and crannies, period furniture and evocative curios. Outside is a vine-hung courtyard with its own garden bar. The inn has a strong reputation for its cooking, from typical pub food in the bar to informal dinners in the saloon bar. There is also a small restaurant for special occasions.

OPEN: 11-11 **BAR MEALS:** L served all week 11-9.30 D served all week Sun 12-6 **RESTAURANT:** L served Wed-Mon 12-2 D served Wed-Mon 7.30-9.30 **BREWERY/COMPANY:** Free House ◖: Larkins Traditional, Harveys Sussex, Young's Ordinary. **CHILDREN'S FACILITIES:** menu, portions, licence, games, high-chairs, food/bottle warming, baby changing **GARDEN:** Patio, lawn, sheltered, bar **NOTES:** Dogs allowed: in bar, in garden, Water

DOVER THE CLYFFE HOTEL

High St, St Margaret's at Cliffe CT15 6AT
☎ 01304 852400 ▤ 01304 851880
e-mail: stay@theclyffehotel.com
Dir: *3m NE of Dover.* ***Map Ref:*** *TR34*

Kentish clapboard building dating from 1584, which has at times been a shoemaker's and an academy for young gentlemen. It is located opposite the parish church, just half a mile from the white cliffs of Dover, and the main bar and neatly furnished lounge lead out into the delightful walled rose garden. Seafood is a speciality of the house, including lobster, bass and mussels as popular options alongside New Romney rack of lamb.

OPEN: 11-3 (Sun 12-10.30) 5-11 **BAR MEALS:** L served all week 11-2 D served all week 6-9.30 Av main course £6.95 **RESTAURANT:** L served all week 12-2 D served all week 6.30-9.30 **BREWERY/COMPANY:** Free House ◖: Shepherd Neame Spitfire, Masterbrew, Fullers London Pride. **CHILDREN'S FACILITIES:** portions, licence, games, high-chairs, food/bottle warming, outdoor play area, playhouse, toys **GARDEN:** Traditional English walled garden **NOTES:** No dogs (ex guide dogs), Parking 20

THE SWINGATE INN & HOTEL ◆◆◆

Deal Rd CT15 5DP
☎ 01304 204043 ▤ 01304 204043
e-mail: terry@swingate.com
Dir: *Telephone for directions.* ***Map Ref:*** *TR34*

Just minutes from Dover's ferry port, this family-run free house makes an ideal touring base. There's a relaxed, friendly atmosphere, and the Thursday jazz evenings are particularly popular. Informal meals are served in the bar or garden, or you can choose from the à la carte menu in the spacious restaurant. Expect mixed grill, rump of lamb with redcurrant jus, grilled red snapper with spinach, and vegetable Wellington with a sun-dried tomato sauce.

OPEN: 11-11 (Sun 12-10.30, Xmas 12-3) **BAR MEALS:** L served all week 12-2.45 D served all week 6-10 **RESTAURANT:** L served all week 12-2.45 D served all week 6.30-10.00 ◖: Fullers London Pride, Abbot Ale, Boddingtons. **CHILDREN'S FACILITIES:** menu, outdoor play area, play area, TV, games, family room **GARDEN:** Large garden with gazebo, aviary **NOTES:** No dogs (ex guide dogs), Parking 60 **ROOMS:** 14 en suite 2 family rooms s£42 d£50

FAVERSHAM SHIPWRIGHTS ARMS

Hollowshore ME13 7TU
☎ 01795 590088
*Dir: A2 through Osprince then R at rdbt. Turn R at T-junct then L opp Davington School & follow signs. **Map Ref:** TR06*

Find this classic pub on the Kent marshes. First licensed in 1738, this was once a haunt of pirates and smugglers. There are numerous nooks and crannies inside and beer is served traditionally by gravity straight from the cask. Frequently changing range of Kent-brewed real ales. Self-sufficient landlord generates his own electricity and draws water from a well. Home-cooked food might include mushroom Stroganoff and sausage and mash. Emphasis on English pies and puddings during the winter. Used as a location in the 1967 Oliver Reed movie 'The Shuttered Room'.

OPEN: 12-3 Summer wknds open all day 6-11 (Sun 12-3, 6-10.30) **BAR MEALS:** L served Tue-Sun 12-2.30 D served Tue-Sat 7-9 Av main course £6
BREWERY/COMPANY: Free House 🍺: Local Beers.
CHILDREN'S FACILITIES: menu, swing, open space, family room **GARDEN:** Large open area adjacent to Faversham Creek **NOTES:** Dogs allowed: in bar, in garden, Parking 30

FOLKESTONE THE LIGHTHOUSE

Old Dover Rd, Capel le Ferne CT18 7HT
☎ 01303 223300 📠 01303 256501
Map Ref: TR23

Breathtaking panoramic sea views and spectacular countryside distinguish this former wine and ale house. The food is good too, and children have their own Jolly Little Sailor menu. Eight comfortable bedrooms.

BAR MEALS: L served all week 12-2.15 D served all week 5.30-9 Sunday 12-8.30 Av main course £7
RESTAURANT: L served all week 12-2.15 D served all week 5.30-9 Sunday 12-8.30 Av 3 course à la carte £17 🍺: Abbot Ale, Greene King IPA, Guest Ales, Ramsgate No5.
CHILDREN'S FACILITIES: menu, portions, games, high-chairs, food/bottle warming, baby changing, outdoor play area, garden area/equipment, family room **GARDEN:** lawn, large patio **NOTES:** No dogs (ex guide dogs), Parking 80
ROOMS: 8 en suite 2 family rooms s£40 d£50 (♦♦♦♦)

FORDCOMBE CHAFFORD ARMS

TN3 0SA
☎ 01892 740267 📠 01892 740703
e-mail: bazzer@chafford-arms.fsnet.co.uk
*Dir: On B2188 (off A264) between Tunbridge Wells & E Grinstead. **Map Ref:** TQ54*

Creeper-clad old-fashioned village pub with an award-winning garden, close to Penshurst Place and Groombridge Place and run by the same landlord for 38 years. Originally built in 1851 for the local paper works that made paper for the Royal Mint. For starters expect local smoked trout with horseradish sauce, avocado vinaigrette or deep-fried mushrooms. Main courses might be lemon sole, home-made prawn Provençale, courgette and aubergine cannelloni, steak or chicken Kiev. There is also a good range of snacks.

OPEN: 11.45-3 6.30-11 (All day Sat)
BAR MEALS: L served all week 12.30-2 D served Tue-Sat 7.30-9 Av main course £7.95 **RESTAURANT:** L served all week 12.30-2 D served Tue-Sat 7.30-9 Av 3 course à la carte £17.50 **BREWERY/COMPANY:** Enterprise Inns 🍺: Larkins Bitter, Marstons Pedigree. 🍷: 9
CHILDREN'S FACILITIES: portions, food/bottle warming, baby changing **GARDEN:** Enclosed garden, patio
NOTES: Dogs allowed: in bar, in garden, Water, Parking 16

LINTON THE BULL INN

Linton Hill ME17 4AW
☎ 01622 743612 🖺 01622 749513
Dir: *A229 through Maidstone to Linton.*
Map Ref: *TQ75*

Traditional 17th-century coaching inn in the heart of the Weald with stunning views from the glorious garden. Popular with walkers and very handy for the Greensand Way. Large inglenook fireplace and a wealth of beams inside, as well as tunnels which once led to the nearby church. A tasty bar menu includes lasagne; spinach and ricotta tortellini; cod and chips; and bubble and squeak, as well as sandwiches, baguettes, and ploughmans. A restaurant menu has the likes of seafood stir fry; salmon and cod duo; trout and almonds; and beef Wellington.

OPEN: 11-3 6-11 (Sun 12-10.30, Sat 11-11)
BAR MEALS: L served all week 12-2.30 D served Mon-Sat 7-9.30 (Sun 12-3.30) Av main course £7.95
RESTAURANT: L served Mon-Sun 12-2.30 D served all week 7-9.30 (Sun 12-3.30) Av 2 course fixed price £11.95
BREWERY/COMPANY: Shepherd Neame 🍺: Shepherd Neame Master Brew & Spitfire, Seasonal Ale.
CHILDREN'S FACILITIES: menu, portions, high-chairs, food/bottle warming **GARDEN:** Lrg garden, ample seating, stunning views **NOTES:** Dogs allowed: in bar, in garden, Parking 30

LITTLEBOURNE KING WILLIAM IV ◆◆◆

4 High St CT3 1UN
☎ 01227 721244 🖺 01227 721244
e-mail: paulharvey@kingwilliam04.fsbusiness.co.uk
Dir: *From A2 follow signs to Howletts Zoo. After zoo & at end of road, pub is straight ahead.*
Map Ref: *TR25*

Located just outside the city of Canterbury, the King William IV overlooks the village green and is well placed for Sandwich and Herne Bay. With open log fires and exposed oak beams, this friendly inn offers a good choice of wholesome food. Seafood choices include seabass on minted ratatouille, and paupiette of plaice and leek with thermidor sauce.

OPEN: 11-3 6-11 (Sat 11-11) **BAR MEALS:** L served all week 12-2.30 D served Mon-Sat 7-9.30 Av main course £12.50
RESTAURANT: L served all week 12-2.30 D served all week 7-9.30 Av 3 course à la carte £20 **BREWERY/COMPANY:** Free House 🍺: Shepherd Neame Master Brew Bitter, Scottish Courage John Smith's, Adnams Bitter. **CHILDREN'S FACILITIES:** portions, games, high-chairs, food/bottle warming, baby changing **GARDEN:** Patio to rear, External seating to front **NOTES:** in bar, in garden, Parking 15 **ROOMS:** 7 en suite s£35 d£50 (◆◆◆)

MAIDSTONE THE RINGLESTONE INN ◆◆◆◆◆ 🍷

Ringlestone Hamlet, Nr Harrietsham ME17 1NX
☎ 01622 859900 🖺 01622 859966
e-mail: bookings@ringlestone.com
Dir: *Take A20 E from Maidstone/at rndbt opp Great Danes Hotel turn to Hollingbourne. Through village, R at crossroads at top of hill.*
Map Ref: *TQ75*

Built 1533, the Ringlestone was a church-owned hospice for monks, and became an ale house in the early 1600s. The promise of a warm welcome - 'A ryghte joyouse greetynge' - is carved into the old English oak sideboard. Today, along with a mind-boggling selection of country fruit wines, ciders and real ales, the hearty home-cooked food brings ample cheer.

OPEN: 12-3 6-11 (Sat-Sun 12-11) Closed: 25 Dec
BAR MEALS: L served all week 12-2 D served all week 7-9.30
RESTAURANT: L served all week 12-2 D served all week 7-9.30 Av 3 course à la carte £24.50 🍺: Shepherd Neame Bishops Finger & Spitfire, Greene King Abbot Ale, Theakston Old Peculiar. 🍷: 40 **CHILDREN'S FACILITIES:** menu, portions, licence, games, high-chairs, food/bottle warming, outdoor play area, 2 acre garden, cots **GARDEN:** Five acres of landscaped gardens, seating **NOTES:** Dogs allowed at manager's discretion, Parking 50 **ROOMS:** 3 en suite s£89 d£99

MARKBEECH THE KENTISH HORSE

Cow Ln TN8 5NT
☎ 01342 850493
Map Ref: TQ44

Surrounded by Kent countryside, this pub is popular with ramblers, cyclists and families. The inn dates from 1340 and is said to have a smuggling history; it boasts a curious street-bridging Kentish sign. The wide-ranging menu offers fresh starters such as Greek feta salad; pint of shell-on prawns; and whitebait. Satisfying main courses include spinach and ricotta cannelloni; sausage and mash with onion gravy; and steak and Guinness pie.

OPEN: 12-11 (Sun 12-10.30) **BAR MEALS:** L served all week 12-2.30 D served Tues-Sat 7-9.30 (Sun L 12-3.30) Av main course £7.95 **RESTAURANT:** L served all week 12-2.30 D served all week 7-9.30 Sun L (12-3.30) ◖: Harvey's Larkins, plus guest ales.
CHILDREN'S FACILITIES: menu, high-chairs, food/bottle warming, outdoor play area, Swings, slide, climbing fort
NOTES: Dogs allowed: Water, biscuits, Parking 40

PLUCKLEY THE DERING ARMS ♆

Station Rd TN27 0RR
☎ 01233 840371 ▤ 01233 840498
e-mail: jim@deringarms.com
Dir: M20 J8 take A20 to Ashford.Then R onto B2077 at Charing to Pluckley. ***Map Ref: TQ94***

Chef/patron James Buss has run this distinctive pub with passion and flair for over 20 years. The impressive building with its curved Dutch gables and uniquely arched windows was formerly a hunting lodge. The interior boasts high ceilings, wood or stone floors, simple antique furniture and winter log fires. The extensive menus feature fresh fish and seafood, and make good use of fresh vegetables from the family farm and herbs from the pub garden.

OPEN: 11-3 6-11 Closed: 26-29 Dec
BAR MEALS: L served all week 12-2 D served all week 7-9.30 Av main course £14 **RESTAURANT:** L served all week 12-2 D served all week 7-9.30 Av 3 course à la carte £24 **BREWERY/COMPANY:** Free House ◖: Goacher's Dering Ale, Maidstone Dark, Gold Star, Old Ale. ♆: 7
CHILDREN'S FACILITIES: portions, high-chairs, food/bottle warming, family room **GARDEN:** Small grassed area with picnic tables **NOTES:** Dogs allowed: in bar, in garden, in bedrooms, Water, Parking 20

SELLING THE ROSE AND CROWN

Perry Wood ME13 9RY
☎ 01227 752214
e-mail: rich-jocie@supanet.com
Dir: A28 to Chilham R at Shottenden turning. R at Old Plough x roads, next R signed Perry Wood.Pub at top of hill. ***Map Ref: TR05***

Set against 150 acres of natural woodland, this traditional 16th-century pub is decorated with local hop garlands and a unique corn dolly collection. Log fires in winter and a very attractive pub garden with fairy lights and an aviary. Wide-ranging menu offers the likes of cod and smoked haddock mornay; Raj curry platter; Fisherman's Fancy; and a selection of ploughmans', filled rolls, and jackets. Specials may include steak and mushroom pudding, liver and bacon casserole, or aubergine and cheese bake. In the garden, try your hand at Bat and Trap, the traditional pub game of Kent.

OPEN: 11-3 6.30-11 Closed: 25-26 Dec pm only, 1 Jan pm only **BAR MEALS:** L served all week 12-2 D served Tue-Sat 7-9.30 Av main course £8 **RESTAURANT:** L served all week 12-2 D served Tue-Sat 7-9.30 **BREWERY/COMPANY:** Free House ◖: Adnams Southwold, Harveys Sussex Best Bitter, Goacher's Real Mild Ale. **CHILDREN'S FACILITIES:** menu, portions, food/bottle warming, outdoor play area, excellent play area in garden, family room **GARDEN:** Prizewinning garden, patio, heaters **NOTES:** Dogs allowed: in bar, in garden, water, biscuit on arrival, Parking 25

SMARDEN THE CHEQUERS INN ◆◆◆◆ ♀

The Street TN27 8QA
☎ 01233 770217 📠 01233 770623
e-mail: charliebullock@lineone.net
Dir: *Through Leeds village, L to Sutton
Valence/Headcorn then L for Smarden. Pub in
village centre.* **Map Ref:** *TQ84*

The Chequers is an atmospheric 14th-century

inn with a clapboard façade situated in the centre of
one of Kent's prettiest villages. The inn has a beautiful
landscaped garden with a large duck pond and an
attractive courtyard - the perfect setting for drinks or a
meal. Bar meals, real ales and a good choice of wines
by the glass are served in the low beamed bars. Two
separate restaurants offer the same delicious food
prepared from fresh local produce.

OPEN: 11-11 (Sun 12-10.30) **BAR MEALS:** L served all
week 12-2.30 D served all week 6-9.30 Av main course £10
RESTAURANT: L served all week 12-2.30 D served all week
6.30-9.30 **BREWERY/COMPANY:** Free House 🍺: Harveys,
Interbrew Bass, Fullers London Pride. ♀: 9
CHILDREN'S FACILITIES: portions, games, high-chairs,
food/bottle warming **GARDEN:** Landscaped garden with
natural pond **NOTES:** Dogs allowed: in bar, Parking 15
ROOMS: 4 en suite 1 family room s£40 d£70

SMARTS HILL THE BOTTLE HOUSE INN 🐑 ♀

Coldharbour Rd TN11 8ET
☎ 01892 870306 📠 01892 871094
e-mail:
info@thebottlehouseinnpenshurst.co.uk
Dir: *From Tunbridge Wells take A264 W then
B2188 N.* **Map Ref:** *TQ54*

Character-laden dining pub of some repute in an
ancient former farmhouse. Built in 1492, it was
granted a licence in 1938. So many old bottles were
found during the subsequent refurbishment that the
pub's name chose itself. The daily-changing menu
offers considerable choice with, as far as possible,
everything made from locally supplied fresh produce.

OPEN: 11-11 (Sun 12-10.30pm) Closed: Dec 25
BAR MEALS: L served all week 12-10 D served all week
12-10 (Sun 12-9.30) **RESTAURANT:** L served all week
12-10 D served all week 12-10 (Sun 12-9.30)
BREWERY/COMPANY: Free House 🍺: Larkins Ale, Harveys
Sussex Best Bitter. ♀: 8 **CHILDREN'S FACILITIES:** menu,
portions, licence, games, high-chairs, food/bottle warming
GARDEN: Front raised terrace garden and side patio
NOTES: Dogs allowed: in bar, in garden, Water, Parking 36

STALISFIELD GREEN THE PLOUGH ♀

ME13 0HY
☎ 01795 890256 📠 01795 890940
Dir: *A20 to Charing, on dual carriageway turn
L for Stalisfield.* **Map Ref:** *TQ95*

Originally a farmhouse, this 15th-century free
house inn has been unspoilt by time, and
boasts a lady ghost among its original beams
and log fires. Set in a pretty village on top of
the North Downs, it is run by Italian owners
who hold regular theme evenings from their
homeland. Interesting menus are
supplemented by the specials, which might
include gravadlax, baked cod fillet with
pancetta and Mozzarella, chicken supreme in
a white wine cream sauce or smoked
haddock with leek mash. The Plough featured

in an episode of the TV series, 'The Darling Buds of
May'.

OPEN: 12-3 7-11 **BAR MEALS:** L served Tue-Sun 12-2.30
D served Tue-Sun 7-9.30 Sun 12-3, 7-10.30 Av main
course £6.95 **RESTAURANT:** L served Tue-Sun 12-3
D served Tue-Sun 7-9.30 Av 3 course à la carte £14.45
BREWERY/COMPANY: Free House 🍺: Adnams Bitter,
Wadworth 6X. ♀: 8 **CHILDREN'S FACILITIES:** menu,
portions, high-chairs, food/bottle warming, baby changing,
family room **GARDEN:** Large beer garden, excellent view
NOTES: Dogs allowed: in bar, in garden, Parking 100

TENTERDEN   WHITE LION INN ♦♦♦♦ ♀

57 High St TN30 6BD
☎ 01580 765077 🖷 01580 764157
e-mail: whitelion@southsurf.com
Dir: *on the A28 Ashford/Hastings road.*
Map Ref: *TQ83*

A 16th-century coaching inn on a tree-lined street of this old Cinque Port, with many original features retained. The area is known for its cricket connections, and the first recorded county match between Kent and London was played here in 1719. The menu offers plenty of choice, from calves' liver and bacon, shoulder of lamb, and Cumberland cottage pie to tuna pasta bake and various ploughman's.

OPEN: 11-11 (Sun 12-10.30) **BAR MEALS:** L served all week 12-2.30 D served all week 6-10 Sun 12-2.30, 6-8.30 **RESTAURANT:** L served all week 12-2.30 D served all week 6-10 **BREWERY/COMPANY:** Lionheart 🍺: Greene King IPA, Adnams Broadside, Bass. **CHILDREN'S FACILITIES:** menu, high-chairs, food/bottle warming **GARDEN:** Patio area with tables and chairs **NOTES:** Dogs allowed: Water, Parking 30 **ROOMS:** 15 en suite 2 family rooms s£59 d£74

TUNBRIDGE WELLS (ROYAL)   THE BEACON ☕ ♀

Tea Garden Ln, Rusthall TN3 9JH
☎ 01892 524252 🖷 01892 534288
e-mail: beaconhotel@btopenworld.com
Dir: *From Tunbridge Wells take A264 towards East Grinstead. Pub 1m on L.* *Map Ref:* *TQ53*

The Beacon was built in 1895 as the home of Sir Walter Harris, a former lieutenant of the

City of London. It sits amid 16 acres of grounds including lakes, woodland and its own chalybeate spring. The building's elegant interior still oozes country house charm. Fresh local ingredients underpin dishes such as roasted rump of lamb on mint and smoked bacon mash.

OPEN: 11-11 (Sun 12-10.30) **BAR MEALS:** L served all week 12-2.30 D served all week 6.30-9.30 **RESTAURANT:** L served all week 12-2.30 D served all week 6-9.30 **BREWERY/COMPANY:** Free House 🍺: Harveys Best, Timothy Taylor Landlord, Breakspear Bitter. ♀: 10 **CHILDREN'S FACILITIES:** menu, portions, licence, high-chairs, outdoor play area, 17 acres **GARDEN:** Decking area, 17 acres of garden **NOTES:** Dogs allowed: in bar, in garden, in bedrooms, Water, Biscuits, Parking 40 **ROOMS:** 3 en suite s£68.50 d£97 (♦♦♦♦)

THE CROWN INN ♀

The Green, Groombridge TN3 9QH
☎ 01892 864742
e-mail: crowngroombridge@aol.com
Dir: *Take A264 W of Tunbridge Wells, then B2110 S.* *Map Ref:* *TQ53*

A cosy and inviting 16th-century inn situated by the village green and once frequented by the Groombridge smugglers, one of whom went on to become a cartographer and surveyor. Sir Arthur Conan Doyle wrote of seeing a ghost at the Crown in his book Valley of Fear. In winter there's a huge open fire in the beamed bar, and in summer the garden is popular. Traditional bar food plus various salads with chips, filled bagels and steak and mushroom pie washed down with local real ales from Harveys or Larkins.

Evening fare in the restaurant may offer diced curried lamb, seared salmon, beef chilli, or sirloin steak.

OPEN: 11-3 6-11 (Summer Fri-Sun open all day) **BAR MEALS:** L served all week 12-3 D served Mon-Sat 7-9 Sun 12-3 Av main course £9 **RESTAURANT:** L served all week 12-3 D served Mon-Sat 7-9 **BREWERY/COMPANY:** Free House 🍺: Harveys IPA, Greene King IPA & Abbot Ale, Larkins. ♀: 8 **CHILDREN'S FACILITIES:** menu, games, high-chairs, food/bottle warming, outdoor play area, Large garden away from road **GARDEN:** Benches, overlooks village green **NOTES:** Dogs allowed: in bar, in garden, Water bowls, Parking 35

Kent continued

WESTERHAM THE FOX & HOUNDS

Toys Hill TN16 1QG
☎ 01732 750328 ▤ 01732 750941
Map Ref: *TQ45*

A traditional family-run country pub high up on Toys Hill, part of the Greensand Ridge overlooking the Weald of Kent. Beautiful gardens, open fires and comfortable old furniture inside. From the menu expect classic roasts, steak and ale pie, beef and Stilton pie, paella, roast cod and sea bass. No music, gaming machines, TV or pool table to disturb the convivial atmosphere. Plenty of good walks locally. Very close to Winston Churchill's home, Chartwell.

OPEN: 11.30-2.30 (open all day, Apr-Oct) 6-11 (Sun 12-4, 7-10.30) Closed: Dec 25 **BAR MEALS:** L served all week 12-2.30 D served Tue-Sat 6-9.30 Av main course £9.25
RESTAURANT: L served all week 12-2.30 D served Tue-Sat 6-9.30 Av 3 course à la carte £18
BREWERY/COMPANY: Greene King ☎: Greene King IPA Abbot Ale. ♀: 9 **CHILDREN'S FACILITIES:** menu, portions, high-chairs, food/bottle warming **GARDEN:** Large, woodland, numerous tables with shade **NOTES:** Dogs allowed: in bar, at discretion of innkeeper, Parking 15

E1 PROSPECT OF WHITBY

57 Wapping Wall E1W 3SH
☎ 020 7481 1095 ▤ 020 7481 9537

Originally known as The Devil's Tavern, this famous 16th-century inn has been a meeting place for sailors and was also a gruesome setting for public executions. Samuel Pepys was a regular here before the tavern was renamed in 1777. Today, old ships timbers retain the seafaring traditions of this venerable riverside inn, which also boasts a rare pewter bar counter. Expect beef Wellington, minted lamb loins, and a good selection of fish dishes.

OPEN: 11.30-11 **BAR MEALS:** L served all week 11.30-9 D served all week Sun 12-9 Av main course £6.45
RESTAURANT: L served Sun-Fri D served Mon-Sat
BREWERY/COMPANY: Scottish & Newcastle ☎: London Pride, Youngs, Speckled Hen, Directors. ♀: 16
CHILDREN'S FACILITIES: portions, high-chairs, food/bottle warming **GARDEN:** Paved, Riverside **NOTES:** Dogs allowed: in bar

E3 THE CROWN

223 Grove Rd E3 5SN
☎ 020 8981 9998 ▤ 020 8980 2336
e-mail: crown@singhboulton.co.uk
Dir: *Nearest tube: Mile End Central Line & District line. Buses 277 to Victoria Park*

A beautifully-restored, listed building spread over two floors, with attractive views across South Hackney's Victoria Park. The open-plan bar is equally suited to lively conversation or some peaceful newspaper reading on quiet afternoons. There are no juke boxes, pin ball machines, or televisions. Upstairs, in a series of dining rooms with balconies, the European cuisine is presented on seasonal, twice-daily changing menus. Brunch is served at weekends and on bank holidays.

OPEN: 12-11 (Mon 5-11, Wknd phone for details) Closed: 25 Dec **BAR MEALS:** L served Tue-Sun 12.30-3.30 D served Mon-Sun 6.30-10.30 Av main course £10.50
RESTAURANT: L served Tue-Sun 12.30-3.30 D served Mon-Sun 6.30-10.30 **BREWERY/COMPANY:** Free House ☎: St Peter's Organic Ale & Best Bitter, Pitfield Eco Warrior & East Kent Goldings. ♀: 12
CHILDREN'S FACILITIES: portions, licence, high-chairs, food/bottle warming, baby changing facilities
GARDEN: Paved area at front of pub **NOTES:** Dogs allowed:

EC1　THE EAGLE

159 Farringdon Rd EC1R 3AL
☎ 020 7837 1353
Dir: *Angel/Farringdon Stn. North end Farringdon Road*

In 1990, The Eagle became the first of the genre of smart eating and drinking establishments we know as the gastropub. Back then London's trendies would not have done their chilling out in the drab Farringdon Road, but a lot of Fleet River water has flowed under its pavements since then, and Clerkenwell is now considered by some the capital's new Soho. The Eagle has remained one of the neighbourhood's top establishments - no mean feat, given the competition today. The airy interior has a wooden-floored bar and dining area, a random assortment of furniture, and an open-to-view kitchen which produces a modern, creative daily-changing menu with a pretty constant Southern European/South American/Pacific Rim theme. Draught and bottled beers, and an international wine list are all well chosen.

OPEN: 12-11 Closed: 1Wk Xmas, BHs
BAR MEALS: L served all week 12.30-3 D served Mon-Sat 6.30-10.30 Sun 12.30-3.30 Av main course £9
RESTAURANT: L served all week D served Mon-Sat
BREWERY/COMPANY: Free House ◖: Wells Eagle IPA & Bombardier. ♀: 14 **CHILDREN'S FACILITIES:** portions, food/bottle warming **NOTES:** Dogs allowed: in bar

THE JERUSALEM TAVERN

55 Britton St, Clerkenwell EC1M 5NA
☎ 020 7490 4281 ▤ 020 7490 4281
e-mail: beers@stpetersbrewery.co.uk
Dir: *100 metres NE of Farringdon tube, 300 metres N of Smithfield*

Named after the Priory of St John of Jerusalem, this historic tavern has been in four different locations since it was established in the 14th century. The current building dates from 1720. Its dark, dimly-lit Dickensian bar, with bare boards, rustic wooden tables, old tiles, candles, open fires and cosy corners, is the perfect film set - and that is what is has been on many occasions. The Jerusalem Tavern, a classic pub in every sense of the description and offers a familiar range of pub fare, including game pie, risotto, sausage and mash and various roasts.

OPEN: 11-11 Closed: 25 Dec & BH Mons
BAR MEALS: L served all week 12-3 D served Sat 6-10 Av main course £6.95 **RESTAURANT:** L served all week D served Sat Av 3 course à la carte £14.85
BREWERY/COMPANY: St Peters Brewery ◖: St Peters (complete range). **CHILDREN'S FACILITIES:** food/bottle warming **NOTES:** No dogs (ex guide dogs)

THE WELL ♀

180 Saint John St, Clerkenwell EC1V 4JY
☎ 020 7251 9363 ▤ 020 7242 9122
e-mail: drink@downthewell.co.uk
Dir: *Telephone for directions*

A gastro-pub where the emphasis is on modern European and Mediterranean-style food served on two floors. The lower ground features the leather-panelled aquarium bar with exotic tropical fish occupying huge tanks set into the walls. Try the crispy pork belly with roasted leeks, Jerusalem artichokes and pied bleu mushrooms with a mustard and brandy cream sauce; or slow-roasted rib eye steak with dauphinoise potatoes, roasted garlic and crispy bacon. Large choice of wines by the glass, and European bottled beers.

OPEN: 11-12 (Sun 11-10.30) **BAR MEALS:** L served Mon-Sun 12-3 D served Mon-Sun 6-10.30 Av main course £11.50 **RESTAURANT:** L served Mon-Sun 12-3 D served Mon-Sun 6-10.30 Av 3 course à la carte £22 ◖: San Miguel, Budvar, Lowenbrau, Paulaner. ♀: 15 **CHILDREN'S FACILITIES:** menu, portions, licence, high-chairs, food/bottle warming, **NOTES:** No dogs (ex guide dogs)

N1 THE COMPTON ARMS ♀

4 Compton Av, Off Canonbury Rd N1 2XD
☎ 0207 3596883
e-mail: 4334@greeneking.co.uk

The best kept secret in N1. A late 17th-century country pub in the middle of town with a peaceful, rural feel. Frequented by a mix of locals, actors and musicians. Real ales from the hand pump, and good value steaks, mixed grill, big breakfast and Sunday roast. Expect a busy bar when Arsenal are at home.

OPEN: 12-6 6-11 Closed: 25 Dec (afternoon) **BAR MEALS:** L served all week 12-2.30 D served all week 6-9 Av main course £5.95 **BREWERY/COMPANY:** Greene King ◖: Greene King IPA, Abbot Ale, Ruddles County, plus guest ale. **CHILDREN'S FACILITIES:** portions, games, family room **GARDEN:** Courtyard

THE DRAPERS ARMS ◉ ♀

44 Barnsbury St N1 1ER
☎ 020 7619 0348 ▤ 020 7619 0413
Dir: *Turn R outside tube st, along Upper Street. Opposite Town Hall*

Smart Islington gastro-pub with one menu serving all areas, but you should book for the upstairs dining room. It attracts a crowd, including a number of household names, for its decent food, interesting wine list, and ales (Old Speckled Hen and Courage). A wide choice of food takes in a big Sunday breakfast, lunchtime sandwiches and fabulous puddings. Typical mains are monkfish and scallop skewer with cardamom rice and muhummra purée, and slow-cooked rabbit with black olives and sherry vinegar.

OPEN: 11-11 (Sun 12-10.30) Closed: 24-27 Dec, 1 & 2 Jan **BAR MEALS:** L served all week 12-3 D served Mon-Sat 7-10 **RESTAURANT:** L served Sun 12-4 D served Mon-Sat 7-10.30 ◖: Old Speckled Hen, Courage, Budvar & Corona. ♀: 20 **CHILDREN'S FACILITIES:** menu, high-chairs, food/bottle warming, baby changing **NOTES:** Dogs allowed: in bar, in garden

THE DUKE OF CAMBRIDGE ♀

30 St Peter's St N1 8JT
☎ 020 7359 3066 ▤ 020 7359 1877
e-mail: duke@singhboulton.co.uk

Running an organic gastro-pub in celeb-laden Islington imposes on owners and childhood friends Geetie Singh and Esther Boulton a tough challenge - to provide the highest quality organic food, wines and beers. Being one of only two Soil Association-certified pubs in the UK proves that they achieve it. Their careful restoration of this 1851 building in 'junkshop minimalist' style involved retaining many original features, and using reclaimed materials and second-hand furniture. Look in vain for juke box, TV and pin-ball machine - there's nothing so intrusive here. The twice-daily-changing blackboard menu is regional European in style, the cooking seasonal and uncomplicated. Examples from the spring seasonal menu include roast beef in a salt crust with beetroot, fennel and horseradish cream; salt cod with rocket, chilli roast potatoes, six-minute egg and aioli; and polenta and gorgonzola fritters with cauliflower, pine nut and raisin salad. All dishes are available as children's portions.

OPEN: 12-11 (Sun 12-10.30) Closed: Dec 25-26, Jan 1 **BAR MEALS:** L served all week 12.30-3 D served all week 7-10.30 (Sun 12.30-3.30, 7-10) Av main course £10 **RESTAURANT:** L served all week 12.30-3 D served all week 6.30-10.30 (Sun 12.30-3.30, 7-10) **BREWERY/COMPANY:** Free House ◖: Pitfield Singhboulton, Eco Warrior, St Peter's Best Bitter, East Kent Golding. ♀: 12 **CHILDREN'S FACILITIES:** portions, licence, high-chairs, food/bottle warming, baby changing **GARDEN:** Small courtyard **NOTES:** Dogs allowed:

THE HOUSE ⊛⊛ ♇

63-69 Canonbury Rd N1 2DG
☎ 020 7704 7410 ▤ 020 7704 9388
e-mail: info@inthehouse.biz

Award-winning gastropub serving
international food with a French slant, though
don't expect anything too fussy or
fashionable. Signature dishes include parfait
of foie gras, and the House shepherd's pie.
Sunday brunch is well patronised.

OPEN: 12-11 (Sun 12-10.30, Mon 5-11) Closed: 24-46 Dec
BAR MEALS: L served Tues-Sun 12-2.30 D served all week
5.30-10.30 (Sat-Sun 12-3.30, Sat 6.30-10.30, Sun 6.30-9.30)
Av main course £13.50 **RESTAURANT:** L served Tues-Sun
12-2.30 D served all week 5.30-10.30 Sat-Sun 12-3.30, Sat
6.30-10.30, Sun 6.30-9.30 Av 3 course à la carte £25
Av 3 course fixed price £14.95 ◖: Adnams. ♇: 8
CHILDREN'S FACILITIES: menu, portions, food/bottle
warming **GARDEN:** Decked terrace & paved front garden
NOTES: No dogs (ex guide dogs)

N6 THE FLASK 🐑 ♇

Highgate West Hill N6 6BU
☎ 020 8348 7346
e-mail: info@theflaskhighgate.co.uk

A 17th-century former school in one of
London's loveliest villages. Dick Turpin hid
from his pursuers in the cellars, and TS Eliot
and Sir John Betjeman enjoyed a glass or two
here. The interior is listed and includes the
original bar with sash windows which lift at
opening time. Enjoy a glass of good real ale,
a speciality bottled beer (choice of 15), or a
hot toddy while you peruse the menu, which
changes twice a day. Choices range through
sandwiches and platters to char-grills and
home-made puddings.

OPEN: 11-11 Nov-Mar open 12 noon Rest: Dec 31 Closed
eve **BAR MEALS:** L served all week 12-3 D served all week
6-10 Sun 12-4, 6-9.30 Av main course £8
BREWERY/COMPANY: ◖: Adnams, Tim Taylor Landlord,
Caledonian IPA, Harveys Sussex. ♇: 12
CHILDREN'S FACILITIES: portions, high-chairs, food/bottle
warming **GARDEN:** A large terrace at the front of the pub
NOTES: Dogs allowed: in bar, in garden, water, doggie snacks

N19 THE LANDSEER ♇

37 Landseer Rd N19 4JU

Sunday roasts are a speciality at this
unpretentious gastro pub. Tucked off the
main road opposite the park, The Landseer is
popular with its local clientele. Well-kept
beers like Marston's Pedigree, Courage
Director's and Kronenbourg are supported by
a range of over a dozen wines served by the
glass. This is an ideal spot to relax with the
weekend papers, or while away an evening
with one of the pub's extensive library of
board games. Weekend lunches and daily
evening meals are served from separate bar
and restaurant menus. Steak and Guinness
sausage with mash and gravy, or pasta penne
with roast vegetables and chilli are typical
choices in the bar. Meanwhile, the restaurant

menu begins with French onion soup, or rabbit rillettes
with sweet pepper coulis. Main courses include roast
cod, chorizo, butter beans and mash; cassoulet; and
herb-crusted rack of lamb with ratatouille.

OPEN: 12-11 Mon-Fri open from 5pm Closed: Christmas Day
BAR MEALS: L served Sat, Sun 12-5 D served all week 6-10
Sun 6-9.30 Av main course £9 **RESTAURANT:** L served
Sat/Sun 12-5 D served all week 6-10 Sun 12.30-5 & 6-9.30
BREWERY/COMPANY: Free House ◖: Marston's Pedigree,
Courage Directors. ♇: 11
CHILDREN'S FACILITIES: portions, licence, food/bottle
warming **GARDEN:** Pavement area between pub and park
NOTES: Dogs allowed: in bar

NW1 THE CHAPEL ♀

48 Chapel St NW1 5DP
☎ 020 7402 9220 📠 020 7723 2337
e-mail: thechapel@btconnect.com
Dir: By A40 Marylebone Rd & Old Marylebone Rd junction. Off Edgware Road by tube station

There's a relaxed, informal atmosphere at this bright and airy gastropub with its stripped floors and pine furniture. The modern, open-plan building derives its name from nothing more than its location, and the daily chalkboard menus give the place a trendy Anglo-Mediterranean feel. Greene King IPA and Adnams ales go side by side with the extensive wine list, and food is served throughout the building and the attractive tree-shaded garden. On any given day expect starters such as courgette, lemon and mint soup; focaccia with roasted vegetables and St Albray cheese; or smoked chicken and vegetable terrine. Follow with pan-fried guinea fowl; baked monkfish with Serrano, aubergine, tomato and anchovy dressing; or stuffed globe artichoke with risotto, smoked Cheddar and tomato coulis. Leave space for banana crème brûlée, or apple tart.

OPEN: 12-11 (Sun 12-10.30) Closed: Dec 24-Jan 2
BAR MEALS: L served all week 12-2.30 D served all week 7-10 (Sun 12.30-3, 7-10) Av main course £11.75
RESTAURANT: L served all week 12-2.30 D served all week 7-10 (Sun 12.30-3, 7-10) Av 3 course à la carte £20
BREWERY/COMPANY: Punch Taverns ◀: Greene King IPA, Adnams. ♀: 8 **CHILDREN'S FACILITIES:** portions, food/bottle warming **GARDEN:** Paved area, shaded by large tree, with tables **NOTES:** Dogs allowed: in bar

NW3 THE HOLLY BUSH 🐑 ♀

Holly Mount, Hampstead NW3 6SG
☎ 020 7435 2892
e-mail: hollybush@btconnect.com

Once the home of English portraitist George Romney, it became a pub after his death in 1802. Recently investigated by real ghostbusters keen to make the acquaintance of a spooky barmaid. The more tangible forms of 21st-century pop and TV celebrities are easier to spot. Staple fare includes pan-roast chicken with paprika; wild boar steak with mash and redcurrant jelly; cured, Cumberland and chorizo sausages with Cheddar mash and gravy; and pies and puddings, together with vegetarian options. Real ales from Adnams and Harveys.

OPEN: 12-11.00 **BAR MEALS:** L served Tue-Sun 12.30-4.00 D served all week 6.30-10.00 Sun 12-9 Av main course £10
RESTAURANT: L served Sat-Sun 12.30-10 D served Wed-Sun Sun 12.30-9 **BREWERY/COMPANY:** ◀: Harveys Sussex Best, Adnams Bitter & Broadside, Lowenbrau, Duvel. ♀: 10 **CHILDREN'S FACILITIES:** portions, games, high-chairs, food/bottle warming **GARDEN:** Small area outside pub with seating & tables **NOTES:** Dogs allowed: in bar, in garden

NW6 THE SALUSBURY PUB AND DINING ROOM 🐑 ♀

50-52 Salusbury Rd NW6 6NN
☎ 020 7328 3286
e-mail: thesalusbury@aol.com
Dir: 100m L out of Queens Park tube & train station

In green, leafy Brondesbury, The Salusbury is a gastropub that attracts its fair share of big names in fashion and media circles. However, lesser mortals not on celebrity A- or even B-lists may eat just as satisfyingly, starting perhaps with smoked goose breast and mushrooms tartare, or papardelle with duck ragú; continuing with pan-fried mackerel, pinenuts and sweet and sour leeks, or broth of Welsh lamb with vegetables and pecorino. A long, cosmopolitan wine list.

OPEN: 12-11 Closed: 25-26 Dec **BAR MEALS:** L served Tues-Sun 12.30-3.30 D served all week 7-11.15 Av main course £11 **RESTAURANT:** L served all week 12.30-3.30 D served all week 7-10.15 Av 3 course à la carte £20 ◀: Broadside. ♀: 7 **CHILDREN'S FACILITIES:** high-chairs, family room **NOTES:** Dogs allowed: in bar

NW10 WILLIAM IV BAR & RESTAURANT ♀

786 Harrow Rd NW10 5JX
☎ 020 8969 5944 ▤ 020 8964 9218
Dir: Telephone for directions

The William IV enjoys a strong local following plus regular visits from pop artistes and TV personalities nipping out from the nearby BBC studios. The daily menu offers an à la carte choice, set lunch, early evening special deal, Saturday brunch (12.30-4pm) and a set two or three course Sunday lunch. Typical dishes are chargrilled sirloin steak with chips and beetroot pesto; baked plaice with green beans; and pea, broad bean and mint tart.

OPEN: 12-11 (Thu-Sat 12-12, Sun 12-10.30) Closed: Dec 25 & Jan 01 **BAR MEALS:** L served all week 12-3 D served all week 6-10.30 Sun 12-4.30 Av main course £10 **RESTAURANT:** L served all week 12-3 D served all week 6-10.30 Av 3 course à la carte £22 Av 2 course fixed price £10 **BREWERY/COMPANY:** Free House 🍺: Fuller's London Pride, Greene King IPA, Interbrew Bass, Brakspear. ♀: 12 **CHILDREN'S FACILITIES:** portions, high-chairs, food/bottle warming, baby changing **GARDEN:** Food served outside **NOTES:** No dogs (ex guide dogs)

SE1 THE BRIDGE HOUSE BAR & DINING ROOM 🐑 ♀

218 Tower Bridge Rd SE1 2UP
☎ 020 7407 5818 ▤ 020 7407 5828
Dir: 5 min walk from London Bridge/Tower Hill tube stations

The nearest bar to Tower Bridge, on the south side, The Bridge House has great views of the river and city. It comprises a bar, dining room and new café, plus facilities for private functions. Dishes range through home-ground beef burger with fat chips and chilli relish; slow roasted Norfolk duck with braised red cabbage, basil mash and red wine gravy; and field mushroom, plum tomato and artichoke tart with mixed leaves and lentil dressing.

OPEN: 11.30-11 (Sun 12-10.30) Closed: 25-26 Dec, 1 Jan **BAR MEALS:** L served all week 11.30-10 D served all week 5-10 Sun 12-9.30 **RESTAURANT:** 12-4 6-10 🍺: Adnams Best Bitter, Adnams Broadside. ♀: 16 **CHILDREN'S FACILITIES:** portions, food/bottle warming, Only in dining room, family room **NOTES:** No dogs (ex guide dogs)

THE FIRE STATION RESTAURANT & BAR ⚙ ♀

150 Waterloo Rd SE1 8SB
☎ 020 7620 2226 ▤ 020 7633 9161
e-mail: firestation@wizardinns.co.uk

Close to Waterloo Station, and handy for the Old Vic Theatre and the Imperial War Museum, this remarkable conversion of a genuine early Edwardian fire station has kept many of its former trappings intact. The rear dining room faces the open kitchen. An interesting menu includes dishes such as Fire Station avocado Caesar salad, baked cod with cheese polenta and pimento and pesto dressing, roast spiced pork belly with sticky rice and pak choi. There are also imaginative midweek and Sunday set-price lunches.

OPEN: 11-11 (Sun 12-10.30) Closed: 25/26 Dec **BAR MEALS:** L served all week 12-5.30 D served all week 5.30-10.30 Av main course £5.95 **RESTAURANT:** L served all week 12-2.45 D served all week 5-11 (Sat 12-11, Sun 12-9.30) Av 3 course à la carte £20 Av 3 course fixed price £13.50 **BREWERY/COMPANY:** 🍺: Adnams Best Bitter & Broadside, Fuller's London Pride, Young's Bitters, Shepherd Neame Spitfire. ♀: 8 **CHILDREN'S FACILITIES:** menu, portions, high-chairs, food/bottle warming, baby changing facilities **NOTES:** No dogs (ex guide dogs)

SE5 THE SUN AND DOVES ♀

61-63 Coldharbour Ln, Camberwell SE5 9NS
☎ 020 7924 9950 📠 020 7924 9330
e-mail: mail@sunanddoves.co.uk

Attractive Camberwell venue known for good food, drink and art - all with a contemporary flavour. For a London pub it also has a decent sized garden, great for the summer months. Drinks options range from Fairtrade coffee and herbal infusions to draught ales and champagne, including plenty of wines by the glass. The menu is stylishly simple, with a daily soup and stew, and snacks like marinated olives and nachos. Otherwise there's a choice of starters/light meals including hot sandwiches, eggs Benedict, and cured meats and pickles. Grills and mains take in speciality skewers - marinaded ingredients (chicken, swordfish, halloumi) grilled on a beech skewer - alongside Cumberland sausage and mash, and fish in beer batter. There are cool side orders too, like fat chips; rocket, Parmesan and pine nut salad, and rustic bread with roast garlic and olive oil. The pub also showcases local artists, many pretty well known.

OPEN: 11-11 Closed: 25/26 Dec **BAR MEALS:** L served all week 12-10.30 D served all week 12-10.30 Sun 12-9 Av main course £8 **RESTAURANT:** L served all week 11-11 D served all week Av 3 course à la carte £18 **BREWERY/COMPANY:** Scottish & Newcastle ◖: Greene King Old Speckled Hen, Scottish Courage John Smith's Smooth. ♀: 8 **CHILDREN'S FACILITIES:** portions, games, high-chairs, food/bottle warming **GARDEN:** Secluded, warm, spacious, S facing **NOTES:** Dogs allowed: in bar, in garden, Water bowl in garden

SE16 MAYFLOWER INN 🐑 ♀

117 Rotherhithe St, Rotherhithe SE16 4NF
☎ 020 7237 4088 📠 020 7064 4710
Dir: *Exit A2 at Surrey Keys roundabout onto Brunel Rd, 3rd L onto Swan Rd, at T jct L, 200m to pub on R*

From the patio of the Mayflower Inn you can still see the renovated jetty from which the eponymous 'Mayflower' embarked on her historic voyage to the New World. The pub has maintained its links with the famous ship through a range of memorabilia, as well as its unusual licence to sell both British and American postage stamps. Pub fare includes stuffed pork loin; Cajun chicken supreme; and fresh pasta with smoked bacon, spinach and mushrooms.

OPEN: 11-3 6-11 (Sun 12-10.30) **BAR MEALS:** L served all week 12-2.30 D served all week 6.30-9.30 (Sun 12-4) Av main course £5.50 **RESTAURANT:** L served Mon-Sun 12-2.30 D served Mon-Sat 6.30-9 (Sun 12-4) **BREWERY/COMPANY:** Greene King ◖: Greene King Abbot Ale, IPA, Old Speckled Hen. ♀: 14 **CHILDREN'S FACILITIES:** portions, high-chairs, food/bottle warming, baby changing **GARDEN:** Jetty over river, Food served outside **NOTES:** Dogs allowed: in bar

SW4 THE WINDMILL ON THE COMMON ★★★ ♀

Clapham Common South Side SW4 9DE
☎ 020 8673 4578 📠 020 8675 1486
e-mail: windmillhotel@youngs.co.uk
Dir: *Nearest tube: Clapham Common or Clapham South*

The windmill on this site in 1655 is long gone, but in more recent times the building has been a popular watering hole for crowds returning from the Epsom races. There are two spacious bars, a conservatory and a back room with a roof shaped like a flattened Byzantine dome. Food ranges from filled baguettes and burgers to crab fishcakes, curries and steak and ale pie. There is separate oak-panelled restaurant and hotel accommodation, and during the hotter months the outside bar opens.

OPEN: 11-11 (Sun 12-10.30) **BAR MEALS:** L served all week 12-2.30 D served all week 6-10 Av main course £7 **RESTAURANT:** L served all week 12-2.30 D served all week 7-10 Sun 12-9 Av 3 course à la carte £15 **BREWERY/COMPANY:** Young & Co ◖: Youngs Bitter, Special, Winter Warmer, Waggledance. ♀: 20 **CHILDREN'S FACILITIES:** portions, licence, high-chairs, food/bottle warming, family room **GARDEN:** Benches, seats approx 50, garden bar **NOTES:** Dogs allowed: in bar, in garden, in bedrooms, Water bowl, Parking 16 **ROOMS:** 29 en suite s£99 d£115

SW6 THE ATLAS

16 Seagrave Rd, Fulham SW6 1RX
☎ 020 7385 9129 📠 020 7386 9113
e-mail: theatlas@btconnect.com
Dir: *2mins walk from West Brompton underground*

In a trendy area of London where so many former pubs have become diners or restaurants, here is an establishment that remains true to its cause. The large bar area - divided into drinking and eating parts - attracts what in a rural village would be called outsiders, but to be a local round here you can even come from Chelsea, Hammersmith or Earl's Court. Mostly Mediterranean dishes - particularly from Italy, Spain, France and North Africa - appear on a twice-daily-changing menu. Dinner menus might feature pan-roast cod fillet and roast garlic mashed potatoes with tarragon Salsa Fresca; grilled leg of lamb with thyme and red wine, spiced black beans with cumin, white wine and parsley; and grilled Tuscan sausages with fennel and black pepper, potato and butternut squash gratin with leek and cream Salsa Crudo. Relatively few London inns have a walled beer garden, but this one does.

OPEN: 12-11 (Sun 12-10.30) Closed: Dec 24-Jan 1, Easter
BAR MEALS: L served all week 12.30-3 D served all week 7-10.30 (Sun 7-10) Av main course £10
BREWERY/COMPANY: Free House ◀: Wells Bombardier, Fuller's London Pride, Brakspear. ♀: 13
CHILDREN'S FACILITIES: food/bottle warming, No children in eve **GARDEN:** Large suntrap, heaters, awning

SW7 THE ANGLESEA ARMS

15 Selwood Ter, South Kensington SW7 3QG
☎ 020 7373 7960 📠 020 7370 5611
e-mail: enquiries@angleseaarms.com
Dir: *Telephone for directions*

This South Kensington pub has an interior little changed since 1827, though the dining area has proved a popular addition. The style is clubby with panelled walls and leather-clad chairs - ideal when matched with the great selection of whiskies. Food ranges from sandwiches to the usual pub staples, backed by daily specials offering pies, fish, meat, and vegetarian options. Great London beers, including Fuller's London Pride and Young's bitter.

OPEN: 11-11 (Sun 12-10.30) Closed: Xmas pm only
BAR MEALS: L served all week 12-3 D served all week 6.30-10 Sat-Sun 12-close Av main course £9
RESTAURANT: L served all week 12-3 D served all week 6.30-10 Sat 12-10, Sun 12-9 **BREWERY/COMPANY:** Free House ◀: Fuller's London Pride, Youngs Bitter, Adnams Bitter, Broadside. ♀: 10 **CHILDREN'S FACILITIES:** menu, portions, food/bottle warming **GARDEN:** Terrace at front and side of the pub **NOTES:** Dogs allowed: in bar, in garden, in bedrooms, Water

SWAG AND TAILS

10/11 Fairholt St SW7 1EG
☎ 020 7584 6926 📠 020 7581 9935
e-mail: theswag@swagandtails.com
Dir: *nearest tube: Knightsbridge*

Tucked away from the hustle and bustle of Knightsbridge, the Swag and Tails is a civilised retreat. The pretty, flower-decked Victorian pub sits in a tiny back street close to Harrods. Over the last fifteen years, the owners have created a successful and welcoming neighbourhood pub-restaurant with a discerning local trade. Real ales and good quality food are served in a warm, relaxing and civilised environment, with high standards of service by efficient staff. Open fires, original panelling and pine tables complement the stripped wooden floors, and create a comfortable setting in which to savour freshly prepared seasonal dishes inspired by Mediterranean cuisine.

OPEN: 11-11 Closed: all BHs **BAR MEALS:** L served Mon-Fri 12-3 D served Mon-Fri 6-10 Av main course £12.50
RESTAURANT: L served Mon-Fri 12-3 D served Mon-Fri 6-10 Av 3 course à la carte £26 **BREWERY/COMPANY:** Free House ◀: Marston's Pedigree, Wells Bombardier Premium Bitter, Scottish Courage John Smiths Smooth. ♀: 11
CHILDREN'S FACILITIES: portions, food/bottle warming
NOTES: Dogs allowed: in bar, In eve

SW11   DUKE OF CAMBRIDGE ♀

228 Battersea Bridge Rd SW11 3AA
☎ 020 7223 5662 ▯ 020 7801 9684
e-mail: info@geronimo-inns.co.uk

An award-winning community pub with an eclectic mix of locals and just a stone's throw from Battersea Park and two of London's most famous Thames crossings - Battersea Bridge and Albert Bridge. Popular Saturday brunch menu and traditional Sunday roasts. The interesting range of dishes includes bacon wrapped venison steaks, sea bass fillet with pesto and tomato roulade and chicken breast stuffed with mushrooms. The Duke of Cambridge supports the Haven trust breast cancer support centres by making a donation every time one its designated dishes, which are healthy and carcinogen free, is sold.

OPEN: 11-11 **BAR MEALS:** L served all week 12-2.30 D served all week 7-9.45 Sun 12-4 Av main course £9.50 **RESTAURANT:** L served all week 12-3 D served all week 7-9.45 Sun 6-9.30 Av 3 course à la carte £16 **BREWERY/COMPANY:** Young & Co ◖: Youngs Bitter & Special, Stella, Fosters, Guiness. ♀: 14 **CHILDREN'S FACILITIES:** portions **GARDEN:** Beer garden, patio, food served outdoors, BBQ **NOTES:** Dogs allowed:

THE FOX & HOUNDS ♀

66 Latchmere Rd, Battersea SW11 2JU
☎ 020 7924 5483 ▯ 020 7738 2678
e-mail: richardmanners@ogh.demon.co.uk
Dir: Nearest station is Clapham Junction. From there turn L down St John's Hill then up Lavender Hill. L at the first set of traffic lights down Latchmere Road. Pub is 200 yards on L

A late 19th-century pub, restored rather than refurbished, with a walled garden, extensive patio planting and a covered and heated seating area. Fresh ingredients are delivered daily from London's markets, and the Mediterranean-style menu changes accordingly. There are a few starters, half a dozen main dishes, one cheese and a couple of desserts. Typical offerings: a plate of antipasti; chicken breast and merguez tagine with fruited couscous, pinenuts, harissa and crème fraîche; and Donald's chocolate and almond cake with cream.

OPEN: 12-3 5-11 (Sat 12-11, Sun 12-10.30, Mon 5-11) Closed: Easter Day, 24 Dec- 01 Jan **BAR MEALS:** L served Tue-Sun 12.30-3 D served all week 7-10.30 Av main course £9.50 **BREWERY/COMPANY:** Free House ◖: Interbrew Bass, Harveys Sussex Best Bitter, Fullers London Pride. ♀: 12 **CHILDREN'S FACILITIES:** portions, food/bottle warming, Children not allowed after 7pm **GARDEN:** Walled garden, covered area with heaters **NOTES:** No dogs (ex guide dogs)

SW18   THE OLD SERGEANT 🐑

104 Garrett Ln, Wandsworth SW18 4DJ
☎ 020 8874 4099 ▯ 020 8874 4099

Traditional, friendly and oozing with character, The Old Sergeant enjoys a good reputation for its beers, but also offers some good malt whiskies. It's a good place to enjoy home-cooked food too: the menu could include salmon fish cakes with a sweet chili sauce, duck and orange sausages with coriander mash and gravy, or Thai fishcakes. One of the first pubs bought by Young's in the 1830s.

OPEN: 11-11 (12-10.30 Sun) **BAR MEALS:** L served all week 12-2.30 D served all week 7-10 (all day Sun) Av main course £7.50 **RESTAURANT:** L served Mon-Fri D served Mon-Fri **BREWERY/COMPANY:** Youngs ◖: Youngs Ordinary, Youngs Special. **CHILDREN'S FACILITIES:** menu, portions, food/bottle warming, baby changing **NOTES:** in bar, dog bowl

W4   THE DEVONSHIRE HOUSE ⊛ ♀

126 Devonshire Rd, Chiswick W4 2JJ
☎ 020 8987 2626 ▤ 020 8995 0152
e-mail: info@thedevonshirehouse.co.uk
*Dir: Off Chiswick High Road. 150 yds from
Hogarth rdbt & A4.* **Map Ref:** *TQ27*

Previously the Manor Tavern, the Devonshire
House was extensively refurbished in 2003
and reopened as a gastro pub offering
excellent food and service to its community
clientele. The two partners have Marco Pierre
White restaurants on their CVs, reflected in
the accomplished but reasonably priced
menus that are changed daily for both lunch
and dinner. At lunch expect starters such as
potted kipper and Irish whiskey terrine; main
courses like roast silver mullet with crushed
new potatoes; and for dessert, Yorkshire
rhubarb hazelnut macaroon crumble with clotted
cream. In the evening, the Mediterranean flavours
become more extrovert, with the likes of marinated
Spanish olives, risotto verde with pangriatta, and mint
tagliatelle with ragout of lamb and mushroom
Bolognese. Most of the popular lagers and spirits are
served, as well as over a dozen wines by the glass.
Outside is a landscaped courtyard where barbecues
are planned.

OPEN: 12-12 (Sun 12-11.30) Closed: 25 Dec, 1 Jan
BAR MEALS: L served Tue-Sun 12-2.30 D served all week
7-10.30 Av main course £12.50 **RESTAURANT:** 12-2.30
D served Tue-Sun 7-10.30 Av 3 course à la carte £24.50
🍺: Stella, Kronenbourg 1664, Hoegaarden, Guinness. ♀: 14
CHILDREN'S FACILITIES: portions, licence, high-chairs,
food/bottle warming **NOTES:** No dogs (ex guide dogs)

W6   THE STONEMASONS ARMS ♀

54 Cambridge Grove W6 0LA
☎ 020 8748 1397 ▤ 020 8748 6086

Trendy yet welcoming London gastro-pub
with warm wooden floors and trestle tables,
serving "modern, but honest British cuisine".
Sample such delights as home-made fish pie
with salad, poached smoked haddock with
creme fraiche and Parmesan sauce, roast new
potatoes and watercress salad, grilled beef
burger with hoummous, salad and chips, and
Hoi Sin chargrilled leg of lamb steak with
sautéed spinach, Puy lentils and raita.
Extensive wine list.

OPEN: 12-11 (Sun 12-10.30) Closed: Dec 25, Jan 1
BAR MEALS: L served all week 12-3 D served all week
6.30-10 (Sun 12-3.30, 6.30-9.30) Av main course £10
RESTAURANT: L served all week 12-4 D served all week
6-10 Av 3 course à la carte £20
BREWERY/COMPANY: Free House 🍺: Adnams, Flowers
Original. **CHILDREN'S FACILITIES:** portions, high-chairs,
food/bottle warming **GARDEN:** Food served outdoors
NOTES: No dogs

W10   PARADISE BY WAY OF KENSAL GREEN ♀

19 Kilburn Ln, Kensal Rise W10 4AE
☎ 020 8969 0098 ▤ 020 8960 9968
e-mail: paradise.bywayof@virgin.net

A truly eclectic pub atmosphere with bare
boards, bric-à-brac, oriental tapestries and
wrought iron chandeliers creating a
Bohemian setting for working artists,
musicians and actors. The unusual name
derives from the last line of G K Chesterton's
poem 'The Rolling English Road', and there
are plenty of original Victorian features in
keeping with its late 19th-century origins. The
food at this lively venue stands up well to the
demands placed on it by weekly live jazz and
special events like weddings, but don't expect
bar snacks or too much flexibility. The self-
styled gastro-pub serves classy food from the
carte, such as Parma ham with rocket and roasted figs,
or crispy fried squid salsa to start, followed by
monkfish and mussels in a creamy garlic sauce with
linguine, and Moroccan spiced haddock with roast
vegetable couscous.

OPEN: 12-11 (Sun 12-10.30) Closed: 25 Dec & Jan 1
BAR MEALS: L served all week 12-4 D served all week
7.30-11 Av main course £12 **RESTAURANT:** L served all
week 12.30-4 D served all week 7.30-11 (Sun 12.30-9)
Av 3 course à la carte £20 Av 2 course fixed price £18
BREWERY/COMPANY: Free House 🍺: Shepherds Neame
Spitfire, Hoegarden, Stella Artois. ♀: 8
CHILDREN'S FACILITIES: menu, portions, licence, games,
high-chairs, baby changing **GARDEN:** Courtyard
NOTES: Dogs allowed: in bar, in garden, Water provided

BLAKENEY THE KINGS ARMS

Westgate St NR25 7NQ
☎ 01263 740341 📠 01263 740391
e-mail:
kingsarms.blakeney@btopenworld.com
Map Ref: TG04

A choice of real ales, Guinness and cider
awaits you inside this Grade II listed free
house on the North Norfolk coast. The Kings
Arms is an ideal centre for walking, or
perhaps a ferry trip to the nearby seal colony
and world-famous bird sanctuaries.
Locally-caught fish and seasonal seafood
feature on the menu, together with local
game, home-made pies and pastas.

OPEN: 11-11 **BAR MEALS:** L served all week 12-9.30
D served all week 12-9.30 Sun 12-9 Av main course £7
BREWERY/COMPANY: Free House 🍺: Greene King Old
Speckled Hen, Woodfordes Wherry Best Bitter, Marston's
Pedigree, Adnams Best Bitter. 🍷: 12
CHILDREN'S FACILITIES: menu, portions, games, high-chairs,
food/bottle warming, baby changing, outdoor play area,
swings, family room **GARDEN:** Very safe large patio and
grass area **NOTES:** Dogs allowed: in bar, in garden,
in bedrooms, Water, Parking 10

WHITE HORSE HOTEL

4 High St NR25 7AL
☎ 01263 740574 📠 01263 741303
e-mail: enquiries@blakeneywhitehorse.co.uk
Dir: From A148 (Cromer to King's Lynn rd)
turn onto A149 signed to Blakeney.
Map Ref: TG04

Blakeney is a delightful fishing village of narrow streets
lined with flint-built cottages, and Blakeney's first pub,
a 17th-century coaching inn, is located just 100 yards
from the tidal quay affording fine views across the
harbour. Not surprisingly, given its proximity to the sea,
seafood is a speciality of the house, including fresh
local mussels, crab, lobster, whitebait, sea bass, Dover
sole and sea trout.

OPEN: 11-3 6-11 (Sun 12-3, 7-10.30) Closed: 7-21 Jan
BAR MEALS: L served all week 12-2 D served all week 6-9
Av main course £9 **RESTAURANT:** D served Tue-Sun 7-9
Av 3 course à la carte £26 **BREWERY/COMPANY:** Free
House 🍺: Adnams Bitter, Adnams Broadside, Woodfordes
Wherry, Woodfordes Nelson. 🍷: 12 **CHILDREN'S FACILITIES:**
menu, portions, high-chairs, food/bottle warming, baby changing,
highchairs, family room **GARDEN:** Courtyard, picnic tables and
umbrellas **NOTES:** No dogs (ex guide dogs), Parking 14

BRANCASTER STAITHE THE WHITE HORSE ★★ ✿

Main Rd PE31 8BY
☎ 01485 210262 📠 01485 210930
e-mail: reception@whitehorsebrancaster.co.uk
Dir: mid-way between King's Lynn &
Wells-next-the-sea on the A149 coastal road.
Map Ref: TF74

Expect a friendly welcome at this stylish dining pub,
which enjoys a wonderful situation in an unspoilt part
of North Norfolk near the coastal path. Scrubbed pine
tables, high-backed settles, an open log fire in winter
and cream-painted walls contribute to the bright,
welcoming atmosphere. But the pub's enviable
reputation is based on its renowned seafood which
can be enjoyed in the airy conservatory restaurant, the
scrubbed bar, or on the sun deck.

OPEN: 11-11 (Sun 12-10.30) **BAR MEALS:** L served all week
11.30-3 **RESTAURANT:** L served all week 12-3 D served all
week 6-10 **BREWERY/COMPANY:** Free House 🍺: Adnams
Best Bitter, Adnams Regatta, Fullers London Pride, Woodfordes
Nelsons Revenge. 🍷: 12 **CHILDREN'S FACILITIES:** menu,
portions, games, high-chairs, food/bottle warming, baby
changing **GARDEN:** Sun deck terrace overlooking tidal
marshes **NOTES:** Dogs allowed: in bar, in garden, Parking 80
ROOMS: 15 en suite 3 family rooms s£72 d£104

BURNHAM THORPE THE LORD NELSON

Walsingham Rd PE31 8HL
☎ 01328 738241 📠 01328 738241
e-mail: david@nelsonslocal.co.uk
Map Ref: TF84

Inside, you'll find a timeless atmosphere of huge high-backed settles, old brick floors and

open fires. Nelson himself drank here, and entertained the whole village to a farewell dinner before returning to sea in 1792. Families are warmly welcomed, and children will enjoy the huge garden with its climbing frame, wooden play area and basketball net.

OPEN: 11-3 6-11 (Sun 12-3 6.30-10.30)
BAR MEALS: L served all week 12-2 D served Mon-Sat 7-9
RESTAURANT: L served all week 12-2 D served Mon-Sat 7-9
BREWERY/COMPANY: Greene King 🍺: Greene King Abbot Ale & IPA, Woodforde's Wherry, Nelsons Revenge, Old Speckled Hen (summer only). ♀: 11
CHILDREN'S FACILITIES: menu, portions, games, high-chairs, food/bottle warming, baby changing, outdoor play area, large wooded play area & equipment; toys inside **GARDEN:** Very large; seating **NOTES:** Dogs allowed: in bar, in garden, Water, Parking 30

CLEY NEXT THE SEA THE GEORGE HOTEL ◆◆◆◆ ♀

High St NR25 7RN
☎ 01263 740652 📠 01263 741275
e-mail: thegeorge@cleynextthesea.com
Dir: On coast road (A149). Centre of village.
Map Ref: TG04

Not far from Cley's famous windmill, the George Hotel is a classic Edwardian Norfolk inn but with a modern twist, located near the sea and marshes, where the first naturalist trust was formed in 1926. The area's wildlife reserves boast abundant birdlife and local seal colonies.

OPEN: 11-3 6-11 (all day Apr-Oct & Bank Hols)
BAR MEALS: L served all week 12-2.30 D served all week 6.30-9.30 Av main course £6.95 **RESTAURANT:** L served all week 12-2.30 D served all week 6.30-9 Av 3 course à la carte £19 **BREWERY/COMPANY:** Free House 🍺: Greene King IPA, Abbot Ale & Old Speckled Hen, Adnams Bitter, Woodforde's Wherry. ♀: 8 **CHILDREN'S FACILITIES:** menu, outdoor play area, high chairs, baby changing, family room **GARDEN:** Mature garden **NOTES:** Dogs allowed: in bar, in garden, in bedrooms, Parking 15 **ROOMS:** 12 en suite s£35 d£40

COLTISHALL KINGS HEAD ◆◆◆ ❀❀ 🐑 ♀

26 Wroxham Rd NR12 7EA
☎ 01603 737426 📠 01603 736542
Dir: A47 Norwich ring road onto B1150 to North Walsham at Coltishall. R at petrol station, follow rd to R past church, on R next to car park.
Map Ref: TG21

Right in the heart of the Norfolk Broads, this 17th-century free house stands on the banks of the River Bure. Cruisers can be hired at nearby Wroxham, and fishing boats are available at the pub. If you prefer to stay on dry land, you'll find a warm welcome at the bar with its real ales and inviting bar menu: sausage and mash; smoked salmon with tagliatelle and a white wine and cream sauce; Thai green chicken curry are usually available, as well as a variety of baguettes and burgers.

A more sophisticated à la carte menu is served both in the restaurant and bar, with a tempting variety of options. Among the starters expect terrine of foie gras, deep fried oysters, local Brancaster mussels, and pan-fried Scottish scallops. The main courses include Scotch beef, French squab pigeon, local venison, and guinea fowl, plus eight different fish dishes.

OPEN: 11-3 6-11 (Sun all day) Closed: 26 Dec
BAR MEALS: L served all week 12-2 D served all week 7-9 Av main course £7.50 **RESTAURANT:** L served all week 12-2 D served all week 7-9 Av 3 course à la carte £21
BREWERY/COMPANY: Free House 🍺: Adnams Bitter, Directors, Marston's Pedigree. ♀: 8
CHILDREN'S FACILITIES: menu, portions, high-chairs, food/bottle warming **NOTES:** No dogs (ex guide dogs), Parking 20 **ROOMS:** 4 bedrooms 2 en suite 1 family room s£25 d£55

DEREHAM YAXHAM MILL ◆◆◆

Norwich Rd, Yaxham NR19 1RP
☎ 01362 851182 🖷 01362 631482
e-mail: traypoch1@aol.com
Map Ref: TF91

A converted windmill, dating back to 1810, situated in open countryside not far from the coast, the Norfolk Broads and Norwich. The new owners have made some changes since taking over, and the bar now features two guest ales, which change every day. Menus cater well for all tastes, with a good selection of fish dishes, as well as favourites such as minted lamb in mint gravy, steak and kidney pie, liver and bacon casserole and ham, egg and chips.

OPEN: 12-3 7-11.30 Summer open all day
BAR MEALS: L served Tue-Sun 12-2 D served all week 7-9 Av main course £6.95 **RESTAURANT:** L served Tue-Sun 12-2 D served all week 7-9 Av 3 course à la carte £12
🍺: Carlsberg, Tetley plus guest ales.
CHILDREN'S FACILITIES: portions, high-chairs, food/bottle warming, outdoor play area, play fort **GARDEN:** Lawn, picnic tables **NOTES:** No dogs (ex guide dogs), Parking 40
ROOMS: 8 en suite 2 family rooms s£35 d£50

FAKENHAM THE WENSUM LODGE HOTEL

Bridge St NR21 9AY
☎ 01328 862100 🖷 01328 863365
e-mail: enquiries@wensumlodge.fsnet.co.uk
Map Ref: TF92

Originally built around 1750 as the grain store to Fakenham Mill, this privately-owned establishment opened as a restaurant in 1983. It later became the Wensum Lodge Hotel, taking its name from the river it overlooks. Friendly service and quality home-cooked food, with two dozen wines to choose from. The à la carte menu may start with warm bacon and avocado salad, and continue with classic dishes like pork tenderloin in mixed herbs, or peppered fillet of lamb. Vegetarians are well catered for, with their own menu of first and main courses.

OPEN: 11-11 **BAR MEALS:** L served all week 11.30-2.30 D served all week 6.30-9.30 Av main course £7.95
RESTAURANT: L served all week 11.30-2.30 D served all week 6.30-9.30 Av 3 course à la carte £25
BREWERY/COMPANY: Free House 🍺: Greene King Abbot Ale & IPA, Adnams. **CHILDREN'S FACILITIES:** menu, portions, games, high-chairs, baby changing facilities
GARDEN: Small garden with stream **NOTES:** No dogs (ex guide dogs), Parking 20 **ROOMS:** 17 en suite 2 family rooms s£55 d£80 (★★)

THE WHITE HORSE INN ◆◆◆◆

Fakenham Rd, East Barsham NR21 0LH
☎ 01328 820645 🖷 01328 820645
e-mail: rsteele@btinternet.com
Map Ref: TF92

Ideally located for birdwatching, walking, cycling, fishing, golf and sandy beaches, this refurbished 17th-century inn offers en suite rooms and a characterful bar with log-burning inglenook. Good range of beers and malt whiskies. Fresh ingredients are assured in daily specials, with fish especially well represented: cod, plaice, scampi, haddock, bream and a seafood platter usually appear on the menu. Enclosed courtyard at rear.

OPEN: 11-3 6-11 **BAR MEALS:** L served all week 12-2 D served all week 7-9.30 **RESTAURANT:** L served all week 12-2 D served all week 7-9.30 **BREWERY/COMPANY:**
🍺: Adnams Best, Adnams Broadside, Tetley, Wells Eagle IPA.
CHILDREN'S FACILITIES: menu, portions, games, high-chairs, food/bottle warming **GARDEN:** Patio area & enclosed courtyard **NOTES:** No dogs (ex guide dogs), Parking 50
ROOMS: 3 en suite 2 family rooms s£35 d£50

GREAT RYBURGH THE BOAR INN 🐑

NR21 0DX
☎ 01328 829212 📠 01328 829421
Dir: *Off A1067 4m S of Fakenham.*
Map Ref: *TF92*

The village, deep in rural Norfolk, has one of the county's unusual round-towered Saxon churches. Opposite is the 300-year-old Boar, dispensing a good variety of food, including beef Madras with rice, sweet and sour chicken with noodles, plaice fillet with prawns in Mornay sauce, scallops, lemon sole, and prime Norfolk steaks. Specials include skate wing with garlic and herb butter, and wild boar steak with cranberry and red wine jus. Bar/alfresco snacks and children's meals.

OPEN: 11-2.30 6.30-11 (All day 1 May-30 Sep)
BAR MEALS: L served all week 12-2 D served all week 7-9.30 **RESTAURANT:** L served all week 12-2 D served all week 7-9.30 Av 3 course à la carte £15
BREWERY/COMPANY: Free House 🍺: Adnams & guest ale.
CHILDREN'S FACILITIES: menu, portions, games, high-chairs, food/bottle warming, pool & games room, family room
GARDEN: Food served outside. **NOTES:** No dogs (ex guide dogs), Parking 30 **ROOMS:** 5 en suite 2 family rooms s£30 d£50 (♦♦♦)

HETHERSETT KINGS HEAD PUBLIC HOUSE 🐑

36 Norwich Rd NR9 3DD
☎ 01603 810206
Dir: *Old Norwich Road just off B1172 Cringleford to Wymondham road. 5m SW of Norwich.* *Map Ref:* *TG10*

Dating back to the 17th century, this former manorial cottage was where killer James Johnson was arrested by local constables for the murder of a glove-maker. He was tried and hanged in 1818. Appetising menu offers the likes of chilli con carne, Cajun salmon, battered cod and home-made lasagne.

OPEN: 11-2.30 5.30-11 (Sun 12-3 7-10.30 all day Sat (Sep-May)) **BAR MEALS:** L served all week 12-2 D served Mon-Sun 6.30-9 (Sun 12-2.30, 7-9) **RESTAURANT:** L served all week 12-2 D served Mon-Sun 6.30-9.30 (Sun 12-2.30, 7-9) Av 3 course à la carte £22.50 **BREWERY/COMPANY:** Unique Pub Co 🍺: Adnams Best Bitter, Greene King Abbot Ale, IPA, Tetley Smoothflow. **CHILDREN'S FACILITIES:** menu, portions, high-chairs, food/bottle warming, outdoor play area, Swings, climbing frame **GARDEN:** Seating surrounded by trees, benches & tables **NOTES:** in bar, Water, No dogs (ex guide dogs), Parking 20

HEVINGHAM MARSHAM ARMS FREEHOUSE ♦♦♦♦ 🐑 ⏳

Holt Rd NR10 5NP
☎ 01603 754268 📠 01603 754839
e-mail: nigelbradley@marshamarms.co.uk
Dir: *4m N of Norwich Airport on B1149 through Horsford.* *Map Ref:* *TG12*

Victorian philanthropist and landowner Robert Marsham built what is now the Marsham Arms as a hostel for poor farm labourers, and some original features remain - including the large open fireplace. Cabaret and live music often feature in the function suite. A good range of traditional pub fare is offered, including roast salmon, chicken in bacon and mushroom sauce, and steak and kidney pie. Plenty of fresh fish.

OPEN: 10-3 6-11 (open All day Summer) Closed: 25 Dec
BAR MEALS: L served all week 11-3 D served all week 6-9.30 **RESTAURANT:** L served all week 12-3 D served all week 6-9.30 **BREWERY/COMPANY:** Free House
🍺: Adnams Best, Woodforde's Wherry Best Bitter, Greene King IPA, Interbrew Bass. **CHILDREN'S FACILITIES:** menu, outdoor play area, high chairs, play area, family room
GARDEN: Large lawn with patio **NOTES:** No dogs, Parking 100 **ROOMS:** 10 en suite (♦♦♦♦)

HORSTEAD Recruiting Sergeant

Norwich Rd NR12 7EE
☎ 01603 737077 ▯ 01603 738827
Dir: on the B1150 between Norwich & North
Walsham. **Map Ref:** TG21

The name of this inviting country pub comes from the tradition of recruiting servicemen by giving them the King or Queen's shilling in a pint of beer. It offers good food, ales and wines in homely surroundings with a patio and lawned garden for alfresco dining. The menu is ever changing, with inventive dishes such as fresh oysters with a tabasco, lime and red onion dressing, duck breast on an apple and potato rosti and chicken breast stuffed with mozzarella and chorizo. There is also a vast daily specials menu, including fish and vegetarian dishes.

OPEN: 11-11 **BAR MEALS:** L served all week 12-2 D served all week 6.30-9.30 Av main course £7.95 **RESTAURANT:** L served all week 12-2 D served all week 6.30-9.30 Av 3 course à la carte £16 **BREWERY/COMPANY:** Free House ▮: Adnams, Woodefordes, Greene King Abbot Ale, Scottish Courage. ▯: 13 **CHILDREN'S FACILITIES:** menu, portions, high-chairs, food/bottle warming, baby changing **GARDEN:** Large patio, seats approx 40, enclosed lawn **NOTES:** Dogs allowed: in bar, in garden, Water, Parking 50

ITTERINGHAM Walpole Arms

NR11 7AR
☎ 01263 587258 ▯ 01263 587074
e-mail: goodfood@thewalpolearms.co.uk
Dir: Leave Aylsham in Blickling direction. After Blickling Hall take 1st R turn to Itteringham. **Map Ref:** TG13

An 18th-century oak-beamed country inn with a romantic restaurant and garden. The Walpole is run by a formidably knowledgeable team. Combining their skills with local products from named suppliers means that the strongly seasonal and daily-changing menu offers a comprehensive selection of dishes for every taste.

OPEN: 12-3 (Summer open all day Sat, Sun) 6-11 (Winter Sun 7-10.30) **BAR MEALS:** L served all week 12-2.00 D served Mon-Sat 7-9.30 Sunday 12.30-2.30 **RESTAURANT:** L served Wkds 12-2.00 D served Mon-Sat 7-9.30 Sun 12.30-2.30 **BREWERY/COMPANY:** ▮: Adnams Broadside & Bitter, Woodfordes Wherry Best Bitter & Walpole. ▯: 12 **CHILDREN'S FACILITIES:** menu, portions, high-chairs, food/bottle warming, outdoor play area, large fully fenced garden **GARDEN:** 2 large grassy areas with tables, patio area **NOTES:** Dogs allowed: in bar, in garden, Water, Parking 100

LARLING Angel Inn

NR16 2QU
☎ 01953 717963 ▯ 01953 718561
Map Ref: TL98

A 17th century former coaching inn of great charm and character which has been in the hands of the same family for three generations. Local produce is used whenever possible and the menus include varied light bites, burgers, salads and sandwiches. Main courses include home-made steak and kidney pie, fresh cod in a crispy Adnams bitter batter, steaks and grills. The largest annual beer festival in Norfolk takes place at the inn in August.

OPEN: 10-11 **BAR MEALS:** L served Sun-Sat 12-2 D served Sun-Sat 6.30-9.30 Fri & Sat 12-2.30, 6.30-10, Sun 12-2.30, 6.30-9.30 Av main course £7.50 **RESTAURANT:** L served all week 12-2 D served all week 6.30-9.30 Fri & Sat 12-2.30, 6.30-10, Sun 12-2.30, 6.30-9.30 Av 3 course à la carte £15 **BREWERY/COMPANY:** Free House ▮: Adnams Bitter, Buffy's Bitter, Wolf Bitter, Caledonian Deuchars IPA. ▯: 7 **CHILDREN'S FACILITIES:** menu, portions, outdoor play area, swings **GARDEN:** Large, garden tables **NOTES:** No dogs (ex guide dogs), Parking 100

LITTLE FRANSHAM THE CANARY AND LINNET

Main Rd NR19 2JW
☎ 01362 687027 📠 01362 687021
e-mail: ben@canaryandlinnet.co.uk
Dir: *Situated on A47 between Dereham and Swaffham.* **Map Ref:** *TF91*

Pretty former blacksmith's cottage with exposed beams, low ceilings, inglenook fireplace and a conservatory dining area overlooking the rear garden. Food is offered in the bar, restaurant or garden from daily specials, carte or bar menu. Typical dishes include cod in beer batter, steak and ale pie, salmon fillet with wholegrain mustard sauce, medallions of pork in a Stilton sauce, or smoked haddock with spinach and cheddar. A selection of malt whiskies.

OPEN: 12-3 6-11 (Sun 12-3 7-10) **BAR MEALS:** L served Mon-Sun 12-2 D served all week 6-9.30 **RESTAURANT:** L served all week 12-2 D served Mon-Sun 6-9.30 **BREWERY/COMPANY:** Free House 🍺: Greene King IPA, Tindall's Best, Adnams Bitter, Wolf. **CHILDREN'S FACILITIES:** menu, portions, high-chairs, food/bottle warming **NOTES:** Dogs allowed: in bar, Parking 70

LITTLE WALSINGHAM THE BLACK LION HOTEL ◆◆◆◆

Friday Market Place NR22 6DB
☎ 01328 820235 📠 01328 821407
e-mail: blacklionwalsingham@btinternet.com
Dir: *From Kings Lynn take A148 and B1105 or from Norwich take A1067 and B1105.*
Map Ref: *TF93*

The northern end of the hotel was built in the 14th century to accommodate King Edward III on his numerous pilgrimages to the shrine of Our Lady at Walsingham. Nowadays the hotel caters for discerning diners and drinkers. Besides a range of appetising bar snacks, the menu offers delicious dishes like venison medallions with Roquefort cheese and walnuts; grilled skate with orange and capers; or sage Derby and baby cauliflower vol-au-vents with Cheddar gratin.

OPEN: 11.30-3 (Easter-Oct 11.30-11) 6-11 (Sat 11.30-11, Sun 12-10.30) **BAR MEALS:** L served all week 12-2 D served all week 7-9.30 Av main course £8.50 **RESTAURANT:** L served all week D served all week 7-9.30 Av 3 course à la carte £18 **BREWERY/COMPANY:** Free House 🍺: Greene King IPA, Carlsberg Tetley Bitter, Abbott Ale. **CHILDREN'S FACILITIES:** menu, portions, high-chairs, food/bottle warming, changing room **GARDEN:** Courtyard garden, picnic tables, well **NOTES:** Dogs allowed: in bar, in garden, in bedrooms, Water, food **ROOMS:** 8 en suite 1 family room s£48.50 d£70 (◆◆◆◆)

MUNDFORD CROWN HOTEL

Crown Rd IP26 5HQ
☎ 01842 878233 📠 01842 878982
Dir: *Take A11 until Barton Mills interception, then A1065 to Brandon & thru to Mundford.*
Map Ref: *TL89*

Dating back to 1652, the Crown was once a famous hunting inn. In later years, the building played host to the local magistrates, with a court held here every second Thursday. At one time it was even a doctors' waiting room. Handy for exploring Thetford Forest and visiting local attractions such as Banham Zoo and Snetterton race circuit. Today's menu includes steak and kidney pie, lamb rogan josh, fillet of salmon, and pan-fried breast of duck.

OPEN: 11-11 **BAR MEALS:** L served all week 12-3 D served all week 7-10 Av main course £7.50 **RESTAURANT:** L served all week 12-3 D served all week 7-10 Av 3 course à la carte £25 **BREWERY/COMPANY:** Free House 🍺: Courage Directors, Courage Best, Greene King IPA & Guest ales. **CHILDREN'S FACILITIES:** menu, portions, high-chairs, food/bottle warming **GARDEN:** beer garden patio, food served outside **NOTES:** Dogs allowed: in bar

REEDHAM   RAILWAY TAVERN ♀

17 The Havaker NR13 3HG
☎ 01493 700340
e-mail: railwaytavern@tiscali.co.uk
Map Ref: TG40

A classic Victorian station pub in the middle
of the Norfolk Broads, with as many summer
visitors arriving by boat as by car. Good home-cooked
meals are served in the restaurant, bar or beer garden,
from a varied and innovative menu. The pub serves
beers brewed in the village, and plays host to beer
festivals in April and September, when real ale lovers
can line their stomachs with roast hog then sample
some of the 70 Norfolk brews on offer.

OPEN: 11-3 (Fri-Sun 11-11) 6-11 **BAR MEALS:** L served all
week 11.30-3 D served all week 6-9 Av main course £8.50
RESTAURANT: L served all week 11.30-3 D served all week
6-9.30 (Fri-Sun all day) Av 3 course à la carte £15
BREWERY/COMPANY: Free House ◀: Adnams, plus guest
ales. ♀: 12 **CHILDREN'S FACILITIES:** menu, portions, licence,
games, high-chairs, food/bottle warming, outdoor play area,
sand pit, Wendy house, family room **GARDEN:** converted
stable block **NOTES:** Dogs allowed: in bar, Water provided,
Parking 20

THE REEDHAM FERRY INN

Ferry Rd NR13 3HA
☎ 01493 700429 ▤ 01493 700999
e-mail: reedhamferry@aol.com
Dir: 6m S of Acle follow signs from Acle or
Loddon (Acle to Beccles rd). *Map Ref:* TG40

Quaint 17th-century inn in lovely Norfolk
Broads country and associated with the last
working chain ferry in East Anglia. With the
same name over the door for more than fifty
years, this is one of the longest running
family inns in East Anglia. Typical fare ranges
from salads, baguettes, sausage and chips or
pizzas, to joint of the day with all the
trimmings, scampi and chips, or steak and ale
pie. The specials boards are always worth
examining.

OPEN: 11-3 6.30-11 (Sun 12-10.30)
BAR MEALS: L served Mon-Sat 12-2 D served all week 7-9
(Sun 12-9) Av main course £6.50 **RESTAURANT:** L served
Mon-Sat 12-2 D served all week 7-9 (Sun 12-9)
BREWERY/COMPANY: Free House ◀: Woodforde's Wherry,
Adnams - Best & Broadside, Greene King Abbot Ale.
CHILDREN'S FACILITIES: menu, high-chairs, puzzles, toys,
blackboards **GARDEN:** Beside the River Yare on the Norfolk
Broads **NOTES:** Dogs allowed: in bar, in garden, Water
provided, Parking 50

SALTHOUSE   THE DUN COW

Coast Rd NR25 7XG
☎ 01263 740467
Dir: On A149 coast road, 3m E of Blakeney,
6m W of Sheringham. *Map Ref:* TG04

Overlooking some of the country's finest
freshwater marshes, the front garden of this
attractive pub is inevitably popular with birdwatchers
and walkers. The bar area was formerly a blacksmith's
forge, and many original 17th-century beams have
been retained. Children are welcome, but there's also
a walled rear garden reserved for adults. The menu
includes snacks, pub staples like burgers and jacket
potatoes, and main courses like gammon steak, pasta
and meatballs, plaice and chips, and lasagne.

OPEN: 11-11 (Sun 12-10.30) **BAR MEALS:** L served all
week 12 D served all week 9 Av main course £7
BREWERY/COMPANY: Pubmaster ◀: Greene King IPA &
Abbot Ale, Adnams Broadside.
CHILDREN'S FACILITIES: menu, high-chairs, food/bottle
warming, baby changing, family room **GARDEN:** Large
garden overlooking marshes **NOTES:** Dogs allowed: in bar,
Parking 15

SCOLE SCOLE INN

Ipswich Rd IP21 4DR
☎ 01379 740481 🖹 01379 740762
e-mail: scole.scole@oldenglishinns.co.uk
Dir: *Telephone for directions.* **Map Ref:** *TM17*

Fine old Grade I listed inn, dating from 1655 and located just off the Ipswich to Norfolk road. It has a striking Dutch façade and a wealth of period detail in the bars and intimate restaurant. Bar food includes sandwiches, fresh Lowestoft plaice, and steak and ale pie, and there's a fixed-price dinner menu in the restaurant. The inn also offers accommodation divided between the main house and converted Georgian stables.

OPEN: 11-11 (Sun 12-10.30) **BAR MEALS:** L served all week 12-2.15 D served all week 7-9.30 **RESTAURANT:** L served Sun-Fri 12-2 D served all week 7-9.30 **BREWERY/COMPANY:** Greene King : Greene King IPA, Abbot Ale, Speckled Hen, Ruddles County. **CHILDREN'S FACILITIES:** menu, high-chairs, food/bottle warming, Highchair **GARDEN:** Basic gardens with benches and tables **NOTES:** Parking 48 **ROOMS:** 23 en suite 1 family room (★★)

SNETTISHAM THE ROSE & CROWN ★★ ⊛ 🐑 ♀

Old Church Rd PE31 7LX
☎ 01485 541382 🖹 01485 543172
e-mail: info@roseandcrownsnettisham.co.uk
Dir: *N from Kings Lynn on A149 signed Hunstanton. Inn in centre of Snettisham between market square and the church.*
Map Ref: *TF63*

Long, low and covered in roses, the family-run Rose and Crown is all a village pub should be. The bars all have timbered ceilings, open fires and marvellous tiled floors. The pub has a growing reputation for exciting, good quality food and a regularly changing menu.

OPEN: 11-11 (Sun 12-10.30) **BAR MEALS:** L served all week 12-2 D served all week 9.30-9 (Sat-Sun 12-2.30, Fri & Sat 9.30) **RESTAURANT:** L served all week 12-2 D served all week 6-9 (Sat-Sun 12-2.30, Fri & Sat 9.30) **BREWERY/COMPANY:** Free House : Adnams Bitter & Broadside, Interbrew Bass, Fuller's London Pride, Greene King IPA. ♀: 20 **CHILDREN'S FACILITIES:** menu, portions, games, high-chairs, food/bottle warming, baby changing, outdoor play area, large play fort, crayons etc, family room **GARDEN:** Lrg walled garden, seating & shade **NOTES:** Dogs allowed: in bar, in garden, in bedrooms, Water, Parking 70 **ROOMS:** 11 en suite 4 family rooms s£50 d£70

STOKE HOLY CROSS THE WILDEBEEST ARMS ⊛⊛ 🐑 ♀

82-86 Norwich Rd NR14 8QJ
☎ 01508 492497 🖹 01508 494353
e-mail: wildebeest@animalinns.co.uk
Map Ref: *TG20*

A passion for fine food underpins the operation of this unusually named dining pub, situated just two miles south of Norwich. Formerly the Red Lion, the pub was renamed after an erstwhile landlord whose nicknames included 'the wild man' and 'beasty'. The old pub was opened up some years ago to create a wonderful space with working fireplaces at both ends and a horseshoe bar in the middle. If the interior is striking and sophisticated, the casual and relaxed atmosphere attracts a good range of clients from country and city alike. Good

quality local produce forms the basis of dishes like chargrilled rib-eye steak with aioli and house chips; twice-baked goats cheese soufflé; and grilled black bream with chorizo bubble and squeak, courgette tagliatelle and red pepper fondue. Desserts are just as appetising, with choices like glazed mango tart, and raspberry and redcurrant parfait.

OPEN: 12-3 6-11 (Sun 12-3 7-10.30) Closed: Dec 25-26 **BAR MEALS:** L served All D served All Av main course £9 **RESTAURANT:** L served all week 12-2 D served all week 7-10 Av 3 course à la carte £22.50 Av 3 course fixed price £14.95 **BREWERY/COMPANY:** Free House : Adnams. ♀: 12 **CHILDREN'S FACILITIES:** menu, portions, games, high-chairs, food/bottle warming **GARDEN:** Beer garden, beautifully landscaped **NOTES:** No dogs (ex guide dogs), Parking 30

SWANTON MORLEY DARBYS FREEHOUSE

1&2 Elsing Rd NR20 4NY
☎ 01362 637647 📠 01362 637987
Dir: *From A47 (Norwich to King's Lynn) take B1147 to Dereham.* **Map Ref:** *TG01*

Converted from two cottages in 1988 but originally built as a large country house in the 1700s, this popular freehouse opened when the village's last traditional pub closed. Named after the woman who lived here in the 1890s and farmed the adjacent land. Stripped pine tables, exposed beams and inglenook fireplaces enhance the authentic country pub atmosphere. Up to eight real ales are available and home-cooked food includes pigeon breast, steak and mushroom pudding, pesto pasta and salmon fillet.

OPEN: 11.30-3 6-11 (Sat 11.30-11, Sun 12-10.30) Rest: Dec 25 Closed Eve **BAR MEALS:** L served all week 12-2.15 D served all week 6.30-9.45 Av main course £7.50 **RESTAURANT:** L served all week 12-2.15 D served all week 6.30-9.45 Av 3 course à la carte £18.50 **BREWERY/COMPANY:** Free House 🍺: Woodforde's Wherry, Badger Tanglefoot, Adnams Broadside, plus three guest beers. **CHILDREN'S FACILITIES:** menu, outdoor play area, toy box, family room **GARDEN:** beer garden, outdoor eating **NOTES:** Dogs allowed: Parking 75

THOMPSON CHEQUERS INN ♦♦♦♦

Griston Rd IP24 1PX
☎ 01953 483360 📠 01953 488092
e-mail: themcdowalls@barbox.net
Dir: *Telephone for directions.* **Map Ref:** *TL99*

Historic 16th-century pub which over the years has been a manor court, doctor's surgery and meeting room. Many original features remain, including exposed beams and a timber and thatched roof swooping almost to the ground. With a growing reputation for exciting, imaginative and good quality food it's hardly surprising that large numbers of drinkers and diners are drawn here.

OPEN: 11.30-2.30 6.30-11 (Sun 12-3, 6.30-10.30) **BAR MEALS:** L served all week 12-2 D served all week 6.30-9.30 Av main course £7.50 **RESTAURANT:** L served all week 12-2 D served all week 6.30-9.30 Av 3 course à la carte £23 **BREWERY/COMPANY:** Free House 🍺: Fuller's London Pride, Adnams Best, Wolf Best, Greene King IPA. **CHILDREN'S FACILITIES:** menu, portions, high-chairs, food/bottle warming, baby changing, outdoor play area **GARDEN:** Childrens climbing frame lawned area **NOTES:** Dogs allowed: in bar, in garden, in bedrooms, Water, Sweeties, Parking 35 **ROOMS:** 3 en suite 1 family room s£40 d£60 (♦♦♦♦)

THORNHAM LIFEBOAT INN ★★ ✺ 🍷

Ship Ln PE36 6LT
☎ 01485 512236 📠 01485 512323
e-mail: reception@lifeboatinn.co.uk
Dir: *A149 to Hunstanton, follow coast rd to Thornham, pub 1st L.* **Map Ref:** *TF74*

A long and colourful history attaches to this

16th-century inn overlooking the salt marshes and Thornham Harbour. There are roaring log fires in winter and fine summer views across open meadows to a sandy beach. The best available fish and game feature on the menus in the form of traditional country fare. Mussels are a speciality, along with fish and chips - fillet of finest fresh cod in a crisp beer batter. Children and well-behaved dogs welcome.

OPEN: 11-11 **BAR MEALS:** L served all week 12-2.30 D served all week 6.30-9.30 Av main course £8.95 **RESTAURANT:** D served all week 7-9.30 Av 3 course fixed price £26 **BREWERY/COMPANY:** Free House 🍺: Adnams, Woodforde's Wherry, Greene King Abbot Ale. 🍷: 10 **CHILDREN'S FACILITIES:** menu, outdoor play area, wooden play fort, family room **GARDEN:** Enclosed wall patio garden **NOTES:** Dogs allowed: in bar, in garden, in bedrooms, Water provided, Parking 100 **ROOMS:** 22 en suite 2 family rooms

TITCHWELL · TITCHWELL MANOR HOTEL ★★ ◎◎ 🐑

PE31 8BB
☎ 01485 210221 ▤ 01485 210104
e-mail: margaret@titchwellmanor.com
Dir: A149 (coast rd) between Brancaster & Thornham. **Map Ref:** TF74

Built at the tail-end of the 19th century as a farmhouse, this family-run hotel is in the centre of a small coastal hamlet. From its pretty walled garden the sea views are glorious. The sea, of course, is a major influence on lunch menus, so fish and seafood lovers will be in their element.

OPEN: 11-11 **BAR MEALS:** L served all week 12-2 D served all week 6.30-9.30 Av main course £10
RESTAURANT: L served all week 12-2 D served all week 6.30-9.30 Av 3 course à la carte £20
BREWERY/COMPANY: Free House 🍺: Greene King IPA & Abbot Ale. **CHILDREN'S FACILITIES:** menu, portions, games, high-chairs, food/bottle warming, baby changing, books, games, TV, VCR, garden **GARDEN:** Large walled garden, summerhouse **NOTES:** Dogs allowed: in bar, in garden, in bedrooms, Water, kennel, Parking 50 **ROOMS:** 16 en suite 6 family rooms

TIVETSHALL ST MARY · THE OLD RAM COACHING INN ★★ 🐑 ⚲

Ipswich Rd NR15 2DE
☎ 01379 676794 ▤ 01379 608399
e-mail: theoldram@btinternet.com
Dir: On A140 approx 15m S of Norwich.
Map Ref: TM18

Sympathetically refurbished with exposed

brickwork and original beams, this 17th-century inn features a terraced garden and comfortably-furnished bedrooms. The main menu offers a very wide selection of meats, fish, salads, pastas, snacks and vegetarian dishes, including dedicated selections for children and the over-60s. Daily specials might include medallions of pork fillet with herb crust on a bed of red cabbage and apple sauce with cider jus.

OPEN: 7.30am-11 Closed: Dec 25-26
BAR MEALS: L served all week 11.30-10 D served all week Av main course £9.95 **BREWERY/COMPANY:** Free House 🍺: Adnams Bitter, Woodforde's Wherry Best Bitter, Coors Bass. ⚲: 28 **CHILDREN'S FACILITIES:** menu, portions, high-chairs, food/bottle warming, baby changing
GARDEN: Terraced, herb garden, patio heaters
NOTES: Water, No dogs (ex guide dogs), Parking 150
ROOMS: 11 en suite 1 family room s£49 d£63

UPPER SHERINGHAM · THE RED LION INN 🐑

The Street NR26 8AD
☎ 01263 825408
Dir: A140(Norwich to Cromer) then A148 to Sheringham/Upper Sheringham.
Map Ref: TG14

About 400 years old, flint-built, with original floors, natural pine furniture, a large wood-burning stove, and a Snug Bar haunted by a female ghost. Local produce is used extensively, with fish, including plaice, haddock, halibut, cod and crab, featuring in a big way. Other options are liver and bacon in port and orange gravy, steak and ale pie; Thai red chicken curry; a half pheasant in cranberry sauce; and chicken stuffed with prawns on a crab sauce.

OPEN: 11.30-3 6.30-11 Summer Hols Open all day Sun
BAR MEALS: L served all week 12-2 D served all week 6.30-9 Av main course £7.50 **RESTAURANT:** L served all week 12-2 D served all week 6.30-9 Av 3 course à la carte £15 **BREWERY/COMPANY:** Free House 🍺: Woodforde's Wherry, Greene King IPA. **CHILDREN'S FACILITIES:** portions, games, food/bottle warming, baby changing, outdoor play area, Not in main bar in eve, family room **GARDEN:** Large lawned area with fruit trees **NOTES:** Dogs allowed: in bar, in garden, in bedrooms, Water, Parking 16, No credit cards

WARHAM ALL SAINTS THREE HORSESHOES

NR23 1NL
☎ 01328 710547
Dir: *From Wells A149 to Cromer, then R onto
B1105 to Warham.* **Map Ref:** *TF94*

This fascinating free house was an alehouse
in 1725, and has remained one ever since. It
has one of the best original interiors in the
area, with gaslights in the main bar, scrubbed
deal tables, and a grandfather clock that was
made in nearby Dereham in 1830. There's a
rare example of a Norfolk 'twister' set into the
ceiling - a curious red and green dial for
playing village roulette. Fascinating
memorabilia and local artefacts are displayed
in the bars. Outside, there's a sheltered lawn
with picnic tables, and an enclosed courtyard.
Local ales are served direct from the cask.

Cooking is in the Mrs Beeton style, using fresh local
produce in shellfish cheese bake; local soused herrings
with herbs and onions; cottage garden bake; and
Norfolk beef pie. Specials might be local cider mussels;
braised local rabbit; fried liver and onions; or
mushroom, nut and wine pie.

OPEN: 11.30-2.30 (Sun 12-3) 6-11 (Sun 6-10.30)
BAR MEALS: L served all week 12-1.45 D served all week
6.00-8.30 Av main course £7.50
BREWERY/COMPANY: Free House ◀: Greene King IPA,
Woodforde's Wherry. **CHILDREN'S FACILITIES:** portions,
food/bottle warming, family room **GARDEN:** Grassed area
with seating; enclosed courtyard **NOTES:** Dogs allowed:
in bar, in garden, in bedrooms, Water, dog food and biscuits,
Parking 50, No credit cards

WELLS-NEXT-THE-SEA THE CROWN HOTEL

The Buttlands NR23 1EX
☎ 01328 710209 ▤ 01328 711432
e-mail: reception@thecrownhotelwells.com
Dir: *10m from Fakenham on B1105.*
Map Ref: *TF94*

There's a warm welcome at this former
coaching inn, overlooking the quiet tree-lined
green known as The Buttlands. Stylish,
uncluttered décor now enhances the
old-world charm of the refurbished
16th-century building. Diners can be sure of
freshly prepared food from the best
ingredients. Half a dozen Brancaster oysters
or a Caesar salad with marinated pork belly
are just two of the lighter options in the lively
bar with its ancient beams and open fire.
There's more formal dining in the elegant

restaurant, where roast quail or marinated herring are
the precursors to main courses such as wild
mushroom and saffron risotto; pan-fried sea bass; or
marinated duck breast. Finish with lemon tart and
crème frâiche or honey-roasted fruit on toasted brioche
with Mascarpone.

OPEN: 11-11 **BAR MEALS:** L served all week 12-2
D served all week 6-9 Av main course £10
RESTAURANT: D served all week 7-9 Av 3 course fixed price
£29.95 **BREWERY/COMPANY:** Free House ◀: Adnams
Bitter, Adnams Broadside, Adnams Guest Ale, Bitburger.
♀: 12 **CHILDREN'S FACILITIES:** menu, portions, games,
high-chairs, food/bottle warming **GARDEN:** Decking area

WINTERTON-ON-SEA FISHERMANS RETURN

The Lane NR29 4BN
☎ 01493 393305 ▤ 01493 393951
e-mail: fishermans_return@btopenworld.com
Dir: *8m N of Gt Yarmouth on B1159.*
Map Ref: *TG41*

This 300-year-old brick and flint pub is within walking
distance of long beaches (sensible shoes essential for
clambering over dunes!), and National Trust land, where
you can enjoy a spot of bird or seal watching. Dogs are
also welcome. There is a vast choice of malts and
ciders, and a good, traditional menu. Dishes might
include a seafood platter, fish pie, and various omelettes
and burgers, as well as a changing specials board.

OPEN: 11-2.30 6.30-11 (Sat 11-11, Sun 12-10.30)
BAR MEALS: L served all week 11.30-2 D served all week
6.30-9 Av main course £8.75 **BREWERY/COMPANY:** Free
House ◀: Woodforde's Wherry & Norfolk Nog, Adnams Best
Bitter & Broadside and Greene King IPA. ♀: 10
CHILDREN'S FACILITIES: menu, portions, high-chairs,
outdoor play area, slide, climbing frame, swing, family room
GARDEN: Large enclosed garden with tables, play equipment
NOTES: Dogs allowed: in bar, in garden, in bedrooms, Water
& chews, Parking 50

ABINGDON THE MERRY MILLER ♀

Cothill OX13 6JW
☎ 01865 390390 ▤ 01865 390040
e-mail: rob@merrymiller.fsbusiness.co.uk
Dir: *1m from the Marcham interchange on the A34.* *Map Ref:* SU49

Beams, flagstones and log fires all feature in this 17th-century pub. Overall, the interior is redolent more of Tuscany than the granary it once was, which at least ensures that the pasta dishes feel at home. But lunch, if not pasta, could just as easily be pie of the day, wholetail scampi and chips, or chicken pistou, while dinner might be characterised by braised half shoulder of lamb, smoked haddock and leek fishcakes, steak and kidney casserole, or Brie and broccoli pithivier.

OPEN: 12-11 (Sun 12-10.30) **BAR MEALS:** L served all week 12-2.45 D served all week 6.30-9.45 Sun all day Av main course £10.95 **RESTAURANT:** L served all week 12-2.45 D served all week 6.30-9.45
BREWERY/COMPANY: Greene King ◖: Greene King IPA & Old Speckled Hen. ♀: 15 **CHILDREN'S FACILITIES:** menu, high-chairs, food/bottle warming **GARDEN:** small patio garden, 20 parasol-covered seats **NOTES:** Dogs allowed: in bar, Parking 60

ARDINGTON THE BOARS HEAD ♀

Church St OX12 8QA
☎ 01235 833254 ▤ 01235 833254
e-mail: info@boarsheadardington.co.uk
Dir: *Off A417 E of Wantage.* *Map Ref:* SU48

Tucked away beside the church, the pretty, 400-year-old Boars Head is situated within the beautifully maintained Lockinge Estate. Although dining is important, it's still very much the village local. Log fires blaze when they should, candles are lit in the evenings, and there are always fresh flowers. The words 'fresh', 'locally grown', and 'seasonal' underpin the innovative, refreshingly unwordy menus, and everything is home made.

OPEN: 12-3 6.30-11 **BAR MEALS:** L served all week 12-2.30 D served all week 7-10 Av main course £9.50 **RESTAURANT:** L served all week 12-2.30 D served all week 7-10 Av 3 course à la carte £25
BREWERY/COMPANY: Free House ◖: Hook Norton Old Hooky, West Berkshire Berwery Dr. Hexter's, Warsteiner, Butts Brewery. ♀: 8 **CHILDREN'S FACILITIES:** menu, portions, games, high-chairs, food/bottle warming, baby changing **GARDEN:** Patio area, three tables **NOTES:** in bar, in garden, Parking 10

BAMPTON THE ROMANY

Bridge St OX18 2HA
☎ 01993 850237 ▤ 01993 852133
e-mail: romany@barbox.net
Map Ref: SP30

A shop until 20 years ago, The Romany is housed in an 18th-century building of Cotswold stone with a beamed bar, log fires and intimate dining room. The choice of food ranges from bar snacks and bar meals to a full à la carte restaurant menu, with home-made specials like hotpot, Somerset pork, or steak and ale pie. There is a good range of vegetarian choices. Regional singers provide live entertainment a couple of times a month.

OPEN: 11-11 **BAR MEALS:** L served all week 12-2 D served all week 6.30-9 Av main course £6 **RESTAURANT:** L served all week 12-2 D served all week 6.30-9 **BREWERY/COMPANY:** Free House ◖: Archers Village, plus guests. **CHILDREN'S FACILITIES:** menu, portions, games, high-chairs, food/bottle warming, outdoor play area **GARDEN:** Food served outside **NOTES:** Dogs allowed: Water, Parking 8

BARNARD GATE THE BOOT INN ♀

OX29 6XE
☎ 01865 881231 🖹 01865 882119
e-mail: info@thebootinn.com
Dir: off the A40 between Witney & Eynsham.
Map Ref: SP41

With a name like The Boot Inn, it's hardly surprising that this Cotswold stone pub is festooned with footwear, much of it donated by household names. Happily the smells are more likely to emanate from the kitchen, which provides brasserie-style food for smart and civilised dining. A typical meal may begin with smoked mackerel, followed by calves' liver and back bacon. Real ales served in spacious quarry-tiled bar.

OPEN: 11-3 6-11 (open all day in summer)
BAR MEALS: L served all week 12-2 D served all week 7-9.30 **RESTAURANT:** L served all week 12-2.30 D served all week 7-9.30 **BREWERY/COMPANY:** Free House
🍺: Hook Norton Best Bitter, Adnams Best Bitter, Fullers London Pride. ♀: 6 **GARDEN:** Courtyard **NOTES:** No dogs (ex guide dogs), Parking 30

BLACK BOURTON THE VINES ♀

Burford Rd OX18 2PF
☎ 01993 843559 🖹 01993 840080
e-mail: vinesrestaurant@aol.co.uk
Dir: From A40 Witney, take A4095 to Faringdon, then 1st R after Bampton to Black Bourton. *Map Ref:* SP20

This traditional Cotswold stone building features a stylish contemporary bar with cosy leather sofas beside an open log fire. The bar menu offers a choice of light bites, salads and pastas in addition to main meals, and generally reflects seasonal changes. The restaurant area was designed and decorated by John Clegg of the BBC's Real Rooms Team; try mains of roasted rump of lamb or pork tenderloin with fruit chutney.

OPEN: 11-2.30 6-11 (Sun 12-10.30) **BAR MEALS:** L served Tue-Sun 12-2 D served Tue-Sun 6.30-9.30
RESTAURANT: L served Tue-Sun 12-2 D served Tue-Sun 6.30-9.30 **BREWERY/COMPANY:** Free House 🍺: Old Hookey, Tetley Smooth, Carlsberg-Tetley.
CHILDREN'S FACILITIES: menu, portions, licence, high-chairs, food/bottle warming **GARDEN:** Large lawn area, seating **NOTES:** No dogs (ex guide dogs), Parking 70

BLOXHAM THE ELEPHANT & CASTLE 🐑

OX15 4LZ
☎ 01295 720383
e-mail: elephant.bloxham@btinternet.com
Dir: Just off A361. *Map Ref:* SP43

The arch of this 15th-century, Cotswold-stone coaching inn still straddles the former Banbury to Chipping Norton turnpike. Locals play darts or shove-ha'penny in the big wood-floored bar, whilst the two-roomed lounge boasts a bar-billiards table and a large inglenook fireplace. The reasonably priced menu starts with a range of sandwiches and crusty filled baguettes, whilst hot dishes include pub favourites like breaded haddock, crispy battered cod, scampi and a seafood platter.

OPEN: 10-3 5-11 (Sat, Sun-open all day)
BAR MEALS: L served Mon-Sat 12-2 Av main course £5.50
RESTAURANT: L served Mon-Sat 12-2
BREWERY/COMPANY: Hook Norton 🍺: Hook Norton Best Bitter, Hook Norton Seasona Ales, Guest Ales.
CHILDREN'S FACILITIES: menu, portions, food/bottle warming, baby changing, outdoor play area, Lawns, family room **GARDEN:** Raised lawn in flower filled garden, patio **NOTES:** in bar, Water, Parking 20

BROADWELL THE FIVE BELLS BROADWELL ◆◆◆

GL7 3QS
☎ 01367 860076
e-mail: trevorcooper@skynow.net
Dir: *A361 from Lechlade to Burford, after 2m R to Kencot Broadwell, then R after 200m, then R at crossrds.* **Map Ref:** SP20

Attractive 16th-century Cotswold stone inn overlooking the manor and parish church. The bars are full of character with beams and flagstones, and the conservatory leads to a pretty garden. An extensive choice of dishes includes salmon and prawn gratin, pheasant in red wine, and steak and kidney pie. Accommodation in five luxury chalets.

OPEN: 11.30-2.30 7-11 (Sun 12-3, 7-10.30) Closed: 25 & 26 Dec, closed Mon except BHs **BAR MEALS:** L served Tue-Sun 12-1.45 D served Tue-Sat 7-9 Av main course £7.50 **RESTAURANT:** L served Tue-Sun 12-1.45 D served Tue-Sat 7-9 Av 3 course à la carte £13.50 **BREWERY/COMPANY:** Free House **◀:** Interbrew Bass Bitter, Archers Village. **CHILDREN'S FACILITIES:** menu, portions **GARDEN:** Quiet, peaceful **NOTES:** Dogs allowed: in bar, in garden, Parking 30 **ROOMS:** 5 en suite d£50

BURFORD GOLDEN PHEASANT ★★ ♀

91 High St OX18 4QA
☎ 01993 823223 ▤ 01993 822621
e-mail: robrichardson.goldenpheasant-burford.co.uk
Dir: *Leave M40 at junction 8 and follow signs A40 Cheltenham into Burford.* **Map Ref:** SP21

Attractive honey-coloured, 17th-century stone inn in the centre of Burford, with cosy log fires bringing warmth in winter. Expect an informal atmosphere in the brasserie-style lounge bar and smart restaurant, where the food has an enthusiastic following. The menu might include braised lamb shank with mint red wine jus or salmon fillet with lemon and parsley butter while the specials board, which changes every couple of days, offers dishes such as saffron and wild mushroom risotto or confit of duck.

OPEN: 9-11 **BAR MEALS:** L served all week 12-2.30 D served all week 6.30-9.30 Av main course £9.95 **RESTAURANT:** D served all week 6.30-9 Av 3 course à la carte £25 **BREWERY/COMPANY:** **◀:** Abbot, IPA. **♀:** 7 **CHILDREN'S FACILITIES:** menu, portions, high-chairs, baby changing **GARDEN:** Patio **NOTES:** Dogs allowed: in bar, in bedrooms, Manager's discretion, Parking 12 **ROOMS:** 10 en suite s£65 d£85

THE INN FOR ALL SEASONS ★★ ♀

The Barringtons OX18 4TN
☎ 01451 844324 ▤ 01451 844375
e-mail: sharp@innforallseasons.com
Dir: *3m W of Burford on A40.* **Map Ref:** SP21

Situated some three miles west of Burford on the A40, just inside Gloucestershire, this 16th-century Grade II listed Cotswold coaching inn has been linked to the stone industry, particularly that used for St Paul's Cathedral. Within the solid walls is a treasure-trove of ancient oak beams, original fireplaces and complementary period furniture. The ten en suite bedrooms are spacious and comfortably furnished.

OPEN: 11-2.30 6-11 (Sun 12-3, 7-10.30) **BAR MEALS:** L served all week 11.30-2.20 D served all week 6.30-9.30 Av main course £8 **RESTAURANT:** L served all week 11.30-2.30 D served all week 6.30-9.30 Av 3 course à la carte £16.75 **BREWERY/COMPANY:** Free House **◀:** Wadworth 6X, Interbrew Bass, Wychwood, Badger. **♀:** 15 **CHILDREN'S FACILITIES:** menu, portions, games, high-chairs, food/bottle warming, baby changing, outdoor play area **GARDEN:** Small grass area, tables, good views **NOTES:** Dogs allowed: in bar, in garden, in bedrooms, Parking 80 **ROOMS:** 10 en suite 2 family rooms s£54 d£90

THE LAMB INN ★★★ 🌸🌸 🐑 ♀

Sheep St OX18 4LR
☎ 01993 823155 🖨 01993 822228
e-mail: info@lambinn-burford.co.uk
Dir: *From M40 J8 follow signs for A40 & Burford. Off High Street.* **Map Ref:** *SP21*

If your idea of a traditional English inn includes stone flagged floors, real ale and log fires, you'll not be disappointed at the Lamb. With its 500 years of history, this honey-coloured stone-built coaching inn lies just off the centre of Burford, whilst still having easy access to the shops. In summer you can visit the walled cottage garden, admire the herbaceous borders and perhaps take lunch on the lawn.

OPEN: 11-2.30 6-11 (Sun 12-4, 7-10.30)
BAR MEALS: L served Mon-Sat 12-2.30 D served Mon-Sun 7-9.30 Sat no bar menu in evening Av main course £12
RESTAURANT: L served Mon-Sun 12.30-2.30 D served Mon-Sun 7-9.30 Av 3 course fixed price £32
BREWERY/COMPANY: Free House 🍺: Wadworth 6X, Hook Norton Best, Badger Dorset Bitter. ♀: 14 **CHILDREN'S FACILITIES:** menu, portions, games, high-chairs, food/bottle warming, baby changing, family room **GARDEN:** walled cottage garden **NOTES:** Dogs allowed: in bar, in garden, in bedrooms, Water **ROOMS:** 15 en suite s£80 d£130

THE MAYTIME INN ♦♦♦ ♀

Asthall OX18 4HW
☎ 01993 822068 🖨 01993 822635
e-mail: timmorgan@themaytime.fsnet.co.uk
Dir: *A361 from Swindon, R onto A40 then onto B4047 to Asthall.* **Map Ref:** *SP21*

Traditional Cotswold pub in the Windrush valley, between the two historical towns of Burford and Witney. The present owners acquired the then derelict local in 1975 and set about transforming it into a character inn. There's a daily fresh fish board.

OPEN: 11-3 6-11 **BAR MEALS:** L served all week 12.15-2.15 D served all week 7-9.15 Av main course £10.95 **RESTAURANT:** L served all week 12.15-2.15 D served all week 7-9.15 Av 3 course à la carte £18.50
BREWERY/COMPANY: Free House 🍺: Timothy Taylor. ♀: 8 **CHILDREN'S FACILITIES:** menu, portions, high-chairs, food/bottle warming **GARDEN:** Patio **NOTES:** Dogs allowed: in bar, in garden, in bedrooms, Water, Parking 100 **ROOMS:** 6 en suite 1 family room s£55 d£72.50

CHADLINGTON   THE TITE INN ♀

Mill End OX7 3NY
☎ 01608 676475 🖨 0870 7059308
e-mail: willis@titeinn.com
Dir: *3m S of Chipping Norton.* **Map Ref:** *SP32*

Nothing can beat the Tite Inn's winter welcome of log fires, mulled wine and home-cooked food. In summer, the garden comes into bloom and the climbing roses help to create a perfect setting for enjoying the inn's five draught beers and hand-pulled cider. Lunchtime brings ploughman's lunches, sandwiches and hot dishes. In the evening, expect lambs kidneys in red wine with mash, salmon fishcakes with hollandaise sauce, or Brazil nut roast with fresh tomato sauce.

OPEN: 12-2.30 6.30-11 (Sun 12-3, 7-10.30) Closed: Dec 25-26 **BAR MEALS:** L served Tue-Sun 12-2 D served Tue-Sun 7-9 Av main course £8.95 **RESTAURANT:** L served Tue-Sun 12-2 D served Tue-Sat 6.30-9 Av 3 course à la carte £12 **BREWERY/COMPANY:** Free House 🍺: Youngs,2 Guest Beers, Hopback, Wyrepiddle. ♀: 8 **CHILDREN'S FACILITIES:** portions, food/bottle warming **GARDEN:** Large beer garden, outstanding views **NOTES:** Dogs allowed: in bar, in garden, Water provided, Parking 30

CHALGROVE THE RED LION INN

The High St OX44 7SS
☎ 01865 890625 🖷 01865 890795
Dir: *B480 from Oxford Ring rd, thru Stadhampton, L then R at mini-rdbt, at Chalgrove Airfield R fork into village.*
Map Ref: *SU69*

A pub owned by the village church? The Red Lion is, and has been since 1637, when it provided free dining and carousing for the 'naughty' church wardens. Parts of this lovely cream-painted and beamed pub even date back to the 11th century. Following a recent change of ownership, the emphasis today is on a warm welcome, a good pint of real ale, and both traditional and imaginative eating.

OPEN: 12-3 6-11 (Winter 12-2.30, 5.30-11, Sun 7-10.30) Closed: 1 Jan **BAR MEALS:** L served all week 12-2 D served Mon-Sat 6-9 No food Sun eve Av main course £6.50 **RESTAURANT:** L served all week 12-2 D served Mon-Sat 7-9 Av 3 course à la carte £18.50 **BREWERY/COMPANY:** Free House 🍺: Fuller's London Pride, Adnams Best, Wadworth 6X. ♀: 6 **CHILDREN'S FACILITIES:** menu, portions, food/bottle warming **GARDEN:** Large, with seating **NOTES:** Dogs allowed: in bar, in garden, Water, Parking 20

CHINNOR SIR CHARLES NAPIER

Spriggs Alley OX39 4BX
☎ 01494 483011 🖷 01494 485311
Dir: *M40 J6 to Chinnor. Turn R at rdbt carry on straight up hill to Spriggs Alley.* **Map Ref:** *SP70*

Situated amongst beech woods and fields in the Chiltern Hills, this is a genuine people's pub. Here you'll find a welcoming atmosphere, excellent real ales, and a serious approach to cooking. Huge winter fires and an eclectic mix of furniture and exhibition sculptures encourage you to linger, and Sunday lunch can go on all day!

OPEN: 12-3.30 6.30-12 (closed Mon, Sun Night) Closed: 25/26 Dec **BAR MEALS:** L served Tue-Sat 12-2.30 D served Tues-Thurs 7-9.30 No bar food Sun Av main course £10.50 **RESTAURANT:** L served Tue-Sun 12-2.30 D served Tue-Sat 7-10 Sun 12-3.30 Av 3 course à la carte £31 Av 2 course fixed price £16.50 **BREWERY/COMPANY:** Free House 🍺: Wadworth 6X. ♀: 10 **CHILDREN'S FACILITIES:** menu, portions, high-chairs, food/bottle warming, Only children over 6 for Dinner **GARDEN:** Large garden and terrace **NOTES:** No dogs (ex guide dogs), Parking 50

CHURCH ENSTONE CROWN INN

Mill Ln OX7 4NN
☎ 01608 677262 🖷 01608 677394
e-mail: tcwarburton@btopenworld.com
Dir: *Telephone for directions.* **Map Ref:** *SP32*

New owners took over this 17th-century, Cotswold-stone free house in 2003. Tony, an award-winning chef/proprietor, and his team prepare all the homemade food, while his wife, Caroline, runs front of house. Lunch and dinner menus change daily, making extensive use of fresh local meats and other produce. Fish, such as Cornish turbot with chive sauce, and seafood are a speciality. The picturesque cottage garden is ideal for sunny days and evenings. Hook Norton and guest ales from the bar.

OPEN: 12-3 6-11 (Sun 12-3, 7-10.30) **BAR MEALS:** L served Tue-Sun 12-2 D served Tue-Sat 7-9 Av main course £9.50 **RESTAURANT:** L served Tue-Sun 12-2 D served Tue-Sat 7-9 Av 3 course à la carte £19.50 **BREWERY/COMPANY:** Free House 🍺: Hook Norton Best Bitter, Shakespeare Spitfire, Timothy Taylor Landlord. **CHILDREN'S FACILITIES:** portions, games, food/bottle warming **GARDEN:** Small cottage garden **NOTES:** Dogs allowed: in bar, in garden, Water, Parking 8

CLIFTON DUKE OF CUMBERLAND'S HEAD

OX15 0PE
☎ 01869 338534 📄 01869 338643
Dir: *A4260 from Banbury, then B4031 from Deddington.* **Map Ref:** *SP43*

Built in 1645, originally as cottages, this stone and thatch pub is situated in the hamlet of Clifton, between the historic villages of Deddington and Aynho. It's named after Prince Rupert who led the king's troops at the Battle of Edge Hill. The themed monthly menu might include roast troncon of turbot with hollandaise sauce, or fillet steak en croute with Madeira jus. There's a large garden and barbeque for use in fine weather.

OPEN: 12-2.30 (w/end 12-3) 6.30-11 (closed Mon Lunch) Closed: Dec 25 **BAR MEALS:** L served Tue-Sun 12-2 D served all week 6-9 Av main course £10 **RESTAURANT:** L served Wed-Sun 12-2 D served Wed-Sat 7-9.30 Av 2 course fixed price £15 **BREWERY/COMPANY:** 🍺: Hook Norton, Adnams, Deuchers Black Sheep. **CHILDREN'S FACILITIES:** portions, high-chairs, food/bottle warming **GARDEN:** beer garden, outdoor eating, BBQ **NOTES:** Dogs allowed: Parking 20

DEDDINGTON DEDDINGTON ARMS ★★★ ◉ 🐑 🍷

Horsefair OX15 0SH
☎ 01869 338364 📄 01869 337010
e-mail: deddarms@aol.com
Dir: *A43 to Northampton, B4100 to Aynho, B4031 to Deddington. M40 J11 to Banbury. Follow signs for hospital, then towards Adderbury & Deddington, on A4260.* **Map Ref:** *SP43*

Fillet of beef with garlic mash, carrot broth, and seared foie gras

The hotel overlooks the market square in Deddington, a gateway to the Cotswolds, and the only English parish with a coat of arms. From its timbered bars, with open fires blazing away when you need them, it has offered a warm welcome to travellers and locals for 400 years. A bar meal could be a sandwich or something hot and more substantial like a chicken curry, lamb cutlets or smoked haddock.

OPEN: 11-11 **BAR MEALS:** L served all week 12-2 D served all week 6.30-9 Av main course £9.50 **RESTAURANT:** L served all week 12-2 D served all week 6.30-10.00 Sun 7-9 Av 3 course à la carte £27 **BREWERY/COMPANY:** Free House 🍺: Carlsberg-Tetleys Tetleys Bitter, Green King IPA. 🍷: 8 **CHILDREN'S FACILITIES:** menu, portions, high-chairs **NOTES:** No dogs (ex guide dogs), Parking 36 **ROOMS:** 27 en suite bedrooms 3 family rooms s£75 d£85

THE UNICORN NEW 🐑

Market Place OX15 0SE
☎ 01869 338838 📄 01869 338592
e-mail: carol@putland.com
Map Ref: *SP43*

A 17th-century Grade II listed coaching inn, 'The Queen' stagecoach would depart from the front every morning as it plied between Oxford and Banbury. A lunch menu served in the Snug or in the restaurant starts at the usual jackets and sandwiches, and progresses through griddles to specials such as hot roast gammon with Cumberland gravy, or whole grilled brill with lemon butter and black pepper; dinner menus continue along traditional lines. Outside is a secret garden with barbecue, lawns, flowerbeds and 'Aunt

Sally' pitch. Local market every fourth Saturday. Under new licensees.

OPEN: 12-11 (Sun 12-10.30) **BAR MEALS:** L served all week 12-2.30 D served all week 6-9 (Sun 12-3.15. No D Sun winter) Av main course £7.25 **RESTAURANT:** L served all week 12-2.15 D served all week 6-9.15 (Sun 12-3.15. No D Sun winter) Av 3 course à la carte £15.50 🍺: Hook Norton, Fullers London Pride. **CHILDREN'S FACILITIES:** menu, portions, high-chairs, food/bottle warming, Lunchtimes/early evening **GARDEN:** Walled, secret garden, lawns, flowerbeds

DORCHESTER (ON THAMES) THE WHITE HART ★★★

High St OX10 7HN
☎ 01865 340074 📠 01865 341082
e-mail: whitehartdorch@aol.com
Dir: *A4074 Oxford to Reading, 5M J7 M40
A329 to Wallingford.* **Map Ref:** *SU59*

Crisp Fried Stuffed Pig's Trotter with parsnip purée, confit of red onion, and balsamic vinegar jus

Providing a warm welcome to travellers for around 400 years, including the many thousands who must have arrived by stage-coach during its coaching inn days. Today it has a noted fresh food restaurant, comfortable bars with old beams and log fires, and 24 individually designed bedrooms, some with four-posters.

OPEN: 11-11 **BAR MEALS:** L served all week 12-2.30 D served all week 6.30-9.30 Av main course £7.95 **RESTAURANT:** L served all week 12-2.30 D served all week 6.30-9.30 Av 3 course à la carte £28 Av 3 course fixed price £12.50 **BREWERY/COMPANY:** Free House ◀: Greene King, Marstons Pedigree, St Austell Tribute, Deucars Caledeonian IPA. ♀: 12 **CHILDREN'S FACILITIES:** menu, portions, high-chairs, food/bottle warming **NOTES:** No dogs (ex guide dogs), Parking 28 **ROOMS:** 28 en suite 4 family rooms s£75 d£95

DUNS TEW THE WHITE HORSE INN ♀

OX25 6JS
☎ 01869 340272 📠 01869 347732
e-mail: whitehorse@dunstew.fsbusiness.co.uk
Dir: *M40 J11, A4260, follow signs to
Deddington and then onto Duns Tew.*
Map Ref: *SP42*

Log fires, oak panelling and flagstone floors create a cosy atmosphere appropriate for a 17th-century coaching inn. The food ranges from baguettes and salads (spinach, bacon and Parmesan, crevettes and hot potatoes) through to main courses such as shoulder of lamb or venison casserole.

OPEN: 12-11 (Sun 12-10.30) Closed: Single Malts **BAR MEALS:** L served all week 12-2.45 D served all week 6-9.45 Av main course £10 **RESTAURANT:** L served all week 12-2.45 D served all week 6-9.45 **BREWERY/COMPANY:** Old English Inns ◀: Greene King IPA, Batemans XXXX, Ruddles County, Abbot Ale. ♀: 10 **CHILDREN'S FACILITIES:** menu, portions, high-chairs, food/bottle warming **GARDEN:** Patio area enclosed by bushes **NOTES:** Dogs allowed: in garden, in bedrooms, Water, Parking 25

EAST HENDRED THE WHEATSHEAF

Chapel Square OX12 8JN
☎ 01235 833229
e-mail: tr@cywilson.freeserve.co.uk
Dir: *2m from the A34 Milton interchange.*
Map Ref: *SU48*

In a pretty village close to the Ridgeway path, this 16th-century beamed coaching Inn was formerly used as a magistrates' court. Home-cooked, freshly prepared food includes traditional pub grub such as steaks, pies and fresh haddock deep fried in lager batter. The extensive specials list might include Tempura prawns with a sweet chilli dip or baked whole sea bass with basil and caper dressing. New owners for 2004.

OPEN: 12-3 6-11 (All day Sat, Sun, BHS) **BAR MEALS:** L served all week 12-2 D served Mon-Sat 6.30-9 Av main course £5.50 **BREWERY/COMPANY:** Greene King ◀: Greene King Abbot Ale, IPA, plus guest ales. **CHILDREN'S FACILITIES:** menu, family room **NOTES:** Dogs allowed: in garden, Water, Parking 12

FARINGDON THE LAMB AT BUCKLAND

Lamb Ln, Buckland SN7 8QN
☎ 01367 870484 🖹 01367 870675
e-mail: enquiries@thelambatbuckland.co.uk
Dir: *Just off A420 3m E of Faringdon.*
Map Ref: *SU29*

Real ales, decent wines and restaurant quality food are offered at this stone-built, 18th-century inn. The Lamb stands on the very edge of the Cotswolds, with spectacular views across the Thames flood plain. The imaginative menu is supplemented by daily specials including fish, and quality local ingredients are to the fore in dishes such as roast rack of lamb with mint and sorrel sauce, and roast breast of duck with Calvados and apple sauce.

OPEN: 10.30-3pm 5.30-11pm Closed: 24 Dec-7 Jan
BAR MEALS: L served Tue, Sun 12-2 D served Tue-Sat 6.30-9.30 **RESTAURANT:** L served Tue-Sun 12-2 D served Tue-Sat 6.30-9.30 **BREWERY/COMPANY:** Free House
🍺: Hook Norton, Adnams Broadside, Arkells 3Bs. 🍷: 12
CHILDREN'S FACILITIES: menu, portions, games, high-chairs, food/bottle warming **GARDEN:** Food served outside.
NOTES: No dogs, Parking 50

FIFIELD MERRYMOUTH INN 🐑 🍷

Stow Rd OX7 6HR
☎ 01993 831652 🖹 01993 830840
e-mail: tim@merrymouthinn.fsnet.co.uk
Dir: *Situated on the A424 between Burford (3M) and Stow on the Wold (4M).*
Map Ref: *SP21*

The Merrymouth takes its name from the Murimouth family who were feudal lords of Fifield. The inn dates back to the 13th century and has a wonderful vaulted cellar, and rumour has it that there was once a secret passage to Bruern Abbey. A blackboard of fresh fish and vegetarian dishes supplements the Merrymouth menu.

OPEN: 12-2.30 6-10.30 (Closed Sun eve in winter)
BAR MEALS: L served all week 12-2 D served all week 6.30-9 Sun 7-8.30 Av main course £9.95
RESTAURANT: L served all week 12-2 D served all week 6.30-9 Av 3 course à la carte £18.50
BREWERY/COMPANY: Free House 🍺: Hook Norton Best Bitter, Adnams Broadside. 🍷: 7
CHILDREN'S FACILITIES: menu, portions, games, high-chairs, food/bottle warming **GARDEN:** Small patio & enclosed garden at pubs front **NOTES:** Dogs allowed: in bar, in garden, in bedrooms, Parking 70

FILKINS THE FIVE ALLS ♦♦♦ 🐑 🍷

GL7 3JQ
☎ 01367 860306 🖹 01367 860776
Dir: *A40 exit Burford, Filkins 4m, A361 to Lechlade.* **Map Ref:** *SP20*

Set in a peaceful Cotswold village just outside Lechlade, this popular pub is offering home-

made fare such as steak and kidney pudding, beef and Guinness pie, jerk chicken, mussels, chicken and mushroom pie, seabass with watercress, prawn curry, various sandwiches, and various steaks. The lawned garden has an over-sized chess set, quoits and a patio for a summer snack outdoors.

OPEN: 11-3 6-11 **BAR MEALS:** L served all week 11.30-2 D served all week 7-9.30 Av main course £9.95
RESTAURANT: L served all week 11.30-2 D served all week 7-9.30 Av 3 course à la carte £20
BREWERY/COMPANY: Free House 🍺: Hook Norton Best, Old Hooky. 🍷: 8 **CHILDREN'S FACILITIES:** menu, portions, high-chairs, food/bottle warming, baby changing, Garden
GARDEN: Large lawned garden with patio **NOTES:** No dogs (ex guide dogs), Parking 100 **ROOMS:** 6 en suite
1 family room s£45 d£60

FRINGFORD THE BUTCHERS ARMS

OX27 8EB
☎ 01869 277363
Map Ref: SP62

Flora Thompson mentioned this traditional village pub in her 1939 novel 'Lark Rise to Candleford', all about life on the Northamptonshire/Oxfordshire border. A good selection of fresh fish and other seafood, including mussels, crab and king prawns, is offered, as well as liver, bacon and onions, peppered fillet steak, half a roast duck, and steak and kidney pie. Pumps display Adnams Broadside and Marston's Pedigree labels. From the patio watch the cricket during the summer.

OPEN: 12-3 (Sun 12-10.30) 6-11 **BAR MEALS:** L served all week 12-2 D served all week 7-10 Av main course £7.95 **RESTAURANT:** L served all week 12-2 D served all week 7-10 Av 3 course à la carte £18 Av 2 course fixed price £9.95 **BREWERY/COMPANY:** Punch Taverns 🍺: Youngs Bitter, Jennings Cumberland, Adnams Broadside, Marstons Pedigree. **CHILDREN'S FACILITIES:** menu, portions, food/bottle warming **NOTES:** Dogs allowed: in bar, Must be on leads, Parking 40

GORING MILLER OF MANSFIELD

High St RG8 9AW
☎ 01491 872829 🖷 01491 874200
Dir: From Pangbourne A329 to Streatley, then R on B4009, 0.5m to Goring. *Map Ref:* SU68

An eighteenth-century, ivy-clad former coaching inn in the Goring Gap, the point where the River Thames flows between the Chilterns and the Berkshire Downs. In addition to the oak-beamed bar, where you can have full meals and snacks, there is a separate restaurant with a substantial menu.

OPEN: 11-11 (Sun 12-10.30) **BAR MEALS:** L served all week 12-2 D served all week 6.30-10 (Sun 12-4, 6.30-9.30) Av main course £9.50 **RESTAURANT:** L served all week 12-2 D served all week 7-10 Av 3 course à la carte £17.50 **BREWERY/COMPANY:** Free House 🍺: Greene King Old Speckled Hen, Brakspear Bitter, Adnams Best. **CHILDREN'S FACILITIES:** menu, portions, games, high-chairs, food/bottle warming, baby changing **NOTES:** Dogs allowed: in bar, Water, Parking 8 **ROOMS:** 10 en suite s£45 d£65 (♦♦♦)

HENLEY-ON-THAMES THE GOLDEN BALL

Lower Assendon RG9 6AH
☎ 01491 574157 🖷 01491 576653
e-mail: Golden.Ball@theseed.net
Dir: A4130, R onto B480, pub 300yds on L.
Map Ref: SU78

Dick Turpin hid in the priest hole at this 400-year-old building tucked away in the Stonor Valley close to Henley. It has a traditional pub atmosphere with well-used furnishings, open fire, exposed timbers, brasses and a collection of old bottled ales. Well-kept beer and home-cooked food are served, and there's a south-facing garden with plenty of garden furniture and undercover accommodation. Favourite fare includes sausage and mash, fish pie and lasagne.

OPEN: 11-3 6-11 **BAR MEALS:** L served all week 12-2.00 D served all week 7-9.00 Av main course £8.95 **BREWERY/COMPANY:** Brakspear 🍺: Brakspear Bitter & Special, 2 monthly seasonal beers. **CHILDREN'S FACILITIES:** menu, portions, games, high-chairs, food/bottle warming, baby changing, outdoor play area, climbing frame, slide, family room **GARDEN:** Large south facing garden **NOTES:** Dogs allowed: in bar, water outside, hitching rail, Parking 50

THE WHITE HART HOTEL

High St, Nettlebed RG9 5DD
☎ 01491 642145 📠 01491 649018
e-mail: Info@whitehartnettlebed.com
Dir: *On the A4130 between Henley-on-Thames and Wallingford.* **Map Ref:** *SU78*

This beautifully restored brick and flint building dating from the 17th century was used as a billeting house for loyalist Cavalier troops during the English Civil War. Chris Barber, former private chef to the Prince of Wales, serves up delicious food in two chic dining venues.

OPEN: 11-11 **BAR MEALS:** L served all week 12-2.30 D served all week 6-10 Av main course £11
RESTAURANT: L served Tue-Sat D served Thu-Sat 7-9 Av 3 course à la carte £45 🍺: Brakspear, Guinness, Stella Artois, Fosters. 🍷: 12 **CHILDREN'S FACILITIES:** menu, portions, licence, games, high-chairs, food/bottle warming, baby changing, outdoor play area, family room
GARDEN: Large lawned area with seating **NOTES:** No dogs (ex guide dogs), Parking 50 **ROOMS:** 12 en suite 3 family rooms d£105

HOOK NORTON   THE GATE HANGS HIGH ◆◆◆◆

Whichford Rd OX15 5DF
☎ 01608 737387 📠 01608 737870
e-mail: gatehangshigh@aol
Dir: *Off A361 SW of Banbury.* **Map Ref:** *SP33*

A charming country pub set in beautiful countryside near the Rollright stones and the idyllic village of Hook Norton, home to the famous brewery and source of the tip-top ales served in the bar. The pub is on the old Wales to Banbury drovers' road and there was once a tollgate outside, which was said to hang high so that all the ducks and geese and small animals could roam freely but large beasts had to stop and pay the toll. It is also said that Dick Turpin frequented the place when he was lying low. The bar has a long, low beamed ceiling, a copper hood over the hearth in the inglenook fireplace and a brick-built bar counter with festoons of hops above. Typical dishes include barbeque ribs, braised rabbit, salmon and prawn fishcakes, and corned beef hash.

OPEN: 12-3 6-11 (Sun, 12-4, 7-10.30)
BAR MEALS: L served all week 12-2.30 D served all week 6-10 Sun 12-3, 7-9 Av main course £7.95
RESTAURANT: L served all week 12-2.30 D served all week 6-10 Sun 12-3, 7-9 Av 3 course à la carte £18 Av 3 course fixed price £12.95 **BREWERY/COMPANY:** Hook Norton 🍺: Hook Norton - Best, Old Hooky, Haymaker & Generation.
CHILDREN'S FACILITIES: menu, portions, high-chairs, food/bottle warming **GARDEN:** Wonderful views overlooking fields, courtyard **NOTES:** Dogs allowed: in bar, in garden, Water, Parking 30 **ROOMS:** 4 en suite 1 family room s£40 d£60

SUN INN 🍷

High St OX15 5NH
☎ 01608 737570 📠 01608 737535
e-mail: enquiries@the-sun-inn.com
Map Ref: *SP33*

Stuart and Joyce Rust have taken over the Sun Inn after a two-year break from the trade - they were at the Gate Hangs High for over fourteen years. It's a traditional Cotswold stone inn with oak beams, flagstone floors and an inglenook fireplace, close to the Hook Norton Brewery. The same menu is offered in the bar or candlelit restaurant, including shank of lamb with mustard mash, and sea bass with spinach and Mediterranean tomato sauce.

OPEN: 11.30-3 6-11.30 **BAR MEALS:** L served all week 12-2 D served all week 7-9.30 Av main course £7.95
RESTAURANT: L served all week 12-2 D served all week 7-9.30 Av 3 course à la carte £17
BREWERY/COMPANY: Hook Norton 🍺: Hook Norton Best Bitter, Old Generation, Mild & Double Stout.
CHILDREN'S FACILITIES: portions, food/bottle warming
GARDEN: Patio area, walled **NOTES:** No dogs, Parking 20

KELMSCOT THE PLOUGH INN

GL7 3HG
☎ 01367 253543 📠 01367 252514
e-mail: plough@kelmscottgl7.fsnet.co.uk
Dir: *From M4 onto A419 then A361 to Lechlade & A416 to Faringdon, pick up signs to Kelmscot.* ***Map Ref:*** *SU29*

A sympathetically restored 17th-century inn, popular with the walking and boating fraternity, in an attractive village close to Kelmscot Manor and the Thames. Expect the likes of grilled cod fillets with ginger and spring onion mash, herb crust and mild curry cream. There is a lawn and patio area for outdoor eating in warmer weather.

OPEN: 11-3 (Sun 12-3, 7-10.30) 7-11
BAR MEALS: L served all week 12-2.30 D served Mon-Sat 7-9 Av main course £11.50 **RESTAURANT:** L served Tue-Sun 12-2.30 D served Tue-Sat 7-9 (Open Mon in summer) Av 3 course à la carte £20
BREWERY/COMPANY: Free House 🍺: Hook Norton, Guest beers, Timothy Taylor. **CHILDREN'S FACILITIES:** portions, games, high-chairs, food/bottle warming **GARDEN:** Grassed area with patio **NOTES:** Dogs allowed: in bar, in garden, in bedrooms, Water provided, Parking 4

KINGSTON LISLE THE BLOWING STONE INN 🍷

OX12 9QL
☎ 01367 820288 📠 01367 821102
e-mail: luke@theblowingstoneinn.com
Dir: *B4507 from Wantage toward Ashbury/Swindon, after 6m R to Kingston Lisle.* ***Map Ref:*** *SU38*

Combining modern times with old-fashioned warmth and hospitality, this attractive country pub derives its name from the Blowing Stone, located on the outskirts of the village. Popular with walkers and horse racing fans, it is run by Radio Five Live racing presenter Luke Harvey and his sister.

OPEN: 12-2.30 (open all day Fri-Sun) 6-11
BAR MEALS: L served Tue-Sun 12-3 D served all week 7-9.30 Av main course £10.50 **RESTAURANT:** L served all week 12-2.30 D served all week 7-9.30
BREWERY/COMPANY: Free House 🍺: Courage Best, Fuller's London Pride & Guest Beers. 🍷: 7
CHILDREN'S FACILITIES: menu, portions, games, high-chairs, food/bottle warming, baby changing **GARDEN:** Large with pond and fountain **NOTES:** Dogs allowed: in bar, in garden, in bedrooms, Water, Parking 30

LEWKNOR THE LEATHERN BOTTEL 🍷

1 High St OX49 5TW
☎ 01844 351482
Map Ref: *SU79*

Run by the same family for more than 25 years, this 16th-century coaching inn is set in the foothills of the Chilterns. Walkers with dogs, families with children, parties for meals or punters for a quick pint are all made equally welcome. In winter there's a wood-burning stove, a good drop of Brakspears ale, nourishing specials and a quiz on Sunday. Summer is the time for outdoor eating, the children's play area, Pimm's and Morris dancers.

OPEN: 10.30-3 6-11 **BAR MEALS:** L served all week 12-2 D served all week 7-9.30 Av main course £6.95
BREWERY/COMPANY: Brakspear 🍺: Brakspear Ordinary, Special. 🍷: 12 **CHILDREN'S FACILITIES:** menu, portions, food/bottle warming, outdoor play area, adventure play area, family room **GARDEN:** Large garden enclosed with hedge
NOTES: Dogs allowed: in bar, Water, Parking 35

LOWER SHIPLAKE THE BASKERVILLE ARMS

Station Rd RG9 3NY
☎ 0118 940 3332 ▤ 0118 940 7235
e-mail: enquiries@thebaskerville.com
Map Ref: SU77

Set on the popular Thames Path, not far from picturesque Henley, the attractive brick-built Baskerville Arms is handy for both the river and the railway station. A good restaurant and a lovely garden add to the appeal. Starters might include tiger prawns tossed in chilli, Stilton soup, Thai crab cakes and old-fashioned prawn cocktail, while typical main courses range from grilled fillet steak set on a potato and parsnip rosti, vegetable crumble, blackened fillet of Cajun-style salmon, and roast breast of corn-fed chicken wrapped in pancetta and stuffed with herbed cheese.

OPEN: 11.30-2.30 (Fri 11.30-2.30, 5.30-11.30) 6-11 (Sun 11.30-2.30, 5.30-11) **BAR MEALS:** L served all week 12-2 D served Mon-Sat 7-9.30 Av main course £9 **RESTAURANT:** L served Mon-Sun 12-2 D served Mon-Sat Av 3 course à la carte £20 Av 3 course fixed price £9.95 ◖: London Pride, Brakspear, Stella Artois, Castlemaine & Hoppit. ♀: 8 **CHILDREN'S FACILITIES:** portions, high-chairs, food/bottle warming, outdoor play area **GARDEN:** Spacious garden with play area & BBQ **NOTES:** Dogs allowed: in bar, in garden, Parking 12

MIDDLETON STONEY THE JERSEY ARMS ★★ ♀

OX25 4AD
☎ 01869 343234 ▤ 01869 343565
e-mail: jerseyarms@bestwestern.co.uk
Map Ref: SP52

Charming family-run hotel, formerly a coaching inn. Cosy bar offering good range of popular bar food with the extensive menu supplemented by daily blackboard specials, including soups, pâtés, pasta dishes and traditional main courses like steak and kidney pie. Beamed and panelled Livingston's restaurant with Mediterranean terracotta decor and cosmopolitan brasserie-style menu.

OPEN: 12-11 **BAR MEALS:** L served all week 12-2.15 D served all week 6.30-9.30 Av main course £9.50 **RESTAURANT:** L served all week 12-2.15 D served all week 6.30-9.30 Av 3 course à la carte £21 **BREWERY/COMPANY:** Free House ◖: Interbrew Flower, Bass. **CHILDREN'S FACILITIES:** menu, high-chairs, food/bottle warming **GARDEN:** Courtyard garden **NOTES:** No dogs (ex guide dogs), Parking 50 **ROOMS:** 20 en suite 4 family rooms s£85 d£96

MURCOTT THE NUT TREE INN ♀

Main St OX5 2RE
☎ 01865 331253 ▤ 01865 331977
Dir: Off B4027 NE of Oxford via Islip & Charlton-on-Moor. **Map Ref:** SP51

14th-century thatched country inn, dating back to 1360. Set in a country idyll (six acres of gardens, a duck pond, donkeys, geese, peacocks and chickens) its interior delivers all the hoped-for rustic charm, with bare beams, inglenooks with wood burning stoves, real ales and home-cooked meals. New management.

OPEN: 12-3 6-11 (Sun 12-5) **BAR MEALS:** L served Tue-Sat 12-2.30 D served Tue-Sat 6-9 Av main course £12 **RESTAURANT:** L served Tue-Sun 12-2.30 D served Tue-Sat 6-9 Av 3 course à la carte £19 Av 2 course fixed price £9.95 **BREWERY/COMPANY:** Free House ◖: Hook Norton, Adnams. ♀: 6 **CHILDREN'S FACILITIES:** licence, outdoor play area, family room **GARDEN:** Fenced and hedged with trees and lawns **NOTES:** Dogs allowed: in garden, Kennel, Parking 40

OXFORD   THE ANCHOR

2 Hayfield Rd, Walton Manor OX2 6TT
☎ 01865 510282
e-mail: anchorhay@aol.com
Dir: *A34 Oxford Ring Road(N), exit Peartree Roundabout, 1.5m then R at Polstead Rd, follow rd to bottom, pub on R.* **Map Ref:** *SP50*

Local resident T E Lawrence (of Arabia) once frequented this friendly 1930s pub. Nowadays you'll find a relaxed atmosphere, and good food and drink. The wide-ranging menu offers pub favourites such as steak and ale pie, sausage and mash, and fish and chips.

OPEN: 12-11 (Mon-Sat 12-11, Sun 12-10.30)
BAR MEALS: L served all week 12-2.30 D served all week 6-9 Av main course £5.95
BREWERY/COMPANY: Wadworth **◀:** Wadworth 6X, Henrys IPA, JCB. **CHILDREN'S FACILITIES:** portions, food/bottle warming, only until 9pm **GARDEN:** Patio at front and rear of pub **NOTES:** Dogs allowed: in bar, in garden, Water, on leads, Parking 15

PISHILL   THE CROWN INN 🐑 ♀

RG9 6HH
☎ 01491 638364 📠 01491 638364
e-mail: jc@capon.fsnet.co.uk
Dir: *On B480 off A4130, NW of Henley-on-Thames.* **Map Ref:** *SU78*

Old maps spell the village's name with an

extra 's', and it probably does therefore mean what you are thinking. The theory is that, having climbed up the steep hill from Henley-on-Thames, waggon drivers would stop at the inn for a drink, giving their horses time to relieve themselves. A long-standing favourite, the building goes back to the 15th century. It has, reputedly, the country's largest priest hole.

OPEN: 11.30-2.30 6-11 (Sun 12-3, 7-10.30) Closed: 25-26 Dec, 1 Jan **BAR MEALS:** L served all week 12-2 D served all week 7-9.30 (Sun 12-3) Av main course £11.50
RESTAURANT: L served all week 12-2 D served all week 7-9.30 Av 3 course à la carte £23.50
BREWERY/COMPANY: Free House **◀:** Archer's Best, Hook Norton. **♀:** 8 **CHILDREN'S FACILITIES:** portions, high-chairs, food/bottle warming, Children in dining room
GARDEN: Extensive gardens overlooking the valley
NOTES: No dogs (ex guide dogs), Parking 60

ROKE   HOME SWEET HOME ♀

OX10 6JD
☎ 01491 838249 📠 01491 835760
Dir: *Just off the B4009 from Benson to Watlington, signed posted on B4009.* **Map Ref:** *SU69*

Long ago converted from adjoining cottages by a local brewer, this pretty 15th-century inn stands in a tiny hamlet surrounded by lovely countryside. A wealth of oak beams and the large inglenook fireplace dominate a friendly bar with an old-fashioned feel. Recently taken over and re-decorated by Andrew Hearn, who also runs The Horns at Crazies Hill, the new menu has a commitment to good, hearty pub eating. Look out for pork and leek sausages with spring onion mash and onion gravy, pan-fried calves liver with bacon and black

pudding, fresh fish of the day, and tuna and chili fish cakes with red Thai cream sauce. Plenty of local ales on tap.

OPEN: 11-2.30 6-11 (Sun 12-3, closed Sun eve) Closed: Dec 25-26 Rest: Sun Closed eve **BAR MEALS:** L served all week 12-2 D served Mon-Sat 6-9 Av main course £9
RESTAURANT: L served Mon-Sun 12-2 D served Mon-Sat 7-9 **BREWERY/COMPANY:** Free House **◀:** London Pride, Loddon Brewery Beers- Hoppit, Feremans Gold. **♀:** 10
CHILDREN'S FACILITIES: menu, portions, high-chairs, food/bottle warming, license **NOTES:** Dogs allowed: Water, Parking 60

SHENINGTON THE BELL ♉

OX15 6NQ
☎ 01295 670274
e-mail: thebell@shenington.freeserve.co.uk
Dir: M40 J11 take A422 towards Stratford. Village is signposted 3m N of Wroxton.
Map Ref: SP34

Nestling amid mellow stone houses, a classic village green and a church with an impressive Tudor tower, the comfortable and welcoming 300-year-old Bell has an open log fire burning in winter, and tables outside in the summer. The pub promises home-cooked food prepared with fresh local ingredients. Expect duck in port and black cherries; foil-baked sea bass with herbs and lemon, pecan cakes with celery sauce, salmon in watercress sauce, and soups and devilled sausages on toast.

OPEN: 12-2.30 7-11 **BAR MEALS:** L served Tue-Sun 12-2 D served all week 7-11 **RESTAURANT:** L served all week 12-2 D served all week 7-11 Av 3 course à la carte £12.50 **BREWERY/COMPANY:** Free House ◖: Hook Norton, Flowers. ♉: 8 **CHILDREN'S FACILITIES:** menu, portions, high-chairs, food/bottle warming **GARDEN:** Beer garden, outdoor eating **NOTES:** Dogs allowed: in bar, Water

SHIPTON-UNDER-WYCHWOOD THE LAMB INN ♉

High St OX7 6DQ
☎ 01993 830465 ▤ 01993 832025
e-mail: lamb@suwychwood.fsbusiness.co.uk
Dir: 4m N of Burford on the A361.
Map Ref: SP21

Whether you're popping in for a quick drink and a snack or planning a romantic weekend away, you'll find a warm welcome at this beautiful old inn. The rustic stone-walled bar is just the place to savour a broad range of home-cooked food. Typical dishes include medallions of monkfish, breast of local pheasant, or spinach and ricotta crêpe farcie.

OPEN: 11-11 (Sun 12-10.30) **BAR MEALS:** L served all week 12-2.30 D served all week 6.30-9.30 (Sun 12-9.30) Av main course £10 **RESTAURANT:** L served all week 12-2.30 D served all week 7-9.30 (Sun 12-9.30) Av 3 course à la carte £22.50 **BREWERY/COMPANY:** Old English Inns ◖: IPA, Abbott Ale, Old Speckled Hen, Wadworth 6X. ♉: 9 **CHILDREN'S FACILITIES:** menu, portions, games, high-chairs, food/bottle warming **GARDEN:** Landscaped formal garden **NOTES:** Dogs allowed: in bar, in garden, in bedrooms, Water, Parking 20

THE SHAVEN CROWN HOTEL ♉

High St OX7 6BA
☎ 01993 830330 ▤ 01993 832136
e-mail: reservations@shavencrown.co.uk
Dir: On A361, halfway between Burford and Chipping Norton opposite village green and church. Map Ref: SP21

Built of honey-coloured Cotswold stone around a medieval courtyard, the Shaven Crown is up to 700 years old in parts, and was originally a hospice to the neighbouring Bruern Monastery. After the Dissolution of the Monasteries, Queen Elizabeth I used it as a hunting lodge before giving it to the village in 1580, when it became the Crown Inn. In 1930, a whimsically-minded brewery changed the name to reflect monkish hairdos.

OPEN: 12-2.30 5-11 **BAR MEALS:** L served all week 12-2 D served all week 5.30-9.30 **RESTAURANT:** L served Sun 12-2 D served all week 7-9 **BREWERY/COMPANY:** Free House ◖: Hook Norton Best, Old Hooky, Speckled Hen & Archers Wychwood. ♉: 10 **CHILDREN'S FACILITIES:** menu, portions, games, high-chairs, food/bottle warming, high chairs, cots, baby listening facilities **GARDEN:** Enclosed courtyard, lawned with trees **NOTES:** Dogs allowed: in bar, in garden, in bedrooms, Water, Parking 15

SOUTH MORETON THE CROWN INN

High St OX11 9AG
☎ 01235 812262
Dir: *From Didcot take A4130 towards Wallingford. Village on R.* **Map Ref:** *SU58*

Located midway between Wallingford and Didcot this friendly pub serves clients from far and wide, in a food-led operation with real ales on tap. The building dates from around 1870, and has been extensively revamped in rustic style. Expect roast half shoulder of lamb, rump and sirloin steaks, cod mornay, haddock in beer batter, and home-made salmon fishcakes.

OPEN: 11-3 5.30-11 (Sun 12-3, 7-10.30) Closed: Dec 25-26 **BAR MEALS:** L served all week 12-2 D served all week 7-9.30 Av main course £8.50 **RESTAURANT:** L served all week 12-2 D served all week 7-9.30 **BREWERY/COMPANY:** Wadworth **◀:** Badger Tanglefoot, Adnams Best, Wadworth 6X & Henrys IPA. **♀:** 8 **CHILDREN'S FACILITIES:** menu, portions, high-chairs, food/bottle warming **GARDEN:** 2 areas with bench style seating **NOTES:** Dogs allowed: in bar, in garden, Water, Parking 30

SOUTH STOKE THE PERCH AND PIKE

RG8 0JS
☎ 01491 872415 ▤ 01491 875852
e-mail: helpdesk@perchandpike.com
Dir: *Between Goring and Wallingford just off B4009.* **Map Ref:** *SU58*

The Perch and Pike was built in the 17th century and soon became the village's foremost beerhouse. The recently refurbished main building, and the rebuilt barn restaurant, both ooze atmosphere. A robust starter like smoked paprika and beef goulash could be followed with something light, such as smoked chicken and bacon salad.

OPEN: 11-3 6-11 (Closed Sun night) **BAR MEALS:** L served all week 12-2.30 D served Mon-Sat 7-9.45 Av main course £10.50 **RESTAURANT:** L served all week 12-2.30 D served Mon-Sat 7-9.45 **BREWERY/COMPANY:** Brakspear **◀:** Brakspear Bitter, Special & Seasonal. **CHILDREN'S FACILITIES:** menu, portions, licence, games, high-chairs, food/bottle warming **GARDEN:** Split on 2 levels **NOTES:** Dogs allowed: in bar, in garden, in bedrooms, Parking 30 **ROOMS:** 4 en suite 4 family rooms s£75 d£75 (♦♦♦♦)

STANTON ST JOHN STAR INN

Middle Rd OX33 1EX
☎ 01865 351277 ▤ 01865 351006
e-mail: stantonstar@supanet.com
Dir: *At A40/Oxford ring road rdbt take Stanton exit, follow rd to T junct, R to Stanton, 3rd L, pub on L 50yds.* **Map Ref:** *SP50*

Although the Star is only a short drive from the centre of Oxford, this popular pub still retains a definite 'village' feel. The oldest part of the pub dates from the early 17th century, and in the past, the building has been used as a butcher's shop and an abattoir. The garden is peaceful and secluded. A varied menu features steak and Guinness pie, lamb in redcurrant and rosemary, deep-fried whitebait, Thai curry, lasagna, and moussaka.

OPEN: 11-2.30 6.30-11 **BAR MEALS:** L served all week 12-2 D served all week 6.30-9.30 Av main course £7.95 **BREWERY/COMPANY:** Wadworth **◀:** Wadworth 6X, Henrys IPA & JCB, Stella. **♀:** 7 **CHILDREN'S FACILITIES:** menu, portions, games, high-chairs, food/bottle warming, outdoor play area, family room **GARDEN:** Large secure garden **NOTES:** Dogs allowed: in bar, in garden, Water bowls, Parking 50

THE TALK HOUSE

Wheatley Rd OX33 1EX
☎ 01865 351648 📠 01865 351085
e-mail: talkhouse@t-f-h.co.uk
Dir: *Stanton-St-John signed from the Oxford ring road.* **Map Ref:** *SP50*

The Talk House is a cleverly converted 17th-century inn located within easy reach of Oxford and the A40. It comprises three bar and dining areas, all with a Gothic look and a welcoming atmosphere. Business, wedding and function bookings are catered for, and The Snug is ideal for private parties of eight to 15, with its own fireplace and private bar. An interesting modern menu reflects global influences with starters such as Thai crab cakes, and chicken satay skewers. Main courses show equal diversity with The Envy of India and Becky's Fur & Feather Casserole. Bed and breakfast accommodation is also offered in four chalet-style rooms situated around the attractive rear courtyard.

OPEN: 12-3 5.30-11 (Open all day in Summer Easter wknd-Oct) **BAR MEALS:** L served all week 12-2 D served all week 7-10 (Sun 12-9) Av main course £10 **RESTAURANT:** L served all week 12-2 D served all week 7-10 (Sun 12-9) Av 3 course à la carte £20 **BREWERY/COMPANY:** Free House 🍺: Hook Norton Best Bitter, Tetley's Cask Ale, Burton Ale. **CHILDREN'S FACILITIES:** menu, food/bottle warming **GARDEN:** Courtyard garden **NOTES:** No dogs (ex guide dogs), Parking 60 **ROOMS:** 4 en suite s£40 d£60 (♦♦♦)

STOKE ROW CROOKED BILLET 🐑 ♥

RG9 5PU
☎ 01491 681048 📠 01491 682231
Dir: *From Henley to Oxford A4130.Turn L at Nettlebed for Stoke Row.* **Map Ref:** *SU68*

A rustic country inn hidden away down a single-track lane in deepest Oxfordshire, still retaining all the original charm of a true country pub. It dates back to 1642, and was once the haunt of the notorious highwayman Dick Turpin. Many of its best features are unchanged. Nowadays this old inn attracts many local celebrities like Kate Winslet, the cast of EastEnders, and Jeremy Paxman.

OPEN: 12-11 (Sun 12-10.30) **BAR MEALS:** L served all week 12-2.30 D served all week 7-10 Av main course £14 **RESTAURANT:** L served all week 12-2.30 D served all week 7-10 All day Sun Av 3 course à la carte £27.50 Av 2 course fixed price £12.95 **BREWERY/COMPANY:** Brakspear 🍺: Brakspear Bitter. ♥: 12 **CHILDREN'S FACILITIES:** portions, food/bottle warming **GARDEN:** Beautiful, rustic, over-looks farmland **NOTES:** No dogs (ex guide dogs), Parking 50

SWALCLIFFE STAG'S HEAD ♥

OX15 5EJ
☎ 01295 780232 📠 01295 788977
e-mail: stagsheadswalcliffe@dial.pipex.com
Dir: *6M W of Banbury on the B4035.* **Map Ref:** *SP33*

Believed to have been built during the reign of Henry VIII, this thatched pub originally housed builders working on the nearby church. It enjoys picture postcard looks and attracts a broad range of customers. An apple tree in the landscaped garden was reputedly grown from a pip brought back from the Crimean War, and its fruit is still used in home-made puddings.

OPEN: 12-2.30 6.30-11 Rest: Sun Closed eve **BAR MEALS:** L served Tues-Sun 12-2.15 D served Tues-Sat 7-9.30 Av main course £13.95 **RESTAURANT:** L served Tues-Sun 12-2.15 D served Tues-Sat 7-9.30 **BREWERY/COMPANY:** Free House 🍺: Brakspears PA, Wychwood Seasonal, Spinning Dog Brewery, Black Sheep. ♥: 7 **CHILDREN'S FACILITIES:** menu, games, high-chairs, food/bottle warming, baby changing, outdoor play area, play area in garden **GARDEN:** Beautiful terraced garden **NOTES:** Dogs allowed: in bar, in garden, in bedrooms, Water, biscuits

SWERFORD THE MASON'S ARMS

Banbury Rd OX7 4AP
☎ 01608 683212 📄 01608 683105
*Dir: Between Banbury and Chipping Norton
A361. Map Ref: SP33*

This 300-year-old pub on the edge of the Cotswolds has been tastefully renovated to provide modern amenities without destroying its traditional charm. With a chef/proprietor who has worked with Marco Pierre White and Gordon Ramsey, the visitor can be assured of wonderful food with a menu that changes fortnightly. A typical meal may include smoked venison, and avocado parfait to start, followed by poached haddock with asparagus and a watercress sauce, or chargrilled rib-eye steak. For smaller appetites there is a good range of sandwiches and light bites, and real ales.

OPEN: 10-3 7-11 Closed: 25 Dec **BAR MEALS:** L served Mon-Sun 12-2.30 D served Mon-Sun 7-9.30 **RESTAURANT:** L served all week 12-2.30 D served all week 7-10 Av 3 course à la carte £20 **BREWERY/COMPANY:** Free House ◖: Hook Norton Best. **CHILDREN'S FACILITIES:** menu, licence, high-chairs, food/bottle warming **GARDEN:** Lrg grassed area, with seating, views **NOTES:** Dogs allowed: in bar, water, Parking 50

WHEATLEY BAT & BALL INN ♦♦♦

28 High St OX44 9HJ
☎ 01865 874379 📄 01865 873363
e-mail: bb@traditionalvillageinns.co.uk
*Dir: Pass through Wheatley towards Garsington, take only L turn, signed Cuddesdon.
Map Ref: SP50*

Do not be surprised to discover that the bar of this former coaching inn is packed to the gunnels with cricketing memorabilia. The comprehensive menu, supplemented by daily specials, is likely to feature steaks, fresh-baked pie of the day, herb-battered fresh cod, and maybe chargrilled Toulouse sausages. Lighter meals include homemade lasagne, lamb Peshwari, and warm spinach and pancetta salad. Oh yes, even the seven letting rooms are named after famous cricketers.

OPEN: 11-11 **BAR MEALS:** L served all week 12-2.45 D served all week 6.30-9.45 (Sun 12-9.45) Av main course £9.50 **RESTAURANT:** L served all week 12-2.45 D served all week 6.30-9.45 (Sun 12-9.45) **BREWERY/COMPANY:** Marstons ◖: Marston's Pedigree & Original, LBW. ♀: 14 **CHILDREN'S FACILITIES:** menu, portions, games, high-chairs, food/bottle warming **GARDEN:** Patio with good views **NOTES:** Dogs allowed: in bar, Water Bowl, Parking 15 **ROOMS:** 7 en suite 1 family room s£50 d£65

WITNEY THE BELL INN ♀

Standlake Rd, Ducklington OX29 7UP
☎ 01993 702514 📄 01993 706822
Dir: One mile south of Witney in Ducklington village off A415 Abingdon road. Map Ref: SP31

Nearly 700 years have passed since the men building the adjacent church also erected their own living accommodation. Their hostel eventually became the Bell, and much extended over the years, it even embraces William Shepheard's former brewery, which closed in 1886. Today it is a popular, traditional village local, with many original features - and an amazing collection of some 500 bells. Home-made pies, stews and burgers are a speciality, and there's a pig roast on Boxing Day.

OPEN: 12-3 5-11 (Fri-Sun 12-11) Rest: 25, 26 Dec & 1 Jan closed eve **BAR MEALS:** L served all week 12-2 D served Mon-Sat 6-9 Av main course £8.50 **RESTAURANT:** L served all week 12-2 D served Mon-Sat 6-9 Av 3 course à la carte £15 ◖: Greene King, IPA & Old Speckled Hen, Morland Original. **CHILDREN'S FACILITIES:** menu, portions, games, high-chairs, food/bottle warming, outdoor play area, climbing frame, swings **GARDEN:** Terrace at front and rear of pub **NOTES:** No dogs, Parking 12

BROCKLEY GREEN THE PLOUGH INN ♀

CO10 8DT
☎ 01440 786789 📠 01440 786710
e-mail: ploughdave@aol.com
Dir: Take B1061 from A143, approx 1.5m beyond Kedington. **Map Ref:** *TL74*

Quality and service are the hallmark of this delightfully situated free house, which has been run by the same family since 1957. The traditional interior retains its oak beams and soft red brickwork, whilst major extensions have added a restaurant. The distinctive bar menu includes steak and kidney pudding, T-bone steak and daily specials such as Mexican chilli beef, whilst restaurant diners could expect duck terrine with caramelised red onion chutney followed by white swordfish loin steak with tomato coulis. Separate seafood specials are available.

OPEN: 12-2.30 5-11 **BAR MEALS:** L served all week 12-2 D served all week 7-9.30 Av main course £9
RESTAURANT: L served all week 12-2 D served all week 7-9.30 **BREWERY/COMPANY:** Free House 🍺: Greene King IPA, Adnams Best, Fuller's London Pride, Woodforde's Wherry Best Bitter. ♀: 12 **CHILDREN'S FACILITIES:** menu, portions, games, high-chairs, food/bottle warming **GARDEN:** a Large lawn bordered by shrubs **NOTES:** Dogs allowed: in bar, in garden, in bedrooms, Water bowls, Parking 50

BROME CORNWALLIS COUNTRY HOTEL ♀

IP23 8AJ
☎ 01379 870326 📠 01379 870051
e-mail: info@thecornwallis.com
Dir: Just off A140 at Brome, follow B1077 to Eye. Pub is 30 metres on the left.
Map Ref: *TM17*

New owners have arrived at this handsome looking building, dating from 1561, the one-time Dower House to Brome Hall. Within its 20 peaceful acres are an avenue of limes, some impressive yew topiary and a pretty water garden, while inside many of the original beams, panels and oak and mahogany settles remain from earliest times. In the log-fired Tudor Bar look into the murky depths of a 60-foot well.

OPEN: 11-11 **BAR MEALS:** L served all week 12-2.30 D served all week 6-9.45 Av main course £9.50
RESTAURANT: L served all week 12-2.30 D served all week 6.30-9.45 Av 3 course fixed price £24
BREWERY/COMPANY: Free House 🍺: Adnams, Greene King IPA, St Peters Best. ♀: 16
CHILDREN'S FACILITIES: menu, high-chairs **GARDEN:** 21 acres of gardens, pond **NOTES:** Water, No dogs (ex guide dogs), Parking 400

BURY ST EDMUNDS THE LINDEN TREE 🐑

7 Out Northgate IP33 1JQ
☎ 01284 754600
Dir: Opposite railway station. **Map Ref:** *TL86*

Built to serve the railway station, this is a big, friendly Victorian pub, with stripped pine bar, dining area, non-smoking conservatory and charming garden. The family-orientated menu ranges from beef curry, home-made pies, and liver and bacon, to crab Thermidor, fresh sea bass, and mushroom and lentil moussaka. Youngsters will go for the burgers, scampi, Quorn or pork chipolatas, all served with a choice of potatoes, peas or beans, and salad. Freshly filled ciabattas at lunchtime.

OPEN: 11-3 5-11 Closed: Xmas for 3 days
BAR MEALS: L served all week 12-2 D served all week 6-9.30 Sun 12-3 & 6-9 Av main course £9
RESTAURANT: L served all week 12-2 D served all week 6-9.30 Sun 12-3 & 6-9 Av 3 course à la carte £16
BREWERY/COMPANY: Greene King 🍺: Greene King, IPA, Abbot Ale, Ruddles County & Old Speckled Hen.
CHILDREN'S FACILITIES: menu, portions, games, high-chairs, food/bottle warming, baby changing, outdoor play area, swing, see-saw **GARDEN:** Large, picnic tables **NOTES:** No dogs (ex guide dogs)

THE THREE KINGS ◆◆◆◆

Hengrave Rd, Fornham All Saints IP28 6LA
☎ 01284 766979 ▤ 01284 723308
e-mail: enquiries@the-three-kings.com
Map Ref: TL86

Plenty of exposed wood and interesting artefacts create a traditional atmosphere at this pretty pub. Bedroom accommodation is also provided in converted Grade II listed outbuildings. Food is served in the bar, conservatory, restaurant and courtyard. There are at least four fresh grilled fish dishes every day, a choice of steaks, and old favourites like steak and ale pie or liver and bacon.

OPEN: 11-11 Sun 12-10.30 **BAR MEALS:** L served all week 11.30-2 D served all week 5.30-9.30 Sun 12-2.30, 6-8.30 Av main course £5.95 **RESTAURANT:** L served Tue-Sun 12-2 D served Tue-Sat 7-8.30 Sun 12-2.30 **BREWERY/COMPANY:** Greene King ◖: Greene King IPA & Abbot. **CHILDREN'S FACILITIES:** menu, portions, licence, high-chairs, food/bottle warming, cot, high chairs, changing area **GARDEN:** Patio area, benches **NOTES:** No dogs (ex guide dogs), Parking 28 **ROOMS:** 9 en suite 2 family rooms s£55 d£75

CAVENDISH   BULL INN ♟

High St CO10 8AX
☎ 01787 280245
Dir: A134 Bury St Edmunds to Long Melford, then R at green, pub 5m on R. **Map Ref:** TL84

A Victorian pub set in one of Suffolk's most beautiful villages, with an unassuming façade hiding a splendid 15th-century beamed interior. Expect a good atmosphere and decent food, with the daily-changing blackboard menu listing perhaps curries, shank of lamb, fresh fish and shellfish, and a roast on Sundays. Outside there's a pleasant terraced garden.

OPEN: 11-3 (Sun 12-10.30) 6-11 **BAR MEALS:** L served Tue-Sun 12-2 D served Tue-Sun 6.30-9 Av main course £7.95 **RESTAURANT:** L served Tue-Sun 12-2 D served Tue-Sun 6.30-9 Av 3 course à la carte £18 **BREWERY/COMPANY:** Adnams ◖: Adnams Bitter & Broadside. **CHILDREN'S FACILITIES:** menu, portions, high-chairs, food/bottle warming **GARDEN:** Terraced Garden **NOTES:** Dogs allowed: Parking 30

CHELMONDISTON   BUTT & OYSTER ♟

Pin Mill Ln IP9 1JW
☎ 01473 780764 ▤ 01473 780764
Map Ref: TM23

The role of this 16th century pub on the eerie Suffolk coast has always been to provide sustenance for the local bargees and rivermen whose thirst for beer is near legendary. Today, with its character still thankfully intact, the Butt & Oyster is a favourite haunt of locals, tourists and yachtsmen. A mixture of seafood and traditional dishes characterises the menu, including toad in the hole, steak and kidney pie and scampi and chips.

OPEN: 11-11 (Sun 12-10.30) Rest: Dec 25-26 Dec 31 Closed eve **BAR MEALS:** L served all week D served all week (Food served all day, Sun 12-9.30) Av main course £8 **BREWERY/COMPANY:** Pubmaster ◖: IPA, Adnams, Flowers Original, Broadside. **CHILDREN'S FACILITIES:** menu, family room **GARDEN:** outdoor eating, riverside **NOTES:** Dogs allowed: Garden only, Water, Parking 40

DUNWICH THE SHIP INN

St James St IP17 3DT
☎ 01728 648219 ▤ 01728 648675
e-mail: shipinn@tiscali.co.uk
Dir: *N on A12 from Ipswich thru Yoxford, R
signed Dunwich.* **Map Ref:** *TM47*

Dunwich, a famous seaport before the sea
swept it away in the Middle Ages, is now
merely an attractive seaside village. All that is
left of its former glory (in 630 it was the seat
of the East Anglian bishopric) are the friary
ruins, and of course the Ship Inn. This old
smugglers' haunt exudes great warmth and
character, and is noted for traditional food
and local ales. As one would expect, fresh
local fish features prominently on the menu,
including cod, mackerel, prawns, scampi, and
fishcakes. The specials board may
supplement these with sole, haddock, sardines and
crab according to availability, and in fine weather the
Dunwich fish can be eaten in the garden. Non-fish
dishes include, bacon and walnut salad, black pudding
with apple cider and wholegrain mustard sauce, steak
and ale casserole, pork in peach and Madeira sauce;
and several salads. Real ales are from Suffolk's own
Adnams and Mauldons breweries.

OPEN: 11-11 Sun 12-10.30 **BAR MEALS:** L served all
week 12-3 D served all week 6-9.00 Av main course £6.85
RESTAURANT: L served all week 12-3 D served all week
7-9.00 **BREWERY/COMPANY:** Free House 🍺: Adnams,
Mauldons. **CHILDREN'S FACILITIES:** menu, portions,
high-chairs, food/bottle warming, high chairs **GARDEN:** Large
terraced area **NOTES:** Dogs allowed: in bar, in garden,
in bedrooms, Parking 10

EARL SOHAM VICTORIA

The Street IP13 7RL
☎ 01728 685758
Dir: *From the A14 at Stowmarket, Earl Soham
is on the A1120 heading towards Yoxford.*
Map Ref: *TM26*

Backing on to the village green, this friendly,
down-to-earth pub has its own brewery
attached to the rear of the building.
Traditional pub fare is on offer, like home-
made chilli, baked gammon, various meat
and game casseroles, curries, and smoked
salmon salad, along with such light lunches
as macaroni cheese, filled jacket potatoes,
toasted sandwiches and various ploughman's.
Home-made desserts include sponge
pudding and treacle, and walnut tart.

OPEN: 11.30-3 6-11 (Sun 12-3, 7-10.30)
BAR MEALS: L served all week 11.30-2 D served all week
6-10 Av main course £7 **BREWERY/COMPANY:** Free
House 🍺: Earl Soham-Victoria Bitter, Albert Ale, & Gannet
Mild (all brewed on site). Earl Soham Porter, Edward Ale.
GARDEN: Benches at front and rear of pub **NOTES:** Dogs
allowed: garden only, Parking 25

ERWARTON THE QUEENS HEAD

The Street IP9 1LN
☎ 01473 787550
Dir: *From Ipswich take B1456 to Shotley.*
Map Ref: *TM23*

Views of the coast and countryside can be
enjoyed from this handsome 16th-century
building in traditional Suffolk style. Low oak-
beamed ceilings make this an atmospheric
stop for a beer. Alternatively, choose from
traditional pub favourites in the conservatory
restaurant overlooking the River Stowe:
prawn cocktail or breaded mushrooms to
start; then steak and kidney pudding or
gammon steak with egg or pineapple; and
finishing with chocolate 'lumpy bumpy' or
Belgian apple pie.

OPEN: 11-3 6.30-11 (Sun 12-3, 7-10.30) Closed: 25 Dec
BAR MEALS: L served all week 12-2.45 D served all week
7-9.30 **RESTAURANT:** L served all week 12-2.45 D served
all week 7-9.30 **BREWERY/COMPANY:** Free House
🍺: Adnams Bitter & Broadside, Greene King IPA.
CHILDREN'S FACILITIES: menu, portions, high-chairs,
food/bottle warming, children welcome in restaurant only
NOTES: No dogs (ex guide dogs), Parking 30

EYE THE WHITE HORSE INN ◆◆◆◆

Stoke Ash IP23 7ET
☎ 01379 678222 📠 01379 678557
e-mail: whitehorse@stokeash.fsbusiness.co.uk
Dir: *On the main A140 between Ipswich &*
Norwich. **Map Ref:** *TM17*

A 17th-century coaching inn set amid lovely Suffolk countryside. The heavily-timbered interior accommodates an inglenook fireplace, two bars and a restaurant. There are seven spacious motel bedrooms in the grounds, as well as a patio and secluded grassy area. An extensive menu is supplemented by lunchtime snacks, grills and daily specials from the blackboard.

OPEN: 11-11 (Sun 11-10.30) **BAR MEALS:** L served all week 11-9.30 D served all week 11-9.30 Av main course £8 **RESTAURANT:** L served all week 11-9.30 D served all week 11-9.30 Av 3 course à la carte £14.50 **BREWERY/COMPANY:** Free House 🍺: Adnams, Greene King Abbot, IPA Smooth. **CHILDREN'S FACILITIES:** menu, portions, licence, games, high-chairs, food/bottle warming **GARDEN:** Patio & grass area **NOTES:** No dogs (ex guide dogs), Parking 60 **ROOMS:** 7 en suite bedrooms 1 family room s£42.50 d£57.50

FRAMLINGHAM THE STATION HOTEL ♉

Station Rd IP13 9EE
☎ 01728 723455
Dir: *Bypass Ipswich heading toward Lowestoft*
on the A12. **Map Ref:** *TM26*

Since trains stopped coming to Framlingham in 1962 the buildings of the former station hotel have been put to good use. One is a vintage motorcycle repair shop, while another is an antique bed showroom. The hotel has established itself as a popular destination, with a good reputation for seafood and locally brewed beers. Check out the menu for roll-mop herrings, seafood platter, Loch Fyne oysters, smoked trout salad, greenlip mussels and corn beef hash with a cheese topping.

OPEN: 12-2.30 5-11 **BAR MEALS:** L served all week 12-2 D served all week 7-9.30 Av main course £6.95 **RESTAURANT:** L served all week 12-2 D served all week 7-9.30 Av 3 course à la carte £11 **BREWERY/COMPANY:** Free House 🍺: Earl Soham Victoria, Albert & Mild. **CHILDREN'S FACILITIES:** family room **GARDEN:** Pond, patio, food served outdoors **NOTES:** Dogs allowed: Water, Biscuits, Parking 20

HADLEIGH THE MARQUIS OF CORNWALLIS ♉

Upper St, Layham IP7 5JZ
☎ 01473 822051 📠 01473 822051
e-mail: marquislayham@aol.com
Dir: *On the A12 between Colchester and*
Ipswich, take B1070 to Hadleigh. Upper Layham
1 mlie before Hadleigh. **Map Ref:** *TM04*

Known locally as the 'Noodle', this late 16th-century inn stands in two acres of gardens overlooking the Brett Valley, and is named after a British military commander defeated in the American War of Independence. Traditional bar snacks and home-made pies are supplemented by dishes which are cooked to order from local Suffolk produce and served in the candlelit restaurant. These include cidered chicken casserole, and spare ribs of pork.

OPEN: 12-3 (Sun 12-10.30) 6-11 **BAR MEALS:** L served all week 12-2.30 D served all week 7-9.30 Av main course £7.25 **RESTAURANT:** L served all week 12-2.30 D served all week 7-9.30 Av 3 course à la carte £14.65 **BREWERY/COMPANY:** Free House 🍺: Adnams & Broadside, Greene King IPA & Abbot Ale. ♉: 9 **CHILDREN'S FACILITIES:** menu, portions, high-chairs, food/bottle warming **GARDEN:** 2 acres, overlooking River Brett & Valley **NOTES:** Dogs allowed: in bar, in garden, Water, Parking 30

HALESWORTH THE QUEEN'S HEAD

The Street, Bramfield IP19 9HT
☎ 01986 784214 📠 01986 784797
e-mail: qhbfield@aol.com
Dir: 2m from A12 on the A144 towards Halesworth. Map Ref: TM37

Located on the edge of the Suffolk Heritage Coast, and only 15 minutes from the historic coastal town of Southwold, the Queen's Head has a beautiful rear garden overlooked by Bramfield's thatched village church with its unusual separate round bell tower. The pub's interior has scrubbed pine tables, exposed beams, vaulted ceiling and huge fireplaces. Over the past five years the owners have developed the establishment's reputation for fine dining. Most of the ingredients are sourced from small local suppliers and organic farms, which are always identified on the menu.

OPEN: 11.45-2.30 6.30-11 (Sun 12-3, 7-10.30) Closed: 26 Dec **BAR MEALS:** L served all week 12-2 D served all week 6.30-10 Sun 7-9 **BREWERY/COMPANY:** Adnams
🍺: Adnams Bitter & Broadside. 🍷: 7
CHILDREN'S FACILITIES: games, high-chairs, food/bottle warming, baby changing, High chairs, books, toys, family room **GARDEN:** Enclosed garden with seating, willow dome **NOTES:** Dogs allowed: in bar, in garden, in bedrooms, Water, Parking 15

HOLBROOK THE COMPASSES

Ipswich Rd IP9 2QR
☎ 01473 328332 📠 01473 327403
Dir: From A137 S of Ipswich, take B1456/B1080. Map Ref: TM13

Holbrook is bordered by the rivers Orwell and Stour, and this traditional country pub, which dates back to the 17th century, is on the Shotley peninsula. For several decades the inn was a staging post between London and Ipswich and the area is still popular with visitors. The menu is varied and appetising; it's also reasonably priced, with only one steak dish topping the £10 mark. Good fish options include grilled or battered cod or haddock, fish pie, and seafood lasagne. Special mains are chicken Alex, a boneless chicken breast in the pub's gourmet sauce of white wine, bacon, mushrooms and cream and kleftico, a large lamb joint slowly cooked in red wine and herbs, served with chive and onion mash. Some courses are offered in smaller portions at lower prices.

OPEN: 11-2.30 (Sun 12-3, 6-10.30) 6-11 Closed: 25-26 Dec, 1 Jan **BAR MEALS:** L served all week 11.30-2.15 D served all week 6-9.15 (Sun food times, 12-2.15, 6-9.15) Av main course £8 **RESTAURANT:** L served all week 11.30-2.15 D served all week 6-9.15 (Sun food times, 12-2.15, 6-9.15) **BREWERY/COMPANY:** Pubmaster
🍺: Carlsberg, Greene King IPA, Adnams Bitter, Kronenbourg & Guest Ales. **CHILDREN'S FACILITIES:** menu, high-chairs, outdoor play area **GARDEN:** Six picnic benches **NOTES:** No dogs (ex guide dogs), Parking 30

HONEY TYE THE LION

CO6 4NX
☎ 01206 263434 📠 01206 263434
Dir: On A134 between Colchester & Sudbury. Map Ref: TL93

Low-beamed ceilings and an open log fire are charming features of this traditional country dining pub on the Essex/Suffolk border. The menu is concise yet offers enticing choices: seared breast of pigeon or deep-fried sardines could lead on to baked breast of chicken filled with green pesto and Mozzarella, or duo of duck sausages with orange-scented sweet potato. Fish such as grilled darne of salmon, baked rainbow trout, or roast fillets of sea bass are also available; a couple of thoughtful vegetarian options complete the picture.

OPEN: 11-3 5-11 (Sun 12-10.30) **BAR MEALS:** L served all week 12-2 D served all week 6-9.30 SUn 12-9.30 Av main course £8.50 **RESTAURANT:** L served all week 12-2 D served all week 6-9.30 Sun 12-9.30
BREWERY/COMPANY: Free House 🍺: Greene King IPA, Adnams Bitter, quest ale. **CHILDREN'S FACILITIES:** menu, portions, high-chairs, food/bottle warming **GARDEN:** Patio with tables and umbrellas **NOTES:** Dogs allowed: in garden, Parking 40

HORRINGER BEEHIVE ♀

The Street IP29 5SN
☎ 01284 735260 ▤ 01638 730416
Dir: *From A14, 1st turning for Bury St Edmunds, sign for Westley & Ickworth Park.*
Map Ref: TL86

Buzzing (what else?) with activity, the Beehive is a converted Victorian flint and stone cottage, close to the National Trust's Ickworth House. Its succession of cosy dining areas is furnished with antique pine tables and chairs. In season, visitors head for the tables on the patio and the picnic benches in the walled beer garden. The proprietors respond to changing customer appetites with seasonal produce and daily changing menus. With these factors in mind therefore they may, for instance, offer starters of salmon and crayfish tail terrine with lemon dressing, or cream of parsnip soup with a hint of curry. And for main courses there could well be seared liver with balsamic jus, home-made pork apple and leek sausages on creamy mash, or steamed monkfish with tomato pesto and saffron rice. If it's just a tasty snack you want, try warm spinach and Parmesan tart with salad, and round off with chocolate and Grand Marnier mousse.

OPEN: 11.30-2.30 7-11 Closed: Dec 25-26
BAR MEALS: L served all week 12-2 D served Mon-Sat 7-9.45 **RESTAURANT:** L served all week 12-2 D served all week 7-9.45 Av 3 course à la carte £18
BREWERY/COMPANY: Greene King 🍺: Greene King IPA & Abbot Ale, Guest beers. **CHILDREN'S FACILITIES:** portions, food/bottle warming **GARDEN:** Patio, picnic benches, walled garden **NOTES:** No dogs (ex guide dogs), Parking 30

ICKLINGHAM THE RED LION ♀

The Street IP28 6PS
☎ 01638 717802 ▤ 01638 515702
e-mail: lizard2020@supernet.com
Dir: *On A1101 between Mildenhall & Bury St Edmunds.* **Map Ref:** TL77

A sympathetically restored 16th-century inn set back from the road behind a lawned area with flower beds and garden furniture. A raised rear terrace overlooks the River Lark and open fields. An attractive thatched country inn, the Red Lion stands back from the A11 between Newmarket and Thetford. The interior, glowing by candlelight in the evening, features exposed beams, wooden floors, rugs and antique furniture.

OPEN: 12-3 6-11 Closed: 25 Dec Rest: 26 Dec & 31 Dec Closed PM **BAR MEALS:** L served all week 12-2.30 D served all week 6-10 Av main course £10 **RESTAURANT:** L served all week 12-2.30 D served all week 6-10 Av 3 course à la carte £20 **BREWERY/COMPANY:** Greene King 🍺: Greene King Abbot Ale & IPA. ♀: 15 **CHILDREN'S FACILITIES:** high chair available **GARDEN:** Large lawn with parasols, river at rear **NOTES:** No dogs, Parking 50

LAVENHAM ANGEL HOTEL ★★ ❀ ♀

Market Place CO10 9QZ
☎ 01787 247388 ▤ 01787 248344
e-mail: angellav@aol.com
Dir: *From A14 take Bury East/Sudbury turn off A143, after 4m take A1141 to Lavenham, Angel is off the High Street.* **Map Ref:** TL94

This fine historic inn, which was originally licensed in 1420, stands amid some 300 listed buildings in England's best-preserved medieval wool town. The building retains many original features. Eight en suite bedrooms enable excellent dinner, bed and breakfast packages to be offered. The warm and friendly atmosphere is helped by the open plan layout; a no-smoking policy applies throughout, and children are well catered for.

OPEN: 11-11 (Sun 12-10.30) Closed: 25-26 Dec
BAR MEALS: L served all week 12-2.15 D served all week 6.45-9.15 Av main course £9 **RESTAURANT:** L served all week 12-2.15 D served all week 6.45-9.15 Av 3 course à la carte £18 **BREWERY/COMPANY:** Free House 🍺: Adnams Bitter, Nethergate, Greene King IPA & Old Growler. ♀: 9
CHILDREN'S FACILITIES: portions, licence, games, high-chairs, food/bottle warming, baby changing, highchairs, toys, cots, baby listening **GARDEN:** Lawn and patio area with tables and seating **NOTES:** No dogs (ex guide dogs), Parking 105 **ROOMS:** 8 en suite 1 family room s£50 d£75

LEVINGTON THE SHIP INN

Church Ln IP10 0LQ
☎ 01473 659573
Dir: *off the A14 towards Felixstowe. Nr Levington Marina.* **Map Ref:** *TM23*

This charming 14th-century thatched pub overlooks the River Orwell, and there are pleasant walks in the surrounding countryside. The Ship is already popular with birdwatchers and yachting folk, and is fast establishing a reputation for fresh, home-made dishes. Fish and seafood both feature strongly; mussels have their own speciality menu, with crevettes, lobster, crab, haddock, tuna and monkfish all making an appearance when available. The main menu changes twice daily.

OPEN: 11.30-3 6.30-11 **BAR MEALS:** L served all week 12-2 D served Mon-Sat 6.30-9.30 (Sun 12-3) Av main course £8.50 **RESTAURANT:** L served all week 12-2 D served all week 6.30-9.30 (Sun 12-3)
BREWERY/COMPANY: Pubmaster ◀: Greene King IPA, Adnams Best & Broadside. ♀: 8
CHILDREN'S FACILITIES: Garden, Patio **GARDEN:** Patio area front and back **NOTES:** No dogs (ex guide dogs), Parking 70

LONG MELFORD THE CROWN HOTEL

Hall St CO10 9JL
☎ 01787 377666 ▤ 01787 379005
e-mail: quincy@crownmelford.fsnet.co.uk
Dir: *from Sudbury take A134 to Bury St Edmunds, at 1st rndbt take 1st L to Long Melford.* **Map Ref:** *TL84*

At the heart of Constable country, Long Melford's pub was built in 1610 yet retains a Tudor cellar and oak beams. In 1885, the Crown was the last place to hear the Riot Act read in West Suffolk. A hearty bar menu includes salads, ploughmans', jacket potatoes, sandwiches, mixed grill, poached salmon, aubergine and mushroom bake, steak and mushroom pie, and fish and chips.

OPEN: 11.30-11 (Sun 12-10.30) **BAR MEALS:** L served all week 12-2.30 D served all week 7-9.30 Av main course £8.50 **RESTAURANT:** L served all week 12-2.30 D served all week 7-9.30 Av 3 course à la carte £16
BREWERY/COMPANY: Free House ◀: Greene King Old Speckled Hen, IPA. ♀: 12 **CHILDREN'S FACILITIES:** menu
GARDEN: Al fresco, large umbrellas, patio area
NOTES: No dogs (ex guide dogs), Parking 6

MELTON WILFORD BRIDGE

Wilford Bridge Rd IP12 2PA
☎ 01394 386141
Dir: *Head to the coast from the A12, follow signs to Bawdsey & Orford, cross railway lines, next pub on L.* **Map Ref:** *TM25*

Fish dishes and chargrills are specialities at this pub, just down the road from the famous Saxon burial ship at Sutton Hoo (NT). Examples include Dover sole, pan- or deep-fried skate wing, deep-fried sprats, chargilled chicken piri piri, rib-eye and T-bone steaks, and lamb cutlets. Other menu choices include home-made steak Guinness and mushroom pie, pure beef burgers, and spinach and ricotta cannelloni. Supreme of pheasant, and sea bass sometimes appear as daily specials.

OPEN: 11-3 food served all day Sat-Sun 6.30-11 Closed: 25-26 Dec **BAR MEALS:** L served all week 11.30-2 D served all week 6.30-9.30 Av main course £9.50
RESTAURANT: L served all week 11.30-2 D served all week 6.30-9.30 Av 3 course à la carte £16
BREWERY/COMPANY: Free House ◀: Adnams Best, Broadside, Scottish Courage John Smith's + guest Ales.
CHILDREN'S FACILITIES: menu, portions, high-chairs, food/bottle warming **GARDEN:** Patio, seats up to 30 people
NOTES: No dogs (ex guide dogs), Parking 40

MONKS ELEIGH THE SWAN INN

The Street IP7 7AU
☎ 01449 741391 ▤ 01449 741391
Dir: *On the B1115 between Sudbury & Hadleigh.* **Map Ref:** *TL94*

Part-14th century, the Swan occupies a prime site in the middle of the village, its thatch and cream façade blending easily with the 'Suffolk pink' wash of its medieval near neighbours. Like Lavenham a few miles to the north west, Monks Eleigh was founded on the prosperous local wool trade, which explains the impressive nature of some of these properties. The original building was open to the roof and evidence still exists of the smoke hole. Wattle and daub panels were discovered in one room during renovations, and the main restaurant, with a magnificent open fireplace, was possibly once used as the manorial court. Menus change daily, making optimum use of seasonal local produce, with game featuring during the permitted months. An example menu begins with home-cured gravadlax, follows with roast duck breast on a compôte of aubergines, cherry tomatoes and basil, served with gratin dauphinoise, and finishes with iced Amaretto spumoni.

OPEN: 12-3 7-11 **BAR MEALS:** L served Wed-Sun 12-2 D served Wed-Sun 7-9.30 Open from 10am Sun (breakfast) Av main course £11 **RESTAURANT:** L served Wed-Sun 12-2 D served Wed-Sun 7-9.30 Av 3 course à la carte £20
BREWERY/COMPANY: Free House 🍺: Greene King IPA, Adnams Bitter & Broadside. ♀: 20
CHILDREN'S FACILITIES: portions, high-chairs, food/bottle warming **NOTES:** No dogs (ex guide dogs), Parking 10

ORFORD KING'S HEAD

Front St IP12 2LW
☎ 01394 450271
e-mail: ian_thornton@talk21.com
Dir: *From Woodbridge follow signs for Orford Castle along the B1084 through Butly and Chillesford onto Orford.* **Map Ref:** *TM45*

Atmospheric 13th-century inn with a smuggling history, located a short walk from the quay. The interior includes a beamed bar serving Adnams ales, and a wood-floored restaurant offering plenty of local produce. Typical starters include locally smoked mackerel with a salad garnish, and deep-fried Brie with a Cumberland sauce, followed perhaps by 'boozy beef' (made with steak and Adnams ale), seafood platter, or Orford-made salmon fish cakes. Bar snacks include sandwiches, burgers and things with chips.

OPEN: 11.30-3 6-11 **BAR MEALS:** L served all week 12-2 D served all week 6-9 Av main course £7.25
RESTAURANT: L served all week 12-2 D served all week 6-9 Av 3 course à la carte £14 **BREWERY/COMPANY:** Adnams
🍺: Adnams Bitter, Adnams Broadside, Adnams Regatta, Adnams Fisherman. **CHILDREN'S FACILITIES:** menu, high-chairs, food/bottle warming **GARDEN:** Large grassed area with flower border **NOTES:** Dogs allowed: in bar, in garden, Water, Parking 20

POLSTEAD THE COCK INN 🐑

The Green CO6 5AL
☎ 01206 263150 ▤ 01206 263150
e-mail: enquiries@the-cock-inn-polstead.fsbusiness.co.uk
Dir: *Colchester/A134 towards Sudbury then R, follow signs to Polstead.* **Map Ref:** *TL93*

A 17th-century pub with a Victorian restaurant extension, the Cock overlooks the green in a lovely village at the heart of Constable country. With some of Suffolk's prettiest landscapes right on the doorstep, it's not surprising that the pub attracts cyclists and ramblers. Originally a farmhouse, the building is characterised by oak beams, quarry-tiled floors and plain painted walls.

OPEN: 11-3 (Open Mon during X-mas, Easter) 6-11 (Sun-BHS 12-3, 6-10.30) **BAR MEALS:** L served Tues-Sun 11.30-2.30 D served Tues-Sun 6.30-9.30 Sun 12-2.30, 6.30-9
RESTAURANT: L served Tue-Sun 11.30-2.30 D served Tues-Sun 6.30-9.30 Sun 12-2.30, 6.30-9 **BREWERY/COMPANY:** Free House 🍺: Greene King IPA, Adnams, Tetley Smooth.
CHILDREN'S FACILITIES: menu, portions, high-chairs, food/bottle warming, outdoor play area, swings, slide, seesaw, climbing frame **GARDEN:** Picnic tables, pretty garden, water feature **NOTES:** Dogs allowed: in bar, in garden, Water, Parking 20

RAMSHOLT RAMSHOLT ARMS

Dock Rd IP12 3AB
☎ 01394 411229
Dir: *End of lane on beach at Ramsholt, signed off B1083 Woodbridge to Bawdsey.*
Map Ref: *TM34*

Enjoying a glorious, unrivalled position on a tidal beach overlooking the River Deben, this 18th-century, pink-washed former farmhouse, ferryman's cottage and smugglers' inn is the perfect summer evening destination for a pint on the terrace to watch the glorious sunset over the river. Expect a civilised atmosphere, picture windows, Adnams ales, and good home-cooked food, in particular fish and seafood in summer and local game in winter. Blackboard dishes could include cod and chips, local lobster, Cromer crab, whole Dover sole, roast partridge and decent pies.

OPEN: 11.30-11 (Sun 12-10.30) **BAR MEALS:** L served all week 12-3 D served all week 6.30-9 Av main course £8
RESTAURANT: L served all week 12-3 D served all week 6.30-9 **BREWERY/COMPANY:** Free House 🍺: Adnams, Greene King, Woodfords, Nethergates.
CHILDREN'S FACILITIES: menu **GARDEN:** Food served outside. Large garden, estuary **NOTES:** Dogs allowed: Water provided, Parking 60

SOUTHWOLD CROWN HOTEL ★★ ❀❀ ♀

The High St IP18 6DP
☎ 01502 722275 📠 01502 727263
e-mail: crown.hotel@adnams.co.uk
Dir: *off A12 take A1094 to Southwold, stay on main road into town centre, hotel on L in High St.* **Map Ref:** *TM57*

A posting inn, dating from 1750, today fulfilling the purposes of pub, wine bar, restaurant and small hotel. As the flagship for Adnams brewery, excellent ales and wines can be sampled - the latter featuring on a menu of more than 20 sold by the glass. Alternatively you can visit the cellar and kitchen store at the rear of the Crown yard for a full selection of wines and bottled beers. Good food is served in either the bar or the restaurant; the Crown's seaside location means fish is well represented on both menus. Typical imaginative dishes in the bar might be steamed mussels with parsley and garlic, or grilled squid with risotto nero.

OPEN: 11-11 6-11 (all day opening during peak times)
BAR MEALS: L served all week 12-2 D served all week 7-9.30 (all day opening Sun) Av main course £11
RESTAURANT: L served all week 12.30-1.45 D served all week 7.30-8.45 **BREWERY/COMPANY:** Adnams
🍺: Adnams. ♀: 20 **CHILDREN'S FACILITIES:** portions, high-chairs, food/bottle warming, baby changing, family room
NOTES: Guide dogs only, No dogs, Parking 18
ROOMS: 14 bedrooms 13 en suite s£77 d£55

THORNHAM MAGNA THE FOUR HORSESHOES ♀

Wickham Rd IP23 8HD
☎ 01379 678777 📠 01379 678134
Dir: *From Diss on A140 turn R and follow signs for Finningham, 0.5m turn R for Thornham Magna.* **Map Ref:** *TM17*

Thornham Magna is a delightful, unspoilt village, close to Thornham Country Park and the interesting thatched church at Thornham Parva. This fine 12th-century inn is also thatched, and has timber-framed walls as well as a well in the bar. Came under new management as this guide went to press, so reader's reports are welcome.

OPEN: 12-11 **BAR MEALS:** L served all week 12.00-9.30 D served all week Av main course £7.50
RESTAURANT: L served all week 12.00-9.30 D served all week **BREWERY/COMPANY:** Greene King 🍺: Greene King IPA, Abbot & Old Speckled Hen. ♀: 20
CHILDREN'S FACILITIES: menu, family room **NOTES:** Dogs allowed: in bar, in garden, Parking 80

TOSTOCK GARDENERS ARMS

IP30 9PA
☎ 01359 270460
Dir: *From A14 follow signs to Tostock (0.5m).*
Map Ref: *TL96*

Parts of this charming pub, at the end of the village green, near the horse chestnut tree, date back 600 years. The basic bar menu - salads, grills, ploughmans', sandwiches, toasties, etc - is supplemented by specials boards that offer six starters and 12 main courses in the evening. Look out for lamb balti, Thai king prawn green curry, steak and kidney pie, or chicken and Stilton roulade. Large grassy garden.

OPEN: 11-3 5.30-11 (Sun 12-3 7-10.30)
BAR MEALS: L served all week 12-2 D served all week 7-9 Av main course £8 **RESTAURANT:** L served Mon-Sat 12-2 D served Wed-Sun 7.15-9.30 Av 3 course à la carte £13
BREWERY/COMPANY: Greene King ◀: Greene King IPA, Greene King Abbot, Greene King seasonal beers.
GARDEN: Food served outside, large grass area
NOTES: Dogs allowed: Parking 20

WANGFORD THE ANGEL INN

High St NR34 8RL
☎ 01502 578636 ▯ 01502 578535
e-mail: enquiries@angelinn.freeserve.co.uk
Map Ref: *TM47*

A traditional green-and-cream-painted inn with a handsome Georgian façade, set in the heart of the pretty village of Wangford. Dating back to the 16th century, and complete with resident ghost, its cosy bar and restaurant are characterised by exposed beams and roaring log fires in winter. Home-made dishes include fresh fish (grilled sea bass steak with citrus butter, baby crayfish tails sautéed in garlic butter), hearty favourites such as steaks, pies and sausages, and good vegetarian options.

OPEN: 12-3 6-11 **BAR MEALS:** L served Tues-Sun 12-2 D served Tues-Sun 6.30-9 Av main course £8
RESTAURANT: L served Tues- Sun 12-2 D served Tues-Sun 6.30-9 Av 3 course à la carte £15
BREWERY/COMPANY: Free House ◀: Adnams Best, Spitfire, Greene King Abbot Ale, Brakspear Bitter.
CHILDREN'S FACILITIES: menu, outdoor play area, slide, swings, family room **GARDEN:** Large walled garden with benches **NOTES:** Dogs allowed: in bar, in garden, in bedrooms, Parking 20

CHIDDINGFOLD THE SWAN INN & RESTAURANT 🐑 🍷

Petworth Rd GU8 4TY
☎ 01428 682073 ▯ 01428 683259
Map Ref: *SU93*

A lovely 14th-century village pub whose sympathetic refurbishment has included bare floors, wooden furniture and big leather sofas. The chef makes impressive use of seafood, fish and local game. A typical menu starts with white bean soup with pesto tortellini and crepe oil, followed by char-grilled rib of beef with garlic fondant, foie gras and shallot confit sauce, or fillets of red mullet with fresh pasta in a rich shellfish sauce, finishing with terrine of summer berries in red wine jelly with vanilla and black pepper syrup. Bar snacks are also available.

OPEN: 11-3 5.30-11 (Sat 11-11, Sun 12-10.30)
BAR MEALS: L served all week 12-2.30 D served all week 6.30-10 (Sat & Sun 12-10) Av main course £8
RESTAURANT: L served all week 12-2.30 D served all week 6.30-10 Av 3 course à la carte £20
BREWERY/COMPANY: Free House ◀: Hogs Back TEA, Ringwood Best, Fuller's London Pride. 🍷: 15
CHILDREN'S FACILITIES: portions, high-chairs, food/bottle warming, baby changing **GARDEN:** Terraced sun trap
NOTES: Dogs allowed: in bar, Water, Parking 25

DORKING ABINGER HATCH

Abinger Ln, Abinger Common RH5 6HZ
☎ 01306 730737
Dir: *A25 from Guildford, L to Abinger Common.*
Map Ref: *TQ14*

Flagged floors, beamed ceilings and open fires are features of this 18th-century coaching inn, classically located opposite the church and duck pond. It's a free house serving Harveys, Fullers London Pride, Badger Tanglefoot, Youngs, Adnams and Chiswick beers, and home-cooked food prepared by the landlord. Options range from hot and kickin' chicken with BBQ dressing to double-baked loin of lamb with rosemary and red wine sauce.

OPEN: 11.30-2.30 5-11 (all day Sat-Sun)
BAR MEALS: L served all week 12-2.15 D served Tue-Sat 6-9.15 Av main course £5 **RESTAURANT:** L served all week 12-2.15 D served all week 6-9.15
BREWERY/COMPANY: Free House 🍺: Harveys, Fuller's London Pride, Chiswick Bitter, Badger Tanglefoot.
CHILDREN'S FACILITIES: menu **GARDEN:** Food served outside **NOTES:** Dogs allowed: Parking 35

EGHAM THE FOX AND HOUNDS ♀

Bishopgate Rd, Englefield Green TW20 0XU
☎ 01784 433098 📠 01784 438775
e-mail: thefoxandhounds@4cinns.co.uk
Dir: *From village green turn L into Castle Hill Rd, then R into Bishops Gate Rd.*
Map Ref: *TQ07*

The Surrey border once ran through the centre of this good English pub, which is on the edge of Windsor Great Park, convenient for walkers and riders. Features include a large garden, handsome conservatory and weekly jazz nights. Menus offer a range of daily-changing fish specials as well as dishes like orange and sesame chicken fillets on coriander and lime noodles, or roast pork with grain mustard glaze and Parmesan crisps.

OPEN: 11-11 (Sun 12-10.30) (Fri-Sun, open all day)
BAR MEALS: L served all week 12-2.30 D served all week 6.30-9.30 Av main course £13.50 **RESTAURANT:** L served all week 12-2.30 D served all week 6.30-10 Av 3 course à la carte £25 🍺: Fullers London Pride, IPA, Courage Best. ♀: 8
NOTES: Dogs allowed: Parking 60

GUILDFORD RED LION 🐷 ♀

Shamley Green GU5 0UB
☎ 01483 892202 📠 01483 894055
Map Ref: *SU94*

Attractive old village pub with large front and rear gardens, ideal for whiling away summer afternoons watching the local cricket team play on the green opposite. In the cosy bar or large comfortable restaurant, peruse no fewer than four varied menus on which everything listed is home prepared including roast half duck with black cherry sauce, vegetable tartlet with Mornay sauce, fresh fish pie, and another four or more fish/seafood dishes. Young's and Adnam's in the bar.

OPEN: 7.30-11.30 **BAR MEALS:** L served all week 12-3 D served all week 7-10 Av main course £10.95
RESTAURANT: L served all week 12-3 D served all week 7-10 Av 3 course à la carte £22.50
BREWERY/COMPANY: Pubmaster 🍺: Youngs Pedigree, Adnams Broadside, Stella Artois. ♀: 6
CHILDREN'S FACILITIES: menu, licence **GARDEN:** Large front and rear garden **NOTES:** No dogs (ex guide dogs), Parking 20

LEIGH   THE PLOUGH ♀

Church Rd, LEIGH RH2 8NJ
☎ 01306 611348 ▤ 01306 611299
Dir: *Telephone for directions.* **Map Ref:** *TQ24*

A welcoming country pub overlooking the village green and situated opposite St Bartholomew's Church. Varied clientele, good atmosphere and quaint low beams which are conveniently padded! A hearty bar menu offers steak sandwiches, burgers, melts, salads, ploughmans' and jacket potatoes, while the restaurant area menu features tomato and artichoke pasta, smoked haddock fillet mornay, or Mexican style tortilla wraps.

OPEN: 11-11 (Sun 12-10.30) **BAR MEALS:** L served all week 12-3 D served all week 7-10 Av main course £8
RESTAURANT: L served all week 12-3 D served all week 7-10 Av 3 course à la carte £15
BREWERY/COMPANY: Hall & Woodhouse ◖: Badger Best, Tanglefoot, Sussex Bitter. ♀: 15 **GARDEN:** Patio/Paved surrounded by climbing roses **NOTES:** Dogs allowed: in bar, in garden, Water, Parking 6

NEWDIGATE   THE SURREY OAKS

Parkgate Rd RH5 5DZ
☎ 01306 631200 ▤ 01306 631200
Dir: *turn off either A24 or A25 and follow signs to Newdigate, The Surry Oaks is 1m E of Newdigate Village on the road towards Leigh/Charwood.* **Map Ref:** *TQ14*

Parts of this country pub date from 1570, the Georgian bar has been converted into a restaurant, and there are two small, beamed bars, one with an inglenook fireplace and stone-flagged floor. Restaurant and bar menus offer a good range of dishes plus a daily choice from the blackboard.

OPEN: 11.30-2.30 (Sat 11.30-3, 6-11) 5.30-11 (Sun 12-3, 7-10.30) **BAR MEALS:** L served all week 12-2 D served Tue-Sat 7-9 Av main course £8.50 **RESTAURANT:** L served all week 12-2 D served Tue-Sat 7-9 Av 3 course à la carte £15 **BREWERY/COMPANY:** Punch Taverns ◖: Harveys Sussex Best, Adnams, rotating guest beers.
CHILDREN'S FACILITIES: menu, portions, games, high-chairs, food/bottle warming, outdoor play area, swings, slide, climbing frame **GARDEN:** Large: pond, aviary, goat paddock
NOTES: Dogs allowed: in bar, in garden, Water, Parking 75

OCKLEY   BRYCE'S AT THE OLD SCHOOL HOUSE ❀ 🐾 ♀

RH5 5TH
☎ 01306 627430 ▤ 01306 628274
e-mail: bryces.fish@virgin.net
Dir: *8m S of Dorking on A29.* **Map Ref:** *TQ14*

A boys' boarding academy until Bill Bryce acquired it in 1982. Bill is into fresh fish in a big way, and given that this is rural Surrey, he manages to obtain a huge range. Non-fish eaters are not forgotten, but the choice is restricted. The restaurant, in the old school gym, offers seven starters and seven main courses - all fish. A good wine list includes plenty available by the glass.

OPEN: 11-3 6-11 (Closed Sun pm Nov, Jan, Feb) Closed: 25 Dec, 1 Jan **BAR MEALS:** L served all week 12-2.30 D served Mon-Sat 6.30-9.30 Av main course £10.50
RESTAURANT: L served all week 12-2.30 D served Mon-Sat 7-9.30 Av 3 course à la carte £27.50 Av 3 course fixed price £27.50 **BREWERY/COMPANY:** Free House ◖: London Pride, GB & Butser, Scottish Courage John Smith's Smooth.
♀: 15 **CHILDREN'S FACILITIES:** portions, high-chairs, food/bottle warming **GARDEN:** Terrace area **NOTES:** Dogs allowed: in bar, in garden, Water, Parking 25

OXTED GEORGE INN ♀

High St RH8 9LP
☎ 01883 713453
Dir: *Telephone for directions.* **Map Ref:** *TQ35*

A 500-year-old pub and restaurant with a friendly family atmosphere, warmed by log fires under the original oak beams. Home-made steak and kidney pudding, braised shank of lamb, sardines and salmon fillets from its seasonal menus epitomise the range of carefully sourced and well-cooked fare that is available on any day. There are decent wines to accompany the food, with Badger beers as alternative supping. A committed team let their quality of service speak for itself.

OPEN: 11-11 12-10.30 (Sun 12-2.30)
BAR MEALS: L served all week 12-9.30 D served all week Av main course £6.50 **RESTAURANT:** L served all week 12-2.30 D served all week 6-9.30
BREWERY/COMPANY: Woodhouse Inns 🍺: Badger Tanglefoot, Badger Best, King & Barnes, Sussex.
CHILDREN'S FACILITIES: menu **GARDEN:** Patio Area
NOTES: Dogs allowed: in bar, in garden, Parking 25

STAINES THE SWAN HOTEL ♀

The Hythe TW18 3JB
☎ 01784 452494 ▤ 01784 461593
e-mail: swan.hotel@fullers.co.uk
Dir: *Just off A308, S of Staines Bridge. Minutes from M25, M4 & M3. 5m from Heathrow.*
Map Ref: *TQ07*

Overlooking the Thames by Staines Bridge, this 18th-century inn was frequented by river bargemen who were paid in tokens which could be exchanged at the Swan for food and drink. The menu consists of traditional English fare - everything from fish and chips to steak and ale pie.

OPEN: 11-11 25 Dec 12-3, Sun 12-10.30
BAR MEALS: L served all week 12-6 D served all week 6-9.30 Sun 12-8 Av main course £7.50
RESTAURANT: L served all week 12-6 D served all week 6-9.30 **BREWERY/COMPANY:** Fullers 🍺: Fuller's London Pride, ESB. ♀: 10 **CHILDREN'S FACILITIES:** menu, high-chairs, food/bottle warming **GARDEN:** Patio with seating. Overlooks River Thames **NOTES:** Dogs allowed: in bar, in garden

---

VIRGINIA WATER THE WHEATSHEAF HOTEL ★★ ♀

London Rd GU25 4QF
☎ 01344 842057 ▤ 01344 842932
e-mail: sales@wheatsheafhotel.com
Dir: *M25 Jct 13, head towards A30 Bracknell.*
Map Ref: *TQ06*

The Wheatsheaf dates back to the second half of the 18th century and is beautifully situated overlooking Virginia Water on the edge of Windsor Great Park. Chalkboard menus offer a good range of freshly prepared dishes with fresh fish as a speciality. Popular options are beer battered cod and chips, roast queen fish with pesto crust, and braised lamb shank on mustard mash.

OPEN: 11-11 **BAR MEALS:** L served all week 12-10 D served all week Av main course £8
RESTAURANT: L served all week 12-10 D served all week Av 3 course à la carte £16 **BREWERY/COMPANY:** 🍺: Guest Ales. **CHILDREN'S FACILITIES:** menu, family room **GARDEN:** beer garden, patio, outdoor eating **NOTES:** No dogs, Parking 90 **ROOMS:** 17 en suite s£90 d£95

ARLINGTON OLD OAK INN

BN26 6SJ
☎ 01323 482072 ▤ 01323 895454
Dir: *N of A27 between Polegate & Lewes.*
Map Ref: *TQ50*

Built in 1733 as the village almshouse, this became a pub in the early 1900s. It is close to Abbots Wood and the Cuckoo Trail - both ideal for walking. The menu offers light bites such as bacon and potato salad, or roasted flat mushrooms with Brie and bacon, as well as standards such as baguettes and jacket potatoes. Hot dishes include poached salmon, home-made fishcakes of the day, and a selection of steaks.

OPEN: (Open all day every day) **BAR MEALS:** L served all week 12-2.30 D served all week 6.30-9.30 (food all day Sat-Sun) Av main course £6.95 **RESTAURANT:** L served all week 12-2.30 D served all week 9.30-9.30 (food all day Sat-Sun) Av 3 course à la carte £16.95
BREWERY/COMPANY: Free House ◀: Harveys, Badger, Adnams Broadside & guest ales.
CHILDREN'S FACILITIES: menu, portions, games, high-chairs, food/bottle warming, outdoor play area, wooden adventure, frame & slide **GARDEN:** Grassed and hedged with tables
NOTES: Dogs allowed: Water provided. To be kept on lead, Parking 40

BARCOMBE THE ANCHOR INN

Anchor Ln BN8 5BS
☎ 01273 400414 ▤ 01273 401029
Dir: *From A26 (Lewes to Uckfield road).*
Map Ref: *TQ41*

On the west bank of the River Ouse, the Anchor was built in 1790 mainly to cater for bargees. It lost its liquor licence in 1895, after the landlord was convicted of smuggling, not regaining it until 1963. Two cosy bars serve real ales, including Harvey's from the county town of Lewes, four miles downstream, and fine wines. Freshly prepared food is served in the bar and in the restaurant. Boats may be hired to explore the river.

OPEN: 11-11 (Sun 12-10.30) Closed: 25 & 31 Dec
BAR MEALS: L served all week 12-3 D served all week 6-9 Av main course £5.95 **RESTAURANT:** L served all week 12-3 D served all week 6-9 **BREWERY/COMPANY:** Free House ◀: Harvey Best, Badger & Tanglefoot.
CHILDREN'S FACILITIES: portions, high-chairs, food/bottle warming, baby changing, family room **NOTES:** No dogs (ex guide dogs), Parking 300

EAST CHILTINGTON THE JOLLY SPORTSMAN

Chapel Ln BN7 3BA
☎ 01273 890400 ▤ 01273 890400
e-mail: thejollysportsman@mistral.co.uk
Dir: *From Lewes take A275, L at Offham onto B2166 towards Plumpton, take Novington Ln, after approx 1m L into Chapel Ln.*
Map Ref: *TQ31*

An isolated pub with a lovely garden set on a quiet no-through road looking out to the South Downs. The small atmospheric bar, with its stripped wooden floor and mix of comfortable furniture, has been sympathetically upgraded to a character Victorian-style dining inn by respected restaurateur Bruce Wass from Thackerays in Tunbridge Wells. Well-sourced food features on the daily-changing menus, served throughout the bar and smart, yet informal restaurant. The vegetarian choice embraces blue cheese and squash risotto, and potato gnocchi with piquillo peppers and capers.

OPEN: 12-2.30 6-11 (Sun 12-4) Closed: 25/26 Dec
BAR MEALS: L served Tue-Sun 12.30-2 D served Tue-Sat 7-9 (Sun 12.30-3, Fri & Sat eve 7-10) Av main course £12
RESTAURANT: L served Tue-Sun 12.30-2 D served Tue-Sat 7-9 (Sun 12.30-3, Fri & Sat eve 7-10) Av 3 course à la carte £26 Av 3 course fixed price £13.75
BREWERY/COMPANY: Free House ◀: Changing guest beers. ♀: 9 **CHILDREN'S FACILITIES:** portions, licence, games, high-chairs, food/bottle warming, baby changing, outdoor play area, Large climbing frame & swings
GARDEN: quiet, secluded, view of South Downs
NOTES: Dogs allowed: in bar, Water, Parking 30

FIRLE THE RAM INN ♀

BN8 6NS
☎ 01273 858222
e-mail: nikwooller@raminnfirle.net
Dir: R off A27 3m E of Lewes. *Map Ref:* TQ40

The oldest part of the Ram dates from 1542, and though added to many times - it has 14 staircases - it has changed little in recent years. Situated at the foot of the South Downs, the inn is part of the Firle Estate, seat of the Gage family. Its flint-walled garden includes picnic tables and children's play equipment. Menu choices range through burgers, pastas and six varieties of ploughman's to fish and chips and rack of pork loin ribs.

OPEN: 11.30-11 (Sun 12-10.30) Rest: Dec 25 Open 12-2
BAR MEALS: L served all week 12-5.30 D served all week (Fri-Sun 12-9) Av main course £6.50
BREWERY/COMPANY: Free House ◖: Harveys Best plus regular changing ales. ♀: 8
CHILDREN'S FACILITIES: menu, licence, outdoor play area, high chairs, changing room, play equipment, family room
GARDEN: Two gardens 1 with picnic benches, 1 orchard
NOTES: Dogs allowed: in bar, in garden, Water, Parking 10

ICKLESHAM THE QUEEN'S HEAD 🐑 ♀

Parsonage Ln TN36 4BL
☎ 01424 814552 ▯ 01424 814766
Dir: Between Hastings & Rye on A259.
Map Ref: TQ81

A distinctive tile-hung pub set near the 12th-century parish church with wonderful views over the Brede Valley to Rye and beyond. The building dates from 1632 and became an alehouse in the 19th century. Inside you'll find high beamed ceilings, large inglenook fireplaces, church pews and a clutter of old farm implements, all of which add to the atmosphere of this friendly, independent free house. There are also stories of a ghost called George and a secret passageway to the church. Hearty home-cooked food is served, including starters/snacks, salads, sandwiches and a choice of steaks and grills. The pub is on the 1066 walk route and has a large garden with outdoor seating, a children's play area and a boules pitch.

OPEN: 11-11 (Sun 12-10.30) Rest: 25-26 Dec Closed evenings **BAR MEALS:** L served all week 12-2.45 D served all week 6.15-9.30 Av main course £7.50
RESTAURANT: L served all week D served all week
BREWERY/COMPANY: Free House ◖: Rother Valley Level Best, Greene King Abbot Ale, Ringwood Old Thumper, Woodforde Wherry. ♀: 10 **CHILDREN'S FACILITIES:** menu, portions, games, high-chairs, food/bottle warming, outdoor play area, Play area, wendy house **GARDEN:** Seating for 60, boules pitch **NOTES:** in bar, in garden, No dogs (ex guide dogs), Parking 50

KINGSTON (NEAR LEWES) THE JUGGS ♀

The Street BN7 3NT
☎ 01273 472523 ▯ 01273 483274
e-mail: juggs@shepherd-neame.co.uk
Dir: E of Brighton on A27. *Map Ref:* TQ30

Named after the women who walked from Brighton with baskets of fish for sale, this rambling, tile-hung 15th-century cottage, tucked beneath the South Downs, offers an interesting selection of freshly cooked food.

OPEN: 11-11 Sunday 12-10.30 **BAR MEALS:** L served all week 12-2.30 D served Mon-Sat 6-9 Sun 12-3.30 Av main course £7.95 **RESTAURANT:** L served all week 12-2 D served Mon-Sat 6-9.30 Sun 12-3.30 Av 3 course à la carte £15 **BREWERY/COMPANY:** Shepherd Neame
◖: Shepherd Neame Spitfire, Best & Oranjeboom.
CHILDREN'S FACILITIES: menu, games, high-chairs, food/bottle warming, family room **GARDEN:** patio, beer garden **NOTES:** Dogs allowed: on lead, Parking 30

LEWES THE SNOWDROP

119 South St BN7 2BU
☎ 01273 471018
Map Ref: *TQ41*

In the mid 19th century this was where Britain's biggest avalanche occurred, hence the pub's rather whimsical, deceptively-gentle name. Specialising in vegetarian and vegan food, the kitchen focuses on locally sourced seasonal fare and offers constantly changing specials. Entertainment is a big feature at the Snowdrop, with such weekly fixtures as jazz and live bands.

OPEN: 11-11 (sun 12-10.30) **BAR MEALS:** L served all week 12-3 D served all week 5-9 Av main course £6.50 **BREWERY/COMPANY:** Free House 🍺: Harveys Best, plus guests. **CHILDREN'S FACILITIES:** menu, portions, games, high-chairs, food/bottle warming **GARDEN:** Beer patio & enclosed garden area **NOTES:** Dogs allowed: in bar, Water & biscuits

MAYFIELD THE MIDDLE HOUSE 🐑

High St TN20 6AB
☎ 01435 872146 📠 01435 873423
Dir: *E of A267, S of Tunbridge Wells.*
Map Ref: *TQ52*

A 16th-century inn with original beams, fireplaces and carved wood panelling, the

Middle House is said to be one of the finest timber-framed buildings in Sussex. It was built in 1575 for Sir Thomas Gresham, Elizabeth I's Keeper of the Privy Purse. Today, Monica and Bryan Blundell own it, son Darren is general manager, daughter Kirsty manages the restaurant, and Mark is the head chef and son-in-law.

OPEN: 11-11 **BAR MEALS:** L served all week 12-2.30 D served all week 7-9.30 Av main course £10 **RESTAURANT:** L served all week 12-2 D served Tue-Sat 7-9.30 Av 3 course à la carte £23 Av 3 course fixed price £17.50 **BREWERY/COMPANY:** Free House 🍺: Harvey Best, Greene King Abbott Ale, Black Sheep Best, Theakston Best. 🍷: 9 **CHILDREN'S FACILITIES:** menu, portions, high-chairs, food/bottle warming, outdoor play area, wooden climbing frame **GARDEN:** Terraced area with flower beds, good views **NOTES:** No dogs (ex guide dogs), Parking 25

RUSHLAKE GREEN HORSE & GROOM 🐑

TN21 9QE
☎ 01435 830320 📠 01435 830320
e-mail: chappellhatpeg@aol.com
Map Ref: *TQ61*

Grade II listed building on the village green with pleasant views from the well-cultivated gardens. Dishes are offered from blackboard menus in the cosy bars: steak, kidney and Guinness pudding; boiled knuckle of gammon with onion stock and butter beans; and rabbit in cider are favourites, along with the excellent fresh fish choice - perhaps monkfish stuffed with chorizo on cherry tomato compôte, or fresh tuna on courgette tagliatelle.

OPEN: 11.30-3 5.30-11 **BAR MEALS:** L served all week 12-2.30 D served all week 7-9.30 **RESTAURANT:** L served all week 12-2.30 D served all week 7-9.30 Av 3 course à la carte £20 **BREWERY/COMPANY:** Free House 🍺: Harveys, Master Brew, Shepherd Neame Spitfire. 🍷: 7 **CHILDREN'S FACILITIES:** Beautiful, gated garden **GARDEN:** Well-tended, views over lake, smart furniture **NOTES:** Dogs allowed: in bar, Parking 20

RYE   MERMAID INN ★★★ ✿ 🐾 ♈

Mermaid St TN31 7EY
☎ 01797 223065 📠 01797 225069
e-mail: mermaidinnrye@btclick.com
Map Ref: TQ92

Once frequented by smugglers, the Mermaid had been trading for 150 years by the time

Elizabeth I paid Rye a visit in 1573. Numerous ghost stories add to the appeal of the place, as do beams hewn from ancient ships' timbers, secret passages and cosy log fires. Bar menu offers traditional dishes such as steak and kidney pudding, baked fish pie, and a choice of baguettes.

OPEN: 11-11 (Sun 12-11) **BAR MEALS:** L served Mon-Sat 12-2.15 D served Sun-Fri 7-9.15 Av main course £8.50 **RESTAURANT:** L served all week 12-2.15 D served all week 7-9.15 Av 3 course à la carte £35 Av 3 course fixed price £20 **BREWERY/COMPANY:** Free House 🍺: Greene King Old Speckled Hen, Scottish Courage Courage Best. **CHILDREN'S FACILITIES:** portions, games, high-chairs, food/bottle warming, high chairs, baby listening, baby sitters **GARDEN:** Paved patio **NOTES:** No dogs (ex guide dogs), Parking 26 **ROOMS:** 31 en suite 6 family rooms s£80 d£160

THE YPRES CASTLE INN 🐾 ♈

Gun Garden TN31 7HH
☎ 01797 223248
e-mail: info@yprescastle.co.uk
Map Ref: TQ92

In a superb location, next to the 13th-century Ypres Tower and Gun Gardens with views to

the coast and marshes, this attractive weather boarded building dates from 1640. It is named after Sir John Ypres and was once something of a smuggling centre. The large garden includes a boules pitch, while inside there are traditional pub games like shove ha'penny.

OPEN: 11.30-11 (Jan-Mar 11.30-3, 6-11, Sat 11-11 Sun 12-4) **BAR MEALS:** L served all week 12-2.30 12-3 in main season Av main course £6 **RESTAURANT:** L served all week 12-2.30 D served Mon-Sat 6.30-9 12-3 in main season Av 3 course à la carte £22 **BREWERY/COMPANY:** Free House 🍺: Harveys Best, Adnams Broadside, Wells Bombardier, Timothy Taylor Landlord. ♈: 12 **CHILDREN'S FACILITIES:** portions, high-chairs, food/bottle warming, No children after 8:30pm, family room **GARDEN:** Lawn, views of river & castle **NOTES:** Dogs allowed: in bar, in garden, Water, not main restaurant

THREE LEG CROSS   THE BULL

Dunster Mill Ln TN5 7HH
☎ 01580 200586 📠 01580 201289
Dir: From M25 exit at Sevenoaks toward Hastings, R at x-rds onto B2087, R onto B2099 through Ticehurst, R for Three Legged Cross.
Map Ref: TQ63

In a peaceful hamlet setting, the Bull is a real country pub, with oak beams and large open fires, based around a Wealden hall house built between 1385 and 1425. The garden features a duck pond, a pétanque court and a children's play area. A typical menu might include strips of chicken breast pan fried with bacon, tagine of lamb, Barbury duck, smoked haddock Florentine, Mediterranean pasta bake, and mushroom tortellini Raphael.

OPEN: 11-11 Closed: Dec 25, 26 (evening) **BAR MEALS:** L served all week 12-2.30 D served all week 6.30-9.30 Sat/Sun 12-3- summer all day Av main course £6 **RESTAURANT:** L served all week 12-2.30 D served all week 6.30-9.30 **BREWERY/COMPANY:** Free House 🍺: Harveys, Spitfire, Speckled Hen, Stella Artois. **CHILDREN'S FACILITIES:** menu, licence, high-chairs, outdoor play area **NOTES:** Dogs allowed: in bar, in garden, Parking 80 **ROOMS:** 4 en suite d£60 (♦♦♦)

WINCHELSEA THE NEW INN 🐑 ♇

German St TN36 4EN
☎ 01797 226252
e-mail: newinnchelsea.co.uk
Map Ref: TQ91

This 18th-century inn is situated in the centre of the beautiful ancient town, which was once one of the seven Cinque Ports. There are no specials, but the menu features popular dishes such as home-made pies, roasts, scallops and bacon in a wine and cream sauce and various fish dishes. To the rear of the pub is a charming garden, where guests may eat or simply relax before taking a stroll in the surrounding countryside.

OPEN: (Open all day every day) **BAR MEALS:** L served all week 12-3 D served all week 6.30-9.30 (Sun 12-9) Av main course £7.95 **RESTAURANT:** L served all week 12-2.30 D served all week 6.30-9.30 (Sun 12-9) Av 3 course à la carte £15 **BREWERY/COMPANY:** Greene King ◖: Morlands Original, Abbots Ale, Greene King Ipa, Fosters. ♇: 10 **CHILDREN'S FACILITIES:** menu, portions, high-chairs, food/bottle warming, family room **GARDEN:** Traditional Old English **NOTES:** Parking 20

AMBERLEY THE BRIDGE INN

Houghton Bridge BN18 9LR
☎ 01798 831619
Dir: 5m N of Arundel on B2139.
Map Ref: TQ01

The Bridge Inn dates from 1650, and has a Grade II listing. It is very popular with cyclists and walkers, and is only a two minute walk from the Amberley chalk pits and museum. Special features are the open fires and display of original oil and watercolour paintings. Campers can arrange pitches in the garden. The menu offers a comprehensive fish choice plus dishes such as braised lamb shank, rack of pork ribs, leek and Stilton crepes, and Lincolnshire sausage.

OPEN: 11-11 (Sun 12-10.30) **BAR MEALS:** L served all week 12-3 D served all week 6-9 Av main course £9 **RESTAURANT:** L served all week 12-3 D served all week 7-9 Av 3 course à la carte £17 **BREWERY/COMPANY:** Free House ◖: Harveys Sussex, Fullers London Pride, Youngs, Bass. **GARDEN:** Food served outside. Well kept garden **NOTES:** Dogs allowed: Water provided, Parking 20

BILLINGSHURST YE OLDE SIX BELLS ♇

76 High St RH14 9QS
☎ 01403 782124 📠 01403 780520
Dir: On the A29 between London & Bognor, 17m from Bognor. *Map Ref:* TQ02

This attractive timbered pub dates from 1436 and features flagstone floors and an inglenook fireplace. Legend has it that a curse will fall on anyone who moves the old fireback, made from a re-used pattern of an iron grave slab. There is also reputed to be a smugglers' tunnel leading to the nearby church. Home-cooked food is served and the pastry is a highlight. The pub has a pretty roadside garden and is part of a Badger Ale Trail.

OPEN: 11-11 (Sun 12-10.30) Rest: 25 Dec closed eve **BAR MEALS:** L served all week 12-2 D served Mon-Sat 7-9 Av main course £6.50 **RESTAURANT:** L served Mon-Sat 12-2 7-9 **BREWERY/COMPANY:** Hall & Woodhouse ◖: Badger Tanglefoot, Best and Sussex Ale. ♇: 8 **CHILDREN'S FACILITIES:** menu, outdoor play area **GARDEN:** Large garden, rose archway, lawned area **NOTES:** Dogs allowed: in bar, in garden, on a lead, Parking 15

CHILGROVE THE WHITE HORSE ◆◆◆◆ ❀❀ ♀

High St PO18 9HX
☎ 01243 535219 ▤ 01243 535301
e-mail: info@whitehorsechilgrove.co.uk
Dir: *On B2141 between Chichester &
Petersfield.* **Map Ref:** *SU81*

Picturesque South Downs hostelry, dating from 1756,
with a team of French chefs and an extensive and
rightly celebrated wine list - in essence a gastronomic
inn, offering a fusion of French cuisine and English
hospitality. Bar lunches are available but it's the
restaurant that earns the culinary plaudits, offering an
eclectic menu with an emphasis on the traditional.
Dishes might include fresh Selsey crab salad, slow
roasted duck or braised oxtail.

OPEN: 11-3 6-11 (Closed Mon Winter mths only)
BAR MEALS: L served all week 11-3 D served all week 6-11
Av main course £10.50 **RESTAURANT:** 11-3 6
BREWERY/COMPANY: Free House 🍺: Ballard's.
CHILDREN'S FACILITIES: portions, food/bottle warming
GARDEN: Downland garden with good views **NOTES:** Dogs
allowed: in bar, Parking 100 **ROOMS:** 8 en suite
2 family rooms

FERNHURST THE KING'S ARMS ♀

Midhurst Rd GU27 3HA
☎ 01428 652005 ▤ 01428 658970
Dir: *On A286 between Haslemere and
Midhurst, 1m S of Fernhurst.* **Map Ref:** *SU82*

Grade II-listed 17th-century free house and
restaurant set amidst rolling Sussex farmland.

Dazzling hanging baskets, flowering tubs, vines and
creepers add a touch of colour to the proceedings.
Inside, the pub has a cosy feel, with an L-shaped bar
and restaurant characterised by beams, lowish ceilings
and a large inglenook fireplace. Owners Michael and
Annabel Hirst have been here since 1996, maintaining
the convivial atmosphere.

OPEN: 11.30-3 5.30-11 q Closed: 25 Dec
BAR MEALS: L served all week 12-2.30 D served Mon-Sat
7-10 **RESTAURANT:** L served all week 12-2.30 D served
Mon-Sat 7-10 Av 3 course à la carte £21
BREWERY/COMPANY: Free House 🍺: Kings Arms Best
Bitter, Ringwood Brewery Best Bitter, Hogsback TEA,
Caledonian IPA. ♀: 10 **CHILDREN'S FACILITIES:** portions,
food/bottle warming **GARDEN:** Large garden with trees
overlooking fields **NOTES:** Dogs allowed: in bar, in garden,
Water, biscuits, Parking 45

HALNAKER ANGLESEY ARMS 🐕

PO18 0NQ
☎ 01243 773474 ▤ 01243 530034
e-mail: angleseyarms@aol.com
Dir: *4m E from centre of Chichester on A285
(Petworth Road).* **Map Ref:** *SU90*

This Georgian hostelry stand in two acres of
landscaped grounds on the Goodwood estate, and is
the nearest pub for the annual 'Festival of Speed'. The
building has always been a pub, and there's a
traditional atmosphere in the wood-floored bar with its
winter fires and Young's and Adnam's ales. Fresh local
ingredients are the foundation of dishes such as game
casserole, or artichoke and butternut squash risotto.
Scrummy puddings, too.

OPEN: 11-3 5.30-11 (Open all day Sat-Sun)
BAR MEALS: L served all week 12-2.30 D served all week
7-10 Av main course £7 **RESTAURANT:** L served all week
12-2 D served all week 7.30-10 Av 3 course à la carte £20
BREWERY/COMPANY: Pubmaster 🍺: Young's Bitter,
Adnams Bitter, Abbot Ale.
CHILDREN'S FACILITIES: portions, high-chairs, food/bottle
warming, baby changing **GARDEN:** Two gardens, one
courtyard for dining **NOTES:** Dogs allowed: in bar, in garden,
Water, Parking 50

HAYWARDS HEATH THE SLOOP ♀

Sloop Ln, Scaynes Hill RH17 7NP
☎ 01444 831219
Map Ref: TQ32

Located next to the tranquil River Ouse and taking its name from the vessels which once worked the adjacent Ouse Canal, the Sloop is surrounded by beautiful countryside. The older part of the building, originally two lock-keepers' cottages, dates back over several centuries and records indicate it has been trading since 1815. Major changes in recent years, have resulted in additional dining areas and a dining/meeting room.

OPEN: 12-3 6-11 (Sun 12-10.30) **BAR MEALS:** L served all week 12-2.30 D served Tue-Sat 6.30-9.30 Sun 12-4 (Sep-Apr), 12-6.30 (May-Aug) Av main course £8.95 **RESTAURANT:** L served all week 12-2.30 D served all week 6.30-9.30 **BREWERY/COMPANY:** Greene King ◖: Greene King IPA, Abbot Ale, Ruddles county, XX Dark Mild & Guest beers. ♀: 8 **CHILDREN'S FACILITIES:** menu, portions **GARDEN:** Two secluded gardens, parkland **NOTES:** Dogs allowed: in bar, in garden, Water, Parking 75

KIRDFORD THE HALF MOON INN

RH14 0LT
☎ 01403 820223 ▤ 01403 820224
e-mail: halfmooninn.kirdford@virgin.net
Dir: Off A272 between Billingshurst & Petworth. At Wisborough Green follow signs 'Kirdford'.
Map Ref: TQ02

Officially one of the prettiest pubs in Southern England, this red-tiled 16th-century village inn is covered in climbing rose bushes, and sits directly opposite the church in this unspoilt Sussex village near the River Arun. Although drinkers are welcome, the Half Moon is mainly a dining pub. New owner Kim Fishlock has already stamped her mark on the pub. The interior, with its low beams and log fires, has been fully redecorated.

OPEN: 11-3 6-11 (Closed Sun eve) **BAR MEALS:** L served Mon-Sun 12-2.30 D served Mon-Sat 6-9.30 Av main course £10 **RESTAURANT:** L served Tue-Sun 12-2 D served Tue-Sat 7-9 Av 3 course à la carte £22 **BREWERY/COMPANY:** ◖: Fuller's London Pride. **CHILDREN'S FACILITIES:** outdoor play area, swings, slide **GARDEN:** 3 separate gardens for families and dining **NOTES:** No dogs, Parking 12

MAPLEHURST THE WHITE HORSE

Park Ln RH13 6LL
☎ 01403 891208
Dir: 5m southeast of Horsham, between the A281 & A272. Map Ref: TQ12

In the tiny Sussex hamlet of Maplehurst, this traditional pub offers a break from modern life: no music, no fruit machines, no cigarette machines… just hearty pub food and an enticing range of ales. Sip Harvey's Best, Welton's Pride and Joy or Dark Star Espresso Stout in the bar or whilst admiring the rolling countryside from the quiet, south-facing garden. Home-made chilli con carne with garlic bread is a speciality.

OPEN: 12-2.30 6-11 (Sun 12-3, 7-10.30)
BAR MEALS: L served all week 12-2 D served all week 6-9 (Sun 12-2.30, 7-9) Av main course £5 ◖: Harvey's Best, Welton's Pride & Joy, Dark Star Expresso Stout, King's Red River. **CHILDREN'S FACILITIES:** menu, portions, licence, games, high-chairs, food/bottle warming, outdoor play area, swings, slide, climbing frame, family room **GARDEN:** Large, great views, quiet & safe **NOTES:** Dogs allowed: in bar, in garden, dog biscuits, Parking 20, No credit cards

MIDHURST THE ANGEL HOTEL ★★★ ◉ ♀

North St GU29 9DN
☎ 01730 812421 📄 01730 815928
Map Ref: *SU82*

An imposing and well-proportioned, late-Georgian façade hides the true Tudor origins of this former coaching inn. Its frontage overlooks the town's main street, while at the rear attractive gardens give way to meadowland and the ruins of Cowdray Castle. Bright yellow paintwork on local cottages means they are Cowdray Estate-owned. Gabriel's is the main restaurant, or try The Halo Bar where dishes range from snacks and pasta to sizzlers and steaks, with additional specials.

OPEN: 11-11 **BAR MEALS:** L served Everyday 12-2.30 D served Everyday 6-9.30 Av main course £10 **RESTAURANT:** L served all week 12-2.30 D served all week 6.30-9.30 Av 3 course à la carte £23 Av 3 course fixed price £16 **BREWERY/COMPANY:** Free House 🍺: Gale's HSB & Best. ♀: 12 **CHILDREN'S FACILITIES:** portions, licence, games, high-chairs, food/bottle warming **GARDEN:** walled garden, pond, views of Cowdray Ruins **NOTES:** Dogs allowed: in bar, in garden, in bedrooms, Parking 75 **ROOMS:** 28 en suite bedrooms 18 family rooms s£80 d£110

NUTHURST BLACK HORSE INN 🐑 ♀

Nuthurst St RH13 6LH
☎ 01403 891272 📄 01403 892656
e-mail: cliveh@henwood.fsbusiness.co.uk
Dir: *4m S of Horsham, between the A281, A24 and the A272.* **Map Ref:** *TQ12*

True to its history as a smuggler's hideout, this lovely old free house is still hidden away

in a quiet backwater, half masked by its impressive window boxes. Built of clay tiles and mellow brick, it originally formed a row of cottages with a forge in the adjoining barn. Plenty of its history remains: inside you'll find stone-flagged floors, an inglenook fireplace and an exposed wattle and daub wall. The place is spotlessly clean, with smoke-free areas.

OPEN: 12-3 6-11 (Sat-Sun, BH's open all day) **BAR MEALS:** L served all week 12-2.30 D served all week 6.30-9.30 All day Sat, Sun & BH's **RESTAURANT:** L served all week 12-2.30 D served all week 6.30-9.30 All day Sat, Sun & BH's **BREWERY/COMPANY:** Free House 🍺: Harveys Sussex, W J King, Weltons, Youngs London Pride and numerous guest ales. ♀: 12 **CHILDREN'S FACILITIES:** menu, portions, games, high-chairs, food/bottle warming **GARDEN:** Front & rear patio area, garden with stream **NOTES:** Dogs allowed: in bar, Water & Biscuits, Parking 28

OVING THE GRIBBLE INN 🐑 ♀

PO20 2BP
☎ 01243 786893 📄 01243 788841
e-mail: brianelderfield@hotmail.com
Dir: *From A27 take A259. After 1m L at roundabout, 1st R to Oving, 1st L in village.* **Map Ref:** *SU90*

Named after local schoolmistress Rose Gribble, the inn retains all of its 16th-century charm. Large open fireplaces, wood burners and low beams set the tone. There's no background music at this peaceful hideaway, which is the ideal spot to enjoy any of the half dozen real ales from the on-site micro-brewery. Liver and bacon, spinach lasagne with red peppers, and special fish dishes are all prepared and cooked on the premises.

OPEN: 11-3 5.30-11 (Sun 12-4, 7-10.30) **BAR MEALS:** L served all week 12-2.30 D served all week 6-9.30 Sun 7-9 Av main course £7.95 **RESTAURANT:** L served all week 12-2.30 D served all week 6-9.30 Sun 7-9 **BREWERY/COMPANY:** Woodhouse Inns 🍺: Gribble Ale, Reg's Tipple, Slurping Stoat, Plucking Pheasant. ♀: 8 **CHILDREN'S FACILITIES:** menu, portions, high-chairs, food/bottle warming, family room **GARDEN:** Large shaded garden with seating for over 100 **NOTES:** Dogs allowed: in bar, in garden, Toys & water provided, Parking 40

PETWORTH   WELLDIGGERS ARMS ♀

Polborough Rd GU28 0HG
☎ 01798 342287
Dir: *1m E of Petworth on the A283.*
Map Ref: *SU92*

Welldiggers once occupied this rustic, 300-year-old roadside pub, which boasts low-beamed bars with open log fires and huge oak tables. It is conveniently located for racing at Goodwood and Fontwell, as well as a visit to Sir Edward Elgar's cottage. Dishes on the menu may include English steaks, butchered on the premises, fresh scallops, lobster and crab and cod with home-made chips.

OPEN: 11-3 6.30-10 (Thu-Sat eve only Sun 12-10.30) Closed: Dec 25 **BAR MEALS:** L served all week 12-2 D served Tues-Sat 6.30-9.30 Av main course £8.50 **RESTAURANT:** L served all week 12-2 D served Tues- Sat 6.30-9.30 Av 3 course à la carte £13.50 **BREWERY/COMPANY:** Free House 🍺: Youngs. **CHILDREN'S FACILITIES:** outdoor play area **GARDEN:** Large lawn & patio, food served outside **NOTES:** Dogs allowed: Parking 35

SUTTON   WHITE HORSE INN

The Street RH20 1PS
☎ 01798 869221 ▤ 01798 869291
Dir: *Turn off A29 at foot of Bury Hill. After 2m pass Roman Villa on R. 1m to Sutton.*
Map Ref: *SU91*

Pretty Georgian inn tucked away in a sleepy village at the base of the South Downs. In the neat bars and dining room expect imaginative food, the daily-changing choice featuring perhaps Stilton and broccoli soup, baked sea bass with lemon basil and tomato, confit of duck, lamb shank with tomatoes and red wine, and French lemon tart.

OPEN: 11-3 5.30-11 (Sun 12-3 7-10.30, summer wknd all day) **BAR MEALS:** L served all week 12-2 D served all week 7-9 Av main course £6.50 **RESTAURANT:** L served all week 12-2 D served all week 7-9 Av 3 course à la carte £30 **BREWERY/COMPANY:** Free House 🍺: Youngs Special, Courage Best, plus guests. **CHILDREN'S FACILITIES:** menu **NOTES:** Dogs allowed: Parking 10

WALDERTON   THE BARLEY MOW 🐑

PO18 9ED
☎ 023 9263 1321 ▤ 023 9263 1403
e-mail: mowbarley@aol.co.uk
Dir: *North Chichester B2146. From Havent B2147. Turn R signed Walderton, the Barley Mow is 100 yds on L.* **Map Ref:** *SU71*

Ivy-clad with hanging baskets, this pretty pub is comfortably set beside the rolling Sussex Downs, and is a magnet for walkers, cyclists and riders with a special tethering pole for horses. Famous locally for its skittle alley, it also has a reputation for good home-made pub food: steak and ale pie, battered fresh cod, lasagne, broccoli and cheese bake, chestnut and parsnip bake, roast partridge, and a Sunday roast.

OPEN: 11-3 6-11.30 (Summer, all day Sun) **BAR MEALS:** L served all week 12-2.15 D served all week 6-9.30 Av main course £4.99 **RESTAURANT:** L served all week 12-2.15 D served all week 6-9.30 **BREWERY/COMPANY:** Free House 🍺: Ringwood Old Thumper & Fortyniner, Fuller's London Pride, Itchen Valley Godfathers, Scottish Courage John Smith's. **CHILDREN'S FACILITIES:** menu, portions, high-chairs, food/bottle warming **GARDEN:** Mature garden, tables, seats, stream **NOTES:** Dogs allowed: in bar, in garden, Parking 50

Sussex, West continued

WARNHAM THE GREETS INN ♈

47 Friday St RH12 3QY
☎ 01403 265047 📠 01403 265047
Dir: *Off A24 N of Horsham.* *Map Ref:* *TQ13*

A fine Sussex hall house dating from about 1350 and built for Elias Greet, a local merchant. Magnificent inglenook fireplace and head-crackingly low beams in the flagstone-floored bar. There is a rambling series of dining areas where diners can sample the wares of the new team. Reports welcome.

OPEN: 11-2.30 (Sun 12-2, 7-10.30) 6-11 Rest: 25-26 Dec 12-2 only **BAR MEALS:** L served all week 12-2 D served all week 7-9 Av main course £9 **RESTAURANT:** L served all week 12-2 D served all week 7-9 Av 3 course à la carte £20 **BREWERY/COMPANY:** 🍺: Interbrew Flowers Original, Fuller's London Pride, Harvey's Sussex. **GARDEN:** Large, food served outside **NOTES:** Dogs allowed: Water, Parking 30

ARRETON THE WHITE LION

PO30 3AA
☎ 01983 528479
e-mail: cthewhitelion@aol.com
Map Ref: *SZ58*

A 300-year-old former coaching inn with oak beams, polished brass, open fires and added summer attractions in the children's playground and aviary. Popular locally for its cosy atmosphere, well-priced bar food and the starting point for the Isle of Wight ghost hunt. Curious visitors can stoke up on hearty venison with fruits of the forest sauce, steak and kidney pie, pork escalope, and a variety of steaks

OPEN: 11-12 (Sun 11-10.30) **BAR MEALS:** L served all week 12-9 D served all week 12-9 Av main course £7 **BREWERY/COMPANY:** 🍺: Badger Best, Fuller's London Pride, Interbrew Flowers IPA. **CHILDREN'S FACILITIES:** menu, outdoor play area, family room **GARDEN:** Patio area in pleasant old village location **NOTES:** Dogs allowed: in bar, in garden, Water, Parking 6

BEMBRIDGE THE CRAB & LOBSTER INN 🐑 ♈

32 Foreland Fields Rd PO35 5TR
☎ 01983 872244 📠 01983 873495
e-mail: allancrab@aol.com
Dir: *Telephone for directions.* *Map Ref:* *SZ68*

Clifftop inn with a large patio area affording superb views across the Solent and English

Channel. Locals and tourists alike seek out the friendly atmosphere in the nautically-themed bars, and walkers find the cliffs and nearby stretches of the 65-mile Isle of Wight Coast Path especially good for exploring on foot. Locally caught seafood forms part of the menu throughout the year, and among the fish dishes are crab cakes and lobster. A full range of chargrilled steaks is also available.

OPEN: 11-3 (Wknds & summer all day) 6-11 **BAR MEALS:** L served all week 12-2.30 D served all week 6.00-9.30 Av main course £10 **RESTAURANT:** L served all week 12-2.30 D served all week 7-9.30 Av 3 course à la carte £25 **BREWERY/COMPANY:** Enterprise Inns 🍺: Interbrew Flowers Original, Goddards Fuggle-Dee-Dum, Green King IPA, John Smiths. ♈: 10 **CHILDREN'S FACILITIES:** menu, portions, licence, games, high-chairs, food/bottle warming, baby changing **GARDEN:** Patio overlooking the beach **NOTES:** Dogs allowed: in bar, in garden, Water, Parking 40

COWES   THE FOLLY ♀

Folly Ln PO32 6NB
☎ 01983 297171
*Dir: A3054. **Map Ref:** SZ49*

Reached by both land and water and very popular with the Solent's boating fraternity, the Folly is one of the island's more unusual pubs. Timber from an old sea-going French barge was used in the construction, and wood from the hull can be found in the nautical theme of the bar. Extensive specials board menu ranging from 'Crewpot' casserole - beef goulash, lamb and vegetable, or spicy sausage - to plaice, mackerel trout and salmon.

OPEN: 9-11 BHs & Cowes Week late opening
BAR MEALS: L served all week 12-9.30 D served all week
BREWERY/COMPANY: 🍺: Interbrew Flowers Original, Bass, Goddards Best Bitter. **CHILDREN'S FACILITIES:** menu, portions, high-chairs, food/bottle warming, baby changing, outdoor play area **NOTES:** Dogs allowed: in bar, Water, Parking 30

NORTHWOOD   TRAVELLERS JOY

85 Pallance Rd PO31 8LS
Map Ref: *SZ49*

Pub deeds suggest that an alehouse first opened on this site some 300 years ago. Today's more elderly locals can remember a talking mynah bird in the bar which so upset a visiting darts team that they set it alight! Home-made steak and kidney pie, beef in black bean sauce with noodles, chicken tikka masala, mixed grill, pasta of the day, ploughman's, jacket potatoes and the curiously named chicken Cyrilburger are on the menu. Isle of Wight beers feature in the bar.

OPEN: 11-2 5-11 Sun Closed 3-7 **BAR MEALS:** L served all week 12-2 D served all week 6-9 sun 12-2 7-9 Av main course £5.25 🍺: Goddardss Special Bitter, Courage Directors, Ventnor Golden Bitter, Deuchars IPA.
CHILDREN'S FACILITIES: menu, portions, games, high-chairs, food/bottle warming, outdoor play area, climbing frame, family room **GARDEN:** Large garden with patio and terrace
NOTES: Dogs allowed: Parking 30

ROOKLEY   THE CHEQUERS

Niton Rd PO38 3NZ
☎ 01983 840314 📠 01983 840820
e-mail: richard@chequersinn-iow.co.uk
Map Ref: *SZ58*

Horses in the neighbouring riding school keep a watchful eye on comings and goings at this 250-year-old family-friendly free house. In the centre of the island, surrounded by farms, the pub has a reputation for good food at reasonable prices. Fish, naturally, features well, with sea bass, mussels, plaice, salmon and cod usually available. Other favourites are mixed grill, pork medallions, T-bone steak, and chicken supreme with BBQ sauce and cheese.

OPEN: 11-11 **BAR MEALS:** L served all week 12-10 D served all week 12-10 Sun 12-9.30 Av main course £8
RESTAURANT: L served all week 12-10 D served all week Sun 12-9.30 **BREWERY/COMPANY:** Free House 🍺: Gale's HSB, Greene King Old Speckled Hen, Scottish Courage John Smiths, Courage Directors. **CHILDREN'S FACILITIES:** menu, portions, licence, games, high-chairs, food/bottle warming, baby changing, outdoor play area, Baby changing, highchairs, family room **GARDEN:** Large garden and patio with seating
NOTES: Dogs allowed: in bar, Water, Parking 70

SEAVIEW SEAVIEW HOTEL & RESTAURANT

High St PO34 5EX
☎ 01983 612711 📠 01983 613729
e-mail: reception@seaviewhotel.co.uk
Dir: *B3330 (Ryde-Seaview rd), turn L via Puckpool along seafront road, hotel on left adjacent to sea.* **Map Ref:** *SZ69*

Set in a picturesque sailing village, this inn was used as a Royal Navy station in the Second World War, with an observation point on the roof. There are stunning views across the sea to Portsmouth naval dockyard, and the naval theme is continued inside, with a collection of artefacts including classic ship models, letters from the Titanic and bills from the Queen Mary. The bar is adorned with old oars, masts and ships wheels. The two restaurants - one a classic dining room, the other modern and stylish - and the bar menu offer contemporary dishes with an emphasis on freshly caught fish and seafood.

OPEN: 11-2.30 6-11 **BAR MEALS:** L served all week 12-2 D served all week 7-9.30 Av main course £8.95
RESTAURANT: L served all week 12-1.30 D served all week 7.30-9.30 Av 3 course à la carte £30
BREWERY/COMPANY: Free House 🍺: Goddards, Greene King Abbot Ale, Adnams ALe.
CHILDREN'S FACILITIES: menu, games, high-chairs, food/bottle warming, baby changing
GARDEN: Courtyard/patio, Food served outside
NOTES: Dogs allowed: in bar, Parking 12
ROOMS: 17 en suite 1 family room s£55 d£95 (★★★)

SHORWELL THE CROWN INN

Walkers Ln PO30 3JZ
☎ 01983 740293 📠 01983 740293
Dir: *From Newport to Carisbrooke High St, then L at rdbt at top of hill, take B3323 to Shorwell.* **Map Ref:** *SZ48*

Attractive village pub with a resident ghost

who strongly disapproves of card playing. When the locals have a winter game, the cards are often found strewn all over the bar the next morning. Home-cooked food uses local produce wherever possible, and antique furniture and solid stone walls add to the pub's appeal.

OPEN: 10.30-3 (Sun 12-3) 6-11 (sun eve 6-10:30)
BAR MEALS: L served all week 12-2.30 D served all week 6-9 Av main course £6.50 **RESTAURANT:** L served all week 12-2.30 D served all week 6-9 Av 3 course à la carte £12
BREWERY/COMPANY: Whitbread 🍺: Interbrew Boddingtons, Flowers Original, Badger Tanglefoot, Wadworth 6X. **CHILDREN'S FACILITIES:** menu, portions, high-chairs, food/bottle warming, baby changing, outdoor play area, swings, slide, wendy house, family room **GARDEN:** Large, sheltered, flower beds, stream, ducks **NOTES:** Dogs allowed: in bar, in garden, on lead, Parking 70

The cliffs at Hunstanton, Norfolk

The West
Country

The only two large cities in the region are Bristol and Plymouth, both major ports with a strong tradition of international trade. The coastline predominates, attracting huge numbers of visitors to fabulous beaches and a congenially mild climate in the English Riviera. The Jurassic Coast of Dorset and East Devon with its rich geology and wealth of fossils is designated a UNESCO World Heritage Site, and the South West Coast Path is the longest of the National Trails, extending 630 miles from Minehead to Poole Harbour.

Other natural features of the region are Exmoor, extending from the Heritage Coast of North Devon and Somerset, and Dartmoor in Devon – both National Parks. Further inland are the Mendips, including Wookey Hole and Cheddar Gorge, and the gentle Cotswolds, studded with pretty stone-built villages. The cathedral towns of Salisbury, Exeter, Gloucester and Wells are well worth exploring, as are the delightful old towns of Bath, Cheltenham, Dorchester and Glastonbury.

Top tourist attractions in the West Country are the Eden Project in Cornwall, the Roman Baths & Pump Room in Bath, Avebury Stone Circle and Stonehenge in Wiltshire.

Top tipples
Cider is the classic West Country drink, produced from the cider apples grown in abundance across the region, and currently enjoying a revival with many independent cider makers producing a wide range of distinctive ciders. Scrumpy is the term coined for 'real cider' (the equivalent of real ale), made from naturally fermented apples and little else. Another regional speciality is apple brandy; a good example being Julian Temperley's, made in Somerset.

Top class English wine producers who welcome visitors are Three Choirs Vineyard in Gloucestershire, and Sharpham Vineyard in Devon, (the Sharpham Estate also produces award-winning cheeses).

If beer is your choice, brewery tours are available at Smiles Brewery in Bristol, where they still use the traditional Victorian tower method of production.

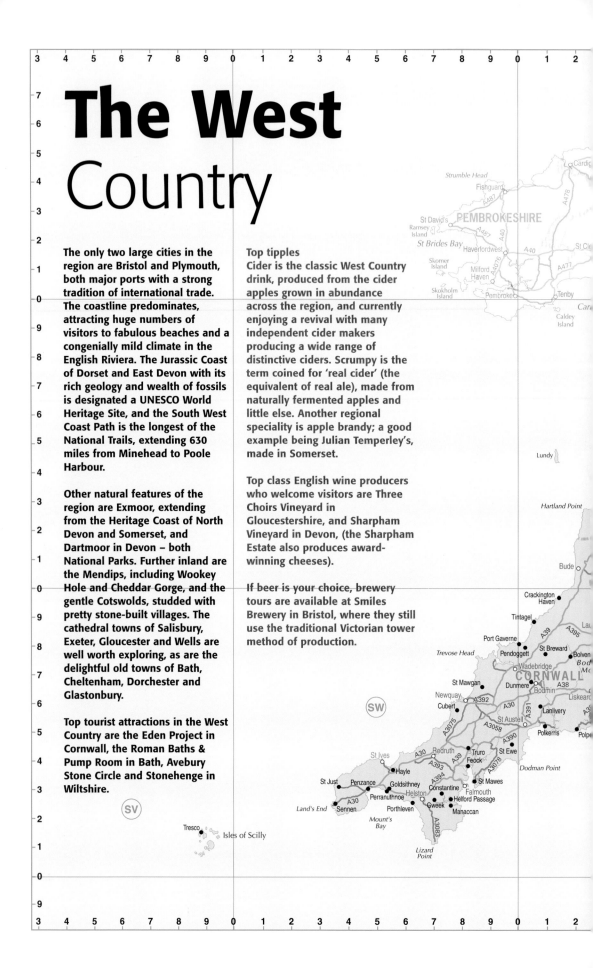

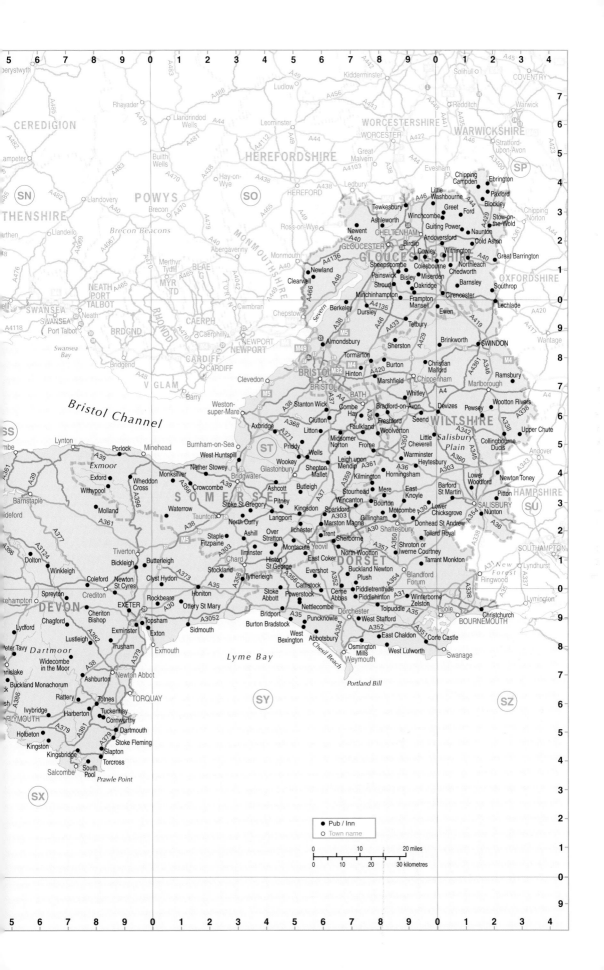

BOLVENTOR JAMAICA INN

PL15 7TS
☎ 01566 86250 ▤ 01566 86177
e-mail: enquiry@jamaicainn.co.uk
Map Ref: *SX17*

With its cobbled courtyard, beamed ceilings and roaring log fires, this mid-eighteenth century former coaching inn set high on Bodmin Moor is steeped in the atmosphere that inspired Daphne du Maurier to write her famous novel of smuggling and intrigue; the Smugglers Museum houses one of the most extensive collections of smuggling artefacts in the UK. Today the inn offers the traveller a warm welcome and a large range of home-cooked food from bar snacks and cold food to steak, fish, and vegetarian meals that can be washed down with a selection of real ales.

OPEN: 9-11 **BAR MEALS:** L served all week 12-2.30 D served all week 2.45-9 Av main course £7
RESTAURANT: L served all week 2.30-9 D served all week 2.45-9 Av 3 course à la carte £16.50 ▆: 4x, Doombar, Budweiser, Stella. ♀: 8 **CHILDREN'S FACILITIES:** menu, licence, high-chairs, food/bottle warming, baby changing, outdoor play area, pirate boat with rope, swings, slide
GARDEN: Lawn area with tables **NOTES:** No dogs (ex guide dogs), Parking 6 **ROOMS:** 6 en suite s£45 d£60 (♦♦♦)

CALLINGTON THE COACHMAKERS ARMS

6 Newport Square PL17 7AS
☎ 01579 382567 ▤ 01579 384679
Dir: *Telephone for directions.* **Map Ref:** *SX36*

Traditional stone-built pub on the A388 between Plymouth and Launceston. Pictures of local scenes, old cars and antique trade advertisements contribute to the atmosphere, as do the fish tank and aviary. Produce is local where possible and most of the food is home made, including soups, lasagne, and the daily pie. Regulars range from the local football team to the pensioners dining club. On Wednesday there's a charity quiz night, and Thursday is steak night.

OPEN: 11-3 (Sun 12-3, 7-10.30) 6-11
BAR MEALS: L served all week 12-2 D served all week 7-9.30 Av main course £4.50 **RESTAURANT:** L served all week 12-2 D served all week 7-9.30 Av 3 course à la carte £15 **BREWERY/COMPANY:** Enterprise Inns ▆: Doombar, Cornish Knocker, Worthing Best Bitter, Abbot Ale. ♀: 7
CHILDREN'S FACILITIES: menu, portions, food/bottle warming **NOTES:** Dogs allowed: in bar, in bedrooms, Water, Parking 10

CONSTANTINE TRENGILLY WARTHA INN ★★ ❀

Nancenoy TR11 5RP
☎ 01326 340332 ▤ 01326 340332
e-mail: reception@trengilly.co.uk
Dir: *SW of Falmouth.* **Map Ref:** *SW72*

The Cornish name means 'settlement above the trees' and, indeed, the old family-run free house and its six acres of gardens and meadows lie in the peaceful wooded valley of Polpenwith Creek, an offshoot of the Helford River. The river supplies the oysters that appear on the menu during the season, while the sea and surrounding farmland supply much else.

OPEN: 11-3 6.30-11 Rest: 25 Dec No Food
BAR MEALS: L served all week 12-2.15 D served all week 6.30-9.30 (Sun 12-2, 7-9.30) Av main course £8
RESTAURANT: D served all week 7.30-9.30 Av 3 course fixed price £27 **BREWERY/COMPANY:** Free House
▆: Sharps Cornish Coaster, St Austell HSD, Skinners, Exmoor Gold. ♀: 15 **CHILDREN'S FACILITIES:** menu, portions, high-chairs, food/bottle warming, baby changing, high chairs, toys, changing room, family room **GARDEN:** Walled garden, benches, pergola, terrace **NOTES:** Dogs allowed: in bar, Parking 50 **ROOMS:** 8 en suite 2 family rooms s£49 d£78

CRACKINGTON HAVEN   COOMBE BARTON INN ♦♦♦ 🐑 ♈

EX23 0JG
☎ 01840 230345 📠 01840 230788
e-mail: info@coombebartoninn.com
Dir: *S from Bude on A39, turn off at Wainhouse Corner, then down lane to beach.*
Map Ref: *SX19*

Originally built for the 'Captain' of the local slate quarry, the Coombe Barton (it means 'valley farm' in Cornish) is over 200 years old and sits in a small cove surrounded by spectacular rock formations. Local seafood is a feature of the menu and includes sea bass, lemon sole, plaice, salmon steaks, and halibut. The kitchen is also known for its vegetarian specials.

OPEN: 11-11 (Winter weekdays closed 3-6)
BAR MEALS: L served all week 11-2.30 D served all week 6.30-9.30 Av main course £8.75 **RESTAURANT:** L served all week 11-2.30 D served all week 6-10
BREWERY/COMPANY: Free House 🍺: St Austell Dartmoor Best & Hick's special Draught, Sharp's Doom Bar Bitter.
CHILDREN'S FACILITIES: menu, portions, games, high-chairs, food/bottle warming, family room **GARDEN:** Patio
NOTES: No dogs, Parking 25 **ROOMS:** 6 bedrooms 3 en suite 1 family room s£30 d£25

CUBERT   THE SMUGGLER'S DEN INN 🐑 ♈

Trebellan TR8 5PY
☎ 01637 830209 📠 01637 830580
e-mail: hankers@aol.com
Dir: *From Newquay take A3075 to Cubert crossroads, then R, then L signed Trebellan, 0.5m.* **Map Ref:** *SW75*

Two miles from the coast in an attractive valley, this thatched 16th-century pub features a long bar, an inglenook wood-burner, and barrel seats. Among other features are a family room, beer garden and well-kept real ales tapped from the cask. Fresh fish is always available, and there are various vegetarian dishes.

OPEN: 11-3 6-11 (Winter 12-2) Rest: Mon, Wed Closed Lunch Winter **BAR MEALS:** L served all week 12-2 D served all week 6-9.30 Av main course £10 **RESTAURANT:** L served all week 12-2 D served all week 6-9.30 Av 3 course à la carte £20 **BREWERY/COMPANY:** Free House 🍺: Skinner's Smugglers Ale, Betty Stogs Bitter, Sharp's Doom Bar, Trebellan Tipple. ♈: 8 **CHILDREN'S FACILITIES:** menu, portions, games, high-chairs, food/bottle warming, outdoor play area, climbing frames, rope nets, slide, seesaw, family room
GARDEN: Small fenced beer garden, tables & chairs
NOTES: Dogs allowed: in bar, in garden, Water, Parking 50

DUNMERE   THE BOROUGH ARMS

PL31 2RD
☎ 01208 73118 📠 01208 76788
e-mail: Borougharms@aol.com
Dir: *From A30 take A389 to Wadebridge, pub approx 1m from Bodmin.* **Map Ref:** *SX06*

Popular with walkers, cyclists, anglers, families and local businesses, this large pub is situated directly on the Camel trail. Traditional pub fare includes a light menu of sandwiches, ploughman's and jacket potatoes; typical pub dishes like grills, a daily curry, lasagne, and jumbo cod, plus daily specials and a fill-your-own-plate carvery.

OPEN: 11-11 (Sun 12-10.30) **BAR MEALS:** L served all week 12-2.15 D served all week 6.30-9.15 Av main course £5.50 **RESTAURANT:** L served all week 12-2.15 D served all week 6.30-9.15
BREWERY/COMPANY: Scottish & Newcastle 🍺: Sharp's Bitter, Skinner's, Scottish Courage John Smith's Smooth.
CHILDREN'S FACILITIES: menu, portions, games, food/bottle warming, baby changing, outdoor play area, high-chairs, baby changing facilities, family room
GARDEN: Large with kids play area **NOTES:** Dogs allowed: in bar, in garden, Water, Parking 150

FEOCK THE PUNCH BOWL & LADLE 🐑 ♀

Penelewey TR3 6QY
☎ 01872 862237 🖹 01872 870401
Dir: *Off A38 Falmouth Road.* **Map Ref:** *SW83*

A traditional thatched roadside inn handy for Truro and Trelissik gardens. It was originally three farm cottages, and there is even a resident ghost! The cosy bar offers real ales from St Austell brewery, and in warmer weather you can enjoy a drink in the walled garden. The new owners offer daily fish and seafood specials using local mussels, salmon and sea bass. Other dishes include lamb shank and ploughman's.

OPEN: 11.30-11 (Sun 12-10.30) **BAR MEALS:** L served all week 12-2 D served all week 6-9 Av main course £7.95 **RESTAURANT:** L served all week 12-2.30 D served all week 6-9 Av 3 course à la carte £18 ◉: IPA Tribute, HSD. ♀: 8 **CHILDREN'S FACILITIES:** menu, portions, high-chairs, baby changing **GARDEN:** lovely views **NOTES:** Dogs allowed: Parking 60

GOLDSITHNEY THE TREVELYAN ARMS ◆◆◆◆

Fore St TR20 9JU
☎ 01736 710453
e-mail: georgecusick@hotmail.com
Dir: *5 miles from Penzance. A394 signed to Goldsithney.* **Map Ref:** *SW53*

The former manor house for Lord Trevelyan, this 17th-century property stands at the centre of the picturesque village just a mile from the sea. It has also been a coaching inn and a bank/post office in its time, but these days is very much the traditional family-run Cornish pub, recently refurbished. Food is fresh and locally sourced, offering good value for money.

OPEN: 12-11 **BAR MEALS:** L served all week 12-2 D served all week 6-9 L Sun 12-2.30 Av main course £6.50 **RESTAURANT:** L served all week 12-2 D served all week 6-9 Av 2 course fixed price £10 ◉: Morland Speckled Hen, Sharps Doombar, Flowers IPA, Guiness. **CHILDREN'S FACILITIES:** menu, portions, games, high-chairs, food/bottle warming **GARDEN:** Front patio **NOTES:** Dogs allowed: in bar, water, Parking 5 **ROOMS:** 2 en suite s£25 d£50 no children overnight

---

GUNNISLAKE THE RISING SUN INN 🐑

Calstock Rd PL18 9BX
☎ 01822 832201
Dir: *From Tavistock take A390 to Gunnislake, pub is through village and 0.25m on L. L at traffic lights and 0.25m on R.* **Map Ref:** *SX47*

A traditional two-roomed picture postcard pub set in award winning terraced gardens overlooking the beautiful Tamar Valley. Great walks start and finish at the Rising Sun, which is understandably popular with hikers and cyclists, locals and visitors. The menu, available in the bar and restaurant, takes in fresh fish (sea bass, John Dory), Thai pork curry, home-baked gammon, chicken enchilada, and stuffed roast pepper.

OPEN: 12-2.30 5-11 (Sun 12-3, 7-10.30) **BAR MEALS:** L served Mon-Sun 12-2 D served Mon-Sun 6-9 (Apr-Oct Sat-Sun 12-9) Av main course £6 **RESTAURANT:** L served Mon-Sun 12-2 D served Mon-Sun 6-9 (Apr-Oct Sat-Sun 12-9) **BREWERY/COMPANY:** Free House ◉: Interbrew Bass, Sharp's Cornish Coaster, Skinner's Betty Stogs Bitter, Timothy Taylor Landlord. **CHILDREN'S FACILITIES:** portions, food/bottle warming **GARDEN:** Large terraced garden, views of Tamar Valley **NOTES:** Dogs allowed: in bar, (Not in restaurant), Parking 14

GWEEK   THE GWEEK INN

TR12 6TU
☎ 01326 221502 🖥 01326 221502
e-mail: info@gweekinn.co.uk
Dir: *2m E of Helston near Seal Sanctuary.*
Map Ref: *SW72*

A traditional family-run village pub at the mouth of the Helford River with a great reputation for quality service and value-for-money food. Nearby tourist attractions include the Lizard Peninsula, Goonhilly Earth Station, and the National Seal Sanctuary is only 100 metres away. Extensive menu offers starters and snacks, jackets and salads, traditional roasts, and children's meals; the chalkboard lists locally-caught seafood and other specials. A good selection of real ales includes Sharp's Doom Bar and Worthington Creamflow.

OPEN: 12-2.30 6.30-11 (Sun Eve 7-10.30)
BAR MEALS: L served all week 12-2 D served all week 6.30-9 (Sun 7-9) Av main course £6.50
RESTAURANT: L served Sun & by reservation 12-2 D served all week 6.30-9 (Sun 7-9) Av 3 course à la carte £15
BREWERY/COMPANY: Punch Taverns 🍺: Interbrew Flowers IPA, Old Speckled Hen, Sharps Doom Bar, 2 guest beers.
CHILDREN'S FACILITIES: menu, high-chairs, food/bottle warming, baby changing, outdoor play area, screened garden area **GARDEN:** BBQ, food served outdoors **NOTES:** Dogs allowed: in bar, in garden, on lead, Parking 70

HAYLE   THE WATERMILL

Old Coach Rd, Lelant Downs TR27 6LQ
☎ 01736 757912
e-mail: watermill@btconnect.com
Dir: *From the A30 take the A3074 towards St Ives take L turns at the next two mini Rdbts.*
Map Ref: *SW53*

The old watermill here was in use until the 1970s. Today the building is a family-friendly free house offering fine Cornish ales and an excellent selection of meals. There is an extensive bar menu, and "Upstairs at the Watermill" is a separate restaurant, open every evening. Expect ham hock glazed in honey and cider, grilled whole lemon sole, smoked chicken and mushroom strudel, or roasted vegetable pancakes with lemon and lime sauce served with saffron rice.

OPEN: 11-3 6-11 (Jul-Sept 11-11) **BAR MEALS:** L served all week 12-2.30 D served all week 6.30-9.30 Av main course £6.95 **RESTAURANT:** L served all week D served all week 6.30-9.30 Av 3 course à la carte £17.50
BREWERY/COMPANY: Free House 🍺: Sharp's Doombar Bitter, Dreckley Ring 'o' Bells, Skinners Betty Stogs.
CHILDREN'S FACILITIES: menu, games, high-chairs, baby changing, outdoor play area, large lawned area
GARDEN: Acre, stream, pergola, ample seating, lawn
NOTES: No dogs (ex guide dogs), Parking 35

HELFORD PASSAGE   FERRYBOAT INN ♀

TR11 5LB
☎ 01326 250625 🖥 01326 250916
e-mail: ronald.brown7@btopenworld.co.uk
Dir: *From A39 at Falmouth, towards River Helford.* **Map Ref:** *SW72*

Beautifully positioned on the north bank of the Helford River, this 300-year-old pub overlooks a safe beach and stands bang on the Cornish coastal path. Enjoy the views from the nautical-themed main bar, whose French windows open onto a spacious terrace. Well-kept St Austell ales are backed by a good range of wines, available by the glass. Food includes chicken salad, ploughmans, daily-changing fish specials and Ferryboat ocean pie.

OPEN: 11-11 Sun 12-10.30pm **BAR MEALS:** L served all week 12-2.30 D served all week 6.30-9 Av main course £6.25 **RESTAURANT:** L served all week 12-2.30 D served all week 6.30-9 Av 3 course à la carte £10.95
BREWERY/COMPANY: St Austell Brewery 🍺: St Austell HSD, Tribute. ♀: 8 **CHILDREN'S FACILITIES:** menu, games, high-chairs, food/bottle warming, baby changing
GARDEN: Patio, food served outdoors **NOTES:** Dogs allowed: in bar, Parking 80

KINGSAND THE HALFWAY HOUSE INN

Fore St PL10 1NA
☎ 01752 822279 📄 01752 823146
e-mail: info@halfwayinn.biz
Dir: From either Torpoint Ferry or Tamar Bridge follow signs to Mount Edgcombe.
Map Ref: SX45

Tucked among the narrow lanes and colour-washed houses of this quaint fishing village is the family-run Halfway House Inn, set right on the coastal path. Locally caught seafood is a feature of the small restaurant, and menus might feature roast garlic monkfish, and scallops and seafood paella. For the casual diner there's a good selection of baguettes and baked potatoes.

OPEN: 12-3 7-11 summer open all day
BAR MEALS: L served all week 12-2.30 D served all week 7-9.30 Winter 12-2, 7-9 **RESTAURANT:** L served all week 12-2 D served all week 7-9 12-2, 7-9 £19
BREWERY/COMPANY: Free House 🍺: Sharp's Doom Bar Bitter, Sharps Own, Marstons Pedigree, Courage Best. 🍷: 6
CHILDREN'S FACILITIES: menu, portions, games, high-chairs, food/bottle warming **NOTES:** Dogs allowed: in bar, in bedrooms, Water, Dog chews **ROOMS:** 6 en suite 1 family room s£30 d£60 (♦♦♦)

LANLIVERY THE CROWN INN

PL30 5BT
☎ 01208 872707 📄 01208 871208
*Dir: From Bodmin take A30 S, follow signs 'Lanhydrock', L at mini rdbt 0.3m take A390, Lanlivery 2nd R. **Map Ref:** SX05*

Built to accommodate masons constructing

the church opposite, this 12th-century longhouse has 3-foot-thick exterior walls, a large inglenook fireplace and a priest hole. The tranquil garden and patio are perfect for the summer months. The lunch, dinner and wine menus are all extensive, with dishes including fish pie, sausage of the day with mash and, by prior arrangement, fresh lobster.

OPEN: 11-3 6-11 open all day during summer season
BAR MEALS: L served all week 12-2.15 D served all week 7-9.15 Av main course £10 **RESTAURANT:** L served all week 12-2.15 D served all week 7-9.15 Av 3 course à la carte £22 **BREWERY/COMPANY:** Free House 🍺: Sharp's Doom Bar, Crown Inn Glory, Coaster, Eden Ale. 🍷: 7
CHILDREN'S FACILITIES: menu, portions, high-chairs, food/bottle warming, baby changing, outdoor play area
GARDEN: Cottage style, wrought iron furniture **NOTES:** Dogs allowed: in bar, in garden, Water, treats, Parking 40

MANACCAN THE NEW INN

TR12 6HA
☎ 01326 231323
e-mail: penny@macace.net
Map Ref: SW72

Thatched village pub, deep in Daphne du Maurier country, dating back to Cromwellian times. Attractions include the homely bars and a large, natural garden full of flowers. At lunchtime you might try a locally made pasty or moules marinière, and in the evening perhaps sea bass and chive fishcakes with tomato coulis and sautéed vegetables, or slow-roasted lamb shank with red wine and redcurrant gravy.

OPEN: 12-3 (Sat-Sun all day in summer) 6-11
BAR MEALS: L served all week 12-2.30 D served all week 6-9.3 (Sun 12-2, 7-9) Av main course £9.50
BREWERY/COMPANY: Pubmaster 🍺: Flowers IPA, Sharps Doom Bar. 🍷: 14 **CHILDREN'S FACILITIES:** menu, portions, games, high-chairs, food/bottle warming **GARDEN:** Large, natural, lots of flowers **NOTES:** Dogs allowed: in bar, very welcome, Water, Parking 20

PENDOGGETT   THE CORNISH ARMS

PL30 3HH
☎ 01208 880263 📠 01208 880335
e-mail: millstjanet@aol.com
Dir: *From A30 Launceston, R onto A395, then L on to A39, then R onto B3314. Pub 7m along this road.* **Map Ref:** *SX07*

Atmospheric 16th-century coaching inn a mile or so from the beautiful and unspoiled Cornish coast. Hidden beaches and secret coves are just a short walk away and nearby is the fishing village of Port Isaac where you can watch the catch being landed. Solid beams and stone-flagged floors characterise the pub's comfortable interior. Salads and snacks are on the menu, as well as bar food which might include steak and ale pie; ham, egg and chips; lamb cutlets; duck pancakes; and fresh local fish.

OPEN: 11-11 (Sun 12-10.30) **BAR MEALS:** L served all week 12.30-2.30 D served all week 6.30-9.30 Sun 12.30-2.30, 6.30-9 **RESTAURANT:** L served all week 12.30-2.30 D served all week 6.30-9.30
BREWERY/COMPANY: Free House 🍺: Bass, Sharp's Doom Bar, John Smiths & Guest ale. ♀: 10
CHILDREN'S FACILITIES: menu, portions, games, high-chairs, food/bottle warming, family room **GARDEN:** Food served outside. Overlooking Port Isaac **NOTES:** Dogs allowed: in bar, Water provided, Parking 50

PENZANCE   THE TURKS HEAD INN 🐑 ♀

Chapel St TR18 4AF
☎ 01736 363093 📠 01736 360215
e-mail: veronica@turkspz.freeserve.co.uk
Map Ref: *SW43*

Dating from around 1233, making it Penzance's oldest pub, it was the first in the country to be given the Turks Head name. Sadly, a Spanish raiding party destroyed much of the original building in the 16th century, but an old smugglers' tunnel leading directly to the harbour and priest holes still exist. Typically available are mussels, sea bass, John Dory, lemon sole, tandoori monkfish, pan-fried venison, chicken stir-fry, pork tenderloin, steaks, mixed grill and salads. A sunny flower-filled garden lies at the rear.

OPEN: 11-3 5.30-11 (Sun 12-3, 5.30-10.30) Closed: Dec 25 **BAR MEALS:** L served all week 11-2.30 D served all week 6-10 Sun 12-2.30, 6-10 Av main course £6.75
RESTAURANT: L served all week 11-2.30 D served all week 6-10 Av 3 course à la carte £18.50
BREWERY/COMPANY: Punch Taverns 🍺: Young's Special, Greene King IPA, Sharp's Doom Bar Bitter, Guest Ale. ♀: 14
CHILDREN'S FACILITIES: menu, portions, high-chairs, food/bottle warming, family room **GARDEN:** Walled garden **NOTES:** No dogs (ex guide dogs)

PERRANUTHNOE   THE VICTORIA INN ♦♦♦ 🐑 ♀

TR20 9NP
☎ 01736 710309 📠 01736 719284
Dir: *Take the A394 Helston- Penzance road and turn down to the village following all the signs for Perranuthnoe.* **Map Ref:** *SW52*

This 12th-century inn is mentioned in the Domesday Book and is reputed to be the oldest hostelry in Cornwall. The pub is idyllically situated close to a sandy beach and the coastal footpath. With its Mediterranean-style patio, good food and en suite accommodation, the Victoria makes a pleasant stopover. Expect daily fresh fish, as well as dishes like braised venison in Burgundy jus; or home-made ratatouille with cheese topping and salad.

OPEN: 11.30-2.30 6.30-11 July&Aug open at 6pm
BAR MEALS: L served all week 12-2 D served all week 6.30-9 **RESTAURANT:** L served all week 12-2 D served all week 6.30-9 Av 3 course à la carte £18
BREWERY/COMPANY: 🍺: Bass, Doom Bar, Abbot Ale.
♀: 8 **CHILDREN'S FACILITIES:** menu, portions, high-chairs, food/bottle warming **GARDEN:** Paved Mediterranean style **NOTES:** Dogs allowed: in garden, Water provided; in bar only, Parking 10 **ROOMS:** 3 en suite s£35 d£55 no children overnight

POLKERRIS   THE RASHLEIGH INN 🐑 ♀

PL24 2TL
☎ 01726 813991 ▤ 01726 815619
e-mail: jonspode@aol.com
Dir: *Off A3082 outside Fowey.* **Map Ref:** *SX05*

A 300-year-old stone built pub that literally stands on a beach in a small, safe cove. The main bar used to be a boathouse and coastguard station. Panoramic views can be enjoyed from the multi-level sun terrace. Real ale selections vary according to season, and there is a good choice of malt whiskies. Although the restaurant menu is a little limited, the pub's location ensures a great catch of fresh fish and seafood every day.

OPEN: 11-11   **BAR MEALS:** L served all week 12-2 D served all week 6-9 snacks 3-5 everyday Av main course £6.75 **RESTAURANT:** L served all week 12-2 D served all week 6-9 Av 3 course à la carte £20   **BREWERY/COMPANY:** Free House ◖: Sharp's Doom Bar, Cotleigh Tawny, Blue Anchor Spingo, Timothy Taylor Landlord. ♀: 8 **CHILDREN'S FACILITIES:** menu, portions, high-chairs, food/bottle warming, baby changing, Baby changing facilities, high chairs **GARDEN:** Multi-level terrace, overlooks Polkerris etc **NOTES:** No dogs (ex guide dogs), Parking 22

POLPERRO   OLD MILL HOUSE INN 🐑

Mill Hill PL13 2RP
☎ 01503 272362 ▤ 01503 272058
e-mail: enquiries@oldmillhouseinn.co.uk
Dir: *Telephone for directions.* **Map Ref:** *SX25*

Log fires and a riverside garden enhance the character of this delightful 17th-century free house. The building was extensively refurbished last year, with new showers and carpets in the bedrooms. Well-kept ales and good home-cooked food attract drinkers and diners alike, with a straightforward selection of dishes that includes slow-cooked lamb shank in natural jus; John Dory fillets in wine and tarragon sauce; and fresh crab salad with crusty bread.

OPEN: 11-11 (Winter open at 12)   **BAR MEALS:** L served Tue-Sun 12-2.30 Sun carvery 12-3   **RESTAURANT:** D served Tue-Sat 7-9.30 Av 3 course à la carte £15 ◖: Sharp's, Special, Sharps Old Mill Ale. **CHILDREN'S FACILITIES:** menu, portions, high-chairs, food/bottle warming, outdoor play area   **GARDEN:** By river, benched, grassed   **NOTES:** Dogs allowed: in bar, in garden, in bedrooms, Water & Bonio, Parking 6

PORT GAVERNE   PORT GAVERNE HOTEL ★★ 🐑

PL29 3SQ
☎ 01208 880244 ▤ 01208 880151
Dir: *Signed from B3314, S of Delabole via B3267 on E of Port Isaac.* **Map Ref:** *SX08*

Just up the road from the sea and a beautiful little cove, this delightful 17th-century inn is a magnet for locals and holidaymakers alike. It is a meandering building with plenty of period detail, evocative of its long association with both fishing and smuggling. Bread is home made and locally supplied produce is to the fore, particularly fresh fish.

OPEN: 11-2.30 6.00-11 (Summer 11-11) Closed: Early Jan - Mid Feb   **BAR MEALS:** L served all week 12-2.30 D served all week 6.30-9.30 Av main course £7 **RESTAURANT:** D served all week 7-9.30 Av 3 course fixed price £25   **BREWERY/COMPANY:** Free House ◖: Sharp's Doom Bar, Bass, Greene King Abbot Ale. **CHILDREN'S FACILITIES:** portions, games, high-chairs, food/bottle warming   **NOTES:** Dogs allowed: in bar, in garden, in bedrooms, Water provided, Parking 15 **ROOMS:** 15 en suite 2 family rooms s£35 d£70

PORTHLEVEN   THE SHIP INN

TR13 9JS
☎ 01326 564204
Map Ref: *SW62*

Built into steep cliffs and approached by a flight of stone steps, this 17th-century smuggling inn has wonderful views over the harbour, especially at night when it is floodlit. Inside is a knocked-through bar with log fires, and a family room converted from an old smithy. Real ales are properly served, and a good choice of food includes seafood platter, moules marinara, home-made chilli, and crab Thermidor. Fresh crab sandwiches jacket potatoes, and ploughman's are popular snacks.

BAR MEALS: L served all week 12-2 D served all week 7-9 Av main course £10 **BREWERY/COMPANY:** Free House ◀: Scottish Courage Courage Best, Sharp's Doom Bar, Old Speckled Hen. **CHILDREN'S FACILITIES:** menu, games, high-chairs, food/bottle warming, toys available, family room **GARDEN:** Terraced. Overlooks the harbour **NOTES:** Dogs allowed: in bar, in garden, Water

ST BREWARD   THE OLD INN

Church Town, Bodmin Moor PL30 4PP
☎ 01208 850711 📠 01208 851671
e-mail: darren@theoldinn.fsnet.co.uk
Dir: *4 miles from A30 near Bodmin, or signed from B3266. Pub next to landmark St Breward church.* **Map Ref:** *SX07*

The Old Inn is located high up on Bodmin Moor in a village surrounded by spectacular scenery. It was constructed in the 11th century by monks who built the parish church next door, and retains its slate floors, wooden beams and log fires. Real ales and home-made dishes are served in the bar and restaurant, including fish, steaks, roasts, venison, and Moorland Grill. Wedding receptions and other functions can also be catered for.

OPEN: 11-3 6-11 (Summer open all day Fri-Sun) **BAR MEALS:** L served all week 11-1.50 D served all week 6-8.50 Av main course £6.95 **RESTAURANT:** L served all week 11-1.50 D served all week 6-8.50 Av 3 course à la carte £22 **BREWERY/COMPANY:** Free House ◀: Bass, Sharp's Doom Bar Bitter, Sharps Special, Guest Ales. ♀: 24 **CHILDREN'S FACILITIES:** menu, high-chairs, food/bottle warming, baby changing, family room **GARDEN:** Garden & decking area **NOTES:** Dogs allowed: in bar, in garden, Water, Parking 35

ST DOMINICK   WHO'D HAVE THOUGHT IT INN

St Dominic PL12 6TG
☎ 01579 350214
Map Ref: *SX46*

The village of St Dominic, well-known for its strawberries and daffodils, can add to its attractions this free house with beams, open fire, antique furnishings, and lovely views across the Tamar Valley. Comfortable disabled access. Handy for Cotehele House (NT). The Silage bar has darts, TV and jukebox, while the Straw bar welcomes dogs on leads; the lounges are a touch more formal. Enjoy the likes of fillet steak, fish, home-made pies and curries.

OPEN: 11.30-2.30 6-11 **BAR MEALS:** L served all week 12-2.30 D served all week 6.30-9.30 Av main course £7.50 **BREWERY/COMPANY:** Free House ◀: Bass, Betty Stoggs, Hicks. ♀: 10 **CHILDREN'S FACILITIES:** menu, portions, high-chairs, food/bottle warming, family room **GARDEN:** Small garden with spectacular views **NOTES:** Dogs allowed: Water provided, Parking 50

ST EWE   THE CROWN INN

PL26 6EY
☎ 01726 843322 📠 01726 844720
Dir: *From St Austell take B3273. At Tregiskey x-rds turn R. St Ewe is signposted on R.*
Map Ref: *SW94*

Hanging baskets add plenty of brightness and colour to this delightful 16th-century inn, just a mile from the famous Lost Gardens of Heligan. The owner helped restore the gardens over a period of ten years. Well-kept St Austell ales complement an extensive menu and daily specials. Expect cod in beer batter, local steaks, rack of lamb, and liver and bacon among other favourites.

OPEN: 12-3 5-11 **BAR MEALS:** L served all week 12-2 D served all week 6-9 Av main course £6.95
RESTAURANT: L served all week 12-2 D served all week 6-9 Av 3 course à la carte £17.50 **BREWERY/COMPANY:** St Austell Brewery 🍺**:** Tribute, Hicks Special, Tinners, plus guest ale. **CHILDREN'S FACILITIES:** outdoor play area, family room **GARDEN:** Two marquees, heated fenced, well lit **NOTES:** Dogs allowed: in bar, in garden, Water, Parking 60

ST JUST (NEAR LAND'S END)   THE WELLINGTON HOTEL ◆◆◆

Market Square TR19 7HD
☎ 01736 787319 📠 01736 787906
e-mail: wellingtonhotel@msn.com
Map Ref: *SW33*

Named after the Iron Duke, who once stayed here, this imposing granite-fronted, family-run hotel overlooks the market square. St Just is on the scenic coastal road between St Ives and Lands End, close to some of Cornwall's finest cliffs, coves and beaches and Cape Cornwall, England's only cape. A hot and cold menu is available at lunchtime and evenings, with fresh, locally caught fish and crab, steaks and daily specials. Large beer garden.

OPEN: 10.30-11 **BAR MEALS:** L served all week 12-2 D served all week 6-9 Av main course £6
RESTAURANT: L served all week 12-2 D served all week 6-9 Av 3 course à la carte £15 **BREWERY/COMPANY:** St Austell Brewery 🍺**:** St Austell Tinners, St Austell Tribute, St Austell Cornish Cream Mild.
CHILDREN'S FACILITIES: menu, high-chairs, food/bottle warming, outdoor play area, slide, wendy house, pool table, family room **GARDEN:** Enclosed by walls, filled with flowers **NOTES:** Dogs allowed: in bar, in garden, in bedrooms, £10 charge if staying, Parking 20 **ROOMS:** 11 en suite 4 family rooms s£30 d£50

ST MAWES   THE VICTORY INN

Victory Hill TR2 5PQ
☎ 01326 270324 📠 01326 270238
Dir: *In centre of village close to the harbour.*
Map Ref: *SW83*

Close to St Mawes Harbour on the Roseland Peninsula is this friendly fishermen's local, named after Nelson's flagship. These days it doubles as a modern dining pub, offering the freshest of local seafood and harbour views. The blackboard specials change daily according to the catch. There's also a choice of pub grub dishes - fresh mussels with fries, pasty and gravy, sausage and mash - while lunchtime snacks include white Cornish crab sandwiches.

OPEN: 11-11 (Sun 12-10.30) **BAR MEALS:** L served all week 12-2.15 D served all week 6.30-9 Av main course £7
RESTAURANT: L served Mon-Sun 12-2.15 D served Mon-Sun 6.30-9 Av 3 course à la carte £20 🍺**:** Sharps, Bass, Ringwood, IPA. **CHILDREN'S FACILITIES:** menu, portions, games, high-chairs, food/bottle warming, darts, Various games **GARDEN:** Food served outside **NOTES:** Dogs allowed: in bar, biscuits, water and toys

ST MAWGAN   THE FALCON INN ◆◆◆◆ 🛏 ♈

TR8 4EP
☎ 01637 860225 📠 01637 860884
e-mail: enquiries@falconinn.net
Dir: *From A30 8m W of Bodmin, follow signs to Newquay/St Mawgan Airport. After 2m turn R into village, pub at bottom of hill.*
Map Ref: *SW86*

Taking its name from a falcon which, at the time of the Reformation, flew over the village to indicate a secret Catholic church service was being held, this 15th-century pub lies in the sheltered Vale of Lanherne. Comprehensive menu and daily specials range from salmon en papillette, to hearty sirloin steaks, and steak and kidney pie.

OPEN: 11-3 6-11 **BAR MEALS:** L served all week 12-2 D served all week 6.30-9.30 **RESTAURANT:** L served all week 12-2 D served all week 6.30-9.30 **BREWERY/COMPANY:** St Austell Brewery 🍺: St Austell HSD, Tinners Ale & Tribute. ♈: 7 **CHILDREN'S FACILITIES:** menu, high-chairs, food/bottle warming, baby changing, outdoor play area, Outdoor slide, swing bridge, climbing frame, family room **GARDEN:** Large garden, sheltered, safe **NOTES:** Dogs allowed: in bar, in garden, in bedrooms, Water, Parking 25 **ROOMS:** 3 bedrooms 2 en suite s£26 d£54

SALTASH   THE CROOKED INN ◆◆◆◆ 🛏

Stoketon Cottage, Trematon PL12 4RZ
☎ 01752 848177 📠 01752 843203
e-mail: info@crooked-inn.co.uk
Map Ref: *SX45*

Originally two cottages, providing accommodation for the cooks and gardeners of Stoketon Manor (the remains of which are still evident across the courtyard), the building was converted into an inn over 15 years ago, and now has adjacent bedroom blocks. It is set in 20 acres of grounds overlooking the Lynher Valley. The range of home-cooked meals includes locally caught fish, traditional pies, vegetarian combo, steaks and curries.

OPEN: 11-11 (Sun 11-10.30) **BAR MEALS:** L served all week 12-2.30 D served all week 6-10 **RESTAURANT:** L served all week 12-2.30 D served all week 6-10 **BREWERY/COMPANY:** Free House 🍺: Hicks Special Draught, Sharp's Eden Ale, Skinner's Cornish Knocker Ale. **CHILDREN'S FACILITIES:** menu, portions, high-chairs, food/bottle warming, outdoor play area, trampoline, animals, treehouse, slide, swings **GARDEN:** 10 acres. Patio and decking with seating **NOTES:** Dogs allowed: in bar, in garden, in bedrooms, Parking 60 **ROOMS:** 18 bedrooms 15 en suite 15 family rooms s£29 d£45

SEATON   SMUGGLERS INN

Tregunnick Ln PL11 3JD
☎ 01503 250646 📠 01503 250646
Map Ref: *SX35*

Dating back to the 17th century, The Smugglers is idyllically located opposite the beach. Inside, the atmosphere is warm and friendly, and the décor in keeping with the pub's age. Local ales are served, and the menu offers such dishes as chargrilled halibut steak; fillet of beef medallions with brandy and wild mushroom cream; and field mushrooms stuffed with wild rice and topped with slivers of smoked cheese. There is an extensive bar menu, and a good choice of children's dishes.

BAR MEALS: L served all week 12-2.30 D served all week 6-9.30 **RESTAURANT:** L served (Varies to season) 12-2.30 D served all week 7-9.30 Av 3 course à la carte £22.50 **BREWERY/COMPANY:** Free House 🍺: Real ales From local brewery. **CHILDREN'S FACILITIES:** menu, high-chairs, baby changing, family room **GARDEN:** Patio area **NOTES:** Dogs allowed: in bar, in garden, Water, Parking 10

SENNEN   THE OLD SUCCESS INN ★★ 🐑

Sennen Cove TR19 7DG
☎ 01736 871232 🖷 01736 871457
e-mail:
oldsuccess@sennencove.fsbusiness.co.uk
Map Ref: SW32

Originally two thatched cottages, this late
17th-century inn was the place where local
fishermen brought their catch and bought
their ale. It was also a rendezvous for
smugglers and wreckers, but now Charlie's
Bar is a focal point for the local lifeboat crew,
whose territory includes nearby Land's End. In
a glorious location with expansive views to
England's only cape - Cape Cornwall. Fresh
local fish, including seafood paella and sea
bass, as well as 'continental style' specials are popular.
Live music every Saturday night all year round.

OPEN: 11-11 **BAR MEALS:** L served all week 12-2.30
D served all week 6.15-9.30 Av main course £6.25
RESTAURANT: L served Sun 12-2.15 D served all week
7-9.30 Av 3 course à la carte £17 Av 3 course fixed price
£16.95 **BREWERY/COMPANY:** Free House 🍺: Doom Bar,
Sharps Special, Skinners. **CHILDREN'S FACILITIES:** menu,
portions, high-chairs, food/bottle warming **GARDEN:** Beer
terrace, stunning views of Whitesand Bay **NOTES:** Dogs
allowed: in bar, Parking 16 **ROOMS:** s£35 d£84

TINTAGEL   THE PORT WILLIAM ◆◆◆◆ ♀

Trebarwith Strand PL34 0HB
☎ 01840 770230 🖷 01840 770936
e-mail: theportwilliam@btinternet.com
Dir: Off B3263 between Camelford & Tintagel.
Map Ref: SX08

Occupying one of the best locations in
Cornwall, this former harbourmaster's house lies
directly on the coastal path. The inn is 50 yards from
the sea and the building dates back about 300 years.
Focus on the daily-changing specials board for such
dishes as artichoke and roast pepper salad, grilled
sardines, warm smoked trout platter, or spinach ricotta
tortelloni.

OPEN: 11-11 (Sun 12-10.30)   12 opening in winter
BAR MEALS: L served all week 12-2.30 D served all week
6.30-9.30 **RESTAURANT:** L served all week 12-2.30
D served all week 6-9.30 **BREWERY/COMPANY:** Free
House 🍺: St Austell Tinners Ale & Hicks, Interbrew Bass.
♀: 8 **CHILDREN'S FACILITIES:** menu, portions, high-chairs,
food/bottle warming, baby changing, Beach, family room
GARDEN: Patio overlooking sea, food served outside
NOTES: Dogs allowed: in bar, Water, Parking 75
ROOMS: 8 en suite s£55 d£75

TORPOINT   THE EDGCUMBE ARMS ◆◆◆◆ ♀

Cremyll PL10 1HX
☎ 01752 822294 🖷 01752 822014
e-mail: edgcumbearms1@btopenworld.com
Dir: Please phone for directions.
Map Ref: SX45

The inn dates from the 15th century and is
located right on the Tamar Estuary, next to
the National Trust park, close to the foot ferry
from Plymouth. Views from the bow window
seats and waterside terrace are glorious,
taking in Drakes Island, the Royal William
Yard and the marina. Real ales from St Austell
and quality home-cooked food are served in
a series of rooms, which are full of character
with American oak panelling and stone
flagged floors. Fresh local seafood and
Cornish beef steaks are a feature of the
menus alongside a daily curry and steak and ale pie. A
good choice of bar snacks is also offered. The inn has a
first floor function room with sea views, and a
courtyard garden; it also holds a civil wedding license.
A bridal suite is included in the range of pretty
bedrooms.

OPEN: 11-11 (Sun 12-10.30) Rest: 6 Jan - 28 Feb Closed
from 3-6 **BAR MEALS:** L served all week 12-2.30 D served
all week 6-9 Av main course £6.95 **RESTAURANT:** L served
all week 12-2.30 D served all week 7-9 Av 3 course à la
carte £16 **BREWERY/COMPANY:** St Austell Brewery 🍺: St
Austell HSD, Tribute HS, IPA, Cornish Cream. ♀: 10
CHILDREN'S FACILITIES: menu, high-chairs, food/bottle
warming, family room **GARDEN:** Large picnic area with
tables **NOTES:** Dogs allowed: in bar, in garden, Water,
Parking 12 **ROOMS:** 6 en suite 2 family rooms s£35 d£50

TREBURLEY THE SPRINGER SPANIEL

PL15 9NS
☎ 01579 370424 ▤ 01579 370113
Dir: *On the A388 halfway between Launceston & Callington.* **Map Ref:** *SX37*

This unassuming roadside hostelry dates from the 18th century, and the old creeper-covered walls conceal a cosy bar with two high-backed wooden settles, farmhouse style chairs, and a wood-burning stove to keep out the chill on cooler days. Blackboards in the bar list the lighter snack options - freshly filled sandwiches and rolls, decent soups and daily specials - as well as the more serious choices that are also served in the separate beamed dining room where the setting is slightly more formal.

OPEN: 11-3 6-11 **BAR MEALS:** L served all week 12-2 D served all week 6.30-9 Av main course £8.50
RESTAURANT: L served all week 12-2 D served all week 6.30-9 Av 3 course à la carte £20 **BREWERY/COMPANY:** Free House ◖: Sharp's Doom Bar, Eden & Cornish, Springer Ale. ♀: 7 **CHILDREN'S FACILITIES:** menu, portions, food/bottle warming, baby changing, family room
GARDEN: Landscaped with seating, food served outside
NOTES: Dogs allowed: in bar, Water & biscuits, Parking 30

TRESCO THE NEW INN ★★ ⦿

New Grimsby TR24 0QQ
☎ 01720 422844 ▤ 01720 423200
e-mail: newinn@tresco.co.uk
Dir: *By New Grimsby Quay.* **Map Ref:** *SV81*

'The Best Pub on Tresco' - well the only one actually, although once there were thirteen.

The Scillies are warmed by the Gulf Stream, and sub-tropical vegetation is everywhere. Not surprisingly, Tresco's day job is tourism, and most people's itineraries include The New Inn. Lunch is sandwiches, fresh fish, a few meat dishes, pasta or something vegetarian. Dinner might be pizzas, home-made seafood lasagne, vegetable Thai-fry, rack of lamb, and more.

OPEN: 11-11 **BAR MEALS:** L served all week 12-2 D served all week 6-9 limited menu available all day Apr-Sept Av main course £8.95 **RESTAURANT:** D served all week 7-9
Av 3 course fixed price £27 **BREWERY/COMPANY:** Free House ◖: Skinner's Betty Stogs Bitter, Tresco Tipple, Ales of Scilly Maiden Voyage, St Austell IPA. ♀: 8
CHILDREN'S FACILITIES: menu, games, high-chairs, food/bottle warming, baby changing **GARDEN:** Patio area with sub-tropical plants **NOTES:** No dogs (ex guide dogs), Assistance dogs by arrangement **ROOMS:** 16 en suite d£138

TRURO THE WIG & PEN INN

Frances St TR1 3DP
☎ 01872 273028 ▤ 01872 277351
Dir: *City centre nr Law Courts, 10 mins from railway station.* **Map Ref:** *SW84*

THE
WIG & PEN

Frances Street, Truro
Cornwall TR1 3DN
Tel: 01872 273028

A listed city centre pub originally known as the Star, that became the Wig & Pen when the county court moved to Truro. There is a ghost called Claire who lives in the cellar, but she is friendly! The choice of food includes such home-made dishes as steak and ale pie, curry, casseroles, steaks and vegetarian dishes, and a range of fish options such as sea bass, John Dory, mullet or monkfish.

OPEN: 11-11 (Sun 12-10.30) **BAR MEALS:** L served all week 12-2.30 D served all week 6-9 Av main course £5
RESTAURANT: D served Summer all, winter Thurs-Sat 6-9.45
Av 3 course à la carte £25 Av 3 course fixed price £25
BREWERY/COMPANY: St Austell Brewery ◖: St Austell Dartmoor & HSD plus guest ales.
CHILDREN'S FACILITIES: menu, games, high-chairs, food/bottle warming **GARDEN:** Patio area with pot plants
NOTES: Dogs allowed: in non eating area

ASHBURTON THE RISING SUN ◆◆◆◆

Woodland TQ13 7JT
☎ 01364 652544 ▤ 01364 653628
e-mail: mail@risingsunwoodland.co.uk
Dir: *E of Ashburton from the A38 take lane signed to Woodland and Denbury pub is on the L approx 1.5m.* **Map Ref:** SX77

Isolated, but all the better for that, in beautiful Devon countryside. The sun rises directly opposite the main building - hence the pub's name - and the sunny south-facing terrace and large garden are both delightful places to eat and drink. Menus are updated daily.

OPEN: 11.45-3 Closed Mon lunch in Summer except BHS 6-11 (Sun 12-3, 7-10.30) Closed: Dec 25 Rest: Mon Closed all day in winter **BAR MEALS:** L served Tue-Sun 12-2.15 D served Tue-Sun 6-9.15 **RESTAURANT:** L served Tue-Sun 12-2.15 D served Tue-Sun 6-9.15 **BREWERY/COMPANY:** Free House ◖: Princetown Jail Ale, IPA, Teignworthy Reel Ale & Changing guest ales. ♀: 10 **CHILDREN'S FACILITIES:** menu, portions, games, high-chairs, food/bottle warming, baby changing, outdoor play area, Toys, childrens books, swings, old tractor, family room **GARDEN:** Patio and lawn with seating **NOTES:** Dogs allowed: in bar, in garden, in bedrooms, Water, Parking 30 **ROOMS:** 2 en suite 1 family room s£38 d£60

BICKLEIGH FISHERMAN'S COT ♀

EX16 8RW
☎ 01884 855237 ▤ 01884 855241
e-mail: fishermanscot.bickleigh@eldridge-pope.co.uk
Map Ref: SS90

Well-appointed inn by Bickleigh Bridge over the River Exe with food all day and large beer garden, just a short drive from Tiverton and Exmoor. The Waterside Bar is the place for snacks and afternoon tea, while the restaurant incorporates a carvery and à la carte menus. Sunday lunch is served, and champagne and smoked salmon breakfast is optional.

OPEN: 11-11 (Sun 12-10.30) **BAR MEALS:** L served all week 12-9.30 D served all week Av main course £7.50 **RESTAURANT:** L served all week 12-10 D served all week **BREWERY/COMPANY:** Eldridge Pope ◖: Wadworth 6X, Bass. ♀: 8 **CHILDREN'S FACILITIES:** menu, high-chairs, baby changing **GARDEN:** Food served outside. **NOTES:** Dogs allowed: Parking 100

BUCKLAND MONACHORUM DRAKE MANOR INN ♀

The Village PL20 7NA
☎ 01822 853892 ▤ 01822 853892
Dir: *Off A386 near Yelverton.* **Map Ref:** SX46

A warm welcome is assured at this mainly 16th-century inn, whose licensee celebrates 15 years at the inn this year. Nestling between the church and the stream, it is named after local resident Sir Francis Drake. Heavy beams and fireplaces with wood-burning stoves are still in evidence, and the pub is renowned for its pretty gardens and award-winning floral displays. Meals include bar snacks and daily specials, with dishes like cajun spiced chicken breast, a selection of steaks, and a good choice of vegetarian dishes.

OPEN: 11.30-2.30 6.30-11 (Sun 12-3, 7-10.30) **BAR MEALS:** L served all week 12-2 D served all week 7-10 (Sun 12-2, 7-9.30) Av main course £6.95 **RESTAURANT:** L served all week 12-2 D served all week 7-10 (Sun 12-2, 7-9.30) Av 3 course à la carte £15 **BREWERY/COMPANY:** ◖: Scottish Courage John Smiths & Courage Best, Wadworth 6X, Greene King Abbott Ale, Sharp's Doom Bar. ♀: 9 **CHILDREN'S FACILITIES:** portions, high-chairs, food/bottle warming, family room **GARDEN:** Pretty cottage garden next to stream **NOTES:** Dogs allowed: in bar, in garden, Water, Parking 4

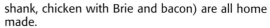

BUTTERLEIGH THE BUTTERLEIGH INN

EX15 1PN
☎ 01884 855407 🖷 01884 855600
Dir: *3m from J 28 on the M5 turn R by The Manor Hotel in Cullompton and follow Butterleigh signs.* **Map Ref:** *SS90*

Dating back 400 years, this was a cider house until the turn of the last century. Today, still tucked away in a sleepy village amid glorious countryside south of Tiverton, the Butterleigh is worth seeking out for its excellent Cotleigh Brewery ales and good food. You can eat and drink outside in two beer gardens, or in the homely bars with their comfortable furniture and open fires. Locally caught fish is served as starters or mains, and the traditional meat courses (pork and cider casserole, game pie, lamb shank, chicken with Brie and bacon) are all home made.

OPEN: 12-2.30 6-11 **BAR MEALS:** L served all week 12-2 D served all week 7-9.15 Av main course £9.95
BREWERY/COMPANY: Free House 🍺: Cotleigh Tawny Ale, Barn Owl Bitter, O'Hanlans "Yellow Hammer", Otter Ale.
CHILDREN'S FACILITIES: menu, portions, licence, games, food/bottle warming, baby changing, outdoor play area, lunch times only **GARDEN:** Seating available for 30 plus
NOTES: Dogs allowed: Parking 50

CHAGFORD RING O'BELLS

44 The Square TQ13 8AH
☎ 01647 432466 🖷 01647 432466
e-mail: info@ringobellschagford.co.uk
Dir: *From Exeter take A30 to Whiddon Down Rdbt, take 1st L onto A382 to Mortonhampstead. After 3.5m to Easton Cross Turn R Signed to Chagford.* **Map Ref:** *SX78*

Twice burnt down during its 500-year history, this traditional West Country inn, in an area popular as a base for walking and tours of Dartmoor, continues to thrive and is now under new ownership. Daily changing menus use local produce as often as possible, with Dartmoor lamb, Devonshire mussels cooked in West Country cider, and a Cornish fish trio featuring. The pudding menu includes traditional favourites; apple and blackcurrant crumble, ginger sponge, treacle tart, and lemon posset.

OPEN: 9-3 5-11 (Sun 9-3, 6-10.30) **BAR MEALS:** L served all week 12-2 D served all week 6-9 Av main course £8.95
RESTAURANT: L served all week 12-2 D served all week 6-9
BREWERY/COMPANY: Free House 🍺: Butcombe Bitter, Exmoor Ale, Devon Cream, Hicks HSD-Cornish Bitter. 🍷: 8
CHILDREN'S FACILITIES: portions, games, high-chairs, food/bottle warming, coloured pencils and paper
GARDEN: Walled courtyard with lawn & covered area
NOTES: Dogs allowed: in bar, in garden, in bedrooms, very dog friendly, water & biscuits provided

THREE CROWNS HOTEL ★★

High St TQ13 8AJ
☎ 01647 433444 & 433441 🖷 01647 433117
e-mail: threecrowns@msn.com
Map Ref: *SX78*

An impressive, 13th-century, granite-built inn with a wealth of historical associations to investigate. Take young poet and Cavalier Sydney Godolphin, for example, who was shot in the hotel doorway in 1643 and who continues to 'appear', making him the hotel's oldest resident. Period features include mullioned windows, sturdy oak beams and a massive open fireplace. Among chef's specialities are sautéed fillet of pork with mango salsa and lemon sole poached in white wine with mixed seafood sauce.

OPEN: 8-11.20 all day **BAR MEALS:** L served all week 12-3 D served all week 6-9.30 Av main course £6
RESTAURANT: L served all week D served all week 6-9.30 Av 3 course à la carte £28.50 Av 3 course fixed price £19.50
BREWERY/COMPANY: Free House 🍺: Flowers Original, Boddingtons, Bass, Whitbread.
CHILDREN'S FACILITIES: menu, portions, licence, high-chairs, food/bottle warming **NOTES:** Dogs allowed: in bar, in bedrooms, Parking 20 **ROOMS:** 17 en suite 3 family rooms s£60 d£74

CHERITON BISHOP THE OLD THATCH INN

EX6 6HJ
☎ 01647 24204 ▤ 01647 24584
e-mail: mail@theoldthatchinn.f9.co.uk
Dir: *Take A30 from M5, about 10m take turn on L signed Cheriton Bishop.* **Map Ref:** SX79

Listed chocolate box inn with plenty of old world charm and modern comforts. Licensed as a pub in 1974, it is close to Fingle Bridge, described by RD Blackmore as 'the finest scene in all England'. Meals range from light snacks to fillet of smoked haddock, wild mushroom and pepper risotto, and West Country lamb shank with a rosemary and garlic jus.

OPEN: 11.30-3 6-11 Closed: 25 Dec
BAR MEALS: L served all week 12-2 D served all week 7-9.30 Av main course £8.50 **RESTAURANT:** L served all week 12-2 D served all week 7-9.30 Av 3 course à la carte £20.50 **BREWERY/COMPANY:** Free House ◖: Sharp's, Otter Ale, Adnam's Broadside, Doombar. ♀: 9
CHILDREN'S FACILITIES: menu, portions, games, high-chairs, food/bottle warming, baby changing, outdoor play area, toy box, family room **GARDEN:** South facing patio garden
NOTES: No dogs, Parking 30

CLYST HYDON THE FIVE BELLS INN

EX15 2NT
☎ 01884 277288 ▤ 01884 277693
e-mail: rshenton@btclick.com
Dir: *B3181 3m out of Cullompton, L to Clyst Hydon then R to Clyst St Lawrence. Pub on R.* **Map Ref:** ST00

New owners Di and Roger Shenton are committed to continuing the long tradition of hospitality at this traditional free house and careful modernisation has left its old-world atmosphere intact. Meals are eaten in the bar, which has designated non-smoking areas, or in the raised side garden with its far-reaching country views.

OPEN: 11.30-3 6.30-11 Closed: Dec 26 & Jan 1 Rest: Dec 25 & Dec 31 Closed eve **BAR MEALS:** L served all week 12-2 D served all week 7-10 Av main course £8.95 **RESTAURANT:** L served all week 12-2 D served all week 7-10 **BREWERY/COMPANY:** Free House ◖: Cotleigh Tawny Ale, Otter Bitter, O'Hanlon's.
CHILDREN'S FACILITIES: menu, high-chairs, food/bottle warming, outdoor play area, ropes, climbing frame, family room **GARDEN:** Large well kept award winning floral display
NOTES: No dogs (ex guide dogs), Parking 40

COLEFORD THE NEW INN ♦♦♦♦

EX17 5BZ
☎ 01363 84242 ▤ 01363 85044
e-mail: new-inn@reallyreal-group.com
Dir: *From Exeter take A377, 1.5m after Crediton turn L for Coleford. Pub in 1.5m.* **Map Ref:** SS70

This 13th-century, thatched free house is built of a mixture of compressed earth, clay and straw known as cob. Original beams and an ancient bar blend well with extensions created from the old barns, there's a ghost, and a resident parrot, Captain, who likes to greet guests. The inn's policy of using fresh local produce wherever possible translates into an extensive fixed menu, topped up with blackboard specials.

OPEN: 12-3 6-11 (Sun 7-10.30) Closed: 25-26 Dec
BAR MEALS: L served all week 12-2 D served all week 7-10 **RESTAURANT:** L served all week 12-2 D served all week 7-10 **BREWERY/COMPANY:** Free House ◖: Wadworth 6X, Otter Ale, Badger Bitter, Shepherd Neame Spitfire.
CHILDREN'S FACILITIES: menu, portions, high-chairs, food/bottle warming **GARDEN:** Terraced, paved, decked area, stream **NOTES:** Parking 50 **ROOMS:** 6 en suite 1 family room s£60 d£70

CORNWORTHY   HUNTERS LODGE INN

TQ9 7ES
☎ 01803 732204
e-mail: rog.liz@hunterslodgeinn.com
Dir: *Off A381 S of Totnes.* *Map Ref:* SX85

Dating from the early 18th century, this country local is tucked away in a quiet village close to the River Dart. The interior is simply furnished and a real fire burns in the smart fireplace. Fresh local produce is used in the cooking, and the water sold originates from a spring in the village. Devon gammon with egg and chips, Angus fillet steak, and Moroccan lamb casserole with apricots are typical dishes. Plenty of good fish and shell fish choices too, with produce coming from Plymouth, Aveton Gifford, and Dartmouth.

OPEN: 11.30-2.30 6.30-11 **BAR MEALS:** L served all week 12-2 D served all week 7-9 Av main course £10 **RESTAURANT:** L served all week 12-2 D served all week 7-9 Av 3 course à la carte £18.50 **BREWERY/COMPANY:** Free House ◖: Teignworthy Reel Ale & Springtide, Guest Ales. ♀: 14 **CHILDREN'S FACILITIES:** menu, portions, food/bottle warming, outdoor play area, games **GARDEN:** Large paddock with shaded seating areas **NOTES:** Dogs allowed: in bar, in garden, Water, dog chews, Parking 18

DARTMOUTH   ROYAL CASTLE HOTEL ★★★

11 The Quay TQ6 9PS
☎ 01803 833033 🖷 01803 835445
e-mail: enquiry@royalcastle.co.uk
Map Ref: SX85

The regal prefix followed visits to the hotel by the Prince of Wales in the late 1870s, when his eldest sons were serving on HMS Britannia. Opposite the bar is the Lydstone Range, forged in Dartmouth over 300 years ago, and on which you can still have your meat roasted during the winter. Tudor fireplaces, spiral staircases, priest holes and period furniture are further evidence of the hotel's history. Fish and seafood dishes are always available, as well as traditional bar food options.

OPEN: 11-11 **BAR MEALS:** L served all week 11.30-6.30 D served all week 6.30-10 Av main course £7.50 **RESTAURANT:** L served all week 12-2 D served all week 7-9.30 Av 3 course fixed price £22.50 **BREWERY/COMPANY:** Free House ◖: Exe Valley Dob's Bitter, Courage Directors, Bass. ♀: 12 **CHILDREN'S FACILITIES:** portions, high-chairs, family room **NOTES:** Dogs allowed: in bar, Water, biscuits, Parking 14 **ROOMS:** 25 en suite 3 family rooms s£55 d£110

DOLTON   THE UNION INN

Fore St EX19 8QH
☎ 01805 804633 🖷 01805 804633
Dir: *From A361 take B3227 to S Moulton, then Atherington. L onto B3217 then 6m to Dalton. Pub on R.* *Map Ref:* SS51

A 17th-century free house built as a Devon longhouse, now under new management. Traditionally constructed of cob, the building was converted to a hotel in the mid-19th century to serve the local cattle markets, and it remains a traditional village pub with a cosy atmosphere. With its large Georgian rooms, sash windows and traditional pub interior, it offers a warm welcome to visitors. There's a homely beamed bar, oak settles and sturdy wooden tables, plus good home cooking, especially Sunday roasts and traditional dishes washed down with West Country ales. In the bar you should find baguettes and toasties, as well as local ham and sausage. Restaurant meals might include marinated rib-eye steak, or braised oxtail will red wine and vegetables.

OPEN: 12-3 6-11 Sun 12-10.30 open Wed in summer Closed: 1st 2 wks Feb **BAR MEALS:** L served Thur-Tue 12-2 D served Thur-Tue 7-10 Sun 12-5 Av main course £4.20 **RESTAURANT:** L served Sun 12-2 D served Thu-Tue 7-9 Sun 12-5 Av 3 course à la carte £17 **BREWERY/COMPANY:** Free House ◖: Sharp's Doom Bar, Jollyboat Freebooter, Clearwater Cavalier, St Austell Tribute. **CHILDREN'S FACILITIES:** menu, portions, licence, games, high-chairs, food/bottle warming **GARDEN:** Small area with three tables **NOTES:** Dogs allowed: in bar, in garden, in bedrooms, dog bed and toys, Parking 15

243

EXETER RED LION INN

Broadclyst EX5 3EL
☎ 01392 461271
Dir: on the B3181 Exeter to Culompton.
Map Ref: SX99

At the centre of a National Trust village, close to Killerton House and Gardens, this renowned 15th-century inn features original beams and antique furniture inside, and a cobbled courtyard outside. Among the kitchen's dishes you may find fisherman's pie; baked aubergine stuffed with Mozzarella, tomatoes and pesto; butternut squash crumble; Moroccan lamb tajine; or old favourites such as steak and ale pie or fish and chips. Special occasions are catered for with impressive buffets.

OPEN: 11-3.00 5.30-11 (Sun 12-3, 7-10.30)
BAR MEALS: L served all week 12-2.30 D served all week 6-9.30 Sun 12-2.30, 7-9 Av main course £5
RESTAURANT: L served all week 12-2.3 D served Mon-Sat 6-9.30 Sun 12-2.3, 7-9 **BREWERY/COMPANY:** Free House
🍺: Bass, Fullers London Pride, O'Hanlons Local Blakelys red, Speckled Hen. ♀: 7 **CHILDREN'S FACILITIES:** menu, portions, games, high-chairs, food/bottle warming, baby changing **GARDEN:** Small garden with three tables
NOTES: 70

EXMINSTER SWANS NEST

Station Rd EX6 8DZ
☎ 01392 832371
Dir: From M5 follow A379 Dawlish Rd.
Map Ref: SX98

A much extended pub in a pleasant rural location whose facilities, unusually, extend to a ballroom, dance floor and stage. The carvery is a popular option for diners, with a choice of meats served with freshly prepared vegetables, though the salad bar is a tempting alternative, with over 39 items, including quiches, pies and home-smoked chicken. A carte of home-cooked fare includes grilled lamb steak, Devon pork chop, and five-bean vegetable curry. Interested diners might like to sample 'Plant Pot Pudding', as well as take a look at a jukebox that once belonged to Sir Elton John.

OPEN: 10.30-2.30 6-11 Closed: Dec 26
BAR MEALS: L served all week 12-2 D served all week 6-9.45 **RESTAURANT:** L served all week 12-2 D served all week 6-9.30 **BREWERY/COMPANY:** Free House 🍺: Otter Bitter, Princetown Jail Ale. **CHILDREN'S FACILITIES:** menu, outdoor play area, children's play park, family room
NOTES: No dogs, Parking 102

EXTON THE PUFFING BILLY

Station Rd EX3 0PR
☎ 01392 877888 🖷 01392 876212
e-mail: the_billy@hotmail.com
Map Ref: SX98

Enjoy estuary views from this 16th-century village pub, popular for its live jazz, real ales and fine wines. Menus include a good range of seafood (cod, lobster, scallops, oysters) and 'big plates' such as mid-Devon pork tenderloin with fondant potato, caramelised apples and cider jus; dry-aged Aberdeen Angus 8oz steak with thyme roasted shallots, red wine glaze and beetroot confit, on a leek and potato cake; or local red mullet fillets with spinach, ratatouille, crushed new potatoes and kalamata olives. Nice collection of desserts.

OPEN: 11-3 5.30-11 Closed: 25 Dec, 1 Jan
BAR MEALS: L served all week 12-3 D served all week 6-7 Av main course £6.50 **RESTAURANT:** L served all week 12-3 D served all week 6-10 Av 3 course à la carte £25 Av 3 course fixed price £13.75 🍺: Cafferys, Dobs, Firefly, Konig Pilsner. ♀: 16 **CHILDREN'S FACILITIES:** portions, licence, games, high-chairs, food/bottle warming, playground opposite **GARDEN:** Sun terrace, small garden
NOTES: No dogs (ex guide dogs), Parking 30

HARBERTON THE CHURCH HOUSE INN

TQ9 7SF

☎ 01803 863707

Dir: *From Totnes take A381 S. Take turn for Harberton on R, adjacent to church in centre of village.* **Map Ref:** *SX75*

Originally built to house masons working on the church next door (in around 1100), the inn has some fascinating historic features, including a Tudor window frame and latticed window with 13th-century glass. The extensive daily menu is supplemented by daily specials and a traditional roast on Sundays. There's plenty of seafood/fish, such as pan-fried crevettes, bouillabaisse and whole plaice, along with rump steak old English style, and lamb with rosemary and port jus. Family room provided.

OPEN: 12-3 6-11 (Sat 12-4, 6-11 Sun 12-3, 7-10.30)
BAR MEALS: L served all week 12-2 D served all week 7-9.30 Av main course £8.95 **RESTAURANT:** L served all week 12-2 D served all week 7-9.30 Av 3 course à la carte £17.50 **BREWERY/COMPANY:** Free House 🍺: Marstons Pedigree, Butcombe, Courage Best, Theakstons XB. 🍷: 14
CHILDREN'S FACILITIES: menu, portions, games, high-chairs, food/bottle warming, family room **NOTES:** Dogs allowed: in bar, in bedrooms, Water, dog biscuits, food, Parking 20

HOLBETON MILDMAY COLOURS INN

PL8 1NA

☎ 01752 830248 📄 01752 830432

e-mail: louise@mildmaycolours.fsnet.co.uk

Dir: *S from Exeter on A38, Yealmpton/Ermington, S past Ugborough & Ermington R onto A379. After 1.5m, turn L, signposted Mildmay Colours/Holbeton.* **Map Ref:** *SX65*

A 17th-century pub, which derives its unusual name from a famous jockey, Lord Anthony Mildmay, whose portrait and silks are hung in the pub. On the racing theme, the pub was used as a location for the film 'International Velvet' with Tatum O'Neal and Oliver Reed. Surrounded by thatched cottages and rolling hills, the inn also has a well-equipped family room. There are simple bar snacks and children's meals, along with daily specials such as nut roast with a sherry cream sauce; Dartmouth smoked chicken salad; local mackerel and salsa sauce; Mildmay Colours beer batter cod; Modbury Stilton & pork sausages, mash & onion gravy; and whole Torbay sole. Try barrel rolling at the August beer festival.

OPEN: 11-3 6-11 (Sun 12-3, 7-10.30)
BAR MEALS: L served all week 12-2 D served all week 6-9
RESTAURANT: L served Sun 12-2 Av 3 course à la carte £12
BREWERY/COMPANY: Free House 🍺: Mildmay Colours Bitter & Mildmay SP, Sharps Eden Ale, Cornish Knocker, Blackawton. **CHILDREN'S FACILITIES:** menu, portions, high-chairs, food/bottle warming, swing, aviary, family room
GARDEN: Nice flower arangements, 10 picnic benches
NOTES: Dogs allowed: in bar, in garden, in bedrooms, Water, Parking 20

HONITON THE OTTER INN 🍷

Weston EX14 3NZ

☎ 01404 42594

Dir: *Just off A30 W of Honiton.* **Map Ref:** *ST10*

On the banks of the idyllic River Otter, this ancient 14th-century inn is set in over two acres of grounds and was once a cider house. Enjoy one of the traditional real ales, try your hand at scrabble, dominoes or cards, or peruse the inn's extensive book collection. A wide-ranging menu caters for all tastes and includes fresh fish, game, steak, vegetarian dishes, bar meals and Sunday lunch.

OPEN: 11-11 (Sun 12-10.30) Rest: Dec 25-26 Closed eve
BAR MEALS: L served all week 12-3 D served all week 6-10 Av main course £5 **RESTAURANT:** L served all week 12-3 D served all week 6-9 Av 3 course à la carte £15
BREWERY/COMPANY: Free House 🍺: Otter Ale, Flowers IPA. 🍷: 7 **CHILDREN'S FACILITIES:** menu, outdoor play area, changing Room, family room **GARDEN:** Food served outside **NOTES:** Dogs allowed: Water, Parking 60

HORNS CROSS   HOOPS COUNTRY INN & HOTEL

'Hoops', nr Clovelly EX39 5DL
☎ 01237 451222 📄 01237 451247
e-mail: reservations@hoopsinn.co.uk
Dir: *On the A39 between Bideford & Clovelly.*
Map Ref: *SS32*

Set in 16 acres of garden and meadow close to the National Trust coastal path, this thatch- roofed, cob-walled 13th-century smugglers' inn combines olde worlde charm with a great range of real ales and hearty modern cooking. Menus use fresh West Country produce from local suppliers. Fresh fish features prominently. Outside, the large patio has a fountain and the landscaped gardens are filled with shrubs and unusual plants.

OPEN: 8-11 (Sun 8.30-10.30) Closed: Dec 25
BAR MEALS: L served all week 12-3 D served all week 6-9.30 Av main course £9.50 **RESTAURANT:** L served all week 12-3 D served all week 7-9.30 Av 3 course à la carte £22 **BREWERY/COMPANY:** Free House **:** Hoops Old Ale, Jollyboat Mainbrace, Cottage, Normans Conquest. **:** 10
CHILDREN'S FACILITIES: menu, licence, games, high-chairs, food/bottle warming, baby changing **GARDEN:** outdoor eating, BBQ **NOTES:** Dogs allowed: water & food, Parking 100 **ROOMS:** 12 en suite s£60 d£90 (★★)

IVYBRIDGE   ANCHOR INN

Lutterburn St, Ugborough PL21 0NG
☎ 01752 892283 📄 01752 897449
e-mail: enquiries@anchorugborough.co.uk
Map Ref: *SX65*

New owner Tim Martin has brought international flavours like ostrich, kangaroo and crocodile to this village free house. Nevertheless, beamed ceilings, open fires and real cask ales maintain the traditional welcome, and the Anchor is ideally located for exploring Dartmoor or the South Devon beaches. Food is served every day with bar menu choices or full à la carte. The pub's trademark dishes are 'Hot Rocks' - steaks cooked at your table with a selection of sauces.

OPEN: 11.30-3 5-11 (Fri-Sat 11.30-11 Sun 12-10.30)
BAR MEALS: L served all week 12-2.30 D served all week 7-9 Av main course £5 **RESTAURANT:** L served all week 12-2 D served all week 7-9 **BREWERY/COMPANY:** Free House **:** Bass, Courage, Directors, local ales.
CHILDREN'S FACILITIES: menu, portions, games, high-chairs, food/bottle warming, Over 14yrs in bar **GARDEN:** Small walled area with two tables **NOTES:** Dogs allowed: in bar, Water & biscuits provided, Parking 15

KINGSBRIDGE   CHURCH HOUSE INN

Churchstow TQ7 3QW
☎ 01548 852237
Dir: *On A379 0.5m W of Kingsbridge.*
Map Ref: *SX74*

Set in some lovely Devon countryside on the way to Salcombe, this historic 15th-century inn was originally the site of a rest house for Cistercian monks during the 13th century. Look out for sea bass, steak and kidney pie, devilled chicken, or smoked salmon. There is also a very popular hot carvery.

OPEN: 11-2 6-11 (Nov-Mar closed Sun eve)
BAR MEALS: L served all week 12-2 D served all week 6.30-9 Av main course £6.75 **RESTAURANT:** L served all week 12-2 D served all week 7-9 Av 3 course à la carte £11 **BREWERY/COMPANY:** Free House **:** Interbrew Bass, Fuller's London Pride, St Austell Dartmoor Best and Guest Ales. **:** 8 **CHILDREN'S FACILITIES:** menu, family room **GARDEN:** Patio with heaters, food served outside **NOTES:** Dogs allowed: Parking 26

THE CRABSHELL INN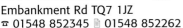

Embankment Rd TQ7 1JZ
☎ 01548 852345 🖹 01548 852262
Map Ref: *SX74*

Located on Kingsbridge estuary with its good sailing, this historic pub was originally a bathing hut for the local barracks. Crab-catching competitions take place along the quay and in the summer there is always plenty of boating activity. Extensive menu with an array of fresh fish detailed on the display boards. Expect oven-baked fillet of salmon and grilled whole lemon sole, as well as the likes of half roast duck, mixed grill, and local pasty. A wide vegetarian choice and a helpful takeaway and picnic menu.

OPEN: 11-11 (Sun 12-10.30) **BAR MEALS:** L served all week 12-2.30 D served all week 6-9.30 Av main course £5.50 **RESTAURANT:** L served all week 12-2.30 D served all week 6-9.30 Av 3 course à la carte £11.75 **BREWERY/COMPANY:** Free House 🍺: Bass Bitter, Crabshell Bitter, Wadworth 6X. **CHILDREN'S FACILITIES:** menu, portions, games, high-chairs, food/bottle warming, outdoor play area, Games room, game machines, pool table, family room **GARDEN:** Patio area with tables & seats **NOTES:** Dogs allowed: in bar, in garden, Water, Parking 40

KINGSTON   THE DOLPHIN INN

TQ7 4QE
☎ 01548 810314 🖹 01548 810314
Map Ref: *SX64*

Built as somewhere to live by stonemasons constructing the neighbouring church, this 16th-century inn retains all the beams,

inglenooks and exposed stonework one would hope to find. A mile from the sea, and only a few to Bigbury Bay where offshore Burgh Island is reachable at high tide only by tractor transport. Homemade dishes making good use of locally caught or grown produce include fisherman's pie, crab bake, liver and onions, bangers and mash, lasagne and steaks.

OPEN: 11-3.00 Jan-Feb, Mon-Fri 12-3 6-11 (Sun 12-3, 7-10.30) **BAR MEALS:** L served all week 12-2 D served all week 6-9.30 Sun 7-9; closed Mon in winter **BREWERY/COMPANY:** 🍺: Ushers, Four Seasons Ale, Courage Best, Sharps Doom Bar. **CHILDREN'S FACILITIES:** menu, portions, games, high-chairs, food/bottle warming, baby changing, outdoor play area, swings and climbing frame, family room **GARDEN:** Small patio area, large garden, seating **NOTES:** No dogs (ex guide dogs), Parking 40

LIFTON   THE ARUNDELL ARMS ★★★ 🌸🌸🌸 ♇

PL16 0AA
☎ 01566 784666 🖹 01566 784494
e-mail: reservations@arundellarms.com
Dir: *2/3m off the A30 dual carriageway, 3m E of Launceston.* ***Map Ref:*** *SX38*

Owned and managed by Anne Voss-Bark for 43 years, this creeper-clad 18th-century

coaching inn is in a delightful village on the edge of Dartmoor. It is a favourite with country sports enthusiasts and has 20 miles of private fishing. The bar menu offers upmarket sandwiches; light dishes such as sweet pepper salad with Parmesan and pesto; and hot dishes like fillets of fresh red mullet in light beer batter. The renowned restaurant features top quality locally-sourced produce.

OPEN: 11.30-3 6-11 **BAR MEALS:** L served all week 12-2.30 D served all week 6-10 Av main course £12.50 **RESTAURANT:** L served all week 12.30-2 D served all week 7.30-9.30 Av 3 course à la carte £40 Av 5 course fixed price £34 **BREWERY/COMPANY:** Free House 🍺: Guest beers. ♇: 9 **CHILDREN'S FACILITIES:** menu, portions, high-chairs, food/bottle warming, baby changing room **GARDEN:** Terraced garden with fountain **NOTES:** Dogs allowed: in bar, in garden, in bedrooms, Parking 70 **ROOMS:** 27 en suite s£52 d£104

LUSTLEIGH   THE CLEAVE ♀

TQ13 9TJ
☎ 01647 277223 📄 01647 277223
e-mail: alisonperring@supanet.com
Dir: *Off A382 between Bovey Tracy and
Moretonhampstead.* ***Map Ref:*** *SX78*

Originally a Devon longhouse, this
15th-century thatched inn, on Dartmoor's
eastern flanks, is a perfect pit-stop for walkers.
It appeared in the 1939 film 'Hound of the
Baskervilles', and was the unofficial waiting-
room for the now long-gone railway station.
The cosy lounge bar has granite walls and a
vast inglenook fireplace; the bigger Victorian
bar has an impressive collection of musical
instruments. The menu includes breast of
chicken stuffed with Stilton and wrapped in
bacon; and a "volcanic" chilli con carne.

OPEN: 11-3 6.30-11 (summer 11-11) Closed: Mon Nov-Feb
BAR MEALS: L served all week 12-2.30 D served all week
6.30-9 Av main course £6.95 **RESTAURANT:** L served all
week 12-2 D served all week 6.30 Av 3 course à la carte £18
BREWERY/COMPANY: Heavitree 🍺: Interbrew Flowers
Original Bitter, Interbrew Bass, Wadworth 6X, Otter Ale. ♀: 12
CHILDREN'S FACILITIES: menu, portions, games, high-chairs,
food/bottle warming, baby changing, outdoor play area, books
crayons & games in family room, family room
GARDEN: Traditional cottage style garden **NOTES:** Dogs
allowed: in bar, in garden, Water, Parking 10

LYDFORD   CASTLE INN & HOTEL ♀

EX20 4BH
☎ 01822 820242 & 820241 📄 01822 820454
Dir: *Off A386 S of Okehampton.*
Map Ref: *SX58*

This pretty, wisteria-clad inn dates from the
16th century, has a castle next door and one

of the nicest beer gardens in the country. No visit
would be complete without a look at the impressive
Lydford Gorge nearby. The interior oozes atmosphere,
with its slate floors, low, lamp-lit beams, decorative
plates and huge ancient fireplace. Fresh fish appears
daily, and main courses include several vegetarian
dishes as well as roasts and a confit of duck. The
shrub-filled garden is a lovely spot to while away time
with a pint, and great for summer dining.

OPEN: 11-11 **BAR MEALS:** L served all week 12-2 D served
all week 6.30-9 Av main course £8 **RESTAURANT:** L served
all week 12-2 D served all week 6.30-9 Av 3 course à la carte
£20 Av 3 course fixed price £17 **BREWERY/COMPANY:**
Heavitree 🍺: Fullers London Pride, 6X, Otter Ale. ♀: 13
CHILDREN'S FACILITIES: menu, outdoor play area, garden
with pets corner **GARDEN:** Food served outside.
NOTES: Dogs allowed: in bar, patio & bedrooms, Parking 10

MOLLAND   THE LONDON INN

EX36 3NG
☎ 01769 550269
Map Ref: *SS82*

Just below Exmoor lies peaceful Molland, and
to find its church is to find this 15th-century
inn. Historic features abound, but try and
picture today's spacious dining room as the
original inn, and the bar as the brewhouse.
Every so often the frequently-changing menu
will feature guinea fowl with red wine sauce
and black cherries, grilled salmon with
parsley butter, and tarragon chicken breast
with wine sauce and grapes. Bar snacks
lunchtime and evenings. No credit cards,
though.

OPEN: 11.30-11 (Sun 12-3, 7-10.30)
BAR MEALS: L served all week 12-2 D served all week 7-9
Av main course £6.50 **RESTAURANT:** L served all week
D served all week Av 3 course à la carte £12
BREWERY/COMPANY: Free House 🍺: Exmoor Ale, Cotleigh
Tawny Bitter. **CHILDREN'S FACILITIES:** menu, portions,
games, high-chairs, food/bottle warming, box of toys
in family room **NOTES:** Dogs allowed: in bar, in garden,
in bedrooms, Water, Parking 12, No credit cards

NEWTON ST CYRES — THE BEER ENGINE

EX5 5AX
☎ 01392 851282 📠 01392 851876
e-mail: enquiries@thebeerengine.co.uk
Dir: From Exeter take A377 towards Crediton, pub is opp train station in Newton St Cyres.
Map Ref: SX89

A pretty, whitewashed free house, where the proprietors have been brewing their own beer for 20 years, making it the longest established Devon brewery. As for food, dishes range from haddock in the landlord's own Brewery Batter (made with wort) through to African spicy lamb, home-made steak pies, monkfish in whisky sauce, and plenty of good vegetarian options. Sunday lunches draw people from far and wide.

OPEN: 11-11 (Sun 12-10.30) **BAR MEALS:** L served all week 12-2 D served all week 6.30-9 (Sun 12-9)
RESTAURANT: L served all week 12-2 D served all week 6.30-9.30 (Sun 12-2, 6.30-9) Av 3 course à la carte £14
BREWERY/COMPANY: Free House 🍺: Beer Engine Ales: Piston Bitter, Rail Ale, Sleeper Heavy.
CHILDREN'S FACILITIES: portions, games, high-chairs, food/bottle warming **GARDEN:** Terraced with paved area, flowers **NOTES:** Dogs allowed: in bar, Parking 30

OTTERY ST MARY — THE TALATON INN

Talaton EX5 2RQ
☎ 01404 822214 📠 01404 822214
Map Ref: SY19

Timber-framed, well-maintained 16th-century inn, run by a brother and sister partnership. A strong seafood emphasis means that the menu may feature poached salmon hollandaise, cod and chips, seafood platter, or scampi. Blackboard specials change regularly, and may include chicken Wellington or fillet steak Rossini, for example. Good selection of real ales and malts.

OPEN: 12-3 7-11 **BAR MEALS:** L served all week 12-2 D served Tue-Sat 7-9.15 Sun no food eve Av main course £7 **RESTAURANT:** L served all week 12-2.15 D served Tue-Sat 7-9.15 Sun no food eve
BREWERY/COMPANY: Free House 🍺: Otter, Fuller's London Pride, O'Hanlon's, Badger Tanglefoot.
CHILDREN'S FACILITIES: menu, portions, high-chairs, food/bottle warming, Over 14's **GARDEN:** Small courtyard with 4 benches **NOTES:** Dogs allowed: in bar only, Parking 30

PETER TAVY — THE PETER TAVY INN ♀

PL19 9NN
☎ 01822 810348 📠 01822 810835
e-mail: Peter.tavy@virgin.net
Dir: Off A386 NE of Tavistock. Map Ref: SX57

A 15th-century inn exemplifying the best of the English tradition, surrounded by lovely countryside on the edge of Dartmoor. The

building was renovated and extended in 1988, though its character remains intact with slate floors, low beams and large fireplaces filled with blazing logs in cold weather. In summer the beautiful garden with its moorland views is a popular spot to sit. The pub is renowned for its good food and well-kept real ales; home-made dishes prepared from fresh local produce are offered from a regularly changing blackboard menu.

OPEN: 12-2.30 6-11 (Sun Eve 6.30-10.30) Closed: 25 Dec
BAR MEALS: L served all week 12-2 D served all week 6.30-9 Av main course £10 **RESTAURANT:** L served all week 12-2 D served all week 6.30-9 Av 3 course à la carte £19 **BREWERY/COMPANY:** Free House 🍺: Princetown Jail Ale, Summerskills Tamar, Tavy Tipple, Blackawton Brewery.
♀: 8 **CHILDREN'S FACILITIES:** menu, portions, licence, games, high-chairs, food/bottle warming, family room
GARDEN: Small garden with views of Dartmoor
NOTES: Dogs allowed: in bar, Water, Parking 40

RATTERY   CHURCH HOUSE INN

TQ10 9LD
☎ 01364 642220 🗎 01364 642220
e-mail: ray12@onetel.net.uk
Map Ref: SX76

Dating from 1028, Devon's oldest inn is also one of the oldest in the UK. Large open fireplaces, sturdy oak beams and loads of nooks and crannies. Traditional English food includes snacks, light meals, sandwiches, lasagne, chicken and cranberry curry, and rump steak. Moussaka features as a special, as do duck, guinea fowl, venison and rabbit. Plaice, sea bass, brill, halibut, lemon and Dover sole are usually available. Always at least three real ales, including local St Austell Dartmoor Best.

OPEN: 11-3 6-11 (Winter 11-2.30, 6.30-10.30)
BAR MEALS: L served all week 12-2 D served all week 7-9
RESTAURANT: L served all week 12-2 D served all week 7-9
BREWERY/COMPANY: Free House ◖: St Austell Dartmoor Best, Greene King Abbot Ale, Morland Speckled Hen, Otter Ale. ♀: 8 **CHILDREN'S FACILITIES:** menu, portions, licence, high-chairs, food/bottle warming **GARDEN:** Large lawn, seating, benches **NOTES:** Dogs allowed: in bar, Water, Parking 30

ROCKBEARE   JACK IN THE GREEN INN

London Rd EX5 2EE
☎ 01404 822240 🗎 01404 823445
e-mail: info@jackinthegreen.uk.com
Dir: From M5 take old A30 towards Honiton, signed Rockbeare. **Map Ref:** SY09

Named after the Green Man, associated with fertility in ancient pagan tradition, the pub is set in four acres of grounds and gardens and is a popular dining venue, whether you're stopping by for a bar snack, or a fuller meal in the restaurant, the quality is evident in everything produced. Consistency, attention to detail and use of fresh local produce is central to the philosophy of the kitchen. In summer you can sit outside and enjoy the view.

OPEN: 11-2.30 6-11 (Sun 12-10.30) Closed: Dec 25 - Jan 2 inclusive **BAR MEALS:** L served all week 11-2 D served all week 6-9.30 **RESTAURANT:** L served all week 11-2 D served all week 6-9.30 **BREWERY/COMPANY:** Free House ◖: Cotleigh Tawny Ale, Thomas Hardy Hardy Country, Otter Ale, Royal Oak. ♀: 12 **CHILDREN'S FACILITIES:** menu, portions, food/bottle warming, baby changing, family room **GARDEN:** Benches **NOTES:** in bar, No dogs (ex guide dogs), Parking 120

SIDMOUTH   THE BLUE BALL

Stevens Cross, Sidford EX10 9QL
☎ 01395 514062 🗎 01395 514062
e-mail: rogernewton@blueballinn.net
Map Ref: SY18

Run by the same family for 90 years, this thatched-roofed pub dates back to the late 14th century and is built of cob and flint. Converted from its farmhouse origins, the bar occupies the old dairy, with beams and log fires inside and a garden with a terrace and playhouse outside. Food centres round fresh fish and other local produce, and options range from ploughman's and sandwiches to steak and kidney pudding and local sausages.

OPEN: 11-11 Closed: 25 Dec eve **BAR MEALS:** L served all week 12-2 D served all week 6-9.30
BREWERY/COMPANY: Pubmaster ◖: Interbrew Bass & Flowers IPA, Otter Bitter, Greene King Old Speckled Hen, Guest ale each week. ♀: 10
CHILDREN'S FACILITIES: menu, outdoor play area, Wendy house, slide, family room **GARDEN:** Large, colourful gardens, quiet areas **NOTES:** Dogs allowed: in bar, in garden, Water, Parking 100

SLAPTON   THE TOWER INN

Church Rd TQ7 2PN
☎ 01548 580216 🖶 01548 580140
e-mail: towerinn@slapton.org
Dir: *Off A379 south of Dartmouth, turn L at Slapton Sands.* **Map Ref:** *SX84*

A charming 14th-century inn tucked away in a delightful historic village. It is in the heart of the South Hams, and is ideally placed for enjoying what is generally regarded as some of the finest coastline in the British Isles. Today's interior is a fascinating series of low-ceilinged interconnecting rooms with stone walls, beams, pillars and pews. Two large stone fireplaces provide comfort and warmth on cooler days.

OPEN: 12-3 6-11 (Sun 7-10.30) Closed: 25 Dec **BAR MEALS:** L served all week 12-2.30 D served all week 6-9.30 **RESTAURANT:** L served all week 12-2.30 D served all week 7-9.30 Av 3 course à la carte £25 **BREWERY/COMPANY:** Free House 🍺: Adnams Southwold, Badger Tanglefoot, St Austell, Tower. 🍷: 8 **CHILDREN'S FACILITIES:** menu, portions, games, high-chairs, food/bottle warming, family room **GARDEN:** Beautiful walled garden **NOTES:** Dogs allowed: in bar, Water, biscuits, Parking 6

SOUTH POOL   MILLBROOK INN 🍷

TQ7 2RW
☎ 01548 531581 🖶 01548 531868
Dir: *Take A379 from Kingsbridge to Frogmore then E.* **Map Ref:** *SX74*

You can arrive here by boat an hour either side of high tide, or why not come by foot? Take the ferry to East Portlemouth, cross over the stepping stones at Waterhead and follow the quiet country lane into South Pool to arrive at this quaint 16th-century village pub. Inside, it is small, cosy and unspoilt, with open fires, fresh flowers, cushioned wheelback chairs, and original beams adorned with old banknotes and clay pipes. Wholesome bar food includes fresh crab sandwiches, fisherman's pie, scallop and bacon salad, and monkfish casserole;

alternatively try Devon rabbit pie with a suet crust; or a local sirloin steak au poivre. Peaceful sunny rear terrace overlooking a stream with ducks.

OPEN: 12-3 (open all day Aug) 6-11 (Sun 12-3, 6-10.30) **BAR MEALS:** L served all week 12-2 D served all week 7-9 Av main course £8 **BREWERY/COMPANY:** Free House 🍺: Bass, Fuller's London Pride, Sharps Doombar, Otter Ale. 🍷: 12 **CHILDREN'S FACILITIES:** menu, high-chairs, food/bottle warming, family room **NOTES:** Dogs allowed: in bar, Water bowls

SPREYTON   THE TOM COBLEY TAVERN

EX17 5AL
☎ 01647 231314
Dir: *From Merrymeet roundabout take A3124 N. Turn R off the Post Inn, the 1st R again over bridge.* **Map Ref:** *SX69*

From this pub one day in 1802 a certain

Thomas Cobley and his companions set forth for Widecombe Fair, recorded and remembered in the famous song. Today, this traditional village local offers a good selection of bar snacks, lighter fare and home-made main meals, including pies, salads, duck and fish dishes, as well as a good vegetarian selection. The garden is in a pretty setting.

OPEN: 12-2 6-11 (Mon open Summer, BHS) **BAR MEALS:** L served Tue-Sun 12-2 D served Tue-Sun 7-9 Av main course £8 **RESTAURANT:** L served Sun 12-2 D served Wed-Sat 7-8.45 **BREWERY/COMPANY:** Free House 🍺: Cotleigh Tawny Ale, Interbrew Bass, Tom Lobely Bitter, Doom Bar Tribute. **CHILDREN'S FACILITIES:** menu, portions, games, high-chairs, food/bottle warming, baby changing **GARDEN:** Wooden seated area, approx 8 benches **NOTES:** No dogs (ex guide dogs), Parking 8 **ROOMS:** 4 bedrooms 1 family room s£22.50 d£22.50 (♦♦♦)

STOCKLAND KINGS ARMS ◆◆◆◆

EX14 9BS
☎ 01404 881361 🖹 01404 881732
e-mail: info@kingsarms.net
Map Ref: *ST20*

By the Great West Way, at the heart of the Blackdown Hills, stands this long, Grade II, thatched and whitewashed 16th-century inn. It boasts an impressive flag-stoned walkway entrance, a medieval oak screen and an original bread oven, as well as an old grey-painted phone box. The atmospheric Farmers bar is a lively and popular meeting place, while the Cotley restaurant bar offers a wide range of blackboard specials: fish choices like pasta marinara, king prawn Madras, Cajun Scotch salmon fillet, along with meaty pork tenderloin and wild mushroom risotto, breast of Quantock duck, ostrich fillet, and Cotley rack of lamb. Mouthwatering desserts include lemon treacle sponge pudding, and blueberry and raspberry cheesecake. The British and classic cooking is complemented by well-kept real ales and an outstanding collection of cheeses.

OPEN: 12-3 6.30-11.30 Closed: Dec 25
BAR MEALS: L served Mon-Sat 12-2 Av main course £10.50 **RESTAURANT:** L served all week 12-2 D served all week 6.30-9 **BREWERY/COMPANY:** Free House ◀: Otter Ale, Exmoor Ale, Scottish Courage John Smiths, O'Hanlon's Yellowhammer. ⚲: 21
CHILDREN'S FACILITIES: menu, portions, high-chairs, food/bottle warming **GARDEN:** Part lawn part patio, seating for 30 **NOTES:** Dogs allowed: in bar, in garden, in bedrooms, Parking 45 **ROOMS:** 3 en suite 1 family room s£40 d£60

STOKE FLEMING THE GREEN DRAGON INN

Church Rd TQ6 0PX
☎ 01803 770238 🖹 01803 770238
e-mail: pcrowther@btconnect.com
Dir: *Telephone for directions.* **Map Ref:** *SX84*

A smugglers tunnel is said to connect this 12th-century pub to Blackpool Sands. Certainly the landlord is drawn to the sea: he's famous for his voyages across the Atlantic. Inside, you'll find a warm atmosphere and deceptively simple cooking. Lunchtime snacks include fresh baguettes and locally made beefburgers, whilst dinner menus allow you to order starters as light bites (perhaps prawn platter with aïoli and bread or Dartmouth smoked mackerel). Main courses include Italian meatloaf, venison pie and lamb shanks.

OPEN: 11-3 5.30-11 **BAR MEALS:** L served Mon-Sun 12-2.30 D served Mon-Sun 6.30-9 Av main course £6.50 **RESTAURANT:** L served Mon-Sun 12-2.30 D served Mon-Sun 6.30-9 Av 3 course à la carte £15
BREWERY/COMPANY: Heavitree ◀: Otter, Flowers IPA, Bass 6x. ⚲: 9 **CHILDREN'S FACILITIES:** menu, portions, games, high-chairs, food/bottle warming, outdoor play area, garden, climbing frame, swing **GARDEN:** Small at rear; covered patio at front **NOTES:** Dogs allowed: in bar, in garden, Parking 6, No credit cards

---

TOPSHAM BRIDGE INN

Bridge Hill EX3 0QQ
☎ 01392 873862 🖹 01392 877497
e-mail: bridge@cheffers.co.uk
Dir: *4 miles from Exeter city centre.*
Map Ref: *SX98*

Four generation of the same family have run this listed 16th-century inn since 1897, and under their management it has remained old-fashioned in the best sense of the word. It sits peacefully beside the River Clyst, where benches are strategically placed to watch the heron, egret and Canada geese. Inside are quirky little rooms filled with atmosphere and interesting local characters, and usually a minimum of eight real ales on tap to help oil the conversation (Triple FFF's I Can't Remember, O'Hanlon's Yellowhammer and Blackawton's Dragonheart are just a few of these). Food is limited to sandwiches (smoked chicken, Stilton cheese), ploughmans, and hot meat and potato pasties, all made freshly to order, but this is mainly a drinker's pub, and the selection of beers changes daily.

OPEN: 12-2 6-10.30 (Sun 7-10.30 Sat 6-11)
BAR MEALS: L served all week 12-1.45
BREWERY/COMPANY: Free House ◀: Branscombe Vale-Branoc, Adnams Broadside, Exe Valley, O'Hanlons.
CHILDREN'S FACILITIES: food/bottle warming
GARDEN: Benches overlooking River Clyst **NOTES:** Dogs allowed: in bar, in garden, Water, Parking 20, No credit cards

TORCROSS   START BAY INN

TQ7 2TQ
☎ 01548 580553 🖷 01548 580941
e-mail: cstubbs@freeuk.com
Dir: *between Dartmouth & Kingsbridge on the
A379.* **Map Ref:** *SX84*

For some great Devonshire fish served in
glorious surroundings, head for this
14th-century thatched pub situated between
Slapton Ley and the panoramic sweep of
Start Bay in the beautiful South Hams. The
landlord dives for plaice, scallops and skate,
and hooks sea bass by rod and line, while
the rest of the catch is freshly delivered from
a local trawler. Arrive soon after opening,
especially in the summer, to sample cod,
haddock and plaice deeply fried in a light
batter, lemon sole, giant prawns, and crab
and seafood platters, along with various steaks,
freshly-roasted chicken, spinach and Mascarpone
lasagne, and plenty of sandwiches, ploughman's
lunches, and other snacks. Treacle sponge pudding,
spotted Dick, and locally made ice cream go down well
whatever the season. The bar and dining areas are
simply furnished and decorated with photographs of
the storm-ravaged pub.

OPEN: 11.30-2.30 6-11 (Summer 11.30-11)
BAR MEALS: L served all week 11.30-2 D served all week
6-10 Sun 12-2.15 Av main course £5
BREWERY/COMPANY: Heavitree 🍺: Interbrew Flowers
Original & Bass, Otter Ale. 🍷: 8
CHILDREN'S FACILITIES: menu, games, high-chairs,
food/bottle warming, baby changing, family room
GARDEN: Patio area overlooks Slapton Sands **NOTES:** Dogs
allowed: On leads, Water, Parking 18

TOTNES   DURANT ARMS ◆◆◆◆

Ashprington TQ9 7UP
☎ 01803 732240
e-mail: info@thedurantarms.com
Dir: *Leave A38 at Totnes Jct, proceed to
Dartington & Totnes, at 1st set of traffic lights R
for Knightsbridge on A381, after 1m L for
Ashprington.* **Map Ref:** *SX86*

Ashprington is a beautiful South Hams village with
lovely views over the Dart valley. Here you will find the
18th-century Durant Arms, ideally placed for touring
this popular area. The award-winning inn is renowned
for its cuisine: all food is freshly cooked to order and
based on a wide variety of locally-sourced meat, fish
and vegetables. A small terrace garden makes a
pleasant alternative to the bars in warm weather.

OPEN: 11.30-2.30 (Sun 12-2.30, 7-10.30) 6.30-11
BAR MEALS: L served all week 12-2.30 D served all week
7-9.15 Av main course £6.95 **RESTAURANT:** L served all
week 12-2.30 D served all week 7-9.15 Av 3 course à la carte
£13 **BREWERY/COMPANY:** Free House 🍺: Dartmoor Bitter,
Tetley, Tribute. 🍷: 8 **CHILDREN'S FACILITIES:** portions,
high-chairs, food/bottle warming, family room **GARDEN:**
Terraced garden with rosewood furniture **NOTES:** Parking 8
ROOMS: 7 en suite s£40 d£35 no children overnight

THE STEAM PACKET INN ◆◆◆◆

St Peter's Quay TQ9 5EW
☎ 01803 863880 🖷 01803 862754
e-mail: steampacket@bucaneer.co.uk
Dir: *Leave A38 at Totnes Junct, proceed to
Dartington & Totnes. Straight across lights & rdbt
following signs for town centre with river on L,
follow The Plains in town centre for 100yds. Pub
on river.* **Map Ref:** *SX86*

The sign for this riverside inn depicts the
Amelia, a steam packet ship that regularly
called here with passengers, parcels and mail
before the days of modern road and rail
transport. The inn has great river views,
particularly from the restaurant. One menu is
served throughout, including fresh fish
according to market availability. Typical dishes
are steaks, oven-roasted cod with goats'
cheese, trio of sausages (also vegetarian), and green
Thai vegetable curry.

OPEN: 11-11 (Sun 12-10.30) **BAR MEALS:** L served all
week 12-2.30 D served all week 6.30-9.30 Av main
course £13 **RESTAURANT:** L served all week 12-2.30
D served all week 7-9.30 Av 3 course à la carte £20
BREWERY/COMPANY: Free House 🍺: Scottish Courage
Directors, Courage Best, Interbrew Bass & Two Real Ales.
CHILDREN'S FACILITIES: menu, portions, food/bottle
warming, board games, high chairs **GARDEN:** Riverside quay,
lights, raised terrace **NOTES:** Dogs allowed: in bar, in garden,
Water, small dogs in bedroom, Parking 16 **ROOMS:** 4 en suite
1 family room s£40 d£65

TRUSHAM   CRIDFORD INN

TQ13 0NR
☎ 01626 853694 📠 01626 853694
e-mail: cridford@eclipse.co.uk
Map Ref: SX88

An archetypal thatched country pub, the
Cridford Inn has been a nunnery and a farm
before finding its present vocation. The
building dates from 825 but was remodelled
in 1081. Features of the atmospheric interior
are rough stone walls, slate floors, and what
is believed to be the oldest domestic window
in Britain. The landlady is a culinary expert
from Kuala Lumpur, so Malaysian specialities
such as beef Rendang are offered alongside
traditional pub fare.

OPEN: 12-3 7-11 Closed: 8 Jan- 13 Feb
BAR MEALS: L served all week 12-2.30 D served all week
7-9.30 Av main course £6.50 **RESTAURANT:** D served all
week 7-9.30 **BREWERY/COMPANY:** Free House
🍺: Sharpes Own, Badger Best, Trusham Ale, Tinners.
CHILDREN'S FACILITIES: menu, garden area, family room
NOTES: Dogs allowed: in bar, in garden, in bedrooms,
Parking 35

TUCKENHAY   THE MALTSTERS ARMS 🐑 ⚲

TQ9 7EQ
☎ 01803 732350 📠 01803 732823
e-mail: pub@tuckenhay.demon.co.uk
Map Ref: SX85

In secluded, wooded Bow Creek off the River
Dart, this splendid 18th-century pub is
accessible only through high-banked Devon
lanes, or by boat for about three hours either
side of high tide. It is noted for real charcoal
barbeques in the summer, live music events
on the quayside, and a daily changing menu
of good local produce imaginatively cooked.
This may feature seafood soup with mussels
and clams; wild Dart salmon in a fennel
crust; and pot roasted local mallard. There is
a good selection of Devonshire real ales.

OPEN: 11-11 (Sun 12-10.30) **BAR MEALS:** L served all
week 12-2.30 D served all week 7-9.30 Av main course £10
RESTAURANT: L served all week 12-2.30 D served all week
7-9.30 Av 3 course à la carte £18
BREWERY/COMPANY: Free House 🍺: Princetown
Dartmoor IPA, Young's Special, Teignworthy Maltsters Ale,
Blackawton Special. ⚲: 20 **CHILDREN'S FACILITIES:** menu,
portions, high-chairs, food/bottle warming, comics, games,
family room **GARDEN:** Riverside paved quay with seating &
tables **NOTES:** Dogs allowed: in bar, in garden, in bedrooms,
dog bowl, biscuits, lots of pals, Parking 50

TYTHERLEIGH   TYTHERLEIGH ARMS HOTEL ⚲

EX13 7BE
☎ 01460 220400 & 220214 📠 01460 220406
e-mail: TytherleighArms@aol.com
Map Ref: ST30

Beamed ceilings and huge roaring fires are
notable features of this family-run,
17th-century former coaching inn. It is a
food-led establishment, situated on the
Devon, Somerset and Dorset borders. Fresh
home-cooked dishes, using local ingredients,
include lamb shank with honey and cider,
steaks and fresh seafood such as West
Country cod and Lyme Bay scallops.
Comprehensive bar snack menu also
available.

OPEN: 11-2.30 6.30-11 **BAR MEALS:** L served all week
12-2.30 D served all week 6.30-9 Av main course £8.95
RESTAURANT: L served all week 12-2.30 D served all week
6.30-9 Av 3 course à la carte £16.95
BREWERY/COMPANY: Free House 🍺: Butcombe Bitter,
Exmoor Fox, Murphy's, Boddingtons.
CHILDREN'S FACILITIES: menu, portions, licence,
high-chairs, food/bottle warming **GARDEN:** Courtyard, very
pretty **NOTES:** Parking 60

WIDECOMBE IN THE MOOR   THE OLD INN

TQ13 7TA
☎ 01364 621207 📠 01364 621407
e-mail: oldinn.wid@virgin.net
Dir: *Telephone for directions.* **Map Ref:** *SX77*

Dating from the 15th century, the Old Inn was partly ruined by fire but rebuilt around the original fireplaces. Two main bars and no fewer than five eating areas offer plenty of scope for visitors to enjoy the home-cooked food. From several menus plus blackboard specials, options range from filled Widecombe granary sticks through salads and steaks to lamb with gin sauce, organic fillet steak, paella and chicken breast filled with soft cheese with a tomato and basil sauce.

OPEN: 11-3 7-11 (Summer 6.30-11) Closed: 25 Dec
BAR MEALS: L served all week 11-2 D served all week 7-10 Av main course £7 **RESTAURANT:** L served all week 11-2 D served all week 7-10 Av 3 course à la carte £15.50
BREWERY/COMPANY: Free House 🍺: Interbrew Flowers IPA & Boddingtons. **CHILDREN'S FACILITIES:** menu, portions, high-chairs, food/bottle warming, baby changing, family room **GARDEN:** Streams, Ponds, Gazebos
NOTES: Dogs allowed: in bar, in garden, Water, Parking 55

WINKLEIGH   THE KINGS ARMS

Fore St EX19 8HQ
☎ 01837 83384
Map Ref: *SS60*

An ancient thatched country inn in Winkleigh's central square. Wood-burning stoves keep the beamed bar and dining rooms warm in chilly weather, and wooden settles and flagstones add to the traditional atmosphere. Great real ales are supplemented by local draught ciders. Darts and dominoes encouraged, no juke box or fruit machines. Food served all day using freshly prepared local produce as available: Lucy's fish pie, steak and kidney parcel, liver and bacon, vegetarian stir-fry, and sticky toffee pudding are some examples. Booking recommended at weekends.

OPEN: 11-11 (Sun 12-10.30) **BAR MEALS:** L served all week 11-9.30 D served all week Sun 12-9 Av main course £8.50 **RESTAURANT:** L served all week 11-9.30 D served all week (Sun 12-9)
BREWERY/COMPANY: Enterprise Inns 🍺: Butcombe Bitter, Flowers IPA, Skinners Cornish Knocker. 🍷: 8
CHILDREN'S FACILITIES: menu, portions, licence, games, high-chairs, food/bottle warming, baby changing
GARDEN: Small courtyard to side of property **NOTES:** Dogs allowed: in bar

ABBOTSBURY   ILCHESTER ARMS

9 Market St DT3 4JR
☎ 01305 871243 📠 01305 871225
Map Ref: *SY58*

Rambling 16th-century coaching inn set in the heart of one of Dorset's most picturesque villages. Abbotsbury is home to many crafts including woodwork and pottery. A good area for walkers, and handy for the Tropical Gardens and Swannery.

OPEN: 11-11 Sun 12-10.30 Rest: 25 Dec 12-3, 7-10.30
BAR MEALS: L served all week 12-2 D served all week 7-9 Sun 12-2.30/3 Av main course £7 **RESTAURANT:** L served all week 12-2.30 D served all week 7-9.30 Sun 12-2.30, 7-9 Av 3 course à la carte £18.50 🍺: Gales HSB, Badger Tanglefoot, Courage Best, Tribute.
CHILDREN'S FACILITIES: menu, portions, licence, games, high-chairs, food/bottle warming **NOTES:** Dogs allowed: in bar, Parking 50

BOURTON   THE WHITE LION INN ♀

High St SP8 5AT
☎ 01747 840866 📠 01747 841529
e-mail:
whitelioninn@bourtondorset.fsnet.co.uk
Dir: Off A303, opposite B3092 to Gillingham.
Map Ref: ST73

This stone-built village inn should certainly
feature in any list of typical English pubs.
Here you'll find old beams and flagstones, log
fires and real ales, as well as home-cooked
English food. Hosts Mike and Scarlett Senior
share decades of catering experience - Mike
has clocked up more than 40 years of
innkeeping, while Scarlett's family has been
in the trade for around 100 years. The single
menu allows diners to choose between
eating in one of the bars, or in the

non-smoking restaurant. Lunchtime brings choices like
rare roast beef and horseradish on farmhouse bread;
and pork, ham and Stilton pie with pease pudding
mash. The main menu includes roasted tomato,
Dolcelatte and chive tart; braised lamb shank in red
wine sauce; and Herefordshire beef and Guinness pie.

OPEN: 12-3 6-11 (Sun 12-10.30) Closed: 26 Dec
BAR MEALS: L served all week 12-2 D served all week 7-9
Av main course £9 **RESTAURANT:** L served all week 12-2
D served all week 7-9 (Sun 12-2.30)
BREWERY/COMPANY: 🍺: Fullers London Pride, Youngs,
Bitter & Guest Beer. ♀: 8 **CHILDREN'S FACILITIES:** menu,
portions, high-chairs, food/bottle warming **GARDEN:** Grassed
with trees, patio area **NOTES:** Dogs allowed: in bar,
in garden, Water, Parking 30

BRIDPORT   SHAVE CROSS INN 🐑 ♀

Shave Cross, Marshwood Vale DT6 6HW
☎ 01308 868358 📠 01308 867064
e-mail: roy.warburton@virgin.net
*Dir: From Bridport take B3162 2m turn L
signed 'Broadoak/Shave Cross' then
Marshwood. Map Ref: SY49*

With its thatched roof and cob and flint walls, this
friendly, family-run inn is every inch the typical Dorset
pub. The restaurant has wonderful old beams and the
inn is home to the oldest thatched skittle alley in the
country. Other ancient traditions including ashen faggot
burning on Twelfth Night are strongly maintained.

OPEN: 10.30-3 5-11 (all day Sat-Sun in Summer, BHs) Rest:
25 Dec Closed eve **BAR MEALS:** L served Tue-Sun 12-3
D served Tue-Sun 5-9.30 Sun 12-3, 6-8
RESTAURANT: L served Tue-Sun 12-3 D served Tue-Sat 7-9.30
Sun 6-8 (summer) **BREWERY/COMPANY:** Free House
🍺: Local guest beers, Branoc (Branscombe Valley), Quay
Brewery Weymouth. **CHILDREN'S FACILITIES:** menu,
portions, licence, games, high-chairs, food/bottle warming,
outdoor play area **GARDEN:** Cottage garden **NOTES:** Dogs
allowed: in bar, in garden, on leads, water available, not in
restaurant, Parking 30

BUCKLAND NEWTON   GAGGLE OF GEESE ♀

DT2 7BS
☎ 01300 345249
e-mail:
gaggle@bucklandnewton.freeserve.co.uk
Dir: On B3143 N of Dorchester.
Map Ref: ST60

In the heart of Hardy's Wessex, this was the
Royal Oak until a former landlord started
keeping geese. From just a simple flock has
evolved a twice-yearly goose auction that
featured in Hugh Fearnley-Whittingstall's
televised rural chronicle, Tales from
Riverside Cottage. Menus include grilled
rump and gammon steaks, roast chicken,
breaded wholetail scampi, langoustines,
macaroni cheese, chicken tikka masala,
lamb rogan josh, pasta, salads and pizza, as

well as children's dishes, ploughman's and
sandwiches.

OPEN: 12-2.30 6.30-11 **BAR MEALS:** L served all week
12-2 D served all week 7-10 Av main course £6.95
RESTAURANT: L served all week 12-2 D served all week
7-10 **BREWERY/COMPANY:** Free House 🍺: Badger Dorset
Best, Ringwood Best & Fortyniner, Butcombe.
CHILDREN'S FACILITIES: menu, portions, food/bottle
warming, outdoor play area **GARDEN:** Pub on 5 acres. Pond
& stream **NOTES:** Dogs allowed: in bar, in garden, Water,
Parking 30

BURTON BRADSTOCK THE ANCHOR INN

High St DT6 4QF
☎ 01308 897228 ▯ 01308 897228
e-mail: sleepingsat@hotmail.com
Dir: *2m SE of Bridport on B3157 in the centre
of the village of Burton Bradstock.*
Map Ref: *SY48*

Tenants would come to this 300-year-old
coaching inn to pay their rent in the days
when the whole village belonged to one
family. In keeping with its name, the Anchor
is full of marine memorabilia; fishing nets are
draped across the ceilings, and old fishing
tools and shellfish art created by the chef can
be seen on the walls. Seafood is the house
speciality with sometimes as many as twenty
different main fish courses on the menu,
especially fresh local scallops, crab and
lobster. You can choose between lobster thermidor or
armoricaine, grilled plaice with lobster and prawn
sauce, or stuffed crab. Meat eaters are not ignored with
platters like Barbary duck, beef Stroganoff, and
peppered pork fillet among others. Several real ales are
on sale, and over 50 different Scottish whiskies.

OPEN: 11-11 Sun 12-10.30 **BAR MEALS:** L served all week
12-2 D served all week 6.30-9 Av main course £14.50
RESTAURANT: L served all week 12-2 D served all week
6.30-9 Av 3 course à la carte £25 **BREWERY/COMPANY:**
🍺: Ushers Best, Flowers IPA, Hobgoblin, Winter Storm. 🍷: 8
CHILDREN'S FACILITIES: menu, portions, licence,
high-chairs, food/bottle warming, outdoor play area, family
room **GARDEN:** Patio **NOTES:** Dogs allowed: in bar, Water,
Parking 24

CATTISTOCK FOX & HOUNDS INN ◆◆◆◆

Duck St DT2 0JH
☎ 01300 320444 ▯ 01300 320444
e-mail: info@foxandhoundsinn.com
Map Ref: *SY59*

An attractive 16th-century inn set in the
beautiful village of Cattistock. Original features
include bare beams, open fires and huge inglenooks,
one with an original bread oven. It's a fascinating
building, full of curiosities such as the 'hidden
cupboard', reached by a staircase that winds around the
chimney in one of the loft areas. Meals are traditional
and home made: cottage pie, pork in cider and apple
sauce, lamb shank on mash, and haddock mornay.

OPEN: 12-2.30 6.30-11 **BAR MEALS:** L served Tue-Sun
12-2 D served Tue-Sat 7-9 **RESTAURANT:** L served Tue-Sun
12-2 D served Tue-Sat 7-9 **BREWERY/COMPANY:** Palmers
Brewery 🍺: Palmers IPA, Copper Ale, Palmers 200, Tally Ho
Ale. **CHILDREN'S FACILITIES:** portions, high-chairs,
food/bottle warming **GARDEN:** Large and well maintained
NOTES: Dogs allowed: in bar, in garden, in bedrooms, Water
and biscuits, Parking 12 **ROOMS:** 3 bedrooms 2 en suite
s£40 d£60

CERNE ABBAS THE ROYAL OAK 🍷

23 Long St DT2 7JG
☎ 01300 341797 ▯ 01300 341797
e-mail: royaloak@cerneabbas.fsnet.co.uk
Dir: *M5/A37, follow A37 to A352 signposted
Cerne Abbas, midway between Sherborne &
Dorchester. Pub in centre of village.*
Map Ref: *ST60*

Thatched, creeper-clad, 16th-century inn, formerly a
coaching inn and blacksmiths, situated in a picturesque
village below the Dorset Downs. Home-cooked food is
served in the cosy, traditional interior. An imaginative
menu includes belly pork with hoi sin apple and
mushroom sauce. Attractive courtyard garden.

OPEN: 11.30-3 Summer close 3.30pm 6-11 Closed:
Dec 25 **BAR MEALS:** L served all week 12-2 D served all
week 7-9.30 Summer 2.30, Sun 9 Av main course £9
RESTAURANT: L served all week 12-2-2.30 D served all
week 7-9.30 Sun last orders 9pm Av 3 course à la carte £18
BREWERY/COMPANY: Free House 🍺: St Austell Brewery,
Tribute, Tinners, Butcombe. 🍷: 13 **CHILDREN'S FACILITIES:**
menu, portions, games, food/bottle warming, baby changing,
Books & games provided before meals. **GARDEN:** attractive
walled garden, decking, furniture **NOTES:** Dogs allowed:
in bar, Water bowl in garden

CHRISTCHURCH   THE SHIP IN DISTRESS

66 Stanpit BH23 3NA
☎ 01202 485123
e-mail: sally@shipindistress.com
Map Ref: SZ19

A 300-year-old smugglers' pub close to Mudeford Quay, specialising in seafood. The

name derives from a smuggling vessel rescued by regulars from a nearby creek where it had run aground. Legend says that the pub's owner, Mother Sellers, warned smugglers of the coastguards' presence by wearing a red dress. Nowadays the food provides the excitement, meat and vegetarian alternatives, bread and wide choice of desserts are all home-made daily.

OPEN: 10-11 **BAR MEALS:** L served all week 12-2 D served all week 7-9.30 (Sun 12-3) Av main course £12 **RESTAURANT:** L served all week 12-2 D served all week 7-9 Av 3 course à la carte £25 **BREWERY/COMPANY:** Inn Partnership ◀: Ringwood Best, Fortyniner, Interbrew Bass, Courage Directors. **CHILDREN'S FACILITIES:** portions, games, food/bottle warming **GARDEN:** Patio **NOTES:** Dogs allowed: in bar, Water, Biscuits, Parking 40

CORFE CASTLE   THE GREYHOUND INN

The Square BH20 5EZ
☎ 01929 480205 ▤ 01929 481483
e-mail: mjml@greyhound-inn.fsnet.co.uk
Dir: W from Bournemouth, take A35, after 5m L onto A351, 10m to Corfe Castle.
Map Ref: SY98

Corfe Castle forms a dramatic backdrop to the 16th-century inn and probably furnished the stones to build it. Seafood platters, chargrilled meat baskets and steaks are features of the menu, plus there's a weekend carvery and a 10-dish buffet feast, based on local ingredients. A recent addition is a coffee and panini deli bar, with a salad buffet and a create-your-own-sandwich section. Beer festivals, barbecues and hog roasts are regular events in summer.

OPEN: 11-3 Summer open all day 6-11.30 **BAR MEALS:** L served all week 12-2.30 D served all week 6-9 Jul-Aug food all day Av main course £12.95 **RESTAURANT:** L served all week 12-2.30 D served all week 6-9 Jul-Aug food all day Av 3 course à la carte £17.95 **BREWERY/COMPANY:** Enterprise Inns ◀: Fuller's London Pride, Adnams, Timothy Taylor Landlord, Black Sheep. ♀: 10 **CHILDREN'S FACILITIES:** menu, games, high-chairs, food/bottle warming, outdoor play area, games, Colouring books, mini football, family room **GARDEN:** BBQ & hog roast in summer; castle views **NOTES:** Dogs allowed: in bar, in garden, in bedrooms, Water

EAST CHALDON   THE SAILORS RETURN

DT2 8DN
☎ 01305 853847 ▤ 01305 851677
Dir: 1m S of A352 between Dorchester & Wool. **Map Ref:** SY78

A splendid 18th-century thatched country pub in the village of East Chaldon (or Chaldon

Herring - take your pick), tucked away in rolling downland near Lulworth Cove. Considerably extended since the 1930 view on the website. Seafood includes whole local plaice, scallop and mussel Stroganoff, and wok-fried king prawns. Alternatives include half a big duck, local faggots, whole gammon hock, and vegetarian dishes. Choose from the blackboard in the beamed and flagstoned bar and eat inside or in a grassy area outside.

OPEN: 11-3 (all day open from Easter-end Sept) 6-11 **BAR MEALS:** L served all week 12-2 D served all week 6.30-9.30 **RESTAURANT:** L served all week 12-2 D served all week 6.30-9.30 **BREWERY/COMPANY:** Free House ◀: Ringwood Best, Hampshire Strongs Best Bitter, Badger Tanglefoot. **CHILDREN'S FACILITIES:** menu, outdoor play area, family room **GARDEN:** Grassed area with wooden tables and benches **NOTES:** Dogs allowed: Parking 100

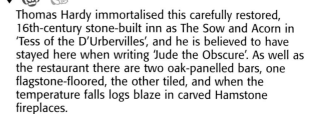

EVERSHOT THE ACORN INN ◆◆◆◆

DT2 0JW
☎ 01935 83228 ▤ 01935 83707
e-mail: stay@acorn-inn.co.uk
Dir: *A303 to Yeovil, Dorchester Rd, on A37 R to
Evershot.* **Map Ref:** *ST50*

Thomas Hardy immortalised this carefully restored,
16th-century stone-built inn as The Sow and Acorn in
'Tess of the D'Urbervilles', and he is believed to have
stayed here when writing 'Jude the Obscure'. As well as
the restaurant there are two oak-panelled bars, one
flagstone-floored, the other tiled, and when the
temperature falls logs blaze in carved Hamstone
fireplaces.

OPEN: 11.30-11 **BAR MEALS:** L served all week 12-2
D served all week 6.30-9.30 Av main course £5
RESTAURANT: L served all week 12-2 D served all week
6.30-9.30 Av 3 course à la carte £21
BREWERY/COMPANY: Free House ◖: Fuller's London Pride,
Butcombe, Guest Ale. **CHILDREN'S FACILITIES:** portions,
high-chairs, food/bottle warming, family room **GARDEN:** Patio
area with benches **NOTES:** Dogs allowed: in bar, Parking 40
ROOMS: 9 en suite 2 family rooms s£75 d£90

GILLINGHAM THE KINGS ARMS INN

East Stour Common SP8 5NB
☎ 01747 838325
e-mail: rayandjannattka@aol.com
Dir: *4m W of Shaftesbury on A30.*
Map Ref: *ST82*

A 200-year-old country inn, the Kings Arms
makes an excellent base for exploring the
delights of Dorset's countryside and coast,
with plenty of well-loved attractions within
reach, including nearby Shaftesbury and the
famous Golden Hill. The pub has recently
changed hands and is now under new family
ownership, offering accommodation and
meals from a single menu plus daily specials
in the bar or restaurant.

OPEN: 12-2.30 Longer hrs summer 5-11 Closed: 25 Dec
BAR MEALS: L served Tue-Sun 12-2 D served Tue-Sat 6-8.45
Av main course £7 **RESTAURANT:** L served Tue-Sun 12-2
D served Tue-Sat 6-8.45 **BREWERY/COMPANY:** Free
House ◖: Cools Worthington's Bitter, Ringwood Best Bitter,
Quay Weymouth Best Bitter, Butcombe Ales & Wye Valley
Ales. **CHILDREN'S FACILITIES:** portions, games, high-chairs,
food/bottle warming, baby changing, outdoor play area, family
room **GARDEN:** Patio & sitting area **NOTES:** No dogs
(ex guide dogs), Parking 40 **ROOMS:** 3 en suite

MOTCOMBE THE COPPLERIDGE INN ◆◆◆◆

SP7 9HW
☎ 01747 851980 ▤ 01747 851858
e-mail: thecoppleridgeinn@btinternet.com
Map Ref: *ST82*

A working farm until 15 years ago, this
traditional, family-run country inn is full of

character, with flagstone floors, stripped pine and
delightful views stretching across the Blackmore Vale,
perfect for touring and exploring. Wide-ranging menus
offer dishes cooked to order from fresh local
ingredients. Extensive choice of snacks.

OPEN: 11-3 5-11 All day Sat & Sun **BAR MEALS:** L served
all week 12-2.30 D served all week 6-9.30 Av main
course £7.50 **RESTAURANT:** L served all week 12-2.30
D served all week 6-9.30 Av 3 course à la carte £17.50
BREWERY/COMPANY: Free House ◖: Butcombe Bitter,
Greene King IPA, Wadworth 6X, Fuller's London Pride. ♀: 7
CHILDREN'S FACILITIES: menu, portions, games, high-chairs,
food/bottle warming, outdoor play area, garden, swings &
slide, family room **GARDEN:** 15 acres including lawns, wood,
pond area **NOTES:** Dogs allowed: in bar, in garden,
Parking 60 **ROOMS:** 10 en suite 3 family rooms s£42.50
d£75 (◆◆◆◆)

NETTLECOMBE MARQUIS OF LORNE ♦♦♦♦ 🐑 ♀

DT6 3SY
☎ 01308 485236 📠 01308 485666
e-mail: julie.woodroffe@btinternet.com
Dir: 3m E of A3066 Bridport-Beaminster rd. From Bridport North to Beaminster after 1.5m turn right signed Powerstock, West Milton & Mill after 3m at a T Jct, pub up hill on left. **Map Ref:** *SY59*

A 16th-century farmhouse converted into a pub in 1871, when the Marquis himself named it to prove land ownership. Membership of the Campaign for Real Food means that much local produce is used. Superb gardens with beautiful views.

OPEN: 11.30-2.30 6.30-11 (Sun all day)
BAR MEALS: L served all week 12-2 D served all week 6.30-9 (Sun 12-9) Av main course £8
RESTAURANT: L served all week 12-2 D served all week 6.30-9 (Sun 12-9) Av 3 course à la carte £15
BREWERY/COMPANY: Palmers 🍺: Palmers Copper, IPA, 200 Premium Ale. ♀: 8 **CHILDREN'S FACILITIES:** menu, portions, games, high-chairs, food/bottle warming, baby changing, outdoor play area, Children over 10 allowed in bedrooms **GARDEN:** Well kept garden with good views & play area **NOTES:** Dogs allowed: in bar, in garden, Water, Parking 50 **ROOMS:** 7 en suite s£45 d£70

NORTH WOOTTON THE THREE ELMS ♀

DT9 5JW
☎ 01935 812881 📠 01935 812881
Dir: From Sherborne take A352 towards Dorchester then A3030. Pub 1m on R.
Map Ref: *ST61*

Real ales and locally produced ciders await you at this family-run free house overlooking Blackmore Vale. There are stunning views from the pub's garden, and the landlord boasts a collection of around 1,300 model cars. The wide-ranging menu includes dishes like shark and bacon cassoulet, royal ocean platter (a mixture of hot and cold fish and seafood), lamb and mango casserole, and Thai-style salmon supreme with noodles and stir-fried vegetables.

OPEN: 11-2.30 6.30-11 (Sun 12-3, 7-10.30) Closed: 25-26 Dec **BAR MEALS:** L served all week 12-2 D served all week 6.30-10 Av main course £8 **RESTAURANT:** L served all week 12-2 D served all week 6.30-10
BREWERY/COMPANY: Free House 🍺: Fuller's London Pride, Butcombe Bitter, Otter Ale. ♀: 10
CHILDREN'S FACILITIES: menu, outdoor play area
NOTES: Dogs allowed: Parking 50

OSMINGTON MILLS THE SMUGGLERS INN ♀

DT3 6HF
☎ 01305 833125 📠 01305 832219
Map Ref: *SY78*

This 13th-century inn was the headquarters of notorious French smuggler Pierre Latour, whose wife (the landlord's daughter) was mistakenly shot during a raid on the pub. Her husband was hiding up the chimney. More famously, John Constable painted the view of Weymouth Bay from what is now the car park. Located bang on the coastal path, with a stream running through the garden and a play area for children, it's a good stop on a sunny day. The interior is cosy, with bare beams and flagstone floors. Food includes seasonal fresh fish in the summer, scrumpy chicken, chargrilled rump steak, stuffed peppers, and steak and Tanglefoot pie.

OPEN: 11-11 Sun 12-10.30 Rest: Nov-Mar Closed Mon-Fri 3-6 **BAR MEALS:** L served all week 12-9.30 D served all week 12-9.30 Sun 12-9 Av main course £6.95
RESTAURANT: L served all week 12 D served all week 9.30 **BREWERY/COMPANY:** Woodhouse Inns 🍺: Badger Best, Tanglefoot. ♀: 12 **CHILDREN'S FACILITIES:** menu, portions, licence, games, high-chairs, food/bottle warming, outdoor play area, swings, slide & assault course, family room
GARDEN: Large lawn with picnic benches & BBQ
NOTES: No dogs (ex guide dogs), Parking 70

PIDDLEHINTON   THE THIMBLE INN

DT2 7TD
☎ 01300 348270
Dir: *A35 westbound, R onto B3143,*
Piddlehinton 4m. **Map Ref:** *SY79*

Good food, open fires and traditional pub games make this friendly village local a favourite spot with visitors. The pub stands in an unspoilt valley on the banks of the River Piddle, and the riverside patio is popular in summer. The extensive menu caters for all tastes, from sandwiches, jacket potatoes and children's meals, to grilled duck breast with pink grapefruit and ginger sauce; game pie which, the menu advises, may contain shot; and a range of fish specials, including fresh Poole plaice.

OPEN: 12-2.30 7-11 (Sun 12-2.30 7-10.30) Closed: 25 Dec **BAR MEALS:** L served all week 12-2 D served all week 7-9 **RESTAURANT:** L served all week 12-2 D served all week 7-9 **BREWERY/COMPANY:** Free House 🍺: Badger Best & Tanglefoot, Palmer Copper Ale & Palmer IPA, Ringwood Old Thumper. **CHILDREN'S FACILITIES:** menu, portions, high-chairs, food/bottle warming, baby changing room area **NOTES:** Dogs allowed: in bar, in garden, Parking 50

PIDDLETRENTHIDE   THE POACHERS INN ◆◆◆◆

DT2 7QX
☎ 01300 348358 🖨 01300 348153
e-mail:
thepoachers@piddletrenthide.fsbusiness.co.uk
Dir: *8m from Dorchester on B3143.*
Map Ref: *SY79*

At the heart of Thomas Hardy country, this free house in a small village by the River Piddle features open fires and traditional pub games, reflecting its identity as a genuine English local, whose riverside patio is especially popular in summer. Home-made soups, steak and ale pie, vegetarian options and an impressive array of steaks and grills.

OPEN: 12-11 Closed: 24-26 Dec **BAR MEALS:** L served all week 12-6.30 D served all week 6.30-9
RESTAURANT: L served all week 12-6.30 D served all week 6.30-9 **BREWERY/COMPANY:** Free House
🍺: Carlsberg-Tetley Bitter, Poachers Ale, Badger Tanglefoot & IPA, Scottish Courage John Smiths Smooth.
CHILDREN'S FACILITIES: menu, portions, high-chairs, food/bottle warming **GARDEN:** Over-looks river, tables, seating **NOTES:** Dogs allowed: in bar, in garden, in bedrooms, Parking 40 **ROOMS:** 18 en suite 1 family room

PLUSH   BRACE OF PHEASANTS ♀

DT2 7RQ
☎ 01300 348357
e-mail: albu@tinyworld.co.uk
Dir: *A35 onto B3143, 5m to Piddletrenthide,*
then R to Mappowder & Plush. **Map Ref:** *ST70*

Tucked away in a fold of the hills east of Cerne Abbas, is this pretty 16th-century

thatched village inn, hidden at the heart of Hardy's beloved county. Beginning life as two cottages then a village smithy, inside the ambience is warm and welcoming, with an open fire, oak beams and fresh flowers. Lunch, dinner and bar meals are available, and the choice of menu reflects the changing of the seasons. Fantastic walking country.

OPEN: 12-2.30 7-11 (Sun 12-3 7-10.30) Closed: Dec 25 Rest: Mon Closed in winter **BAR MEALS:** L served Tues-Sun 12.30-2.30 D served Tues-Sun 7.30-9.30 Av main course £10.50 **RESTAURANT:** L served Tues-Sun 12-1.30 D served Tues-Sun 7-9.30 Av 3 course à la carte £22
BREWERY/COMPANY: Free House 🍺: Fuller's London Pride, Butcombe Bitter, Ringwood Best, Adnams. ♀: 12
CHILDREN'S FACILITIES: portions, licence, facilities by arrangement, family room **GARDEN:** Large, food served outside **NOTES:** Dogs allowed: in bar, Water, Parking 30

POWERSTOCK THREE HORSESHOES INN ◆◆◆◆ ♀

DT6 3TF
☎ 01308 485328 ▯ 01308 485229
e-mail: info@threehorseshoesinn.com
Dir: E of A3066 (Bridport/Beaminster rd).
Map Ref: SY59

The honeyed stone façade of The 'Shoes blends effortlessly into a streetscape beloved of film companies seeking that 'English village' location. Powerstock is popular with walkers and cyclists too who enjoy the glorious coastal views from the garden. Visitors seeking warmth will find the traditional bar or cosy wood-panelled restaurant, both with open fireplaces, perfect. Boasting a reputation for excellent cuisine, the inn makes extensive use of fresh local produce for its light lunch menu and evening carte which, although short, still manage to offer terrific choice.

OPEN: 11-3 6.30-11.30 (Sun 12-3 6.30-11.30)
BAR MEALS: L served all week 12-2.30 D served all week 7-9 Summer 7-9.30, Sun 12-3, 7-8.30 Av main course £8
RESTAURANT: L served all week 12-2.30 D served all week 7-9 Summer 7-9.30, Sun 12-3, 7-8.30 Av 3 course à la carte £17 **BREWERY/COMPANY:** Palmers ◖: Palmer's IPA, Copper Ale. ♀: 9 **CHILDREN'S FACILITIES:** portions, games, high-chairs, food/bottle warming, outdoor play area, Lrg garden with swings&climbing frame, family room
GARDEN: Patio leading to terraced garden **NOTES:** Dogs allowed: in bar, in garden, in bedrooms, Water, food, toys, blankets, Parking 30 **ROOMS:** 3 en suite 1 family room s£50 d£70 (◆◆◆◆)

PUNCKNOWLE THE CROWN INN ♀

Church St DT2 9BN
☎ 01308 897711 ▯ 01308 898282
Dir: From A35, into Bridevally, through Litton Cheney. From B3157, inland at Swyre.
Map Ref: SY58

Picturesque 16th-century thatched inn retaining a traditional atmosphere within its rambling, low-beamed bars, which were once the haunt of smugglers from nearby Chesil Beach on their way to visit prosperous customers in Bath. Food ranges from light snacks and sandwiches to steak and kidney pie cooked in Guinness; pork and pepper casserole cooked in cider; trout with toasted almonds; or bean and ratatouille hot pot. A children's menu offers all the usual favourites.

OPEN: 11-3 (Sun 12-3, 7-10.30) 7-11 (Summer 6.30 opening) Closed: 25 Dec **BAR MEALS:** L served all week 12-2 D served all week 7-9 Summer weekdays from 6.30pm Av main course £8 **BREWERY/COMPANY:** Palmers ◖: Palmers IPA, 200 Premium Ale, Copper Tally Ho!. ♀: 10 **CHILDREN'S FACILITIES:** menu, portions, high-chairs, family room **GARDEN:** Large garden with raised patio area **NOTES:** Dogs allowed: in bar, in garden, in bedrooms, Water, Parking 12, No credit cards

SHERBORNE WHITE HART

Bishops Caundle DT9 5ND
☎ 01963 23301 ▯ 01963 23301 (by arrangement)
Dir: On A3030 between Sherborne & Sturminster Newton. Map Ref: ST61

Walkers who come to pretty Bishops Caundle owe a debt of thanks to whoever waymarked the route to start and end here. The 16th-century pub was once a monks' brewhouse, and later used by the notorious Judge Jeffreys. An extensive menu ranges through snacks, children's and vegetarian dishes, steaks and chef's specialities. Favourites include grilled duck with port and orange, and spicy sizzling pork. There's also a six-activity play trail and two sunken trampolines.

OPEN: 11.30-3 6.30-11 (Sun 12-3, 7-10.30)
BAR MEALS: L served all week 12-2 D served all week 6.45-9.30 Av main course £6.10 **RESTAURANT:** L served all week 12-2 D served all week 6.30-9.30
BREWERY/COMPANY: Hall & Woodhouse ◖: Badger Best, Tanglefoot, Golden Champion, Sussex Golden Glory.
CHILDREN'S FACILITIES: menu, portions, high-chairs, outdoor play area, Activity play trail, 2 trampolines, family room **GARDEN:** Patio area, 6 benches **NOTES:** Dogs allowed: Water provided, Parking 32

SHROTON OR IWERNE COURTNEY THE CRICKETERS ◆◆◆◆◆ ♀

DT11 8QD

☎ 01258 860421 📠 01258 861800

Dir: *Off the A350 Shaftesbury to Blandford.*
Map Ref: *ST81*

Built at the turn of the 20th century, The Cricketers is to be found nestling under Hambledon Hill, and comprises a main bar, sports bar and den, all light and airy rooms leading to the restaurant at the rear. This overlooks a lovely garden, well stocked with trees and flowers. In fine weather, eat outside beneath the clematis-covered pergola. An extensive menu, serving both the bar and restaurant, offers a good choice of interesting dishes featuring unusual combinations.

OPEN: 11.30-2.30 6.30-11 Winter Sun eve 7-
BAR MEALS: L served all week 12-2 D served all week 6.30-9 Sun from7 £5 **RESTAURANT:** L served all week 12-2 D served all week 6.30-9 Sun from 7 **BREWERY/COMPANY:** Free House 🍺: Ringwood 49er, Butcombe Bitter, Shepherds Neame Spitfire, Marstons Pedigree. ♀: 10 **CHILDREN'S FACILITIES:** portions, games, high-chairs, food/bottle warming, baby changing **GARDEN:** Bordered by trees and hedges, herb garden **NOTES:** No dogs (ex guide dogs), Parking 19 **ROOMS:** 1 en suite s£45 d£65 no children overnight

STOKE ABBOTT THE NEW INN 🐑 ♀

DT8 3JW

☎ 01308 868333

e-mail:
webbs@newinnstokeabbott.fsnet.co.uk
Map Ref: *ST40*

This welcoming 17th-century village inn, with its thatched roof, log fires and beautiful garden was once a farmhouse. It offers three real ales, and the extensive menu includes light meals such as grilled black pudding with caramelised apples; cold smoked duck breast with plum chutney; and a good choice of baguettes, sandwiches and vegetarian dishes. Specials might include medallions of pork with Stilton sauce or fresh whole grilled sea bass. Listen out for the singing chef!

OPEN: 11.30-3 (Winter Mon-Thur 7-10.30) 7-11 (Sun 12-3, 7-10.30) **BAR MEALS:** L served all week 12-2 D served all week 7-9.30 **RESTAURANT:** L served all week 12-2 D served all week 7-9.30 Av 3 course à la carte £25 **BREWERY/COMPANY:** Palmers 🍺: Palmers IPA & 200 Premium Ale, Tally Ho. **CHILDREN'S FACILITIES:** menu, portions, games, high-chairs, food/bottle warming **GARDEN:** Large, comfortable, beautiful views **NOTES:** Dogs allowed: in bar, Parking 25

TARRANT MONKTON THE LANGTON ARMS ◆◆◆◆ ♀

DT11 8RX

☎ 01258 830225 📠 01258 830053

e-mail: info@thelangtonarms.co.uk

Dir: *A31 from Ringwood, or A357 from Shaftesbury, or A35 from Bournemouth.*
Map Ref: *ST90*

Well regarded in this neck of the woods for its good food, here is a 17th-century thatched free house in a peaceful spot in the village centre. Items on the Stables Restaurant menu change frequently and usually feature traditionally made faggots in rich onion sauce; game pie (season permitting) cooked in red wine and redcurrant gravy; braised wild rabbit; fillet of battered pearl snapper; baked aubergine, with ratatouille and mozzarella; and four-bean stew. A children's adventure play area and skittle alley add to the pub's wider appeal.

OPEN: 11.30-11 (Sun 12-10.30) **BAR MEALS:** L served all week 11.30-2.30 D served all week 6-9.30 Av main course £7 **RESTAURANT:** L served Sun 12-2 D served Wed-Sat 7-9 Av 3 course à la carte £25 Av 3 course fixed price £16.95 **BREWERY/COMPANY:** Free House 🍺: Hop Back Best, Guest Beers. ♀: 6 **CHILDREN'S FACILITIES:** menu, portions, high-chairs, baby changing, outdoor play area, adventure playground, family room **GARDEN:** Large beer garden **NOTES:** No dogs (ex guide dogs), Parking 100 **ROOMS:** 6 en suite s£50 d£70

TOLPUDDLE   THE MARTYRS INN ♀

DT2 7ES
☎ 01305 848249 ▤ 01305 848977
e-mail: martyrs@scottz.co.uk
Dir: *Off A35 between Bere Regis (A31/A35 Junction).* **Map Ref:** *SY79*

Tolpuddle is the somewhat unlikely birthplace of the Trades Union Congress. Its seeds were sown in 1834 by six impoverished farm labourers who tried to bargain with local landowners for better conditions. Their punishment was transportation to Australia. Martyrs' memorabilia abounds in the pub. Home-made starters include chicken liver and wild mushroom pâté, and garlic mushrooms en croûte; main courses include Tolpuddle sausages with mash and onion gravy, country vegetable pasta bake, and spicy chicken curry with rice and naan bread. There is a play area to keep the children amused.

BAR MEALS: L served all week 12-3 D served all week 6.30-9 **RESTAURANT:** L served all week D served all week **BREWERY/COMPANY:** Hall & Woodhouse ◖: Badger Dorset Best & Tanglefoot. **CHILDREN'S FACILITIES:** menu, portions, games, high-chairs, food/bottle warming, baby changing, outdoor play area, large garden **NOTES:** Dogs allowed: Parking 25

TRENT   ROSE & CROWN INN

DT9 4SL
☎ 01935 850776 ▤ 01935 850796
e-mail: ian@roseandcrowntrent.fsnet.co.uk
Dir: *W on A30 towards Yeovil. 3m from Sherborne R to Over Compton/Trent, 1.5m downhill, then R. Pub opp church.*
Map Ref: *ST51*

Workers building the 15th-century church constructed the oldest part of this thatched pub, which has been considerably added to over the centuries. The France-bound Charles II reputedly hid here, while in the mid 20th-century it was a favoured watering hole of Lord Fisher, the Archbishop of Canterbury who crowned Queen Elizabeth II. Today's visitors can enjoy the likes of moules mariniere, seafood mornay or herb-crusted lamb cutlets, while the children play on the climbing frame, swings and slide.

OPEN: 12-3 7-11 (Sun 12-3 only) Closed: 1 Jan **BAR MEALS:** L served all week 12-2 D served all week 7-9 Av main course £8.50 **RESTAURANT:** L served all week 12-2 D served all week 7-9 **BREWERY/COMPANY:** Free House ◖: Doombar, Butcombe Bitter, Exmoor, Guiness. **CHILDREN'S FACILITIES:** menu, portions, high-chairs, food/bottle warming, outdoor play area, wooden climbing frame, swings and a slide, family room **GARDEN:** table seating, fish pond, south facing **NOTES:** Dogs allowed: in bar, in garden, on lead only, water, Parking 30

WEST BEXINGTON   THE MANOR HOTEL ★★

DT2 9DF
☎ 01308 897616 ▤ 01308 897035
e-mail: themanorhotel@btconnect.com
Dir: *On B3157, 5m E of Bridport.*
Map Ref: *SY58*

Just 500 yards from spectacular Chesil Beach and the clear waters of Lyme Bay lies this 16th-century manor house, featuring Jacobean oak panelling and flagstone floors. It makes an excellent base for exploring Dorset's numerous delights and enjoying stunning coastal walks. The menu offers starters such as Thai style fish balls cooked in coconut milk; or air dried Dorset ham with fresh figs; perhaps followed by baked lemon sole with a pale sherry sauce; or stir-fried loin of lamb with ginger, garlic and sesame.

OPEN: 11-11 (Sun 12-10.30) **BAR MEALS:** L served all week 12-2 D served all week 6.30-9.30 Av main course £9.95 **RESTAURANT:** L served all week 12-2 D served all week 7-9.30 Av 3 course fixed price £19.50 **BREWERY/COMPANY:** Free House ◖: Butcombe Gold, Harbour Master. **CHILDREN'S FACILITIES:** menu, portions, high-chairs, food/bottle warming, outdoor play area, playing field, family room **GARDEN:** Large garden with sea views **NOTES:** in bar, water bowls, No dogs, Parking 40 **ROOMS:** 13 en suite 3 family rooms s£70 d£110

WEST LULWORTH THE CASTLE INN

Main Rd BH20 5RN
☎ 01929 400311 ▤ 01929 400415
Dir: *on the Wareham to Dorchester Rd, L
approx 1m from Wareham.* **Map Ref:** *SY88*

Picturesque thatched and beamed inn with a
delightful setting near Lulworth Cove, close to
plenty of good walks and popular attractions. The wide-
ranging menu offers a number of mouth-watering
dishes, including chicken, ham and mushroom pie; fillet
steak with oysters; liver and bacon casserole; seafood
stew; sesame chicken with ginger and onion sauce;
plus a variety of flambé dishes cooked at the table.

OPEN: 11-2.30 (Winter 12-2.30, 7-11) 6-11 Closed: 25 Dec
BAR MEALS: L served all week 11-2.30 D served all week
6-10.30 Av main course £6 **RESTAURANT:** L served all
week D served Fri & Sat 7-9.30 Av 3 course à la carte £15
BREWERY/COMPANY: Free House ◀: Ringwood Best,
Gales, Courage, John Smith. ♀: 8 **CHILDREN'S FACILITIES:**
menu, portions, licence, games, high-chairs, food/bottle
warming, baby changing, outside chess/draughts, board
games, family room **GARDEN:** Large tiered garden, lots of
plants, flowers **NOTES:** Dogs allowed: in bar, in garden,
in bedrooms, Water/Food, Parking 30

WEST STAFFORD THE WISE MAN INN ♀

DT2 8AG
☎ 01305 263694
Dir: *2m from A35.* **Map Ref:** *SY78*

Set in the heart of Thomas Hardy country, this thatched
16th-century pub was originally the village shop and
off-licence. It is now a regular stopping off point for
those on the Hardy trail. The menu makes full use of
good local produce - fresh fish and vegetables, and
organic meat. There is a children's menu, and a large
secluded garden with ample seating.

OPEN: 11-3 6.30-11 (Summer 6-11)
BAR MEALS: L served all week 12-2.30 D served Mon-Sat
7-9.30 Av main course £7 **RESTAURANT:** L served all week
12-2.30 D served Mon-Sat 7-9.30
BREWERY/COMPANY: Pubmaster ◀: Ringwood, 3 casked
ales each week. ♀: 6 **CHILDREN'S FACILITIES:** menu,
portions, games, high-chairs, outdoor play area, family room
GARDEN: Large, plenty of seating, secluded **NOTES:** Dogs
allowed: in bar, in garden, in bedrooms, Water & biscuits
provided, Parking 25

WINTERBORNE ZELSTON BOTANY BAY INNE

DT11 9ET
☎ 01929 459227
Map Ref: *SY89*

An obvious question: how did the pub get its
name? Built in the 1920s as The General
Allenby, it was changed about 17 years ago in
belated recognition of prisoners from
Dorchester jail who were required to spend a
night nearby before transportation to
Australia. Since no such fate awaits anyone
these days, meals to enjoy at leisure include
bacon-wrapped chicken breast; steak and
kidney pudding; roasted Mediterranean
vegetable Wellington; and fish catch of the
day. Real ales are locally brewed.

OPEN: 12-3 6-11 Mon-Sat summer open 10-
BAR MEALS: L served all week 12-2.15 D served all week
6.30-9.30 **RESTAURANT:** L served all week 12-2.15
D served all week 6.30-9.30 Av 3 course à la carte £16
◀: Badger Best Bitter, Tanglefoot, Botany Bay Bitter, Fursty
Ferret. **CHILDREN'S FACILITIES:** menu, portions, licence,
games, high-chairs, family room **GARDEN:** Paved area with
flowers overlooking fields **NOTES:** Dogs allowed: in bar only;
water, Parking 60

ALMONDSBURY THE BOWL ★★

16 Church Rd BS32 4DT
☎ 01454 612757 📠 01454 619910
e-mail: reception@thebowlinn.co.uk
Map Ref: *ST68*

Dating back to 1550, this picturesque whitewashed pub on the edge of the Severn

Vale was originally a terrace of three cottages. The inn gets its name from its interesting geographical location in the escarpment of the south-western vale of the Severn. Bar menu with pies and casserole, pasta, freshly baked baguettes, and fish. In Lilies Restaurant try duck leg confit, pan-fried lemon sole, fillets of lamb, or roasted monkfish.

OPEN: 11-3 5-11 (Sun 12-10.30) Rest: 25 Dec Closed eve **BAR MEALS:** L served all week 12-2.30 D served all week 6-10 Sun 12-8 Av main course £8 **RESTAURANT:** L served all week 12-2.30 D served all week 7-10 Av 3 course à la carte £27 **BREWERY/COMPANY:** Free House 🍺: Scottish Courage Courage Best, Smiles Best, Wickwar BOB, Moles Best. 🍷: 9 **CHILDREN'S FACILITIES:** menu, portions, games, high-chairs, food/bottle warming **GARDEN:** Patio area at rear. Seating on frontage **NOTES:** Dogs allowed: in bar, in garden, in bedrooms, Parking 50 **ROOMS:** 13 en suite s£44.50 d£71

ANDOVERSFORD THE ROYAL OAK INN

Old Gloucester Rd GL54 4HR
☎ 01242 820335
e-mail: bleninns@clara.net
Dir: *200metres from A40, 4m E of Cheltenham.* **Map Ref:** *SP01*

The Royal Oak stands on the banks of the River Coln, one of a small chain of popular

food-oriented pubs in the area. Originally a coaching inn, its main dining room, galleried on two levels, occupies the converted former stables. Lunchtime bar fare of various sandwiches, lasagne and ham, egg and chips (for example), extends in the evening to Chinese crispy duck with lime and soy noodles or roast pork fillet with rosti potato and creamy cider sauce.

OPEN: 11-2.30 5.30-11 **BAR MEALS:** L served all week 12-2.30 D served all week 7-9.30 Av main course £6.50 **RESTAURANT:** L served all week 12-2.30 D served all week 7-9.30 Av 3 course à la carte £15 **BREWERY/COMPANY:** Free House 🍺: Hook Norton Best, Tetleys Bitter, Draught Bass. 🍷: 8 **CHILDREN'S FACILITIES:** menu, portions, high-chairs, food/bottle warming **GARDEN:** Patio area with tables on banks of the river **NOTES:** Dogs allowed: in bar, in garden, Water, Parking 44

ASHLEWORTH THE QUEENS ARMS

The Village GL19 4HT
☎ 01452 700395
Map Ref: *SO82*

An 18th-century inn with Victorian additions set in the centre of a delightful village. The pretty front garden is dominated by two

beautifully clipped 200-year-old yew trees, and at the back a flagstoned patio area is graced with white cast iron garden furniture and hanging baskets. The restaurant comprises two intimate rooms retaining a warm, pubby atmosphere. Dishes based on local produce are listed on prominently placed chalkboards at lunch and dinner.

OPEN: 12-2.30 7-11 Closed: Dec 25-26 **BAR MEALS:** L served all week 12-2 D served all week 7-9 Fri-Sat 7-10 Av main course £11.50 **RESTAURANT:** L served all week 12-2 D served all week 7-9 Fri-Sat 7-10 Av 3 course à la carte £19.50 **BREWERY/COMPANY:** Free House 🍺: Shepherd Neame Spitfire, Donnington BB, S A Brain & Company Rev James, Young's Special. 🍷: 12 **CHILDREN'S FACILITIES:** food/bottle warming **GARDEN:** Garden with rose bushes, yew trees, patio **NOTES:** No dogs (ex guide dogs), Parking 50

BARNSLEY   THE VILLAGE PUB

GL7 5EF
☎ 01285 740421 ▤ 01285 740929
e-mail: reservations@thevillagepub.co.uk
Dir: *On B4425 4m NE of Cirencester.*
Map Ref: *SP00*

There is plenty of atmosphere in the beautifully restored dining rooms at the Village Pub, with their eclectic mix of furniture, flagstone floors, exposed beams and open fires. But despite the mellow-stoned country pub setting, this distinctive dining venue is light years away from the average local. This is an exemplary pub restaurant, perennially busy and renowned locally as one of the best places to eat in the area. The food starts with quality ingredients as the basic premise - locally sourced produce, traceable or organic meats, and fresh seasonal fish from Cornwall - offered from a daily changing menu. Starters might include oxtail soup, smoked chicken and vegetable salad or steamed mussels; mains could be fillet of bream with sweet and sour vegetables or rib eye steak with roast mushrooms. If the New York cheesecake's on the menu don't fail to order it!

OPEN: 11-3.30 6-11 **BAR MEALS:** L served all week 12.00-3.00 D served all week 7-10 **RESTAURANT:** L served all week 12-3 D served all week 7-10
BREWERY/COMPANY: Free House ◀: Hook Norton Bitter, Wadworth 6X. ♀: 17 **CHILDREN'S FACILITIES:** menu, portions, licence, high-chairs, food/bottle warming **GARDEN:** Walled terrace **NOTES:** Dogs allowed: in bar, in garden, Parking 35

BERKELEY   THE MALT HOUSE ★★

Marybrook St GL13 9BA
☎ 01453 511177 ▤ 01453 810257
e-mail: the-malthouse@btconnect.com
Dir: *From A38 towards Bristol from exit 13 or 14 of M5, after approx 8m Berkeley is signposted, the Malthouse is situated on the main road heading towards Sharpness.* **Map Ref:** *ST69*

Close by the Severn Way is this century-old former slaughterhouse which has developed over the years into a comfortable and welcoming inn with a range of menus to suit all tastes and pockets. At lunchtime, snacks are available and there is a special menu with good choices at a give-away price for "mature students" (60 years plus!). Sunday carvery; skittle alley available.

OPEN: 12-11 (Sun 12-4, Mon 4-11) **BAR MEALS:** L served Tues-Sat 11-2 D served Mon-Sat 6-9.00 Sun 12-2
RESTAURANT: L served Tues-Sat 12-2.00 D served Mon-Sat 6-9 Sun 12-2 Av 3 course à la carte £15
BREWERY/COMPANY: Free House ◀: Pedigree, Theakstons.
CHILDREN'S FACILITIES: menu, portions, high-chairs, food/bottle warming **GARDEN:** Small garden; Food served outside in summer **NOTES:** No dogs (ex guide dogs), Parking 40 **ROOMS:** 9 en suite 1 family room s£49 d£69

BIRDLIP   THE GOLDEN HEART ♀

Nettleton Bottom GL4 8LA
☎ 01242 870261 ▤ 01242 870599
Dir: *on the main road A417 Gloucester to Cirencester.* **Map Ref:** *SO91*

Glorious country views are afforded from the terraced gardens of this Cotswold stone inn, while inside you will find real fires, real ales and a wide selection of wines. The regular menu is supplemented by a daily blackboard choice, and dishes range from the traditional - bubble and squeak with lamb and mint sausages - to more exotic options like ostrich, bacon and mushroom pudding. A meeting room and private dining areas can be arranged.

OPEN: 11-3 5.30-11 (Fri-Sat 11-11, Sun 12-10.30)
BAR MEALS: L served all week 12-3 D served all week 6-10 Sun 12-10 Av main course £10 **RESTAURANT:** L served all week 12-3 D served all week 6-10 Sun 12-10
BREWERY/COMPANY: Free House ◀: Interbrew Bass, Timothy Taylor Landlord & Golden Best, Archers Bitter, Young's Special. ♀: 10 **CHILDREN'S FACILITIES:** menu, portions, games, high-chairs, food/bottle warming, garden, family room **GARDEN:** Terrace, 3 levels, large patio area, seating **NOTES:** Dogs allowed: in bar, in garden, in bedrooms, water, Parking 60

BISLEY THE BEAR INN

George St GL6 7BD
☎ 01452 770265
Dir: *E of Stroud off B4070.* **Map Ref:** *SO90*

Constructed as a courthouse with meeting rooms for the village in the 16th century, The Bear became an inn around 1766 and has continued as such ever since. Its outstanding features include a huge inglenook fireplace, a bread oven and an old priest hole; though the rock-hewn cellars, including a 60-ft well, are more likely Tudor. Menu items include bear burgers, bear necessities (sauté potatoes with various ingredients mixed in) and bear essentials such as steak, kidney and Guinness pie.

OPEN: 11.30-3 Sun 12-3 6-11 Sun 7-10.30 Closed: 25-26 Dec **BAR MEALS:** L served all week 12-2 D served Mon-Sat 7-9 No food Sun pm Av main course £9.45
BREWERY/COMPANY: Pubmaster 🍺: Tetley, Flowers IPA, Charles Wells Bombardier, Marstons.
CHILDREN'S FACILITIES: portions, food/bottle warming, family room **GARDEN:** Food served outside **NOTES:** Dogs allowed: in bar, Parking 20

BLOCKLEY THE CROWN INN & HOTEL ★★★

High St GL56 9EX
☎ 01386 700245 📠 01386 700247
e-mail: info@crown-inn-blockley.co.uk
Map Ref: *SP13*

In an area often awash with tourists, the 'hidden', National Trust-protected Cotswold village of Blockley wisely keeps its head down. Most visitors come because of the Crown, with Virginia creepers covering its mellow stone walls, and old beams, log fires and exposed stone walls inside. Rafter's Restaurant offers a blend of traditional and modern food, including steaks, roast of the day, and pan-fried shark steak Creole. Duggan's Brasserie is ideal for either a light lunch or an evening meal.

OPEN: 12-11 **BAR MEALS:** L served all week 12-2.30 D served all week 6.30-9.30 Av main course £8
RESTAURANT: L served all week 12-2.30 D served all week 7-9.30 Av 3 course à la carte £25 **BREWERY/COMPANY:** Free House 🍺 Hook Norton Best, Scottish Courage John Smith's, Wadworth 6X. **CHILDREN'S FACILITIES:** high-chairs, food/bottle warming **NOTES:** Dogs allowed: in bar, in garden, in bedrooms, Water, Parking 40 **ROOMS:** 24 en suite 4 family rooms s£54.95 d£39.95

CHEDWORTH SEVEN TUNS ♀

Queen St GL54 4AE
☎ 01285 720242 📠 01285 720242
Dir: *A40 then A429 towards Cirencester, after 5m R for Chedworth, 3m then 3rd turning on R.*
Map Ref: *SP01*

Traditional village inn dating back to 1610, and the ideal place to relax in after an exhilarating walk in the Cotswolds. Handy also for visiting nearby Chedworth Roman villa which can be reached on foot. Directly opposite the inn, which takes its name from seven chimney pots, are a waterwheel, a spring and a raised terrace for summer drinking. The freshly prepared daily-changing menu might feature braised rabbit, cheese and walnuts with a Stilton sauce, steak and kidney pie and ravioli. Well-kept real ales.

OPEN: 11-11 (Nov-Mar 11-3, 6-11, Sun 12-10.30)
BAR MEALS: L served all week 12-3 D served Mon-Sat 7-10 Av main course £6.50 **RESTAURANT:** L served all week 12-3 D served all week 6-10 Av 3 course à la carte £16.50
BREWERY/COMPANY: Free House 🍺: Young's Bitter, Youngs Special, Winter Warmer. ♀: 12
CHILDREN'S FACILITIES: menu, family room **NOTES:** Dogs allowed: Water, biscuits, Parking 30

CHIPPING CAMPDEN   THE BAKERS ARMS

Broad Campden GL55 6UR
☎ 01386 840515
Map Ref: SP13

Small Cotswold inn with a great atmosphere - visitors are welcomed and regulars are involved with the quiz, darts and crib teams. The traditional look of the place is reflected in its time-honoured values, with good meals at reasonable prices and a choice of four or five real ales. Typical main courses are chicken curry, mariner's pie, cottage pie, and liver and bacon; these are backed by specials such as breaded salmon fishcakes and pork chops cooked in cider.

OPEN: 11.30-2.30 Fri-Sat 11.30-11 4.45-11 (Sun 12-10.30, Summer 11.30-11) Closed: 25 Dec Rest: 26 Dec closed evening **BAR MEALS:** L served all week 12-2 D served all week 6-9 Apr-Oct 12-9 **RESTAURANT:** L served all week 12-2 D served all week 6-9 **BREWERY/COMPANY:** Free House 🍺: Hook Norton, Stanway Bitter, Bombardier, Timothy Taylor Landlord. **CHILDREN'S FACILITIES:** menu, portions, high-chairs, food/bottle warming, outdoor play area, Swings **GARDEN:** Large grassed area **NOTES:** Dogs allowed: Garden only. Water provided, Parking 30, No credit cards

EIGHT BELLS INN ♀

Church St GL55 6JG
☎ 01386 840371 📠 01386 841669
e-mail: neilhargreaves@bellinn.fsnet.co.uk
Map Ref: SP13

This tiny, stone-built free house has two atmospheric bars where the original oak beams, open fireplaces and even a priest's hole still survive. In summer the pub is hung with attractive flower baskets, and guests arrive through the cobbled entranceway where the bars lead on to the more recently opened dining room. There is also an enclosed courtyard for drinking and dining in fine weather, plus a beautiful terraced garden overlooking the almshouses and the church. In these delightful surroundings, freshly prepared local food is offered from a daily-changing seasonal menu that reflects a serious approach to food.

OPEN: 11-3 5.30-11 (all day Jul-Aug) Closed: 25 Dec **BAR MEALS:** L served all week 12-2.30 D served all week 6.30-9.30 Av main course £9.50 **RESTAURANT:** L served all week 12-2.30 D served all week 6.30-9.30 Av 3 course à la carte £20 **BREWERY/COMPANY:** Free House 🍺: Hook Norton Best & Guest Beers, Goff's Jouster. ♀: 8 **CHILDREN'S FACILITIES:** menu, portions, games, high-chairs, food/bottle warming, colouring competition on menus, family room **GARDEN:** Terrace, courtyard, great views **NOTES:** Dogs allowed: in bar, in garden, in bedrooms, Water **ROOMS:** 4 en suite 1 family room s£50 d£85 (♦♦♦)

THE NOEL ARMS HOTEL ★★★ ❀

High St GL55 6AT
☎ 01386 840317 📠 01386 841136
e-mail: reception@noelarms.com
Dir: Telephone for directions. *Map Ref:* SP13

A 14th-century inn renowned for accommodating Charles II in 1651 after his defeat by Cromwell at Worcester. As a reminder, Civil War weaponry festoons the grand stone hall. Light meals are served in both the historic beamed Dover's bar and the modern conservatory. In the Gainsborough restaurant (booking essential) your choice may start with peppered asparagus spears wrapped in crispy prosciutto; followed by honey-glazed breast of duck, or flash-fried fillet of red mullet; and finishing perhaps with warm tart of chocolate marmalade.

OPEN: 11-11 (Sun 12-10.30) **BAR MEALS:** L served all week 12-2 D served all week 7-9 Av main course £8 **RESTAURANT:** L served Sun 12-2 D served all week 7-9 **BREWERY/COMPANY:** Free House 🍺: Hook Norton, Scottish Courage John Smith's. **CHILDREN'S FACILITIES:** menu, portions, high-chairs **NOTES:** Dogs allowed: in bar, Parking 25 **ROOMS:** 26 en suite 1 family room s£90 d£120

CIRENCESTER BATHURST ARMS

North Cerney GL7 7BZ
☎ 01285 831281 ▤ 01285 831155
Dir: *The Bathurst Arms is setback from the Cheltenham Rd (A435).* **Map Ref:** *SP00*

Former coaching inn with bags of period charm - antique settles on flagstone floors, stone fireplaces, beams and panelled walls. The pretty garden stretches down to the River Churn, and a large barbecue is in use most summer weekends. Local delicacies include grilled Cerney goats' cheese with mixed leaves and walnuts, and trio of organic sausages with garlic mash and red onion gravy.

OPEN: 11-3 (Sun 12-3, 7-10.30) 6-11
BAR MEALS: L served all week 12-2 D served all week 7-9 Av main course £10 **RESTAURANT:** L served all week 12-2 D served all week 7-9.30 Av 3 course à la carte £20
BREWERY/COMPANY: Free House ◧: Hook Norton, Cotswold Way, rotating guest beers.
CHILDREN'S FACILITIES: menu, portions, high-chairs, food/bottle warming, baby changing **GARDEN:** Riverside with boules pitch **NOTES:** Dogs allowed: in bar, dog bowl, Parking 40

CLEARWELL WYNDHAM ARMS ★★★ 🐑 ♈

GL16 8JT
☎ 01594 833666 ▤ 01594 836450
e-mail: nigel@thewyndhamhotel.co.uk
Dir: *In village centre on B4231.*
Map Ref: *SO50*

The quintessentially English village of Clearwell in the Royal Forest of Dean takes its name from the Dunraven Well on the hotel boundary. The building itself dates back to the 14th century when it was a manor house; over the centuries has evolved into a highly civilised small hotel, run with great style and enthusiasm. Eat in either the bustling bar or the quieter restaurant.

OPEN: 11-11 (Sun 12-10.30) **BAR MEALS:** L served all week 12-2 D served all week 6.45-9 Av main course £9.95
RESTAURANT: L served all week 12-2 D served all week 6.45-9.30 Av 3 course à la carte £17.50
BREWERY/COMPANY: Free House ◧: Speculation Bitter, Freeminer Bitter. ♈: 7 **CHILDREN'S FACILITIES:** menu, portions, games, high-chairs, food/bottle warming, baby changing **NOTES:** Dogs allowed: Field for exercise, Parking 50 **ROOMS:** 18 en suite 2 family rooms s£45 d£65

COLD ASTON THE PLOUGH INN

GL54 3BN
☎ 01451 821459 ▤ 824000
Dir: *village signed from A436 & A429 SW of Stow-on-the-Wold.* **Map Ref:** *SP11*

A delightful 17th-century pub standing at the heart of this lovely Cotswold village close to Stow-on-the-Wold, at a convergence point of four major Cotswold walks. Full of traditional character such as old beams and flagstone floors, the pub is reputedly haunted. Typical menu includes home-made steak and ale pie, spinach and ricotta cannelloni and a selection of steaks. Patio and garden for summer al fresco drinking.

OPEN: 12-3 6.30-11 (Sun 12-3, 7-10.30)
BAR MEALS: L served all week 12-2.30 D served all week 6.30-9.30 Av main course £7.95
BREWERY/COMPANY: Free House ◧: Hook Norton, Donningtons, Tetleys. **CHILDREN'S FACILITIES:** portions, high-chairs **GARDEN:** Food served outside **NOTES:** Dogs allowed at owners' discretion, Parking 30

COLESBOURNE THE COLESBOURNE INN ♆

GL53 9NP
☎ 01242 870376 📠 01242 870397
e-mail: info@colesbourneinn.com
Dir: *On A435 (Cirencester to Cheltenham road).* **Map Ref:** *SP01*

Large log fires, beams, and a large garden overlooking wooded hills are all features of this 17th-century coaching inn. The interior is decorated with a wealth of bric-à-brac, and there are cask ales to sup and traditional food in both lounge bar and dining room. Lunch might offer boiled gammon and wild boar sausages, with favourites at night that take in pan-fired king prawns and scallops, and lamb or beef sizzlers.

OPEN: 11.30-3 6.30-11 **BAR MEALS:** L served Wed-Sun 12-2 D served Mon-Sat 7-9 Av main course £10.95 **RESTAURANT:** L served Wed-Sun 12-2.30 D served Mon-Sat 7-9.30 **BREWERY/COMPANY:** Wadworth 🍺: Wadworth 6X, Henrys IPA. ♆: 6 **CHILDREN'S FACILITIES:** portions, high-chairs **GARDEN:** Views overlooking Cotswold country side **NOTES:** Dogs allowed: in bar, Water, toys, Parking 40

COWLEY THE GREEN DRAGON INN

Cockleford GL53 9NW
☎ 01242 870271 📠 01242 870171
Map Ref: *SO91*

A handsome stone-built inn dating from the 17th century and located in the Cotswold hamlet of Cockleford. Very popular at weekends. The fittings and furniture are the work of the 'Mouse Man of Kilburn' (so-called for his trademark mouse) who lends his name to the popular Mouse Bar, with its stone-flagged floors, beamed ceilings and crackling log fires. The weekly menu includes sandwiches at lunchtime, children's favourites, and a choice of starters/light meals such as smoked haddock chowder or Caesar salad. Typical fare includes salads such as Brie and bacon, or smoked duck and chorizo; steak and kidney pudding; or tournedos of pork, garnished with sausage and set on a white bean purée. Fish may include sea bass; red mullet; or crayfish tails cooked en papillote with white wine, basil and baby vegetables. Other important features are the choice of real ales, with a monthly guest beer; the heated dining terrace; the comfortable courtyard bedrooms; and the function room/skittle alley.

OPEN: 11-11 **BAR MEALS:** L served all week 12-2.30 D served all week 6.30-10.30 (Sat & Sun 12-10) Av main course £9 **BREWERY/COMPANY:** Free House 🍺: Hook Norton, Scottish Courage Courage Best, Directors & Theakston, Smiles Best Bitter.
CHILDREN'S FACILITIES: menu, portions, high-chairs, food/bottle warming **NOTES:** Dogs allowed: in bar, in garden, in bedrooms, Water, Parking 100

DURSLEY PICKWICK INN

Lower Wick GL11 6DD
☎ 01453 810259 📠 01453 810259
e-mail: enquiries@thepickwickinn.com
Dir: *From Gloucester A38, turn L opposite Berkeley turnoff, pub on L.* **Map Ref:** *ST79*

Built in 1762, this has always been an inn, but has also doubled as a barber's and a slaughterhouse. The restaurant was built on in the mid-1980s, and the bar has an Old Codger Corner especially reserved for elderly regulars. Log burners warm the building in cooler months. Typical menu includes Tracy Tupman's Honey Glazed Duck Breast, Stilton and walnut pie, mushroom and red pepper stroganoff, Pickwick special mixed grill, steak and ale pie, and plenty of fish options. Lots of live music.

OPEN: 11.30-3 (Sun 12-3,7-10.30) 6-11
BAR MEALS: L served all week 11.30-2.30 D served all week 6.30-10 Sun 12-3 Av main course £10
RESTAURANT: L served all week 11.30-2.30 D served all week 6.30-10 Av 3 course à la carte £15
BREWERY/COMPANY: Youngs 🍺: Youngs Bitter, Youngs Special, Waggle Dance, Youngs Winter Warmer.
CHILDREN'S FACILITIES: menu, games, high-chairs, food/bottle warming, outdoor play area, large adventure playground **GARDEN:** Food served outside. Lawn & flower beds **NOTES:** Dogs allowed: in bar, Water, Parking 80

EBRINGTON   EBRINGTON ARMS

Ebrington GL55 6NH
☎ 01386 593223 📠 01386 593763
Dir: *Telephone for directions.* **Map Ref:** *SP14*

A charmingly down-to-earth Cotswold village pub dating from the mid-18th century. Stone flagfloors, large open fires and beautiful surrounding countryside give it plenty of character. Walkers frequent the pub for its locally-brewed ales and good home-cooked food, including butterflied breast of chicken with chilli butter and Mediterranean vegetables and cod with deep-fried leeks.

OPEN: 11-2.30 (open all day from Etr) 6-11
BAR MEALS: L served Tue-Sun 12-2 D served Tue-Sat 6-9 Av main course £8 **RESTAURANT:** L served Tue-Sun 12-2 D served Tue-Sat 6-9 **BREWERY/COMPANY:** Free House 🍺: Hook Norton Best, Fullers London Pride & Bombadier.
CHILDREN'S FACILITIES: menu, portions, licence, games, high-chairs, food/bottle warming, family room
GARDEN: Lawn and patio area **NOTES:** Dogs allowed: in bar, Water, Parking 12

EWEN   THE WILD DUCK ★★

Drakes Island GL7 6BY
☎ 01285 770310 📠 01285 770924
e-mail: wduckinn@aol.com
Dir: *From Cirencester take A429, at Kemble take L turn to Ewen, pub in village centre.*
Map Ref: *SU09*

An Elizabethan inn of mellow Cotswold stone, the Wild Duck is in many ways a typical local inn, with an abundance of exposed beams, oak panelling, open fires, and ancestral portraits adorning the walls. The enclosed courtyard is an ideal place for summer eating. The country-style dining room offers fresh seasonal food, including game in winter and fresh fish from Brixham delivered overnight.

OPEN: 8-11 (Sun 12-10.30) Rest: 25 dec Closed eve
BAR MEALS: L served all week 12-2 D served all week 7-10
RESTAURANT: L served all week 12-2 D served all week 7-10
BREWERY/COMPANY: Free House 🍺: Scottish Courage Theakston Old Peculier, Wells Bombardier, Greene King Old Speckled Hen, Smiles Best. 🍷: 25 **CHILDREN'S FACILITIES:** menu, portions, games, high-chairs, food/bottle warming, baby changing **GARDEN:** Enclosed courtyard, giant chess board
NOTES: Dogs allowed: in bar, in garden, in bedrooms, Parking 50 **ROOMS:** 11 en suite s£60 d£80

FORD   PLOUGH INN ♦♦♦♦

GL54 5RU
☎ 01386 584215 📠 01386 584042
e-mail: info@theploughinnatford.co.uk
Dir: *4m from Stow-on-the-Wold on the Tewkesbury road.* **Map Ref:** *SP02*

The new management of this 16th-century inn, steeped in history and character, continue to provide all that one associates with a traditional English pub; flagstone floors, log fires, sturdy pine furnishings and lively conversation. Meals made from local produce are cooked to order and the inn is renowned for its fresh, seasonal asparagus. The area is popular with lovers of the Cotswolds, racing, and Britain's sporting heritage.

OPEN: 11-11 (Sun 12-10.30) Closed: Dec 25
BAR MEALS: L served all week 12-2 D served Mon-Sun 6.30-9 weekends food all day 12-9 Av main course £8.95
RESTAURANT: L served all week 11.30-2.00 D served all week 6.30-9.00 **BREWERY/COMPANY:** 🍺: Donnington BB & SBA, Bottled Double Donnington.
CHILDREN'S FACILITIES: menu, portions, games, high-chairs, outdoor play area, play fort in garden **GARDEN:** Large court, beer garden with heat lamps **NOTES:** No dogs, Parking 50
ROOMS: 3 en suite 1 family room s£35 d£55

FRAMPTON MANSELL THE CROWN INN

GL6 8JG
☎ 01285 760601 ▤ 01285 760681
Dir: *A49 halfway between Cirencester and Stroud.* **Map Ref:** *SO90*

The Crown is peacefully located in the middle of a charming village in the heart of Stroud's Golden Valley. It is a 17th-century inn, full of old world charm, with honey-coloured stone walls, beams and open fireplaces, where log fires are lit in winter. Fresh local food, real ales and a good choice of wines by the glass are served in the restaurant and three inviting bars. Representative dishes include fresh Brixham sole with a garnish of seafood, chef's home-made stew with fresh vegetables and herby dumplings, and filo tarts with Brie, cherry tomatoes and spinach. There are some wonderful walks and cycling routes in the surrounding countryside, and the royal residences of Highgrove and Gatcombe Park are in the neighbourhood. Visitors should also look out for otters at the nearby mill.

OPEN: 12-2.30 6.30-11 **BAR MEALS:** L served all week 12-2 D served all week 6.30-9.30 Fri-Sat 6.30-10 Av main course £8.95 **RESTAURANT:** L served all week 12-2.30 D served all week 6.30-9.30 Av 3 course à la carte £18 🍺: Courage & real ales. ♀: 8
CHILDREN'S FACILITIES: menu, portions, games, high-chairs, food/bottle warming, family room **GARDEN:** Patio, garden overlooking valley **NOTES:** No dogs (ex guide dogs), Parking 100 **ROOMS:** 12 en suite s£69 d£89 (♦♦♦♦)

GREAT BARRINGTON THE FOX

OX18 4TB
☎ 01451 844385
e-mail: info@foxinnbarrington.co.uk
Map Ref: *SP21*

Picturesquely set pub with a delightful patio and large beer garden overlooking the River Windrush - on warm days a perfect summer watering hole. Built of mellow Cotswold stone and characterised by low ceilings and log fires, the inn offers a range of well-kept Donnington beers and a choice of food which might include beef in ale pie, local pigeon breasts casseroled with button mushrooms, chicken piri-piri, Thai tuna steak, and spinach, leek and chestnut pie.

OPEN: 11-11 **BAR MEALS:** L served all week 12-2.30 D served all week 6.30-9.30 **RESTAURANT:** L served all week 12-2.30 D served all week 6.30-9.30
BREWERY/COMPANY: 🍺: Donnington BB, SBA. ♀: 7
CHILDREN'S FACILITIES: portions, high-chairs, food/bottle warming **GARDEN:** Very large by river & lake, seats 100 people **NOTES:** Dogs allowed: in bar, in garden, in bedrooms, Parking 60

GREET THE HARVEST HOME ♀

Evesham Rd GL54 5BH
☎ 01242 602430
e-mail: sworchardbarn@aol.com
Dir: *M5 J9 take A435 towards Evesham, then B4077 & B4078 towards Winchcombe. 200yds from station.* **Map Ref:** *SP03*

Set in the beautiful Cotswold countryside, this traditional country inn draws steam train enthusiasts aplenty, as a restored stretch of the Great Western Railway runs past the end of the garden. Built around 1905, the pub is handy for Cheltenham Racecourse and Sudeley Castle. Expect a good range of snacks and mains, including locally-reared beef and tempting seafood dishes.

OPEN: 12-3 6-11 (Sun 6-10.30) Rest: 25 & 31 Dec closed eve **BAR MEALS:** L served all week 12-2 D served all week 6-9 Av main course £8 **RESTAURANT:** L served all week 12-2 D served all week 6-9 Av 3 course à la carte £16 Av 2 course fixed price £5.95
BREWERY/COMPANY: Enterprise Inns 🍺: Old Speckled Hen, Goffs Jouster, Deuchars IPA. ♀: 7
CHILDREN'S FACILITIES: menu, portions, licence, high-chairs, food/bottle warming, large garden
GARDEN: Grass area, picnic tables, countryside views
NOTES: Dogs allowed: in bar, in garden, Water, Parking 30

GUITING POWER   THE HOLLOW BOTTOM ◆◆◆◆ 🐑 ♀

GL54 5UX
☎ 01451 850392 ▤ 01451 850945
e-mail: hello@hollowbottom
Dir: *Telephone for directions.* **Map Ref:** *SP02*

An 18th-century Cotswold stone pub with a horse-racing theme, frequented by the racing fraternity associated with Cheltenham. Its nooks and crannies lend themselves to an intimate drink or meal, and there's a separate dining room plus tables outside for fine weather. Freshly made dishes include calves' liver, grilled seabass, marlin, and fillet steak, as well as exotic treats such as kangaroo and crocodile tail.

OPEN: 11-11   **BAR MEALS:** L served all week 12 D served all week 9.30 Av main course £9.50   **RESTAURANT:** L served all week 12 D served all week 9.30 Av 3 course à la carte £19.50   **BREWERY/COMPANY:** Free House ◖: Hook Norton Bitter, Goff's Jouster, Timothy Taylor Landlord, Fullers London Pride. ♀: 7 **CHILDREN'S FACILITIES:** menu, portions, licence, games, high-chairs, food/bottle warming, baby changing, cots **GARDEN:** Bench, table, patio heaters   **NOTES:** Dogs allowed: in bar, in garden, in bedrooms, Parking 15   **ROOMS:** 4 bedrooms 3 en suite s£45   d£65

HINTON   THE BULL INN

SN14 8HG
☎ 0117 9372332 ▤ 0117 937 2332
Dir: *From M4 Junc 18, A46 to Bath for 1m then R, 1m down hill, Bull on R.* **Map Ref:** *ST77*

Converted to an inn about 100 years ago, a 15th-century farmhouse off the old London to Bath road with a traditional pub atmosphere. In the evening, the bars and a non-smoking area are candlelit.

OPEN: 11.30-3 6-11 (Sun 6.30-10.30)   **BAR MEALS:** L served all week 11.30-2 D served all week 6-9 Av main course £8.95   **RESTAURANT:** L served all week 11.30-2 D served all week 6-9   **BREWERY/COMPANY:** Wadworth ◖: Wadworth 6X & Henrys IPA. **CHILDREN'S FACILITIES:** menu, outdoor play area, swings, climbing frames, family room   **GARDEN:** Very large garden   **NOTES:** Dogs allowed: in bar, in garden, Parking 30

LECHLADE   THE TROUT INN ♀

St Johns Bridge GL7 3HA
☎ 01367 252313 ▤ 01367 252313
e-mail: chefpjw@aol.com
Dir: *From A40 take A361 then A417. From M4 to Lechlade then A417 to the Trout Inn.* **Map Ref:** *SU29*

Dating from around 1220, a former almshouse with a large garden on the banks of the Thames. Things are generally humming here, with tractor and steam events, and jazz and folk festivals. The interior is all flagstone floors and beams in a bar that overflows into the old boat-house. The extensive menus offer a wide choice.

OPEN: 10-3 6-11 open all day Summer Closed: Dec 25   **BAR MEALS:** L served all week 12-2 D served all week 7-10 Sun 7-9.30pm   **RESTAURANT:** L served all week 12-2pm D served all week Av 3 course à la carte £16   **BREWERY/COMPANY:** ◖: Courage Best, John Smiths, Bass, Smiles. ♀: 16 **CHILDREN'S FACILITIES:** menu, portions, games, high-chairs, food/bottle warming, outdoor play area, family room   **GARDEN:** Food served outside, overlooking Weir Pool   **NOTES:** Dogs allowed: in bar, Water, Parking 30

LITTLE WASHBOURNE HOBNAIL'S INN ♀

GL20 8NQ
☎ 01242 620237 ▯ 01242 620458
e-mail: info@hobsnailsinn.com
Dir: *From J9 of the M5 take A46 towards Evesham then B4077 to Stow on Wold. Hobnails is 1.5 m on the L.* **Map Ref:** *SO93*

15th-century exposed beams, a log fire and various other character features complement this charming old inn which, until recently, had been owned by the same family for about 250 years. The menu offers the likes of Hobnails lamb - a half-shoulder slowly roasted until tender and laced with a minted port and red wine sauce; chicken cous-cous; and house risotto with sun-dried tomatoes, onions, peppers, mushrooms and basil.

Lighter bites include filled baps and burger with salad and chips.

OPEN: 12-3 6-11 (Easter-Sept 11-11)
BAR MEALS: L served all week 12-2 D served closed Monday (Easter-Sep) 6.30-9.30 (Sun 12-9) Av main course £6.25 **RESTAURANT:** D served all week 6.30-9.30 Av 3 course à la carte £18
BREWERY/COMPANY: Enterprise Inns ◀: London Pride, Flowers IPA, Bass, 6X. **CHILDREN'S FACILITIES:** menu, portions, licence, games, high-chairs, food/bottle warming
GARDEN: Large patio area with tables **NOTES:** Dogs allowed: in bar, Parking 80

MARSHFIELD THE CATHERINE WHEEL

39 High St SN14 8LR
☎ 01225 892220
e-mail: info@thecatherinewheel.co.uk
Dir: *Telephone for directions.* **Map Ref:** *ST77*

A friendly country pub that appeals equally to locals and visitors from further afield. The old-

style inn serves a good range of food including fresh fish dishes like sea bass with salmon mousse, and luxury fish stew, as well as chicken stuffed with smoked cheese served with mango coulis, lamb shanks with mint and redcurrant gravy, and duck breast with plum sauce. Roasted Mediterranean tartlet in a smoked cheese sauce is one of several vegetarian choices.

OPEN: 11-3 6-11 Rest: Mon Closed lunch
BAR MEALS: L served Tue-Sun 12-2 D served Mon-Sat 7-10 Av main course £8 **RESTAURANT:** L served Tue-Sun 12-2 D served Mon-Sat 7-10 Av 3 course à la carte £18
BREWERY/COMPANY: Free House ◀: Scottish Courage Courage Best, Abbey Ales Bellringer, Buckleys Best.
CHILDREN'S FACILITIES: portions, high-chairs, food/bottle warming **GARDEN:** Patio area **NOTES:** Dogs allowed: in bar, in garden, Parking 10

THE LORD NELSON INN ♀

1 & 2 High St SN14 8LP
☎ 01225 891820 & 891981
e-mail: clair.vezey@btopenworld.com
Map Ref: *ST77*

Family-run 17th-century coaching inn located in the Cotswolds, in a village on the outskirts of Bath. A friendly atmosphere, various real ales and cosy open fires add to the appeal and character of the place. The Cotswolds is also a haven for hikers and countryside lovers. Appetising menu features the likes of monkfish, fresh salmon, Thai King prawns, and prime fillet of beef garnished with Mont D'or potatoes and a rich Madeira reduction.

OPEN: 12-2.30 Summer: Sun 12-10.30 5.30-11 Winter: Sun 12-3, 6.30-10.30 **BAR MEALS:** L served all week 12-2 D served all week 6-9 Sun 12-3, 6-9 Av main course £9.75
RESTAURANT: L served all week 12-2 D served all week 6-9 Sun 12-3, 6-9 Av 3 course à la carte £22.50 ◀: Courage Best, Butcombe. ♀: 7 **CHILDREN'S FACILITIES:** menu, portions, games, high-chairs, food/bottle warming
GARDEN: small patio area with seating **NOTES:** Dogs allowed: in bar

MINCHINHAMPTON   THE WEIGHBRIDGE INN ♀

GL6 9AL
☎ 01453 832520 ▤ 01453 835903
e-mail: enquiries@2in1pub.co.uk
Dir: Situated between Nailsworth and Avening on the B4014. Map Ref: SO80

This historic 17th-century free house stands beside the original packhorse trail to Bristol,

now a quiet footpath and bridleway. The building has been carefully renovated behind the scenes, but the original features of the bars and restaurant remain unspoilt. The atmosphere is redolent of the past, with massive roof beams reaching nearly to the floor in the upstairs restaurant. The drinking areas are just as cosy whilst, outside, the various patios and arbours make the most of the surrounding Cotswold scenery.

OPEN: 12-11 (Sun 12-10.30) **BAR MEALS:** L served all week 12-9.30 D served all week 12-9.30 Av main course £6.20 **RESTAURANT:** L served all week 12-9.30 D served all week 12-9.30 Av 3 course à la carte £15 **◀:** Wadworth 6X, Uley Old Spot & Laurie Lee. ♀: 16 **CHILDREN'S FACILITIES:** menu, portions, high-chairs, food/bottle warming, baby changing facilities **GARDEN:** Two large patios, heaters, awnings, arbors **NOTES:** Dogs allowed: in bar, in garden, Water, Parking 50

MISERDEN   THE CARPENTERS ARMS 🐑 ♀

GL6 7JA
☎ 01285 821283
e-mail: bleninns@clara.net
Dir: Leave A417 at Birdlip, take B4010 toward Stroud, after 3m Miserden signed.
Map Ref: SO90

Named after the carpenter's workshop on the Miserden Park Estate, this old inn retains its inglenook fireplaces and original stone floors. Worn benches still carry the nameplates used by the locals a century ago to reserve their seats at the bar. Supplemented with daily specials, the main menu includes beer battered cod, chicken breast in honey mustard sauce, and salmon with parsley sauce. Good range of vegetarian dishes.

OPEN: 11.30-2.30 (Sun 12-3, 7-10.30) 6.30-11 **BAR MEALS:** L served all week 12-2.30 D served all week 7-9.30 Av main course £5.50 **RESTAURANT:** L served all week 12-2.30 D served all week 7-9.30 Av 3 course à la carte £13 **BREWERY/COMPANY:** Free House **◀:** Greene King IPA, Wadworths, Guest Beer. ♀: 8 **CHILDREN'S FACILITIES:** menu, portions, licence, high-chairs, food/bottle warming **GARDEN:** Patio area and gardens **NOTES:** Dogs allowed: in bar, in garden, Water, Parking 22

NAUNTON   THE BLACK HORSE

GL54 3AD
☎ 01451 850565
Map Ref: SP12

Renowned for its home-cooked food, Donnington real ales and utterly peaceful bed and breakfast, this friendly inn enjoys a typical Cotswold village setting beloved of ramblers and locals alike. Under new ownership, the inn provides a traditional English menu featuring liver and bacon, cottage pie, scampi and broccoli and cheese bake.

OPEN: 11.30-3 (open all day Sat & Sun) 6-11 **BAR MEALS:** L served all week 12-2 D served all week 6.30-9.30 **RESTAURANT:** L served all week 12-2 D served all week 6.30-9.30 **BREWERY/COMPANY:** **◀:** Donnington BB, SBA. **CHILDREN'S FACILITIES:** menu, portions, high-chairs **GARDEN:** Food served outside **NOTES:** Dogs allowed: in bar, Parking 12

NEWENT THE YEW TREE ♀

Clifford Mesne GL18 1JS
☎ 01531 820719
Dir: *Follow A40 to Ross on Wye, 2m, past Huntley turn R sign Mayhill/Cliffords Mesne, pass Glass House, turn L Yew Tree 50 Yds.*
Map Ref: *SO72*

Once a 16th-century cider press, The Yew Tree can be found on the side of May Hill in a delightful rural setting. The restaurant is the fulfilment of chef/patron Paul Hackett's dream of a high-class, cosmopolitan restaurant in the country, serving haute cuisine at reasonable prices. Ideally situated for walking the Gloucestershire Way.

OPEN: 12-2 6.30-11 Closed: 2-16 Jan
BAR MEALS: L served Tue-Sun 12-3 D served Tue-Sun 6.30-10.50 Av main course £13 **RESTAURANT:** L served Tue-Sun 12-3 D served Tue-Sun 6.30-10.30 Av 3 course à la carte £24.50 Av 3 course fixed price £24.50
BREWERY/COMPANY: Free House ◀: Shepherds Neame Spitfire, Wye Valley Butty Bach, Fuller's London Pride. ♀: 8
CHILDREN'S FACILITIES: portions, games, high-chairs, food/bottle warming, swing, slide, animals **GARDEN:** Spacious garden, furniture and parasols **NOTES:** Dogs allowed: in bar, in garden, in bedrooms, toys, water, Parking 30

NEWLAND THE OSTRICH INN

GL16 8NP
☎ 01594 833260 ▯ 01594 833260
e-mail: kathryn@theostrichinn.com
Dir: *Follow Monmouth signs from Chepstow (A466), Newland is signed from Redbrook.*
Map Ref: *SO50*

An early 13th-century inn situated opposite the fine church known as the 'Cathedral of the Forest'. Huge open fireplace, old furniture, and friendly pub dog. In the bar expect the likes of olde English sausages, Ostrich Inn pasta, steak and ale pie, sizzling ribs, three cheese tart, and Forester's Feast. The restaurant offers fillet steak with a rich wild mushroom and port sauce, butterflied boneless trout with a chive butter sauce, tarte tatin of caramelized red onions, goat's cheese and coriander, or rack of lamb with creamy garlic potato and caramelized shallots. Specials board changes weekly. Eight constantly changing ales always available.

OPEN: 12-3 6.30-11 (Sat/BH's 6-11)
BAR MEALS: L served all week 12-2.30 D served all week 6.30-9.30 Av main course £9.50 **RESTAURANT:** L served all week 12-2.30 D served all week 6.30-9.30 (Sat 6-9.30) Av 3 course à la carte £22 **BREWERY/COMPANY:** Free House ◀: Timothy Taylor Landlord, Pitchfork, Butty Bach, Old Speckled Hen. **CHILDREN'S FACILITIES:** portions, games, food/bottle warming **GARDEN:** Food served outside. Lawn & patio areas **NOTES:** Dogs allowed: in bar, Water & companions to play with

NORTHLEACH WHEATSHEAF INN ♦♦♦♦ ♀

GL54 3EZ
☎ 01451 860244 ▯ 01451 861037
e-mail:
enquiries@wheatsheafatnorthleach.com
Map Ref: *SP11*

This 16th-century Cotswold stone coaching inn has comfortable bedrooms, a real ale bar, a dining room and a function room overlooking the garden. The menu, which changes daily, offers the likes of Gloucestershire Old Spot sausages with bubble and squeak, or butternut squash and feta cheese gratin. There is a good wine list, and a selection of malt whiskies.

OPEN: 12-11 **BAR MEALS:** L served all week 12-3 D served all week 7-10 Sun 12-3, 7-9 Av main course £11 **RESTAURANT:** L served all week 12-3 D served all week 7-10 Sun 12-3, 7-9 Av 3 course à la carte £15
BREWERY/COMPANY: Free House ◀: Wadsworth 6X, Hook Norton Best Bitter, Hobgoblin. ♀: 10
CHILDREN'S FACILITIES: portions, licence, high-chairs, food/bottle warming **GARDEN:** Terraced with beautiful flowers & trees **NOTES:** Dogs allowed: in bar, Parking 15
ROOMS: 8 en suite 1 family room s£50 d£60

OAKRIDGE THE BUTCHER'S ARMS

GL6 7NZ
☎ 01285 760371 ▤ 01285 760602
Dir: *From Stroud take A419 turn L for Eastcombe. Then follow signs for Bisley. Just before Bisley turn R to Oakridge. Look out for brown tourist sign "Butchers Arms".*
Map Ref: *SO90*

Traditional Cotswold country pub with stone walls, beams and log fires in the renowned Golden Valley. Once a slaughterhouse and butchers shop. A full and varied restaurant menu offers steak, fish and chicken dishes, while the bar menu ranges from ploughman's lunches to home-cooked daily specials.

OPEN: 11-3 6-11 Closed: 25-26 Dec, 1 Jan
BAR MEALS: L served Tue-Sun 12-2 D served Tue-Sat 6.30-9
RESTAURANT: L served Sun 12-3 D served Tue-Sat 7-9
BREWERY/COMPANY: Free House 🍺: Greene King Abbot Ale, Wickwar BOB, Archers Best, Youngs Bitter.
CHILDREN'S FACILITIES: portions, food/bottle warming, baby changing, family room **GARDEN:** Food served outside. Overlooks Golden Valley **NOTES:** Dogs allowed: in bar, in garden, except in restaurant, Parking 50

PAINSWICK THE FALCON INN 🛏 🍷

New St GL6 6UN
☎ 01452 814222 ▤ 01452 813377
e-mail: bleninns@clara.net
Dir: *On A46 in centre of Painswick.*
Map Ref: *SO80*

Boasting the world's oldest known bowling green in its grounds, the Falcon dates from 1554 and stands at the heart of a conservation village. For three centuries it was a courthouse, but today its comfy accommodation and friendly service extends to a drying room for walkers' gear. The seasonal menu might offer game terrine or Greek salad to start, then venison en croute, chicken korma or Irish stew to follow.

OPEN: 11-4 5.30-11 (Sun 12-4, 6-10.30)
BAR MEALS: L served all week 12-2.30 D served all week 7-9.30 Av main course £6.50 **RESTAURANT:** L served all week 12-2.30 D served all week 7-9.30 Av 3 course à la carte £16 **BREWERY/COMPANY:** Free House 🍺: Hook Norton Best, Old Hooky, Wadworth 6X, Greene King IPA.
🍷: 10 **CHILDREN'S FACILITIES:** menu, portions, licence, high-chairs, food/bottle warming **GARDEN:** Courtyard and large bowling green to rear **NOTES:** Dogs allowed: in garden, in bedrooms, Water, Parking 35
ROOMS: 12 en suite 4 family rooms s£42 d£68

THE ROYAL OAK INN 🛏 🍷

St Mary's St GL6 6QG
☎ 01452 813129
e-mail: bleninns@clara.net
Dir: *In the centre of Painswick on the A46 between Stroud & Cheltenham.* **Map Ref:** *SO80*

Tucked away behind the church of this conservation village, the Royal Oak features very low ceilings, old paintings and artefacts, and a huge, open fire. In summer, a sun-trap rear courtyard contributes to its atmosphere. Food takes a solidly 'Olde English' approach using fresh produce delivered daily. Good range of snacks, too.

OPEN: 11-2.30 5.30-11 **BAR MEALS:** L served all week 12-2.30 D served all week 7-9.30 Av main course £5.50
RESTAURANT: L served all week 12-2.30 D served all week 7-9.30 Av 3 course à la carte £12.50
BREWERY/COMPANY: Free House 🍺: Hook Norton Best, Wadworth 6X, Black Sheep Bitter plus Guest Ales. 🍷: 8
CHILDREN'S FACILITIES: menu, portions, high-chairs, food/bottle warming **GARDEN:** Patio and courtyard
NOTES: Dogs allowed: in bar, in garden, Water

PAXFORD THE CHURCHILL ARMS ❀ ♈

GL55 6XH
☎ 01386 594000 🖷 01386 594005
e-mail: info@thechurchillarms.com
Dir: *2m E of Chipping Campden, 4m N of Moreton-in-Marsh.* **Map Ref:** *SP13*

In the heart of a picturesque north Cotswolds village, the Churchill Arms enjoys glorious views over rolling countryside. Popular with walkers and lovers of outdoor pursuits, the pub offers refreshing ales including Hook Norton bitter, a wide range of wines, and interesting modern pub food. Menus change daily: starters might include cod fishcake with pickled cucumber and avocado; game terrine with home-made green tomato chutney; or vanilla risotto with gruyere, smoked haddock and pancetta. For your main course, try grilled flounder, sherry, rosemary and tomato; monkfish with sweet and sour sauce and okra; or one of several vegetarian options. Puddings such as cappuccino mousse with marmalade, poached pear and coffee parfait or white chocolate and raspberry iced terrine will make your meal even more memorable. The Churchill Arms deservedly continues to attract discerning custom.

OPEN: 11-3 6-11 **BAR MEALS:** L served all week 12-2 D served all week 7-9 Av main course £11 **RESTAURANT:** L served all week 12-2 D served all week 7-9 Av 3 course à la carte £22 **BREWERY/COMPANY:** Free House ◖: Hook Norton Bitter, Arkells, Moonlight. ♈: 8 **CHILDREN'S FACILITIES:** portions, high-chairs, food/bottle warming **GARDEN:** 25 covers, parasols **NOTES:** in garden, No dogs (ex guide dogs)

SHEEPSCOMBE THE BUTCHERS ARMS 🐑 ♈

GL6 7RH
☎ 01452 812113 🖷 01452 814358
e-mail: bleninns@clara.net
Dir: *1.5m south of A46 (Cheltenham to Stroud road), N of Painswick.* **Map Ref:** *SO81*

Once used to hang and butcher deer hunted by Henry VIII from his Royal deer park, this friendly hostelry boasts a sunny sheltered terrace and panoramic views. A varied menu includes braised lamb shank, or whole over-roasted trout with garlic butter, and several steak options, while specials could be whole roast partridge or beef Wellington. Snacks might include rolls, bagels or tortilla wraps.

OPEN: 11.30-2.30 (Sun 12-3, 7-10.30) 6-11.30 **BAR MEALS:** L served all week 12-2.30 D served all week 7-9.30 Av main course £5.50 **RESTAURANT:** L served all week 12-2.30 D served all week 7-9.30 Av 3 course à la carte £15 **BREWERY/COMPANY:** Free House ◖: Hook Norton Best, Uley old Spot, Wye Valley, Dorothy Goodbodys Summer Ale. ♈: 10 **CHILDREN'S FACILITIES:** menu, portions, licence, high-chairs, food/bottle warming, safe garden away from road **GARDEN:** Beer garden, food served outdoors, patio **NOTES:** Dogs allowed: in garden and on terrace only, water, Parking 16

SOUTHROP THE SWAN

GL7 3NU
☎ 01367 850205 🖷 01367 850555
Dir: *Off A361 between Lechlade and Burford.* **Map Ref:** *SP10*

At the end of 2003, new owners arrived at this creeper-clad, 16th-century Cotswold pub, one coming from another Oxfordshire hostelry, the other from London's Bibendum restaurant. The public bar, with an old skittle alley, has a menu with plenty to choose from, while in the restaurant you may find braised pork belly with soy, ginger, garlic, chilli and sticky jasmine rice; grilled entrecôte with béarnaise sauce; escargots de Bourgogne; and smoked haddock, saffron and spring onion risotto.

OPEN: 11.30-3.30 6.30-11 **BAR MEALS:** L served all week 12-2 D served all week 7-9 **RESTAURANT:** L served all week 12-2.30 D served all week 7-10 Sun pm closed (winter) Av 3 course à la carte £22.50 **BREWERY/COMPANY:** Free House ◖: Hook Norton, Greene King IPA, Old Hooky, Abbot Ale. **CHILDREN'S FACILITIES:** portions, games, food/bottle warming **NOTES:** Dogs allowed: in bar

STOW-ON-THE-WOLD THE EAGLE AND CHILD ♀

C/o The Royalist Hotel, Digbeth St GL54 1BN
☎ 01451 830670 ▯ 01451 870048
e-mail: info@theroyalisthotel.co.uk
*Dir: From the A40 take the A429 towards Stow
on the Wold turn into town and pub is situated
by the green on the L. **Map Ref:** SP12*

Historic pub accessed through reception of
the Royalist Hotel, which is certified as the oldest inn
in England. The Eagle and Child has a long and
colourful history. Discoveries include a tunnel leading
from the bar to the church across the street, witches'
marks visible in the rooms, a bear pit, ancient timbers
and a frieze. The pub has two dining areas, one with a
beamed ceiling, exposed brickwork and an open fire,
the other a bright conservatory.

OPEN: 11-11 (Winter open at 12) **BAR MEALS:** L served all
week 12-2.30 D served all week 6.30-10
RESTAURANT: L served all week 12-2.30 D served all week
6.30-10 **BREWERY/COMPANY:** Free House ◀: Hook
Norton Best, Greene King Abbot Ale, Timothy Taylor Landlord.
♀: 8 **CHILDREN'S FACILITIES:** menu, portions, games,
high-chairs, food/bottle warming, baby changing
GARDEN: Small paved terraced garden **NOTES:** Dogs
allowed: in bar, in garden, in bedrooms, Parking 8

STROUD THE RAM INN

South Woodchester GL5 5EL
☎ 01453 873329 ▯ 01453 873329
e-mail: drink@raminn.com
*Dir: A46 from Stroud to Nailsworth, R after 2m
into S.Woodchester (brown tourist signs).*
***Map Ref:** SO80*

From the terrace of the 400-year-old
Cotswold-stone Ram there are splendid views
over five valleys, although proximity to the
huge fireplace may prove more appealing in
winter. Rib-eye steak, at least two fish dishes,
home-made lasagne and Sunday roasts can
be expected, washed down by regularly
changing real ales such as Uley Old Spot,
Wickwar BOB and Archer's Golden. The
Stroud Morris Men regularly perform.

OPEN: 11-11 (Sun 12-10.30) **BAR MEALS:** L served all
week 12-2.30 D served all week 6.00-9.30 Sun 12-2.30,
6-8.30 Av main course £7 **RESTAURANT:** L served all week
12-2.30 D served all week 6-9.30 Sun 12-2.30, 6-8.30
Av 3 course à la carte £11 Av 2 course fixed price £9.95
BREWERY/COMPANY: Free House ◀: Scottish Courage,
John Smiths, Uley Old Spot, Wickwar BOB.
CHILDREN'S FACILITIES: menu, portions, high-chairs,
food/bottle warming, baby changing **GARDEN:** 2 large patio
areas, seats approx 120 people **NOTES:** Dogs allowed:
in bar, in garden, Water, Parking 60

TETBURY GUMSTOOL INN ♀

Calcot Manor GL8 8YJ
☎ 01666 890391 ▯ 01666 890394
e-mail: reception@calcotmanor.co.uk
*Dir: In Calcot (on jct of A4135 & A46, 3m W of
Tetbury). **Map Ref:** ST89*

The Gumstool is the pub at Calcot Manor Hotel, a
charmingly converted English farmhouse set around a
flower-filled courtyard of ancient barns and stables. Built
in the 14th century by Cistercian monks, the inn provides
a cosy contrast to the manor, with a real English pub
atmosphere. An eclectic menu offers a wide choice of
interesting dishes to suit all tastes and appetites; most
portions can be either 'ample' or 'generous'.

OPEN: 11.30-2.30 5.30-11 (Sat 11.30-11, Sun 12-10.30)
BAR MEALS: L served all week 12-2 D served all week 7-9.30
Av main course £9.50 **RESTAURANT:** L served all week 12-2
D served all week 7-9.30 Av 3 course à la carte £20
BREWERY/COMPANY: Free House ◀: Scottish Courage
Courage Directors, Best & Theakston XB, Greene King Spitfire,
Wickwar BOB. ♀: 16 **CHILDREN'S FACILITIES:** menu, games,
high-chairs, food/bottle warming, OFSTED registered playzone,
family room **NOTES:** No dogs, Parking 100

TEWKESBURY THE FLEET INN

Twyning GL20 6DG
☎ 01684 274310 🖹 01684 291612
e-mail: fleetinn@hotmail.com
Dir: 0.5m Junction 1 - M50. *Map Ref:* SO83

Idyllically located on the banks of the River Avon, this 15th-century pub with restaurant has lawns and patios that can seat up to 350. Fishing, boules, play area, pet's corner, bird garden, craft shop, tea room and a Japanese water garden are all to hand. The traditional bars and themed areas provide a wide range of dishes.

OPEN: 11-11 **BAR MEALS:** L served all week 12-2.30 D served all week 6-9.30 **RESTAURANT:** 12-2.30 6.00-9.30 **BREWERY/COMPANY:** Whitbread 🍺: Boddingtons, Greene King Abbot Ale, Bass, Fullers London Pride. **CHILDREN'S FACILITIES:** menu, high-chairs, baby changing, outdoor play area, Changing room, play area **GARDEN:** Patios and water front garden **NOTES:** No dogs (ex guide dogs), Parking 50

TORMARTON COMPASS INN ★★ ☟

GL9 1JB
☎ 01454 218242 🖹 01454 218741
e-mail: info@compass-inn.co.uk
Dir: From M4 take A46 towards Stroud for 100yds then R. *Map Ref:* ST77

A former coaching inn, extended to offer accommodation and easily accessible from the M4 (J18), the Compass Inn stands in four acres of grounds; a unique enclosed orangery allows guests to enjoy the best of the weather. Light bites include a range of jacket potatoes and sandwiches, while the Vittles bar food includes traditional home-cooked dishes. The restaurant has main dishes such as loin of Welsh lamb with its own shepherd's pie, buttered sugar snaps and red wine sauce. Horse riding, hot air ballooning and clay pigeon shooting can be arranged.

OPEN: 7-11 Closed: 25-26 Dec **BAR MEALS:** L served all week 11-10 D served all week 7-10 **RESTAURANT:** L served all week D served all week 7-10 **BREWERY/COMPANY:** Free House 🍺: Interbrew Bass & Sussex, Badger, Butcombe Gold. ☟: 7 **CHILDREN'S FACILITIES:** menu, portions, high-chairs, food/bottle warming, baby changing **GARDEN:** Beer garden several terraces **NOTES:** Dogs allowed: in bar, in garden, in bedrooms, Water, Parking 200 **ROOMS:** 26 en suite 4 family rooms s£65 d£75

WINCHCOMBE ROYAL OAK

Gretton GL54 5EP
☎ 01242 604999 🖹 01242 602387
Map Ref: SP02

Dating back to the 1830s, this classic Cotswold pub has plenty of original character, including flagstone floors, old pine tables, and exposed beams. The pub is owned by Goff's Brewery so plenty of real ales are on tap, and there is also a huge selection of bottled beers. Lovely views across to the Malvern Hills can be enjoyed from the conservatory and gardens - at the bottom of which is a restored steam railway line. The lunchtime bar menu is traditional pub fare, and can be eaten anywhere in the building. In the evening, a more sophisticated menu is served in the restaurant, presenting a diverse choice including game, fish and vegetarian dishes.

OPEN: 12-3 6-11 (Sun 12-5, 7-10.30) Closed: Dec 25 **BAR MEALS:** L served all week 12-2.30 D served all week 6-7 **RESTAURANT:** L served all week 12-2.30 D served all week 6-9.30 (Sun 12-4) **BREWERY/COMPANY:** Free House 🍺: Goff's Jouster & White Knight, Mighty Oak Burntwood, RCH East Street Cream, Tournament. **CHILDREN'S FACILITIES:** menu, portions, high-chairs, food/bottle warming, outdoor play area, swings, climbing frame **GARDEN:** Orchard, patio, tennis court **NOTES:** Dogs allowed: in bar, in garden, Water

Gloucestershire continued

WITHINGTON THE MILL INN

GL54 4BE

☎ 01242 890204 📠 01242 890195

Dir: *3m from the A40 between Cheltenham & Oxford.* **Map Ref:** *SP01*

This traditional inn has been serving travellers for over 400 years and is set beside the River Coln in a deep Cotswold valley. Inside is stone-flagged floors, oak panelling and log fires, whilst outside is a lawned garden with 40 tables, providing a peaceful setting for a drink or meal. The menu comprises of English dishes, including steak and ale pie, scampi, tuna steaks and smoked salmon salad.

OPEN: 11.30-3 6.30-11 (Sun 12-3, 6.30-10.30) **BAR MEALS:** L served all week 12-2 D served all week 6.30-9 **BREWERY/COMPANY:** Samuel Smith 🍺: Samuel Smith Old Brewery Bitter, Samuel Smith Sovereign. **CHILDREN'S FACILITIES:** menu, high-chairs, baby changing facilities, family room **GARDEN:** Lawned with 40 tables, Trees and river **NOTES:** Dogs allowed: in garden, in bedrooms, Water, biscuits, Parking 80

ASHCOTT ASHCOTT INN

50 Bath Rd TA7 9QQ

☎ 01458 210282 📠 01458 210282

Dir: *M5 J23 follow signs for A39 to Glastonbury.* **Map Ref:** *ST43*

Dating back to the 16th century, this former coaching inn has an attractive bar with beams and stripped stone walls, as well as quaint old seats and an assortment of oak and elm tables. Outside is a popular terrace and a delightful walled garden. A straighforward menu offers 'Home Favourites' such as Cumberland sausages, pasta carbonara, Spanish omelette and steak baguette, while poultry and seafood choices include chicken provençal, tuna steak with salad, or chicken tikka masala. Vegetarians may enjoy

mushroom stroganoff with gherkins and capers, or Stilton and walnut salad.

OPEN: 11-11 **BAR MEALS:** L served all week D served all week Av main course £7 **RESTAURANT:** L served all week 12-2.45 D served all week 5.30-9.30 Av 3 course à la carte £17 **BREWERY/COMPANY:** Heavitree 🍺: Otter. ☿: 12 **CHILDREN'S FACILITIES:** menu, outdoor play area, play equipment **GARDEN:** Large seclude area, shaded with large trees **NOTES:** No dogs (ex guide dogs), Parking 50

ASHILL SQUARE & COMPASS

Windmill Hill TA19 9NX

☎ 01823 480467

Dir: *Turn off A358 at Stewley Cross service station (Ashill) 1m along Wood Road, behind service station.* **Map Ref:** *ST31*

Beautifully located overlooking the Blackdown Hills in the heart of rural Somerset, a traditional country pub with a warm, friendly atmosphere. Lovely gardens make the most of the views, and the refurbished bar area features hand-made settles and tables. Good choice of food includes pasta, steaks, fish such as breaded plaice, battered cod, and seafood crêpes, and specials like tenderloin of pork with an apple and cider sauce, or cauliflower cheese topped with mushrooms or bacon.

OPEN: 12-2.30 6.30-11 (Sun 7-11) Rest: Tues-Thur Closed lunchtime **BAR MEALS:** L served all week 12-2.30 D served all week 7-10 **BREWERY/COMPANY:** Free House 🍺: Exmoor Ale & Gold Moor Withy Cutter, Wadworth 6X, Branscombe Bitter, Exmoor Ale. **CHILDREN'S FACILITIES:** menu, outdoor play area, Swings, slides, climbing frame **GARDEN:** Very large garden, patio area, amazing views **NOTES:** Dogs allowed: in bar, in garden, Parking 30

AXBRIDGE   THE OAK HOUSE ♟

The Square BS26 2AP
☎ 01934 732444 📠 01934 733112
Dir: *From M5 J22, take A38 to Bristol. Turn onto A371 to Cheddar/Wells, then L at Axbridge. Town centre.* **Map Ref:** *ST45*

Parts of the house date back to the 11th century, with exposed beams, massive inglenook fireplaces and an ancient well linked to the Cheddar Caverns. The bar is small and intimate, while in the bistro food is served in an informal atmosphere. Sirloin and gammon steaks, Cumberland sausages and Cajun chicken share the menu with 'family favourites' comprising fisherman's pie, pork and cider casserole, leek and potato bake and specials on the chalkboard.

OPEN: 11-3 6.30-11 (Sun 11-10.30)
BAR MEALS: L served all week 12-2.30 D served all week 6.30-9.30 Av main course £7.95 **RESTAURANT:** 12-3 7-9 (Sun 6-9) Av 3 course à la carte £12.95
BREWERY/COMPANY: 🍺: Timothy Taylor, Butcombe. ♟: 8
CHILDREN'S FACILITIES: menu **NOTES:** No dogs

BUTLEIGH   THE ROSE & PORTCULLIS

Sub Rd BA6 8TQ
☎ 01458 850287 📠 01458 850120
Dir: *Telephone for directions.* **Map Ref:** *ST53*

A 16th-century free house, drawing its name from the local lord of the manor's coat of arms. Thatched bars and an inglenook fireplace are prominent features of the cosy interior. Large bar and dining room menus are on offer daily. Typical hot food choices include omelettes, burgers, fish, curry, steaks, hot baguettes, jacket potatoes, ploughman's, salads, and vegetarian choices.

OPEN: 12-3 6-11 **BAR MEALS:** 12-2 7-9
RESTAURANT: 12-2 7-9 **BREWERY/COMPANY:** Free House 🍺: Interbrew Flowers IPA, Butcombe Bitter, Wadworth 6X. **CHILDREN'S FACILITIES:** menu, outdoor play area **NOTES:** Dogs allowed: Parking 50

CLUTTON   THE HUNTERS REST ♦♦♦♦ ♟

King Ln, Clutton Hill BS39 5QL
☎ 01761 452303 📠 01761 453308
e-mail: info@huntersrest.co.uk
Dir: *Follow signs for Wells A37 through village of Pensford, at large rdbt turn L towards Bath, after 100 meters R into country lane, pub 1m up hill.* **Map Ref:** *ST65*

This inn, built as a hunting lodge for the Earl of Warwick around 1750, later became a smallholding and tavern for the local north Somerset coal-mining community.

OPEN: 11.30-3 6-11 (All day Sun in summer)
BAR MEALS: L served all week 12-2 D served all week 6.30-9.45 (Sun 12-2.30, 6.30-9) **RESTAURANT:** L served all week 12-2 D served all week 6.30-9.45
BREWERY/COMPANY: Free House 🍺: Interbrew Bass, Smiles Best, Emoor Ale, Wadworth 6X. ♟: 12
CHILDREN'S FACILITIES: menu, portions, games, high-chairs, food/bottle warming, baby changing, outdoor play area, Play area with swing, slides etc, family room **GARDEN:** Large landscaped areas with country views **NOTES:** Dogs allowed: in bar, in garden, Water, Parking 80 **ROOMS:** 5 en suite 2 family rooms s£57.50 d£80

COMBE HAY   THE WHEATSHEAF

BA2 7EG
☎ 01225 833504   📠 01225 833504
e-mail: jakica@btclick.com
Dir: *Take A369 Exeter rd from Bath to Odd Down, turn L at park towards Combe Hay. Follow lane for approx 2m to thatched cottage & turn L.* **Map Ref:** *ST75*

Nestling on a hillside overlooking a peaceful valley, 2 miles south of Bath off the A367, the 17th-century Wheatsheaf is a pretty, black and white timbered pub, adorned with flowers in summer, and featuring an attractively landscaped terraced garden, an ideal spot for summer imbibing. The unspoilt character of the rambling bar has been maintained, with massive solid wooden tables, sporting prints and open log fire. Food on the varied carte features home-cooked dishes, notably local game in season and fresh fish. Typical choices may include ploughman's lunches, terrines, and locally caught trout, in addition to roast rack of lamb, breast of pheasant stuffed with cream cheese, mushrooms and garlic, and chicken filled with crab and prawns and wrapped in bacon.

OPEN: 11-3 6-11 (Sat 11-11, Sun 12-10.30) Closed: 25-26 Dec, Jan 1 **BAR MEALS:** L served all week 12-2.30 D served all week 6.30-9.30 Av main course £7
RESTAURANT: L served all week 12-2 D served all week 6.30-9.30 Av 3 course à la carte £18
BREWERY/COMPANY: Free House 🍺: John Smith, Guest Ales. **CHILDREN'S FACILITIES:** menu, Large area in pub field **NOTES:** Dogs allowed: on leads, Parking 100

CROWCOMBE   CAREW ARMS ♀

TA4 4AD
☎ 01984 618631
e-mail: info@thecarewarms.co.uk
Dir: *Village is 10 miles from both Taunton and Minehead, off A358.* **Map Ref:** *ST13*

Set in glorious Somerset countryside this friendly pub offers local beers, including Exmoor and Otter Ales, which accompany hearty meals such as tender belly pork with mashed potatoes, pan-fried lambs' liver and kidneys with grilled bacon, ruby red fillet mignon, and chicken Dolcelatte. Fresh fish choices usually include mussels, king scallops and sea bass. Eat inside or enjoy the views from the garden in summer.

OPEN: 11-3 6-11 **RESTAURANT:** L served all week 12-2.30 D served Mon-Sat 7-10 Av 3 course à la carte £22
BREWERY/COMPANY: Free House 🍺: Exmoor Ale, Otter Ale, Cotleigh Ales. ♀: 8 **CHILDREN'S FACILITIES:** menu, high-chairs **GARDEN:** Beautiful garden with countryside views **NOTES:** Dogs allowed: in bar, in garden, in bedrooms, Parking 40

EAST COKER   THE HELYAR ARMS ◆◆◆◆ ❀ ♀

Moor Ln BA22 9JR
☎ 01935 862332 📠 01935 864129
e-mail: info@helyar-arms.co.uk
Dir: *from Yeovil, take A30 or A37, follow signs for East Coker.* **Map Ref:** *ST51*

Reputedly named after Archdeacon Helyar, a chaplain to Queen Elizabeth I, this Grade II listed country inn and restaurant dates back in part to 1468. Log fires warm the old world bar, while the separate restaurant was restored from an original apple loft. Superior cooking and wine list here, with local suppliers all given credits on the menus, which propose dishes such as bresaola (with air-cured Somerset beef); honey-glazed home-baked ham; and roast fillet of Dartmoor venison. These are backed by steaks, pork and sausages from the grill, and up to ten daily specials on the blackboard.

OPEN: 11-3 6-11 (Sun 12-3,6-10.30)
BAR MEALS: L served all week 12-2.30 D served all week 6.30-9.30 Sun 12-4.30 Jan-Apr Av main course £11
RESTAURANT: L served all week 12-2.30 D served all week 6.30-9.30 Sun 12-4.30 Jan-Apr Av 3 course à la carte £20 Av 3 course fixed price £16.95
BREWERY/COMPANY: Pubmaster 🍺: Bass, Flowers Original, Fullers London Pride. ♀: 16
CHILDREN'S FACILITIES: menu, games, high-chairs, food/bottle warming, basket of toys/books, family room
GARDEN: Grassed area seats 40, BBQ in the summer
NOTES: Dogs allowed: in bar, in garden, in bedrooms, Parking 40 **ROOMS:** 6 en suite 3 family rooms s£59 d£70

EXFORD   THE CROWN HOTEL ★★★ 🌸🌸 ♀

TA24 7PP
☎ 01643 831554 🖹 01643 831665
e-mail: info@crownhotelexmoor.co.uk
Dir: *From M5 J25 follow signs for Taunton.
Take A358 then B3224 via Wheddon Cross to
Exford.* **Map Ref:** *SS83*

A warm welcome awaits customers at Exmoor's oldest
coaching inn. The 17th-century building is set in three
acres of gardens and woodland, with its own stabling
and stretch of salmon fishing. The cosy bar and smart
non-smoking dining-room are both served by a single
menu that makes imaginative use of quality local
produce.

OPEN: 11-3 6-11 **BAR MEALS:** L served all week 12-2
D served all week 6.30-9.30 Av main course £8.95
RESTAURANT: L served Sun 12-2 D served all week 7-9
Av 3 course à la carte £32.50 Av 4 course fixed price £27.50
BREWERY/COMPANY: Free House 🍺: Exmoor Ale, Gold &
Stag, Cotleigh Tawny, Guest ales. ♀: 8
CHILDREN'S FACILITIES: menu, portions, high-chairs,
food/bottle warming **GARDEN:** Water garden, next to stream
NOTES: Dogs allowed: in bar, in garden, in bedrooms, Water,
Parking 20 **ROOMS:** 17 en suite 1 family room s£55 d£95

FAULKLAND   THE FAULKLAND INN ♀

BA3 5UH
☎ 01373 834312
e-mail: enquiries@faulkland-inn.co.uk
Dir: *On the A366 between Radstock and
Trowbridge, 17M from Bristol & the M4/M5.*
Map Ref: *ST75*

Former coaching inn, under new ownership, set in a
village complete with a green, stocks, standing stones
and pond. There is a bar menu offering light ans
simple dishes, combined with more traditional
favourites, and a carte serving larger dishes in the
evening. Typical dishes include beef wellington with
red wine jus, grilled calves liver and smoked bacon
with parsnip bubble and squeak, and a range of
specials and vegetarian options are available.

OPEN: 12-3 6-11 (Sun 12-3, 7-10.30)
BAR MEALS: L served all week 12-2 D served all week
7-9.30 Av main course £6 **RESTAURANT:** L served all week
12-2 D served all week 7-9.30 Av 3 course à la carte £22
BREWERY/COMPANY: Free House 🍺: Butcombe. ♀: 8
CHILDREN'S FACILITIES: menu, portions, high-chairs,
food/bottle warming **GARDEN:** Food served outside
NOTES: No dogs (ex guide dogs), Parking 30

FRESHFORD   THE INN AT FRESHFORD 🐑 ♀

BA2 6EG
☎ 01225 722250 🖹 01225 723887
e-mail: dwill60632@aol.com
Dir: *1m from A36 between Beckington &
Limpley Stoke.* **Map Ref:** *ST76*

With its 15th-century origins, and log fires
adding to its warm and friendly atmosphere,
this popular inn in the Limpley Valley is an
ideal base for walking, especially along the
Kennet & Avon Canal. Extensive gardens. The
à la carte menu changes weekly to show the
range of food available, and a daily specials
board and large children's menu complete
the variety. Typical home-made dishes are
pâtés, steak and ale pie, lasagne and
desserts; a nice selection of fish dishes
includes fresh local trout.

OPEN: 11-3 6-11 **BAR MEALS:** L served all week 12-2
D served all week 6-9 Av main course £6.25
RESTAURANT: L served all week 12-2 D served all week 6-9
Av 3 course à la carte £16.95
BREWERY/COMPANY: Latona Leisure 🍺: Wadworth 6X,
Butcombe Bitter, Interbrew Bass, Scottish Courage Courage
Best. ♀: 8 **CHILDREN'S FACILITIES:** menu, portions,
food/bottle warming, baby changing **GARDEN:** Large
terraced garden **NOTES:** Dogs allowed: in bar, in garden,
Water, Parking 60

FROME THE TALBOT 15TH-CENTURY COACHING INN ◆◆◆◆

Selwood St, Mells BA11 3PN
☎ 01373 812254 🖷 01373 813599
e-mail: roger@talbotinn.com
Dir: *From A36(T), R onto A361 to Frome, then*
A362 towards Radstock, 0.5m then L to Mells
2.5m. **Map Ref:** *ST74*

Rambling stone coaching inn entered through an
archway into an informally planted cobbled courtyard.
Inside are lots of little stone-floored bars and eating
areas, including a restaurant with low oak-beamed
ceilings, stripped pews, wheelback chairs, candles in
bottles, and fresh flowers on the tables. English/
French-influenced menus offer a good selection of largely
locally sourced meat, fish, game and vegetarian dishes.

OPEN: 12-2.30 6.30-11 (Sun 12-3 7-10.30) Closed: 25-26
Dec **BAR MEALS:** L served all week 12-2 D served all week
7-9 **RESTAURANT:** L served all week 12-2 D served all week
7-9 **BREWERY/COMPANY:** Free House 🍺: Butcombe Bitter
& guest ales. **CHILDREN'S FACILITIES:** menu, Cottage
Garden **GARDEN:** Cottage garden **NOTES:** Dogs allowed:
in bar, in garden, in bedrooms, Water, Parking 10
ROOMS: 8 en suite 2 family rooms s£75 d£95

HINTON ST GEORGE THE LORD POULETT ARMS ◆◆◆◆

High St TA17 8SE
☎ 01460 73149
e-mail: shill@datrix.co.uk
Dir: *2m N of Crewkerne, 1.5m S of A303.*
Map Ref: *ST41*

Owners Michelle Paynton and Stephen Hill
are progressively restoring the 17th-century,
thatched Ham-stone inn with its pretty
garden featuring fruit trees full of mistletoe.
Original flagstone floors have been revealed,
and when the garden is done the pub's
new/old look will be complete. Real ales are
served from the barrel, and the monthly-
changing menu places a strong emphasis on
local fresh, seasonal and often organic
produce. Choices might include Parma ham
wrapped chicken parcel, "Proper" steak and
kidney pie, stone baked pizza, filo pastry encased
artichokes in creamy saffron and green olive pesto, and
mushroom and pine-nut kibbe.

OPEN: 12-3 6.30-11 (Sun-Mon 7-10.30) Rest: Mon Closed
lunch **BAR MEALS:** L served Tue-Sun 12-2 D served Tue-Sat
7-9 Av main course £8.50 **RESTAURANT:** L served Tue-Sun
12-2 D served Tue-Sat 7-9 Av 3 course à la carte £17
BREWERY/COMPANY: Free House 🍺: Butcombe Bitter,
Hopback, Otter, Branscombe.
CHILDREN'S FACILITIES: menu, portions, high-chairs,
food/bottle warming **GARDEN:** Garden with fruit trees and
Poleta wall **NOTES:** Dogs allowed: in bar, in garden, Water
bowl, Parking 10 **ROOMS:** 4 en suite 1 family room s£48
d£72

ILCHESTER ILCHESTER ARMS ◆◆◆◆ ♆

The Square BA22 8LN
☎ 01935 840220 🖷 01935 841353
e-mail: enquiries@ilchesterarms.co.uk
Dir: *From A303 take A37 to Ilchester/Yeovil, L*
towards Ilchester at 2nd sign marked Ilchester.
Hotel 100yds on R. **Map Ref:** *ST52*

First licensed in 1686, this elegant Georgian
building dominates the old town square. Lucy
and Brendan McGee have been here over a
year now and made considerable changes.
Brendan, as head chef, has created an
extensive bistro menu with dishes such as
calves' liver, onion and bacon or medallions
of venison with hot and sour red cabbage
and red wine and game sauce. Bar meals
encompass sandwiches, salads, the house
burger, and beef and ale pie.

OPEN: 11-11 Closed: 26 Dec **BAR MEALS:** L served all
week 12-2.30 D served Mon-Sat 7-9.30 (Sun 12-2.30)
Av main course £7 **RESTAURANT:** L served all week
12-2.30 D served Mon-Sat 7-9.30 (Sun 12-2.30) Av 3 course
à la carte £20.50 Av 3 course fixed price £14.50
BREWERY/COMPANY: Free House 🍺: Carling, Stella Artois,
Buttcombe, Flowers IPA & regularly changing ales from local
breweries. **CHILDREN'S FACILITIES:** menu, portions, games,
high-chairs, food/bottle warming, baby changing, outdoor play
area, Wendy house in garden with toys **GARDEN:** Enclosed,
walled English garden **NOTES:** No dogs (ex guide dogs),
Parking 15 **ROOMS:** 7 en suite 1 family room s£60 d£70

ILMINSTER NEW INN

Dowlish Wake TA19 0NZ
☎ 01460 52413
Dir: *From Ilminster follow signs for Kingstone then Dowlish Wake.* **Map Ref:** *ST31*

A 350-year-old stone-built pub tucked away in a quiet village close to Perry's thatched cider mill. There are two bars with woodburning stoves, bar billiards and a skittle alley. The menu features local produce and West Country specialities, including fish, steaks and home-made pies.

OPEN: 11-3 (Sun 12-3, 7-10.30) 6-11 Rest: 25 Dec Closed eve **BAR MEALS:** L served all week 12-2.30 D served Mon-Sat 7-9.30 Av main course £6.50
BREWERY/COMPANY: Free House 🍺: Butcombe Bitter + guest beers. **CHILDREN'S FACILITIES:** menu, outdoor play area, slide and climbing frame, family room **GARDEN:** Beer garden, food served outdoors **NOTES:** Dogs allowed Parking 50

KINGSDON KINGSDON INN ♟

TA11 7LG
☎ 01935 840543
Dir: *From A303 take A372 towards Langport then B3151 toward Street, 1st R and R again.* **Map Ref:** *ST52*

Plenty of wooden seating makes the front garden a lovely spot in summer from which to absorb the peaceful Somerset scene, while the rambling bars are an all-year-round delight. The warmly decorated original front rooms have low beamed ceilings, stripped and scrubbed pine furniture, and a huge, but sadly only decorative, stone inglenook, although a log fire may well be blazing on a raised hearth in the lower bar. Good value lunch dishes include poached salmon in parsley sauce; lamb's liver, bacon and onions;

braised oxtail in Guinness; and grilled goat's cheese salad on ciabatta bread. In the evening you might start with crab and prawn mornay, or wild boar pâté, then follow with half a roast duck in scrumpy cider sauce; trio of cod, salmon and sole in a prawn sauce; or mushroom parcel with wild mushroom sauce.

OPEN: 11-3 6-11 **BAR MEALS:** L served all week 12-2 D served all week 7-10 Sun 7-9 Av main course £9.20
BREWERY/COMPANY: Free House 🍺: Cotleigh Barn Owl, Otter Bitter, Cottage Golden Arrow, Butcombe Best. ♟: 10
CHILDREN'S FACILITIES: portions, high-chairs, food/bottle warming **GARDEN:** Lawn at front, picnic benches etc
NOTES: No dogs (ex guide dogs), Parking 18

LANGPORT THE OLD POUND INN ♦♦♦

Aller TA10 0RA
☎ 01458 250469 ▤ 01458 250469
Map Ref: *ST42*

Built as a cider house, the Old Pound Inn dates from 1571 and retains plenty of historic character with oak beams, open fires and a garden that used to be the village pound. It's a friendly pub with a good reputation for its real ale and home-cooked food, but also provides function facilities for 200 with its own bar. Whimsically named dishes include portly venison, horsy wild boar, and fruit 'n' nut trout.

OPEN: 11-11 **BAR MEALS:** L served all week 12-2.45 D served all week 6-9.45 Av main course £5.50
RESTAURANT: L served all week 12-2.45 D served all week 6-9.45 Av 3 course à la carte £20 🍺: Butcombe, Butcombe Gold, Yorkshire Bitter, Courage Best.
CHILDREN'S FACILITIES: menu, portions, high-chairs, food/bottle warming, baby changing **GARDEN:** The old village pound **NOTES:** Dogs allowed: in bar, Parking 30
ROOMS: 6 en suite s£35 d£55

ROSE & CROWN

Huish Episcopi TA10 9QT

☎ 01458 250494

Dir: *Telephone for directions.* *Map Ref:* ST42

Boasting an 80-year-old licensee who was born on the premises, this charming thatched pub is better known locally as 'Eli's' - the name of the owner's father who ran it for 55 years. In the same family for 130 years, few changes have taken place here and the pub still has flagstones and a wide selection of old pub games. Local ales, farm cider and cider brandy accompany dishes like shepherd's pie, steak and ale pie, spinach lasagne, or delicious home-made soups and filled jacket potatoes. Local produce is used, including some fruit and vegetables from the pub garden.

OPEN: 11.30-2.30 5.30-11 (Fri-Sat 11.30-11, Sun 12-10.30) Rest: 25 Dec closed eve **BAR MEALS:** L served all week 12-2 D served all week 6-7.30 **BREWERY/COMPANY:** Free House ◖: Teignworthy Reel Ale, Mystery Tor, Hop Back Summer Lightning, Butcombe Bitter.
CHILDREN'S FACILITIES: games, food/bottle warming, outdoor play area, outside play area with sand pit & slide, family room **GARDEN:** Mainly lawns, seating, play area **NOTES:** Dogs allowed: in bar, in garden, Water, Parking 50, No credit cards

---

LEIGH UPON MENDIP   THE BELL INN 🐑 ⅋

BA3 5QQ

☎ 01373 812316

Dir: *head for Bath, then twrds Radstock following the Frome Rd, turn twrds Mells and then Leigh-upon-Mendip.* *Map Ref:* ST64

The Bell is a 17th-century inn located in the centre of the village on the edge of the Mendip Hills. It was built by the masons who constructed the parish church and who donated the fireplace in the main bar while they were lodging here. Home-cooked dishes include lamb shank, Normandy pork, chicken Parmigiana and wild mushroom carbinara. A three-mile walk around the lanes starts and finishes as the pub.

OPEN: 12-3 6-11 **BAR MEALS:** L served all week 12-2 D served all week 6.30-9.30 (Sun 12-2.30) Av main course £8 **RESTAURANT:** L served all week 12-2 D served all week 6.30-9 (Sun 12-2.30) Av 3 course à la carte £15 **BREWERY/COMPANY:** Wadworth ◖: Wadworth 6X, Butcombe Bitter, Wadworths JCB, Henrys IPA. ⅋: 9
CHILDREN'S FACILITIES: menu, portions, games, high-chairs, food/bottle warming, outdoor play area, slide, swings, family room **GARDEN:** Patio, grassed area with flower borders **NOTES:** No dogs (ex guide dogs), Parking 24

LITTON   THE KINGS ARMS

BA3 4PW

☎ 01761 241301

Map Ref: ST55

Full of nooks and crannies, this 15th-century local at the heart of the Mendips has a large garden with a stream running through it, and boasts a separate children's play area and outdoor eating. Menus offer smoked haddock fish pie, homemade chilli, and steak, mushroom and Guinness pie. Kings Arms Platters include Pigman's Platter - jumbo pork Lincolnshire sausage with eggs and chips.

OPEN: 11-2.30 6-11 (Sun 12-3 7-10.30)
BAR MEALS: L served all week 12-2.30 D served all week 6.30-10 Av main course £8 **BREWERY/COMPANY:** Free House ◖: Bass, Butcombe, Wadworth 6X, Flowers.
CHILDREN'S FACILITIES: menu, outdoor play area, family room **NOTES:** Dogs allowed: (In garden only. On lead at all times.), Parking 50

MARSTON MAGNA   THE MARSTON INN

BA22 8BX
☎ 01935 850365 📄 01935 850397
*Dir: Telephone for directions. **Map Ref:** ST52*

Grade II listed building close to Yeovilton Air Museum, and handy for the link road to the West Country. The oldest parts of the inn are reputed to be haunted, and there's a skittle alley for the energetic. The menu offers rump steak with Stilton sauce, chicken breast grilled with mushrooms, seafood fettuccine, and ham and eggs, washed down with seasonal guest ales.

OPEN: 12-2.30 Jun-Sep open 3pm 6-11 Open all day Sat, Sun 12-10.30 **BAR MEALS:** L served all week 12-2 D served Mon-Sat 6-9.30 Av main course £5.95 **RESTAURANT:** L served all week 12-2 D served Mon-Sat 6-9.30 Av 3 course à la carte £15 **BREWERY/COMPANY:** 🍺: Banks Bitter, Worthington Cream Flow, Stella Artois, Seasonal Guest Ale. **CHILDREN'S FACILITIES:** menu, skittle alley, family room **GARDEN:** Walled patio area, secure play area **NOTES:** in bar, water & toys, Parking 16

MIDSOMER NORTON   OLD STATION

Wells Rd, Hallatrow, nr Paulton BS39 6EN
☎ 01761 452228
Map Ref: ST65

This former Station Hotel stands opposite Hallatrow's old railway station, with a bar full of railway memorabilia. An old railway carriage now houses the 'Orient Express' style restaurant with its views of the large, well-maintained garden. The range of West Country ales takes in Brains SA and Butcombe, and home-made menu choices include griddled steaks, vegetarian Balti, and fish specials like red snapper with prawns.

OPEN: 12-3 5-11 (Open all day Fri-Sun) **BAR MEALS:** L served all week 12-2 D served all week 6.30-9 (Sun 12-2.30, 6.30-9) Av main course £7.75 **RESTAURANT:** L served all week 12-2 D served all week 6.30-9 (Sun 12-2.30, 6.30-9) Av 3 course à la carte £16 🍺: Brains S.A, Rev James, Draught Bass, Butcombe. **CHILDREN'S FACILITIES:** menu, portions, high-chairs, food/bottle warming, outdoor play area, swings, football pitch **GARDEN:** Large well maintained garden, 20 benches **NOTES:** No dogs (ex guide dogs), Parking 40

MONKSILVER   THE NOTLEY ARMS ♀

TA4 4JB
☎ 01984 656217 📄 01984 656576
*Dir: Telephone for directions. **Map Ref:** ST03*

An English country dining pub on the edge of Exmoor with some interesting African influences. The owners are from Zimbabwe where they farmed and ran a country club.

Ingredients are locally sourced, from Somerset lamb to Exmoor sirloin steaks, mussels from the River Exe, and fresh fish for their daily changing selection. They offer some Zimbabwean and South African dishes such as ostrich fillet (reared in Devon). All the meals are freshly prepared on the premises, and there is nothing fried, which means no chips! Children will be happily occupied in the garden or children's room with books and games.

OPEN: 11.30-2.30 6.30-11 **BAR MEALS:** L served all week 12-2 D served all week 7-9.30 Weekdays in winter 7-9 Av main course £7.25 **BREWERY/COMPANY:** Unique Pub Co 🍺: Exmoor Ale, Wadworth 6X, Smiles Best. ♀: 10 **CHILDREN'S FACILITIES:** portions, games, high-chairs, food/bottle warming, outdoor play area, children's room with books & games, family room **GARDEN:** well tended, bordered by stream **NOTES:** Dogs allowed: in bar, on lead, water provided, Parking 26

MONTACUTE KINGS ARMS INN

TA15 6UU
☎ 01935 822513 ▤ 01935 826549
e-mail: Kingsarmsinn@realemail.co.uk
Dir: *Turn off A303 at A3088 roundabout
signposted Montacute. Hotel by church in village
centre.* *Map Ref:* ST41

At the foot of a steep hill, or the Mons Acutus
that gave the village its name, the
17th-century, ham stone-built King's Arms
offers a relaxed, country house atmosphere.
Daily changing menus can be perused in
either of two restaurants, or the bar. Often
available will be tender lamb shank, baked
breast of duck, steak and kidney pie, soft
filled pancakes, liver and bacon, honey roast
ham and Stilton salad, and crab and prawn
risotto.

OPEN: 11-11 (Sun 12-10.30) **BAR MEALS:** L served all
week 12-2.30 D served all week 7-9 Av main course £10.95
RESTAURANT: L served all week 12-2.30 D served all week
7-9 Av 3 course à la carte £23.90 Av 3 course fixed price
£21.95 🍺: Greene KIng Abbot & IPA, Old Speckled Hen,
Ruddles County. ♀: 15 **CHILDREN'S FACILITIES:** menu,
high-chairs, food/bottle warming **GARDEN:** Large lawn,
orchard **NOTES:** Dogs allowed: in bar, in garden,
in bedrooms, Water, Parking 12

NETHER STOWEY THE COTTAGE INN

Keenthorne TA5 1HZ
☎ 01278 732355
Dir: *M5 J23 follow A39 signs for
Cannington/Minehead. Inn on A39.*
Map Ref: ST13

Dating from the 16th century, the Cottage is
an old coaching inn and traditional cider
house where cider was made until about 15
years ago. The walls of the bar are original
cob-stone and wattle, around one metre thick
at its base. Hearty eating options include a
carvery with four roasts and five veg, cottage
pies, curries, steaks, and braised shoulder of
lamb. Plenty of fish options.

OPEN: 11-11 (sun 12-10.30) **BAR MEALS:** L served all
week 12-2.30 D served all week 6-9
RESTAURANT: L served all week 12-2.30 D served Tue-Sun
6-9.30 Av 3 course à la carte £13
BREWERY/COMPANY: Free House 🍺: Bass, Butcombe
Bitter, Doom Bar, Otter. **CHILDREN'S FACILITIES:** menu,
portions, high-chairs, food/bottle warming, outdoor play area,
Fenced area **GARDEN:** Food served outside. Patio area
NOTES: Dogs allowed: in the garden only Parking 60

NORTH CURRY THE BIRD IN HAND

1 Queen Square TA3 6LT
☎ 01823 490248
Map Ref: ST32

A friendly 300-year-old village inn with large
stone inglenook fireplaces, flagstone floors,
exposed beams and studwork. Cheerful staff
make you feel at home. Blackboard specials
concentrate on local produce.

OPEN: 12-3 7-11 Rest: 25 Dec Closed eve
BAR MEALS: L served Mon-Sun 12-2 D served Mon-Sun
7-9.30 Av main course £5 **RESTAURANT:** L served
Mon-Sun 12-2 D served Mon-Sun 7-9.30 Av 3 course à la
carte £20 **BREWERY/COMPANY:** Free House 🍺: Badger
Tanglefoot, Exmoor Gold, Otter Ale, Cotleigh Barn Owl.
CHILDREN'S FACILITIES: menu **NOTES:** Dogs allowed:
Parking 20

OVER STRATTON THE ROYAL OAK

TA13 5LQ
☎ 01460 240906 ▤ 01460 242421
e-mail: chris&jill@the-royal-oak.net
Dir: *A3088 from Yeovil, L onto A303, Over Stratton on R after S Petherton.* **Map Ref:** *ST41*

A welcoming old thatched inn built from warm Hamstone, full of blackened beams, flagstones, log fires, pews and settles - with the added attraction of a garden, children's play area and barbecue. Real ales, including Tanglefoot, from the Badger brewery in Blandford Forum, supplement traditional menus of fish pie, salmon with saffron hollandaise, and game cobblers with chive and horseradish scones. Traditional Sunday roast.

OPEN: 11-3 6-11 (wkds all day) **BAR MEALS:** L served all week 12-2.30 D served all week 6.30-9.30 **RESTAURANT:** L served all week 12-2.30 D served all week 6.30-9.30 **BREWERY/COMPANY:** Woodhouse Inns ◖: Badger Best, Tanglefoot, Sussex Best Bitter. **CHILDREN'S FACILITIES:** menu, high-chairs, outdoor play area, play area, family room **NOTES:** Dogs allowed: in bar, in garden, Water, Parking 70

PITNEY THE HALFWAY HOUSE

TA10 9AB
☎ 01458 252513
Dir: *on B3153 between Langport and Somerton.* **Map Ref:** *ST42*

This is a pub largely dedicated to the promotion of real ale as produced by the many excellent micro-breweries in Somerset, Devon and Wiltshire. There are always six to ten of these available in tip-top condition. There is also an excellent choice of bottled Continental beers. This delightfully old-fashioned rural pub draws customers from a huge area. Three homely rooms boast open fires, books and games, but no music or electronic games. Home-cooked meals (except Sundays when it is too busy with drinkers) include soups, local sausages,

sandwiches and a good selection of curries and casseroles in the evening.

OPEN: 11.30-3 5.30-11 (Sun 12-3, 7-10.30) Closed: 25 Dec **BAR MEALS:** L served Mon-Sat 12-2 D served Mon-Sat 7-9.30 **BREWERY/COMPANY:** Free House ◖: Butcombe Bitter, Teignworthy, Otter Ale, Cotleigh Tawny Ale. **CHILDREN'S FACILITIES:** portions, games, food/bottle warming, outdoor play area **NOTES:** Dogs allowed: Water, Parking 30

PORLOCK THE SHIP INN 🐑

High St TA24 8QD
☎ 01643 862507 ▤ 01643 863224
e-mail: mail@shipinnporlock.co.uk
Dir: *A358 to Williton, then A39 to Porlock.*
Map Ref: *SS84*

Coleridge and even Nelson's press gang. Nestling at the foot of Porlock's notorious hill, where Exmoor tumbles into the sea, its thatched roof and traditional interior provide an evocative setting for a meal or drink. Meals range through ploughman's, light bites and dishes such as home-made steak, mushroom and ale pie.

OPEN: 11-11 (Sun 12-11) **BAR MEALS:** L served all week 12-2 D served all week 6.30-9.00 Sundays 12.30-2.30 Av main course £5.95 **RESTAURANT:** L served Sun 12-2 D served all week 7-9 Sun 12.30-2.30, 7-9 Av 3 course fixed price £10 **BREWERY/COMPANY:** Free House ◖: Cotleigh Barn Owl, Bass, Courage Best, Regular Guest Ales eg Snowy (Cotleigh). **CHILDREN'S FACILITIES:** menu, portions, games, high-chairs, food/bottle warming, outdoor play area, swings, climbing frame **NOTES:** Dogs allowed: in bar, water provided, Parking 40 **ROOMS:** 10 bedrooms 8 en suite 3 family rooms (♦♦♦)

Many travellers have been welcomed to this 13th-century inn, including Wordsworth,

PRIDDY NEW INN ♀

Priddy Green BA5 3BB
☎ 01749 676465
Dir: From M4 J18 take A39 R to Priddy 3m before Wells. From J19 through Bristol onto A39. From M5 J21 take A371 to Cheddar, then B3371. **Map Ref:** *ST55*

Overlooking the village green high up in the Mendip Hills, this former farmhouse is popular with walkers, riders and cavers, and once served beer to the local lead miners. Expect liver and bacon, chargrilled steaks and Brixham plaice. Plus New Inn pies, including a vegetarian version, jacket potatoes, omelettes and toasties. Priddy hosts the 'friendliest folk festival in England' every July.

OPEN: 11.30-2.30 7-11 (Sun & Mon 12-2.30)
BAR MEALS: L served all week 12-2 D served all week 7-9.30
RESTAURANT: L served all week 12-2 D served all week 7-9.30 **BREWERY/COMPANY:** Free House ◀: Interbrew Bass, Fuller's London Pride, Wadworth 6X, New Inn Priddy.
CHILDREN'S FACILITIES: menu, outdoor play area, slide, see-saw, play equipment, family room **GARDEN:** Large garden
NOTES: Dogs allowed: in bar, Water, Parking 30

SHEPTON MALLET THE THREE HORSESHOES ♀

Batcombe BA4 6HE
☎ 01749 850359 🖷 01749 850615
Dir: Take A359 from Frome to Bruton. Batcombe signed on R. **Map Ref:** *ST64*

Diners can expect a warm welcome and good hospitality from the friendly owners of this

delightful pub. Built of honey-coloured stone, their 16th-century coaching inn is tucked away in a pretty village. Exposed stripped beams, and a fine stone inglenook with log fire are to be found in the long and low-ceilinged main bar, where good real ales make a suitable accompaniment to the food. The menus change weekly offering a wide range of home-cooked dishes.

OPEN: 12-3 6.30-11 Closed: 25-26 Dec
BAR MEALS: L served all week 12-2 D served all week 7-9.30 Av main course £9 **RESTAURANT:** L served all week 12-2 D served all week 6.30-9.30 Av 3 course à la carte £16
BREWERY/COMPANY: Free House ◀: Butcombe Bitter, Wadworth 6X, Adnams Bitter, Interbrew Bass.
CHILDREN'S FACILITIES: menu, outdoor play area, adventure playground **GARDEN:** Food served outside
NOTES: Dogs allowed: Water, Parking 25

SPARKFORD THE SPARKFORD INN

High St BA22 7JH
☎ 01963 440218 🖷 01963 440358
e-mail: sparkfordinn@sparkford.fsbusiness.co.uk
Dir: just off A303, 400yds from rdbt at Sparkford. **Map Ref:** *ST62*

A picturesque 15th-century former coaching inn characterised by its popular garden, beamed bars and fascinating old prints and photographs. Nearby are the Haynes Motor Museum and the Yeovilton Fleet Air Arm Museum. A varied menu offers a selection of traditional meals and home-cooked favourites, including salmon and spinach pie, deep-fried breaded plaice, jumbo sausages, spinach and ricotta cannelloni, cottage pie with cheese topping, and a good lunchtime carvery.

OPEN: 11-11 **BAR MEALS:** L served all week 12-2 D served all week 7-9.30 **RESTAURANT:** L served all week 12-2 D served all week 7-9.30 **BREWERY/COMPANY:** Free House ◀: Interbrew Bass, Otter Ale, Butcombe Bitter, Greene King Abbot. **CHILDREN'S FACILITIES:** menu, portions, high-chairs, food/bottle warming, baby changing, outdoor play area **NOTES:** Dogs allowed: in bar, in garden, in bedrooms, Parking 50

STANTON WICK THE CARPENTERS ARMS

BS39 4BX
☎ 01761 490202 ▤ 01761 490763
e-mail: carpenters@buccaneer.co.uk
Dir: From A37(Bristol to Wells rd) take A368 towards Weston-Super-Mare, take 1st R.
Map Ref: ST66

In its tranquil hamlet overlooking the Chew Valley, this charming stone-built free house was formerly a row of miners' cottages. Behind the pretty façade with its climbing roses and colourful flower tubs, you'll find a comfortable bar with low beams and a chatty, music-free atmosphere. There are warming winter fires and, in summer, guests can enjoy the delights of al fresco meals on the spacious garden patio. The Cooper's Parlour, with an extensive daily chalkboard, is the focus of imaginative snacks and bar food.

OPEN: 11-11 Sun 12-10.30 Closed: 25/26 Dec
BAR MEALS: L served all week 12-2 D served all week 7-10 Sun 7-9 Av main course £11 **RESTAURANT:** L served all week 12-2 D served all week 7-10 Sun 7-9 Av 3 course à la carte £22 **BREWERY/COMPANY:** Buccaneer Holdings
🍺: Interbrew Bass, Butcombe Bitter, Scottish Courage Courage Best, Wadworth 6X. ♀: 12 **CHILDREN'S FACILITIES:** menu, portions, high-chairs **GARDEN:** Landscaped. Patio area, pond, heaters **NOTES:** in bar, in garden, Water, No dogs (ex guide dogs), Parking 200 **ROOMS:** 12 en suite 1 family room s£64.50 d£89.50 (♦♦♦♦)

STAPLE FITZPANE THE GREYHOUND INN ♦♦♦♦

TA3 5SP
☎ 01823 480227 ▤ 01823 481117
e-mail: ivor-lucy@the-greyhoundinn.com
Dir: From M5, take A358 E, signed Yeovil, after 4m follow sign to R, signed Staple Fitzpaine.
Map Ref: ST21

Nestling in a picturesque village, this 16th-century coaching inn takes its name from the men on horseback who dispatched news before the days of the Royal Mail. Weather permitting, enjoy the surrounding garden or alternatively, take refuge in rambling rooms characterised by flagstone floors, old timbers and natural stone walls. A good selection of traditional ales and seasonal, freshly prepared dishes awaits: perhaps fillet steak with Roquefort butter and port jus or pork tenderloin stuffed with mushrooms in a herb crust with Madeira sauce.

OPEN: 12-3 6-11 (Summer open all day)
BAR MEALS: L served all week 12-2 D served all week 7-9.30 Av main course £10.50 **RESTAURANT:** D served Thur-Sat 7-9 **BREWERY/COMPANY:** Free House 🍺: Otter, Adnams Broadside, London Pride, Castle Eden.
CHILDREN'S FACILITIES: menu, portions, games, high-chairs, food/bottle warming, family room **GARDEN:** Split level, all round the Inn **NOTES:** Dogs allowed: in bar, in garden, On leads. Water/Food provided, Parking 60 **ROOMS:** 4 en suite s£49.95 d£75.90

STOKE ST GREGORY ROSE & CROWN

Woodhill TA3 6EW
☎ 01823 490296 ▤ 01823 490996
e-mail: ron.browning@virgin.net
Dir: M5 J25, A358/A378 then 1st L through North Curry to Stoke St Gregory church on R. Pub 0.5m on L. Map Ref: ST32

Just off the famous and sometimes bleak Somerset Levels, this picturesque, 17th-century cottage-style pub still has a 60-ft well. The attractive dining room used to be a skittle alley, but it undoubtedly gives pleasure to many more people now, given the excellent dinner menu that lists a wide range of steaks and accompanying sauces, as well as skate wings meunière; grilled Brixham plaice fillets; roast Somerset chicken; and vegetable Stroganoff. The Luncheon Bar menu offers a splendid choice too.

OPEN: 11-3 7-11 Rest: Dec 25 Closed eve
BAR MEALS: L served all week 12.30-2 D served all week 7-9.30 **RESTAURANT:** L served all week 12.30-2 D served all week 7-10 **BREWERY/COMPANY:** Free House
🍺: Exmoor Fox, & Stag, Guest Ales.
CHILDREN'S FACILITIES: menu **GARDEN:** Pretty patio area with tables **NOTES:** No dogs (ex guide dogs), Parking 20

WATERROW   THE ROCK INN ◆◆◆ ♀

TA4 2AX
☎ 01984 623293 ▯ 01984 623293
Dir: *From Taunton take B3227. Waterrow approx 14m W.* **Map Ref:** *ST02*

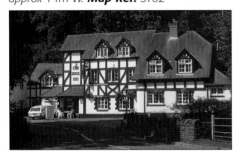

A 400-year-old former smithy and coaching inn built into the rock face, in a lovely green valley beside the River Tone. Sit in the peaceful bar, with the winter log fire and traditional furnishings, and sample the appetising menu including steaks and various home-made dishes.

OPEN: 11.30-3 6-11 (Sun close 10.30) Closed: 25-26 Dec Rest: (Open L 25 Dec) **BAR MEALS:** L served all week 12-2.30 D served all week 7-9.30 Av main course £7.50 **RESTAURANT:** L served all week 11-2.30 D served all week 7-9.30 Av 3 course à la carte £15 **BREWERY/COMPANY:** Free House ◀: Cotleigh Tawny, Exmoor Gold, monthly guest ales. ♀: 15 **CHILDREN'S FACILITIES:** menu **NOTES:** No dogs (ex guide dogs), Parking 20 **ROOMS:** 7 en suite 1 family room s£24 d£48

WELLS   THE CITY ARMS NEW ♀

69 High St BA5 2AG
☎ 01749 673916 ▯ 01749 672901
e-mail: query@thecityarmsatwells.co.uk
Map Ref: *ST54*

At the heart of the historic cathedral city; in Tudor times this used to be the jail. Today, as a free house, it provides a warm welcome, offering a range of fine ales, and a menu featuring freshly cooked, often seasonal, local produce. Favourite dishes include salmon and spinach fishcakes; calves' liver with fried onions and smoked bacon; and organic pork chops on mash with a local cider and apple sauce. City Arms burger, and sausage and mash are popular bar snacks.

OPEN: 9-11 **BAR MEALS:** L served all week 9 D served all week 10 **RESTAURANT:** L served all week 12 D served all week 6-9 Av 3 course à la carte £15 Av 3 course fixed price £17.50 ◀: Butcombe, Greene King, Sharps. ♀: 16 **CHILDREN'S FACILITIES:** menu, portions, licence, games, food/bottle warming, family room **NOTES:** Dogs allowed: in bar

WEST HUNTSPILL   CROSSWAYS INN 🐑 ♀

Withy Rd TA9 3RA
☎ 01278 783756 ▯ 01278 781899
e-mail: crossways.inn@virgin.net
Dir: *On A38 3.5m from M5 J22/23.*
Map Ref: *ST34*

A 17th-century coaching inn on the old Taunton to Bristol route provides a roomy yet intimate space to enjoy home-made food and a good range of national and local real ales, without the distraction of piped music, pool or darts. Part-panelled walls and the large fireplace in the central bar set the tone, and the visitor is assured of a warm welcome from the owners and a young, enthusiastic team.

OPEN: 12-3 5.30-11 (Sun 12-4.30, 7-10.30) Closed: 25 Dec **BAR MEALS:** L served all week 12-2 D served all week 6.30-9 (Sun; roast served 12-2.30, full menu 12-2, 7-9) Av main course £5.80 **RESTAURANT:** L served all week 12-2 D served all week 6.30-9.00 Av 3 course à la carte £10.50 **BREWERY/COMPANY:** Free House ◀: Interbrew Bass, Flowers IPA, Fuller's London Pride, Greene King Abbot Ale. **CHILDREN'S FACILITIES:** menu, portions, high-chairs, food/bottle warming, baby changing, Indoor games, skittles, family room **GARDEN:** Seating, food served outside **NOTES:** Dogs allowed: water, Parking 60

WHEDDON CROSS THE REST AND BE THANKFUL INN ◆◆◆◆ 🐾 ♀

TA24 7DR
☎ 01643 841222 📠 01643 841813
e-mail: enquiries@restandbethankful.co.uk
Dir: *5m S of Dunster.* **Map Ref:** *SS93*

Wonderful views of the moors can be enjoyed from this old coaching inn, located in the highest village on Exmoor. Old world charm blends with friendly hospitality in the cosy bar and spacious restaurant, where both traditional and contemporary food is served. Bar snacks from ploughman's to pies join vegetable lasagne, macaroni cheese, duckling à l'orange, scampi and rump steak, with perhaps profiteroles or apple and blackberry pie to round off.

OPEN: 9.30-3 6.30-11 Winter (7pm Opening)
BAR MEALS: L served all week 12-2 D served all week 7-9.30 **RESTAURANT:** L served all week 12-2 D served all week 7-10 **BREWERY/COMPANY:** Free House 🍺: Tawny, Otter Ale, Worthington Bitter, Abbott Ale. ♀: 7
CHILDREN'S FACILITIES: menu, high-chairs, food/bottle warming, outdoor play area, family room **GARDEN:** Paved patio **NOTES:** No dogs, Parking 50 **ROOMS:** 5 en suite s£30 d£60

WINCANTON BULL INN ♀

Hardway, nr Bruton BA10 0LN
☎ 01749 812200
Map Ref: *ST72*

A regular in this 17th-century free house is enjoying free beer for life after betting landlord Martin Smith that he could promote the pub on TV during England's World Cup matches in Korea and Japan. Luckily, says Martin, he's not a big drinker. Meals in the bar or restaurant include sirloin, rump and fillet steaks, ostrich steak, curries, home-made pies, chicken supreme, sea bass, red mullet, smoked haddock, and salmon and cod fish cakes. A gentle stream runs alongside the suntrap beer garden.

OPEN: 11.30-2.30 6-11 **BAR MEALS:** L served all week 12-2 D served Mon-Sat 6-10 **RESTAURANT:** L served all week 12-2 D served Mon-Sat 7-9.30
BREWERY/COMPANY: Free House 🍺: Butcombe Bitter, Greene King IPA & Old Speckled Hen, Shepherd Neame-Spitfire, Bass. **CHILDREN'S FACILITIES:** menu, outdoor play area **GARDEN:** Beer garden with tables & chairs
NOTES: Dogs allowed: in bar, Water tap outside, Parking 30

WITHYPOOL ROYAL OAK INN ★★ 🌸

TA24 7QP
☎ 01643 831506 📠 01643 831659
e-mail: enquiries@royaloakwithypool.co.uk
Dir: *From M5 through Taunton on B3224, then B3223 to Withypool.* **Map Ref:** *SS83*

With an ever-growing reputation as a sporting hotel for its hunting, shooting, and walking in the Exmoor National Park, this 300-year-old inn continues to generate its own long and colourful history. The two bars reflect Exmoor's sporting life. The Rod Room is full of fishing memorabilia and in both beamed bars, warmed by open fires, a wealth of good food created from local produce is available. You can dine in the bar or in the strikingly decorated dining room. As many of the ingredients as possible are sourced locally.

OPEN: 11-2.30 6-11 Closed: 25 Dec **BAR MEALS:** L served all week 12-2 D served all week 6.30-9.30 Av main course £12.50 **RESTAURANT:** L served Sun 12-2 D served all week 7-9.30 Av 3 course à la carte £26
BREWERY/COMPANY: Free House 🍺: Exmoor Ale & Exmoor, Stag, Grolsch. **CHILDREN'S FACILITIES:** portions, food/bottle warming **NOTES:** Dogs allowed: in bar, in garden, Kennels if needed, Parking 20 **ROOMS:** 8 bedrooms 7 en suite s£65 d£100

Somerset continued

WOOKEY   THE BURCOTT INN ♀

Wells Rd BA5 1NJ
☎ 01749 673874
Map Ref: ST54

A convenient stop for visitors to Wells or the Mendip Hills, this stone-built roadside inn sits opposite a working water mill, and is characterised by beams, open fires, pine tables and settles. Freshly prepared food is available in the bars, restaurant or large garden. The menu includes such dishes as salmon and prawns in garlic butter; grilled lamb cutlets with honey, mint and berry sauce; mixed fish grills, and various home-made pasta dishes. French sticks, sandwiches and salads are also available. Try your hand at the traditional pub games.

OPEN: 11.30-2.30 6-11 Closed: 25/26 Dec, 1 Jan
BAR MEALS: L served all week 12-2.30 D served Tue-Sat 6.30-9.30 Av main course £8.45 **RESTAURANT:** L served all week 12-2.30 D served Tue-Sat 6.30-9.30 Av 3 course à la carte £16 **BREWERY/COMPANY:** Free House
◀: Teignworthy Old Moggie, Cotleigh Barn Owl Bitter, RCH Pitchfork, Branscombe BVB.
CHILDREN'S FACILITIES: food/bottle warming, family room
GARDEN: Large garden, beautiful views **NOTES:** No dogs (ex guide dogs), Parking 30

WOOLVERTON   RED LION ♀

Bath Rd BA2 7QS
☎ 01373 830350 ▤ 01373 831050
Dir: On the A36 between Bath & Warminster.
Map Ref: ST75

Once a court room, with possible connections to Hanging Judge Jeffries, this 400-year-old building has lovely slate floors and an open fire. It is decorated in Elizabethan style and is an ideal place to enjoy real ales, country wines and good home cooking. Look out for steak and 6X ale pie, roasted lamb shoulder, ocean lasagne, smoked haddock and asparagus tart, butterflied chicken fillet, and a selection of hot rolls, jacket potatoes and sandwiches.

OPEN: 11.30-11 (Sun 12-10.30) **BAR MEALS:** L served all week 12-2.30 D served all week 6-9 Av main course £6.75 **BREWERY/COMPANY:** Wadworth ◀: Wadworth 6X, Henry's IPA, Wadworth JCB & Seasonal, Guest Beers. ♀: 30
CHILDREN'S FACILITIES: menu, outdoor play area, play area, high chairs **GARDEN:** Large garden, benches
NOTES: Dogs allowed: in bar, in garden, water, Parking 40

BARFORD ST MARTIN   BARFORD INN ♀

SP3 4AB
☎ 01722 742242 ▤ 01722 743606
e-mail: ido@barfordinn.co.uk
Dir: On A30 5m W of Salisbury.
Map Ref: SU03

Customer satisfaction and service are the keynotes in this 16th-century former coaching inn five miles outside Salisbury. A welcoming lounge, lower bar area and intimate snug have greeted visitors for generations - during World War II the Wiltshire Yeomanry dedicated a tank to the pub, known then as The Green Dragon. The varied menu includes freshly cut ciabattas, chargrilled medallions of beef, seafood linguini, or vegetarian stuffed Creole-style aubergine, and there's a range of exotic coffees to finish.

OPEN: 11-11 Closed: Dec 25 **BAR MEALS:** L served all week 12-2.30 D served all week 7-9.30 Av main course £9 **RESTAURANT:** L served all week 12-2.30 D served all week 7-9.30 **BREWERY/COMPANY:** Hall & Woodhouse
◀: Badger Dorset Best & Tanglefoot. ♀: 12
CHILDREN'S FACILITIES: menu **NOTES:** No dogs (ex guide dogs), Parking 40 **ROOMS:** 4 en suite s£50 d£55 (♦♦♦♦)

BRADFORD-ON-AVON THE CROSS GUNS FREEHOUSE RESTAURANT ♀

Avoncliff BA15 2HB
☎ 01225 862335 & 867613
e-mail: enquiries@crossedguns.com
Map Ref: *ST86*

A beautiful 16th-century inn nestling between the canal and the river. Exposed stone walls, low beamed ceilings and inglenook fireplaces deliver bags of rustic charm, whilst the idyllic riverside terraces provide a perfect location to enjoy a sunny day. Don't forget to sample the acclaimed food: typical dishes include steak and ale pie, chicken stuffed with Stilton and wrapped in bacon, and salmon and monkfish lattice with white wine and cucumber sauce.

OPEN: 10-11 **BAR MEALS:** L served all week 12-9 D served all week 12-9 Av main course £8
RESTAURANT: L served all week 12-2 D served all week 6.30-9 **▣:** Millworkers, Token Ale, Worthington, Bass. ♀: 12
CHILDREN'S FACILITIES: menu **GARDEN:** Seats 300 people, external heaters **NOTES:** Dogs allowed: in bar, in garden, in bedrooms, Parking 16

THE KINGS ARMS ♀

Monkton Farleigh BA15 2QH
☎ 01225 858705 ▤ 01225 858999
e-mail: enquiries@kingsarms-bath.co.uk
Dir: *Follow A4 from Bath to Bradford, At Bathford join A363, turning L to Monkton Farleigh.* **Map Ref:** *ST86*

Dating back to the 11th century, this historic Bath stone building is situated in a most attractive village five minutes' drive from Bradford-on-Avon. It was originally a monks' retreat attached to the nearby and now ruined monastery, and one of their number is said to be among several ghosts at the pub. In the 17th century the building was converted into a public house but many original features remain, including mullioned windows, flagged floors and a vast inglenook

in the medieval-style Chancel restaurant, which is hung with tapestries and pewter plates. Approached by way of an arboreal courtyard, the pub leads through to an enclosed garden with parasol-shaded tables and two aviaries - home to golden pheasants, lovebirds and Spook, the resident long-eared eagle owl.

OPEN: 12-3.00 5.30-11.00 (Sat 12-1, Sun 12-10.30)
BAR MEALS: L served all week 12-2.45 D served all week 6.30-9.30 (12-9.30 Sat & Sun) Av main course £7.50
RESTAURANT: L served all week 12-2.45 D served all week 6.30-9.30 (12-9.30 Sat & Sun) Av 3 course à la carte £21
BREWERY/COMPANY: **▣:** Greene King Old Speckled Hen, Wadworth 6X, Buttcombe Bitter, Wychwood Hobgoblin. ♀: 10
CHILDREN'S FACILITIES: menu, high-chairs, baby changing
GARDEN: Aviaries over-looking countryside **NOTES:** Dogs allowed: in bar, in garden, Parking 45

BRINKWORTH THE THREE CROWNS ♀

SN15 5AF
☎ 01666 510366 ▤ 01666 510303
Dir: *A3102 to Wootton Bassett, then B4042, 5m to Brinkworth.* **Map Ref:** *SU08*

The owner's research tells him that his pub acquired its name in 1801, but did it have an earlier name? The search continues. It stands on the village green by the church and, although deceptively small from the outside, opens up in a way Dr Who would have appreciated into a large, bright conservatory, a garden room and then out to a heated patio. In winter, an open log fire heats the traditional bars. All menus are written on large blackboards, where among the chicken supreme, rack of lamb, Somerset wild boar and home-made seafood pie, are crocodile

and Taste of the Wild - marinated slices of kangaroo, venison and ostrich, served with a brandy-based sauce. Other main meals include various pies, and a satisfying number of fish dishes. Lunchtime snacks such as ploughman's, filled rolls and jacket potatoes, are generously proportioned.

OPEN: 11-3 6-11 Closed: 25-26 Dec
BAR MEALS: L served all week 12-2 6-9.30 Av main course £15 **RESTAURANT:** L served all week 12-2 D served all week 6.15-9.30 Av 3 course à la carte £20
BREWERY/COMPANY: Enterprise Inns **▣:** Wadworth 6X, Bass, Castle Eden, Fullers London Pride. ♀: 10
CHILDREN'S FACILITIES: outdoor play area, childrens menu, activity sheets **GARDEN:** Sheltered patio with heaters, well maintained **NOTES:** Dogs allowed: in bar, in garden, Parking 40

BURTON THE OLD HOUSE AT HOME ♀

SN14 7LT
☎ 01454 218227 ▤ 01454 218227
Dir: *On B4039 NW of Chippenham.*
Map Ref: *ST87*

A soft stone, ivy-clad pub with beautiful landscaped gardens and a waterfall. Inside there are low beams and an open fire. Overseen by the same landlord for nearly twenty years, the crew here are serious about food. The kitchen offers a good fish choice, vegetarian and pasta dishes, and traditional pub meals. Favourites include lamb cutlets with champ, salmon and crab cakes, Woodland duck breast with stuffing, butterfly red mullet, and king scallops in Cointreau.

OPEN: 11.30-2.30 7-11 (w/end 11.30-3, Sun 7-10.30) (closed Tue lunch) **BAR MEALS:** L served Mon-Sun 12-2 D served Mon-Sun 7-10 Av main course £12
BREWERY/COMPANY: Free House **◖:** Wadworth 6X, Interbrew Bass. **♀:** 20 **GARDEN:** 3 tiered, landscaped
NOTES: No dogs, Parking 25

CHRISTIAN MALFORD THE RISING SUN 🐾 ♀

Station Rd SN15 4BL
☎ 01249 721571 ▤ 01249 721571
e-mail: risingsun@tesco.net
Dir: *From M4 J 17 take B4122 towards Sutton Benger, turn L on to the B4069, pass through after 1m to Christian Malford, turn R into village (station road) pub is the last building on the L.*
Map Ref: *ST97*

The characteristics of a convivial, unspoilt country inn have been preserved by new owner, Simon Woodhead. Particularly popular are the slow-roasted lamb shank, Barbary duck breast, pork medallions, and the wide variety of fish dishes, including lemon sole, red bream and tuna loin. The malty, hoppy Archers Village Bitter from Swindon, plus guest ales, are on tap in the bar. Dogs are offered water and 'treats'.

OPEN: 12-2.30 6.30-11 **BAR MEALS:** L served Tue-Sun 12-2 D served Mon-Sun 6.30-10 Av main course £7
RESTAURANT: L served Tue-Sun 12-2 D served Mon-Sun 6.30-10 Av 3 course à la carte £18
BREWERY/COMPANY: Free House **◖:** Archers Village, IPA & Two guest beers. **♀:** 9 **CHILDREN'S FACILITIES:** menu, food/bottle warming **GARDEN:** Food served outside, lawn
NOTES: Dogs allowed: in bar, in garden, Water & Treats, Parking 15

COLLINGBOURNE DUCIS THE SHEARS INN & COUNTRY HOTEL ♀

The Cadley Rd SN8 3ED
☎ 01264 850304 ▤ 01264 850220
Dir: *On A338 NW of Andover & Ludgershall.*
Map Ref: *SU25*

A thatched 16th-century building that used to function as a shearing shed for market-bound sheep. Now a thriving country inn, it owes some of its popularity to fresh seafood specials, including roast monkfish in Parma ham, seared tuna with quails' eggs and fresh anchovies, and gâteau of lobster, sole and salmon with basil and tomato dressing. Venison, rack of lamb, and various steaks, all with a delicious sauce or jus, are among other contributory factors.

OPEN: 11-11 **BAR MEALS:** L served all week 12-2.30 D served all week 6.30-9.30 (No meals Sun eve) Av main course £6.95 **RESTAURANT:** L served all week 12-2.30 D served all week 6.30-9.30 Av 3 course à la carte £20
BREWERY/COMPANY: Free House **◖:** Breakspear's Bitter & Guest Ales. **♀:** 31 **CHILDREN'S FACILITIES:** menu
GARDEN: Small area with 10 picnic tables **NOTES:** Dogs allowed: in bar, in garden, Parking 50

DEVIZES THE BEAR HOTEL ★★★ ♀

The Market Place SN10 1HS
☎ 01380 722444 ▤ 01380 722450
e-mail: info@thebearhotel.net
Map Ref: SU06

Right in the centre of Devizes, home of Wadworth's brewery, this old coaching inn dates from at least 1559 and lists Judge Jeffreys, George III, and Harold Macmillan amongst its notable guests. You'll find old beams, log fires, fresh flowers - and a menu with starters like grilled black pudding with apple and cider vinaigrette; and main courses such as pot-roasted partridge, or broccoli and mushroom strudel. For desserts (all home made) expect elderflower and gooseberry torte, or profiteroles with chocolate sauce.

OPEN: 9.30-11 Closed: 25-26 Dec **BAR MEALS:** L served all week 11.30-2.30 D served all week 7-9.30 Av main course £4.50 **RESTAURANT:** L served Sun-Fri 12.15-1.45 D served Mon-Sat 7-9.30 Av 3 course à la carte £21.95 Av 2 course fixed price £18
BREWERY/COMPANY: Wadworth ◀: Wadworth 6X, Wadworth IPA, Wadworth JCB, Old Timer. ♀: 18
CHILDREN'S FACILITIES: portions, high-chairs, food/bottle warming **GARDEN:** Courtyard **NOTES:** Dogs allowed: in bar, in garden, in bedrooms **ROOMS:** 25 en suite 3 family rooms s£50 d£75

THE SOUTHGATE INN ♀

Potterne Rd SN10 5BY
☎ 01380 722872 ▤ 01380 722872
e-mail: southgateinn@supanet.com
Map Ref: SU06

Friendly blues/jazz oriented pub serving an interesting choice of imported beers (from 21% ABV to 3.5% ABV in strength), many of them on draft. It also claims to be the only pub in the county serving kosher beer acceptable to the Jewish faith. The Southgate proudly proclaims its 'friendly food and fantastic staff', and the house speciality is ciabatta toasties. In summer you can sit outside in The Secret Garden (it is very small).

OPEN: 11-12 **BAR MEALS:** 11-10 ◀: GFB, Summer Lightning, Best. ♀: 45 **CHILDREN'S FACILITIES:** licence, high-chairs, food/bottle warming **GARDEN:** Very small, known as 'Secret Garden' **NOTES:** Dogs allowed: in bar, Parking 15

DONHEAD ST ANDREW THE FORESTER INN ♀

Lower St SP7 9EE
☎ 01747 828038
Dir: Near Shaftsbury, 4.5 miles on A30 to Salisbury. Map Ref: ST92

An attractive 14th-century thatched inn, recently refurbished to add a modern feel to its rustic charm. The interior still includes an inglenook fireplace and traditional wooden furnishings, and the pub retains a good local trade. There's an increased emphasis on home-cooked food such as warm chicken, bacon and cashew nut salad; tagliatelle of oyster mushrooms, artichokes and tomatoes in a cream sauce; and crab fishcakes. Other charms include an attractive garden and lunchtime bar snacks such as ciabattas and ploughman's platters. An old well is now a central part of the terrace.

OPEN: 12-3 6.30-11 **BAR MEALS:** L served all week 12-2 D served all week 7-9.30 **RESTAURANT:** L served all week 12-2 D served all week 7-9.30 ◀: 6X, Adnams, Bass, Ringwood. ♀: 10 **CHILDREN'S FACILITIES:** menu, portions, licence, games, high-chairs, food/bottle warming, baby changing **GARDEN:** Large patio area and garden **NOTES:** Dogs allowed: in bar, in garden, Parking 30

EAST KNOYLE   THE FOX AND HOUNDS

The Green SP3 6BN
☎ 01747 830573 📄 01747 830865
Dir: *Off A303 onto A350 for 200yds, then R.
Pub 1 0.5m on L.* **Map Ref:** *ST83*

Originally three cottages, dating from the late
15th century, this thatched pub overlooks the
Blackmore Vale with fine views for up to 20
miles. East Knoyle is the birthplace of Sir
Christopher Wren, and was also home to
Lady Jane Seymour.

OPEN: 11-2.30 6-11 **BAR MEALS:** L served all week
12-2.30 D served all week 7-10 🍺: Fullers London Pride,
Wadworth 6X, Smiles Golden, Butts Barbus Barbus.
CHILDREN'S FACILITIES: family room **NOTES:** Dogs
allowed: Parking 10

HEYTESBURY   THE ANGEL INN

High St BA12 0ED
☎ 01985 840330 📄 01985 840931
e-mail: Angelheytesbury@aol.com
Dir: *From A303 take A36 toward Bath, 8m,
Heytesbury on L.* **Map Ref:** *ST94*

With all the charm and character of a
traditional coaching inn, the Angel is a dining
pub in the modern idiom. This charming free
house is tucked away in a tiny village in the
lovely Wylye Valley, close to the edge of
Salisbury Plain. Heytesbury was a
parliamentary borough for several hundred
years until 1831, and the Angel was used as a
polling station. The pub has a reassuringly
civilised atmosphere, with relaxed and
friendly service that makes for a pleasurable
dining experience. The beamed bar features scrubbed
pine tables, warmly decorated walls and an attractive
fireplace with a wood-burning stove. In summer,
guests spill out into the secluded courtyard garden,
which is furnished with hardwood tables and cotton
parasols. Good quality local ingredients feature strongly
in a range of seasonal menus that combine modern
flavours with the best of traditional cuisine.

OPEN: 12-11 Sun (12-10.30) **BAR MEALS:** L served all
week 12-2.30 D served all week 7-9.30 Av main
course £9.95 **RESTAURANT:** L served all week 12-2.30
D served all week 7-9.30 Av 3 course à la carte £25
BREWERY/COMPANY: Free House 🍺: Ringwood Best,
Marstons Pedigree, Old Hooky, Ringwood Boondoogle.
CHILDREN'S FACILITIES: licence **NOTES:** Dogs allowed:
in bar, in garden, in bedrooms, Water, Parking 12

HORNINGSHAM   THE BATH ARMS ♈

BA12 7LY
☎ 01985 844308 📄 01985 844150
Dir: *Off B3092 S of Frome.* **Map Ref:** *ST84*

An impressive, creeper-clad stone inn
occupying a prime position at one of the
entrances to Longleat Estate. Purchased from
Glastonbury Abbey and converted into a pub
in 1763, the Bath Arms has been comfortably
refurbished and features a fine beamed bar
with settles and old wooden tables, and a
terracotta painted dining-room with open fire.
Menus offer traditional fish and chips, tuna
with mango salsa and herb oil, poussin with
bacon and braised Savoy cabbage, rib-eye
steak with red wine jus, and snacks like
Longleat ploughman's.

OPEN: 12-3 6-11 (1 May-31 Oct all day)
BAR MEALS: L served all week 12-2.30 D served Mon-Sat
7-9.30 Av main course £8.50 **RESTAURANT:** L served all
week 12-2.30 D served Mon-Sat 7-9.30 Av 3 course à la
carte £16 **BREWERY/COMPANY:** Young & Co 🍺: Youngs
Bitter, Special, Waggle Dance, Winter Warmer. ♈: 18
CHILDREN'S FACILITIES: menu **GARDEN:** Food served
outside **NOTES:** Dogs allowed: Parking 15

KILMINGTON THE RED LION INN

BA12 6RP
☎ 01985 844263
Dir: B3092 off A303 N towards Frome. Pub 2.5m from A303 on R on B3092 just after turning to Stourhead Gardens. **Map Ref:** ST73

This 14th-century coaching inn once provided two spare horses to assist coaches in the climb up nearby White Sheet Hill. The interior, unchanged over decades, features flagstone floors, oak beams, antique settles and blazing log fires. The landlord has been here for 25 years, and as well as being a champion of real ale, he supervises his kitchen to ensure that all produce - much of it local - is served in prime condition. A typical menu includes meat or vegetable lasagne, chicken casserole and game pie, as well as a selection of pasties, baked potatoes and toasted sandwiches.

OPEN: 11.30-2.30 6.30-11 (Sun 12-3, 7-10.30) (25 Dec Closed eve) **BAR MEALS:** L served all week 12-1.50 Av main course £4.95 **BREWERY/COMPANY:** Free House ◖: Butcombe Bitter, Jester, Guest Ale.
CHILDREN'S FACILITIES: portions, food/bottle warming
GARDEN: Large with picnic tables **NOTES:** Dogs allowed: in bar, in garden, in bedrooms, Not between 12-2, Parking 25, No credit cards

LITTLE CHEVERELL THE OWL

Low Rd SN10 4JS
☎ 01380 812263 📄 01380 812263
e-mail: jamie@theowl.info
Dir: A344 from Stonehenge, then A360, after 10m L onto B3098, R after 0.5m, Owl signposted. **Map Ref:** ST95

A 19th-century local situated in a tiny hamlet surrounded by farmland, with views of Salisbury Plain and plenty of good walks. The pretty split-level garden runs down to the Cheverell Brook. Quiz on first Wednesday of month in aid of a local charity. Holds three beer festivals during the year, with one in August also hosting a soap-box derby - again in aid of charity. Typical dishes include sizzling fajitas, Thai green chicken curry, and pan-fried skate wing. Opens for lunch on Christmas day.

OPEN: 11-3 6.30-11 (After April Sat/Sun 11-11, Mon-Fri 11-4 5.30-11) **BAR MEALS:** L served all week 12-3 D served all week 7-10.30 Sun 12-4, 7-9.30 Av main course £8.95 **RESTAURANT:** L served all week 12-3 D served all week 7-10.30 Sun 12-4, 7-9.30 Av 3 course à la carte £17.95 **BREWERY/COMPANY:** Free House
◖: Wadworth 6X, Hook Norton Best, Cotleigh Tawney Owl, Scottish Courage Courage Directors. ♀: 23
CHILDREN'S FACILITIES: menu, portions, licence, games, high-chairs, food/bottle warming, outdoor play area, swings
GARDEN: Decked area, brook, benches **NOTES:** Dogs allowed: in bar, in garden, in bedrooms, Water, Parking 28

LOWER CHICKSGROVE COMPASSES INN ◆◆◆◆

SP3 6NB
☎ 01722 714318 📄 01722 714318
e-mail: thecompasses@aol.com
Dir: A30 W from Salisbury, after 10m R signed Chicksgrove. **Map Ref:** ST92

An idyllic 14th-century thatched pub deep in beautiful Wiltshire countryside, offering the very best in real ale, fine wines and freshly prepared food. Not that easy to find, but worth negotiating the narrow lanes for. Inside the latched door, there's a long, low-beamed bar with high-backed stools, stone walls, worn flagstone floors and a large inglenook fireplace with a wood-burning stove. The blackboard menu changes daily, depending on the time of year and local availability. Everything is freshly made, including the popular steak and kidney pie with suet pastry; duck breast with a Chinese jus; pork tenderloin with Blue Vinny cheese, cider and cream sauce; and monkfish marinated in Thai spices with rice. A good range of filled onion loaves, salads and jacket potatoes is available at lunchtime. Puddings include wild strawberry Alexander, and chocolate and Kahlua mousse.

OPEN: 12-3 6-11 Closed: 25, 26 Dec **BAR MEALS:** L served Tue-Sun 12-2 D served Tue-Sat 7-9 (No food Sun eve) Av main course £12 **RESTAURANT:** L served Tues-Sun 12-2 D served Tues-Sat 7-9 (No food Sun eve) Av 3 course à la carte £20 **BREWERY/COMPANY:** Free House ◖: Interbrew Bass, Wadworth 6X, Ringwood Best, Chicksgrove Churl. ♀: 7
CHILDREN'S FACILITIES: menu, portions, games, high-chairs, food/bottle warming, outdoor play area, swings & see-saw, rope ladder **GARDEN:** Large grass area **NOTES:** Dogs allowed: in bar, Water, Parking 30 **ROOMS:** 4 en suite 3 family rooms s£45 d£65

LOWER WOODFORD THE WHEATSHEAF ♀

SP4 6NQ
☎ 01722 782203
Dir: *Take A360 N of Salisbury. Village
signposted 1st R.* **Map Ref:** *SU13*

Once a farm and brewhouse, now a thriving
country pub in the Avon Valley. A rustic decor
gives the interior a contemporary twist.
Expect dishes like seared tuna steak with
lemon and coriander butter, salmon and dill
fishcakes, and traditional cod and chips. Steak
and Tanglefoot ale pie, Cumberland sausage
and mash, and slow-roasted lamb shank
should also be available.

OPEN: 11-11 (Sun 12.10.30) **BAR MEALS:** L served all
week 12-9.30 D served all week Av main course £7.50
RESTAURANT: L served all week 12-2.30 D served all week
7-9.30 **BREWERY/COMPANY:** Hall & Woodhouse
🍺: Badger Dorset Best & Tanglefoot, plus guest ales.
CHILDREN'S FACILITIES: menu, outdoor play area, baby
change facility **GARDEN:** Food served outside. Enclosed
garden **NOTES:** Dogs allowed: In the garden only,
Parking 50

MERE THE GEORGE INN ♦♦♦

The Square BA12 6DR
☎ 01747 860427 ▤ 01747 861978
Dir: *Follow signs from A303 into village.*
Map Ref: *ST83*

Following extensive but careful refurbishment,
the former Talbot Hotel has been reborn as
the George. It was built about 1580 and, in
1651, Charles II dined here en route to exile
in France. Today's diners, however, are
unlikely to be looking over their shoulders as
they enjoy home-made soups and gratin
dishes, Scottish sirloin, steak and ale pie,
succulent local pork, lamb, poultry and game,
traditional Sunday roasts and West Country
cheeses.

OPEN: 11-11 (Mon-Tue 11-3, 6-11; Sun 12-3, 7-10.30)
BAR MEALS: L served all week 12-2.30 D served all week
6.30-9 Av main course £6.50 **RESTAURANT:** L served all
week 12-2 D served all week 6.30-9 Av 3 course à la carte
£16 **BREWERY/COMPANY:** Hall & Woodhouse
🍺: Champion Ale, Badger IPA, Tanglefoot, Badger Best.
CHILDREN'S FACILITIES: menu, high chair, family room
GARDEN: Patio area **NOTES:** No dogs, Parking 20
ROOMS: 7 en suite s£32.50 d£50

NEWTON TONEY THE MALET ARMS ♀

SP4 0HF
☎ 01980 629279 ▤ 01980 629459
e-mail: Malet@doghouse.co.uk
Dir: *8 miles NE of Salisbury on A338, 5 miles
SW of A303.* **Map Ref:** *SU24*

Built around 350 years old, the Mallet stands
on the banks of the River Bourne. Originally
the bake house for a long gone Elizabethan
manor, it's now a village pub with a lively bar
scene, an enthusiastic cricket team, and a
'Flying Mallet' facility providing outside
catering and beer tents for local events. Food
is all home made - beef burgers, fish, curries
and lots of game in season, and special
culinary evenings are a regular occurrence.

OPEN: 11-3 6-11 Closed: 26 Dec, 1 Jan
BAR MEALS: L served all week 12-2.30 D served all week
6.30-10 Av main course £8.95 **RESTAURANT:** L served all
week 12-2.30 D served all week 6.30-10 Av 3 course à la
carte £19 **BREWERY/COMPANY:** Free House
🍺: Wadworth 6X, Stonehenge Heelstone, Butts Barbus
Barbus & local guest ales. ♀: 8
CHILDREN'S FACILITIES: menu, high-chairs, food/bottle
warming **GARDEN:** paved with seating area, large paddock
NOTES: Dogs allowed: in bar, Water, Parking 30

NUNTON THE RADNOR ARMS

SP5 4HS
☎ 01722 329722
Dir: *From Salisbury ring road take A338 to Ringwood. Nunton signposted on R.*
Map Ref: *SU12*

A popular pub in the centre of the village

dating from around 1750. In 1855 it was owned by the local multi-talented brewer/baker/grocer. Bought by Lord Radnor in 1919. Bar snacks supplemented by an extensive fish choice and daily specials, which might include braised lamb shank, wild mushroom risotto, tuna with noodles, turbot with spinach or Scotch rib-eye fillet. Hosts an annual local pumpkin competition.

OPEN: 11-3 6-11 (Sun 12-3, Sun 7-10.30)
BAR MEALS: L served all week 12-2.30 D served Mon-Sat 7-9.30 Av main course £10 **RESTAURANT:** L served all week 12-2.30 D served all week 7-9.30 Av 3 course à la carte £17.50 **BREWERY/COMPANY:** Hall & Woodhouse
🍺: Badger Tanglefoot, Best & Golden Champion.
CHILDREN'S FACILITIES: menu, portions, high-chairs, food/bottle warming, outdoor play area, childrens license, family room **GARDEN:** Food served outside **NOTES:** Dogs allowed: in bar, Parking 40

PEWSEY THE FRENCH HORN

Marlborough Rd SN9 5NT
☎ 01672 562443 📠 01672 562785
e-mail: info@french-horn.co.uk
Dir: *A338 thru Hungerford, at Burbage take B3087 to Pewsey.* **Map Ref:** *SU16*

Popular local pub set beside historic Pewsey

Wharf on the Kennet & Avon Canal. Napoleonic prisoners of war working on the canal were summoned to the inn for meals by the sound of a French horn. Quality food is served in the restaurant - duck in cherry sauce, smoked haddock rarebit, pan-fried rib-eye steak, and the bar - vegetable quiche, beef stew and dumplings, ploughman's platter.

OPEN: 11.30-3 6-11 (Fri-Sat open all day.) (Sun 12-3 and 7-10.30) 25 Dec Closed evening **BAR MEALS:** L served all week 12-2.30 D served all week 6.30-9 Sunday dinner 7-9 Av main course £6.80 **RESTAURANT:** L served all week 12-2.30 D served all week 6.30-9 Av 3 course à la carte £25 **BREWERY/COMPANY:** Wadworth 🍺: Wadworth 6X, Henry's Original IPA, JCB. 🍷: 8 **CHILDREN'S FACILITIES:** menu, portions, high-chairs, food/bottle warming, baby changing, outdoor play area **GARDEN:** Canalside beer garden **NOTES:** Dogs allowed: in bar, Water, Parking 20

THE WOODBRIDGE INN

North Newnton SN9 6JZ
☎ 01980 630266 📠 01980 630457
e-mail: woodbridgeinn@btconnect.com
Dir: *2m SW on A345.* **Map Ref:** *SU16*

Variously a toll house, bakery and brewhouse, this Grade II-listed, 16th-century building stands in over four acres of beautiful grounds by the Wiltshire/Hampshire Avon, and was established as a coaching inn in 1850. Eating options are described as "Traditional home-made pub food", and a new tenant aims to please. Reports welcome.

OPEN: 12-11 (Sun 12-10.30) **BAR MEALS:** L served all week 12-9 D served all week 12-9 Av main course £6.50 **RESTAURANT:** L served all week 12-9 D served all week 12-9 **BREWERY/COMPANY:** Wadworth 🍺: Wadworth 6X, Henrys IPA, Summersault & Old Timer.
CHILDREN'S FACILITIES: menu, portions, games, outdoor play area, swings, slides, play area **GARDEN:** Large grassed with flower beds **NOTES:** Dogs allowed: in bar, in garden, Water, Parking 60

PITTON   THE SILVER PLOUGH ♀

White Hill SP5 1DU
☎ 01722 712266 📄 01722 712266
Dir: *From Salisbury take A30 towards Andover, Pitton signposted (approx 3m).* **Map Ref:** *SU23*

Surrounded by rolling countryside and with a peaceful garden, this popular pub is at the heart of a village full of thatched houses. Converted from a farmstead around 60 years ago, inside you will find beams strung with antique glass rolling pins - said to bring good luck - along with bootwarmers, Toby jugs and various other artefacts. It also features a skittle alley adjacent to the snug bar and there are darts and board games available. It is within easy reach of many lovely downland and woodland walks. Hughen and Joyce Riley took over as hosts at The Silver Plough in late 2002 and offer a range of dishes both lunchtime and evening, including children's meals. House specialities include half a roast shoulder of lamb with mint and garlic gravy, and red bream fillet with caramelised onions, prosciutto and pesto sauce.

OPEN: 11-3 6-11 (Sun 12-3, 6-10.30) 25-26 Dec, 1 Jan Closed eve **BAR MEALS:** L served all week 12-2.30 D served all week 6-9.30 Av main course £8 **RESTAURANT:** L served all week 12-2.30 D served all week 7-9.30 Av 3 course à la carte £18 **BREWERY/COMPANY:** Hall & Woodhouse 🍺: Badger Tanglefoot, Badger Best, IPA & King & Barnes Sussex + guest ales. ♀: 32 **CHILDREN'S FACILITIES:** menu, skittle alley, darts, board games, family room **GARDEN:** Lots of bench tables **NOTES:** Dogs allowed: in bar, in garden, water, biscuits, Parking 50

RAMSBURY   THE BELL 🐑 ♀

The Square SN8 2PE
☎ 01672 520230
Map Ref: *SU27*

This 300-year-old Wiltshire village inn has had a contemporary makeover but still retains a traditional feel with features like the old church pews and the pretty garden to the rear. Fish is the house speciality. Try the grilled red mullet with roasted pepper, almond parfait and pesto oil or the gilthead bream baked with olive oil. The kitchen happily combines classical techniques with global inspiration. It's rare to find a restaurant menu that offers stuffed Lebanese peppers with a spicy tomato coulis, and stacked medallions of venison and haggis with a red wine reduction.

OPEN: 12-3 6-11 (Sun 12-3, 7-10.30) **BAR MEALS:** L served Tues-Sun 12-2 D served Mon-Sat 7-9 Av main course £9 **RESTAURANT:** L served all week 12-2 D served Mon-Sat 7-9 Av 3 course à la carte £25 **BREWERY/COMPANY:** Free House 🍺: Butts, Wadworth 6X & Henry's Original IPA, West Berkshire, Arkells. ♀: 15 **CHILDREN'S FACILITIES:** family room **GARDEN:** Country garden **NOTES:** Dogs allowed: in bar, in garden, Parking 20

SALISBURY   THE OLD MILL HOTEL ♀

Town Path, West Harnham SP2 8EU
☎ 01722 327517 📄 01722 333367
Dir: *near city centre, on River Avon.*
Map Ref: *SU12*

Listed building which became Wiltshire's first papermaking mill in 1550. Tranquil meadow setting with classic views of Salisbury Cathedral. Crystal clear water diverted from the River Nadder cascades through the restaurant.

OPEN: 11-11 **BAR MEALS:** L served all week 12-2.30 D served all week 7-9 Av main course £4.95 **RESTAURANT:** L served all week 12-2 D served all week 7-9 Av 3 course à la carte £18 **BREWERY/COMPANY:** Old English Inns 🍺: Greene King IPA, Old Speckled Hen. **CHILDREN'S FACILITIES:** menu **GARDEN:** Food served outside **NOTES:** Dogs allowed: Parking 10

SEEND THE BARGE INN

Seend Cleeve SN12 6QB
☎ 01380 828230 ▯ 01380 828972
Dir: *Off A365 between Melksham & Devizes.*
Map Ref: *ST96*

Delightfully situated Victorian barge-style pub, converted from a wharf house, on the Kennet and Avon Canal between Bath and Devizes. Note the delicately painted Victorian flowers adorning the ceilings and upper walls. Once upon a time it was home to 8'2" Fred Kempster, the 'Wiltshire Giant'. In addition to the lunchtime menu of snacks and hot dishes there's a seasonal carte supported by blackboard specials.

OPEN: 11-3 6-11 All day Sat-Sun **BAR MEALS:** L served all week 12-2 D served all week 7-9.30 Av main course £9 **RESTAURANT:** L served all week 12-2 D served all week 7-9.30 Av 3 course à la carte £16 **BREWERY/COMPANY:** Wadworth 🍺: Wadworth 6X & Henry's IPA, Badger Tanglefoot, Butcombe Bitter. ♈: 10 **CHILDREN'S FACILITIES:** menu, portions, games, high-chairs, food/bottle warming **GARDEN:** canal side **NOTES:** Dogs allowed: Water, Parking 50

BELL INN

Bell Hill SN12 6SA
☎ 01380 828338
e-mail: Bellseend@aol.com
Map Ref: *ST96*

Local tradition has it that Oliver Cromwell and his troops breakfasted here on 18 September 1645, when advancing from Trowbridge to attack Devizes Castle. The pub has been extended to include the old brewhouse, a two-floor restaurant with wonderful views over the valley. House specialities include mini lamb shoulder, Thai green chilli chicken, beef and Stilton pie, chicken cacciatore, and feta cheese lasagne. A good choice of fish includes breaded plaice stuffed with prawns and mushrooms. Closed all day Tuesdays.

OPEN: 11-3 5.30-11 **BAR MEALS:** L served Wed-Mon 11.45-2.15 D served Wed-Mon 6.15-9.30 Sun 12-2.15 Av main course £7 **RESTAURANT:** 11.45-2.15 6.15-9.30 **BREWERY/COMPANY:** Wadworth 🍺: Wadworth 6X, Henry's IPA & Henrys Smooth. **CHILDREN'S FACILITIES:** menu, portions, high-chairs, food/bottle warming, outdoor play area, climbing frame with swings **GARDEN:** seating for 60 people, beautiful views **NOTES:** Dogs allowed: in bar, in garden, Water, Parking 30

SHERSTON CARPENTERS ARMS ♈

SN16 0LS
☎ 01666 840665
Dir: *On the B4040 W of Malmesbury.*
Map Ref: *ST88*

A locals' pub of whitewashed Cotswold stone dating from the 17th century. It has four interconnecting rooms, with low, beamed ceilings, a wood-burner and a cosy old-world atmosphere. The sunny conservatory restaurant overlooks the garden - a plantsman's delight with its large variety of shrubs, climbers, specimen roses, acers and herbaceous perennials. Seasonal fish dishes are served alongside pies, venison sausages, smoked salmon crêpes, and mushroom and paprika parcels.

OPEN: 12-2.30 5-11 (Sat 10-2.30, Sun 7-10.30) **BAR MEALS:** L served all week 12-2 D served Mon-Sat 7-9 Av main course £7.50 **RESTAURANT:** L served all week 12-2 D served Mon-Sat 7-9 Av 3 course à la carte £12.50 **BREWERY/COMPANY:** Enterprise Inns 🍺: Interbrew Flowers IPA & Whitbread Best, Guest Ales. ♈: 7 **CHILDREN'S FACILITIES:** menu, portions, high-chairs, food/bottle warming, outdoor play area, swings, slide, climbing frame **GARDEN:** Plantsmans garden, array of plants **NOTES:** No dogs (ex guide dogs), Parking 12

THE RATTLEBONE INN 🍷

Church St SN16 0LR
☎ 01666 840871 📠 01666 840871
e-mail: rattleboneinn@youngs.co.uk
Dir: *M4 J18 take A46 towards Stroud, then R onto B4040 through Acton Turville & onto Sherston. Or N from M4 J17 & follow signs.*
Map Ref: *ST88*

A 16th-century village inn standing where, according to legend, local hero John Rattlebone died of his wounds after the Battle of Sherston in 1016. The rambling series of beamed rooms have kept their existing character, but a new team has taken the operation. Reports on the direction they take are welcome.

OPEN: 12-11 **BAR MEALS:** L served all week 12-2.30 D served all week 6-9.30 Sun 6-9 Av main course £7
RESTAURANT: L served all week 12-2.30 D served all week 6-9.30 Av 3 course à la carte £15
BREWERY/COMPANY: Young & Co 🍺: Youngs Special, Bitter, Smiles Best, Youngs Triple A. 🍷: 18
CHILDREN'S FACILITIES: portions, high-chairs, food/bottle warming **GARDEN:** Food served outside **NOTES:** No dogs (ex guide dogs)

STOURHEAD   SPREAD EAGLE INN 🍷

BA12 6QE
☎ 01747 840587 📠 01747 840954
e-mail: thespreadeagle@aol.com
Dir: *N of A303 off B3092.* **Map Ref:** *ST73*

This charming inn was built at the beginning of the 19th century in the heart of the 2,650-acre Stourhead Estate, now one of the country's most visited National Trust properties. Before or after a walk through the magnificent gardens and landscapes there is plenty on offer here, including guinea fowl or wood pigeon supreme; beef stir-fry; wild boar and herb sausages; swordfish steak; and Mediterranean stuffed peppers. The bar menu embraces inexpensive hot meals, filled jackets, ploughman's, salads and sandwiches.

OPEN: 9-11 **BAR MEALS:** L served all week 12-3 D served all week 6-9 Av main course £5.50
RESTAURANT: D served all week 6-9 Av 3 course à la carte £19 **BREWERY/COMPANY:** Free House 🍺: Courage Best, Wadworth 6X. **CHILDREN'S FACILITIES:** portions, high-chairs, food/bottle warming **NOTES:** No dogs (ex guide dogs), Parking 200

SWINDON   THE SUN INN 🍷

Lydiard Millicent SN5 3LU
☎ 01793 770425 📠 01793 778287
e-mail: thesuninnlm@yahoo.co.uk
Dir: *3 miles to the W of Swindon, 1.5 miles from Junct 16 of M4.* **Map Ref:** *SU18*

18th-century inn located in the conservation area of Lydiard Millicent. Originally in the same family for 100 years, the pub's history is illustrated through photographs and pictures. The setting sun over the fields at the back of the inn might have inspired its name. Popular choices include chef's beer battered fish and chips, liver and bacon, salmon steak, Jamaican chicken, and vegetable Wellington.

OPEN: 11.30-3 5-11 (Sat 11.30-3, 6-11, Sun 12-4, 6.30-10.30) (Mar-Sep all day Sun) **BAR MEALS:** L all week 12-2.30 D all week 6.30-9.30 (Sun 12-2.30 6.30-9) Av main course £6.50 **RESTAURANT:** L all week 12-2.30 D all week 6.30-9.30 Av 3 course à la carte £14.50
BREWERY/COMPANY: Free House 🍺: Interbrew Flowers original, Wadworth 6X, Moles Bitter, Abbot Ale. 🍷: 8
CHILDREN'S FACILITIES: menu, portions, games, high-chairs, food/bottle warming, baby changing, outdoor play area
GARDEN: BBQ, suntrap **NOTES:** Dogs allowed, Parking 50

TOLLARD ROYAL KING JOHN INN

SP5 5PS
☎ 01725 516207
Dir: *On B3081 (7m E of Shaftesbury).*
Map Ref: *ST91*

Named after one of King John's hunting lodges, this Victorian building was opened in 1859. A friendly and relaxing place, it is today perhaps better known as 'Madonna's local' after she and husband Guy Ritchie moved in close by. Also nearby is a 13th-century church, and the area is excellent rambling country. A typical menu offers old English favourites such as bangers and apple mash; bacon, liver and kidney casserole; Dorset lamb cutlets; Wiltshire gammon with peaches; and Dover sole.

OPEN: 12-2.30 6.30-11 (Sun 12-10.30)
BAR MEALS: L served all week 12-2 D served all week 7-9 (All day Sun summer) **RESTAURANT:** L served all week 12-2 D served all week 7-9 **BREWERY/COMPANY:** Free House ◀: Courage Best, John Smith's, Wadworth 6X, Ringwood. **CHILDREN'S FACILITIES:** menu, portions, high-chairs, food/bottle warming **GARDEN:** Terrace, food served outside **NOTES:** Dogs allowed: in bar, Water, Parking 18

UPPER CHUTE THE CROSS KEYS ♀

SP11 9ER
☎ 01264 730295 ▤ 01264 730679
Dir: *Near Andover.* **Map Ref:** *SU25*

Located in a walkers' paradise on top of the North Wessex Downs, this free house adjoins a village shop and post office and boasts commanding views from its south-facing terrace and garden. People flock here by foot, bike and car to enjoy the views, the welcome and of course good home-cooked food: perhaps cottage pie, Irish stew, Sunday roast or cod and chips.

OPEN: 11-3 6-11 (Sun 12-4, 7-10.30)
BAR MEALS: L served all week 12-2 D served all week 6-9 Av main course £7.50 **RESTAURANT:** L served all week 12-2 D served all week 6-9 Av 3 course à la carte £15
BREWERY/COMPANY: Free House ◀: Fuller's London Pride, Hampshire Strong's Best, Greene King IPA, Ringwood Best. ♀: 10 **CHILDREN'S FACILITIES:** menu, licence, outdoor play area, swings, Wendy House **GARDEN:** Large, picnic tables, patio area, chairs **NOTES:** Dogs allowed: in bar, in garden, water, doggie treats, Parking 40

WARMINSTER THE ANGEL INN ♀

Upton Scudamore BA12 0AG
☎ 01985 213225 ▤ 01985 218182
e-mail: theangelinn.uptonscudamore
@btopenworld.com
Map Ref: *ST84*

A relaxed and unpretentious old inn in a small village with a name Agatha Christie might have made up. Freshly prepared lunch could be Cumberland sausage with horseradish mash and blackcurrant sauce, or game casserole with juniper berries and bacon dumplings. Dinner candidates include honey-glazed breast of duck with cumin and sweet potato pancake and pineapple sauce, or bacon-wrapped gilthead fillet of sea bream with saffron mash, roasted almonds and red curry sauce. Walled terrace garden.

OPEN: 11-3 6-11 Closed: 25-26 Dec, 1 Jan
BAR MEALS: L served all week 12-2 D served all week 7-9.30 Av main course £13 **RESTAURANT:** L served all week 12-2 D served all week 7-9.30 Av 3 course à la carte £20 **BREWERY/COMPANY:** Free House ◀: Wadworth 6X, Butcombe, John Smith's Smooth, Guest Ales. ♀: 8
CHILDREN'S FACILITIES: menu **GARDEN:** Walled terrace **NOTES:** Dogs allowed: in bar, in garden, Water provided, Parking 30

WHITLEY THE PEAR TREE INN

Top Ln SN12 8QX
☎ 01225 709131 📠 01225 702276
Dir: *A365 from Melksham toward Bath, at Shaw R on B3353 into Whitley, 1st L in lane, pub is at end of lane.* ***Map Ref:*** *ST86*

The Pear Tree is a delightful pub/restaurant in an attractive rural setting surrounded by parkland studded with great oak trees. Well-planted gardens surround the buildings and there is an extensive patio area with solid teak furniture and cream parasols. The pub dates back to 1750 when it was a cider house or farmstead.

OPEN: 11-3 6-11 Closed: 25/26 Dec, 1 Jan
BAR MEALS: L served all week 12-2 D served all week 6.30-9.30 Av main course £11.07 **RESTAURANT:** L served all week 12-2 D served all week 6.30-9.30 Av 3 course à la carte £24 Av 3 course fixed price £14 **BREWERY/COMPANY:** Free House **:** Wadworth 6X, Oakhill Best, Bath Ales Gem, Smiles Best. **:** 10 **CHILDREN'S FACILITIES:** menu
GARDEN: Cottage garden with views over parkland
NOTES: No dogs (ex guide dogs), Parking 60
ROOMS: 8 en suite 2 family rooms s£60 d£90

WOOTTON RIVERS ROYAL OAK

SN8 4NQ
☎ 01672 810322 📠 01672 811168
e-mail: royaloak35@hotmail.com
Dir: *3m S from Marlborough.* ***Map Ref:*** *SU16*

Set in one of Wiltshire's prettiest villages, a thatched and timbered 16th-century inn just 100 yards from the Kennet and Avon Canal, and close to Savernake Forest - a wonderful area for canal and forest walks. Menus are flexible, with light basket meals, ploughman's and sandwiches, and specials like partridge with game sauce and rich beef and Burgundy casserole.

OPEN: 10.30-3.30 6-11 (Close Sun 10.30)
BAR MEALS: L served all week 11.30-2.30 D served all week 6-9.30 Av main course £10 **RESTAURANT:** L served all week 11.30-2.30 D served all week 6-9.30 Av 3 course à la carte £20 Av 3 course fixed price £12.50
BREWERY/COMPANY: Free House **:** Wadworth 6X, London Pride + guest ales. **:** 6 **CHILDREN'S FACILITIES:** menu, family room **GARDEN:** Large lawn area. Raised terrace with seating **NOTES:** Dogs allowed: in bar, in garden, in bedrooms, Parking 20

Hay Tor on Dartmoor, Devon

Scotland

Go west and north for grandeur: the broad beaches where Atlantic waves crash after a 3,000-mile journey; classic mountains (the highest in Britain); islands of romance and unparalleled beauty; and remote, haunting landscapes.

Spread across the centre of the country and up the east coast are the commercial and cultural dynamos of Scotland – Dundee, Edinburgh, Glasgow and Aberdeen – thrust by the Enlightenment and the Industrial Revolution onto the forefront of the world stage. Nowadays, Scottish cities jostle for attention, with multitudes of attractions, with Edinburgh Castle still top of the list. Everywhere, high-tech businesses such as oil and electronics are comfortable bedfellows with the legacy of a dramatic past.

Further south lie the relatively unvisited Southern Uplands, great rolling ranges where turbulent times of border tension between powerful neighbours cannot be forgotten.

Top tipples

Whisky is obviously the national drink. Scotland has the greatest concentration of malt whisky distilleries in the world, making the most of its natural assets: pure water, peat and barley. Most distilleries offer tours to visitors: the Malt Whisky Trail takes in seven Speyside distilleries and other household names with visitor centres are the Glenlivet, Glenfiddich, Dhallas Dhu, Strathisla, Glenfarclas, Glen Grant, Edradour and Isle of Arran distilleries. There's also the Scotch Whisky Heritage Centre in Edinburgh, Dewar's World of Whisky in Aberfeldy, and The Famous Grouse Experience at Crieff.

The Scottish brewing tradition should not be forgotten, either. Scottish water was found to be ideal for producing India Pale Ale (IPA), a brew which kept well on the long voyage to India in colonial days. Strong Scottish ale, the 'wee heavy' was another popular export, with an alcohol content as high as 9% by volume. Scottish beer was traditionally categorised by the price per hogshead, from 40 to 90 shillings, according to strength. Hence, for example, the 60/- ale.

Above: Buachaille Etive Beag reflected in the still waters of Lochan na Fola in Glen Coe

ABERDEEN   OLD BLACKFRIARS

52 Castle Gate AB11 5BB
☎ 01224 581922 📄 01224 582153
Map Ref: NJ90

Traditional city centre pub with many fascinating features, including stone and wooden interior and original stained glass window display. Built on the site of property owned by Blackfriars Dominican monks. Battered haddock, home-made beefburgers and mixed grills feature among the popular bar meals. Breakfasts, toasted sandwiches and freshly prepared daily specials.

OPEN: 11-12 (Sun 12.30-11) Closed: Dec 25 & Jan 1
BAR MEALS: L served all week 11-9 D served all week (Fri-Sat 11-8) **BREWERY/COMPANY:** Belhaven
🍺: Belhaven 80/-, Belhaven St Andrews, Caledonian IPA, Caledonian 80/-. **CHILDREN'S FACILITIES:** menu, licence, high chairs, changing facilities **NOTES:** No dogs

STONEHAVEN   MARINE HOTEL ♀

9/10 Shorehead AB39 2JY
☎ 01569 762155 📄 01569 766691
Dir: 15m south of Aberdeen on A90.
Map Ref: NO88

Ironically, this harbour-side bar was built from the remains of Dunnottar Castle as a temperance hotel in the 19th century. A number of 500-year-old gargoyles are visible on the front. A choice of six real ales is offered - 800 different brews over the years - including Dunnottar Ale especially brewed for the establishment. There are also around a hundred malts at the bar. Seasonal dishes feature game, seafood and fish, maybe venison rump with mustard mash, dressed crab with coriander cream, and herring in oatmeal.

OPEN: 10-12 Closed: 25 Dec, 1 Jan **BAR MEALS:** L served all week 12-2 D served all week 5-8 (Fri 5-9, Sat & Sun 12-9) Av main course £8 **RESTAURANT:** L served all week 12-2 D served all week 5-9 Av 3 course à la carte £16
BREWERY/COMPANY: Free House 🍺: Timothy Taylor Landlord, Caledonian Deuchars IPA, Fuller's London Pride, Moorhouses Black Cat. ♀: 7
CHILDREN'S FACILITIES: menu, Baby changing facilities
NOTES: Dogs allowed

CLACHAN-SEIL   TIGH AN TRUISH INN

PA34 4QZ
☎ 01852 300242
Dir: 14m S of Oban, take A816, 12m turn off B844 toward Atlantic Bridge. *Map Ref:* NM71

Loosely translated, Tigh an Truish is Gaelic for 'house of trousers'. After the Battle of Culloden in 1746, kilts were outlawed and anyone caught wearing one was executed. In defiance of this edict the islanders wore their kilts at home. However, if they went to the mainland, they would stop en route at the Tigh an Truish and change into the hated trews before continuing their journey. Handy for good walks and lovely gardens, and particularly popular with tourists and members of the yachting fraternity, the Tigh an Truish offers a good appetising menu based on the best local produce. Home-made seafood pie, salmon steaks, and mussels in garlic cream sauce feature among the fish dishes, while other options might include meat or vegetable lasagne, beef or nut burgers, steak and ale pie, venison in a pepper cream and Drambuie sauce, and chicken curry. Round off your meal by sampling syrup sponge, apple crumble or chocolate puddle pudding.

OPEN: 11-3 5-11 (May-Sept all day) Closed: 25 Dec & Jan 1 **BAR MEALS:** L served all week 12-2 D served all week 6-8.30 **RESTAURANT:** L served all week 12-2 D served all week 6-8.30 **BREWERY/COMPANY:** Free House
🍺: McEwans 80/- plus guest beers.
CHILDREN'S FACILITIES: menu, family room
GARDEN: Tables beside the sea in garden with lawn
NOTES: Dogs allowed: in bar, in garden, Parking 35, No credit cards

CRINAN   CRINAN HOTEL

PA31 8SR
☎ 01546 830261 ▤ 01546 830292
e-mail: nryan@crinanhotel.com
Map Ref: NR79

The hotel, which dates back 200 years, is at the heart of community life in Crinan, a tiny fishing village at the north end of the Crinan Canal, connecting Loch Fyne to the Atlantic Ocean. The location is fabulous with views across the sound of Jura to the islands of Mull and Scharba from the hotel's Westward Restaurant. The Panther Arms and Mainbrace Bar are located at ground floor level, with a patio where guests can sit outside and watch the comings and goings at the sealock. Wherever you choose to eat, the seafood is superb. Dishes from the bar menu include whole Loch Crinan langoustines with herb aïoli, or warm tart of Loch Crinan scallops with smoked bacon and sun-dried tomatoes. Main courses take in grilled fillet of West Coast mackerel with parsley mash and shrimp butter, or hand-made Barbrek lamb and rosemary sausages with cassoulet.

OPEN: 11-11 Closed: Xmas & New Year
BAR MEALS: L served all week 12.30-2.30 D served all week 6.30-8.30 **RESTAURANT:** 12-2.30 D served all week 7-9 Av 3 course à la carte £22.60
BREWERY/COMPANY: Free House 🍺: Belhaven, Interbrew Worthington Bitter, Tenants Velvet.
CHILDREN'S FACILITIES: menu, portions, licence, games, high-chairs, food/bottle warming, baby changing
GARDEN: Patio available **NOTES:** Dogs allowed: in bar, Water, Parking 30

KILBERRY   KILBERRY INN

PA29 6YD
☎ 01880 770223 ▤ 01880 770223
e-mail: relax@kilberryinn.com
Dir: From Lochgilphead take A83 south. Take B8024 signposted Kilberry. **Map Ref:** NR76

A traditional Highland building way off the beaten track, on a scenic single-track road with breathtaking views An original 'but 'n' ben' cottage with quarried walls, beams and log fires, today the inn is renowned for its fine food. The dining room is welcoming and everything served here, including bread and cakes, is home made.

OPEN: 11-3 6.30-10.30 Closed: Nov-Easter
BAR MEALS: L served Tue-Sun 12.30-2 D served Tue-Sat 7-8.30 Sun 12.30-1.30 **RESTAURANT:** L served Tue-Sun 12.30-2 D served Tue-Sat 6.30-8.30 12.30-1.30
BREWERY/COMPANY: Free House 🍺: Arran Blonde, Arran Dark, Fyne Ales Maverick, Tennents Velvet.
CHILDREN'S FACILITIES: portions, high-chairs, food/bottle warming, baby changing, family room **NOTES:** Dogs allowed: in bedrooms, Water, Parking 8 **ROOMS:** 3 en suite 1 family room s£42.50 d£85 (★★★)

LOCHGILPHEAD   CAIRNBAAN HOTEL & RESTAURANT ★★★ ⊛ ♈

Cairnbaan PA31 8SJ
☎ 01546 603668 ▤ 01546 606045
e-mail: cairnbaan.hotel@virgin.net
Dir: 2m N, take A816 from Lochgilphead, hotel off B841. **Map Ref:** NR88

This late 18th-century coaching inn used to be well patronised by fishermen on the Crinan Canal in flat-bottomed boats called puffers, but today's waterborne clientele is almost entirely sailing for pleasure. The hotel offers high standards of hospitality and smart accommodation. It's owned by ex-QE2 catering officer Darren Dobson, ashore now for some 20 years, and wife Christine, a former teacher, who plans the menus and does all the baking.

OPEN: 11-11 **BAR MEALS:** L served all week 12-2.30 D served all week 6-9.30 Av main course £9
RESTAURANT: D served all week 6-9.30 Av 3 course à la carte £28 **BREWERY/COMPANY:** Free House 🍺: Local Ales. **CHILDREN'S FACILITIES:** menu **GARDEN:** Food served outside. Pation area **NOTES:** In the garden only, No dogs, Parking 50 **ROOMS:** 12 en suite s£72.50 d£92.50

Argyll & Bute continued

TARBERT LOCH FYNE   VICTORIA HOTEL ◆◆◆

Barmore Rd PA29 6TW
☎ 01880 820236 📠 01880 820638
e-mail: victoria.hotel@lineone.net
Map Ref: NR86

Centrally situated in a picturesque fishing village on the Kintyre peninsula, this 18th-century hotel is renowned for its restaurant, which enjoys romantic views over Loch Fyne. Bar and restaurant menus provide a good choice, featuring local game and seafood.

OPEN: 11-12 (Sun 12-12) (Closed 3-5.30 in winter) Closed: 25 Dec **BAR MEALS:** L served all week 12-2.30 D served all week 6-9.30 (Sun 12.30-2.30, 6-9.30) Av main course £7.95 **RESTAURANT:** L served all week 12-2.30 D served all week 6.30-9.30 **BREWERY/COMPANY:** Free House ◖: Scottish Courage John Smiths, 80 Shilling, Tartan Special. **CHILDREN'S FACILITIES:** menu, portions, licence, high-chairs, food/bottle warming, baby changing facility **GARDEN:** Patio area **NOTES:** Dogs allowed: in bar, in garden, in bedrooms, Water provided **ROOMS:** 5 en suite 1 family room s£32 d£64

TAYNUILT   POLFEARN HOTEL ★★ 🐑 🍷

PA35 1JQ
☎ 01866 822251 📠 01866 822251
Dir: *turn off A85, continue 1.5m through village down to loch shore.* **Map Ref:** NN03

Close to the shores of Loch Etive, with stunning all-round views, this friendly family-run hotel sits at the foot of Ben Cruachen. Originally a Victorian fishing villa, it was converted to a hotel in 1960. Whether you're working, walking, cycling, riding, shooting or fishing in the area, the proprietors will store things, dry things, feed, water and warm you with little formality.

OPEN: 12-2 6-11 Closed: 25-26 Dec Rest: Nov-May Closed lunch **BAR MEALS:** L served all week 12-1.45 D served all week 6-8.45 Av main course £9 **RESTAURANT:** 12-1.45 D served all week 5.30-8.45 Av 3 course à la carte £22 **BREWERY/COMPANY:** Free House ◖: Weekly changing guest ale. 🍷: 15 **CHILDREN'S FACILITIES:** menu, food/bottle warming **GARDEN:** Nice lawn, sea view & mountains **NOTES:** Dogs allowed: in bar, Water, Food, Parking 50 **ROOMS:** 14 en suite 2 family rooms s£30 d£55

EDINBURGH   THE SHORE BAR & RESTAURANT 🐑 🍷

3 Shore, Leith EH6 6QW
☎ 0131 553 5080 📠 0131 553 5080
e-mail: enquiries@the.shore.ukf.net
Map Ref: NT27

Overlooking the Water of Leith and only a stone's throw from the busy Port of Leith, this historic 18th-century pub has a fine reputation for Scottish fish and seafood. Blackboard menu changes with every sitting. Have a drink in the small bar, a popular folk music venue, before enjoying a meal like chargrilled swordfish steak with strawberry and peach salsa in the intimate dining room with its white linen and fresh flowers.

OPEN: 11-12 (Sun 12-11) Closed: 25, 26 Dec, 1,2 Jan **BAR MEALS:** L served all week 12-2.30 D served all week 6.30-10 (Sun 12.30-3) Av main course £12 **RESTAURANT:** L served all week 12-2.30 D served all week 6.30-10 (Sun 12.30-3) Av 3 course à la carte £22.50 ◖: Belhaven 80/-, Deuchars IPA, Guiness, Carlsberg. 🍷: 7 **CHILDREN'S FACILITIES:** portions, games, high-chairs, food/bottle warming **GARDEN:** Pavement tables **NOTES:** Dogs allowed: in bar, Water

RATHO THE BRIDGE INN

27 Baird Rd EH28 8RA
☎ 0131 3331320 ▯ 0131 333 3480
e-mail: info@bridgeinn.com
Dir: *From Newbridge B7030 junction, follow signs for Ratho.* **Map Ref:** *NT17*

Dating back to about 1750, the Bridge Inn was originally a farmhouse before it became an important staging-post during the construction of the Union Canal. The present owner restored and re-opened it in the early 1970s. It is now a thriving and award-winning family attraction at the heart of the city's Canal Centre.

OPEN: 12-11 (Sat 11-12, Sun 12.30-11) Closed: 26 Dec, 1 & 2 Jan **BAR MEALS:** L served all week 12-9 Av main course £7 **RESTAURANT:** L served all week 12-2 D served all week 6.30-9 Av 3 course à la carte £22 **BREWERY/COMPANY:** Free House ◖: Belhaven 80/- & Belhaven Best, Deuchars IPA. **CHILDREN'S FACILITIES:** menu, portions, licence, games, high-chairs, food/bottle warming, baby changing, outdoor play area, Victorian carousel, toy box, family room **GARDEN:** Landscaped, Patio, enclosed, ducks roaming **NOTES:** in bar, No dogs (ex guide dogs), Parking 60

GLASGOW RAB HA'S

83 Hutchieson St G1 1SH
☎ 0141 572 0400 ▯ 0141 572 0402
Dir: *City centre.* **Map Ref:** *NS56*

Victorian building, recently refurbished, housing a pub, and restaurant. Expect a traditional pub atmosphere and some innovative cooking. Choices include fajitas, tempura, Thai curries and organic beef burger in the bar. The restaurant offers fusion cooking with dishes from the ocean, the earth and from home.

OPEN: 11-12 Closed: Jan 1 **BAR MEALS:** L served all week 12-10 D served all week Av main course £5.90 **RESTAURANT:** D served all week 5.30-10 Av 3 course à la carte £16 **BREWERY/COMPANY:** Free House ◖: McEwans 70/- & 80/-, Theakstons. **NOTES:** Dogs allowed

AULDGIRTH AULDGIRTH INN ♀

DG2 0XG
☎ 01387 740250 ▯ 01387 740694
e-mail: auldgirthinn@aol.com
Dir: *8m NE of Dumfries on A76 Kilmarnock Rd.*
Map Ref: *NX98*

This 500-year-old riverside inn with its prominent chimneystack featuring a distinctive cross was originally a stopping-off place for monks and pilgrims walking across Scotland. Later Robert Burns, who lived nearby, made it his local. David and Beverly Brown took over this free house in 2002. Their menu includes Celtic chicken breast stuffed with whisky-soaked haggis, salmon and asparagus crêpes, and traditional favourites such as steak and ale pie, liver and bacon, and fish and chips.

OPEN: 11.30-11 (Open all day everyday)
BAR MEALS: L served all week 12-9 D served all week 12-9 Av main course £6 **RESTAURANT:** L served all week 12-9 D served all week 12-9 **BREWERY/COMPANY:** Free House ◖: Belhavens Best, Guest Ale. ♀: 12
CHILDREN'S FACILITIES: menu **GARDEN:** Small grass area, picnic benches **NOTES:** Dogs allowed: in bar, in garden, in bedrooms, Water, food if required, Parking 30
ROOMS: 3 bedrooms 2 en suite 1 family room s£40 d£55 (★★★)

DALBEATTIE ANCHOR HOTEL

Main St, Kippford DG5 4LN
☎ 01556 620205 ▌ 01556 620205
*Dir: A711 to Dalbeattie. follow Solway Coast
sign to Kippford.* **Map Ref:** *NX86*

Overlooking the Marina and Urr Water
estuary, this charming hotel has a Seafarers'
Bar which is a sailor's haven. The area is also
ideal for walkers and bird watchers. The
menu includes such specialities as swordfish
steaks, haddock and cod in butter, chicken
tikka, game casserole, and Solway salmon.
Bedrooms are comfortable and some
overlook the Marina.

OPEN: 11-3 5-12 (all day opening-peak season) Closed:
25 Dec **BAR MEALS:** L served all week 12-2.30 D served all
week 6-9.30 **RESTAURANT:** L served all week 12-2
D served all week 6-9 (extended hours in summer)
BREWERY/COMPANY: Free House ◀: Local Ales-Criffel Cuil
Hill, Knockendoch, John Smiths McEwans 80.
CHILDREN'S FACILITIES: menu, portions, licence, games,
high-chairs, food/bottle warming, games room
GARDEN: Tables out the front **NOTES:** Dogs allowed:
in bar, in bedrooms, Water Bowls **ROOMS:** 6 en suite s£30
d£60 (★★)

ISLE OF WHITHORN THE STEAM PACKET INN

Harbour Row DG8 8LL
☎ 01988 500334 ▌ 01988 500627
e-mail: steampacketinn@btconnect.com
*Dir: From Newton Stewart take A714, then
A746 to Whithorn, then Isle of Whithorn.*
Map Ref: *NX43*

Situated on the quayside overlooking the
harbour, this 18th-century inn is only 20 miles
from the main A75 Stranraer to Dumfries
Euroroute. The attractively modernised bar
and 40-seat conservatory dining area add to
the charm. Lunch and dinner are served
throughout both bars and in the lower dining
room and conservatory restaurants. The
emphasis is on the freshest of Scottish
produce, especially seafood that is often
bought straight from the boats. Expect

scampi, curry, venison haunch steak, and seared
chicken supreme along with a good choice of hot and
cold filled rolls.

OPEN: 11-11 (Winter open Mon-Thu, 11-3, 6-11) Closed:
Dec 25 **BAR MEALS:** L served all week 12-2 D served all
week 6.30-9 Av main course £6 **RESTAURANT:** L served all
week 12-2 D served all week 6.30-9
BREWERY/COMPANY: Free House ◀: Scottish Courage
Theakston XB, Caledonian Deuchars IPA, Black Sheep Best
Bitter. **CHILDREN'S FACILITIES:** menu, portions, licence,
games, high-chairs, food/bottle warming, baby changing
NOTES: Dogs allowed: in bar, in garden, in bedrooms,
Parking 4

KIRKCUDBRIGHT SELKIRK ARMS HOTEL ★★★ ♀

Old High St DG6 4JG
☎ 01557 330402 ▌ 01557 331639
e-mail: reception@selkirkarmshotel.co.uk
Map Ref: *NX65*

A traditional white-painted pub on street
corner, with nice gardens to the rear. It has
associations with the Scottish poet Robert
Burns, and T E Lawrence (of Arabia), who
lived nearby. Good choice of beers, including
Solway Criffel and Youngers Tartan.

OPEN: 11-12 **BAR MEALS:** L served all week 12-2
D served all week 6-9.30 Av main course £6.50
RESTAURANT: L served all week 12-2 D served all week
7-9.30 Av 3 course à la carte £25 ◀: Youngers Tartan, John
Smiths Bitter, Criffel, Old Speckled Hen. ♀: 8
CHILDREN'S FACILITIES: menu, portions, licence,
high-chairs, food/bottle warming, baby changing
GARDEN: Beautiful **NOTES:** Dogs allowed: in bar, in garden,
dog bones/biscuits, Parking 50 **ROOMS:** 16 en suite
3 family rooms s£55 d£80

MOFFAT   BLACK BULL HOTEL ♀

Churchgate DG10 9EG
☎ 01683 220206 📄 01683 220483
e-mail: hotel@blackbullmoffat.co.uk
Map Ref: *NT00*

The main building dates from the 16th century and was used by Graham of Claverhouse as his headquarters. Graham and his dragoons were sent to quell Scottish rebellion in the late 17th century. Scottish bard Robert Burns was a frequent visitor around 1790. The Railway Bar is the place for drinking and pub games, while the Burns Room or restaurant are for eating or relaxation. Traditional fare includes steak pie, seafood platter, macaroni cheese, Black Bull hot pot, Eskdale venison sausage with wine and onion gravy, and Moffat ram pie. Also look out for haggis with tatties and neeps, a selection of tempting sizzlers, and 'Dishes from Around the World.'

OPEN: 11-11 (Thu-Sat 11-12) **BAR MEALS:** L served all week 11.30-2.15 D served all week 6-9.15 Av main course £7.25 **RESTAURANT:** L served all week 11.30-2.15 D served all week 6-9.15 **BREWERY/COMPANY:** Free House 🍺: McEwans, Scottish Courage Theakston 80/-. ♀: 6
CHILDREN'S FACILITIES: menu, portions, games, high-chairs, food/bottle warming **GARDEN:** Courtyard with eight tables
NOTES: Dogs allowed: in bar, Parking 4
ROOMS: 13 en suite 2 family rooms s£39 d£59 (★★★)

NEW ABBEY   CRIFFEL INN

2 The Square DG2 8BX
☎ 01387 850305 850244 📄 01387 850305
Dir: *M/A74 leave at Gretna, A75 to Dumfries, A710 S to New Abbey.* ***Map Ref:*** *NX96*

A former 18th-century coaching inn set on the Solway Coast in the historic conservation village of New Abbey close to the ruins of the 13th-century Sweetheart Abbey. The Graham family ensures a warm welcome and excellent home-cooked food using local produce. Dishes include chicken wrapped in smoked Ayrshire bacon served with Loch Arthur mature creamy cheese sauce, fish dishes feature sea trout and sea bass among several others. Lawned beer garden overlooking corn-mill and square; ideal for touring Dumfries and Galloway.

OPEN: 12-2.30 (Sat 12-12) 5-11 (Sun 12-11)
BAR MEALS: L served all week 12-2 D served all week 5.30-8 (Sun 12-8) Av main course £7
RESTAURANT: L served all week 12-2 D served all week 5-8 (Sun 12-8) Av 3 course à la carte £14
BREWERY/COMPANY: Free House 🍺: Belhaven Best, McEwans 60-. **CHILDREN'S FACILITIES:** menu, portions, games, high-chairs, food/bottle warming, family room
GARDEN: Garden overlooking historic Cornmill & Square
NOTES: Dogs allowed: in bar, in garden, in bedrooms, Water, Parking 8

NEW GALLOWAY   CROSS KEYS HOTEL NEW

High St DG7 3RN
☎ 01644 420494 📄 01644 420672
e-mail: info@crosskeysng.fsnet.co.uk
Dir: *Located at N end of Loch Ken; 10m from Castle Douglas, 40m from Ayr on A713 Galloway Tourist Route.* ***Map Ref:*** *NX67*

Dates back to 1760, and part of it was once the police station and local jail - you can eat bar meals in the restored stone-walled cell. Alternatively, the à la carte restaurant with its innovative clown theme serves hearty food with a strong Scottish accent - haggis, neeps and tatties, Marbury smoked salmon, Buccleuch steaks, Wigtown lamb, and Loch Arthur organic cheese. Try a Sulwath real ale - a young Castle Douglas brewery blending the area's soft water, quality malts and Hereford hops into a flavoursome mellow pint; or join the connoisseurs in the specialist whisky lounge.

OPEN: 12-11 (Oct-Apr 12-12 Fri-Sat Apr-Oct 12-12 all wk)
BAR MEALS: L served all week 12-2 D served all week 6-8 (Oct-Apr no food Mon-Tues. Sun 5.30-7.30) Av main course £7 **RESTAURANT:** D served Apr-Oct Tues-Sun 6.30-8.30 (Sun 5.30-7.30. Oct-Apr Thur-Sun) Av 3 course à la carte £18 🍺: Sulworth real ales, guest real ales.
CHILDREN'S FACILITIES: menu, portions, high-chairs, food/bottle warming, baby changing, In restaurant 8yrs
GARDEN: Small enclosed garden, good views
NOTES: No dogs (ex guide dogs), Parking 6

Dumfries & Galloway continued

NEWTON STEWART CREEBRIDGE HOUSE HOTEL 🐑 ♀

Minnigaff DG8 6NP
☎ 01671 402121 📠 01671 403258
e-mail: info@creebridge.co.uk
Dir: From A75 into Newton Stewart, turn right over river bridge, hotel 200yds on left.
Map Ref: NX46

This country house hotel is a listed building dating from 1760. It was formerly the Earl of Galloway's shooting lodge and part of his estate. The River Cree runs nearby, and the hotel nestles in grounds at the foot of Kirroughtree Forest. Bridge's Bar and Brasserie offers malt whiskies, real ales and an interesting menu with an emphasis on fresh Scottish produce. Typical examples are Creebridge game pâté, home-made ravioli filled with local lobster in seafood broth, and steaks cut from Buccluech beef. There is also a range of speciality breads made in house. The Garden Restaurant, overlooking the landscaped grounds, presents a short, fixed-price menu of modern Scottish cooking.

OPEN: 12-2.30 6-11 (Sun, all day) **BAR MEALS:** L served all week 12-2 D served all week 6-9.30 Av main course £8 **RESTAURANT:** D served all week 7-9 Av 3 course à la carte £25 Av 3 course fixed price £25 **BREWERY/COMPANY:** Free House 🍺: Fuller's London Pride, Tenants, Real Ales, Deuchers. ♀: 8 **CHILDREN'S FACILITIES:** menu, portions, licence, high-chairs, food/bottle warming, baby changing **GARDEN:** Garden with Rose Beds, Fish Pond and Lawns **NOTES:** Dogs allowed: in garden, in bedrooms, Kennels, Water, Parking 40 **ROOMS:** 19 en suite 1 family room s£61 d£102 (★★★)

DALRYMPLE THE KIRKTON INN ◆◆◆ 🐑

1 Main St KA6 6DF
☎ 01292 560241 📠 01292 560835
e-mail: kirkton@cqm.co.uk
Dir: Between A77 & A713 approx 5m from Ayr signed from both roads. *Map Ref: NS31*

Village centre inn situated a short stroll from the River Doon where the salmon leap. Well situated for a visit to the Burns Centre and Cottage, the beach at Ayr or Blairquhan Castle. The restaurant has open fires, and the menu offers such delights as grilled Ayrshire ham steak, haddock mornay, salmon topped with capers and bacon in a delicious lemon cream.

OPEN: 11am-midnight Closed: Christmas Day, New Years Day **BAR MEALS:** L served all week 11-9 D served all week 11-9 Av main course £6 **RESTAURANT:** L served all week 11-9 D served all week 11-9 Av 3 course à la carte £14 Av 3 course fixed price £6 **BREWERY/COMPANY:** Free House 🍺: Belhaven Best & St Andrews. **CHILDREN'S FACILITIES:** menu, portions, games, high-chairs, food/bottle warming, baby changing **GARDEN:** Red chipped area **NOTES:** Dogs allowed: in bar, in garden, in bedrooms, Water, Parking 50 **ROOMS:** 11 en suite 3 family rooms s£36 d£80

GATEHEAD THE COCHRANE INN

45 Main Rd KA2 0AP
☎ 01563 570122
Dir: From Glasgow A77 to Kilmarnock, then A759 to Gatehead. *Map Ref: NS33*

The emphasis is on contemporary British food at this village centre pub, just a short drive from the Ayrshire coast. Friendly, bustling atmosphere inside. Good choice of starters may include soused herring and grilled goat's cheese, while main courses might feature stuffed pancake, pan-fried trio of seafood with tiger prawns, or smoked haddock risotto.

OPEN: 12-2 5.30-11 Closed: 1 Jan **BAR MEALS:** L served all week 12-2 D served all week 6-9 Av main course £7.95 **RESTAURANT:** L served all week 12-2 D served all week 6-9 Av 3 course à la carte £15 **BREWERY/COMPANY:** Free House 🍺: John Smith's. **NOTES:** No dogs (ex guide dogs), Parking 30

EAST LINTON **DROVERS INN** ♀

5 Bridge St EH40 3AG
☎ 01620 860298 📋 01620 860205
Dir: *Off A1 5m past Haddington, follow rd under railway bridge, then L.* ***Map Ref:*** *NT57*

Herdsmen used to stop here as they drove their livestock to market. Those old drovers are long gone but the bar, with wooden floors, beamed ceilings and half-panelled walls, retains an old-world charm. Upstairs, though, is more sumptuous with rich colours, low-beamed ceilings and antique furniture. The menus change every six weeks or so, but may include grilled halibut and black tiger prawns with chervil and garlic butter.

OPEN: 11.30-11 11.30-1 Closed: 25 Dec, 1 Jan
BAR MEALS: L served all week 11.30-2 D served Mon-Fri 6-9.30 (All day Sat-Sun) **RESTAURANT:** L served all week 11.30-2 D served all week 6-9.30
BREWERY/COMPANY: Free House ◀: Adnams Broadside, Deuchars IPA, Old Speckeled Hen, Burton Real Ale. ♀: 6
CHILDREN'S FACILITIES: portions, Baby change facilities
GARDEN: Small enclosed beer garden **NOTES:** in bar

GIFFORD **GOBLIN HA' HOTEL** ♀

EH41 4QH
☎ 01620 810244 📋 01620 810718
e-mail: douglasmuir@btconnect.com
Dir: *On A846, 100yrds from main village square on shore side of the road.*
Map Ref: *NT56*

Traditional hotel with a large patio for summer eating and a good garden with a play area and a dolls' house for children. Members of the Walt Disney company stayed here when they were filming scenes for Greyfriars Bobby in the hills to the south of the village.

OPEN: 11-2.30 5-11 (Jun-Sep all day)
BAR MEALS: L served all week 12.30-2 D served all week 6.30-9 Av main course £7.50 **RESTAURANT:** L served all week 12.30-2 D served all week 6.30-9 Av 3 course à la carte £15 **BREWERY/COMPANY:** Free House ◀: Hop Back Summer lightning, Timothy Taylor Landlord, Caledonian Deuchers IPA, Fuller's ESB. ♀: 12
CHILDREN'S FACILITIES: menu, licence, outdoor play area, changing area, three play areas **GARDEN:** Two acres of garden, seats 80 **NOTES:** Dogs allowed: in garden, in bedrooms **ROOMS:** 7 bedrooms 6 en suite 2 family rooms s£37.50 d£75 (★)

ANSTRUTHER **THE DREEL TAVERN**

16 High St West KY10 3DL
☎ 01333 310727 📋 01333 310577
e-mail: dreeltavern@aol.com
Map Ref: *NO50*

Complete with a local legend concerning an amorous encounter between James V and a local gypsy woman, the 16th-century Dreel Tavern has plenty of atmosphere. Its oak beams, open fire and stone walls retain much of the distant past, while home-cooked food and cask-conditioned ales are served to hungry visitors of the present. Expect to savour steak pie, roast beef and Yorkshire pudding, and plenty of local fish dishes including smoked fish pie, and local crab. Peaceful gardens overlook Dreel Burn. Beers changed weekly.

OPEN: 11-12 (Sun 12.30-12) **BAR MEALS:** L served all week 12-2 D served all week 5.30-9 (Sun 12.30-2) Av main course £6.50 **RESTAURANT:** L served all week 12-2 D served all week 5.30-9 **BREWERY/COMPANY:** Free House ◀: Carlsberg-Tetley Tetley's Imperial, Harviestoun Bitter & Twisted, Greene King IPA, London Pride.
CHILDREN'S FACILITIES: menu, portions, high-chairs, food/bottle warming, family room **GARDEN:** Enclosed area, seats approx 20 **NOTES:** Dogs allowed: in bar only; water, biscuits, Parking 3

AUCHTERMUCHTY FOREST HILLS HOTEL

23 High St KY14 7AP
☎ 01337 828318 ▤ 01337 828318
e-mail: info@theforesthillshotel.com
Dir: *Telephone for directions.* **Map Ref:** *NO21*

Popular inn located in the village square, with an oak-beamed bar, Flemish murals, a cosy lounge, and en suite bedrooms. The town of Auchtermuchty is well known as home to TV series Dr Finlay's Casebook, acoustic duo The Proclaimers, and accordionist extraordinare Jimmy Shand.

OPEN: 11.30-2.30 5-10 **BAR MEALS:** L served all week 12-2 D served all week 6-9 **RESTAURANT:** L served all week 12.30-2 D served Mon-Thu 7-9
BREWERY/COMPANY: Free House
CHILDREN'S FACILITIES: menu **NOTES:** Dogs allowed: in bar, in bedrooms

---

CRAIL THE GOLF HOTEL

4 High St KY10 3TD
☎ 01333 450206 ▤ 01333 450795
e-mail: enquiries@thegolfhotelcrail.com
Dir: *Telephone for directions.* **Map Ref:** *NO60*

Rooted in the 14th century, this is the site of one of Scotland's oldest licensed inns, though the current building dates from the early 18th century. The Crail Golfing Society, formed in the public bar in 1786, is believed to have given the inn its name; it's the seventh oldest club in Scotland. The emphasis here is on traditional Scottish produce, hospitality, and value for money. An entire menu is dedicated to seafood, with dishes such as grilled haddock in a garlic and herb butter, and home-made salmon and smoked haddock

fishcakes. Traditional high tea with home baking is also a speciality.

OPEN: 11-12 **BAR MEALS:** L served all week 12-7 D served all week 7-9 Av main course £6
RESTAURANT: L served all week 12-7 D served all week 7-9
BREWERY/COMPANY: Free House ◖: Scottish Courage McEwans 80/-, 70/-, Tetleys, Belhaven Best.
CHILDREN'S FACILITIES: menu, portions, high-chairs, food/bottle warming **NOTES:** Dogs allowed: in bar, in garden, in bedrooms, Parking 10 **ROOMS:** 5 en suite 1 family room s£37 d£30 (★★★)

DUNFERMLINE THE HIDEAWAY LODGE & RESTAURANT ♇

Kingseat Rd, Halbeath KY12 0UB
☎ 01383 725474 ▤ 01383 622821
e-mail: enquiries@thehideaway.co.uk
Dir: *Telephone for directions.* **Map Ref:** *NT08*

Originally built in the 1930s as a miners' welfare institute, this pleasant country inn enjoys a rural setting on the outskirts of Dunfermline. Each room is named after a Scottish loch, and the extensive menu makes good use of fresh local produce. A typical meal may begin with grilled goats' cheese salad or Oban mussels, then move on to chargrilled tuna steak, Scottish seafood crumble or fillet of Highland venison, and finish with summer fruit pudding or steamed ginger pudding.

OPEN: 12-3 5-11 (Sun 12-9) **BAR MEALS:** L served all week 12-2 D served all week 5-9.30
RESTAURANT: L served all week 12-2 D served all week 5-9.30 **BREWERY/COMPANY:** Free House ◖: John Smith, 80 Special. **CHILDREN'S FACILITIES:** menu
NOTES: No dogs, Parking 35

LOWER LARGO CRUSOE HOTEL

2 Main St KY8 6BT
☎ 01333 320759 📠 01333 320865
Dir: *A92 to Kirkcaldy East, A915 to Lundin Links, then R to Lower Largo.* ***Map Ref:*** *NO40*

This historic inn is located on the sea wall in Lower Largo, the birthplace of Alexander Selkirk, the real-life castaway immortalised by Daniel Defoe in his novel, Robinson Crusoe. In the past the area was also the heart of the once-thriving herring fishing industry. Today it is a charming bay ideal for a golfing break. A typical menu may include 'freshly shot' haggis, Pittenweem haddock and a variety of steaks.

OPEN: 12-12 (Fri 11-1am) **BAR MEALS:** L served all week 12-3 D served all week 6-9 Av main course £6 **RESTAURANT:** 12-3 D served all week 6.30-9 Av 3 course à la carte £22 **BREWERY/COMPANY:** Free House **🍺:** Belhaven 80/-, Best, Caledonian IPA, Deuchars. **CHILDREN'S FACILITIES:** menu, outdoor play area **NOTES:** Dogs allowed: in bar, in garden, in bedrooms, Parking 30

ACHILTIBUIE SUMMER ISLES HOTEL & BAR

IV26 2YG
☎ 01854 622282 📠 01854 622251
e-mail: info@summerisleshotel.co.uk
Dir: *Take A835 N from Ullapool for 10m, Achiltibuie signed on L, 15m to village, hotel 1m on L.* ***Map Ref:*** *NC00*

Situated in a stunningly beautiful and unspoilt landscape, it is difficult to find a more relaxing place to drink, dine or stay. The emphasis is on locally caught and home-produced quality food, and there's a wide choice of malts and real ale. Smoked salmon, langoustines, hummous and a tempting seafood platter all feature on the menu, along with a casserole of the day, and various snacks.

OPEN: 12-11 (4-11 in winter) **BAR MEALS:** L served all week 12-2.30 D served all week 6.30-9.30 Av main course £9 **RESTAURANT:** L served all week 12.30-2 D served all week 8 **BREWERY/COMPANY:** Free House **🍺:** Orkney Dark Island, Raven & Red Macgregor. **CHILDREN'S FACILITIES:** baby changing **NOTES:** Dogs allowed: in bedrooms, Parking 20

APPLECROSS APPLECROSS INN 🍷

Shore St IV54 8LR
☎ 01520 744262 📠 01520 744400
e-mail: applecrossinn@globalnet.co.uk
Dir: *From Lochcarron to Kishorn then L onto unclassifed rd to Applecross over 'Bealach Na Ba'.* ***Map Ref:*** *NG74*

The drive to Judith Fish's door at Applecross Inn will take you through some of Scotland's most awe-inspiring scenery, crossing the Bealach nam Bo rising to 2053 feet with triple hairpin bends before descending through forests into Applecross (A Chromraich, meaning sanctuary). The traditional white-painted inn is set on a sandy cove.

OPEN: 11-11 (Sun 12.30-11) Closed: 25 Dec, 1 Jan **BAR MEALS:** L served all week 12-9 D served all week Av main course £7.95 **RESTAURANT:** L served by appointment D served all week 6-9 **BREWERY/COMPANY:** Free House **🍺:** Scottish Courage John Smith's, Cask Ale, Red Cullin, Millers. **🍷:** 6 **CHILDREN'S FACILITIES:** menu, portions, licence, games, high-chairs, food/bottle warming, baby changing, outdoor play area **GARDEN:** Grassed area on the beach, six tables **NOTES:** Dogs allowed: in garden, in bedrooms, Water, Parking 30 **ROOMS:** 7 bedrooms 3 en suite 2 family rooms s£30 d£60 (★★)

CAWDOR   CAWDOR TAVERN

The Lane IV12 5XP
☎ 01667 404777 📄 01667 404777
e-mail: cawdortavern@btopenworld.com
Dir: *From A96 (Inverness-Aberdeen) take B9006 & follow signs for Cawdor Castle. Tavern in village centre.* **Map Ref:** NH85

A former joinery workshop for the Cawdor Estate, the Tavern is located close to the famous castle in a beautiful conservation village. Oak panelling from the castle, a gift from the late laird, is used to great effect in the bar. Roaring log fires keep the place cosy and warm on long winter evenings.

OPEN: 11-3 5-11 (May-Oct 11-11) Closed: 25 Dec, 1 Jan
BAR MEALS: L served all week 12-2 D served all week 5.30-9 (Sun 12.30-3, 5.30-9) Av main course £8.95
RESTAURANT: L served all week 12-2 D served all week 6.30-9 (Sun 12.30-3, 5.30-9) Av 3 course à la carte £19.95
BREWERY/COMPANY: Free House 🍺: Tennents 80/-, Tomintoul Stag. 🍷: 8 **CHILDREN'S FACILITIES:** menu, portions, licence, games, high-chairs, food/bottle warming, baby changing, Baby changing, Games, Books, family room
GARDEN: Patio area at front of Tavern **NOTES:** Dogs allowed: in bar, Water provided, Parking 60

DUNDONNELL   DUNDONNELL HOTEL ★★★ ✿

IV23 2QR
☎ 01854 633204 📄 01854 633366
e-mail: selbie@dundonnellhotel.co.uk
Dir: *From Inverness W on the A835, at Braemore junct take A382 for Gairloch.*
Map Ref: NH08

Under new ownership after more than 40 years, Dundonnell is one of the leading hotels in the Northern Highlands. Originally a small inn accommodating the occasional traveller to Wester Ross, it has been considerably extended over the years. Its fine location, however, can never change. Sheltered beneath the massive An Teallach range (one of 21 Munros in the area), the views down Little Loch Broom are superb. The Broom Beg bar and bistro is the 'local',

offering a wide range of beers and casual dining, while the Cocktail Bar is the place for a quiet aperitif while mulling over what to eat in the spacious restaurant.

OPEN: 11-11 (reduced hours Nov-Mar, please phone)
BAR MEALS: L served all week 12-2 D served all week 6-8.30 Av main course £5 **RESTAURANT:** D served all week 7-8.30 Av 3 course à la carte £27.50
BREWERY/COMPANY: Free House 🍺: John Smith's.
CHILDREN'S FACILITIES: menu, portions, licence, high-chairs, food/bottle warming **GARDEN:** overlooking Little Loch Broom, seating **NOTES:** Dogs allowed: except in eating area, Parking 60 **ROOMS:** 28 en suite 3 family rooms s£45 d£90

FORT AUGUSTUS   THE LOCK INN

Canalside PH32 4AU
☎ 01320 366302
Dir: *On banks of Caledonian Canal in Fort Augustus.* **Map Ref:** NH30

Built in 1820, this former bank and post office building, replete with flagstone floors and original beams, stands on the banks of the Caledonian Canal close to Loch Ness. A thousand Celtic welcomes are extended to regulars and visitors who come to enjoy the regular Scottish folk music evenings. A new team will hopefully retain all the Scottish charm this inn has come to be known for.

OPEN: 11-11 Closed: 25 Dec, 1 Jan **BAR MEALS:** L served all week 12-3 D served all week 6-9.30 Av main course £6 **RESTAURANT:** L served all week 12-3 D served all week 6-10 Av 3 course à la carte £20 **BREWERY/COMPANY:** Free House 🍺: Caledonian 80/-, Orkney Dark Island, Black Isle. **CHILDREN'S FACILITIES:** menu, family room **GARDEN:** Food served outside **NOTES:** No dogs

FORT WILLIAM MOORINGS HOTEL ★★★ ⊛ 🐑

Banavie PH33 7LY
☎ 01397 772797 🖷 01397 772441
e-mail: reservations@moorings-
fortwilliam.co.uk
Dir: *From A82 in Fort William follow signs for
Mallaig, then L onto A830 for 1m. Cross canal
bridge then 1st R signposted Banavie.*
Map Ref: *NN17*

This striking modern hotel lies hard by the
famous Neptune's Staircase, longest of the
three lock-flights on the coast-to-coast
Caledonian Canal. Most bedrooms and the
Upper Deck lounge bar have good views of
Ben Nevis (1344m) and Aonach Mor
(1219m).

OPEN: 12-11.45 (Thurs-Sat til 1am) **BAR MEALS:** L served all
week 12-9.30 D served all week **RESTAURANT:** D served all
week 7-9.30 **BREWERY/OMPANY:** Free House 🍺: Calders
70/-, Teltley Bitter. **CHILDREN'S FACILITIES:** menu, portions,
games, high-chairs, food/bottle warming **GARDEN:** Small patio,
food served outdoors **NOTES:** Dogs allowed: Water, Parking 80
ROOMS: 28 en suite bedrooms 1 family room s£51 d£82

GAIRLOCH THE OLD INN ◆◆◆◆ 🐑 ♀

IV21 2BD
☎ 01445 712006 🖷 01445 712445
e-mail: info@theoldinn.net
Dir: *just off main A832, near harbour at S end
of village.* **Map Ref:** *NG87*

The Old Inn is a fine old establishment dating from
1792, standing at the foot of Flowerdale Glen. It has
been carefully restored to reveal and retain original
fireplaces and two-foot thick stone walls.

OPEN: 11-12 Rest: Nov-Feb Closed in the afternoon
BAR MEALS: L served all week 12-9.30 D served all week
5-9.30 **RESTAURANT:** L served all week 12-5 D served all
week 5-9.30 **BREWERY/COMPANY:** Free House
🍺: Adnams Broadside, Scottish Courage Courage Directors,
Isle of Skye Red Cullin & Blind Piper, Houston Meters Well.
♀: 8 **CHILDREN'S FACILITIES:** menu, portions, licence,
games, high-chairs, food/bottle warming, baby changing,
outdoor play area, family room **GARDEN:** Large grassy area
with picnic tables **NOTES:** Dogs allowed: in bar, in garden,
in bedrooms, Rugs, water bowls, baskets, Parking 20
ROOMS: 14 en suite bedrooms 3 family rooms s£32 d£45

GARVE INCHBAE LODGE HOTEL 🐑

IV23 2PH
☎ 01997 455269 🖷 01997 455207
e-mail: stay@inchbae.com
Dir: *On A835, hotel 6m W of Garve.*
Map Ref: *NH36*

Originally a 19th-century hunting lodge, Inchbae Lodge
is situated on the banks of the River Blackwater, with
an elegant dining room offering panoramic views. An
ideal base for those keen walkers wishing to take on
Ben Wyvis and the Fannich Hills. Typical dishes include
chicken stuffed with pâté, seafood linguine, and
lasagne.

OPEN: 8-11 Closed: 2 wks in November, Christmas
BAR MEALS: L served all week 10.30-9 D served all week
9.30 **RESTAURANT:** L served all week 12-2 D served all
week 7-9.30 Av 3 course à la carte £15 Av 3 course fixed
price £10 **BREWERY/COMPANY:** Free House 🍺: Belhaven
plus guest ale. **CHILDREN'S FACILITIES:** menu, games,
high-chairs, food/bottle warming, outdoor play area, 7 acres,
toy box, books, jigsaws, puzzles, family room **GARDEN:** Food
served outdoors **NOTES:** Dogs allowed: Parking 30
ROOMS: 15 en suite s£30 d£50 (★★★)

GLENCOE CLACHAIG INN

PH49 4HX
☎ 01855 811252 ▤ 01855 812030
e-mail: inn@clachaig.com
*Dir: In the heart of Glen Coe itself, just off the A82, 20m S of Fort William and 2m E of Glencoe village. **Map Ref:** NN15*

Situated in the heart of Glencoe, this 300-year-old inn is hugely popular with mountaineers and stands a short forest walk from Signal Rock, where the sign was given for the infamous massacre of 1692. Scenes for the third Harry Potter film were shot just 200 yards from the doorstep. The pub is renowned for its real ales, 120 malt whiskies, and warming food which includes such classic local dishes as haggis, Clachaig chicken, venison casserole, and prime Scotch steaks. Outside is a paved terrace to the front and informal grass area by the Boots bar.

OPEN: 11-11 (Fri 11-12, Sat 11-11.30, Sun 12.30-11))
Closed: 24-26 Dec **BAR MEALS:** L served all week 12-9
D served all week 12-9 Av main course £8.50
BREWERY/COMPANY: Free House ◖: Fraoch Heather Ale,
Houston Peter's Well, Atlas 3 Sisters, Atlas Brewery-Latitude.
CHILDREN'S FACILITIES: menu, portions, licence,
high-chairs, food/bottle warming, baby changing, family room
GARDEN: Grassed area, patio at front **NOTES:** Dogs
allowed: in bar, in garden, in bedrooms, Parking 40
ROOMS: 23 en suite 5 family rooms s£32 d£60 (★★)

GLENELG GLENELG INN

IV40 8JR
☎ 01599 522273 ▤ 01599 522283
e-mail: christophermain7@glenelg-inn.com
*Dir: From Shiel Bridge (A87) take unclassified road to Glenelg. **Map Ref:** NG81*

Very much a home from home, this village inn occupies a 200-year-old stable mews and commands stunning views across the Glenelg Bay from its splendid waterside garden. Folk singers and musicians are frequent visitors to the bar where at times a ceilidh atmosphere prevails. The menu offers traditional Scottish fare based on local produce, including mussels, oysters, prawns and wild salmon, white fish, hill-bred lamb, venison and seasonal vegetables. The bar and restaurant selection may include, a tart of locally smoked salmon and black pepper chowder, chargrilled lemon chicken on courgette fritters, served with fresh basil and chilli dressing, fajitas of pan-fried fresh Loch Hourn scallops and coriander, served with an avocado salsa and baby leaves. A choice of vegetarian dishes and home-baked puddings also feature.

OPEN: 12-11 (Bar closed lunchtimes during winter)
BAR MEALS: L served all week 12.30-2 D served all week
6-9.30 **RESTAURANT:** 12.30-2 7.30-9
BREWERY/COMPANY: Free House
CHILDREN'S FACILITIES: menu, portions **GARDEN:** Large
garden going down to the sea **NOTES:** Dogs allowed

LYBSTER THE PORTLAND ARMS HOTEL

KW3 6BS
☎ 01593 721721 ▤ 01593 721722
e-mail: info@portlandarms.co.uk
Dir: Beside A99. From Inverness to Wick, hotel on left, 200yds from sign for Lybster.
***Map Ref:** ND23*

Long a favoured stop-off point for the many Lands End to John O'Groats travellers, the Portland Arms was built as a coaching hotel in the 19th century. It's grown in size since then to become a large hotel whose bar and dining areas cater for every mood: dine in the informal Jo's Kitchen, whose Aga sets a relaxed, farmhouse tone, the Bistro Bar, or the more formal Library. Maximum use is made of fresh local produce, and the menus offer such dishes as fresh haddock in beer batter, home-made steak pie, medallions of beef, and Aga baked ham.

OPEN: 7.30-11 Closed: Dec 31-Jan 3
BAR MEALS: L served all week 12-3 D served all week 5-9
Av main course £8.50 **RESTAURANT:** L served all week
11.30-3 D served all week 5-9 Av 3 course à la carte £18.50
BREWERY/COMPANY: Free House ◖: Tennants Lager,
Velvet, Belhaven Best. **CHILDREN'S FACILITIES:** menu,
portions, licence, games, high-chairs, food/bottle warming,
baby changing, toys, dining area **GARDEN:** Food served
outside **NOTES:** No dogs, Parking 20 **ROOMS:** 22 en suite
4 family rooms s£50 d£80 (★★★★)

NORTH BALLACHULISH   LOCH LEVEN HOTEL

Old Ferry Rd, Onich PH33 6SA
☎ 01855 821236 📠 01855 821550
e-mail: reception@lochlevenhotel.co.uk
Dir: *Off the main A82 at N of Ballachulish Bridge.* **Map Ref:** *NN06*

Over 350 years old, this was a working farm up to 50 years ago, as well as accommodating travellers from the Ballachulish ferry. On the northern shore of Loch Leven by the original slipway, it is ideally placed for touring the Western Highlands.

OPEN: 11-12 (Fri-Sat 11-1, Sun 12.30-11.45)
BAR MEALS: L served all week 12-3 D served all week 6-9 Av main course £7.95 **RESTAURANT:** L served all week 12-3 D served all week 6-9 Av 3 course à la carte £16 **BREWERY/COMPANY:** Free House 🍺: John Smith's, McEwan's 80/-. 🍷: 12 **CHILDREN'S FACILITIES:** menu, portions, games, high-chairs, food/bottle warming, baby changing, outdoor play area, family room **GARDEN:** Terrace with trees & shrubs overlooking loch **NOTES:** Dogs allowed: in bar, Water, Parking 30

PLOCKTON   THE PLOCKTON HOTEL ★★

Harbour St IV52 8TN
☎ 01599 544274 📠 01599 544475
e-mail: info@plocktonhotel.co.uk
Dir: *On A87 to Kyle of Lochalsh take turn at Balmacara. Plockton 7m N.* **Map Ref:** *NG83*

A logo featuring a palm tree for a Scottish hotel? Well yes, when the hotel in question stands on the Gulf Stream-warmed shores of Loch Carron in the Northwest Highlands. Fans of TV's 'Hamish Macbeth' will recognise this location. The Plockton Hotel is rather distinctively painted in black pitch and pointed in white - the traditional way of weatherproofing coastal buildings.

OPEN: 11-11.45 (Sun 12.30-11) **BAR MEALS:** L served all week 12-2.15 D served all week 6-9.15 (Sun 12.30-2.15) Av main course £6.25 **RESTAURANT:** L served all week 12-2.15 D served all week 6-9.15 Av 3 course à la carte £23.75 **BREWERY/COMPANY:** Free House 🍺: Caledonian Deuchars IPA. **CHILDREN'S FACILITIES:** menu, portions, high-chairs, food/bottle warming, baby changing, beside sea-shore, family room **GARDEN:** Beer garden, summer house, amazing views **NOTES:** No dogs (ex guide dogs) **ROOMS:** 15 en suite 1 family room s£45 d£60

PLOCKTON INN & SEAFOOD RESTAURANT

Innes St IV52 8TW
☎ 01599 544222 📠 01599 544487
e-mail: stay@plocktoninn.co.uk
Dir: *On A87 to Kyle of Lochalsh take turn at Balmacara. Plockton 7m N.* **Map Ref:** *NG83*

This attractive, stone-built free house stands just 50 metres from the sea, at the heart of the picturesque fishing village that formed the setting for the 'Hamish Macbeth' TV series. Formerly a church manse, the Plockton Inn is today run by a local family. The atmosphere is relaxed and friendly, with winter fires in both bars, and the prettily decorated bedrooms offering well-equipped comfort.

OPEN: 11-1am (Sun 12.30-11pm) **BAR MEALS:** L served all week 12-2.30 D served all week 5.30-9.30 **RESTAURANT:** L served all week 12-2.30 D served all week 5.30-9.30 **BREWERY/COMPANY:** Free House 🍺: Greene King Abbot Ale & Old Speckled Hen, Fuller's London Pride, Isle Of Skye Blaven, Caledonian 80/-. **CHILDREN'S FACILITIES:** menu, portions, licence, games, high-chairs, food/bottle warming, baby changing, outdoor play area, swings, sandpit, trampoline, ball games etc **GARDEN:** 2 gardens, sloping grass space at rear, trees **NOTES:** Dogs allowed: in bar, in garden, in bedrooms, Parking 10 **ROOMS:** 14 bedrooms 13 en suite 4 family rooms s£38 d£70 (★★★)

Highland continued

SHIELDAIG SHIELDAIG BAR ★ 🌼🌼 ♀

IV54 8XN
☎ 01520 755251 🖷 01520 755321
e-mail:
tighaneileanhotel@shieldaig.fsnet.co.uk
Dir: *5m S of Torridon off A896 on to village road signposted Shieldaig, bar on Loch front.*
Map Ref: NG85

All the seafood in this popular loch-front bar in a charming fishing village is caught locally. Not only that, but the prawn-fishing grounds have won a sustainable fishery award from the Marine Stewardship Council, and are now the model for similar locations in Sweden and elsewhere. You can expect a friendly welcome here, the views across Loch Torridon to the sea beyond are stunning

OPEN: 11-11 (Sun 12.30-10) Closed: Dec 25 & Jan 1
BAR MEALS: L served all week 12-2.30 D served all week 6-8.30 Av main course £6.50 **RESTAURANT:** D served all week 7-8.30 Av 3 course fixed price £32
BREWERY/COMPANY: Free House 🍺: Black Isle Ales, Tenants Superior Ale. ♀: 8 **CHILDREN'S FACILITIES:** menu, licence, Highchairs **GARDEN:** Open courtyard on Lochside with umbrellas **NOTES:** No dogs **ROOMS:** 11 en suite 1 family room s£52.50 d£115

BALLYGRANT BALLYGRANT INN & RESTAURANT 🐑

PA45 7QR
☎ 01496 840277 🖷 01496 840277
e-mail: info@ballygrant-inn.co.uk
Dir: *NE of Isle of Islay, 3m from ferry terminal at Port Askaig.* **Map Ref:** NR36

Variously a farm, an inn, a mine boss's house, and finally, 200 years later in 1967, an inn again. Set in two and a half acres of grounds and enclosed by heather-clad hills, it's close to two of Islay's seven malt whisky distilleries, and within easy reach of Port Askaig ferry terminal. Food is served all day from breakfast through morning coffee, snacks and lunch, to dinner. Scottish ales and all the island's malts are served in the bar, along with bar meals such as grilled trout, beef and orange casserole, lamb patia curry, and a

vegetarian dish of the day. Fresh Islay crab, oysters and scallops are a must whenever they're available.

OPEN: 11-11 (Wkds 11-1am) **BAR MEALS:** L served all week 12-3 D served all week 7-10 Av main course £8.95
RESTAURANT: L served all week 12-3 D served all week 7-10 **BREWERY/COMPANY:** Free House 🍺: Belhaven Best, calders 80/-, Calders 70/-.
CHILDREN'S FACILITIES: portions, games, high-chairs, food/bottle warming, baby changing, family room
GARDEN: Patio, grassed area overlooking woodland
NOTES: Dogs allowed: in bar, Parking 35
ROOMS: 3 en suite 1 family room s£27.50 d£55 (★★)

FOCHABERS GORDON ARMS HOTEL 🐑

80 High St IV32 7DH
☎ 01343 820508 🖷 01343 820300
e-mail: info@gordonarmshotel.com
Map Ref: NJ35

This 200-year old former coaching inn, close to the River Spey and within easy reach of Speyside's whisky distilleries, is understandably popular with salmon fishers, golfers and walkers. Its public rooms have been carefully refurbished, and the hotel makes an ideal base from which to explore this scenic corner of Scotland. The cuisine makes full use of local produce: venison, lamb and game from the uplands, fish and seafood from the Moray coast, beef from Aberdeenshire and salmon from the Spey - barely a stone's throw from the kitchen!

OPEN: 11-3 5-11 (Sun 12-3, 6-10.30)
BAR MEALS: L served all week 12-2 D served all week 5-7 Av main course £5.50 **RESTAURANT:** L served all week 12-2 D served all week 7-9 **BREWERY/COMPANY:** Free House 🍺: Caledonian Deuchars IPA, Scottish Courage John Smith's Smooth, Marsdons Pedigree.
CHILDREN'S FACILITIES: menu, portions, licence, games, high-chairs, food/bottle warming **NOTES:** Dogs allowed: in bar, Parking 40

CARINISH   CARINISH INN

North Uist HS6 5EJ
☎ 01876 580673 🖹 01876 580665
e-mail: carinishinn@btconnect.com
Map Ref: NF86

Modern-style refurbished inn at Carinish, North Uist, convenient for the RSPB Balranald Nature Reserve and local archaeological sites. Fish features prominently on the set-price menu, including roast fillet of West Coast salmon, stuffed monkfish tail wrapped in bacon with stewed tomatoes and polenta, and seafood casserole in a creamy wine and herb sauce. Local artists perform every Saturday night.

OPEN: 11-11 (Thu-Sat 11-1, Sun-Wed 11-11)
BAR MEALS: L served all week 12-2.30 D served all week 6.30-9.30 Av main course £6.50 **RESTAURANT:** L served all week 12-2.30 D served all week 6.30-9.30 Av 3 course à la carte £17 **BREWERY/COMPANY:** Free House
CHILDREN'S FACILITIES: menu **NOTES:** No dogs, Parking 50 **ROOMS:** 8 en suite s£50 d£70 (★★★)

ABERFELDY   AILEAN CHRAGGAN HOTEL ♀

Weem PH15 2LD
☎ 01887 820346 🖹 01887 829009
Dir: A9 N to junct at Ballinluig then A827 onto Aberfeldy, R onto B846. **Map Ref:** NN84

A small, friendly hotel set in two acres of grounds, including a large garden and two terraces with views over the River Tay to the hills beyond. Quality local produce is a feature of the menus. Daily specials include fish from the west coast including Loch Etive whole prawns, king scallops, and Loch Creran oysters. Game in season could include Perthshire venison steak, whole roast grouse, or pheasant. A rare treat is the stuffed Scottish lamb en croute. Cosmopolitan wine list runs to several pages, and over 100 malts.

OPEN: 11-11 Closed: 25-26 Dec, 1-2 Jan
BAR MEALS: L served all week 12-2 D served all week 6.30-9.30 (6.30-8.30 Winter) **RESTAURANT:** L served all week 12-2 D served all week 6.30-9.30
BREWERY/COMPANY: Free House
CHILDREN'S FACILITIES: menu, portions, licence, games, high-chairs, food/bottle warming, baby changing, outdoor play area **GARDEN:** Patio's, lawn **NOTES:** Dogs allowed: in bar, in garden, in bedrooms, Parking 40 **ROOMS:** 5 en suite s£45 d£90 (★★★)

ALMONDBANK   ALMONDBANK INN

31 Main St PH1 3NJ
☎ 01738 583242 🖹 01738 582471
Dir: From Perth take A85 towards Crieff. 3m to Almondbank. **Map Ref:** NO02

A family-run pub a little way out of Perth. From its neat rear garden the views are wonderful, including of the River Almond whose waters once powered the local textile industry, but which is now famous for its fishing. As well as snacks and high teas, there's a dinner menu featuring steaks, chicken, fish, pastas and Mexican dishes, and specials such as duck with wild berries. Owner Tommy Campbell, a retired Scottish football manager, has decorated his bar with football strips bearing famous players' signatures.

OPEN: 11-3 5-11 (Thu-Sun 11-12.30)
BAR MEALS: L served all week 12-2 D served Wed-Sun 5-10 Av main course £4 **RESTAURANT:** L served all week 12-3 D served Wed-Sun 5-10 Av 3 course à la carte £12
BREWERY/COMPANY: Belhaven 🍺: Belhaven Best, Tennants. **CHILDREN'S FACILITIES:** menu, licence, family room **GARDEN:** 6 tables, water fountain **NOTES:** Dogs allowed: in bar, in garden, Water, biscuits

BURRELTON   THE BURRELTON PARK INN

High St PH13 9NX
☎ 01828 670206 ▤ 01828 670676
Map Ref: NO23

Ideally situated for touring the highlands, this long roadside inn is characterised by its typical Scottish vernacular style. Spacious lounge bar and conservatory offering steamed mussels, braised lambs' liver and farmhouse mixed grill, and a well appointed restaurant featuring stuffed supreme of chicken and vension fillet - among other more elaborate dishes. Fresh catch of the day and special high teas served.

OPEN: 12-2.30 5-11 (Sat-Sun 12-11.45)
BAR MEALS: L served all week 12-8.30 D served all week 12-8.30 (No meals 2.30-5) **RESTAURANT:** L served all week 12-8.30 D served all week 12-8.30
BREWERY/COMPANY: Free House 🍺: Changing guest ales Tennents "YO", Velvet and Lager, Guinness, Bellhaven Best.
CHILDREN'S FACILITIES: menu **NOTES:** Dogs allowed: Parking 30

PITLOCHRY   THE OLD MILL INN ♀

Mill Ln PH16 5BH
☎ 01796 474020
e-mail: r@old-mill-inn.com
Dir: In the centre of Pitlochry, along Mill Lane. Behind the post office. *Map Ref:* NN95

Set at the gateway to the Highlands, this converted old mill still boasts a working water wheel, now with a patio overlooking it. Visitors are assured of a good choice of real ales, malts and wine by the glass to accompany an eclectic cuisine: smoked haddock chowder, Stornaway black pudding, steamed mussels, salmon stir-fry, plus burgers, bacon and brie ciabatta, and smoked salmon bagel.

OPEN: 10-11 **BAR MEALS:** L served all week 10-10 D served all week Av main course £7.95
RESTAURANT: L served all week 10-10 D served all week Av 3 course à la carte £15 **BREWERY/COMPANY:** Free House 🍺: Carlsberg-Tetley Tetley Bitter, Orkney Dark Island, Kettle Ale. **CHILDREN'S FACILITIES:** menu **GARDEN:** Food served outside **NOTES:** No dogs, Parking 10

POWMILL   GARTWHINZEAN HOTEL

FK14 7NW
☎ 01577 840595 ▤ 01577 840779
Dir: A977 to Kincardine Bridge road, for approx 7m to the vilage of Powmill, hotel at the end of village. *Map Ref:* NT09

Located between two of Scotland's finest cities, Edinburgh and Perth, and handy for exploring the nearby Ochil and Cleish Hills, this attractive hotel overlooks Perthshire's picturesque countryside. A large selection of malt whiskies and a cosy open fire add to the attractions. Traditional steak pie, lightly grilled fillet of salmon and noisettes of lamb feature among the dishes on the interesting, regularly changing menu.

OPEN: 11-11 (Sun 12.30-10.30) **BAR MEALS:** L served all week 12-1.45 D served all week 5-8.45 Av main course £8
RESTAURANT: L served all week 12-1.45 D served all week 5-8.45 Av 3 course à la carte £20 Av 3 course fixed price £17.50 **BREWERY/COMPANY:** Free House 🍺: Tetley Smoothflow, 70/-. **CHILDREN'S FACILITIES:** menu, Highchairs, Cot **GARDEN:** Food served outside **NOTES:** Dogs allowed: Parking 100 **ROOMS:** 23 en suite s£50 d£70 (★★★)

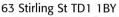

GALASHIELS ABBOTSFORD ARMS ★★

63 Stirling St TD1 1BY
☎ 01896 752517 ▤ 01896 750744
e-mail: roberts750@aol.com
Dir: *Turn off A7 down Ladhope Vale, turn L opposite the bus station.* **Map Ref:** *NT43*

Handy for salmon fishing in the nearby Tweed and visiting Melrose Abbey, this family-run, stone-built 19th-century coaching inn offers comfortable accommodation and traditional bar food. The lunchtime choice runs from filled croissants, salads and baked potatoes to breaded haddock, chicken curry and sirloin steak, bolstered in the evening by roast lamb shank, duck and orange sausages, and quails in cranberry and port. A function room holds up to 150, and there are plenty of good local golf courses.

OPEN: 11.30-11 **BAR MEALS:** L served all week 2-6 D served all week 6-9 (Sun 12-6, 6-8) Av main course £6.50 **RESTAURANT:** L served all week 12-6 D served all week 6-9 (Sun 12-6, 6-8) Av 3 course à la carte £12.50 **BREWERY/COMPANY:** 🍺: John Smith's, Miller, McEwans 70/-. **CHILDREN'S FACILITIES:** menu, portions, games, high-chairs, food/bottle warming, baby changing, high chairs, cot **GARDEN:** Paved area with grass **NOTES:** No dogs (ex guide dogs), Parking 10 **ROOMS:** 14 en suite 3 family rooms s£10 d£60

KINGSKNOWLES HOTEL ★★★

1 Selkirk Rd TD1 3HY
☎ 01896 758375 ▤ 01896 750377
e-mail: enquiries@kingsknowles.co.uk
Dir: *Off A7 at Galashiels/Selkirk rdbt.*
Map Ref: *NT43*

In over three acres of grounds on the banks of the Tweed, a splendid baronial mansion built in 1869 for a textile magnate. Meals are available in two restaurants and the Courtyard Bar. Fresh local or regional produce is used in dishes such as Borders beefsteak casserole, braised lamb steak, half a roast honey-glazed duck, and deep-fried fillet of haddock in breadcrumbs.

OPEN: 12-12 **BAR MEALS:** L served all week 11.45-2 D served all week 5.45-9.30 **RESTAURANT:** L served all week 11.45-2 D served all week 5.45-9.30 **BREWERY/COMPANY:** Free House 🍺: McEwans 80/-, Scottish Courage John Smith's. **CHILDREN'S FACILITIES:** menu, portions, games, high-chairs, food/bottle warming, baby changing, outdoor play area **GARDEN:** 3.5 acres, lawn, rockery **NOTES:** Dogs allowed: in garden, in bedrooms, Parking 60 **ROOMS:** 12 en suite bedrooms 3 family rooms s£54 d£89

INNERLEITHEN TRAQUAIR ARMS HOTEL ◆◆◆

Traquair Rd EH44 6PD
☎ 01896 830229
e-mail: traquair.arms@scotborders.com
Dir: *6m E of Peebles on A72. Hotel 100metres from junc with B709.* **Map Ref:** *NT33*

This traditional stone-built inn is in a village setting close to the River Tweed, surrounded by lovely Borders countryside and offering en suite bedrooms, a dining room and cosy bar. Real ales include Traquair Ale from nearby Traquair House, and the food has a distinctive Scottish flavour with dishes of Finnan savoury, salmon with ginger and coriander, and fillet of beef Traquair. Also a selection of omelettes, salads, and baked potatoes are available.

OPEN: 11-12 (Sun 12-12) Closed: 25& 26 Dec, 1-3 Jan **BAR MEALS:** L served all week 12-9 D served all week Av main course £6.50 **RESTAURANT:** L served all week D served all week 12-9 Av 3 course à la carte £18 Av 4 course fixed price £20 **BREWERY/COMPANY:** Free House 🍺: Traquair Bear, Broughton Greenmantle, plus seasonal guest. **CHILDREN'S FACILITIES:** menu **NOTES:** Dogs allowed: Parking 75 **ROOMS:** 15 en suite s£45 d£58

ST BOSWELLS BUCCLEUCH ARMS HOTEL ★★

The Green TD6 0EW
☎ 01835 822243 ▤ 01835 823965
e-mail: info@buccleucharmshotel.co.uk
Dir: On A68, 8m N of Jedburgh.
Map Ref: NT53

Perfectly placed at the heart of the Scottish Borders, a warm welcome and pleasant atmosphere is assured at this 16th-century inn. The varied supper menu includes pheasant casserole, fresh breaded haddock, and sirloin steak. Afternoon tea, high tea and a snack menu are available. The new landlord has made many allowances for children to dine, with a separate menu or smaller portions from the regular carte.

OPEN: 7.30-11 Closed: 25 Dec **BAR MEALS:** L served all week 12-2 D served all week 6-9 (Jan/Feb last orders 8.30 on Mon/Tue/Wed) **RESTAURANT:** L served all week 12-2 D served all week 6-9 **BREWERY/COMPANY:** Free House 🍺: Calders 70/-, 80/- & Calders Cream Ale, Broughton Greenmantle Ale. **CHILDREN'S FACILITIES:** menu, portions, games, high-chairs, food/bottle warming, baby changing, outdoor play area **GARDEN:** Quiet, spacious & peaceful garden **NOTES:** Dogs allowed: in bar, in garden, in bedrooms, £5 Supplement per night, Parking 80 **ROOMS:** 19 en suite 1 family room s£46 d£38.50

SWINTON WHEATSHEAF HOTEL 🏵🏵 🏠 🔔 🍷

Main St TD11 3JJ
☎ 01890 860257 ▤ 01890 860688
e-mail: reception@wheatsheaf-swinton.co.uk
Dir: 6m N of Duns on A6112. **Map Ref:** NT84

New owners Chris and Jan Winson are continuing to create gastronomic delights at the Wheatsheaf with locally-reared meats, salmon from the Tweed, game from the Borders and seafood from the Berwickshire coast. The hotel can be found in the picturesque village of Swinton on the Scottish Borders. Dinner is served in either the pine conservatory or more traditional dining room.

OPEN: 11-2.30 6-11 (Closed Sun eve in winter)) Closed: 24-26, 31 Dec, 1 Jan **BAR MEALS:** L served all week 12-2 D served all week 6-9 (Sun 6-8.30) **RESTAURANT:** L served all week 12-2 D served all week 6-9 **BREWERY/COMPANY:** Free House 🍺: Caledonian 80/- & Deuchers IPA, Broughton Greenmantle Ale, Caledonian 70/-. 🍷: 8 **CHILDREN'S FACILITIES:** portions, licence, high-chairs, food/bottle warming, In garden **NOTES:** Dogs allowed: in garden, in bedrooms, Parking 6 **ROOMS:** 7 en suite s£62 d£95

TIBBIE SHIELS INN TIBBIE SHIELS INN ◆◆◆

St Mary's Loch TD7 5LH
☎ 01750 42231 ▤ 01750 42302
Dir: From Moffat take A708. Inn is 14m on R.
Map Ref: NT22

On the isthmus between St Mary's Loch and the Loch of the Lowes, this waterside Inn is named after the woman who first opened it in 1826 and expanded the inn from a small cottage to a hostelry capable of sleeping around 35 people, many of them on the floor! Famous visitors during her time included Walter Scott, Thomas Carlyle and Robert L. Stevenson. Tibbie Shiels herself is rumoured to keep watch over the bar, where the selection of over 50 malt whiskeys will sustain you for ghost watching! Meals can be enjoyed either in the bar or the non-smoking dining room; the Inn also offers packed lunches for your walking, windsurfing or fishing expedition (residents fish free of charge). The menu offers a wide range of vegetarian options as well as local fish and game: highlights include Yarrow trout and Tibbies mixed grill.

OPEN: 11-11 (Sun 12.30-11) Rest: 1Nov-Easter closed Mon, Tue & Wed **BAR MEALS:** L served all week 12.30-8.15 D served all week 12.30-8.15 Av main course £6.50 **RESTAURANT:** L served all week 12.30-8.15 D served all week 12.30-8.15 Av 3 course à la carte £11.25 **BREWERY/COMPANY:** Free House 🍺: Broughton Greenmantle Ale, Belhaven 80/-. **CHILDREN'S FACILITIES:** menu, portions, licence, high-chairs, food/bottle warming, baby changing **GARDEN:** 6 acres of Lochside **NOTES:** No dogs (ex guide dogs), Parking 50 **ROOMS:** 5 en suite 2 family rooms s£30 d£52

TWEEDSMUIR   THE CROOK INN ♉

ML12 6QN
☎ 01899 880272 📄 01899 880294
e-mail: thecrookinn@btinternet.com
Map Ref: NT12

First licensed in 1604 and transformed into the art deco style in the 1930s, the Crook nestles deep in the Tweed Valley. Once a haunt of Rabbie Burns, the pub is an ideal base for country pursuits. Broad Law, the second highest peak in southern Scotland, is only five miles away. Elsewhere there are magnificent gardens, golf courses and fishing.

OPEN: 9-12 Closed: Dec 25, 3rd week in Jan
BAR MEALS: L served all week 12-2.30 D served all week 5.30-8.30 Av main course £7 **RESTAURANT:** L served all week 12-2.30 D served all week 7-9 Av 3 course à la carte £16 **BREWERY/COMPANY:** Free House 🍺: Broughton Greenmantle & Best, Scottish Courage John Smith's. ♉: 9
CHILDREN'S FACILITIES: menu, portions, high-chairs, food/bottle warming, baby changing, family room
GARDEN: Large grass area surrounded by trees, garden
NOTES: Dogs allowed: in bar, Water bowls, Parking 60
ROOMS: 8 en suite bedrooms 2 family rooms s£38.50 d£60

BRAE   BUSTA HOUSE HOTEL ★★★ 🐑 ♉

Busta ZE2 9QN
☎ 01806 522506 📄 01806 522588
e-mail: reservations@bustahouse.com
Map Ref: HU26

A 16th-century laird's residence, Busta House is Britain's most northerly country house hotel offering superb sea views and boasting some of Shetland's few trees in its garden. Home-cooked food specialising in fresh Shetland and Scottish produce is served in both the cosy beamed bar and the restaurant.

OPEN: 11.30-11 12.30-11 (Mon-Sat 11.30-11, Sun 12.30-11) **BAR MEALS:** L served all week 12-2.30 D served all week 6-9.30 Av main course £9 **RESTAURANT:** L served Sun 12.30-2 D served all week 7-9.30 Av 4 course fixed price £30 **BREWERY/COMPANY:** Free House 🍺: Valhalla Auld Rock, Simmer Dim & White Wife, Belhaven Best. ♉: 8
CHILDREN'S FACILITIES: menu, portions, licence, games, high-chairs, food/bottle warming **GARDEN:** Private harbour
NOTES: No dogs (ex guide dogs), Parking 50
ROOMS: 20 en suite 1 family room s£75 d£100

ARDVASAR   ARDVASAR HOTEL ★★ ♉

IV45 8RS
☎ 01471 844223 📄 01471 844495
e-mail: richard@ardvasar-hotel.demon.co.uk
Dir: From ferry terminal, 50yds & turn L.
Map Ref: NG60

The second oldest inn on Skye, this well-appointed white-painted cottage-style hotel offers a warm, friendly welcome and acts as an ideal base for exploring the island, spotting the wildlife and enjoying the stunning scenery. Overlooking the Sound of Sleat, the Ardvasar is within walking distance of the Clan Donald Centre and the ferry at Armadale.

OPEN: 12-12 (Sun close 11) **BAR MEALS:** L served all week 12-2.30 D served all week 5.30-9 Av main course £6.50 **RESTAURANT:** D served all week 7-9 Av 3 course à la carte £22.50 **BREWERY/COMPANY:** Free House 🍺: 80/-, Deuchars, IPA, Isle of Skye Hebridean Gold. ♉: 6 **CHILDREN'S FACILITIES:** licence **NOTES:** Dogs allowed: Parking 30 **ROOMS:** 10 en suite s£55 d£80

Skye, Isle of continued

CARBOST THE OLD INN

IV47 8SR
☎ 01478 640205 🖷 01478 640450
e-mail: oldinn@carbost.f9.co.uk
Dir: *Telephone for directions.* **Map Ref:** *NG33*

Once a croft house, this Highland inn is a perfect base for hill walkers and climbers. Rents used to be collected here and a local dentist pulled teeth in one of the upstairs rooms! The patio offers splendid views of Loch Harport and the Cuillins, while inside is a charming mix of wooden floors and original stone walls. Traditional bar food includes the likes of Scottish sausage hotpot, haggis, neeps and tatties, pasta bake, 8oz sirloin steak garni, baked salmon, and sole and prawns in Pernod sauce.

OPEN: 11-12 (hours change in winter - please ring) **BAR MEALS:** L served all week 12-2 D served all week 6.30-9 Av main course £7.50 **BREWERY/COMPANY:** Free House **CHILDREN'S FACILITIES:** menu, portions, licence, games, high-chairs, food/bottle warming, family room **GARDEN:** Shoreside Patio **NOTES:** Dogs allowed: in bar, Parking 20 **ROOMS:** 6 en suite 1 family room s£28 d£55 (★)

ISLE ORNSAY HOTEL EILEAN IARMAIN ★★ ◉◉

IV43 8QR
☎ 01471 833332 🖷 01471 833275
e-mail: hotel@eilean-iarmain.co.uk
Dir: *A851, A852 right to Isle Ornsay harbour front.* **Map Ref:** *NG71*

This award-winning Hebridean hotel overlooks the Isle of Ornsay harbour and Sleat Sound. The old-fashioned character of the hotel remains intact, and décor is mainly cotton and linen chintzes with traditional furniture. More small private hotel than pub, there are some similarities. A bar and restaurant ensure that the standards of food and wine served here - personally chosen by the owner Sir Iain Noble - are exacting.

OPEN: 12-12 (Winter Mon-Sun12-2.30, 5-12) **BAR MEALS:** L served all week 12.30-2 D served all week 6.30-9 Av main course £5.50 **RESTAURANT:** L served all week D served all week 7.30-9 Av 3 course à la carte £25 Av 5 course fixed price £31 **BREWERY/COMPANY:** Free House 🍺: McEwans 80/-. **CHILDREN'S FACILITIES:** menu, High chairs **GARDEN:** Food served outside **NOTES:** Dogs allowed: Parking 30 **ROOMS:** 12 en suite s£90 d£120

SYMINGTON WHEATSHEAF INN 🐑

Main St KA1 5QB
☎ 01563 830307 🖷 01563 830307
Dir: *Telephone for directions.* **Map Ref:** *NS33*

This 17th-century inn lies in a lovely village setting close to the Royal Troon Golf Course, and there has been a hostelry here since the 1500s. Log fires burn in every room and the work of local artists adorns the walls. Seafood highlights the menu - maybe pan-fried scallops in lemon and chives - and alternatives include honey roasted lamb shank, haggis, tatties and neeps in Drambuie and onion cream, and the renowned steak pie.

OPEN: 11-12 Closed: 25 Dec, 1 Jan **BAR MEALS:** L served all week 12-4 D served all week 4-9.30 Av main course £8 **RESTAURANT:** L served all week 12-9.30 D served all week Av 3 course à la carte £14 **BREWERY/COMPANY:** Belhaven 🍺: Belhaven Best, St Andrews Ale, Tennents & Stella. **CHILDREN'S FACILITIES:** menu, Highchairs avalible **NOTES:** No dogs, Parking 20

KILMAHOG THE LADE INN

FK17 8HD
☎ 01877 330152 ▤ 01877 331878
e-mail:
steve@theladeinnscotland.freeserve.co.uk
Map Ref: NS57

Detached white-painted building set in its own grounds on the Leny Estate west of Callander, named afer a mill lade - a stream created from the River Leny to power the mills at Kilmahog. The cosy bar has an open fire and collection of brasses, and the separate dining area offers real Scottish cooking. Expect haggis, neeps and tatties; Trossachs trout, rolled in oats and pan-fried with lemon and herb butter; or local burgers made from grass-fed beef.

OPEN: 12-3 5.30-10.30 (all day Sat/Sun/BH Mon) Closed: 1 Jan **BAR MEALS:** L served all week 12-2.30 D served all week 5.30-9 (Sat 12-9, Sun 12.30-9) Av main course £7.25 **RESTAURANT:** L served all week 12-2.30 D served all week 5.30-9 (Sat 12-9, Sun 12.30-9) Av 3 course à la carte £25 **BREWERY/COMPANY:** Free House ◖: Broughton Greenmantle Ale, Caledonian 80/-, local ales. ♀: 7 **CHILDREN'S FACILITIES:** licence, menu, portions, cutlery, activities, high chairs, food-warming, baby-changing **GARDEN:** seated area **NOTES:** Dogs allowed, Parking 40

KIPPEN CROSS KEYS HOTEL

Main St FK8 3DN
☎ 01786 870293 ▤ 01786 870293
e-mail: crosskeys@kippen70.fsnet.co.uk
Map Ref: NS69

The village of Kippen, situated in the Fintry Hills overlooking the Forth Valley, has strong

associations with Rob Roy. The pub dates from 1703, retains its original stone walls, and enjoys real fires in winter. Nearby Burnside Wood is managed by a local community woodland group, and is perfect for walking and nature trails.

OPEN: 12-2.30 5.30-11 (Fri-Sat 5.30-12 Sun 12.30-11) Closed: 25 Dec, 1 Jan **BAR MEALS:** L served all week 12-2 D served all week 5.30-9 (Sun 12.30-9) Av main course £6.95 **RESTAURANT:** L served all week 12-2 D served all week 5.30-9 (Sun 12.30-9) **BREWERY/COMPANY:** Free House ◖: Belhaven Best, IPA, 80/-, Harviestoun Bitter & Twisted. **CHILDREN'S FACILITIES:** menu, portions, games, high-chairs, food/bottle warming, baby changing, family room **GARDEN:** Small garden with water feature, good views **NOTES:** Dogs allowed: in bar, in garden, Water, Biscuits, Parking 5

STRATHBLANE KIRKHOUSE INN

Glasgow Rd G63 9AA
☎ 01360 771771 ▤ 01360 771711
e-mail: kirkhouse@cawleyhotels.com
Dir: A81 Aberfoyce rd from Glasgow city centre through Bearsden & Milngavie, Strathblane on junct with A891. **Map Ref:** NS57

17th-century coaching inn nestling beneath the jagged scarp of the Campsie Fells, a rolling patchwork of green volcanic hills and picturesque villages. Interesting menu offers international cuisine as well as traditional British dishes. A selection from the menu includes tournedos rossini, roast Burkhill duck, sirloin steak Jacobean, and fillet of salmon Gartness.

OPEN: 10-midnight (Fri-Sat 10-1) **BAR MEALS:** L served all week 12-7 Av main course £5 **RESTAURANT:** L served all week 12-5 D served all week 5-10 Av 3 course à la carte £27.50 **BREWERY/COMPANY:** ◖: Belhaven, Tennants 70/-. **CHILDREN'S FACILITIES:** menu, family room **NOTES:** No dogs, Parking 300 **ROOMS:** 16 en suite s£49.50 d£79 (★★★★)

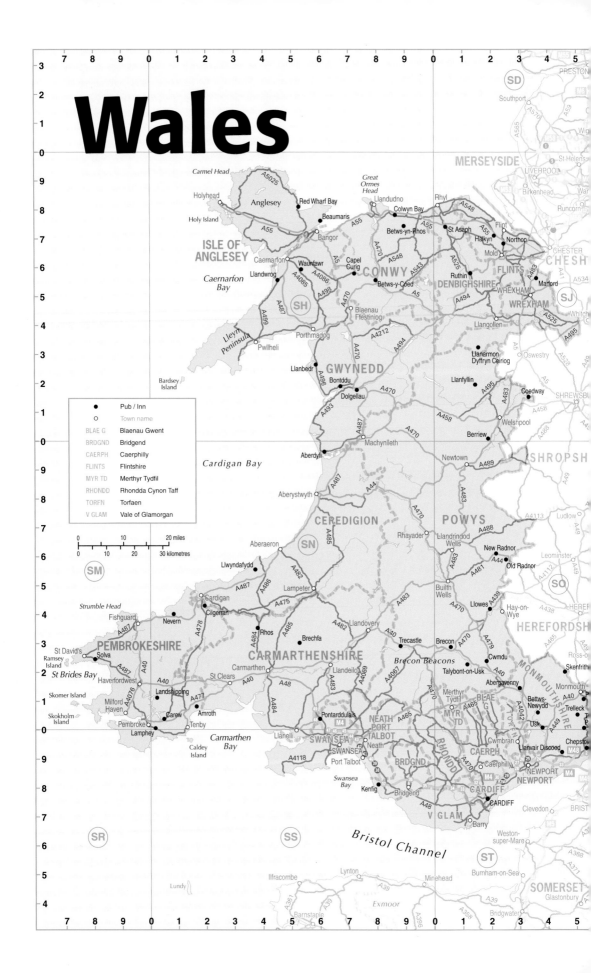

A country fiercely proud of its culture and identity, Wales is known both for its wild natural beauty and its cosmopolitan city life. The glorious coastline of Wales offers the largest concentration of award-winning beaches in the UK, and its mountainous landscapes, cut with lakes and rivers, are breathtakingly scenic.

The seaside and mountain resorts that sprung up when the railways brought Victorian holidaymakers from the factories of England retain a special charm, particularly along the north coast and into Snowdonia. Train lovers today can relish the sights, sounds and smells of more steam railways here than anywhere else in the UK.

Minerals made the country: slate from the monumental quarries and caverns of the north; iron and coal from the mines in the south, where the valleys run steeply down to the major ports of Swansea and Cardiff.

Tourist attractions centre on the castles and gardens of Wales, the industrial heritage sites and Portmeirion, the romantic Italianate village built by Clough Williams-Ellis between 1925 and 1975 on the coast of Snowdonia.

Top tipples

S A Brains & Co Ltd has the reputation for being the national brewery of Wales, founded in Cardiff in 1713. In 1997 it merged with Crown Buckley, another leading independent brewery in South Wales, and the whole range of Brains and Buckley beers are still brewed in the traditional way in Cardiff.

Whisky distillation has recently returned to Wales after an absence of century in the form of Penderyn, a Welsh single malt made in the Gwalia Distillery in the Brecon Beacons National Park. Wales has a long history of distilling spirits, like most Celtic countries, but the tradition was unable to withstand the religious Non-conformism of the 19th century, with its emphasis on temperance.

Above: The majestic Llanberis Pass in Snowdonia National Park

KENFIG PRINCE OF WALES INN ♀

CF33 4PR
☎ 01656 740356
Dir: *M4 J37 into North Cornelly & follow signs for nature reserve, Kenfig.* **Map Ref:** *SS88*

Dating from 1440, this stone-built inn has been many things in its time including a school, guildhall and courtroom. Why not sip some real cask ale in the bar by an inviting log fire? Typical menu includes steak and onion pie, lasagne, chicken and mushroom pie, and a variety of fish dishes. Look out for today's specials on the blackboard.

OPEN: 11.30-4 6-11 (Sun 12-10.30)
BAR MEALS: L served all week 12-2.30 D served Tue-Sat 7-9.30 Av main course £5.95 **RESTAURANT:** L served all week 12-22.30 D served Tue-Sat 7-9.30 Av 3 course à la carte £14 **BREWERY/COMPANY:** Free House ◄: Bass Triangle, Worthington Best. **CHILDREN'S FACILITIES:** menu **GARDEN:** Food served outside **NOTES:** Dogs allowed: Water, toys, Parking 30

CARDIFF CAYO ARMS

36 Cathedral Rd CF11 9HL
☎ 02920 391910
e-mail: celticinns@twpubs.co.uk
Dir: *From Cardiff take Kingsway West turn R into Cathedral Road.* **Map Ref:** *ST17*

Wales's newest brewery company has moved into Cardiff at this nationally-known bilingual pub on a leafy thoroughfare leading to the new stadium and city centre. In front is a large patio garden with umbrella-ed tables and patio heaters that add to the draw on Match Days of Tomos Watkins's ales. The same brew is used in a steak and ale pie and the batter for their celebrated fish and chips. Bedroom accommodation, though modest, is useful to know in the area.

OPEN: 12-11 (Sun 12-10.30) **BAR MEALS:** L served all week 12-3 D served all week 5-8 Av main course £5.95 ◄: Watkins Brewery Bitter, OSB, Whoosh, Merlin Stout. **CHILDREN'S FACILITIES:** menu **GARDEN:** Food served outside **NOTES:** Dogs allowed: Parking 30

BRECHFA FOREST ARMS

SA32 7RA
☎ 01267 202339 ▤ 01267 202339
Map Ref: *SN53*

Grade II-listed, early 19th-century stone-built inn in a pretty village in the beautiful Cothi Valley. A mile or so away, its own stretch of river yields salmon, sea and brown trout, which sometimes feature on the specials menu. Battered cod and scampi, and home-made chicken curry, spaghetti Bolognese, chilli con carne, and steak and mushroom pie are usually available. Fly-fishing mementoes adorn the unspoilt, traditional bars. The rear garden is a registered helipad.

OPEN: 12-2 6.30-11 (closed Sun) Rest: Tuesday & Sunday
BAR MEALS: L served all week 12-2 D served Mon-Sat 6.30-9 Av main course £5.75 **RESTAURANT:** L served Mon-Sat 12-2 D served Mon-Sat 6-9
BREWERY/COMPANY: Free House ◄: Dylan's, Brains Buckleys Best, Buckleys Dark.
CHILDREN'S FACILITIES: outdoor play area
GARDEN: Food served outdoors **NOTES:** No dogs, Parking 15, No credit cards

RHOS LAMB OF RHOS ♀

SA44 5EE
☎ 01559 370055
Map Ref: *SN33*

Country inn with flagstone floors, beamed ceilings and open fires - as well as its own jail and the 'seat to nowhere'. A menu of traditional pub fare includes steaks, chops, mixed grill, vegetarian and vegan dishes all cooked on the premises.

OPEN: 12-2.30 5-11 (Fri-Sun-all day Jul-Aug all day)
BAR MEALS: L served all week 12-2.3 D served all week 6-9 Av main course £5.50 **RESTAURANT:** L served Sun 12-2 D served Fri-Sat 7-9 Av 3 course à la carte £16
BREWERY/COMPANY: Free House 🍺: Worthington Cream Flow, Banks Original. **CHILDREN'S FACILITIES:** menu
GARDEN: beer garden, outdoor eating, patio
NOTES: No dogs, Parking 50, No credit cards

LLWYNDAFYDD CROWN INN & RESTAURANT

SA44 6BU
☎ 01545 560396 📄 01545 560857
Dir: *Off A487 NE of Cardigan.* **Map Ref:** *SN35*

Traditional 18th-century Welsh longhouse with original beams and open fireplaces, close to Cardigan Bay. The delightful, award-winning garden attracts many customers with its tree-sheltered setting, pond and colourful flowers, and it's an easy walk down the lane to a cove where there are caves and National Trust cliffs. Plenty of bar dishes including various grills, pizzas, and steak and kidney pie, or vegetarian omelette. The pretty restaurant offers crab tartlet, pork tenderloin, and chocolate meringue nest.

OPEN: 12-3 6-11 Rest: Nov-Easter closed Sun eve (Oct-Easter) **BAR MEALS:** L served all week 12-2 D served all week 6-9 Av main course £6.50 **RESTAURANT:** L served By appointment only 12-2.30 D served all week 6.30-9 Av 3 course à la carte £21 **BREWERY/COMPANY:** Free House 🍺: Interbrew Flowers Original & Flowers IPA, Tomos Watkins OSB, Greene King Old Speckled Hen.
CHILDREN'S FACILITIES: menu, outdoor play area, climbing frames, slides, swings, family room **GARDEN:** Large terraces
NOTES: No dogs, Parking 80

BETWS-Y-COED WHITE HORSE INN ◆◆◆◆ ♀

Capel Garmon LL26 0RW
☎ 01690 710271 📄 01690 710721
e-mail: whitehorse@supanet.com
Dir: *Telephone for directions.* **Map Ref:** *SH75*

Picturesque Capel Garmon perches high above Betws-y-Coed, with spectacular views

of the Snowdon Range, a good 20 kilometres away. To make a detour to find this cosy 400-year-old inn is to be rewarded not just by a striking collection of Victorian pottery and china, but by a menu featuring fresh local produce such as shoulder of Welsh lamb, traditional cottage pie, and horseshoe gammon steak. Apparently William Hague allegedly proposed to Ffion here!

OPEN: 11-3 6-11 Closed: 2 wks Jan **BAR MEALS:** L served Sat-Sun 12-2 D served all week 6.30-9.30 (Sun 7-9)
Av main course £7.50 **RESTAURANT:** L served Sat-Sun 12-2 D served all week 6.30-9.30 (Sun 7-9) Av 3 course à la carte £7.50 **BREWERY/COMPANY:** Free House 🍺: Tetley Imperial, Tetley Smoothflow, Greene King, Abbot Ale. ♀: 23
CHILDREN'S FACILITIES: menu, portions, high-chairs, baby changing, family room **NOTES:** Dogs allowed: in bar, in garden, Water, Parking 30 **ROOMS:** 6 en suite s£35 d£58 no children overnight

BETWS-YN-RHOS THE WHEATSHEAF INN

LL22 8AW
☎ 01492 680218 🗎 01492 680666
e-mail: perry@jonnyp.fsnet.co.uk
Dir: *A55 to Abergele, take A548 to Llanrwst
from the High St. 2m turn R-B5381, 1m to
Betws-yn-Rhos.* **Map Ref:** *SH97*

Built in the 13th century as an alehouse, the
Wheatsheaf became licensed in 1640 as a
coaching inn on the Conwy to Chester road.
Splendid oak beams studded with horse
brasses, old stone pillars and an original
hayloft ladder add to its cosy charm. Food in
the lounge bar or restaurant is good British
traditional, with starters like garlic
mushrooms, mains like the speciality Welsh
lamb joint slow-roasted with rosemary and
thyme, and several home-made sweets.

OPEN: 12-3 6-11 **BAR MEALS:** L served all week 12-2
D served all week 6-9 (Sun 12-3) **RESTAURANT:** L served
all week 12-2 D served all week 6-9 (Sun 12-3) Av 3 course
à la carte £14.20 🍺: Greene King IPA, Wadworth 6X,
Courage Directors, Worthington Smooth.
CHILDREN'S FACILITIES: menu, portions, games, high-chairs,
food/bottle warming **GARDEN:** Paved beer garden with
Wendy house & BBQ **NOTES:** No dogs (ex guide dogs),
Parking 30

CAPEL CURIG COBDENS HOTEL ★★

LL24 0EE
☎ 01690 720243 🗎 01690 720354
e-mail: info@cobdens.co.uk
Dir: *On A5, 4m N of Betws-Y-Coed.*
Map Ref: *SH75*

Situated in a beautiful mountain village in the
heart of Snowdonia, this 250-year-old inn is a
popular centre for outdoor pursuits.
Wholesome food prepared from fresh local
ingredients satisfies the needs of the
mountaineer as well as the tourist. Welsh
lamb and beef is well represented, as are fish
and pasta dishes. Light bites and sandwiches
are also available plus real ales and guest
beers. A Mountain Bar and sauna are new
attractions.

OPEN: 11-11 (Sun 12-10.30) Closed: 6-26 Jan
BAR MEALS: L served all week 12-2.30 D served all week
6-9 Av main course £8 **RESTAURANT:** L served all week
12-2 D served all week 6-9 Av 3 course à la carte £15
BREWERY/COMPANY: Free House 🍺: Greene King Old
Speckled Hen, Brains, Tetley's cold, Rev James Tetleys.
CHILDREN'S FACILITIES: menu, games, food/bottle
warming **GARDEN:** Part of Snowdonia National Park
NOTES: Dogs allowed: in bar, in garden, in bedrooms,
Parking 35 **ROOMS:** 17 en suite 3 family rooms s£29.50
d£59

COLWYN BAY PEN-Y-BRYN

Pen-y-Bren Rd LL29 6DD
☎ 01492 533360 & 535808 🗎 01492 536127
e-mail: pen.y.bryn@brunningandprice.co.uk
Map Ref: *SH87*

The wonderful view to the headlands and sea
was a major selling point when this large
1970s-built pub came on the market. It
reopened in June 2001 after a substantial
refit, juke boxes and fruit machines having
been banished (as have children in the
evenings). Now it offers old furniture, open
fires, oak floors, rugs and newspapers to
provide an ambience conducive to the
enjoyment of excellent real ales and good
food. Reasonably priced fare ranges from
sandwiches and light bites through to mains

such as twice-roasted pork with Colcannon mash,
black pudding and honey.

OPEN: 11.30-11 (Sun 12-10.30) Xmas/New Year times
differ **BAR MEALS:** L served all week 12-9.30 D served all
week Av main course £8.95 🍺: Timothy Taylors Landlord,
Fullers London Pride, Thwaites Best Bitter, Phoenix Arizona.
🍷: 13 **CHILDREN'S FACILITIES:** food/bottle warming, After
7pm 12yrs **GARDEN:** Terraced garden, views over Rhos on
Sea **NOTES:** Dog park outside, No dogs (ex guide dogs),
Parking 80

RUTHIN WHITE HORSE INN

Hendrerwydd LL16 4LL
☎ 01824 790218
e-mail: vintr74@hotmail.com
Map Ref: SJ15

Drovers used to stop at this traditional 17th-century inn, before driving their flocks east over the Clwydian Range to the markets of Chester and beyond. Viewed through its protective row of tall trees, the simple, whitewashed free house looks welcoming, and indeed this promise is fulfilled by Czech emigré Vit Vintr, and his wife, Ruth. The majority of dishes fall into the modern European category, giving us shoulder of Greek-style lamb (although it actually comes from Llanbedr), Chianti chicken, sea bass with saffron and wild mushrooms, and

stuffed aubergine with vegetarian mince. All main courses are served with a generous accompaniment of julienne of carrots, olive oil-fried mixed bell peppers and courgettes, cauliflower, new potatoes, mange tout and colcannon.

OPEN: 12-2.30 6-11 **BAR MEALS:** L served all week 12-2.30 D served all week 6-9.15 (Sun 6-8.30) **RESTAURANT:** L served all week 12-2.30 D served all week 6-9.15 (Sun 6-8.30) 🍺: Regular changing guest ales. **CHILDREN'S FACILITIES:** menu, portions, high-chairs, food/bottle warming **GARDEN:** Front&back, lovely views, trees, potted plants **NOTES:** Dogs allowed: in bar, Water, Parking 50

ST ASAPH THE PLOUGH INN ♀

The Roe LL17 0LU
☎ 01745 585080 📠 01745 585363
Dir: Rhyl/St Asaph turning from A55, L at rdbt, pub 200yds on L. **Map Ref:** SJ07

A very different kind of establishment including a real ale pub, two restaurants and a wine shop in the UK's smallest cathedral city. An 18th-century former coaching inn, the Plough has been transformed over a period of years. The ground floor retains the traditional pub concept, while upstairs there are an up-market bistro and an Italian-themed art deco restaurant, divided by a wine shop.

OPEN: 12-11 **BAR MEALS:** L served all week 12-9.30 D served all week Sun 12-10 Av main course £8.50 **RESTAURANT:** L served all week 12-3 D served all week 6-10 **BREWERY/COMPANY:** Free House 🍺: Greene King Old Speckled Hen, Shepherds Neame Spitfire. **CHILDREN'S FACILITIES:** menu **NOTES:** No dogs, Parking 200

HALKYN BRITANNIA INN

Pentre Rd CH8 8BS
☎ 01352 780272
e-mail:
sarah.pollitt@britanniainn.freeserve.co.uk
Dir: Off A55 on B5123. **Map Ref:** SJ27

On the old coach route between Chester and Holyhead, a 500-year-old stone pub with lovely views over the Dee estuary and the Wirral. It features a family farm with chickens, ducks and donkeys, and the large patio is ideal for alfresco eating and drinking on warm days. Typical dishes range from rump steak sandwich to pork escalope in pepper sauce, chicken tikka masala, three bean bake, and stuffed salmon roast.

OPEN: 11-11 (Sun 12-10.30) **BAR MEALS:** L served all week 12-2.30 D served all week 6.30-9 Av main course £5.50 **RESTAURANT:** L served all week 12-2.30 D served all week 6.30-9 Av 3 course à la carte £9 **BREWERY/COMPANY:** J W Lees 🍺: J W Lees Bitter, GB Mild, Golden Original. **CHILDREN'S FACILITIES:** menu, Petting farm **GARDEN:** Large patio area **NOTES:** No dogs, Parking 40

Flintshire continued

NORTHOP STABLES BAR RESTAURANT

CH7 6AB
☎ 01352 840577 📠 01352 840382
e-mail: info@soughtonhall.co.uk
Dir: *From A55, take A5119 through Northop village.* **Map Ref:** *SJ26*

Opened in 1997, this magnificent destination pub was made from the Grade I listed stables of Soughton Hall, the former Bishop of Chester's Palace. Superbly converted under massive oak beams, the building maintains its horse-based links. The original brick floor and some of the stalls have been retained, and tables are named after famous racecourses; placing bets by mobile phone, however, is discouraged. The ground floor contains a real ale bar, and upstairs diners will find an open-plan kitchen with an adjacent, fully stocked wine shop. Menu items are split between those for 'punters', with the more expensive for 'owners and trainers'. Choose your own fresh fish, seafood or steaks and watch them cooked to order, accompanied by fresh breads, hand-cut chips and a self-served salad.

OPEN: 11-11 6-11.30 **BAR MEALS:** L served all week 12-9.30 D served all week 7-9.30 Av main course £12 **RESTAURANT:** L served all week 12-3 D served all week 7-10 **BREWERY/COMPANY:** Free House 🍺: Shepherds Neame Spitfire, Shepherd Neame Bishops Finger, Coach House Honeypot. 🍷: 8 **CHILDREN'S FACILITIES:** menu, portions, high-chairs, outdoor play area, family room **GARDEN:** Food served outdoors, patio **NOTES:** Water, No dogs (ex guide dogs), Parking 150

ABERDYFI DOVEY INN ★★ 🍷

Seaview Ter LL35 0EF
☎ 01654 767332 📠 01654 767996
e-mail: info@doveyinn.com
Map Ref: *SN69*

Historic inn on the estuary of the River Dovey, only 20 yards from the sea and the fine sandy beach. The village clings to the hills above the estuary, once a major slate port and now a sailing centre. An extensive seafood menu includes Thai spiced shark steak, fish pie, Bantry Bay mussels, chargrilled swordfish, and tuna steak with red wine fish gravy. Plenty of other options including sandwiches, light bites, vegetarian, meat dishes, pasta, and pizza.

OPEN: 11-11 (Sun 12-10.30) **BAR MEALS:** L served all week 12-2.30 D served all week 6-9.30 **BREWERY/COMPANY:** Free House 🍺: Hancock HB, Bass, Carling Black Label. 🍷: 14 **CHILDREN'S FACILITIES:** menu, licence, family area in bar, family room **GARDEN:** Patio area **NOTES:** Dogs allowed: **ROOMS:** 8 en suite

PENHELIG ARMS HOTEL & RESTAURANT ★★ 🌸 🐾 🍷

Terrace Rd LL35 0LT
☎ 01654 767215 📠 01654 767690
e-mail: info@penheligarms.com
Dir: *On A493 (coastal rd) W of Machynlleth.* **Map Ref:** *SN69*

The inn was built in 1870 facing Penhelig Harbour, where ocean-going schooners were once built. It is now part of the pretty little resort of Aberdyfi, and offers spectacular views over the tidal Dyfi estuary. Guests experience a warm welcome in the bar with its central log-burning hearth and in fine weather can lounge on the sea wall opposite.

OPEN: 11.30-3.30 5.30-11 (Sun 12-3.30, 6-10.30) Closed: Dec 25-26 **BAR MEALS:** L served all week 12-2.30 D served all week 6.30-9.30 Av main course £10.50 **RESTAURANT:** L served all week 12-2.30 D served all week 7-9.30 Av 3 course fixed price £26 **BREWERY/COMPANY:** Free House 🍺: Carlesberg-Tetley Tetley Bitter, Greene King Abbot Ale, Adnams Broadside, Brains Reverend James & SA. 🍷: 30 **CHILDREN'S FACILITIES:** portions, licence, high-chairs, food/bottle warming **GARDEN:** Seating opposite hotel on sea wall **NOTES:** Dogs allowed: in bar, in bedrooms, Parking 12 **ROOMS:** 14 en suite 4 family rooms s£45 d£78

BONTDDU THE HALFWAY HOUSE

LL40 2UE
☎ 01341 430635
e-mail: sheerkahn@aol.com
Dir: On A436 between Dolgellau & Barmouth.
Map Ref: SH61

Dating from the early 1700s, the Halfway House has mellow pine chapel pews and fireplaces, giving the place a welcoming, cosy atmosphere. Situated near the Mawddach estuary, much loved by Wordsworth, the pub is on the route of several popular local walks. Good range of cask conditioned ales, several of which are from local breweries. Food, which can be served in the garden if the weather permits, offers traditional pub fare such as steak, mushroom and ale pie.

OPEN: 11-11 (Sun 12-10.30) 6-11 (Winter 11-3, 6-11)
BAR MEALS: L served all week 12-2.30 D served all week 6-9.30 Av main course £5.95 **RESTAURANT:** L served all week 12-2.30 D served all week 6-9.30
BREWERY/COMPANY: 🍺: Robinsons, Hartleys Cumbria Way. **CHILDREN'S FACILITIES:** menu, high-chairs, food/bottle warming **GARDEN:** Patio, food served outside
NOTES: Dogs allowed: Water, Parking 30

DOLGELLAU GEORGE III HOTEL

Penmaenpool LL40 1YD
☎ 01341 422525 🖷 01341 423565
e-mail: reception@george-3rd.co.uk
Dir: 2m West of A493 beyond RSPB Centre.
Map Ref: SH71

Superbly situated at the head of the Mawddach Estuary, where it was built about 1650. New owners offer both traditional and speciality main courses, but with space limited we'll focus on the latter, such as briam, a slow-baked dish of Mediterranean vegetables with olive oil and garlic, prime Welsh black beef fillet with grilled tomato and mushrooms, and roasted local sea bass with chilli couscous and baked vegetables. Running past the hotel is the Mawddach Trail,

once part of the Cambrian Coast railway line until Dr Beeching closed it in 1964.

OPEN: 11-11 **BAR MEALS:** L served all week 12-2.30 D served all week 6.30-9.30 Av main course £7
RESTAURANT: L served Sun 12-2 D served all week 7-9
🍺: Ruddles Best, John Smiths Cask, Guest Beers: Theakstons, Pedigree and Directors. **CHILDREN'S FACILITIES:** menu, portions, licence, high-chairs, food/bottle warming, baby changing, family room **NOTES:** Dogs allowed: in bar, in garden, in bedrooms, Parking 40

LLANBEDR VICTORIA INN ◆◆◆◆

LL45 2LD
☎ 01341 241213 🖷 01341 241644
e-mail: junebarry@lineone.net
Dir: Telephone for directions. *Map Ref:* SH52

Heavily beamed and richly atmospheric, the Victoria is ideal for the pub enthusiast seeking authentic features like flagged floors, an ancient stove, and unusual circular wooden settle. Good food is served in the bars and restaurant, including tasty filled baguettes, and lamb shoulder shank, fish pie, steak and kidney pie, and Welsh dragon pie. A well-kept garden is inviting on warmer days.

OPEN: 11-11 (Sun 12-10.30) **BAR MEALS:** L served all week 12-9 D served all week 6-9 Av main course £7
RESTAURANT: L served all week 12-3 D served all week 6-9 Av 3 course à la carte £15 **BREWERY/COMPANY:**
🍺: Robinson's Best Bitter, Hartleys XB, Carling Black Label.
CHILDREN'S FACILITIES: menu, outdoor play area, Climbing frame and slide **GARDEN:** Riverside garden, pond, trees & plants **NOTES:** Dogs allowed: in bar, in garden, in bedrooms, Parking 50 **ROOMS:** 5 en suite 1 family room s£42.50 d£72.50

Gwynedd continued

LLANDWROG THE HARP INN

Tyn'llan LL54 5SY
☎ 01286 831071 📠 01286 830239
e-mail: management@theharp.globalnet.co.uk
*Dir: A55 from Chester bypass, signed off A487
Pwllhelli rd.* **Map Ref:** *SH45*

A long established haven for travellers, the inn is located in the historic home village of the nearby Glynllifon Estate, between the mountains of Snowdonia and the beautiful beaches of Dinas Dinlle. A proudly Welsh menu offers Welsh favourites, a Welsh language menu is supplied.

OPEN: 12-3 6-11 (Times vary ring for details, Sat 12-11) Closed: Jan 1 Rest: Oct 1- Easter Closed Sun, Mon
BAR MEALS: L served Tue-Sun 12-2 D served Tue-Sun 6.30-8.30 Av main course £7.95 **RESTAURANT:** L served Tue-Sun 12-2 D served Tue-Sun 6.30-8.30 Av 3 course à la carte £15 Av 3 course fixed price £9.95
BREWERY/COMPANY: Free House 🍺: Interbrew Bass, Black Sheep Best, Wyre Piddle Piddle in the Wind, Plassey Bitter. **CHILDREN'S FACILITIES:** menu, Games for all ages, family room **GARDEN:** 6 tables **NOTES:** Dogs allowed: in bar, in garden, Water, Parking 20 **ROOMS:** 4 bedrooms 1 en suite 1 family room s£25 d£50 (★★★)

WAUNFAWR SNOWDONIA PARC HOTEL & BREWPUB NEW 🐑

LL55 4AQ
☎ 01286 650409 & 650218 📠 01286 650409
e-mail: karen@snowdonia-park.co.uk
Map Ref: *SH55*

A village brewpub and campsite in an idyllic mountain setting, 400 feet above sea level with a river running by. It's situated at Waunfawr Station on the Welsh Highland Railway, with steam trains on site (the pub was originally the station master's house). The pub offers home-brewed beer and home-made food prepared from local produce - Welsh lamb casserole and roast Welsh beef. Children and dogs are welcome and a children's playground is provided.

OPEN: 11-11 **BAR MEALS:** L served all week 11-8.30 D served all week 5-8.30 Av main course £6 🍺: Marston's Bitter & Pedigree, Welsh Highand Bitter (ownbrew), Mansfield Dark Mild, Stella. **CHILDREN'S FACILITIES:** menu, games, high-chairs, food/bottle warming, baby changing, outdoor play area, swings, roundabout, Bouncy Castle Apr-Sep, family room **NOTES:** Dogs allowed: in bar, in garden, Parking 100

BEAUMARIS YE OLDE BULLS HEAD INN ★★ 🏵🏵

Castle St LL58 8AP
☎ 01248 810329 📠 01248 811294
e-mail: info@bullsheadinn.co.uk
Dir: From Brittannia Road Bridge follow A545.
Map Ref: *SH67*

A short walk from Beaumaris Castle and the Menai Straits, this traditional watering hole dates back to 1472. Famous guests have included Samuel Johnson and Charles Dickens. There's a traditional bar leading on to the popular brasserie which offers lighter pasta and vegetarian dishes and the occasional spatchcocked poussin or grilled mullet. Or it's up the stairs to the smartly decorated, first-floor restaurant which offers a more formal menu.

OPEN: 10-11 (Sun-12-10.30) Closed: 25 Dec
BAR MEALS: L served all week 12-2 D served all week 6-9 Av main course £8 **RESTAURANT:** D served Mon-Sat 7.30-9.30 Av 3 course à la carte £30
BREWERY/COMPANY: Free House 🍺: Bass, Hancocks, Worthington. **CHILDREN'S FACILITIES:** menu, No chlldren in restaurant under 7 **NOTES:** No dogs, Parking 10 **ROOMS:** 13 en suite s£67 d£95

RED WHARF BAY   THE SHIP INN ♀

LL75 8RJ
☎ 01248 852568 📠 01248 851013
Map Ref: SH58

At low tide, the sands of Red Wharf Bay stretch for miles, attracting large numbers of waterfowl and wading birds. Before the age of steam, sailing ships arrived with cargoes from all over the world, and sailors drank in the then Quay Inn from six in the morning. Today, Conwy Bay fish and seafood are landed here, before making the short journey via the kitchen to the plates of diners in the bars and non-smoking restaurant. Possible starters include deep fried Perl Wen cheese with fig and plum chutney, or filo basket of Menai mussels with leeks and Gorau Glas cheese. Sandwiches and salads are also available. The waterside beer garden is a big attraction on warm days.

OPEN: 11-3.30 6.30-11 (Sat 11-11, Sun 12-10.30)
BAR MEALS: L served all week 12-2.30 D served all week 6.30-9 (Sun 12-8.30) Av main course £8.50
RESTAURANT: L served Sun 12-2.30 D served Fri-Sat 7-9.30
BREWERY/COMPANY: Free House 🍺: Imperial, Adnams, Greene King, Pedigree. ♀: 8
CHILDREN'S FACILITIES: menu, portions, high-chairs, food/bottle warming, outdoor play area, family room
GARDEN: on water's edge **NOTES:** No dogs (ex guide dogs), Parking 45

ABERGAVENNY   THE SKIRRID MOUNTAIN INN

Lanvihangel Crucorney NP7 8DH
☎ 01873 890258
e-mail: mistyspooks@aol.com
Dir: A465 4 miles outside Abergavenny, well signposted. *Map Ref:* SO21

Reputedly the oldest pub in Wales, the building dates from 1100 and was originally a courthouse (over 180 people met their deaths at the 'hanging beam'). Food served in the bar and restaurant includes Skirrid loaf (vegetarian), game casserole, and traditional Sunday roasts of local beef and lamb. From its location on the edge of the Brecon Beacons, there are great walks up Skirrid or down to Llanthony Priory and the Offa's Dyke footpath.

OPEN: 11-11 **BAR MEALS:** L served all week 12-2 D served Mon-Sat 7-9 Av main course £10
RESTAURANT: L served all week 12-2 D served Mon-Sun 7-9 Sun 12-2 Av 3 course à la carte £12
BREWERY/COMPANY: 🍺: Usher's Best, Marston's Pedigree, Hobgoblin. **CHILDREN'S FACILITIES:** menu, portions, licence, high-chairs, food/bottle warming
GARDEN: patio/terrace, BBQ, floral displays **NOTES:** Dogs allowed: in bar, Parking 20

BETTWS-NEWYDD   BLACK BEAR INN 🐕

NP15 1JN
☎ 01873 880701
Dir: Off B4598 N of Usk. *Map Ref:* SO30

Dating back to the 16th century and situated in a tiny hamlet surrounded by delightful Monmouthshire countryside, the Black Bear retains many of its original features. Owners Gill and Stephen Molyneux have improved and extended the inn since they took over its running 10 years ago, but their upgrading has not in any way detracted from its character. The River Usk, renowned for its salmon and sea and brown trout fishing, is only a quarter of a mile away, and both the Black Mountains and the Table Top Mountain are part of the scenery.

OPEN: 12-2 6-12 **BAR MEALS:** L served Tue-Sun 12-2 D served Mon-Sat 6-10 Av main course £10
RESTAURANT: L served Tue-Sun 12-2 D served Mon-Sat 6-10 **BREWERY/COMPANY:** Free House 🍺: Fuller's London Pride, Timothy Taylor Landlord, Interbrew Bass, Greene King Old Speckled Hen. **CHILDREN'S FACILITIES:** portions, food/bottle warming **GARDEN:** Shrubs, fruit trees, hen house, seating **NOTES:** Dogs allowed: in bar, in garden, in bedrooms, Water tap, Parking 20, No credit cards

CHEPSTOW THE BOAT INN ♀

The Back NP16 5HH
☎ 01291 628192 🖺 01291 628193
Map Ref: ST59

Standing on the banks of the River Wye, The Boat Inn's front terrace is a perfect place to relax on a summer's day and watch the ever-changing scenery. This is a pub which manages to effortlessly combine the virtues of a popular local with an honest approach to providing good bar and restaurant food. Salmon fisheries were once sited virtually next door: the boats would moor in the tide with deep nets stretching across the tidal flow below Brunel's tubular bridge. Today's revitalised pub is an attractive whitewashed building brightened by hanging baskets of flowers.

OPEN: 11-11 Mon-Sat (12-10.30 Sun) Closed: 25 Dec **BAR MEALS:** L served all week 12-3 D served all week 7-9.30 (Sun-Thu 6-7.30) **RESTAURANT:** L served all week 12-3 D served all week 6.30-10 **BREWERY/COMPANY:** Unique Pub Co 🍺: Interbrew Bass, Smiles, Wadworth 6X. **CHILDREN'S FACILITIES:** menu, family room **NOTES:** No dogs, Parking 20

LLANVAIR DISCOED THE WOODLAND RESTAURANT & BAR ♀

NP16 6LX
☎ 01633 400313 🖺 01633 400313
Dir: Telephone for directions. **Map Ref:** ST49

An old inn, extended to accommodate a growing number of diners, the Woodland is located close to the Roman fortress town of Caerwent and Wentworth's forest and reservoir. It remains at heart a friendly village local, serving a good range of beers. A varied menu of freshly prepared dishes caters for all tastes from ciabatta bread with various toppings to Welsh lamb loin wrapped in spinach and filo pastry on a bed of wild mushroom and rosemary risotto. Meat is sourced from a local butcher, who slaughters all his own meat, and the fish is mostly from Cornwall, maybe sea bass cooked in rock salt and lemon. Outside there's a large, well-equipped garden with plenty of bench seating.

OPEN: 11-3 6-11 (Sun 12-3, closed Sun eve) **BAR MEALS:** L served Tue-Sun 12-2 D served Tue-Sat 6-10 (Sun 12-2) Av main course £13.95 **RESTAURANT:** L served Tue-Sun 12-2 D served Tue-Sat 6-9.30 Av 3 course à la carte £25 **BREWERY/COMPANY:** Free House 🍺: Reverend James, H.B Spitfire, Brains & Spitfire. ♀: 8 **CHILDREN'S FACILITIES:** menu, portions, high-chairs, food/bottle warming, outdoor play area, swings, slide **GARDEN:** Plenty of bench seating, play area **NOTES:** Dogs allowed: in bar, in garden, Water, Parking 30

PENALLT THE BOAT INN

Lone Ln NP25 4AJ
☎ 01600 712615 🖺 01600 719120
Dir: From Monmouth take A466. In Redbrook the pub car park is signposted. Park & walk across rail bridge over R Wye. **Map Ref:** SO51

Dating back over 360 years, this riverside pub has served as a hostelry for quarry, mill, paper and tin mine workers, and even had a landlord operating a ferry across the Wye at shift times. The unspoilt slate floor is testament to the age of the place. The excellent selection of real ales and local ciders complement the menu well, with choices ranging from various ploughman's to lamb steffados or the charmingly-named pan haggerty. Ideal for walkers taking the Offa's Dyke or Wye Valley walks.

OPEN: 11-11 (Sun 12-10.30) **BAR MEALS:** L served all week 12-2.30 D served all week 6-9 Sun 12-3 (winter), Sat & Sun 12-9 **BREWERY/COMPANY:** Free House 🍺: Freeminer Bitter, Wadworth 6X, Greene King IPA, Abbot Ale & Old Speckled Hen. **CHILDREN'S FACILITIES:** menu, portions, food/bottle warming **GARDEN:** Rustic tables and benches with waterfalls **NOTES:** Dogs allowed: in bar, Water, Parking 20

SKENFRITH THE BELL AT SKENFRITH

NP7 8UH
☎ 01600 750235 ▤ 01600 750525
e-mail: enquiries@skenfrith.co.uk
Map Ref: SO42

This 17th-century coaching inn is located just inside the Welsh border, on what is now a mere B road, but which was once a main route from England into the Principality. Standing on the banks of the water by the historic arched bridge over the River Monnow, it has beautiful views across to Skenfrith Castle. A few years ago it was AA Pub of the Year and AA Wine Award winner for Wales.

OPEN: 11-11 (Sun 12-10.30) Closed: 1st 2 wks of Feb Rest: Closed Mon Nov-Mar **BAR MEALS:** L served all week 12-2.30 D served all week 7-9.30 Sun 7-9 Av main course £14 **RESTAURANT:** L served all week 12-2.30 D served all week 7-9.30 Sun 7-9 Av 3 course à la carte £27 **BREWERY/COMPANY:** Free House ◀: Freeminer Best Bitter, Hook Norton Best Bitter, Timothy Taylor Landlord. ♀: 13 **CHILDREN'S FACILITIES:** menu, portions, games, high-chairs, food/bottle warming, baby changing **GARDEN:** Lawn, terrace, tables & chairs **NOTES:** Dogs allowed: in bar, in garden, in bedrooms, Parking 36 **ROOMS:** 8 en suite s£70 d£90 (★★★★★)

TINTERN PARVA FOUNTAIN INN ♦♦♦ ♀

Trellech Grange NP16 6QW
☎ 01291 689303 ▤ 01291 689303
e-mail: dmaachi@aol.com
Dir: J2, M48 (8 miles), Grid Ref: SO 502013.
Map Ref: SO50

A fire nearly destroyed this fine old inn, but the thick 17th-century walls survived the flames, and its character remains unspoilt. It enjoys open views of the Wye Valley, and is close to Tintern Abbey. Food in the bar ranges from sandwiches and pies to Hungarian goulash, grills and steaks, and asparagus lasagne, with specials like beef Stroganoff, and duck à l'orange. A couple of well-kept ales are always on tap, plus a good selection of lagers.

OPEN: 12-3 6-10.30 **BAR MEALS:** L served all week 12-2 D served all week 7-10 Av main course £7 **RESTAURANT:** L served all week 12-2 D served all week 7-10 Av 3 course fixed price £15 **BREWERY/COMPANY:** Free House ◀: Wye Valley Butter Bach, Freeminers, Interbrew Flowers, Timothy Taylor Landlord. ♀: 10 **CHILDREN'S FACILITIES:** menu, family room **GARDEN:** Open views of Wye Valley countryside **NOTES:** Dogs allowed: in bar, in garden, in bedrooms, Water, open fields for walks, Parking 30 **ROOMS:** 5 bedrooms 2 en suite s£32 d£48

TRELLECK THE LION INN

NP25 4PA
☎ 01600 860322 ▤ 01600 860060
e-mail: tom@lioninn.co.uk
Dir: From A40 just south of Monmouth take B4293 and follow signs for Trelleck.
Map Ref: SO50

This popular and well-established free house stands opposite the church and is said to be haunted. Guests are greeted by real fires in the winter months, whilst in summer meals can be served in the garden overlooking the Wye valley. Uniquely, the former brew and coach house has now won the South Wales Argus pub restaurant of the year award for three years in succession. The on-site Lion Inn holiday cottage has been tastefully converted from a 400 year-old ruin.

OPEN: 12-3 6-11 (Mon 7-11; closed Sun eve) **BAR MEALS:** L served all week 12-2 D served Mon-Sat 6-9.30 Av main course £8 **RESTAURANT:** L served all week 12-2 D served Mon-Sat 6-9.30 Av 3 course à la carte £20 **BREWERY/COMPANY:** Free House ◀: Bath Ales, Wadworth 6X, Fuller's London Pride, Wye Valley Butty Bach. **CHILDREN'S FACILITIES:** menu, games, food/bottle warming **GARDEN:** Overlooks fields, stream. Large aviary **NOTES:** Dogs allowed: in bar, in garden, Water, biscuits, Parking 40

Monmouthshire continued

USK THE NAGS HEAD INN ♀

Twyn Square NP15 1BH
☎ 01291 672820 🖹 01291 672720
Dir: *On A472.* **Map Ref:** *SO30*

A warm welcome is assured in this 15th-century coaching inn, where the same family has been in charge for nearly forty years. Overlooking the square and just a short stroll from the River Usk, the flower-adorned pub has undoubtedly played a key role in the town winning Wales in Bloom awards for the last three years. Friendly staff work in the traditional bar with polished tables and chairs; lots of horse brasses, farming tools and lanterns hang from exposed oak beams. You know you're in for a treat when you see the good selection of house wines and starters like half a dozen snails in garlic butter, and frogs' legs in hot Provençal sauce. These can be followed by hearty dishes of local game in season, including wild boar steak in an apricot and brandy sauce, pheasant cooked in port, whole stuffed partridge, and rabbit pie. Vegetarian options include Glamorgan sausage, filled with cheese and leek and served with a chilli relish.

OPEN: 10-3 5.30-11 Closed: Dec 25
BAR MEALS: L served all week 10-2 D served all week 5.30-10.30 Av main course £7.50 **RESTAURANT:** L served all week 11.30-2 D served all week 5.30-10.30
BREWERY/COMPANY: Free House 🍺: Brains Bitter, Dark, Buckleys Best & Reverend James. ♀: 8
CHILDREN'S FACILITIES: menu, portions, games, high-chairs, food/bottle warming **NOTES:** No dogs (ex guide dogs)

AMROTH THE NEW INN

SA67 8NW
☎ 01834 812368
Dir: *A48 to Carmarthen, A40 to St Clears, A477 to Llanteg then L.* **Map Ref:** *SN10*

A 400-year-old inn, originally a farmhouse, belonging to Amroth Castle Estate. It has old world charm with beamed ceilings, a Flemish chimney, a flagstone floor and an inglenook fireplace. It is close to the beach, and local lobster and crab are a feature, along with a popular choice of home-made dishes including steak and kidney pie, soup and curry. Enjoy food or drink outside on the large lawn complete with picnic benches.

OPEN: 11.30-3 5.30-11 (closed Nov-Mar) Closed: Nov-Mar
BAR MEALS: L served all week 12-2 D served all week 6-9
RESTAURANT: L served all week 12-2 D served all week 6-9
BREWERY/COMPANY: Free House 🍺: Burton, Carlsberg-Tetley Tetley Bitter.
CHILDREN'S FACILITIES: menu, family room
GARDEN: Large lawn with picnic benches **NOTES:** Dogs allowed: Parking 100, No credit cards

CAREW CAREW INN

SA70 8SL
☎ 01646 651267 🖹 01646 650126
e-mail: mandy@carewinn.co.uk
Dir: *From A477 take A4075. Inn 400yds opp castle & Celtic cross.* **Map Ref:** *SN00*

A traditional stone-built country inn situated opposite the Carew Celtic cross and Norman castle, which is a regular venue for activities by The Sealed Knot. Enjoy the one-mile circular walk around the castle and millpond before settling in the pub. Typical meals include chicken, leek and mushroom pie, pork tenderloin in mustard sauce or chicken in white wine and mustard sauce. Live music every Thursday night under the marquee.

OPEN: 11.30-2.30 4.30-11 (Summer & wknd 11-11)
Closed: Dec 25 **BAR MEALS:** L served all week 11.30-2 D served all week 6-9 Av main course £6.95
RESTAURANT: L served all week 12-2 D served all week 6-9 Av 3 course à la carte £15 Av 2 course fixed price £6.95
BREWERY/COMPANY: Free House 🍺: Worthington Best, SA Brains Reverend James & Guest Ales.
CHILDREN'S FACILITIES: menu, outdoor play area, small climbing frame, slide, see-saw **GARDEN:** overlooks Carew Castle **NOTES:** Dogs allowed: in bar, in garden, Water provided, Parking 20

CILGERRAN   PENDRE INN

Pendre SA43 2SL
☎ 01239 614223
Dir: *Off A478 south of Cardigan.*
Map Ref: *SN14*

Dating back to the 14th century, this is a pub full of memorabilia and featuring exposed interior walls, old beams, slate floors and an inglenook fireplace. An ancient ash tree grows through the pavement in front of the white stone, thick-walled building. Typical menu includes lamb steaks with red wine and cherries, rump and sirloin steaks, pork loin with honey and mustard glaze, and salmon with hollandaise sauce.

OPEN: 12-3 6-11 (closed Sun eve) **BAR MEALS:** L served Mon-Sat 12-2 D served Mon-Sat 6-8 Av main course £6.95 **RESTAURANT:** L served Mon-Sat 12-2 D served Mon-Sat 6-8 **BREWERY/COMPANY:** Free House ◖: Thomas Watkins. **CHILDREN'S FACILITIES:** portions, games, high-chairs, food/bottle warming **GARDEN:** Lawn/patio with large trees and water feature **NOTES:** No dogs (ex guide dogs), Parking 6, No credit cards

LAMPHEY   THE DIAL INN

Ridegway Rd SA71 5NU
☎ 01646 672426 ▤ 01646 672426
Dir: *Just off A4139 (Tenby to Pembroke rd).*
Map Ref: *SN00*

The Dial started life around 1830 as the Dower House for nearby Lamphey Court, and was converted into a pub in 1966. It immediately established itself as a popular village local, and in recent years the owners have extended the dining areas. Food is a real strength, and Pembrokeshire farm products are used whenever possible. You can choose from traditional bar food, the imaginative restaurant menu, or the daily blackboard. Here you'll find specials such as sautéed pheasant and spinach in an almond sauce, wild boar cooked in a honey, ginger and Calvados sauce; Lamphey lamb in tender chunks, with leeks, apricots, thyme, rosemary and a red wine jus, pot-roasted partridge with juniper stuffing, and duo of guinea fowl and pheasant, served with mashed potato, green beans, swede and finished in a rich onion gravy. There's a family room, with darts, pool and other pub games; and a patio for al fresco dining when the weather permits.

OPEN: 11-3 6-12 **BAR MEALS:** L served all week 12-3 D served all week 6.30-10 Av main course £10.50 **RESTAURANT:** L served all week 12-3 D served all week 6.30-10 **BREWERY/COMPANY:** Free House ◖: Hancocks, Interbrew Bass, Worthington. ♇: 8 **CHILDREN'S FACILITIES:** menu, portions, licence, games, high-chairs, food/bottle warming, Family room, games (darts/pool) **GARDEN:** Patio area **NOTES:** No dogs (ex guide dogs), Parking 50

LANDSHIPPING   THE STANLEY ARMS ♇

SA67 8BE
☎ 01834 860447
Dir: *Off A40 at Canaston Bridge onto A4075, R at Cross Hands, next to Canaston Bowls.*
Map Ref: *SN01*

Built as a farmhouse around 1765, first licensed in 1875, the pub has its own mooring on the Cleddau Estuary and is popular with sailors. There's an attractive garden with fine views across the water to Picton Castle, and the area is good for walking. Freshly-cooked pub food includes marinated chicken breast, gammon with egg or pineapple, grilled Milford plaice, Welsh dragon sausage in mustard sauce, home-made curries and Welsh steaks, as well as salads and a children's menu.

OPEN: 12-3 (all day Thur-Sun, Jul-Sept 06) 6-11 (Sun 7-10.30) Rest: Mon-Tue (winter) Closed Lunch **BAR MEALS:** L served all week 12-2.30 D served all week 6-9.30 **RESTAURANT:** L served all week 12-2.30 D served all week 6-9.30 **BREWERY/COMPANY:** Free House ◖: Worthington, Fuller's London Pride, Everards Tiger, Hancocks HB. ♇: 7 **CHILDREN'S FACILITIES:** menu, licence, outdoor play area, children's license, slide and play centre **GARDEN:** Large garden with swings annd sandpit **NOTES:** Dogs allowed: Water, Parking 20

Pembrokeshire continued

NEVERN   TREWERN ARMS ★★

SA42 0NB
☎ 01239 820395 ▤ 01239 820173
Dir: *On the A487 between Cardigan and Fishguard.* **Map Ref:** *SN04*

Ivy-clad 16th century inn set in attractive grounds astride the River Nevern. The Brew House bar is a popular local, with flagstone floors and old settles. Dishes might include broccoli cream cheese, breaded cod, pork Normandy, lemon sole with Penclawdd cockles, roast pheasant marinated in port, or Preseli lamb in redcurrant and rosemary sauce.

OPEN: 11-3 (Sun 12-3,7-10.30) 6-11 Closed: None Rest: None **BAR MEALS:** L served all week 12-2 D served all week 6-9 Av main course £7.50 **RESTAURANT:** D served Thu-Sat 7-9 Av 3 course à la carte £18.50
BREWERY/COMPANY: Free House ◖: Flowers Original, Castle Eden Ale, Wadworth 6X, Worthington.
GARDEN: Lawn/Patio **NOTES:** No dogs, Parking 80
ROOMS: 10 en suite 4 family rooms s£30 d£60

SOLVA   THE CAMBRIAN INN 🐑

Main St SA62 6UU
☎ 01437 721210
Dir: *13m from Haverfordwest on the St David's Rd.* **Map Ref:** *SM82*

Something of an institution in this pretty fishing village is a Grade II listed 17th-century inn that attracts local and returning visitors alike. A sample restaurant menu offers diners many traditional dishes, with a good selection of fish dishes, as well as sirloin steak, duck and pork. Readers reports welcome.

OPEN: 12-3 6-11 (Winter 12-2:30, 7-11) Closed: 2 wks Nov, Dec 25-26 **BAR MEALS:** L served all week 12-2 D served all week 6.30-9.30 Av main course £6.75
RESTAURANT: L served all week 12-2 D served all week 7-9.30 Av 3 course à la carte £20
BREWERY/COMPANY: Free House ◖: Reverend James, Worthington Cream Flow. **GARDEN:** patio, beer garden, outdoor eating **NOTES:** No dogs (ex guide dogs), Parking 12

BERRIEW   LION HOTEL 🐑

SY21 8PQ
☎ 01686 640452 ▤ 01686 640604
Dir: *5m from Welshpool on A483, R to Berriew. Centre of village next to church.* **Map Ref:** *SJ10*

17th-century black and white inn with exposed beams throughout and plenty of character. Welcoming and friendly atmosphere inside. Food options include a variety of starters or light meals and main courses ranging from fillet of salmon to baked goats' cheese salad, steak, mushroom and ale pie, and curry. A range of specials, sandwiches and home-made puddings is also available.

OPEN: 12-3 6-11 (Fri 5.30-11, Sat 7-11, Sun 7-10.30) Closed: Dec 25 **BAR MEALS:** L served all week 12-2 D served all week 7-9 Av main course £9.95
RESTAURANT: L served all week 12-2 D served Mon-Sat 7-9
BREWERY/COMPANY: Free House ◖: Worthington Bitter, Woods Shropshire Lad, Brains Reverend James, Woods Wonderful. **CHILDREN'S FACILITIES:** menu, portions, licence, high-chairs, food/bottle warming, baby changing, family room **GARDEN:** Patio area surrounded by plants
NOTES: Dogs allowed: in bar, in garden, in bedrooms, Water, Parking 6 **ROOMS:** 7 en suite 1 family room s£55 d£70 (★★★)

BRECON THE USK INN ♦♦♦♦ 🏵 ⚱

Talybont-on-Usk LD3 7JE
☎ 01874 676251 🖶 01874 676392
e-mail: stay@uskinn.co.uk
Dir: *6m E of Brecon, just off the A40 towards Abergavenny & Crickhowell.* **Map Ref:** *SO02*

This recently refurbished free house has long been welcoming weary travellers with a good range of real ales. The traditional open fire and flagstone floors remain, and offers just a little more style. Food is taken seriously, with imaginative menus that make good use of fresh local produce.

OPEN: 8am-11pm Closed: Dec 25-26
BAR MEALS: L served all week 12-3 D served all week 6.30-10 **RESTAURANT:** L served all week 12-3 D served all week 7-9.30 **BREWERY/COMPANY:** Free House
🍺: Reverend James & Buckleys Best, Felinfoel Double Dragon, Hancocks HB, Buckleys IPA. ⚱: 8
CHILDREN'S FACILITIES: menu, highchairs, toy basket
GARDEN: Lawned area with mature planting **NOTES:** Dogs allowed: in bar, in garden, Water, Parking 35
ROOMS: 11 en suite 1 family room s£45 d£70

COEDWAY THE OLD HAND AND DIAMOND

SY5 9AR
☎ 01743 884379 🖶 01743 884267
Map Ref: *SJ31*

Close to the Shropshire border and the River Severn, this 17th-century inn still retains much of its original character. Large open log fires burn in the winter and autumn. Typical menu includes chicken in mushroom and Stilton cream sauce, pork chops with cider and apple sauce, fresh sea bass, roast beef and Yorkshire pudding, and vegetable cannelloni. Recent change of management.

OPEN: 11-11 **BAR MEALS:** L served all week 12-10 D served all week Av main course £6.95
RESTAURANT: L served all week 12-10 D served all week **BREWERY/COMPANY:** Free House 🍺: Bass, Worthington, Shropshire Lad + Guest beers.
CHILDREN'S FACILITIES: menu, outdoor play area
GARDEN: Food served outside **NOTES:** Guide Dogs Only, Parking 90

CWMDU THE FARMERS ARMS

NP8 1RU
☎ 01874 730464 🖶 01874 730988
e-mail: cwmdu@aol.com
Dir: *From A40 take A479 signed Builth Wells, Cwmdu is 3m along this road.* **Map Ref:** *SO12*

A traditional country Inn in a quiet valley on the edge of the Black Mountains. The 18th-century building is warmly welcome, with a wood-burning stove when the weather requires it, bar games and a broad selection of real ales. Fresh local ingredients are used to create dishes such as smoked haddock and Welsh onion fishcakes, puff pastry pillows of leeks, and grilled supreme of chicken with sautéed wild mushrooms. Tempting desserts include sticky toffee fudge Pavlova.

OPEN: 12-2.30 6.30-11 (Mon 6.30-11, open BH Mon all day) Closed: Two weeks in Nov **BAR MEALS:** L served Tue-Sun 12-2.15 D served Tue-Sun 7-9.30 Av main course £8 **RESTAURANT:** L served Tue-Sun 12-2.15 D served Tue-Sun 7-9.30 Av 3 course à la carte £22 Av 3 course fixed price £19 **BREWERY/COMPANY:** Free House 🍺: Uley Old Spot Prize Ale, Tomos Watkin OSB, Greene King Old Speckled Hen, Sheperd Neame Spitfire Premium Ale. **CHILDREN'S FACILITIES:** menu, portions, outdoor play area **GARDEN:** Views over the Brecon Beacons
NOTES: Dogs allowed: in bar, in garden, in bedrooms, Water, food, secured penned area, Parking 30

LLANFYLLIN   CAIN VALLEY HOTEL ★★

High St SY22 5AQ
☎ 01691 648366 ▤ 01691 648307
e-mail: info@cainvalleyhotel.co.uk
Dir: *from Shrewsbury & Oswestry follow signs
for Lake Vyrnwy & onto A490 to Llanfyllin.Hotel
on R.* **Map Ref:** *SJ11*

Family run coaching inn dating from the 17th
century, with a stunning Jacobean staircase,
oak-panelled lounge bar and a heavily beamed
restaurant, where the walls have been
exposed to show off the hand-made bricks. A
full bar menu is available at lunchtime and in
the evening, alongside a choice of real ales.
Home-made soup, mixed seafood, Welsh
lamb, steaks and curries are offered. Llanfyllin
is set amid green hills, offering wonderful
walks and breathtaking views.

OPEN: 11.30-11 (Sun 12-10.30) Closed: 25 Dec
BAR MEALS: L served all week 12-2 D served all week 7-9
RESTAURANT: D served all week 7-9
BREWERY/COMPANY: Free House 🍺: Carlsberg-Tetley
Ansells Best Bitter, Interbrew Bass & Worthingtons.
CHILDREN'S FACILITIES: menu, portions, high-chairs, cot,
high chair **NOTES:** Dogs allowed: in bedrooms, Parking 12
ROOMS: 13 en suite 3 family rooms s£42 d£69

THE STUMBLE INN

Bwlch-y-Cibau SY22 5LL
☎ 01691 648860 ▤ 01691 648955
Dir: *A458 to Welshpool, B4393 to Four Crosses
and Llansantfraid, A495 Melford, A490 to
Bwlch-y-Cibau.* **Map Ref:** *SJ11*

Located opposite the church in a peaceful farming
community in unspoilt mid-Wales countryside close to
Lake Vyrnwy, this popular stone-built 18th-century inn
offers a traditional pub atmosphere. Ideal base for
walkers and cyclists. The menu changes frequently and
might feature duck with orange sauce, lamb shank,
whole Dover sole, pork with lemon and mustard
sauce, sizzling Chinese steak, mushroom Stroganoff,
and Mediterranean risotto.

OPEN: 12-3 6-12 (Closed Sun nights Dec-Mar) Closed: 2
Wks Jan **BAR MEALS:** L served Sun 12-2 D served Wed-Sat
6-9 Av main course £8.95 **RESTAURANT:** L served Sun
12-2 D served Wed-Sat 6-10 **BREWERY/COMPANY:** Free
House 🍺: Coors Worthington's, Changing Ales.
CHILDREN'S FACILITIES: menu, games, high-chairs,
food/bottle warming **NOTES:** No dogs (ex guide dogs),
Parking 20

NEW RADNOR   RED LION INN 🐑

Llanfihangel-nant-Melan LD8 2TN
☎ 01544 350220 ▤ 01544 350220
e-mail: enquiries@theredlioninn.net
Dir: *A483 to Crossgates then R onto A44.*
Map Ref: *SO26*

Lying in the bowl-shaped head of a valley, the inn was
built in the 16th century as a pit stop for drovers. Today
motorists, walkers and cyclists all stop here to be well
looked after by the new owners, who even provide a
facility for washing muddy bikes. Most produce is local.

OPEN: 12-2.30 (Winter, 12-2.30, 6-11) 6-11 (Open all day
summer) Rest: Winter Closed Tue **BAR MEALS:** L served
Wed-Mon 12-2.15 D served Mon-Sun 6.30-9.45 Av main
course £10.50 **RESTAURANT:** L served Wed-Mon 12-2.15
D served Wed-Mon 6.30-9.45 Av 3 course à la carte £16.50
BREWERY/COMPANY: Free House 🍺: Randor Ale, Chase
My Tail, Real Ales. **CHILDREN'S FACILITIES:** menu, portions,
games, high-chairs, food/bottle warming, family room
GARDEN: Country garden overlooking mid Wales Hills
NOTES: Dogs allowed: in bar, in garden, Parking 30

OLD RADNOR — HARP INN

LD8 2RH
☎ 01544 350655 🖷 01544 350655
Dir: *A44 from Leominster to Gore, then L to Old Radnor.* **Map Ref:** *SO25*

This charming inn dates back to the 15th-century, yet has been sympathetically renovated, taking great care to retain as much of its original period character as possible. The slate-flagged floor, exposed stone walls and ancient bread oven still remain, as do traditional standards of hospitality and good food. Charles I complained about the food here centuries ago, but he could scarcely do so today. A typical menu includes 10oz Herefordshire steaks, steak and mushroom pie, salmon steak in dill sauce, breast of chicken in Stilton sauce, and pork steak in mustard sauce. Vegetarian options always available.

OPEN: 12-2 6-11 (Sat-Sun 12-3, 6-10.30)
BAR MEALS: L served Sat-Sun 12-2 D served Tue-Sun 6-9
RESTAURANT: L served Sat-Sun 12-2 D served Tue-Sun 7-9
BREWERY/COMPANY: Free House 🍺: Shepherd Neame, Six Bells Brewery, Bishops Castle, Big Nevs.
CHILDREN'S FACILITIES: menu, portions, food/bottle warming, outdoor play area **GARDEN:** Large lawn in front of pub **NOTES:** No dogs (ex guide dogs), Parking 18

TALYBONT-ON-USK — STAR INN

LD3 7YX
☎ 01874 676635
Dir: *Telephone for directions.* **Map Ref:** *SO12*

With its pretty riverside garden, this traditional 250-year-old inn stands in a picturesque village within the Brecon Beacons National Park. The pub, unmodernised and with welcoming fireplace, is known for its constantly changing range of well-kept real ales, and it's an excellent centre for walking and outdoor pursuits. Quiz night on Monday, live bands on Wednesday. Hearty bar food with dishes such as chicken in leek and Stilton sauce, Hungarian pork goulash, traditional roasts, salmon fish cakes, and vegetarian chilli.

OPEN: 11-3 6.30-11 (Sat all day) **BAR MEALS:** L served Mon-Sun 12-2.15 D served Mon-Sun 6.30-9 Av main course £6 **BREWERY/COMPANY:** Free House 🍺: Felinfoel Double Dragon, Theakston Old Peculiar, Hancock's HB, Bullmastiff Best. **CHILDREN'S FACILITIES:** menu, portions, high-chairs, food/bottle warming **GARDEN:** Shaded backed by canal **NOTES:** Dogs allowed: in bar, in garden, in bedrooms

TRECASTLE — CASTLE COACHING INN ♉

LD3 8UH
☎ 01874 636354 🖷 01874 636457
e-mail: guest@castle-coaching-inn.co.uk
Dir: *On A40 W of Brecon.* **Map Ref:** *SN82*

A Georgian coaching inn on the old London to Carmarthen coaching route, now the main A40 trunk road. Family-owned and run, the hotel has been carefully restored in recent years, and has lovely old fireplaces and a remarkable bow-fronted bar window. Ten en suite bedrooms make staying over an attractive possibility, and the inn also offers a peaceful terrace and garden.

OPEN: 12-3 6-11 **BAR MEALS:** L served Mon-Sun 12-2 D served Mon-Sat 6.30-9.00 (Sun 7-9) Av main course £7 **RESTAURANT:** L served Mon-Sun 12-2 D served Mon-Sat 6.30-9 (Sun 7-9) Av 3 course à la carte £16 **BREWERY/COMPANY:** Free House 🍺: Fuller's London Pride, Breconshire Brewery Red Dragon, Timothy Taylor Landlords. ♉: 15 **CHILDREN'S FACILITIES:** menu, portions, licence, high-chairs, food/bottle warming, baby changing **GARDEN:** Paved sun terrace **NOTES:** in bar, in garden, in bedrooms, No dogs (ex guide dogs), Parking 25 **ROOMS:** 10 en suite 2 family rooms s£45 d£60 (★★★)

PONTARDDULAIS THE FOUNTAIN INN

111 Bologoed Rd SA4 1JP
☎ 01792 882501 📠 01792 879972
e-mail: bookings@fountaininn.com
Dir: *A48 from M4 to Pontlliw then on to Pontarddulais, inn on R.* **Map Ref:** *SN50*

Memorabilia from Swansea's industrial past fill this carefully modernised old free house. The chef uses fresh local ingredients to produce an extensive and interesting range of dishes. Expect cockle, bacon and laverbread crêpe, stuffed Welsh saltmarsh lamb, cheese and leek crusted cod, or hake and monkfish in prawn and watercress sauce. Round off your meal with bara brith bread and butter pudding.

OPEN: 12-2 5.30-11.30 Closed: 25-26 Dec
BAR MEALS: L served all week 12-2 D served all week 5.30-9.30 Av main course £9.50 **RESTAURANT:** L served all week 12-2.30 D served all week 5.30-9.30
BREWERY/COMPANY: Free House 🍺: Greene King Old Speckled Hen, Fuller's London Pride, Batemans XXXX.
CHILDREN'S FACILITIES: menu, baby changing table, high chairs **NOTES:** No dogs, Parking 30

LLANARMON DYFFRYN CEIRIOG THE WEST ARMS HOTEL ★★ ❀ 🐾

LL20 7LD
☎ 01691 600665 📠 01691 600622
e-mail: gowestarms@aol.com
Dir: *Leave A483 at Chirk, follow signs for Ceiriog Valley B4500, hotel is 11m from Chirk.* **Map Ref:** *SJ13*

Sixteenth century in origin and a hotel since 1670, the West Arms is at the head of a long, winding valley in the Berwyn foothills. Cattle drovers heading for faraway markets would meet here, and shooting parties have been regulars for centuries. Very much a locals' bar, warmth and character ooze from its slate floors, timberwork and inglenook fireplaces.

OPEN: 8am-11 **BAR MEALS:** L served all week 12-2 D served all week 7-9 **RESTAURANT:** L served Sun 12-2 D served all week 7-9 **BREWERY/COMPANY:** Free House 🍺: Interbrew Flowers IPA, Smooth, Trophy Real Ale, Boddingtons. **CHILDREN'S FACILITIES:** menu, portions, games, high-chairs, food/bottle warming, baby changing, baby changing facilities **GARDEN:** Large lawned area view of Berwyn Mountains **NOTES:** Dogs allowed: in bar, in garden, in bedrooms, Water, 3 Kennels, Parking 30 **ROOMS:** 15 en suite bedrooms 3 family rooms s£52.50 d£85

MARFORD TREVOR ARMS HOTEL 🐾 🍷

LL12 8TA
☎ 01244 570436 📠 01244 570273
e-mail: info@trevorarmsmarford.fsnet.co.uk
Dir: *Off A483 onto B5102 then R onto B5445 into Marford.* **Map Ref:** *SJ35*

Haunted 19th-century coaching inn that was once the scene of public hangings. It takes its name from Lord Trevor of Trevallin, who was killed in a duel. Grisly past notwithstanding, the Trevallin is a charming inn, offering a varied menu. Bar specials might include lamb hotpot, chicken balti, cod and chips, or a three course carvery.

OPEN: 11-11 **BAR MEALS:** L served all week 11-11 D served all week Av main course £6.50
RESTAURANT: L served all week 11-11 D served all week Av 3 course à la carte £15 Av 3 course fixed price £8.25
BREWERY/COMPANY: Scottish Courage 🍺: Greenalls, Scottish Courage, Bombadier & John Smiths, Greene King Old Speckled Hen. 🍷: 12 **CHILDREN'S FACILITIES:** menu, portions, high-chairs, food/bottle warming, outdoor play area, swings and a pets corner, family room **GARDEN:** Large lawn area **NOTES:** No dogs (ex guide dogs), Parking 70